TH

E

DICTIONARY

CW01650451

MINSTER BOOKS

First published in 1976 by
The Hamlyn Publishing Group Limited.
Published in 1983 by Newnes Books.
Michelin House, 81 Fulham Road,
London SW3 6RB

© Copyright Reed International Books

This 1992 edition reprinted exclusively for MINSTER BOOKS

All rights reserved. No part of this publication may be reproduced, stored in a retrieval system or transmitted in any form or by any means, electronic, mechanical, photocopying, recording or otherwise, without the permission of the Publisher.

ISBN 0 600 37091 7

Printed at Thomson Press (India) Ltd.
Faridabad (Haryana)

Foreword

The Newnes Pocket English Dictionary gives concise and accurate definitions of about 12 000 of the most important words in current use in English. Special attention has been taken to cover modern, technical, and informal meanings. An additional feature is the inclusion of over 2000 idioms and idiomatic phrasal verbs (such as *take off*). Distinct senses of words are numbered separately, with the most common or important meaning placed first. Easy-to-read pronunciations based on the International Phonetic Alphabet have been given only for words that might cause some difficulty (see *Key to symbols used in pronunciation* below).

The wide coverage of this dictionary with its emphasis on modernity, together with its compact size and clear typeface, will make it an invaluable aid at school, at the office and in the home.

Abbreviations used in the Dictionary

adj	adjective	*infin*	infinitive	*pt*	past tense
adv	adverb	*interj*	interjection	*r*	reflex ve
aux	auxiliary	*n*	noun	*s*	singular
cap	capital	*neg*	negative	*sl*	slang
conj	conjunction	*pl*	plural	*tab*	taboo
def art	definite article	*poss*	possessive	*Tdmk*	trademark
esp	especially	*pp*	past participle	*US*	United States
f	feminine	*prep*	preposition	*v*	verb
indef art	indefinite article	*pres*	present tense	*vi*	verb intransitive
inf	informal	*pron*	pronoun	*vt*	verb transitive

Key to symbols used in pronunciation

Vowels

iː	m*ee*t	u	p*u*t	ai	fl*y*
i	b*i*t	uː	sh*oo*t	au	h*ow*
e	g*e*t	ʌ	c*u*t	ɔi	b*oy*
æ	h*a*t	ə	*a*go	iə	h*ere*
ɑː	h*ear*t	əː	s*ir*	ɛə	*air*
ɔ	h*o*t	ei	l*a*te	uə	p*oor*
ɔː	*ough*t	ou	g*o*		

Consonants

θ	*th*in	ʃ	*sh*ip
ð	*th*en	ʒ	mea*s*ure
ŋ	si*ng*	tʃ	*ch*in
j	*y*es	dʒ	*g*in

ˈ indicates that the following syllable is stressed, as in ago (əˈgou)

ˌ placed under an *n* or *l* indicates that the *n* or *l* is pronounced as a syllable, as in *button* (ˈbʌtn̩) and *flannel* (ˈflænl̩)

Irregular verbs

Infinitive	Past Tense	Past Participle	Infinitive	Past Tense	Past Participle
abide	abode *or* abided	abode *or* abided	**beware**[2]		
arise	arose	arisen	**bid**	bid	bidden *or* bid
awake	awoke *or* awaked	awoke *or* awaked	**bind**	bound	bound
be	was	been	**bite**	bit	bitten *or* bit
bear[1]	bore	borne *or* born	**bleed**	bled	bled
beat	beat	beaten	**blow**	blew	blown
become	became	become	**break**	broke	broken
begin	began	begun	**breed**	bred	bred
bend	bent	bent	**bring**	brought	brought
bet	bet	bet	**build**	built	built
			burn	burnt *or* burned	burnt *or* burned

Infinitive	Past Tense	Past Participle
burst	burst	burst
buy	bought	bought
can	could	
cast	cast	cast
catch	caught	caught
choose	chose	chosen
cling	clung	clung
come	came	come
cost	cost	cost
creep	crept	crept
crow	crowed *or* crew	crowed
cut	cut	cut
deal	dealt	dealt
dig	dug *or* digged	dug *or* digged
do	did	done
draw	drew	drawn
dream	dreamed *or* dreamt	dreamed *or* dreamt
drink	drank	drunk
drive	drove	driven
dwell	dwelt	dwelt
eat	ate	eaten
fall	fell	fallen
feed	fed	fed
feel	felt	felt
fight	fought	fought
find	found	found
flee	fled	fled
fling	flung	flung
fly	flew	flown
forbid	forbade *or* forbad	forbidden *or* forbid
forget	forgot	forgotten *or* forgot
forgive	forgave	forgiven
forsake	forsook	forsaken
freeze	froze	frozen
get	got	got
give	gave	given
go	went	gone
grind	ground	ground
grow	grew	grown
hang[3]	hung *or* hanged	hung *or* hanged
have	had	had
hear	heard	heard
hide	hid	hidden *or* hid
hit	hit	hit
hold	held	held
hurt	hurt	hurt
keep	kept	kept
kneel	knelt	knelt
knit	knitted *or* knit	knitted *or* knit
know	knew	known
lay	laid	laid
lead	led	led
lean	leant *or* leaned	leant *or* leaned
leap	leapt *or* leaped	leapt *or* leaped
learn	learnt *or* learned	learnt *or* learned
leave	left	left
lend	lent	lent
let	let	let
lie	lay	lain
light	lit *or* lighted	lit *or* lighted
lose	lost	lost
make	made	made
may	might	
mean	meant	meant
meet	met	met
mow	mowed	mown
must		
ought		
panic	panicked	panicked
pay	paid	paid
picnic	picnicked	picnicked
put	put	put
quit	quitted *or* quit	quitted *or* quit
read	read	read
rid	rid *or* ridded	rid *or* ridded
ride	rode	ridden
ring	rang	rung
rise	rose	risen
run	ran	run
saw	sawed	sawn *or* sawed
say	said	said
see	saw	seen
seek	sought	sought
sell	sold	sold

Irregular verbs

Infinitive	Past Tense	Past Participle
send	sent	sent
set	set	set
sew	sewed	sewn *or* sewed
shake	shook	shaken
shall	should	
shear	sheared	sheared *or* shorn
shed	shed	shed
shine	shone	shone
shoe	shod	shod
shoot	shot	shot
show	showed	shown
shrink	shrank *or* shrunk	shrunk *or* shrunken
shut	shut	shut
sing	sang	sung
sink	sank	sunk
sit	sat	sat
sleep	slept	slept
slide	slid	slid
sling	slung	slung
slink	slunk	slunk
slit	slit	slit
smell	smelt *or* smelled	smelt *or* smelled
sow	sowed	sown *or* sowed
speak	spoke	spoken
speed	sped *or* speeded	sped *or* speeded
spell	spelt *or* spelled	spelt *or* spelled
spend	spent	spent
spill	spilt *or* spilled	spilt *or* spilled
spin	spun	spun
spit	spat *or* spit	spat *or* spit
split	split	split
spread	spread	spread
spring	sprang	sprung
stand	stood	stood
steal	stole	stolen
stick	stuck	stuck
sting	stung	stung
stink	stank *or* stunk	stunk
stride	strode	stridden
strike	struck	struck
string	strung	strung
strive	strove	striven
swear	swore	sworn
sweep	swept	swept
swell	swelled	swollen *or* swelled
swim	swam	swum
swing	swung	swung
take	took	taken
teach	taught	taught
tear	tore	torn
tell	told	told
think	thought	thought
throw	threw	thrown
thrust	thrust	thrust
traffic	trafficked	trafficked
tread	trod	trodden *or* trod
wake	woke	woken
wear	wore	worn
weave	wove	woven *or* wove
weep	wept	wept
will	would	
win	won	won
wind	wound	wound
wring	wrung	wrung
write	wrote	written

[1] when *bear* means *give birth to* the past participle is always *born*.

[2] used only in the infinitive or as an imperative.

[3] the preferred form of the past tense and past participle when referring to death by hanging is *hanged*.

A

a, an *indef art* one; each; every; any; some.

aback *adv* **taken aback** taken by surprise; disconcerted; flabbergasted.

abandon *vt* **1** leave behind with no intention of returning; desert; forsake. **2** give up; fail to complete. **abandon oneself (to)** yield, submit, or give in (to).

abashed *adj* ashamed; embarrassed.

abate *vi* lessen; die down. *vt* reduce; subdue; suppress. **abatement** *n*.

abattoir ('æbətwɑ:) *n* slaughterhouse.

abbess *n* female head of nuns in an abbey or nunnery.

abbey *n* **1** community of monks or nuns. **2** buildings occupied by such a community. **3** church attached to such a community.

abbot *n* male head of monks in an abbey or monastery.

abbreviate *vt* shorten (a word or phrase). **abbreviation** *n*.

abdicate *vi,vt* renounce or relinquish (the throne, one's powers, etc.). **abdication** *n*.

abdomen *n* lower part of the body between the diaphragm and pelvis; belly. **abdominal** *adj*.

abduct *vt* take (a person) away unlawfully; kidnap. **abduction** *n*. **abductor** *n*.

aberration *n* deviation from the usual, right, or natural course, condition, etc. **aberrant** *adj*.

abet *vt* (-tt-) assist or encourage in crime or wrongdoing.

abeyance *n* **in abeyance** in a state of inactivity; suspended.

abhor *vt* (-rr-) have an intense horror of; loathe; detest. **abhorrence** *n*. **abhorrent** *adj*.

abide *vt* (abode *or* abided) tolerate; bear. *vi* **1** stay; remain. **2** reside; dwell. **abide by** keep to; remain close or faithful to.

ability *n* **1** power; capacity; means. **2** competence; skill.

abject *adj* **1** downcast; humiliated. **2** despicable; shocking. **3** humble. **abjectly** *adv*.

ablaze *adj* **1** on fire; in flames; burning fiercely. **2** displaying strong passion or ardour.

able *adj* **1** having the power, capacity, opportunity, or means (to). **2** competent; skilled. **ably** *adv*. **able-bodied** *adj* physically fit; strong.

abnormal *adj* irregular; unnatural; deviant. **abnormality** *n*. **abnormally** *adv*.

aboard *adv,prep* on or in(to) a ship, aircraft, etc.

abode[1] *n* place of residence; dwelling; home.

abode[2] *v* a *pt* and *pp* of **abide.**

abolish *vt* do away with; put an end to; ban. **abolition** *n*.

abominable *adj* loathsome; detestable; dreadful. **abominably** *adv*.

Aborigine (æbə'ridʒini) *n also* **Aboriginal** person belonging to a race of original native inhabitants, esp. of Australia. **Aboriginal** *adj*.

abort *vt* **1** terminate (a pregnancy); perform an abortion on. **2** cancel or destroy (a project, mission, etc.) before completion. *vi* **1** miscarry. **2** fail to function successfully; terminate before completion. **abortive** *adj*. **abortion** *n* **1** operation carried out to remove a foetus from the womb. **2** miscarriage. **3** disastrous failure.

abound *vi* exist or have in great quantity; be plentiful.

about *prep* **1** of; concerning; relating to; connected with. **2** near or close to; around. **about to** ready or preparing to; on the point of. ~*adv* **1** approximately. **2** nearby; close at hand. **3** around; here and there; to and fro.

above *adv* higher up; overhead. *prep* **1** over; higher than. **2** more or greater than. **3** in authority over; superior to. **4** beyond (suspicion, reproach, etc.). *adj also* **above-mentioned** mentioned or written above or before. **above all** more than anything. **aboveboard** *adv* openly; without deception. *adj* open; straightforward; honest; legal.

abrasion *n* **1** wearing down by rubbing. **2** graze on the skin. **abrasive** *adj* **1** producing abrasion. **2** harsh; grating. *n* something used for wearing down or smoothing a surface.

abreast *adv* side by side; level with. **keep abreast of** keep up or up-to-date with.

abridge *vt* cut (a novel, play, etc.); condense. **abridgement** *n*.

abroad *adv* **1** in or to a foreign country. **2** in circulation; at large.

abrupt *adj* **1** unexpected and sudden. **2** curt; short; brusque. **abruptly** *adv*. **abruptness** *n*.

abscess *n* pus-filled sore.

abscond *vi* leave without permission; run away, esp. after committing a crime. **absconder** *n*.

absent *adj* ('æbsənt) **1** away; not in attendance. **2** lacking; missing; not present. *v* **absent oneself** (əb'sent) stay away. **absence** *n*. **absentee** *n* person, such as an employee or landlord, who is absent. **absenteeism** *n*. **absent-minded** *adj* forgetful or vague, esp. when preoccupied. **absent-mindedly** *adv*. **absent-mindedness** *n*.

absolute *adj* total; utter; complete. **absolutely** *adv*.

absolve *vt* release from blame, sin, obligation, etc.; pardon; exonerate. **absolution** *n*.

absorb *vt* **1** take in or soak up. **2** assimilate. **3** engross; engage fully. **absorbent** *adj*. **absorbing** *adj*. **absorption** *n*.

abstain *vi* **1** refrain from registering one's vote. **2** refrain from indulging in certain pleasures, such as drinking alcohol. **abstention** *n* withholding of one's vote. **abstinence** *n* state or period of self-denial.

abstract *adj* ('æbstrækt) having no material existence; not concrete; conceptual. *n* ('æbstrækt) brief account; summary; résumé. *vt* (əb'strækt) take away; remove. **abstraction** *n*. **abstract art** *n* art depicting ideas or objects through form, colour, and line rather than natural or actual representation.

absurd *adj* ridiculous; silly; ludicrous. **absurdity** *n*. **absurdly** *adv*.

abundant *adj* plentiful. **abundance** *n*. **abundantly** *adv*.

abuse *vt* (ə'bju:z) **1** use or treat badly or unfairly; misuse. **2** insult; be rude to. *n* (ə'bju:s) **1** ill-treatment; misuse; violation. **2** insulting behaviour or language. **abusive** *adj*.

abyss (ə'bis) *n* deep bottomless pit or gulf. **abysmal** (ə'bizməl) *adj* **1** bottomless; deep. **2** dreadful; shocking. **abysmally** *adv*.

academy *n* **1** school or college offering specialized training. **2** association of distinguished scholars. **academic** *adj* **1** relating to a university, college, etc. **2** theoretical or intellectual rather than practical or technical. *n* university teacher or researcher. **academically** *adv*.

accelerate *vt,vi* make or become faster; speed up. **acceleration** *n*. **accelerator** *n* control pedal in a motor vehicle that is used for regulating speed; throttle.

accent *n* ('æksent) **1** type of pronunciation associated with a particular region, social class, etc. **2** stress placed on a syllable or word. **3** written or printed symbol occurring in some languages to indicate stress, vowel quality, etc. **4** emphasis. *vt* (ək'sent) stress; mark with an accent. **accentuate** *vt* emphasize; draw attention to. **accentuation** *n*.

accept *vt* **1** take something that is offered; receive. **2** agree (to); admit. **3** tolerate; put up with. **acceptable** *adj*. **acceptance** *n*.

access *n* **1** way in or to; approach. **2** opportunity, means, or permission to enter, reach, use, etc. **accessible** *adj* reachable; approachable.

accessory *n* **1** one of an additional set of items. **2** person who assists in or conceals knowledge of a crime.

accident *n* unforeseen event or occurrence, often having unpleasant consequences. **by accident** by chance; unexpectedly. **accidental** *adj*. **accidentally** *adv*.

acclaim *vt* show approval by cheering; applaud; hail; praise. *n also* **acclamation** enthusiastic approval; applause; praise.

acclimatize *vt,vi* make or become conditioned or used (to). **acclimatization** *n*.

accommodate *vt* **1** provide room or space for; house; shelter. **2** adjust (to); reconcile. **accommodation** *n*.

accompany *vt* go with; escort; join in or take part in with. **accompaniment** *n* **1** something that belongs or occurs with something else. **2** music that is played to support a solo performance.

accomplice *n* partner in crime or wrongdoing.

accomplish *vt* achieve; attain; complete successfully. **accomplished** *adj* talented; skilful; proficient, esp. in social graces; refined. **accomplishment** *n* **1** successful completion; achievement. **2** skill; refinement; proficiency.

accord *vt,vi* agree; correspond; match up (to). *n* harmony; agreement. **of one's own accord** on one's own initiative; voluntarily. **accordance** *n*. **in accordance with** in agreement with; conforming to. **according** *adv* **according to 1** as laid down or stipulated by. **2** as stated or shown by; on the evidence of. **3** in relation to; dependent on. **accordingly** *adv* **1** therefore; so. **2** as the situation demands.

accordion *n* portable box-shaped musical instrument with bellows and keys.

accost *vt* **1** approach (someone) in order to converse, question, etc. **2** solicit.

account *n* **1** report of an event, etc. **2** explanation. **3** banking service or a credit service at a store, etc. **4** sum of money deposited at a bank. **5** statement of money transactions. **6** importance; esteem. **on account** on credit. **on account of** because of. **on any/no account** for no reason whatever. **take into account** *or* **take account of** allow for. *vi* **account for 1** give reasons for; explain. **2** make a reckoning of; count. **3** capture; kill. **accountable** *adj* responsible (for). **accountant** *n* professional person who investigates the business and financial transactions of an individual or organization. **accountancy** *n*.

accumulate *vt,vi* amass or collect over a period of time; pile up. **accumulation** *n*. **accumulative** *adj*.

accurate *adj* precise; correct; exactly right. **accuracy** *n*. **accurately** *adv*.

accuse *vt* charge (a person) with a crime, mistake, fault, etc.; blame. **accusation** *n*.

accustom *vt* familiarize; acquaint; acclimatize.

ace *n* **1** playing card having a single pip. **2** pilot who has destroyed a large number of enemy aircraft. **3** champion. *adj sl* first-rate; excellent.

ache *vi* **1** feel a steady dull pain. **2** yearn; long (for). *n* steady dull pain.

achieve *vt* accomplish; attain; gain. **achievement** *n*.

acid *n* sour-tasting chemical compound that turns litmus red and dissolves in water to produce hydrogen ions. *adj* **1** sharp; sour-tasting. **2** sarcastic; caustic. **acidic** *adj*. **acidity** *n*.

acknowledge *vt* **1** recognize that something is true or right; admit. **2** respond to. **acknowledgment** *or* **acknowledgement** *n*.

acne ('ækni) *n* skin disorder affecting mainly the face and upper part of the body, which become covered with pimples and blackheads.

acorn *n* nut that is the fruit of the oak.

acoustic *adj* relating to sound or the sense of hearing. **acoustics** *n* **1** *s* branch of physics concerned with the study of sound-waves. **2** *pl* properties of a concert hall, room, etc., that affect the way sounds are heard.

acquaint *vt* inform; familiarize; introduce. **acquaintance** *n* **1** someone one knows, but not as a close or intimate friend. **2** personal knowledge. **acquaintanceship** *n*.

acquiesce *vi* agree tacitly; assent; comply. **acquiescence** *n*. **acquiescent** *adj*.

acquire *vt* obtain, esp. gradually or with some effort; take possession of; get. **acquisition** *n*. **acquisitive** *adj* eager to possess.

acquit *vt* (-tt-) pronounce not guilty; discharge. **acquit oneself** perform; behave; conduct oneself.

acre *n* unit of land area equal to approx. 4000 sq m (4840 sq yds). **acreage** *n* total number of acres in any given area.

acrobat *n* performer on a trapeze, tightrope, etc., gymnast. **acrobatic** *adj*. **acrobatics** *n s or pl* gymnastic feats or exercises.

across *prep,adv* **1** from one side to another. **2** over on the other side (of). **come across** meet or discover unexpectedly.

acrylic *adj* relating to a type of synthetic fibre.

act *vi* **1** operate; function; behave; perform; do (something). **2** perform in a play. **3** pretend; feign. *vt* take the role of; play. *n* **1** single deed; action. **2** law passed by Parliament. **3** major division of a play, opera, etc., consisting of a number of scenes. **4** performer(s) in a show, circus, etc., or the performance itself.

action *n* **1** process of doing something; act; deed. **2** gesture; movement. **3** mechanism; movement of mechanical parts. **4** lawsuit.

activate *vt* make active; stir; agitate; cause to react.

active *adj* **1** in operation; functioning. **2** taking a positive part. **3** lively; busy. **actively** *adv*. **activist** *n* person working for a particular political cause.

activity *n* **1** movement; motion. **2** something that keeps one occupied or busy.

actor *n* performer in the theatre, on television, or in films. **actress** *f n*.

actual *adj* having real existence; not imaginary. **actually** *adv* really; as a matter of fact; in fact.

actuary *n* expert adviser on insurance, pensions, etc. **actuarial** *adj*.

acupuncture *n* Eastern method of medical treatment using sharp needles to puncture certain areas of the skin.

acute *adj* **1** having a keen sense of hearing, smell, etc. **2** perceptive; quick-witted; shrewd. **3** severe; critical. **4** *med* reaching crisis point; not chronic. **acute accent** *n* symbol placed over certain vowels in some languages, as in *café*. **acute angle** *n* angle of less than 90°. **acutely** *adv*. **acuteness** *n*.

adamant *adj* insistent; firm. **adamantly** *adv*.

Adam's apple *n* popular name for the thyroid cartilage of the larynx.

adapt *vt* modify to suit a different purpose or situation. *vi* adjust to a new environment or set of conditions. **adaptable** *adj*. **adaptation** *n*. **adaptor** *n*.

add *vt,vi* **1** put together; join; give as something extra. **2** calculate the sum (of); total. **3** state further, go on to say. **add to** supplement; increase. **addition** *n*. **additional** *adj* extra. **additive** *adj,n*.

adder *n* viper.

addict *n* ('ædikt) **1** person who has become physically dependent on something, esp. a drug. **2** enthusiast; fanatic. **be(come) addicted to** (ə'diktid) be(come) totally dependent on. **addiction** *n*. **addictive** *adj*.

address *n* **1** postal location of a house, office, etc. **2** speech given before an audience. *vt* **1** write the address on. **2** speak directly to. **addressee** *n*.

adenoids *pl n* mass of enlarged tissue in the pharynx.

adept *adj* skilful; adroit; deft. **adeptly** *adv*. **adeptness** *n*.

adequate *adj* **1** sufficient; just enough; acceptable; satisfactory. **2** able to cope; capable. **adequacy** *n*. **adequately** *adv*.

adhere *vi* stick; hold. *vt* stick; glue; gum. **adhere to** keep to; uphold; observe strictly; abide by. **adherent** *adj*. **adhesion** *n*. **adhesive** *n* substance such as glue, gum, or paste, used for sticking things together. *adj* relating to such a substance.

ad hoc *adj* used for a specified purpose.

adjacent *adj* adjoining; situated beside; next to.

adjective *n* part of speech qualifying a noun. **adjectival** *adj*.

adjoin *vt* be situated next to; border on. **adjoining** *adj*.

adjourn *vt,vi* discontinue or suspend (a meeting, court session, etc.) with the intention of resuming at a later time. **adjournment** *n*.

adjudicate *vi,vt* judge; settle; select (a winner). **adjudication** *n*. **adjudicator** *n*.

adjust *vt* make a minor alteration to; modify; change. *vi* change to fit in with new requirements; adapt. **adjustable** *adj*. **adjustment** *n*.

ad-lib *vi* (-bb-) compose (a speech, lines in a play, etc.) without previous preparation; improvise.

administer *vt* **1** *also* **administrate** govern; control as an official. **2** dispense; hand out; issue. **administrative** *adj*. **administrator** *n*. **administration** *n* **1** management; control; process of governing. **2** body of managers, governors, etc.

admiral *n* highest ranking naval officer. **admiralty** *n* state department responsible for naval affairs.

admire *vt* have a high regard for; respect; look up to; approve of. **admirable** *adj*. **admiration** *n*. **admirer** *n*.

admit *vt* (-tt-) **1** grant entry to. **2** confess; accept blame for. **3** accept as true; agree to. **admissible** *adj* acceptable; allowable. **admission** *n* **1** permission or opportunity to enter. **2** fee charged for entrance. **3** confession. **4** acknowledgment; acceptance. **admittance** *n* right of entry; access.

ado *n* fuss; confused excitement; commotion.

adolescence *n* period between puberty and adulthood. **adolescent** *n,adj*.

adopt *vt* **1** take (another person's child) into one's own family as a legal guardian. **2** take up (someone else's suggestion, plan, etc.). **3** give formal approval to; choose. **adoption** *n*.

adore *vt* love ardently; worship; have great affection for. **adorable** *adj*. **adoration** *n*.

adorn *vt* decorate; embellish; enhance. **adornment** *n*.

adrenaline *n* hormone secreted in the body or produced synthetically that is used to accelerate heart action, raise blood sugar levels, etc.

adrift *adj* **1** cut loose from a mooring; unattached; drifting. **2** off the point; not concise.

adroit *adj* skilfully quick; resourceful; adept. **adroitly** *adv*. **adroitness** *n*.

adulation *n* **1** unqualified or uncritical praise. **2** flattery. **3** unquestioning devotion.

adult *n* **1** person who is grown up or mature. **2** fully grown animal or plant. *adj* **1** mature; of age; fully grown. **2** intended for adults. **adulthood** *n*.

adultery *n* extra-marital sexual intercourse.

advance *vi* **1** move forwards or upwards; proceed. **2** show improvement; progress. *vt* **1** take further; move ahead. **2** pay out (money) before it is due. *n* **1** movement forwards. **2** progress. **3** amount paid before payment is due. *adj* issued in advance. **advancement** *n*. **in advance** beforehand; ahead.

advantage *n* favourable position, circumstances, etc.; privilege; benefit. **advantageous** *adj*.

adventure *n* exciting journey or experience, usually involving risks or hazards. **adventurous** *adj* daring; bold; willing to take risks. **adventurously** *adv*.

adverb *n* part of speech qualifying a verb. **adverbial** *adj*.

adverse *adj* hostile; in opposition; antagonistic. **adversity** *n* distressing circumstances; misfortune.

advertise *vt,vi* give public information (of goods for sale, vacancies, etc.); announce. **advertiser** *n*. **advertisement** *n* public announcement in the press, on televison, etc.; note of goods for sale, etc.

advice *n* opinion or recommendation given in order to help someone make a decision.

advise *vt,vi* give advice (to); recommend. **adviser** *n*. **advisable** *adj* wise; worth recommending.

advocate *vt* ('ædvəkeit) recommend; urge. *n* ('ædvəkət) **1** supporter; believer. **2** (in Scotland) barrister.

aerial *n* system of conducting rods for receiving or transmitting radio or television signals; antenna. *adj* of, in, or from the air. **aerially** *adv*.

aerodynamics *n* study of the behaviour of aircraft, missiles, etc., in relation to airflow. **aerodynamic** *adj*. **aerodynamically** *adv*.

aeronautics *n* study of flight. **aeronautic** *or* **aeronautical** *adj*.

aeroplane *n* aircraft propelled by jet engines or propellers and kept aloft by aerodynamic forces.

aerosol *n* container dispensing a fine spray of pressurized liquid, gas, etc.

aesthetic (i:s'θetik) *adj* **1** pleasing to one's sense of beauty. **2** relating to aesthetics. **aesthetics** *n* branch of philosophy concerned with the concept and study of beauty, esp. in art.

afar *adv* far away; from or at a distance.

affair *n* **1** matter; concern; business. **2** sexual relationship, esp. an extra-marital one; liaison. *pl n* personal, business, or political matters.

affect[1] *vt* **1** influence; alter; cause to change. **2** move; arouse emotionally.

affect[2] *vt* feign; simulate; pretend. **affectation** *n* falseness of manner or style; insincerity.

affection *n* fondness; love; strong liking. **affectionate** *adj*. **affectionately** *adv*.

affiliate *vt,vi* join or unite (with) as a member; associate. **affiliation** *n*.

affinity *n* **1** relationship, esp. by marriage. **2** close connection; resemblance. **3** empathetic attraction; strong liking.

affirm *vt,vi* testify as to truth or validity; substantiate; assent. **affirmation** *n*. **affirmative** *adj* positive; assertive. *n* the answer 'yes'.

affix *vt* (ə'fiks) fasten; attach. *n* ('æfiks) prefix or suffix.

afflict *vt* cause distress, pain, or suffering; torment. **affliction** *n* **1** torment; grief. **2** disease; sickness; disability.

affluent *adj* wealthy; prosperous; rich. **affluence** *n*.

afford *vt* **1** have money, time, etc., to spare (for). **2** be able to risk. **3** offer; provide; allow.

affront *vt* insult or offend, esp. publicly. *n* public insult; display of disrespect.

afield *adv* far away; a long way off.

afloat *adj,adv* **1** floating. **2** solvent.

afoot *adj,adv* under way; in the offing.

aforesaid *adj also* **aforementioned** previously referred to.

afraid *adj* **1** frightened; apprehensive; fearful. **2** sorry; regretful.

afresh *adv* from the beginning; again; anew.

aft *adv* towards or at the stern.

after *prep* **1** following; later than. **2** in pursuit of. **3** in spite of; in view of. **4** concerning. **5** in imitation of. **after all** when everything is considered. ~*adv* **1** behind. **2** subsequently. **take after** resemble. ~*conj* subsequent to the time that. **after-care** *n* help, treatment, supervision, etc., given to a person discharged from hospital or prison. **after-effect** *n* delayed effect, esp. of a drug. **afterlife** *n* life after death. **aftermath** *n* **1** period of devastation following a war, disaster, etc. **2** disastrous consequence. **afternoon** *n* period between midday and evening. **afterthought** *n* thought or idea that occurs later or incidentally. **afterwards** *adv* at a later time; subsequently.

again *adv* **1** once more; any more. **2** additionally; further; besides. **again and again** repeatedly; many times.

against *prep* **1** in contact with; next to; close to; up as far as. **2** in opposition to; competing with. **3** not in favour of. **4** contrasting with. **5** in order to prevent.

age *n* **1** period of time during which a person or thing has existed. **2** era; epoch; period. **3** *also pl inf* a long time. *vi,vt* grow or cause to grow or look old(er). **aged** *adj* **1** ('eidʒid) very old. **2** (eidʒd) of the age of.

agenda *n* list of items to be discussed or dealt with; programme.

agent *n* **1** person representing or working on behalf of a client. **2** something that produces a change or effect. **agency** *n* **1** company providing services or goods and operating on behalf of a client. **2** influence; mediating power.

aggravate *vt* **1** make worse; exacerbate. **2** irritate; annoy. **aggravation** *n*.

aggression *n* feeling or display of hostility, anger, etc. **aggressive** *adj*. **aggressively** *adv*. **aggressor** *n*.

aggrieved *adj* suffering from injustice; feeling unfairly treated.

aghast *adj* horrified; dumbfounded; shocked.

agile *adj* quick; alert; nimble. **agility** *n*.

agitate *vt* **1** shake or stir violently. **2** worry; make anxious; trouble. *vi also* **agitate for** publicly campaign and fight for. **agitator** *n*.

aglow *adj* glowing; shining; alight.

agnostic *n* person who believes that an immaterial being such as God cannot be the subject of real knowledge. **agnosticism** *n*.

ago *adv* in the past.

agog *adj* eager and excited.

agony *n* intense and prolonged pain or suffering; torment; anguish. **agonize** *vi,vt* suffer or cause agony or extreme distress.

agrarian *adj* relating to agricultural land or landed property.

agree *vi* **1** consent. **2** correspond; match; tally. **3** think or feel the same (as). **4** make a joint decision. **5** suit; go well with. *vt* **1** settle; arrange terms of. **2** acknowledge; concede; consent to. **agreeable** *adj* **1** willing to consent. **2** pleasant. **agreement** *n* **1** consent; permission. **2** deal or contract between parties. **3** accordance; harmony.

agriculture *n* practice or study of farming. **agricultural** *adj*. **agriculturalist** *n*.

ahead *adv* further on; in front; in advance. **go ahead** continue; proceed; advance.

aid *vt,vi* help; assist; facilitate. *n* help; assistance; support. **in aid of** for; in order to help.

ailment *n* particular illness or disease.

aim *vt,vi* **1** point or direct (a gun, etc.) towards a target. **2** direct (one's efforts, remarks, etc.) towards a particular object. **aim at** *or* **for 1** try to achieve; strive for. **2** mean or intend for. ~*n* **1** act of aiming. **2** goal; target; purpose. **aimless** *adj* having no particular goal or purpose. **aimlessly** *adv*. **aimlessness** *n*.

air *n* **1** mixture of gases, consisting chiefly of nitrogen (78 per cent) and oxygen (21 per cent), that is essential for respiration. **2** layer of air surrounding the earth; atmosphere. **3** light breeze. **4** impression or aura. **5** bearing; manner. **6** tune; melody. **by air** transported by aircraft. **clear the air** remove tension or discord. **in the air** not yet settled. **into thin air** without a trace; completely. **on/off the air** being/not being broadcast. **walk** *or* **tread on air** feel elated. **airs** *pl n* affectations. ~*vt* **1** expose to fresh air; ventilate. **2** declare openly; make public. *vt,vi* dry in warm air. **airborne** *adj* in or supported or carried by air. **airtight** *adj* preventing the passage of air into or out of; impermeable. **airy** *adj* **1** open to the fresh air; well ventilated. **2** carefree; unconcerned. **3** light as air; graceful. **4** insubstantial; speculative. **airily** *adv*. **airiness** *n*.

air-conditioning *n* system for controlling flow and humidity of air within a building.

aircraft *n* machine, such as an aeroplane, helicopter, or glider, that is capable of flight through the air.

aircraft carrier *n* warship with special decks for operational aircraft.

airfield *n* extensive level area for take-off and landing of aircraft.

airforce *n* branch of a nation's armed services concerned with military aircraft.

airgun *n* gun discharged by compressed air.

air hostess *n* stewardess on an aircraft.

airlift *n* transportation by air of people, food, etc., esp. in an emergency when surface routes are cut. *vt* transport using an airlift.

airline *n* organization offering transportation by scheduled flights for people and cargo. **airliner** *n*.

airmail *n* **1** letters and parcels conveyed by

aircraft. **2** system for sending such mail. *vt* send (mail) by air.

airport *n* system of buildings, runways, hangars, etc., providing facilities for aircraft, passengers, and cargo.

air-raid *n* military attack by enemy aircraft.

airship *n* self-propelled aircraft kept aloft by buoyancy.

aisle *n* **1** gangway or open passageway separating blocks of seats in a theatre, church, etc. **2** area on either side of a church, usually separated from the nave by a series of pillars and arches.

ajar *adj,adv* partially open.

alabaster *n* form of gypsum that is white and opaque or translucent, used for statues, ornaments, etc.

alarm *n* **1** warning signal, such as a bell or shout. **2** sudden fear or anxiety; panic; fright. *vt* **1** frighten; shock; horrify. **2** alert to possible danger.

alas *interj* expression of regret, sadness, etc.

albatross *n* large sea-bird with webbed feet.

albeit *conj* even though; although.

albino *n* person or animal with unnatural colouring in skin and eyes.

album *n* **1** book used for the display of photographs, stamps, etc. **2** long-playing record.

alcohol *n* **1** intoxicating substance produced by fermenting sugar in a liquid. **2** any drink containing such a substance. **alcoholic** *adj* containing alcohol. *n* person addicted to alcohol. **alcoholism** *n* addiction to alcohol.

alcove *n* recess or niche.

alderman *n* senior councillor of a city or borough.

ale *n* type of light-coloured beer.

alert *adj* watchful; quick to respond. **alertness** *n*.

algebra *n* branch of mathematics in which numbers, quantities, and variables are represented by symbols whose manipulation is governed by generalized rules and relationships. **algebraic** *adj*.

alias *adv* also known as. *n* assumed name; pseudonym.

alibi *n* claim that someone accused of a crime was elsewhere at the time that it was committed.

alien *adj* **1** foreign; strange. **2** not part of; contrary. *n* foreigner. **alienate** *vt* estrange; cast out; cause to become indifferent or detached, esp. from society. **alienation** *n*.

alight[1] *adj* **1** on fire; lit up. **2** bright; shining.

alight[2] *vi* (alighted *or* alit) **1** dismount; get down (from). **2** settle or perch (on). **alight on** find unexpectedly; seize; light on.

align *vt,vi* **1** bring into line (with); line up; straighten. **2** form an alliance (with); cooperate. **alignment** *n*.

alike *adj* similar; appearing the same; resembling. *adv* similarly; in the same way.

alimentary canal (æli'mentəri) *n* system of organs in the body, including the stomach and intestines, through which food passes.

alimony *n* allowance paid to one marriage partner by the other following a legal separation.

alive *adj* **1** living; existing. **2** active; vigorous.

alkali ('ælkəlai) *n* chemical base that is soluble in water. **alkaline** *adj*.

all *adj* **1** every one of; the whole of. **2** complete; total. *adv* entirely; completely; totally. **all but** very nearly; almost. **all in all** taking everything into consideration. **in all** altogether; in total.

allay *vt* alleviate; assuage; appease; relieve.

allege (ə'ledʒ) *vt* claim as true; assert; avow. **allegation** (æli'geiʃən) *n*.

allegiance (ə'li:dʒəns) *n* loyalty, esp. to a sovereign; fidelity.

allegory ('æligəri) *n* story, painting, etc. in which moral values and other qualities are personified. **allegorical** (æli'gɔrikḷ) *adj*.

alleluia *interj,n* hallelujah.

allergy ('ælədʒi) *n* physical reaction of the body caused by extreme sensitivity to certain substances. **allergic** (ə'lə:dʒik) *adj*.

alleviate *vt* relieve (pain or suffering); allay. **alleviation** *n*.

alley *n* **1** *also* **alleyway** narrow passageway or street. **2** lane used in skittles, ten-pin bowling, etc.

alliance *n* **1** treaty of mutual friendship and help between nations. **2** relationship so formed. **3** nations so involved. **4** close relationship; union. **allied** *adj* **1** joined by alliance; united. **2** related; connected.

alligator *n* large reptile, chiefly of the southern US, related to the crocodile but having a shorter broader snout.

alliteration *n* repetition of the initial sound, usually a consonant, in a group of words.

allocate *vt* assign; distribute; share out. **allocation** *n*.

allot *vt* (-tt-) allocate. **allotment** *n* **1** plot of rented land for cultivation. **2** assignment.

allow *vt* **1** permit; let. **2** set aside. **3** grant; permit to have; concede. **allow for** make provision for. **allowable** *adj* permissible. **allowance** *n* **1** regular amount of money paid to a dependant. **2** sum of money allocated for certain tasks, responsibilities, etc. **3** concession; toleration. **make allowances for 1** excuse. **2** take into account.

alloy *n* metallic material consisting of a mixture of metals, as in bronze and brass, or of metals and nonmetals, as in steel.

allude *v* **allude to** refer indirectly to.

allure *vt* entice; attract; fascinate. *n* attraction; fascination. **allurement** *n*.

ally *n* ('ælai) **1** member of an alliance. **2** sympathetic person; supporter. *vt,vi* (ə'lai) unite; join (with).

almanac ('ɔ:lmənæk) *n* book containing a calendar, with astronomical and astrological information, etc., for the year.

almighty *adj* **1** omnipotent; supremely or divinely powerful. **2** *sl* tremendous; great. **the Almighty** *n* God.

almond *n* **1** tree related to the plum and peach. **2** smooth oval nut in a hard shell produced by this tree. *adj* of an oval shape like an almond.

almost *adv* nearly; close to; not quite.

alms (ɑ:mz) *pl n* money or gifts donated as charity to the poor. **almshouse** *n* building founded to provide accommodation and food for the poor and aged.

aloft *adj,adv* high up; overhead.

alone *adj,adv* by oneself; by itself; apart; isolated; separate; unaccompanied.

along *prep* **1** from one end to the other. **2** on any part of the length of. *adv* **1** onwards; forwards. **2** together (with); accompanying. **all along** all the time. **alongside** *adv,prep* along the side of; beside; parallel to.

aloof *adj* distant; haughty or reserved; uninvolved. *adv* at a distance; with reserve.

aloud *adv* using a normal speaking voice; not silently; out loud.

alphabet *n* system of letters or other symbols used for writing in a particular language. **alphabetical** *adj* following the order of the letters of the alphabet. **alphabetically** *adv*.

alpine *adj* relating to mountains or a mountainous region.

already *adv* by now, by then; previously.

Alsatian *n* breed of dog resembling a wolf in appearance and often used by the police or as a guard dog.

also *adv* in addition; as well; too; besides.

altar *n* **1** table in a Christian church at which the Eucharist is celebrated. **2** table or platform used for offerings or sacrifices to a deity.

alter *vt,vi* change; give or take on a new form or appearance; modify. **alteration** *n*.

alternate *adj* (ɔl'tə:nət) every other or second one; first one then the other. *vi,vt* ('ɔltəneit) switch repeatedly from one to the other; take or arrange in turn. **alternately** *adv*. **alternation** *n*. **alternative** *n* the second of two possibilities or choices. *adj* offering a choice between two things.

although *conj* though; even though; in spite of the fact that.

altitude *n* height of an aircraft, mountain, etc., esp. that above sea level.

alto *n* **1** male singing voice or musical instrument with a range between tenor and treble. **2** contralto.

altogether *adv* **1** completely; totally; absolutely; all; utterly; entirely. **2** on the whole. **3** added together; in total.

aluminium *n* silvery metallic element extracted mainly from bauxite and widely used in lightweight alloys.

always *adv* all the time; without exception; regularly.

am *v* 1st person singular form of **be** in the present tense.

amalgamate *vi,vt* join together; merge; unite; combine. **amalgamation** *n*.

amass *vt,vi* bring or come together; accumulate; collect.

amateur *n* person who is an unpaid participator in an activity such as sport or the arts. *adj* **1** not professional. **2** *also* **amateurish** lacking in skill or polish; of a rather low standard.

amaze *vt* fill with surprise or wonder; astonish; astound. **amazement** *n*. **amazingly** *adv*.

ambassador *n* minister or diplomat sent abroad by the Government as an official representative.

amber *n* yellowish-brown fossil resin often used for jewellery. *adj* **1** of a yellowish-brown or dull orange colour. **2** made of amber.

ambidextrous *adj* able to use either hand with equal skill. **ambidexterity** *n*.

ambiguous *adj* having more than one possible meaning; open to interpretation. **ambiguity** *n*. **ambiguously** *adv*.

ambition *n* **1** desire or will to achieve fame, power, position, etc. **2** desired object or goal; aim. **ambitious** *adj*. **ambitiously** *adv*.

ambivalent (æm'bivələnt) *adj* having conflicting or uncertain feelings; undecided. **ambivalence** *n*. **ambivalently** *adv*.

amble *vi* **1** walk at an easy and leisurely pace; stroll; saunter. **2** (of a horse) move slowly lifting both legs on the same side of the body together. *n* leisurely pace.

ambulance *n* vehicle designed and equipped to convey sick or injured people to hospital.

ambush *n* **1** act of lying in wait in order to make a surprise attack. **2** such an attack, the concealed place from which such an attack is launched, or the attackers themselves. *vt* attack (an enemy) by ambush.

amen *interj* word meaning 'so be it' spoken or sung at the end of a prayer, hymn, etc.

amenable *adj* **1** willing; agreeable; responsive. **2** legally responsible; answerable. **3** capable of being tested or judged.

amend *vt* rectify; correct; modify. **make amends** make up (for); compensate. **amendment** *n*.

amenity *n often pl*. useful service or facility intended to make life easier or more comfortable.

amethyst *n* precious stone of crystallized quartz that is usually purple or mauve.

amiable *adj* pleasant; likeable; friendly. **amiability** *n*. **amiably** *adv*.

amicable *adj* friendly; not hostile. **amicably** *adv*.

amid *or* **amidst** *prep* among or amongst; in the midst of.

amiss *adj* faulty; defective; wrong. *adv* wrongly; incorrectly. **take amiss** feel wronged or hurt (by), often unjustifiably.

ammonia *n* colourless pungent gas, containing nitrogen and hydrogen, used in the manufacture of fertilizers and of other chemicals.

ammunition *n* **1** bullets, missiles, etc., that can be fired from a gun or other offensive weapon. **2** information or points of argument used against someone in debate, criticism, etc.

amnesty *n* general pardon given esp. to political prisoners.

amoeba *n* microscopic single-celled animal having a constantly changing shape.

among *or* **amongst** *prep* **1** in the middle of; surrounded by; in company with; together with. **2** between; shared by.

amoral (ei'mɔrəl) *adj* outside the sphere of morality. **amorality** *n*.

amorous *adj* concerned with or displaying love; affectionate. **amorously** *adv*. **amorousness** *n*.

amorphous *adj* having no distinct form, shape, or structure.

amount *n* **1** quantity; extent; whole. **2** sum; total. *v* **amount to 1** add up to; come to. **2** be equal or equivalent to; have the same function as.

ampere *n* unit used to measure electric current.

amphetamine *n* drug that stimulates the central nervous system, used for the relief of nasal congestion, hay fever, etc.

amphibian *n* **1** cold-blooded animal, such as the frog or newt, that usually lives on land as an adult but breeds in water. **2** vehicle able to function both on land and water. **amphibious** *adj*.

amphitheatre *n* large arena enclosed by rising tiers of seats.

ample *adj* **1** plenty; more than enough; sufficient. **2** of generous proportions; large. **amply** *adv*.

amplify *vt* increase the intensity of (an electrical signal). *vt,vi* explain in greater detail; expand (on). **amplification** *n*. **amplifier** *n* electrical device, used in radios, televisions, etc., for reproducing a signal at increased intensity.

amputate *vt,vi* sever (a limb or part of a limb) usually by surgery. **amputation** *n*.

amuse *vt* **1** entertain, esp. by speaking or acting in a humorous way. **2** keep pleasantly busy or occupied. **amusement** *n*.

an *indef art* used before an initial vowel sound and sometimes *h*. See **a**.

anachronism *n* **1** representation of an object, event, etc., in too early a historical period; chronological error. **2** something no longer useful or suitable in the present age. **anachronistic** *adj*.

anaemia *n* deficiency of red blood cells causing pale appearance of the skin, fatigue, etc. **anaemic** *adj*.

anaesthetic (ænis'θetik) *n* substance administered before an operation to produce loss of sensation or unconsciousness. **anaesthetist** *n* (ə'ni:sθətist) person trained to administer anaesthetics. **anaesthetize** *vt* (ə'ni:sθətaiz) administer anaesthetics to.

anagram *n* word or phrase whose letters can be transposed to form a new word or phrase.

anal ('einəl) *adj* relating to the anus.

analogy (ə'nælədʒi) *n* comparison that serves to draw attention to a similarity between things. **analogous** (ə'næləgəs) *adj*.

analyse ('ænəlaiz) *vt* break down (a substance, situation, etc.) into constituent parts or stages for examination. **analysis** *n, pl* **analyses** (ə'nælisi:z). **analytic** (ænə'litik) *or* **analytical** *adj*. **analyst** ('ænəlist) *n* **1** person who analyses. **2** psychoanalyst.

anarchy ('ænəki) *n* **1** form of society in which established forms of government and law are not recognized. **2** disorder; lawlessness. **anarchist** *n* supporter of anarchy.

anatomy (ə'nætəmi) *n* study or science of the physical structure of animals and plants. **anatomical** (ænə'tɔmikəl) *adj*. **anatomist** (ə'nætəmist) *n*.

ancestor ('ænsestə) *n* person from whom one is descended; forefather. **ancestral** (æn'sestrəl) *adj*. **ancestry** ('ænsəstri) *n*.

anchor *n* **1** heavy steel or iron object used for holding fast a vessel in the water. **2** something that offers security and stability. *vt,vi* hold fast with the anchor. **anchorage** *n* **1** place where a vessel may be anchored or the fee charged. **2** stability; firm or sound basis.

anchovy ('æntʃəvi) *n* small fish of the herring family with a strong salty flavour.

ancient *adj* **1** relating to a very early or remote historical period. **2** very old.

ancillary *adj* auxiliary; secondary; subsidiary.

and *conj* **1** as well as; in addition to. **2** then; after. **3** also; too.

anecdote ('ænikdout) *n* short witty account or story.

anemone (ə'neməni) *n* **1** woodland plant producing white, red, or deep blue flowers. **2** sea anemone.

anew *adv* afresh; again.

angel *n* **1** spiritual being in the Christian religion who is one of God's attendants and messengers, usually depicted as having human form with wings. **2** sweet kind-hearted person. **angelic** (æn'dʒelik) *adj*.

anger *n* feeling of intense annoyance or irritation; rage. *vt* make angry; enrage; infuriate.

angle[1] *n* **1** difference in direction between two intersecting lines or planes, measured in degrees. **2** shape formed by such lines or planes. **3** projecting corner. **4** point of view; aspect. *vt* **1** move or place at an angle; bend into an angle. **2** direct at a particular audience; bias.

angle[2] *vi* **1** fish with a rod, line, and bait. **2** *also* **angle for** seek (compliments, favours, etc.), esp. by devious means. **angler** *n*.

Anglican *adj* relating to the Church of England. *n* member of the Church of England. **Anglicanism** *n*.

angry *adj* **1** extremely cross or annoyed; enraged. **2** sore and inflamed. **angrily** *adv*.

anguish *n* intense anxiety and distress; agony; torment.

angular *adj* **1** having sharp corners or many angles. **2** bony; gaunt.

animal *n* living organism capable of spontaneous movement; creature. *adj* **1** relating to an animal or animals. **2** physical as opposed to spiritual; carnal.

animate *adj* ('ænimət) living; capable of spontaneous movement. *vt* ('ænimeit) give life or movement to; make active. **animation** *n*.

aniseed *n* seed yielding an aromatic oil with a strong liquorice flavour, used in medicines, drinks, etc.

ankle *n* joint that connects the foot and the leg.

annex *vt* (ə'neks) **1** take possession of by conquest. **2** join; attach; incorporate. *n* ('æneks) *also* **annexe** additional building usually set apart from the main block of a hotel, hospital, etc.

annihilate *vt* wipe out completely; destroy; obliterate. **annihilation** *n*.

anniversary *n* **1** date of a significant event which occurred in some previous year. **2** celebration of this.

announce *vt* declare; proclaim; make known. **announcement** *n*. **announcer** *n* person who introduces programmes, reads news bulletins, etc., on radio or television.

annoy *vt,vi* irritate; bother; vex. **annoyance** *n*.

annual *adj* **1** occurring once a year. **2** valid for one year. **3** lasting for one growing season. *n*

1 plant that lasts for one growing season only. 2 book or periodical published in a new edition each year. **annually** *adv*.

annuity (ə'nju:iti) *n* sum of money paid out in instalments at regular intervals.

annul (ə'nʌl) *vt* (-ll-) declare (a law, marriage contract, etc.) invalid or no longer binding; revoke.

anoint *vt* rub or smear with oil, esp. ritually as an act of consecration. **anointment** *n*.

anomaly (ə'nɔməli) *n* something that is out of place or deviates from the common rule. **anomalous** *adj*.

anonymous (ə'nɔniməs) *adj* **1** *sometimes shortened to* **anon** having no acknowledged author. **2** faceless; unknown. **anonymity** (ænə'nimiti) *n*.

anorak *n* waterproof jacket with a hood.

another *adj* **1** additional; further. **2** different; separate. *pron* **1** one more. **2** a different or new one. **3** a comparable or similar one.

answer *n* **1** reply or response (to a question). **2** solution (to a problem). *vt,vi* reply or respond (to); acknowledge. *vt* solve. **answer for** accept responsibility or blame for. **answer to** match or correspond to (a description). **answerable** *adj* responsible; liable; accountable.

ant *n* small insect that typically lives in a complex highly organized colony.

antagonize *vt* provoke; incite; arouse hostility by attacking. **antagonism** *n*. **antagonist** *n*. **antagonistic** *adj*.

antelope *n* deer-like animal with hollow horns such as the gazelle or springbok.

antenatal *adj* relating to the period of pregnancy; before birth.

antenna (æn'tenə) **1** *pl* **antennae** (æn'teni:) one of a pair of sensitive organs on the head of an insect, crustacean, etc.; feeler. **2** *pl* **antennas** radio aerial.

anthem *n* patriotic song; hymn of praise.

anthology *n* collection of poems, stories, articles, etc.

anthropology *n* study of mankind and man's social and cultural relationships. **anthropological** *adj*. **anthropologist** *n*.

anti-aircraft *adj* designed for defence against enemy aircraft.

antibiotic (æntibai'ɔtik) *n* chemical substance, such as penicillin, used to destroy certain bacteria. *adj* relating to an antibiotic.

antibody *n* protein in the blood that counteracts harmful bacteria.

anticipate *vt* **1** realize or recognize beforehand; predict; foresee. **2** expect; look forward to; await. **anticipation** *n*.

anticlimax *n* drop in mood from excitement to flatness, seriousness to absurdity, etc.

anticlockwise *adj,adv* moving in a direction opposite to that followed by the hands of a clock.

antics *pl n* playful jokes, tricks, or gestures.

anticyclone *n* area of high atmospheric pressure producing calm settled weather.

antidote ('æntidout) *n* substance or agent used to counteract harmful effects; remedy.

antifreeze *n* substance that lowers the freezing point of a liquid, used esp. in car radiators.

antique *n* valuable piece of furniture, work of art, etc., belonging to an earlier period. *adj* **1** old and valuable. **2** antiquated. **antiquated** *adj* obsolete; out-of-date; old-fashioned. **antiquity** (æn'tikwiti) *n* **1** quality of being very old. **2** period before the Middle Ages; distant past.

anti-Semitic (æntisə'mitik) *adj* discriminating against Jews. **anti-Semite** (ænti'semait) *n*. **anti-Semitism** (ænti'semitizəm) *n*.

antiseptic *adj* relating to the destruction of undesirable microorganisms; preventing decay. *n* an antiseptic substance.

antisocial *adj* **1** contrary to the norms of society. **2** unsociable; shunning the company of others.

antithesis (æn'tiθisis) *n, pl* **antitheses** (æn'tiθisi:z) direct contrast; opposite. **antithetical** (ænti'θetikəl) *adj*.

antler *n* branched bony outgrowth on the head of a male deer or similar animal.

anus *n* opening at the lower end of the rectum.

anvil *n* iron or steel block on which metal is hammered and shaped.

anxious *adj* **1** nervous; worried; uneasy; apprehensive; tense. **2** keen; eager. **anxiety** *n*. **anxiously** *adv*.

any *adj* **1** some; several. **2** whichever; no matter which. **3** one of many; every. **at any rate/in any case** anyway; moreover; besides; anyhow; however. ~*pron* **1** anybody; anything. **2** some. *adv* at all; to an extent. **anybody** *pron, n* a person; no matter who; anyone. **anyhow** *adv* **1** besides; anyway. **2** haphazardly; with no particular care or organization; not systematically. **anyone** *pron,n* anybody. **anything** *pron,n* a thing; no matter what or which; something. ~*adv* at all; remotely. **anyway** *adv* **1** in any case; well; besides; anyhow; after all. **2** carelessly; anyhow. **anywhere** *adv* **1** to or at any place. **2** at all; anything.

apart *adv* **1** separately; independently. **2** into parts or pieces. **3** at a distance; away. **apart from** after considering; aside from; other than.

apartheid (ə'pɑːtaid) *n* system of racial segregation, esp. in South Africa.

apartment *n* **1** *chiefly US* flat, usually in a block. **2** suite of rooms.

apathy *n* lack of sympathy, feeling, interest, etc.; listlessness; complete indifference. **apathetic** *adj*.

ape *n* short-tailed or tailless primate, such as the chimpanzee or gorilla.

aperture *n* **1** opening or slit. **2** diaphragm in a lens system that limits the diameter of a light beam entering a camera, etc. **3** diameter of such a diaphragm.

apex ('eipeks) *n, pl* **apexes** *or* **apices** ('æpisiːz) highest point; vertex; tip; pinnacle.

aphid ('eifid) *n* small insect that feeds on plant juices.

apiece *adv* each; for each one.

apology *n* **1** statement expressing regret for an offence, error, failure, etc. **2** poor substitute. **apologetic** *adj* sorry; making an apology. **apologetically** *adv*. **apologize** *vi* make an apology or excuse.

apostle (ə'pɔsəl) *n* one of Christ's twelve disciples.

apostrophe (ə'pɔstrəfi) *n* written or printed symbol (') used to show omission of a letter or letters, or to denote the possessive case.

appal *vt* (-ll-) fill with abhorrence; shock; horrify; disgust.

apparatus *n* equipment, machinery, tools, etc., required for a particular purpose.

apparent *adj* **1** seeming; ostensible. **2** evident; clear; obvious. **apparently** *adv*.

appeal *vi* **1** apply to a higher authority for the reversal of a decision. **2** plead; beseech; call (for). **3** appear attractive (to); please. *n* **1** application to a higher authority. **2** plea; request; entreaty. **3** attractiveness; ability to arouse interest. **appealing** *adj* attractive; arousing interest, sympathy, pity, etc.

appear *vi* **1** come into view; become visible. **2** arrive. **3** seem; give the impression (of). **4** become clear or obvious; emerge. **5** give a public performance. **6** become available. **7** present oneself in court, before a tribunal, etc. **appearance** *n* **1** coming into view. **2** arrival. **3** outward manifestation; impression; aspect; look. **4** public performance. **5** attendance in court. **keep up appearances** maintain an outward show of respectability, affluence, etc.

appease *vt* **1** pacify; soothe. **2** assuage; ease; allay; relieve. **appeasement** *n*.

appendix *n, pl* **appendixes** *or* **appendices** (ə'pendisiːz) **1** small blind functionless tube attached to the lower abdomen. **2** section containing supplementary information at the end of a book. **appendicitis** *n* inflammation of the appendix.

appetite *n* **1** desire to satisfy bodily needs, esp. for food. **2** craving; capacity. **appetizing** *adj* able to stimulate the appetite; tasty.

applaud *vi,vt* **1** show appreciation (of) by clapping. **2** commend; praise. **applause** *n*.

apple *n* edible round fruit with a red, green, or yellow skin.

apply *vt* **1** use in a practical or appropriate way; employ; put into practice. **2** cover with; put on. **3** concentrate; give attention to. *vi* **1** make a formal request (for a job, money, etc.). **2** be appropriate; have a bearing (on). **appliance** *n* piece of equipment; tool; machine; instrument. **applicable** *adj* relevant; appropriate; able to be applied. **applicant** *n* person applying for a job, place, etc.; candidate. **application** *n* **1** formal request; claim. **2** putting into practice (of relevant knowledge, skills, etc.). **3** act of applying (paint, ointment, etc.). **4** close attention; concentration.

appoint *vt* **1** select for a job, position, etc. **2** assign; allocate. **3** arrange for a particular time; fix. **appointment** *n* **1** fixed meeting; engagement. **2** selection or nomination for a job, position, etc. **3** job or position for which a person is selected.

apportion *vt* share out; allot; distribute. **apportionment** *n*.

appraise *vt* estimate the quality or value of; assess. **appraisal** *n*.

appreciate *vt* **1** be grateful for; recognize the worth of. **2** realize; understand; be aware of. *vi* increase in value. **appreciation** *n*. **appreciable** *adj* considerable; large enough to be assessed.

apprehend *vt* **1** arrest and take into custody. **2** be anxious about; fear; dread. *vt,vi* comprehend; grasp. **apprehension** *n* **1** anxiety; fear; caution; dread. **2** understanding; conception. **3** arrest. **apprehensive** *adj* worried; anxious; cautious; uneasy; doubtful.

apprentice *n* person under contract to an employer whilst learning a trade. *vt* engage or place as an apprentice.

approach *vt,vi* draw close or closer (to); near; advance. *vt* **1** make contact with in order to obtain advice, a favour, etc. **2** begin to tackle; start working on; deal with. **3** approximate; come close to being. *n* **1** act of drawing near; advance. **2** initial contact; overture. **3** method of working, acting, thinking, etc. **4** approximation. **5** way in or to; access. **approachable** *adj* **1** accessible; able to be contacted. **2** friendly; easy to get on with.

appropriate *adj* (ə'proupriət) suitable for a particular purpose or set of circumstances; relevant; apt. *vt* (ə'prouprieit) **1** take possession of; take for one's own use. **2** set aside; allocate. **appropriately** *adv*. **appropriation** *n*.

approve *vt* give consent for; sanction. **approve of** have a favourable opinion of; believe to be good or right. **approval** *n* **1** consent; permission. **2** favourable opinion. **on approval** on free trial before deciding whether or not to buy.

approximate *adj* (ə'prɔksimət) roughly calculated; estimated; about right. *vt,vi* (ə'prɔksimeit) come close to what is required or expected; be roughly right. **approximately** *adv*.

apricot *n* small fleshy fruit that is similar to the peach, with a soft reddish-orange skin.

April *n* fourth month of the year.

apron *n* **1** loose covering worn over the front of the body to protect one's clothes and tied round the waist. **2** part of a stage that projects in front of the curtain.

apse *n* semicircular domed recess situated at the east end of a church.

apt *adj* **1** fitting; appropriate; to the point. **2** likely; inclined; liable. **3** quick to learn; clever. **aptly** *adv*. **aptitude** *n* talent, skill, or ability; flair.

aquarium *n, pl* **aquariums** *or* **aquaria** (ə'kwɛəriə) tank or pool for fish and aquatic plants.

Aquarius (ə'kwɛəriəs) *n* eleventh sign of the zodiac represented by the water carrier.

aquatic *adj* relating to or living in water.

aqueduct *n* channel constructed to direct a flow of water, esp. one built as a bridge.

arable *adj* (of land) able to be ploughed in order to produce crops.

arbitrary *adj* **1** not fixed by law; discretionary. **2** impulsive; capricious. **arbitrarily** *adv*.

arbitrate *vt,vi* settle (a dispute); mediate (between). **arbiter** *or* **arbitrator** *n*. **arbitration** *n*.

arc *n* **1** curved segment of a circle. **2** something shaped like an arc, such as a rainbow. **3** luminous electrical discharge between two electrodes. *vi* form an arc.

arcade *n* **1** series of arches and columns. **2** covered passageway or gallery, esp. one lined with shops.

arch^1 *n* **1** curved structure built to bear a load over an opening. **2** *also* **archway** opening, passageway, gateway, etc., with an arch. **3** curve; bow. **4** part of the sole of the foot between the ball and heel. *vt,vi* **1** span with an arch; curve over. **2** produce or form into a curve or bow.

arch^2 *adj* **1** chief; principal. **2** mischievous; cunning.

archaeology (ɑːki'ɔlədʒi) *n* scientific study of ancient remains and artefacts. **archaeological** (ɑːkiə'lɔdʒikəl) *adj*. **archaeologist** (ɑːki'ɔlədʒist) *n*.

archaic (ɑː'keiik) *adj* no longer in current use; out-of-date; old; belonging to the past.

archbishop *n* bishop having jurisdiction over an ecclesiastical province.

archduke *n* prince of the imperial dynasty of Austria. **archduchess** *n* **1** wife or widow of an archduke. **2** princess of the imperial dynasty of Austria. **archduchy** (ɑːtʃ'dʌtʃi) *n* territory ruled by an archduke or archduchess.

archery *n* art of shooting with a bow and arrows. **archer** *n*.

archetype ('ɑːkitaip) *n* **1** prototype. **2** ideal or completely typical example or model; standard type. **archetypal** *or* **archetypical** (ɑːki'tipikəl) *adj*.

archipelago (ɑːki'peləgou) *n* chain or scattered group of islands.

architecture *n* **1** art of designing buildings and other constructions. **2** style of building or design. **3** buildings taken collectively.

architect *n* **1** person trained in architecture. **2** planner; organizer; mastermind.

archives ('ɑːkaivz) *pl n* **1** collection of historical records and documents. **2** place where such a collection is kept. **archivist** ('ɑːkivist) *n* person in charge of archives.

arctic *adj* **1** relating to regions surrounding the earth's North Pole. **2** extremely cold.

ardent *adj* fervent; zealous; vigorously enthusiastic; earnest; passionate. **ardently** *adv.* **ardour** *n.*

arduous *adj* hard and laborious; extremely difficult; exhausting; requiring great effort. **arduously** *adv.*

are *v* plural form of **be** in the present tense.

area *n* **1** extent of a specific surface, piece of ground, geometric figure, etc. **2** open space; region; locality. **3** section or part. **4** range or scope of something.

arena *n* **1** central area for performers in an amphitheatre, stadium, etc. **2** scene of activity.

argue *vi* quarrel; attack verbally. *vi,vt* debate; have a heated discussion (about); present (a case) for or against; reason. **argument** *n.* **argumentative** *adj* quarrelsome; inclined to argue.

arid *adj* **1** extremely dry and infertile; parched. **2** dull; not stimulating. **aridity** *n.*

Aries ('ɛəriːz) *n* first sign of the zodiac represented by the ram.

arise *vi* (arose; arisen) **1** rise; get up; stand up. **2** come about; occur; happen; start.

aristocracy *n* **1** class of privileged people of the highest rank; nobility. **2** government by such a class. **aristocrat** *n.* **aristocratic** *adj.*

arithmetic *n* (ə'riθmətik) **1** manipulation of numbers by addition, subtraction, multiplication, and division. **2** mathematical calculations. *adj* (æriθ'metik) *also* **arithmetical** relating to arithmetic.

arm[1] *n* **1** upper limb extending from the shoulder to the wrist. **2** sleeve. **3** support for the arm on a chair or seat. **4** anything resembling an arm in appearance or function. **armchair** *n* easy chair with supports for the arms. **armhole** *n* opening in a garment for the arm to pass through. **armpit** *n* hollow under the arm where it joins the shoulder.

arm[2] *vt,vi* **1** equip (with weapons and ammunition). **2** prepare (for a confrontation, discussion, etc.). **arms** *pl n* weapons; firearms.

armament *n* **1** equipment for fighting; weaponry. **2** armed force. **3** preparation for a war or battle.

armour *n* **1** protective covering of metal formerly worn in battle. **2** hard protective shell or covering of certain animals. **armour-plated** *adj also* **armoured** fitted with a protective covering of steel against bullets, shells, torpedoes, etc.

army *n* **1** organized military force. **2** horde; large organized group.

aroma *n* distinctive smell given off by food, wine, perfume, etc. **aromatic** *adj.*

arose *v pt* of **arise.**

around *prep* **1** round the outside of; surrounding; enclosing. **2** from place to place within; about; at various points on. **3** round rather than straight across. **4** at approximately; about. *adv* **1** on all sides; in a circle. **2** somewhere near; in the vicinity; about. **3** round; with a circular movement. **get around** travel widely; circulate.

arouse *vt* stimulate; provoke interest, anger, etc., in; awake. *vt,vi* rouse; wake. **arousal** *n.*

arrange *vt* **1** put into some kind of order or pattern; form. **2** fix; make plans for. **3** come to agreement about; settle on. **4** adapt (music) for a different instrument. **arrangement** *n.* **arranger** *n.*

array *n* **1** arranged selection or display; assortment. **2** dress; clothing. *vt* **1** dress lavishly; adorn. **2** arrange in order; set out.

arrears *pl n* outstanding payments; accumulated debts. **in arrears** behind in one's payments.

arrest *vt* **1** seize and detain by lawful authority; apprehend. **2** hinder; check; stop. *n* **1** act of arresting or state of being arrested. **2** hindrance; check; stoppage. **under arrest** held in detention. **arresting** *adj* attracting attention.

arrive *vi* **1** reach a destination. **2** happen; occur. **3** *inf* achieve success. **arrive at** reach. **arrival** *n.*

arrogant *adj* proud; haughty; conceited. **arrogance** *n.* **arrogantly** *adv.*

arrow *n* **1** slender pointed missile shot from a bow. **2** symbol used to indicate direction, etc.

arsenic *n* poisonous brittle grey metallic element.

arson *n* crime of maliciously setting fire to property.

art *n* **1** process of creative activity, esp. painting and drawing. **2** works resulting from such a process. **3** creative or practical skill. **arts** *n pl or s* university course(s) such as modern languages, literature, history, and philosophy.

artefact *n also* **artifact** man-made object.

artery *n* **1** thick-walled tubular vessel that conveys oxygenated blood from the heart. **2** major road, railway, or other channel of communication. **arterial** *adj*.

artful *adj* cunning; crafty; ingenious. **artfully** *adv*.

arthritis *n* painful inflammation of a joint or joints. **arthritic** *adj*.

artichoke *n* **1** *also* **globe artichoke** thistle-like plant with large edible fleshy flower heads. **2** *also* **Jerusalem artichoke** sunflower with an edible tuber.

article *n* **1** small object; item. **2** newspaper or magazine report. **3** clause or section in a document. **4** the words *a* or *an (indefinite articles)* or *the (definite article)* preceding a noun or noun phrase. **articled** *adj* bound by written contract; apprenticed.

articulate *v* (ɑːˈtikjuleit) *vt,vi* speak clearly. *vt* express precisely or coherently. *adj* (ɑːˈtikjulit) **1** fluent; coherent. **2** able to speak. **articulated** *adj* having two or more jointed or pivoted sections. **articulation** *n*.

artifact *n* artefact.

artificial *adj* **1** man-made; synthetic. **2** feigned; not spontaneous. **artificial respiration** *n* method for restoring natural breathing. **artificially** *adv*.

artillery *n* **1** large-calibre guns; cannon. **2** troops or military units trained in their use.

artist *n* **1** creative person, esp. a painter or sculptor. **2** skilful practitioner of a craft, etc. **3** professional performer. **artistic** *adj* **1** creative; skilled. **2** beautiful; aesthetically pleasing. **3** relating to art. **artistically** *adv*.

as *conj* **1** when; just at the time that. **2** in the manner that; like. **3** that which; what; whatever. **4** because; since. *prep,conj* to the extent (that); of the same amount (that). *prep* in the role or capacity of.

asbestos *n* any of several incombustible fibrous minerals used for thermal insulation and in flameproof and building materials.

ascend *vt,vi* climb; mount; rise. **ascent** *or* **ascension** *n*. **the Ascension** ascent of Christ into heaven.

ascertain *vt* determine by inquiry; discover; find out.

ascribe *vt* attribute (a work of art, blame, etc.); assign.

ash[1] *n* widespread deciduous tree with compound leaves, winged seeds, and a durable wood used as timber.

ash[2] *n* **1** grey powdery residue of something that has been burnt. **2** fine material thrown from an erupting volcano. **ashes 1** human remains after cremation. **2** ruins. **ashen** *adj* pallid. **ashtray** *n* receptacle for cigarette ends, ash, etc.

ashamed *adj* **1** full of shame (for); remorseful. **2** reluctant or refusing (to).

ashore *adv,adj* towards or on land.

aside *adv* **1** on or to one side. **2** into a secluded place. **3** out of one's thoughts, consideration, etc. **4** in reserve. **aside from** apart from. ~*n* confidential or seemingly confidential statement.

ask *vt,vi* **1** put a question to (concerning). **2** make a request for. *vt* **1** enquire about. **2** invite. **ask after** request news of. **ask for trouble/it** behave provocatively.

askew *adv* at an angle; awry. *adj* crooked.

asleep *adj* sleeping. **fall asleep** pass into a state of sleep.

asparagus *n* young edible shoots of a plant of the lily family.

aspect *n* **1** direction towards which something faces; outlook. **2** appearance. **3** point of view; angle.

asphalt *n* dark naturally occurring material used in road surfacing and roofing materials. *vt* cover with asphalt.

aspire *vi* have ambitious plans, desires, etc.; yearn for. **aspiration** *n*.

aspirin *n* mild pain-relieving drug, usually taken in tablet form.

ass *n* **1** donkey. **2** fool; stupid person.

assail *vt* attack; assault. **assailant** *n,adj*.

assassinate *vt* murder (a public figure), esp. for political reasons. **assassin** *n* murderer; hired killer. **assassination** *n*.

assault *n* **1** violent or sudden attack. **2** *law* threat of attack. *vt* **1** make an assault on. **2** rape.

assemble *vt,vi* **1** come or bring together; collect. **2** fit together; construct. **assembly** *n*.

assent *n* **1** agreement; acceptance. **2** consent. *vi* agree to; accept.

assert *vt* **1** declare as true. **2** insist upon; maintain. **assert oneself** act authoritatively or boldly. **assertion** *n*. **assertive** *adj*.

assess *vt* **1** determine the value or amount of; evaluate. **2** judge the worth or importance of. **assessment** *n*.

asset *n* possession, quality, etc., that is useful or of value. **assets** *pl n* capital; property.

assign *vt* **1** allot; give to; set apart for; fix. **2** nominate; select for; appoint to. **assignation** *n* arrangement to meet secretly or illicitly; tryst. **assignment** *n*.

assimilate *vt,vi* **1** absorb or become absorbed; incorporate. **2** adjust or become adjusted. *vt* digest (food). **assimilation** *n*.

assist *vt,vi* help; give support (to); work in a subordinate capacity (for). **assistance** *n*. **assistant** *n*.

associate *v* (ə'sousieit) **associate with** *vt* link or connect (with). *vi* keep company (with). *n* (ə'sousiit, -eit) **1** partner; colleague. **2** acquaintance; companion. *adj* (ə'sousiit) **1** having equal or nearly equal status with others. **2** having only partial rights. **association** *n* **1** connection. **2** organized group; society.

assorted *adj* **1** of various kinds; miscellaneous. **2** classified; sorted. **ill-assorted** badly matched. **assortment** *n*.

assuage *vt* make less severe; ease; lessen.

assume *vt* **1** take for granted; accept; suppose. **2** undertake; take on. **3** adopt; feign; affect. **assumed** *adj* **1** false; fictitious. **2** taken for granted. **assumption** *n*.

assure *vt* **1** make certain; ensure. **2** inform confidently; promise; guarantee. **assurance** *n* **1** promise; guarantee. **2** certainty. **3** self-confidence. **4** life or endowment insurance. **assuredly** *adv* definitely.

asterisk *n* symbol (*) used in print to indicate an omission, cross reference, etc. *vt* mark with an asterisk.

asthma ('æsmə) *n* disorder, often allergic, causing difficulty in breathing, wheezing, etc. **asthmatic** *adj,n*.

astonish *vt* fill with surprise or wonder; amaze; astound. **astonishment** *n*.

astound *vt* surprise greatly; astonish.

astray *adv,adj* away from what is right or expected.

astride *adv,adj,prep* with a leg on each side (of).

astrology *n* prediction of human characteristics, activities, etc., based on the motion and relative positions of celestial bodies. **astrological** *adj*. **astrologer** *n*.

astronaut *n* person trained and adapted to space travel. **astronautical** *adj*. **astronautics** *n*.

astronomy *n* study of the universe and the celestial bodies contained in it. **astronomer** *n*. **astronomical** *or* **astronomic** *adj* **1** relating to astronomy or the celestial bodies. **2** huge; immense.

astute *adj* cunning; sly; clever; perceptive; quick. **astutely** *adv*. **astuteness** *n*.

asunder *adv,adj* apart; in(to) pieces.

asylum *n* **1** temporary refuge; place of shelter; sanctuary. **2** mental hospital.

at *prep* **1** in; close to; next to. **2** towards; in the direction of. **3** towards or around a specified time. **4** in a state of; engaged in. **5** during. **6** in exchange for; for the price of. **7** about; concerning.

ate *v pt* of **eat.**

atheism *n* disbelief in the existence of God. **atheist** *n*.

athlete *n* person skilled in running, hurdling, shot putting, or other track and field sports. **athletics** *n* track and field sports. **athletic** *adj*.

atlas *n* book containing maps.

atmosphere *n* **1** gaseous layer surrounding the earth or other celestial body. **2** air in an enclosed space. **3** gaseous medium. **4** prevailing mood; feeling. **5** unit of pressure. **atmospheric** *adj*.

atom *n* **1** minute entity of which chemical elements are composed, consisting of a central nucleus around which electrons orbit. **2** very small amount. **atom bomb** *n also* **atomic bomb** bomb in which energy is derived from nuclear fission. **atomic** *adj*. **atomic energy** *n* energy derived from nuclear fission or fusion. **atomize** *vt* reduce (a liquid, such as perfume) to a fine spray by forcing it through a nozzle. **atomizer** *n*.

atone *vi* make amends (for a sin, error, etc.); expiate. **atonement** *n*.

atrocious *adj* **1** extremely cruel; wicked; appalling; horrifying. **2** *inf* of very poor quality. **atrociously** *adv*. **atrocity** *n* cruel and appalling act or behaviour.

attach *vt,vi* join; connect; fasten. *vi* **1** attribute;

ascribe. **2** adhere; be inherent in. **attached to 1** fond of; devoted to. **2** assigned or brought in as a specialist. **attachment** *n*.

attaché *n* member of staff of an embassy or legation. **attaché case** *n* small rectangular case for carrying documents, etc.

attack *vt* **1** make a physical or verbal assault on, assail; set upon. **2** seize upon; take up with vigour. **3** act or play offensively. **4** affect adversely. *n* **1** physical or verbal assault. **2** offensive action. **3** bout of illness.

attain *vt,vi* succeed in reaching; achieve; obtain; get. **attainable** *adj*. **attainment** *n*.

attempt *vt* try (to do or accomplish something); endeavour. *n* **1** effort, often unsuccessful. **2** attack.

attend *vt,vi* be present (at); go regularly (to). *vi* pay attention (to); listen (to). **attend to 1** deal with; handle; manage. **2** look after; tend; minister. **attendance** *n* **1** act of attending; presence. **2** number of persons present. **attendant** *n* person employed to assist, guide, look after, etc. *adj* associated or accompanying. **attention** *n* **1** concentrated thought. **2** observation; notice. **call** *or* **bring attention to** point out. **pay attention to 1** take notice of; attend. **2** take care of. **stand to attention.** adopt a formal alert stance, esp. on military occasions. **attentive** *adj* **1** listening carefully; observant. **2** thoughtful; polite.

attic *n* room just below the roof; garret.

attitude *n* **1** opinion; judgement; policy; disposition. **2** position of the body; pose. **strike an attitude** assume a theatrical pose.

attorney *n* **1** person with legal authority to act for another. **2** *US* lawyer.

attract *vt* **1** excite pleasure, anticipation, etc., in; fascinate. **2** cause to approach; draw towards. **attraction** *n*. **attractive** *adj* **1** pleasing to look at; alluring; appealing. **2** interesting; pleasing.

attribute *vt* (ə'tribju:t) **attribute to** consider as produced by, resulting from, or belonging to; ascribe to. *n* ('ætribju:t) property; quality; feature. **attribution** *n*.

atypical (ei'tipikəl) *adj* not typical; unrepresentative.

aubergine *n* tropical plant with a deep purple egg-shaped fruit, eaten as a vegetable.

auburn *n,adj* reddish-brown.

auction *n* public sale in which items are sold to the highest bidder. *vt* sell by auction. **auctioneer** *n* person conducting an auction.

audacious *adj* **1** fearlessly bold. **2** impudent; forward.

audible *adj* able to be heard. **audibly** *adv*.

audience 1 group of spectators, listeners, etc. **2** formal hearing or interview granted by someone in authority.

audiovisual *adj* involving both hearing and sight.

audit *n* professional examination of business accounts. *vt,vi* examine by or perform audit(s). **auditor** *n*.

audition *n* trial in which an actor, singer, musician, etc., demonstrates his ability or his aptitude for a role. *vt,vi* give a trial hearing (to).

auditorium *n, pl* **auditoriums** *or* **auditoria** part of a theatre, hall, etc., where the audience is seated.

augment *vt,vi* increase; enlarge; extend. **augmentation** *n*.

August *n* eighth month of the year.

aunt *n* **1** sister of one's mother or father. **2** wife of one's uncle.

au pair *n* foreign girl who undertakes housework, etc., in return for board and lodging. *adv* as an au pair.

aura *n* **1** distinctive air or quality of a person or thing; charisma. **2** apparent emanation surrounding an object, etc.

aural *adj* relating to hearing.

austere *adj* severe; strict; harsh; not luxurious. **austerely** *adv*. **austerity** *n*.

authentic *adj* genuine; real; not faked; from a reliable source. **authentically** *adv*. **authenticity** *n*.

author *n* **1** writer of a book, script, article, etc. **2** originator; creator. **authorship** *n*.

authoritative *adj* possessing, exercising, or claiming authority. **authoritatively** *adv*. **authorize** *vt* empower; sanction; give permission for. **authorization** *n*.

authority *n* **1** power or right to command and enforce obedience. **2** official body or group having such power. **3** position commanding such power. **4** delegated power. **5** acknowledged expert or trustworthy written work. **6** power or influence. **authoritarian** *adj* favouring the enforcement of obedience; opposed to individual freedom; nondemocratic. *n* an authoritarian person.

autistic *adj* living in a fantasy world; abnormally introspective. **autism** *n*.

autobiography *n* person's biography written by that person; personal biography. **autobiographical** *adj*.

autograph *n* handwritten signature. *vt* write an autograph in; sign.

automatic *adj* **1** operated or regulated by mechanical means; self-acting. **2** performed or produced without conscious thought or effort. **3** inevitable. *n* self-loading weapon firing continuously on depression of the trigger. **automatically** *adv*. **automation** *n* automatic operation of industrial processes or equipment.

autonomous *adj* self-governing; self-sufficient; independent. **autonomously** *adv*. **autonomy** *n*.

autumn *n* season between summer and winter.

auxiliary *adj* additional; supporting; extra; ancillary. *n* helper; assistant. **auxiliary verb** verb used to express tense, mood, etc., of another verb.

avail *n* **to** *or* **with no avail** in vain; without success. *v* **avail oneself of** make use of; help oneself to.

available *adj* obtainable; ready for use; accessible. **availability** *n*.

avalanche *n* **1** heavy fall of snow and ice down a mountainside. **2** large pile or heap that has accumulated suddenly and rapidly.

avenge *vt,vi* seek vengeance (for); punish in retaliation.

avenue *n* **1** wide road or drive, esp. one lined with trees. **2** means of achieving; way; opening.

average *n* **1** sum of a set of numbers or quantities divided by their total number; mean value. **2** representative or typical amount, value, etc. **on average** typically; usually. ~*adj* **1** typical; representative; usual. **2** constituting or worked out as an average. *vt* **1** perform or receive an amount calculated as an average. **2** calculate an average. *vi* amount to an average.

averse *adj* disinclined; unwilling; against. **aversion** *n* strong dislike; repulsion.

aviary *n* enclosure or large cage for birds.

aviation *n* art or science of flying aircraft. **aviator** *n* airman; pilot.

avid *adj* eager; enthusiastically dedicated or keen. **avidity** *n*. **avidly** *adv*.

avocado (ævəˈkɑːdou) *n also* **avocado pear** fleshy pear-shaped tropical fruit with a dark green or purple skin.

avoid *vt* keep away from or out of; evade; refrain from. **avoidable** *adj*. **avoidance** *n*.

avow *vt* declare; claim; admit openly. **avowal** *n*.

await *vt* **1** wait for; expect. **2** be ready or in store for.

awake *v* (awoke *or* awaked; awaked) *vt,vi* wake; wake up; rouse. *vt* arouse; stir; stimulate.

awaken *vt,vi* awake.

award *vt* give as a prize; grant. *n* prize; grant.

aware *adj* conscious (of); having knowledge; well-informed. **awareness** *n*.

away *adv* **1** to or at a place further off. **2** apart; at a distance; separately. **3** out of one's possession. **4** without hesitation; immediately. **5** until there is nothing left. **do away with 1** abolish; get rid of. **2** murder; kill. **get away with** do without being noticed or caught. ~*adj* absent; not at home.

awe *n* feeling of absolute wonder, fear, reverence, etc. *vt* fill with awe; dumbfound. **awe-inspiring** *adj* overwhelming; magnificent; tremendous. **awesome** *adj* capable of producing awe. **awe-struck** *adj also* **awe-stricken** filled with awe.

awful *adj* terrible; dreadful; very bad. **awfully** *adv inf* very; extremely.

awhile *adv* briefly; for a while.

awkward *adj* **1** clumsy, ungainly. **2** difficult to deal with; tricky; inconvenient. **awkwardly** *adv*. **awkwardness** *n*.

awl *n* small tool used for boring holes in leather, wood, etc.

awning *n* sheet of canvas attached to a frame to provide cover and protection from the weather.

awoke *v pt* of **awake.**

awry (əˈraɪ) *adj* **1** crooked; askew. **2** wrong; amiss.

axe *n* chopping tool with a long handle and a broad blade. **have an axe to grind** act from selfish motives or a vested interest. ~*vt* **1** chop or fell with an axe. **2** cut back or reduce drastically.

axis *n, pl* **axes** (ˈæksiːz) **1** line about which something rotates or is symmetrical. **2** reference line on a graph by which a point is located. **3** main central stem of a plant.

axle *n* rod or shaft that allows an attached wheel to revolve.

azalea *n* flowering shrub related to the rhododendron.

B

babble *vi,vt* **1** speak incoherently and continuously; chatter. **2** burble; murmur. *n* **1** fast incoherent speech. **2** burbling sound; murmur.

babe *n* baby.

baboon *n* large monkey.

baby *n* **1** newborn child; infant. **2** newborn animal. *vt* treat as a baby; lavish care on. **babyish** *adj*. **baby-sit** *vi* (-tt-) look after a baby for a short time while the parents are out. **baby-sitter** *n*.

bachelor *n* **1** unmarried man. **2** person who holds a first degree from a university or college.

bacillus *n* any of various rod-shaped bacteria.

back *n* **1** that part of the body extending from the base of the neck to the buttocks. **2** corresponding part of an animal. **3** spine; backbone. **4** side or part that is opposite the front; reverse. **5** place furthest away from the front; rear. **6** part of a garment that covers the back. **7** defence player in football, hockey, etc. **behind one's back** without one's knowledge; deceitfully. **get/put one's back up** antagonize; provoke; anger. ~*vt* **1** bet on to win. **2** support; sponsor. **3** provide a musical accompaniment for. *vt,vi* move backwards; reverse. **back down** withdraw a claim, challenge, etc.; admit fault. **back onto** have the back or rear bordering on. **back out** withdraw one's support. **back up** support; encourage; confirm. ~*adv* **1** backwards; towards the rear. **2** in or into the past. **3** to a previous or earlier place, state, condition, owner, etc. **4** in reply; in return. **back to front** with the back and front reversed. **go back on** break (a promise). **take back** revoke; cancel. ~*adj* **1** situated behind. **2** from the past; overdue; not current.

backbencher *n* British member of Parliament without a ministerial position.

backbone *n* **1** spine. **2** stamina; courage; spirit.

backdate *vt* make effective from an earlier date.

backfire *vi* **1** produce an explosion of fuel mixture in an internal-combustion engine. **2** have unintended and unfortunate consequences.

backgammon *n* board game for two players, each using fifteen pieces, which are moved according to the throws of two dice.

background *n* **1** place, setting, scene etc., at the back or in the distance. **2** person's class, education, experience, etc. **3** context through which historical, political, or social events may be understood.

backhand *n* stroke in tennis made with the back of the hand facing the direction of the shot. **backhanded** *adj* **1** relating to a backhand. **2** with underlying sarcasm.

backing *n* **1** sponsorship; support. **2** musical accompaniment.

backlash *n* **1** recoil occurring when machinery parts are badly worn or faulty. **2** hostile reaction; repercussions.

backlog *n* accumulated work, arrears, etc., requiring attention.

backside *n inf* buttocks; bottom.

backstage *adv* **1** behind the stage, esp. in the wings, dressing-rooms, etc. **2** at the back of the stage. *adj* taking place behind or at the back of the stage.

backstroke *n* type of stroke made when swimming on one's back.

backward *adj* **1** slow to learn or progress; underdeveloped. **2** directed towards the back or rear. **3** towards or fixed in the past. **4** bashful; shy. *adv* backwards. **backwardness** *n*.

backwards *adv* **1** towards the back or rear. **2** in reverse. **3** into the past. **4** back to a poorer state or condition. **know backwards** know thoroughly.

backwater *n* **1** stretch of water cut off from the main stream. **2** isolated place unaffected by changes occurring elsewhere.

bacon *n* cured meat from the back or sides of a pig.

bacteria *pl n* group of microscopic vegetable organisms causing putrefaction, fermentation, disease, etc. **bacterial** *adj*.

bad[1] *adj* **1** not good; below standard; poorer than average. **2** disobedient; naughty. **3** harmful; injurious. **4** sinful; wicked. **5** sick; unwell. **6** not fresh; rotten. **7** distressing; upsetting. **8** unpleasant; distasteful. **badly** *adv* **1** unsatisfactorily; poorly. **2** very much; urgently; seriously. **bad-tempered** *adj* cross; irritable.

bad^2 *v* a *pt* of **bid.**

bade (beid, bæd) *v* a *pt* of **bid.**

badge *n* **1** emblem worn or displayed to indicate rank, membership, etc. **2** distinguishing mark or characteristic.

badger *n* nocturnal burrowing animal with a black and white striped head. *vt* pester.

badminton *n* game similar to tennis played with lightweight rackets and a shuttlecock.

baffle *vt* perplex; bewilder; stump; mystify.

bag *n* **1** container of leather, paper, etc., used for carrying things in. **2** loose or sagging fold of skin. *v* (-gg-) *vt* **1** put into a bag. **2** *inf* claim; seize first. *vi* hang loosely; sag; bulge. **baggage** *n* luggage. **baggy** *adj* hanging loosely; not tight. **bagginess** *n*. **bagpipes** *pl n* musical instrument consisting of a set of reed pipes and a wind-bag. **bagpiper** *n*.

bail^1 *n* **1** sum of money that is pledged to secure the release of a person from custody on condition that he appears in court on a specified date. **2** procedure allowing such a sum of money to be pledged. *vt* **bail out** rescue (a person, company, etc.) esp by giving financial assistance.

bail^2 *n* small wooden bar placed across the stumps of a wicket.

bail^3 *vt,vi also* **bail out** remove (water) from the bottom of a boat with a bucket or can.

bailiff *n* **1** official employed by a sheriff to serve writs, collect fines, summon juries, etc. **2** landowner's agent.

bait *n* **1** things such as worms, maggots, etc., used by an angler to lure and catch fish. **2** food or other enticement used to lure animals into a trap. **3** enticement; temptation. *vt* **1** prepare (a line or trap) with bait. **2** lure; entice. **3** taunt; persecute.

bake *vi,vt* cook (bread, cakes, etc.) in an oven. **baker** *n* person who bakes or sells bread, cakes, etc. **bakery** *n* **1** room where bread, cakes, etc., are baked. **2** baker's shop.

balance *n* **1** apparatus for weighing consisting of two pans suspended from either end of a horizontal bar, which has a central pivot. **2** equilibrium. **3** emotional or mental stability; rationality. **4** compatibility; equality of distribution; harmony. **5** equality between credit and debit totals. **6** remainder; amount left over. **in the balance** not yet decided. ~*vt* **1** weigh on a balance. **2** keep or put in a state of balance. **3** calculate the totals of. *vi* have equal totals. *vt,vi* place in or achieve equilibrium. **balance sheet** *n* statement of accounts showing a company's financial position for a given period.

balcony *n* **1** enclosed platform built on to the outside of a wall of a building usually with access from within. **2** gallery of seats above the circle in a theatre.

bald *adj* **1** having no hair, esp. on the head. **2** threadbare; badly worn. **3** bare; having no vegetation. **4** plainly expressed; blunt. **baldly** *adv*. **baldness** *n*.

bale^1 *n* large bundle or package. *vt* pack into a bale.

bale^2 *vi* **bale out** make an emergency parachute jump.

ball^1 *n* **1** spherical object used in games such as football, golf, or tennis. **2** any spherical object. **3** rounded fleshy part of the thumb, sole of the foot, etc. **balls** *pl n sl* testicles. **on the ball** aware; quick to react.

ball^2 *n* grand social event with music and dancing, refreshments, etc. **have a ball** enjoy oneself enormously. **ballroom** *n* hall or large room used for dancing.

ballad *n* narrative poem that is usually set to music.

ballast *n* **1** any heavy material used to stabilize a ship, balloon, etc. **2** mixture of gravel and sand used in building.

ballerina *n* female ballet dancer.

ballet *n* **1** theatrical dance form requiring a conventional and highly developed technique. **2** performance in which a story is told through dance and mime. **3** music written for such a performance. **4** company of dancers.

ballistics *n* study of the motion of projectiles. **ballistic** *adj* relating to projectiles or ballistics.

balloon *n* **1** inflatable coloured rubber bag used as a toy or for decoration. **2** large impermeable bag filled with gas lighter than air that enables it to rise in the air, often having a basket for passengers, scientific instruments, etc. *vi* fly in a balloon. *vt,vi* inflate or swell.

ballot *n* **1** system of voting using tickets, cards, slips, etc. **2** tickets or cards used in voting. **3** number of votes cast. *vt,vi* vote or put to the vote by ballot.

bamboo *n* tropical treelike grass with hard hollow stems, which are often used for making furniture.

ban *vt* (-nn-) prohibit; declare to be illegal;

forbid. *n* order or rule prohibiting certain goods, behaviour, etc.

banal (bəˈnɑːl) *adj* commonplace; trite; mundane.

banana *n* tropical fruit that is long or crescent shaped with a thick yellow skin.

band[1] *n* **1** small group of people. **2** group of musicians, esp. one playing woodwind, brass, and percussion instruments for dancing or marching. *v* **band together** form into a united group.

band[2] *n* **1** flat strip of cloth, rubber, metal, etc., used as a fastening or for decoration. **2** coloured stripe. **3** waveband.

bandage *n* strip of cloth used to keep a dressing in place over a wound, support a sprain, etc. *vt* cover with a bandage.

bandit *n* outlawed robber.

bandy *adj* bow-legged. *vt* **1** exchange (words, blows, etc.). **2** throw or pass to and fro.

bang *n* **1** loud noise as of an explosion; report. **2** knocking noise. **3** slam. **4** sharp hit or blow. *vt,vi* **1** make a loud explosive sound. **2** knock loudly; rap. **3** slam. **4** hit; strike. **banger** *sl* **1** sausage. **2** old car. **3** firework that explodes with a bang.

bangle *n* ornamental band worn as a bracelet.

banish *vt* **1** exile; expel. **2** dispel. **banishment** *n*.

banister *n* support rail on a staircase.

banjo *n* long-necked instrument of the guitar family with a circular body.

bank[1] *n* **1** slope; embankment. **2** large mound or pile. *vt also* **bank up** form into a mound; heap up.

bank[2] *n* **1** institution dealing in deposits and withdrawals of money, loans, exchange of currencies, etc. **2** building occupied by such an institution. **3** place reserved for the safekeeping of some valuable commodity. *vt* deposit in a bank. *vi* have an account with a bank. **bank on** rely on. **bankbook** *n* book containing a record of a person's financial transactions with a bank. **banker** *n* professional expert in banking; financier. **banking** *n* business of running a bank or similar institution. **bank holiday** *n* public holiday on which banks are traditionally closed. **banknote** *n* paper note issued by a bank as money. **Bank Rate** *n* rate of interest charged by the Bank of England to the banking system.

bankrupt *adj* insolvent. *n* person who is declared bankrupt by a court. **bankruptcy** *n*.

banner *n* **1** flag or ensign, esp. one carried in a procession. **2** something that represents a principle, particular cause, etc.

banquet *n* lavish entertainment and feast given for a large number of guests.

baptize *vt,vi* initiate into the Christian faith with the rite of immersing in or sprinkling with water. **baptism** *n*. **Baptist** *n* member of a Christian denomination believing in baptism as an expression of personal faith. *adj* relating to such a denomination.

bar *n* **1** straight piece of wood, metal, etc., used as part of an enclosure, lever, etc. **2** stripe; band. **3** slab of chocolate, soap, etc. **4** barrier; obstruction. **5** counter from which drinks or refreshments are served. **6** room in a hotel or public house where alcoholic drinks are served. **7** *also* **barline** vertical stroke on a stave in a musical score. **8** notes or music occurring between such strokes. **the Bar** professional body of barristers. **barmaid** *n* woman employed to serve drinks in a hotel or public house. **barman** *n*.

barbarian *n* savage or uncivilized person. *adj* uncivilized; not cultured. **barbaric** *adj also* **barbarous** cruel; savage; brutal; inhuman. **barbarism** *n also* **barbarity** cruelty; brutality; uncivilized behaviour.

barbecue (ˈbɑːbikjuː) *n* **1** grid or grill used on an open fire for cooking meat, vegetables, etc. **2** party held in the open air at which barbecued food is served. *vt* cook on a barbecue.

barber *n* person who cuts men's hair, trims beards, etc.

barbiturate *n* drug used as a sedative.

bare *adj* **1** unclothed; naked. **2** uncovered; unadorned. **3** plain; undecorated. **4** having no vegetation. **5** mere; hardly sufficient. *vt* uncover; make bare. **bareness** *n*. **barefoot** *adj,adv* having no covering on the foot. **barely** *adv* **1** hardly; only just; scarcely. **2** austerely; not elaborately.

bargain *n* **1** agreement between parties; deal. **2** something bought cheaply; good buy. **into the bargain** moreover; besides. ~*vi* barter; haggle; make a deal. **bargain for** be prepared for; expect.

barge *n* large flat-bottomed boat used esp. for carrying cargo on canals. *vi* **1** bump (into); collide; push rudely. **2** interrupt; enter noisily.

baritone *n* male singing voice or musical instrument with a range between bass and tenor.

bark[1] *n* **1** loud cry of a dog or wolf. **2** gruff angry voice. *vi,vt* **1** (of a dog or wolf) utter a loud harsh cry. **2** speak in a gruff voice.

bark[2] *n* outer covering of the trunk and branches of a tree. *vt* scrape the skin or outer layer of.

barley *n* cereal plant with spiked ears used for food and to make malt for brewing and distilling. **barley-sugar** *n* boiled sweet made from sugar.

barn *n* farm building used for storing hay, housing livestock, etc.

barnacle *n* crustacean that attaches itself to rocks, the timber of boats, etc.

barometer *n* **1** instrument for measuring atmospheric pressure. **2** anything that indicates or warns of change.

baron *n* **1** nobleman of the lowest rank. **2** *inf* magnate. **baronial** *adj*. **baroness** *n* **1** wife or widow of a baron. **2** woman of a rank that is equivalent to that of a baron. **baronet** *n* man of a rank between that of a baron and a knight. **baronetcy** *n*.

barracks *n pl or s* building used for the accommodation of soldiers.

barrel *n* **1** cylindrical wooden or metal container. **2** tube of a gun through which the bullet or shell is discharged. *vt* put into a barrel.

barren *adj* **1** infertile; sterile. **2** unproductive; bare. **3** dull; uninteresting. **barrenness** *n*.

barricade *n* obstruction hastily set up as a barrier against an advancing enemy. *vt* block with a barricade.

barrier *n* **1** gate, fence, etc., intended to prevent access. **2** something that screens or protects. **3** hindrance; impediment.

barrister *n* lawyer having the right to practise in a court of law.

barrow[1] *n* cart pushed by hand; wheelbarrow.

barrow[2] *n* burial mound.

barter *vi,vt* trade by exchanging goods or commodities. *vi* haggle. *n* exchange of goods by bartering.

base[1] *n* **1** bottom; support on which something is constructed or rests. **2** foundation; basis. **3** main ingredient or element. **4** starting point. **5** headquarters. **6** establishment set up by the armed forces. **7** marked position on a baseball pitch. **8** sour-tasting chemical substance that turns litmus blue. *vt* **1** take as a foundation or starting point. **2** locate; situate. **baseball** *n* game for two sides of nine players each, on a diamond-shaped pitch using a hard ball and wooden bat. **basement** *n* room or set of rooms built below ground level.

base[2] *adj* **1** mean; despicable. **2** inferior; worthless. **baseness** *n*.

bash *inf vt* hit hard; slog. *n* rough blow. **have a bash** try; attempt.

bashful *adj* shy; embarrassed. **bashfully** *adv*. **bashfulness** *n*.

basic *adj* **1** fundamental; main. **2** elementary; primary. **3** relating to a chemical base. **basics** *pl n* fundamental or underlying principles. **basically** *adv*.

basin *n* **1** bowl used for mixing foods, holding liquids, etc. **2** sink; washbasin. **3** area of land drained by a river.

basis *n, pl* **bases** ('beisi:z) **1** underlying principle; foundation. **2** main part.

bask *vi* **1** expose oneself to the warmth of the sun, a fire, etc. **2** display enjoyment of publicity, glory, etc.

basket *n* **1** receptacle made of cane, straw, etc. **2** metal hoop with a net attached used as the goal in basketball. **basketball** *n* game for two sides of five or six players each, using a large ball which must be shot through a metal hoop fixed to a board in order to score. **basketry** *n* art of making baskets.

bass[1] (beis) *n* **1** lowest range of male singing voice. **2** musical instrument having the lowest range of its type. **3** double bass.

bass[2] (bæs) *n, pl* **bass** sea fish with a spiny dorsal fin; perch.

bassoon *n* woodwind instrument that is lower in tone than an oboe and having a mouthpiece fitted with a double reed. **bassoonist** *n*.

bastard *n* **1** illegitimate child. **2** *inf* unpleasant or cruel person.

bat[1] *n* wooden implement used for hitting a ball in various games. **off one's own bat** unassisted and on one's own initiative. ~*vi,vt* (-tt-) strike or play with a bat. **batsman** *n, pl* **-men** person who bats in cricket.

bat[2] *n* small nocturnal mammal that is able to fly.

batch *n* **1** quantity of loaves, cakes, etc., baked at the same time. **2** set; group.

bath *n* **1** large tub that is filled with water and used for washing the whole body. **2** act of sitting or lying in a bath in order to wash oneself. **3** water in a bath. **baths** *pl n* building housing public baths, swimming pool, etc. ~*vi,vt* wash in a bath. **bathroom** *n* room containing a bath and often a toilet and washbasin.

bathe *vi* **1** swim. **2** have a bath. *vt* **1** wash in order to cleanse or soothe. **2** cover with light, colour, etc. **bathing costume** *n* garment worn when bathing, swimming, etc.

baton *n* **1** small stick used to conduct an orchestra. **2** stick carried by the runner in a relay race. **3** staff of office.

battalion *n* military unit of three or four companies.

batter¹ *vt,vi* beat severely and repeatedly; pound.

batter² *n* mixture of flour, eggs, and milk used in cooking.

battery *n* **1** electrical device used as the source of current in radios, torches, vehicles, etc. **2** collection of cages for intensive rearing of chickens, turkeys, etc. **3** unlawful attack on a person. **4** prepared position for artillery, the artillery itself, or a military unit operating it. **5** array; number.

battle *n* **1** fighting between organized forces or armies. **2** hard struggle; fight. *vi* **1** fight in a battle. **2** struggle; strive. **battlefield** *n* site of a battle. **battleship** *n* large armoured warship.

battlement *n* parapet with indentations, used for defence.

bauxite *n* claylike substance that is the chief ore of aluminium.

bawl *vt,vi* shout or cry loudly; howl; bellow *n* howl.

bay¹ *n* coastal inlet.

bay² *n* **1** window area projecting beyond the face of a building. **2** recess; alcove. **3** area set aside for parking or loading and unloading a vehicle. **4** storage area in an aircraft.

bay³ *n* type of laurel tree whose aromatic leaves are used as a seasoning.

bay⁴ *n* bark or deep cry of a hound. **at bay 1** facing and warding off a pursuer. **2** in check; at a distance. ~*vt,vi* bark; howl.

bay⁵ *n* horse with a reddish-brown body and black mane and tail. *adj,n* reddish-brown.

bayonet *n* short blade attached to the muzzle of a rifle. *vt* stab with a bayonet.

be *vi* (*pres t s* am, are, is; *pl* are. *pt s* was, were, was; *pl* were. *pp* been) **1** exist. **2** occur; take place. **3** equal; have the character of. **4** remain; stay. **5** continue to do or act. *v aux* (used to form the passive).

beach *n* expanse of sand, pebbles, etc., on the seashore. **beachcomber** *n* person who makes a living by collecting things washed ashore by the sea.

bead *n* **1** small ball strung together with others to make a necklace, rosary, etc. **2** small drop; globule. *vt* decorate with beads.

beak *n* horny jaw of a bird; bill.

beaker *n* **1** glass for drinking from; tumbler. **2** small glass cylinder used in chemical experiments.

beam *n* **1** thick piece of timber or steel used to support a floor or roof; joist; girder. **2** shaft of light; ray. **3** radio or radar signal. **4** radiant smile. *vt,vi* **1** send out (a ray of light, radio signal, etc.). **2** smile radiantly.

bean *n* **1** type of plant producing pods containing seeds. **2** pod or seeds of such a plant often eaten as a vegetable. **full of beans** cheerful and energetic; ebullient.

bear¹ *v* (bore; borne) *vt* **1** take the weight of; support. **2** hold; carry. **3** accept responsibility for. **4** *pp* **born** give birth to. **5** yield (fruit); produce. **6** tolerate; endure. **7** display; wear. **8** possess; have. **9** conduct (oneself). *vi* follow or move in the direction of. **bring to bear** exert influence; effect. **bear on 1** push or press against. **2** be relevant to; relate to. **bear out** confirm; furnish proof of. **bear up** cope cheerfully; manage. **bearer** *n*.

bear² *n* **1** large carnivorous mammal with black, brown, or white shaggy fur. **2** person who sells stocks and buys them back after the price has dropped.

beard *n* **1** hair growth on the chin and sides of the face. **2** tuft or growth resembling a beard.

bearing *n* **1** person's carriage, posture, deportment, etc. **2** relevance; significance. **3** angle measured from north or some other fixed direction. **4** machine part that supports or guides another moving part. **bearings** *pl n* **1** position or direction determined by reference to fixed points. **2** awareness of one's situation; orientation.

beast *n* **1** animal, esp. when distinguished from man. **2** brutal person. **beastly** *inf adj* disgusting, nasty. **beastliness** *n*.

beat *v* (beat; beaten) *vt* **1** strike hard; hit. **2**

thrash; flog. **3** hammer; bang. **4** whisk; stir vigorously. **5** flap; move up and down. **6** defeat in a contest. **7** do better than; surpass. **8** overcome. *vi* **1** throb; pulsate. **2** pound; bang. **3** produce a rhythmical sound. **4** move up and down. **beat up** assault and injure severely. ~*n* **1** throb; pulsation. **2** blow; bang; stroke. **3** rhythmical sound. **4** basic unit by which the duration of musical notes is measured. **5** stressed syllable or note in poetry or music. **6** type of popular music with a strongly marked rhythm and beat.

beauty *n* **1** quality or qualities appealing to the senses or intellect and conforming to a certain standard of excellence, attractiveness, etc. **2** exceptionally lovely woman. **3** exceptionally good example of something. **beautiful** *adj*. **beautifully** *adv*.

beaver *n* **1** aquatic rodent with webbed feet and a strong broad tail. **2** fur of the beaver. *vi* work hard and enthusiastically.

because *conj* for the reason that; since. **because of** on account of; due to.

beckon *vi,vt* summon with a gesture of the hand or head. *n* summoning gesture.

become *v* (became; become) *vi* **1** grow, change, or develop into; start to be. **2** happen (to); befall. *vt* suit; make attractive. **becoming** fetching; attractive.

bed *n* **1** piece of furniture designed for sleeping on. **2** small plot of ground for growing flowers or vegetables. **3** bottom of the sea, a river, etc. **4** layer of rock. *vt* (-dd-) **1** plant in a bed. **2** *sl* have sexual intercourse with. **bed down** find a place to sleep. **bedclothes** *pl n* covers used on a bed. **bedding** *n* mattress, covers, pillows, etc., used on a bed. **bedridden** *adj* confined to bed, esp. through illness. **bedroom** *n* room used for sleeping in. **bed-sitter** *n also* **bed-sit** one-roomed accommodation, usually with cooking and washing facilities. **bedspread** *n* top cover for a bed.

bedraggled *adj* spattered with mud or dirt.

bee *n* insect that produces wax and converts nectar into honey. **have a bee in one's bonnet** be obsessed or fanatical. **beehive** *n* box-like or domed construction for keeping bees in.

beech *n* deciduous tree with a smooth bark and shiny oval leaves.

beef *n* **1** meat from a cow, bull, etc. **2** cow, bull, etc., used for its meat. **beefy** *adj* **1** containing or having the flavour of beef. **2** muscular and strong.

been *v pp* of **be.**

beer *n* alcoholic drink made from malt and flavoured with hops.

beet *n* **1** *also* **beetroot** plant with a round red root, which is eaten as a vegetable. **2** *also* **sugar beet** plant with a whitish root, which is used as a source of sugar.

beetle *n* insect with wings, which are modified to form a hard protective shell.

befall *vi,vt* (befell; befallen) happen (to); occur, esp. by chance.

befit *vt,vi* (-tt-) be right or suitable (for).

before *adv* on a previous occasion; earlier. *prep* **1** previous to. **2** in front of. **3** in the presence of. *conj* **1** until or up to the time that. **2** rather than; sooner than. **beforehand** *adj,adv* early; in advance.

befriend *vt* take care of as a friend.

beg *vt,vi* (-gg-) **1** ask for (money, food, etc.). **2** beseech; implore; plead (with). **beggar** *n*.

begin *vt,vi* (-nn-) (began; begun) start; commence; bring into being. **beginner** *n* person at an early stage of learning; novice. **beginning** *n* start; starting place; early stage; outset. **beginnings** *pl n* **1** origin; early background. **2** early indication of potential or development.

begonia *n* plant with showy red, green, or greyish leaves and red, yellow, or white flowers.

begrudge *vt* resent; wish to deny; grudge.

beguile *vt,vi* charm; bewitch; hoodwink.

behalf *n* **on behalf of** in the name of; representing.

behave *vi* **1** act; react; function. **2** conduct (oneself). **behaviour** *n*.

behead *vt* execute by severing the head; decapitate.

behind *adv,adj* **1** following; after. **2** in a place that is further back. **3** behindhand. *prep* **1** at the back of; beyond. **2** not so advanced as. **3** remaining; left over. *n inf* buttocks. **behindhand** *adj,adv* in arrears; late.

behold *vt,vi* (beheld) see; look (at). *interj* look!

beige *adj,n* light greyish-brown; fawn.

being *n* **1** living creature. **2** existence; living state.

belated *adj* arriving or happening too late. **belatedly** *adv*.

belch *vi,vt* **1** expel wind noisily fron the stomach

through the mouth. **2** send out in large quantities; gush. *n* **1** act of belching. **2** blast; burst.

belfry *n* tower in which bells are hung.

belie *vt* **1** give the wrong impression of. **2** show to be false.

believe *vt,vi* **1** consider to be true or right; accept. **2** think; assume. *vi* subscribe to a particular faith. **believe in** have faith in, trust; be convinced of the existence of. **believable** *adj.* **believer** *n.* **belief** *n* **1** something believed; opinion. **2** creed; faith. **3** trust; acceptance.

belittle *vt* undervalue, disparage.

bell *n* **1** hollow metal instrument that produces a ringing sound when struck. **2** electrical device that produces a ringing or buzzing sound. **ring a bell** seem vaguely familiar.

belligerent *adj* warlike; aggressive. **belligerence** *n.* **belligerently** *adv.*

bellow *vi,vt* roar loudly; bawl. *n* deep-throated roar or shout.

bellows *n pl or s* device that expands and contracts to produce a strong draught of air.

belly *n* **1** abdomen. **2** stomach. **3** part of something that bulges.

belong *v* **belong to 1** be owned by. **2** be a member of. **3** be part of a set with, go with, fit. *vi* have an allotted place. **belongings** *pl n* personal possessions.

below *adv* at a place lower down; underneath. *prep* lower or further down than; under.

belt *n* **1** strip of leather, cloth, etc., worn round the waist. **2** band; strip. **3** region or zone with specific characteristics. **4** slap; blow; sharp hit. **below the belt** unfairly; against the rules. ~*vt* **1** fasten with a belt. **2** *sl* strike; beat. **3** *also* **belt out** sing, play, or shout loudly. *vi* race; travel fast. **belt up** *sl* stop talking.

bemoan *vt,vi* moan (about); lament; deplore.

bemused *adj* **1** lost in thought. **2** dazed; confused.

bench *n* **1** long wooden or stone seat. **2** work table; counter. **3** seat occupied by a judge or magistrate.

bend *v* (bent) *vt* **1** make into a bow or curved shape. **2** turn or curve in a particular direction. **3** subdue; coerce. *vi* **1** curve. **2** stoop; bow. *n* curve. **round the bend** mad; crazy.

beneath *adv* underneath; below. *prep* **1** concealed under; lower than. **2** in an inferior or subordinate position than. **3** unacceptable to.

benefactor *n* person who donates a large sum of money; patron.

benefit *n* **1** advantage; privilege; good. **2** welfare or insurance payment. *vt,vi* do good to or be good for. **beneficial** *adj* advantageous; helpful. **beneficiary** *n* recipient of a legacy, annuity, etc.

benevolent *adj* **1** kindly; good-natured. **2** charitable; generous. **benevolence** *n.* **benevolently** *adv.*

benign (bi'nain) *adj* **1** gentle; friendly. **2** not malignant.

bent *v pt* and *pp* of **bend.** *adj* **1** crooked; curved. **2** *sl* dishonest, corrupt. **bent on** determined to. ~*n* inclination; penchant.

benzene *n* colourless sweet-smelling liquid containing carbon and hydrogen and used as a solvent.

bequeath *vt* leave (money, property, etc.) esp by will. **bequest** *n* something bequeathed.

bereaved *adj* deprived (of) by death. **bereavement** *n.*

bereft *adj* deprived; completely lacking (in).

beret ('berei) *n* flat circular cap of wool, felt, etc.

berry *n* soft stoneless fruit of various trees or bushes.

berserk (bə'zə:k) *adj* in a frenzy; wild and violent.

berth *n* **1** sleeping place in a ship, train, caravan, etc. **2** mooring place. *vi,vt* moor; dock.

beseech *vt* implore; entreat.

beset *vt* (besetting; beset) **1** trouble; plague. **2** attack; assail.

beside *prep* at the side of; adjacent to; by. **beside oneself** overcome; out of control. **besides** *adv* **1** moreover; furthermore; anyway. **2** additionally, as well. *prep* in addition to; apart from.

besiege *vt* **1** surround and attack (a city, fortress, etc.). **2** assail with demands, requests, etc.

best *adj* **1** of the highest quality. **2** most suitable or desirable. *adv* in the best way. *n* the highest possible standard; utmost. **best man** *n* man who looks after a bridegroom. **best-seller** *n* book or other product that sells exceptionally well.

bestial *adj* **1** brutal; coarse and savage; carnal. **2** relating to a beast.

bestow *vt* give; confer; endow. **bestowal** *n*.

bet *n* **1** pledge between parties to pay a sum of money to the one who successfully predicts the outcome of a future event. **2** sum of money pledged. **3** predicted outcome. **4** course of action. *vt,vi* (-tt-; bet) **1** place a bet (on); gamble. **2** *inf* predict. **betting shop** *n* premises of a bookmaker.

betray *vt* **1** disclose information about or expose to an enemy. **2** be unfaithful or disloyal to. **3** show signs of; reveal inadvertently. **betrayal** *n*.

better *adj* **1** of a higher quality; superior. **2** more suitable or desirable. **3** no longer sick; recovering. **better off** richer; having a greater advantage. *adv* more; to a greater extent. **had better** ought to; should. ~*n* **1** the more excellent or desirable. **2** superior; person of higher worth. **get the better of** outwit; defeat. ~*vt* improve upon. **betterment** *n* improvement.

between *prep* **1** in a space or interval separating two places, moments in time, etc. **2** shared by. **3** through joint effort or contribution. *adv* in or towards the middle.

beverage *n* any drink except water.

beware *vt,vi* be wary (of); take heed (of).

bewilder *vt* puzzle; confuse; perplex. **bewilderment** *n*.

bewitch *vt* charm as if by a spell; enchant.

beyond *prep* **1** farther away than; on the far side of. **2** outside the control or limits of. *adv* farther away.

biannual *adj* occurring twice a year. **biannually** *adv*.

bias *n* **1** prejudice; distorted outlook. **2** tendency; inclination. **3** diagonal line or cut. **biased** *adj* partial; prejudiced.

bib *n* **1** piece of cloth worn under the chin by a baby whilst eating. **2** part of an apron, pinafore, etc., that covers the front of the body above the waist.

Bible *n* collection of sacred writings of the Christian Church. **biblical** *adj*.

bibliography *n* list of works relating to a particular subject, author, etc. **bibliographical** *adj*. **bibliographer** *n*.

biceps *pl n* muscles of the upper arm.

bicker *vi* squabble; quarrel, esp. over trivial matters.

bicycle *also* **cycle** *or* **bike** *n* vehicle with two wheels propelled by pedalling. *vi* ride a bicycle.

bid *v* (-dd-; bad, bade, *or* bid; bidden *or* bid) *vt,vi* **1** offer to buy for a certain sum, esp. at an auction. **2** ask; command. *vt* express in greeting. **bidder** *n*.

bidet ('bi:dei) *n* small bath used for washing the genital area.

biennial *adj* occurring once every two years or lasting for two years. *n* plant with a two-year life cycle. **biennially** *adv*.

big *adj* **1** large; great; not small. **2** important; substantial. **3** generous. *adv* with authority; in a big way.

bigamy *n* crime of marrying another partner when a former marriage is still valid. **bigamist** *n*., **bigamous** *adj*.

bigot *n* offensively intolerant or prejudiced person. **bigoted** *adj*. **bigotry** *n*.

bike *n,vi* short for **bicycle.**

bikini *n* woman's two-piece bathing costume.

bile *n* fluid secreted by the liver. **bilious** *adj* suffering from excessive secretion of bile in the liver.

bilingual *adj* able to speak two languages.

bill[1] *n* **1** statement of money owed; invoice. **2** law or act of Parliament in draft form. **3** poster or notice. **4** programme of events. **5** *US* banknote. *vt* **1** present an account to; invoice. **2** put on a programme; schedule.

bill[2] *n* bird's beak.

billiards *n* game played with a long cue and a number of balls on a table usually fitted with pockets.

billion *n* **1** (in Britain) one million million. **2** (esp. in the US) one thousand million.

billow *n* **1** large sea-wave. **2** surging mass. *vi, vt* swell up; surge.

bin *n* storage container.

binary *adj* **1** composed of two parts. **2** relating to the number two.

bind *v* (bound) *vt,vi* **1** tie or entwine; wrap round tightly. **2** cohere; stick. *vt* **1** restrict; place under an obligation or contract. **2** confine; trap; constrain. **3** fasten together (pages) inside a cover. **4** sew the edge of to prevent fraying, for decoration, etc. *n inf* restricting circumstance; constraint. **binder** *n* folder with clasps for holding together loose sheets of paper. **binding** *n* **1** cover of a book. **2** edging material or tape *adj* restricting;

obligatory. **bindweed** *n* plant that twines round a support or the stems of other plants.

bingo *n* gambling game in which players match up numbers on a chart with those picked out at random.

binoculars *pl n* optical instrument consisting of a pair of small telescopes joined together.

biochemistry *n* study of the chemical compounds occurring in plants and animals. **biochemical** *adj*. **biochemist** *n*.

biography *n* account of a person's life written by someone else. **biographical** *adj*. **biographer** *n*.

biology *n* study of living organisms. **biological** *adj*. **biologically** *adv*. **biologist** *n*.

birch *n* **1** tree with a slender grey or white trunk. **2** bundle of birch twigs used as a whip. *vt* flog; thrash.

bird *n* warm-blooded feathered egg-laying vertebrate with forelimbs modified as wings.

birth *n* **1** act of being born or producing offspring. **2** origin; beginning. **3** descent; lineage. **birth certificate** *n* official document issued when a child's birth is registered. **birth control** *n* method or practice of contraception. **birthday** *n* anniversary of a person's birth. **birthmark** *n* blemish on the skin formed before birth. **birth rate** *n* ratio of live births in relation to a given population.

biscuit *n* crisp flat cake made from baked dough.

bisect *vt* **1** divide into two equal parts. **2** split; cut across. **bisection** *n*.

bisexual *adj* able to respond sexually to a person of either sex. *n* person who is bisexual.

bishop *n* **1** high-ranking clergyman with authority over a diocese. **2** chess piece able to move diagonally across squares of the same colour.

bison *n* N American animal of the ox family with a shaggy coat and humped back; buffalo.

bistro ('bi:strou) small restaurant or bar.

bit[1] *n* **1** small piece or amount. **2** short while. **a bit** a little; somewhat; rather. **bit by bit** gradually. **do one's bit** do one's duty; contribute. **every bit as** equally as. **not a bit** not at all.

bit[2] *n* **1** mouthpiece attached to a bridle for controlling a horse. **2** metal drill used with a brace.

bitch *n* **1** female dog. **2** *sl* malicious woman. *vi* speak maliciously; grumble. **bitchy** *adj*. **bitchiness** *n*.

bite *vt,vi* (bit; bitten) **1** press, cut, or sink into with the teeth. **2** have a tendency to attack with the teeth, fangs, etc. **3** sting; smart. **4** corrode; eat into. **5** take bait. **6** grip; hold fast. *n* **1** act of biting. **2** piece bitten off; morsel. **3** mark or swelling caused by biting. **4** something to eat; snack. **5** strong grip. **biting** *adj* **1** harsh; keen. **2** sarcastic; hurtful.

bitter *adj* **1** having a harsh taste. **2** resentful; rancorous; deeply hostile. **3** distressing; hard to bear. **4** extremely cold; icy. *n* type of beer with a strong flavour of hops. **bitterly** *adv*. **bitterness** *n*.

bivalve *n* mollusc having two shells hinged together.

bizarre *adj* weird; odd; strange.

black *adj* **1** of the colour of coal, jet, etc. **2** extremely dark; unlit. **3** extremely dirty. **4** grim; bleak. **5** enraged; angry. **6** dark-skinned. **black market** *n* system of illicit trading. **black pudding** sausage made from pork fat and blood. ~*n* **1** dark colour having no hue. **2** darkness. **3** *cap* Negro; dark-skinned person. **black and blue** heavily bruised. ~*vt* **1** blacken. **2** *inf* boycott; ban. **black out 1** obliterate. **2** extinguish; plunge into darkness. **3** pass out; lose consciousness. **blackout** *n* **1** power failure. **2** extinguishing of lights in cities, etc., in order to prevent identification by enemy aircraft. **3** temporary loss of consciousness or memory. **blackness** *n*. **blacken** *vt,vi* make or become black; darken. *vt* defame.

blackberry *n* edible purplish-black fruit of the bramble.

blackbird *n* songbird in which the male has black plumage with a yellow beak and the female is brown.

blackboard *n* large board that can be written on with chalk.

blackcurrant *n* small round edible black berry that grows on a cultivated bush.

blackguard ('blægɑ:d) *n* scoundrel; rogue.

blackhead *n* spot with a black surface that clogs a pore on the skin.

blackleg *n* person who acts against the interests of a trade union, esp. by refusing to strike. *vi* (-gg-) act as a blackleg.

blackmail *n* crime of demanding payment in exchange for not disclosing discreditable information. *vt* threaten by means of blackmail. **blackmailer** *n*.

blacksmith *n* craftsman who works with iron.

bladder *n* sac in the body that functions as a receptacle for urine.

blade *n* **1** sharp-edged or cutting part of a knife, sword, etc. **2** long flat leaf of grass. **3** shoulder blade. **4** flat broad end of a propeller, oar, etc.

blame *n* responsibility for a crime, error, fault, etc. *vt,vi* attribute blame (to); find fault (with). **blameless** *adj* innocent; faultless.

blanch *vt* **1** make lighter in colour; bleach. **2** plunge (vegetables, meat, etc.) into boiling water. *vi* become pale with fear, nausea, etc.

blancmange (blə'mɔndʒ) *n* dessert made from milk, cornflour, and flavouring.

bland *adj* **1** not highly flavoured or seasoned. **2** mild; temperate. **3** unemotional; without passion. **blandly** *adv*. **blandness** *n*.

blank *adj* **1** not written on or filled in. **2** bare; undecorated. **3** uncomprehending; expressionless. **4** uninspired. **blank verse** unrhymed verse. ~*n* **1** empty space. **2** mental confusion. **3** written or printed dash. **4** gun cartridge having powder but no bullet. **draw a blank** fail to obtain the required information during an investigation. *v* **blank out** blot out; obliterate.

blanket *n* **1** woollen bed cover. **2** thick layer; cover. *vt* cover up.

blare *vt,vi* **1** shout or sound loudly; proclaim. **2** shine harshly. *n* **1** loud noise; blast. **2** blinding light; glare; blaze.

blasé ('blɑːzei) *adj* no longer capable of being shocked, excited, etc.; cool and sophisticated.

blaspheme *vi* curse; swear; utter profanities. *vt* act irreverently towards. **blasphemous** *adj*. **blasphemy** *n*.

blast *n* **1** explosion. **2** loud explosive noise; blare. **3** strong sudden rush of air, flames, water, etc. *interj sl* exclamation of anger, frustration, etc. *vt,vi* **1** blow up; destroy by explosion. **2** produce a sudden loud noise. **3** force an opening (in); breach. **blastoff** *n* launching of a rocket.

blatant *adj* flagrant; conspicuous; undisguised. **blatancy** *n*. **blatantly** *adv*.

blaze *n* **1** roaring fire; bright flame. **2** bright light; glare. **3** passionate display; outburst. *vi* **1** burn vigorously; flare. **2** glare; shine harshly.

blazer *n* jacket, esp. one worn as part of a school or club uniform.

bleach *vt,vi* whiten through heat or the action of chemicals. *n* substance used for bleaching clothes, the hair, etc.

bleak *adj* **1** desolate and exposed. **2** grim; dismal; unfavourable. **bleakly** *adv*. **bleakness** *n*.

bleat *vt,vi* **1** (of a sheep or goat) utter a high-pitched cry. **2** moan plaintively; whine; complain. *n* cry of a sheep or goat.

bleed *v* (bled) *vi* **1** lose blood. **2** suffer extreme anguish. *vt* **1** drain blood from. **2** draw off (liquid, gas, etc.). **bleeding** *adj* utter. *adv sl* extremely; very.

bleep *n* noise produced by an electronic device. *vi* make a short high-pitched sound.

blemish *n* **1** discoloured mark on the skin. **2** stain or flaw. *vt* spoil; mar; tarnish.

blend *vt,vi* **1** mix (different varieties of tea, tobacco, etc.). **2** combine (colours). **3** merge; form a mixture. *vi* harmonize; mix well. *n* blended mixture. **blender** *n* machine for blending vegetables, liquids, etc.

bless *vt* **1** make holy; consecrate. **2** call for God's aid or protection for. **blessed with** (blest) endowed or favoured with; granted. **blessed** ('blesid) *adj* holy; sacred. **blessing** *n* **1** statement or ceremony invoking God's aid or protection. **2** divine gift; sanction. **3** good fortune.

blew *v pt* of **blow** .

blight *n* **1** plant disease caused by fungi, insects, etc. **2** something that mars or impedes growth. *vt* **1** cause blight in. **2** spoil; destroy.

blind *adj* **1** deprived of the power of sight. **2** unable or unwilling to understand or tolerate. **3** made reckless by passion. **4** concealed; unseen. **5** closed at one end. *adv also* **blindly** **1** without being able to see. **2** without proper information or preparation. *vt* **1** make blind. **2** dazzle. **3** deprive of reason or judgment. *n* length of material on a roller used as a shade for a window. **blindness** *n*. **blindfold** *n* strip of cloth placed over the eyes and tied at the back of the head. *vt* place a blindfold over (the eyes).

blink *vt,vi* **1** rapidly open and shut (the eyes). **2** flash on and off. *n* **1** rapid opening and shutting of the eyes. **2** flash; twinkle. **blinkers** *pl n* **1** direction indicators on a motor vehicle. **2** part of a horse's bridle that prevents sideways vision.

bliss *n* state of ecstatic happiness. **blissful** *adj*. **blissfully** *adv*.

blister *n* **1** small swelling or bubble on the skin produced by friction, burning, etc. **2** bubble of paint. *vt,vi* produce blisters.

blithe *adj* **1** carefree; light-hearted. **2** thoughtless; casual. **blithely** *adv*. **blitheness** *n*.

blitz *n* heavy attack, such as an air-raid. *vt* make an intensive attack on.

blizzard *n* violent snowstorm.

bloat *vt,vi* swell; inflate.

blob *n* **1** drop of liquid, dirt, etc. **2** blurred shape or form. *vt* (-bb-) splash or mark with blobs.

bloc *n* united group of countries, political parties, etc.

block *n* **1** solid piece of stone, wood, etc.; slab; brick; chunk. **2** building comprising a number of offices, flats, etc. **3** group of things fastened together or arranged in rows. **4** obstruction; obstacle; blockage. **5** psychological or mental barrier. *vt also* **block up 1** obstruct; cause a blockage in; stop up. **2** veto; impede; prevent. **blockade** *n* obstruction, esp. of a port or harbour by military forces. *vt* obstruct with a blockade. **blockage** *n* something that blocks, obstructs, or impedes.

bloke *n inf* man.

blond *adj* fair-haired. *n* man with fair hair. **blonde** *f n*. **blondness** *n*.

blood *n* **1** red fluid circulating through the veins and arteries of the body. **2** lineage; descent. **in cold blood** ruthlessly; in a calculated way. **bloodcurdling** *adj* terrifying; ghastly. **blood pressure** *n* pressure of the blood against the inner walls of the arteries. **bloodshed** *n* violent killing; slaughter. **bloodstream** *n* flow of blood through the body. **bloodthirsty** *adj* sadistic; delighting in violence. **bloodthirstiness** *n*. **bloody** *adj* covered or stained with blood; gory. *adj,adv sl* damned; extremely. *vt* stain with blood. **bloodiness** *n*. **bloody-minded** *adj* obstinate; pig-headed; perverse. **bloody-mindedness** *n*.

bloom *n* **1** flower(s); blossom. **2** healthy glow. **3** shiny surface of various fruits. *vi* **1** flower; blossom. **2** flourish; develop vigorously.

blossom *n* flower(s), esp. of a fruit tree. *vi* **1** flower; produce blossom. **2** begin to grow or develop.

blot *n* **1** ink stain. **2** eyesore. **3** damage to one's character or reputation. *vt* (-tt-) **1** stain; mark. **2** use an absorbent material to soak up. **blot out** obscure completely; obliterate. **blot one's copybook** spoil one's reputation or record; blunder. **blotting paper** *n* absorbent paper used esp. to soak up excess ink.

blotch *n* stain; discolouration; patch. *vt,vi* produce stains or patches. **blotchy** *adj*.

blouse *n* woman's garment that is similar to a shirt.

blow[1] *v* (blew; blown) *vt,vi* **1** send out (air) through the mouth or nose; exhale. **2** move through or by air or wind. **3** produce the sound of a whistle, trumpet, the wind, etc. **4** fuse; burn out. **blow out** extinguish or be extinguished. **blow over** subside; pass. **blow up 1** explode or cause an explosion. **2** lose one's temper. **3** inflate. **4** enlarge (a photograph). ~*n* **1** expulsion of air; puff. **2** act of blowing or sound produced by a whistle, trumpet, etc. **blowy** *adj* windy; blustery.

blow[2] *n* **1** heavy stroke or hit with the hand or a weapon. **2** sudden shock or disappointment; setback. **come to blows** start to fight.

blubber *n* thick layer of subcutaneous fat of a whale, seal, etc. *vt,vi* sob; cry noisily.

blue *n* colour in the spectrum that is the colour of a clear sky. **out of the blue** suddenly; without warning; from nowhere. **the blues 1** state of depression; dejectedness. **2** type of music created by Black Americans. ~*adj* **1** of the colour blue. **2** depressed; unhappy. **3** *inf* obscene. **bluebell** *n* woodland plant with blue bell-shaped flowers. **blue-blooded** *adj* of royal or aristocratic descent. **blueprint** *n* **1** photocopy of plans or drawings. **2** original model; prototype.

bluff *vt,vi* feign confidence in order to deceive about one's true motives, resources, etc. *n* act of deception. **call someone's bluff** act in a way that forces someone to reveal his true motives, resources, etc.; challenge.

blunder *n* stupid, tactless, or clumsy mistake. *vi* **1** make a stupid or tactless mistake. **2** move clumsily; stumble.

blunt *adj* **1** not sharp; unable to cut well. **2** outspoken; forthright; direct. *vt,vi* make or become blunt(er). *vt* make less sensitive; dull. **bluntly** *adv*. **bluntness** *n*.

blur *vt,vi* (-rr-) **1** make or become hazy, indistinct, or vague. **2** smear; smudge. *n* **1** something that is indistinct in outline or vague. **2** smudge.

blurt *vt,vi also* **blurt out** reveal (a secret), esp. when confused or under pressure.

blush *vi* become red in the face with embarrassment, shame, etc.; flush. *n* **1** reddening of the cheeks. **2** hint of redness on a flower, fruit, etc.

bluster *vt,vi* speak or act in a forceful and often boastful manner; swagger. *vi* blow strongly; be windy. **blustery** *adj.*

boar *n* **1** wild pig. **2** uncastrated male domestic pig.

board *n* **1** plank of wood. **2** shaped piece of wood or other material designed for a specific purpose, such as an ironing board or chess board. **3** cardboard. **4** notice board or blackboard. **5** body of directors, governors, or other officials; committee. **6** meals provided for residents in a hotel, hostel, etc. **go by the board** be ignored or rejected. **on board** on a ship, aircraft, etc.; aboard. ~*vt,vi* go on to a ship, aircraft, etc.; embark. *vt also* **board up** enclose or cover with boards of wood. *vt* provide lodgings for. *vi* live in lodgings. **boarder** *n* **1** child at boarding school. **2** lodger. **boarding house** *n* small private establishment offering cheap accommodation. **boarding school** *n* school with living accommodation for pupils. **board room** *n* committee room where a board meets.

boast *vi* exaggerate or speak proudly of one's own achievements or qualities; brag. *vt* be the proud possessor of. *n* exaggerated or proud statement. **boastful** *adj.* **boastfully** *adv.* **boastfulness** *n.*

boat *n* small vessel for travelling on water. **in the same boat** in the same situation or predicament. **miss the boat** miss an opportunity. ~*vi* travel in a boat, esp. for pleasure.

bob *vt,vi* (-bb-) **1** move up and down esp. in a liquid. **2** nod or jerk (the head). **3** bow or curtsy. *n* **1** jerky movement. **2** bow or curtsy.

bodice *n* top part of a woman's dress.

body *n* **1** the whole physical structure of a human being or other vertebrate. **2** torso; trunk. **3** corpse. **4** main or central part. **5** mass; expanse. **6** corporate group of people. **7** object or solid. **8** consistency or fullness, esp. of wine. **bodily** *adj* physical; corporeal. *adv* by lifting or using the body. **bodyguard** *n* person giving physical protection to another. **bodywork** *n* covering for the shell or framework of a vehicle.

bog *n* **1** area of waterlogged land, usually of peat. **2** *sl* lavatory. **bogged down** unable to make progress; hindered. **boggy** *adj.*

bogus *adj* fake; sham.

boil[1] *vt,vi* **1** produce gas or vapour from a liquid by the action of heat. **2** cook by heating in liquid. *vi* seethe; become agitated. **boil down** reduce in quantity by boiling. **boil down to** amount to; result in. **boil over** overflow or spill whilst boiling. *n* **on the boil 1** approaching boiling point. **2** in operation; functioning well. **boiler** *n* vessel producing steam to drive an engine. **boiling point** *n* **1** temperature at which a liquid boils. **2** moment at which one loses one's temper or a situation becomes explosive.

boil[2] *n* inflamed pus-filled sore on the skin.

boisterous *adj* unruly; noisy and unrestrained. **boisterously** *adv.* **boisterousness** *n.*

bold *adj* **1** courageous; unafraid; daring. **2** clear; distinct. **boldly** *adv.* **boldness** *n.*

bolster *n* long pillow or cushion. *vt also* **bolster up** reinforce; encourage; boost.

bolt *n* **1** metal bar used to fasten a door, window, etc. **2** screw or pin used with a nut. **3** clap of thunder or flash of lightning. **make a bolt for it** run away quickly. ~*vt* **1** secure or fasten with a bolt. **2** eat hurriedly; gulp down. *vi* **1** jump up suddenly. **2** run off unexpectedly. *adv* **bolt upright** with one's back straight and rigid.

bomb *n* explosive device. **go like a bomb 1** travel at high speed. **2** be highly successful. ~*vt,vi* attack with bombs. **bombard** *vt* **1** attack repeatedly with bombs, missiles, etc. **2** direct series of questions, complaints, etc., at. **bombardment** *n.* **bombardier** (bɔmbə'diə) *n* noncommissioned officer below a sergeant in the Royal Artillery. **bomber** *n* **1** aircraft designed to carry bombs. **2** person who attacks with bombs. **bombshell** *n* unexpected event causing great shock or distress.

bond *n* **1** something that binds, such as a rope or chain. **2** close intimate relationship; tie. **3** obligation; duty. **4** company or government certificate issued as a guarantee of repayment of money lent. **bonded warehouse** warehouse storing imported goods until duty is paid. **bondage** *n* slavery.

bone *n* hard tissue that makes up the skeleton of the body. **have a bone to pick** have something to criticize or quarrel about. **make**

no bones about have no hesitation or doubt about. ~*vt* remove the bones from (meat). **bonemeal** *n* animal food or fertilizer made from crushed bones. **bony** *adj* **1** having many bones. **2** having prominent bones. **3** resembling a bone.

bonfire *n* fire lit out of doors.

bonnet *n* **1** hat kept in place with ribbons tied under the chin. **2** hinged section at the front of a vehicle that covers the engine or luggage compartment.

bonus *n* additional payment, dividend, etc.

booby trap *n* **1** concealed or disguised explosive device intended to blow up when touched. **2** object or trap used by a practical joker to surprise or scare an unsuspecting victim. **booby-trap** *vt* (-pp-) set up a booby trap in or for.

book *n* **1** set of printed pages bound together; volume. **2** written work, such as a novel or textbook. **3** pack of stamps, tickets, etc. **by the book** strictly according to the rules. ~*vt,vi* reserve (a seat, ticket, etc.) in advance. *vt* record (a person's name) prior to prosecution on a minor charge. **bookkeeping** *n* accounting system or practice of keeping records of business transactions. **bookkeeper** *n*. **booklet** *n* small book; brochure. **bookmaker** *n* person running a business to accept bets, esp. in horseracing.

boom *vi* **1** produce a deep resonant sound. **2** thrive; prosper. *n* **1** deep resonant sound. **2** period or state of prosperity.

boomerang *n* curved piece of wood used as a missile and designed to follow a course back to the user when thrown.

boor *n* uncouth coarse person. **boorish** *adj*

boost *n* **1** push or shove upwards. **2** increase; rise. **3** encouragement; help. *vt* **1** lift up with a push. **2** increase; expand. **3** improve; promote. **booster** *n*.

boot *n* **1** type of footwear usually covering the leg up to the knee. **2** stout shoe worn for walking, climbing, playing football, etc. **3** luggage compartment in a vehicle, usually situated at the rear. **4** *inf* kick. **the boot** *sl* dismissal; sack. ~*vt* **1** kick. **2** *also* **boot out** expel or dismiss unceremoniously.

booth *n* **1** enclosed cubicle. **2** covered stall at a market or fair.

booze *inf n* alcoholic drink. *vi* drink heavily.

border *n* **1** stretch of land constituting a frontier or boundary. **2** edge; margin. **3** flower bed along the edge of a lawn, path, etc. *vt,vi* function as a border or boundary (to). **border on 1** lie adjacent to. **2** verge on; come close to. **borderline** *n* **1** boundary line. **2** intermediate area or category. *adj* marginal; in between.

bore[1] *vt,vi* **1** drill (a hole) in. **2** dig or make (a tunnel, shaft, etc.), esp. in order to extract oil, minerals, etc. *n* **1** tunnel or shaft. **2** hollow part of a gun barrel. **3** calibre of a gun.

bore[2] *vt* exhaust or frustrate by being dull, repetitious, etc. *n* tedious or dreary person, task, etc. **boredom** *n*.

bore[3] *v pt* of **bear**[1].

born *v pt* of **bear**[1] (def 4) when used in the passive. *adj* possessing a specified innate quality.

borne *v pp* of **bear**[1].

borough *n* **1** town or district represented in Parliament. **2** area having its own local council.

borrow *vt,vi* **1** take or accept on loan. **2** incorporate into one's own language; adopt. **borrower** *n*.

borstal *n* establishment for young offenders.

bosom *n* **1** breast or chest, esp. of a woman; bust. **2** centre of love or comfort.

boss *inf n* employer, manager, or foreman. *vt,vi* control or manage, esp. domineeringly. **bossy** *adj* overbearing; inclined to dominate. **bossiness** *n*.

botany *n* science or study of plants. **botanical** *adj*. **botanist** *n*.

botch *vt,vi* bungle; make a bad job of. *n* mess; clumsy repair.

both *pron,adj* each of two taken together. *conj* **both...and...** firstly...and secondly...

bother *vt* disturb; worry; annoy; trouble. *vi* concern oneself; take trouble or care. *n* **1** fuss; commotion. **2** trouble; anxiety. *interj* exclamation of mild impatience or annoyance. **bothersome** *adj*.

bottle *n* long glass or plastic vessel with a narrow neck, for holding liquids. *vt,vi* pour into a bottle. **bottle up** repress or hide (emotions). **bottleneck** *n* something that restricts the flow of traffic, goods on a production line, etc.

bottom *n* **1** lowest part; base; foot. **2** seabed, riverbed, etc. **3** worst or most inferior position. **4** *inf* buttocks. **at bottom** fundamentally;

basically. **get to the bottom of** investigate the truth or cause of. ~*adj* lowest. **bottomless** *adj* **1** extremely deep. **2** seemingly endless or inexhaustible. **bottommost** *adj* **1** very lowest. **2** most basic.

bough *n* branch of a tree.

bought *v pt* and *pp* of **buy.**

boulder *n* large stone or rock.

bounce *vi,vt* **1** rebound or cause to spring back after striking or being thrown. **2** jump or throw up and down; jerk. *vi* (of a cheque) be returned by a bank as unacceptable. *n* **1** rebound; springing back. **2** jump; jerk. **3** exuberance; ebullience. **bouncing** *adj* very healthy or robust. **bouncy** *adj* exuberant; high-spirited. **bounciness** *n*.

bound[1] *v pt* and *pp* of **bind.** *adj* **bound to** certain to; sure to. **bound up with** *or* **in** closely involved with.

bound[2] *vi* leap; spring. *n* jump; bounce; leap.

bound[3] *vt* restrict; limit. *n* boundary; limit. **boundless** *adj* inexhaustible; limitless.

bound[4] *adj* heading towards; destined for.

boundary *n* something that marks the edge or limit of an area of land.

bouquet *n* **1** (bou'kei, bu:-) bunch of flowers, esp. one elaborately arranged or displayed. **2** (bu:'kei) aroma of a wine.

bourgeois ('buəʒwa:) *adj* of the middle class, esp. when regarded as conservative and materialistic. *n* member of the middle class. **bourgeoisie** (buəʒwa:'zi:) *n* middle class.

bout *n* **1** boxing contest; fight. **2** short period; spell.

boutique *n* small shop, esp. one selling clothes.

bow[1] (bau) *vt,vi* bend (the body or head) forwards as an act of respect, submission, etc. *vi* yield; submit; comply. **bow down 1** yield. **2** submit. ~*n* bending of the body or lowering of the head.

bow[2] (bou) *n* **1** weapon from which arrows are shot, consisting of a supple piece of wood pulled into a curved shape by a taut string. **2** rod strung with horsehair used for playing a violin, cello, etc. **3** decorative knot having two loops and two loose ends. **4** curve; arc. *vi,vt* **1** draw a bow across (a violin, cello, etc.). **2** curve; bend. **bow-legged** (bou'legid, -'legd) *adj* having the legs curving outwards; bandy.

bow[3] (bau) *n* front or forward end of a ship or boat.

bowels *pl n* **1** intestines. **2** deepest or innermost part.

bowl[1] *n* shallow basin or dish. **bowler** *n also* **bowler hat** hat with a hard rounded crown and narrow brim.

bowl[2] *n* heavy ball used in bowls, tenpin bowling, etc. *vt,vi* **1** roll (a ball) or travel smoothly along the ground. **2** deliver (a ball) to the batsman in cricket. **bowl along** travel fast and comfortably. **bowl over 1** knock to the ground. **2** overwhelm; astound. **bowler** *n* person who bowls in cricket. **bowling** *n* tenpin bowling or skittles. **bowls** *n* game played with weighted balls on a level grass pitch.

box[1] *n* **1** flat-bottomed container sometimes with a lid. **2** compartment for a small number of spectators, situated at the side of an auditorium. **3** cubicle; booth. **4** horsebox. **5** witness box. **6** section of printed matter enclosed within a border. **the box** *sl* television. ~*vt* pack into a box. **box in 1** enclose; board up. **2** corner or jam so as to prevent movement. **Boxing day** *n* first weekday after Christmas day. **box office** *n* booking office in a theatre, cinema, etc.

box[2] *vi,vt* **1** fight in a boxing match (against). **2** punch; hit with the fist. *n* blow of the fist; punch; cuff. **boxer** *n* **1** person who fights in a boxing match. **2** breed of smooth-haired dog, similar to a bulldog. **boxing** *n* sport in which two opponents fight with the fists using padded gloves.

boy *n* male child. **boyhood** *n*. **boyish** *adj*. **boyfriend** *n* male friend, esp. one with whom one has a romantic relationship.

boycott *vt* refuse to deal with (another nation, group, etc.) or buy (goods). *n* practice or instance of boycotting.

bra *n also* **brassiere** woman's undergarment worn to support the bosom.

brace *n* **1** tool into which a drill or bit is fitted for boring holes. **2** beam or girder used for strengthening or supporting a wall. **3** metal band fixed to the teeth to correct their alignment. **4** pair, esp. of game birds. **braces** *pl n* pair of straps worn over the shoulders and fastened to the waistband of a pair of trousers. ~*vt* strengthen or support with a brace. *vt,vi* invigorate; freshen. **brace oneself** prepare oneself for impending pain, shock, etc.

bracelet *n* ornamental chain or band worn round the wrist.

bracken *n* type of large fern.

bracket *n* **1** right-angled support for a shelf. **2** one of a pair of written or printed symbols used to enclose additional information, etc. **3** classified group of people, esp. an income group. *vt* **1** fix with a bracket. **2** enclose within brackets. **3** place in the same category.

brag *vi* (-gg-) boast. *n* card game similar to poker. **braggart** *n* boastful person.

braid *n* **1** plait. **2** band of material made from plaited or twisted threads. *vt* plait; interweave (strands).

Braille *n* system of writing using embossed dots enabling the blind to read by touch.

brain *n* **1** mass of nerve fibre situated inside the skull, forming the main part of the central nervous system. **2** *also* **brains** intelligence. *vt inf* kill by striking violently on the head. **brainwash** *vt* indoctrinate or condition totally. **brainwave** *n* **1** voltage and current waves produced by the brain. **2** brilliant idea or inspiration. **brainy** *adj inf* intelligent.

braise *vt,vi* cook in a small amount of liquid in an airtight container.

brake *n* device on a vehicle that stops or slows down the motion of the wheels. *vi,vt* stop or slow down by applying the brake.

bramble *n* bush with thorny stems, esp. a blackberry bush.

branch *n* **1** limb of a tree or shrub that grows from the trunk or main stem; bough. **2** subdivision; offshoot. **3** local shop, bank, etc., that is part of a larger organization. *vi* **1** produce branches. **2** *also* **branch off** subdivide, diverge; fork. **branch out** extend one's interests.

brand *n* **1** class of product, esp. one marketed under a trademark. **2** type, variety; sort. **3** identifying mark on cattle, sheep, etc. **4** *also* **branding iron** iron rod that is heated and used for marking animals for identification. **5** stigma. *vt* **1** mark with a brand. **2** denounce as; label. **3** impress permanently on the mind; scar. **brand-new** *adj* absolutely new and unused.

brandish *vt* hold or wave (a weapon) threateningly or defiantly. *n* triumphant wave; flourish.

brandy *n* spirit distilled from the fermented juice of grapes.

brash *adj* **1** coarse; loud. **2** reckless, impetuous. **brashly** *adv.* **brashness** *n.*

brass *n* **1** yellowish-gold alloy of copper and zinc. **2** family of musical instruments that includes the trumpet and trombone. **3** engraved memorial tablet made of brass. **get down to brass tacks** start to consider or discuss the most important aspects of an issue or situation. **brassy** *adj* **1** of or like brass. **2** vulgar and showy; shameless.

brassiere *n* bra.

brave *adj* courageous, not cowardly; bold. *vt* face or tackle courageously; defy. *n* warrior of an American Indian tribe. **bravely** *adv.* **bravery** *n.*

brawl *n* noisy uncontrolled fight. *vi* fight or quarrel noisily.

brawn *n* **1** well-developed muscles. **2** muscular strength. **3** dish made of chopped meat from the head of a pig or calf and compressed into a mould.

bray *n* **1** harsh cry of a donkey. **2** shout or harsh laugh. *vi,vt* **1** (of a donkey) utter a harsh cry. **2** shout or laugh harshly.

brazen *adj* **1** shamelessly defiant; bold. **2** made of or like brass; brassy. *v* **brazen out** face or carry out boldly or defiantly.

brazil *n also* **brazil nut** nut with an edible kernel and hard rough shell that grows in a cluster inside a large capsule.

breach *n* **1** infringement or violation of the terms of a contract or agreement. **2** split between factions or parties. **3** gap; hole; crack. *vt* **1** infringe; violate. **2** break open; make a hole in.

bread *n* **1** food made from flour, milk, yeast, etc., baked in the form of loaves or rolls. **2** *sl* money. **breadwinner** *n* person responsible for earning money to support a family.

breadth *n* **1** measurement or extent from one side to another; width; broadness. **2** extent. **3** open-mindedness; tolerance.

break *v* (broke; broken) *vt,vi* **1** shatter or separate into pieces; fragment; smash; burst. **2** damage or cease to function. **3** pause; adjourn; stop for a while. *vt* **1** fail to keep (a promise, agreement, etc.). **2** bankrupt; ruin financially. **3** destroy; crush. **4** fracture (a bone). **5** reveal or disclose (news, a secret, etc.). **6** succeed in giving up (a habit). **7** surpass or improve on (a previous record, achievement, etc.). **8** reduce the impact of. *vi*

1 become known; be made public. **2** change; come to an end. **3** be overcome or overwhelmed with grief, strain, etc. **4** (esp. of the male voice at puberty) undergo a change. *n* **1** fracture; split; crack. **2** pause; recess; interval. **3** disconnection; discontinuation. **4** change of routine or habit. **5** sudden escape. **6** *inf* opportunity; stroke of luck. **break away 1** escape. **2** form or join a new group. **breakaway** *n* **1** escape. **2** split. **break down 1** stop functioning because of mechanical failure. **2** fail. **3** collapse with emotion. **4** analyse. **breakdown** *n* **1** failure. **2** mental collapse; nervous breakdown. **3** analysis; detailed account. **break even** cover one's expenses with neither profit nor loss. **break in(to) 1** force entry, esp. in order to steal. **2** interrupt. **3** tame and train (a horse). **break-in** *n* forced entry. **break off 1** detach a piece (from). **2** discontinue (a relationship). **3** stop abruptly, esp. when speaking. **break out 1** escape (from prison). **2** begin suddenly or violently. **3** develop (a rash, pimples, etc.). **break through 1** penetrate. **2** achieve after a long struggle. **breakthrough** *n* important discovery or achievement. **break up 1** disintegrate. **2** split up; separate; part. **break-up** *n* **1** disintegration. **2** split; separation. **breakable** *adj*. **breakage** *n* **1** act of breaking. **2** the thing broken or its value.

breakfast *n* first meal of the day. *vi* eat breakfast.

breast *n* **1** front part of the body from the neck to the abdomen; chest. **2** mammary gland. **3** centre of affection, patriotic feelings, etc. **make a clean breast of** confess. **breaststroke** *n* stroke in swimming performed face downwards with the arms and legs making circular movements.

breath *n* **1** inhalation and exhalation of air. **2** air inhaled or exhaled. **3** slight gust of air or wind. **4** hint; suggestion; vague rumour. **out of breath** unable to breathe properly. **take one's breath away** dumbfound; astound. **under one's breath** in a low voice or whisper. **breathless** *adj* out of breath. **breathy** *adj*. **breathtaking** *adj* amazing; thrilling.

breathe *vt,vi* **1** inhale and exhale (air). **2** whisper; murmur; blow gently. **breather** *n inf* pause for rest. **breathing space** *n* sufficient room to move or function.

breed *vt,vi* (bred) **1** bear and produce (offspring). **2** propagate; reproduce. **3** generate; give rise to. *n* **1** group within a species, having common characteristics. **2** type; variety; brand. **breeder** *n*. **breeding** *n* **1** reproduction; propagation. **2** socially acceptable upbringing or background.

breeze *n* light wind. *vi inf* move about in a carefree manner. **breezy** *adj*.

brethren *n pl* of **brother,** esp. in a religious context.

brevity *n* briefness; conciseness.

brew *vt,vi* **1** make (beer) by fermentation. **2** make (tea, coffee, etc.) by infusion. *vt* concoct. *vi* **1** undergo fermentation or infusion. **2** be in the process of formation. *n* **1** brand of beer. **2** concoction. **brewery** *n* establishment where beer is brewed.

bribe *n* payment offered in order to influence a person to act in one's favour, esp. illegally. *vt,vi* persuade with a bribe. **bribery** *n*.

brick *n* **1** block of stone or baked clay used in building. **2** small block of wood used as a toy. **3** slab. *vt also* **brick up** seal or enclose with bricks. **bricklayer** *n* person skilled in building with bricks. **bricklaying** *n*. **brickwork** *n* construction with bricks.

bride *n* woman preparing for marriage or recently married. **bridegroom** *n* husband of a bride. **bridesmaid** *n* female attendant who looks after the bride.

bridge[1] *n* **1** construction spanning a river, valley, etc. **2** top part of the nose. **3** platform from which a ship is piloted or navigated. **4** small block supporting the strings of a violin, guitar, etc. **5** something that serves to connect. *vt* **1** place a bridge over; span. **2** form a connection between.

bridge[2] *n* card game developed from whist.

bridle *n* part of a harness, including the headpiece, bit, and reins, for controlling a horse. *vt* **1** fit or control with a bridle. **2** curb; check. *vi* express contempt, anger, etc., by drawing in the chin or jerking the head. **bridlepath** *n* narrow track that is suitable for horses.

brief *adj* **1** lasting a short time. **2** concise. **3** curt; abrupt. *n* **1** document in which a solicitor sets out details of his client's case for a barrister. **2** set of instructions. **briefs** *pl n* short underpants or knickers. ~*vt* prepare or instruct with a brief. **briefly** *adv*. **briefness** *n*. **briefcase** *n* bag or case used to hold papers, documents, etc. **briefing** *n* meeting at which information and instructions are given, esp. for a military operation.

brigade *n* **1** military unit forming part of a division. **2** group of people trained to perform a special task. **brigadier** (brigə'diə) *n* army officer holding a rank below that of major general and above a colonel and usually in command of a brigade.

bright *adj* **1** giving off a strong light. **2** of a strong colour; vivid. **3** shiny; gleaming. **4** cheerful. **5** *inf* clever; intelligent. *adv also* **brightly** in a bright manner. **brightness** *n*. **brighten** *vt,vi* make or become bright(er).

brilliant *adj* **1** shining brightly; glittering. **2** extremely clever or talented. **3** displaying great imagination. **4** outstanding. **brilliance** *n*. **brilliantly** *adv*.

brim *n* **1** rim of a cup, dish, etc. **2** edge of a hat projecting from the crown. *vt,vi* (-mm-) fill or be full so as to overflow.

bring *vt* (brought) **1** carry or convey (to or towards). **2** accompany. **3** produce; yield. **4** cause. **5** force or persuade. **bring about** cause to happen. **bring back** reintroduce; restore. **bring down 1** force down. **2** reduce. **3** humiliate or depress. **bring forward 1** produce; present. **2** fix for an earlier time. **bring in 1** introduce; initiate. **2** yield; earn. **3** include. **bring off** achieve by striving or by taking risks. **bring on 1** cause to start; induce. **2** help to develop; encourage. **bring out 1** cause to show or appear. **2** publish. **bring round 1** make conscious again, esp. after fainting. **2** persuade; convert; convince. **bring up 1** rear; educate from an early age. **2** vomit. **3** introduce or mention.

brink *n* **1** edge of a high or steep place, body of water, etc. **2** threshold; verge.

brisk *adj* **1** quick; lively. **2** invigorating; fresh. **briskly** *adv*. **briskness** *n*.

bristle *n* **1** short tough hair of an animal such as the pig. **2** hair, wire, fibre, etc., of a brush. **3** hair of a man's beard; stubble. *vi* **1** (of fur, hair, etc.) stand on end; be stiff or rigid. **2** display signs of annoyance, indignation, etc. **bristle with** be crowded or overrun with. **bristly** *adj*.

brittle *adj* **1** easily broken, shattered, or cracked. **2** irritable; short-tempered. **brittleness** *n*.

broach *vt* **1** introduce or suggest tentatively. **2** pierce or open in order to draw off liquid; tap.

broad *adj* **1** wide; not narrow. **2** extensive. **3** from one side to another; across; in width. **4** general; not specific. **5** direct; not subtle. **6** crude; coarse; vulgar. **7** displaying features of dialect or non-standard speech. **8** tolerant. **in broad daylight** openly; without attempting to conceal. **broad bean** *n* bean having large flat seeds, which are eaten as a vegetable. **broaden** *vt,vi* make or become broad(er); widen. **broad-minded** *adj* having tolerant or liberal views; not bigoted. **broad-mindedness** *n*.

broadcast *v* (-cast *or* -casted) *vt,vi* transmit via radio or television. *vi* appear on a radio or television programme. *vt* **1** publicize. **2** sow (seed) by hand. *n* radio or television transmission or programme. **broadcaster** *n*. **broadcasting** *n*.

brocade *n* heavy fabric woven with embossed designs.

broccoli *n* type of cabbage having edible green or purple flower heads.

brochure *n* pamphlet or booklet containing information, advertisements, etc.

broke *v pt* of **break.** *adj* penniless; bankrupt.

broken *v pp* of **break. broken-hearted** *adj* overwhelmed with grief, sorrow, disappointment, etc.

broker *n* agent for insurance, shares, securities, loans, etc.

bronchi ('brɔŋkai) *pl n, s* **bronchus** ('brɔŋkəs) *also* **bronchial tubes** two main branches of the windpipe. **bronchial** *adj*. **bronchitis** *n* inflammation of the bronchi.

bronze *n* **1** reddish-gold alloy of copper and tin, sometimes with zinc and lead added. **2** statue or ornament of bronze. *adj* **1** reddish-gold. **2** *also* **bronzed** suntanned. *vt,vi* make or become suntanned.

brooch *n* ornamental pin or clasp fastened to the front of the clothing.

brood *n* **1** group of young birds hatched at the same time. **2** *inf* children in a family; offspring. *vt,vi* **1** sit on and hatch (eggs). **2** think or worry (about) for a long time. **broody** *adj*.

brook *n* small stream.

broom *n* **1** implement for sweeping with a head of bristles or fibres and a long handle. **2** evergreen shrub with bright yellow flowers, that is able to grow on poor soil.

brother *n* **1** son of the same parents as another **2** fellow member; comrade. **3** unordained or lay male member of a religious order. **brotherhood** *n* **1** relationship as a brother. **2** fraternity; fellowship. **3** religious community of men. **brother-in-law** *n, pl* **brothers-in-law** **1** husband of one's sister. **2** brother of one's wife or husband. **3** husband of the sister of one's wife or husband. **brotherly** *adj* affectionate or loyal as a brother.

brought *v pt* and *pp* of **bring.**

brow *n* **1** eyebrow. **2** forehead. **3** crest of a hill. **browbeat** *vt* (-beat; -beaten) intimidate; oppress; bully.

brown *n* the colour of earth; very dark orange or yellow. *adj* **1** of the colour brown. **2** suntanned. *vt,vi* make or become brown. **browned off** *adj* disillusioned; bored; fed up. **brownish** *adj*.

browse *vi* **1** look through or examine a book, items for sale, etc., unhurriedly or casually. **2** feed on vegetation; graze.

bruise *n* rupture of the blood vessels causing discoloration of the skin. *vt,vi* **1** produce a bruise. **2** offend; hurt the feelings (of).

brunette *n* woman or girl with dark hair. *adj* dark; brown.

brunt *n* full impact of force, shock, etc.

brush *n* **1** implement with a head of bristles or fibres and a handle. **2** stroke made with a brush. **3** light touch. **4** short unpleasant meeting or contact. **5** fox's tail. *vt* **1** wipe, clean, apply, etc., with a brush. **2** touch lightly. **brush aside** dismiss as irrelevant; disregard. **brush up** **1** revise; refresh the memory. **2** make neat and tidy.

brusque *adj* curt; brisk; abrupt. **brusquely** *adv*. **brusqueness** *n*.

Brussels sprout *n* type of cabbage having small edible heads of tightly overlapping leaves growing on one stem.

brute *n* **1** animal, esp. when contrasted with man; beast. **2** cruel, tyrannical, or ignorant person. *adj* **brute force/strength** sheer physical force/strength; brawn. **brutal** *adj* cruel; savage; barbaric. **brutality** *n*. **brutally** *adv*.

bubble *n* **1** globule of air or gas contained within a film of liquid. **2** gurgling sound. *vt,vi* form bubbles; effervesce. *vi* gurgle.

buck *n* male of animals such as the rabbit, hare, or deer. *vi* rear in an attempt to unseat a rider. *vt* unseat; throw off. **buck up** **1** hurry. **2** cheer up.

bucket *n* container with a circular bottom and a handle. **kick the bucket** die.

buckle *n* **1** clasp with a prong used for securing a belt or strap. **2** distorted curve; bulge; twist. *vt,vi* **1** fasten with a buckle. **2** force or be forced out of shape through stress, heat, etc.; warp.

bud *n* undeveloped flower or leaf shoot. **nip in the bud** prevent the development of. ~*vi* (-dd-) produce buds. **budding** *adj* beginning to show talent; promising.

Buddhism ('budizəm) *n* Eastern religion, founded by Buddha, that teaches self-awareness through the denial of passion or desire. **Buddhist** *n,adj*.

budge *vt,vi* move; shift.

budget *n* **1** estimate of expected income and expenditure. **2** money allocated for a project. *vt,vi* **1** allow for or include in a budget. **2** spend according to a budget; economize (on).

buffalo *n* **1** African animal of the ox family having curved horns. **2** bison.

buffer *n* **1** shock absorber fitted to a train or placed at the end of a railway track. **2** person or thing that serves to reduce the threat of attack or lessen the impact of a collision.

buffet[1] ('bʌfei) *n* **1** counter or table from which refreshments are served. **2** refreshments set out for guests to help themselves.

buffet[2] ('bʌfit) *vt* **1** blow or toss about; batter. **2** fight or push through.

bug *n* **1** type of insect that feeds on plant juices or the blood of animals. **2** *inf* infection caused by certain microorganisms. **3** concealed device, such as a microphone, used to obtain secret information. **4** *sl* obsession; craze. *vt* (-gg-) **1** annoy; bother; nag. **2** conceal a microphone in.

bugle *n* brass instrument similar to the trumpet but without valves. *vi* play a bugle.

build *vt,vi* (built) **1** construct using materials such as brick, stone, or wood. **2** commission or finance a construction. *vt* **1** establish and develop (a business, etc.). **2** create or design for a particular purpose. **build up** **1** work on in order to strengthen, increase, or enhance. **2** accumulate. **build-up** *n* **1** gradual increase. **2** promotion of a commodity. **builder** *n*. **building** *n* **1** construction having walls and a roof. **2** business or process of constructing houses, shops, etc. **building society** *n* company advancing loans for mortgages using funds deposited by investors. **built-in** *adj* constructed as an integral part.

bulb *n* **1** rounded organ of a plant, such as the tulip or onion, that grows underground. **2** plant growing from such an organ. **3** light bulb. **bulbous** *adj*.

bulge *n* swelling; protuberance. *vi* swell; stick out.

bulk *n* **1** large quantity or volume. **2** greater part. **3** cargo, esp. before packaging. **4** human body, esp. when large or fat. **bulky** *adj* large and cumbersome. **bulkiness** *n*.

bull *n* **1** adult male member of the ox family. **2** male of animals such as the elephant or seal. **3** person who buys stocks and sells them after the price has risen. **4** *sl also* **bullshit** nonsense; exaggerated statement. **bulldog** *n* breed of short-haired dog with a sturdy body, muscular legs, and a large head. **bulldoze** *vt* **1** demolish or clear with a bulldozer. **2** barge through; shove. **bulldozer** *n* heavy tractor used for clearing rubble, earth, etc. **bullfight** *n* public entertainment common in Spain, Portugal, and S America in which a matador fights a bull. **bullfighter** *n*. **bullring** *n* arena used for a bullfight.

bullet *n* projectile discharged from a gun. **bullet-proof** *adj* able to protect from bullets.

bulletin *n* public notice or announcement giving official news or information.

bullion *n* gold or silver, esp. before it has been minted.

bully *vt,vi* threaten or act violently towards someone weaker; intimidate. *n* person who bullies.

bum *n sl* buttocks.

bump *vt,vi* **1** collide (with); bang (into); knock. **2** injure or hurt by banging. *vi also* **bump along** jolt; travel jerkily. **bump into** meet unexpectedly. **bump off** *sl* murder. ~*n* **1** collision; jolt; knock. **2** swelling; lump. **3** small mound; bulge. **bumpy** *adj*. **bumper** *n* protective bar fitted to either end of a vehicle.

bun *n* **1** small sweet baked roll. **2** hair coiled into a knot at the back of the head.

bunch *n* **1** number of things growing or arranged in a cluster. **2** group of people; set. *vt,vi also* **bunch up** gather together; cluster; huddle.

bundle *n* pile of things loosely wrapped or tied together. *vt* **1** *also* **bundle up** make into a bundle. **2** push hurriedly out of sight.

bung *n* stopper for a bottle, barrel, etc. *vt* **1** *also* **bung up** stop up or seal with a bung; block. **2** *sl* throw; chuck.

bungalow *n* single-storeyed house.

bungle *vt,vi* spoil by acting clumsily or incompetently; botch.

bunk *n* **1** narrow bed, esp. on a ship. **2** *also* **bunk bed** one of a pair of beds fitted one above the other in a single framework.

bunker *n* **1** storage container for coal, oil, etc. **2** sand-filled hollow functioning as a hazard on a golf course. **3** fortified underground shelter.

buoy *n* anchored float used as a navigation guide or for mooring a vessel. *v* **buoy up 1** keep afloat. **2** sustain optimism or cheerfulness in. **buoyant** *adj* **1** able to float. **2** optimistic; light-hearted. **buoyancy** *n*. **buoyantly** *adv*.

burble *vt,vi* gurgle; babble. *n* gurgling sound.

burden *n* **1** heavy load. **2** responsibility, suffering, etc., that is hard to cope with. *vt* **1** overload; weigh down with. **2** oppress, cause to suffer. **burdensome** *adj*.

bureau ('bjuərou) *n, pl* **bureaux** ('bjuərou) *or* **bureaus 1** agency or government department dealing in employment, tourist information, etc. **2** writing desk fitted with drawers, pigeonholes, etc.

bureaucracy (bjuə'rɔkrəsi) *n* **1** system of government or administration by paid officials rather than elected representatives. **2** officials working within such a system. **3** excessive use of official administrative procedures; red tape. **bureaucrat** *n*. **bureaucratic** *adj*.

burglary *n* crime of breaking into a building at night with intent to commit certain offences. **burglar** *n*. **burgle** *vt,vi* commit burglary (in or on).

burial *n* burying, esp. of a body at a funeral.

burn *v* (burnt *or* burned) *vt,vi* damage or become damaged by fire, heat, or acid. *vi* **1** be combustible or inflammable. **2** produce heat or light; blaze; glow. **3** feel painfully hot or sore; smart. **4** be consumed with desire, anger, jealousy, etc. *vt* **1** use in order to produce heat or light. **2** make (a hole, mark, etc.) by fire, heat, or acid; scorch. **burn out 1** wear out by heat or friction. **2** use up one's energy; become exhausted. ~*n* **1** injury caused by fire, heat, or acid. **2** mark or hole caused by burning. **burning** *adj* **1** urgent; vital. **2** intense; passionate.

burrow *n* underground hole or tunnel dug by an animal for shelter. *vt,vi* tunnel or dig deeply (into). *vi* delve; search.

burst *vt,vi* (burst) break or split open, esp. under pressure; explode. **burst in(to) 1** enter noisily. **2** interrupt rudely. **burst into song/tears, etc.** start to sing, cry, etc., loudly and suddenly. ~*n* **1** split; rupture. **2** sudden loud noise; explosion. **3** spurt of activity, energy, etc.; surge.

bury *vt* **1** place (a corpse) in a grave or tomb; inter. **2** place underground. **3** conceal by covering. **4** embed; stick into. **5** engross. **6** repress; forget.

bus *n, pl* **buses** *or* **busses** large motor vehicle scheduled to carry passengers along a fixed route. *vi,vt* (-ss-) travel or carry by bus.

bush *n* **1** large plant with woody stems; shrub. **2** thick mass. **the bush** area of rough uncultivated land, esp. in Australia or S Africa; scrubland. **beat about the bush** act evasively; prevaricate. **bushy** *adj* **1** thick and shaggy. **2** covered with bushes.

bushel *n* unit of capacity equal to 2219 cubic inches. **hide one's light under a bushel** be modest about one's abilities or skills.

business *n* **1** commerce; trade. **2** occupation; profession. **3** commercial company; trading organization; firm. **4** affair; matter; concern. **business-like** *adj* conforming to certain standards of business procedure; efficient. **businessman** *n, pl* **-men** man engaged in commerce or trade, esp. as an executive. **businesswoman** *f n.*

bust[1] *n* **1** bosom or breast. **2** sculpture depicting a person's head and shoulders.

bust[2] *vt,vi* (busted *or* bust) **1** break; smash. **2** ruin; make or become bankrupt. **3** *sl* raid or search, esp. in order to arrest. **bust up 1** disrupt. **2** split or part after a quarrel. **bust-up** *n* **1** brawl. **2** separation after a quarrel.

bustle *vt,vi* hurry; be or make busy. *n* busy activity; commotion.

busy *adj* **1** fully occupied; active; engaged. **2** crowded; bustling. *v* **busy oneself** take up time with; occupy oneself. **busily** *adv.* **busybody** *n* person who gossips or meddles.

but *conj* **1** however; yet; nevertheless. **2** except; apart from; other than. *prep* with the exception of. **but for** without; were it not for. ~*adv* merely, just. **all but** almost; nearly.

butane *n* flammable hydrocarbon gas used as a fuel.

butcher *n* **1** person who prepares and sells meat. **2** savage murderer. *vt* **1** slaughter and prepare (meat). **2** murder, esp. with a knife, axe, etc.; slaughter; slay. **butchery** *n.*

butler *n* male servant, usually having special responsibility for wines.

butt[1] *n* **1** blunt thick end of a rifle, tool, etc. **2** cigarette end; stub.

butt[2] *n* **1** person who bears the brunt of ridicule, scorn, etc. **2** mound situated behind the target on a shooting range. **3** target.

butt[3] *vt,vi* push hard with the head or horns; ram. **butt in** interrupt; interfere. ~*n* violent push with the head or horns.

butter *n* yellowish-white solid fat produced by churning cream. *vt* spread with butter. **butter up** flatter. **buttercup** *n* wild flower with bright yellow petals. **butterscotch** *n* brittle toffee made with butter and sugar.

butterfly *n* **1** insect with large wings, which are often brightly coloured or patterned. **2** person who is unable to settle or sustain interest in anything for very long.

buttocks *pl n* fleshy lower part of the body on which a person sits; bottom.

button *n* **1** small disc sewn on to a garment and able to pass through a buttonhole or loop as a fastening, or used for decoration. **2** small knob that is pushed to operate a machine, doorbell, etc. **3** anything small and round that resembles a button. *vt also* **button up** fasten with a button. **buttonhole** *n* **1** hole edged with stitching, through which a button is passed. **2** flower or spray worn in a buttonhole. *vt* **1** stitch round a buttonhole. **2** corner in order to engage in conversation.

buttress *n* **1** structure of stone or brick built to support a wall. **2** source of strength or support. *vt* **1** strengthen with a buttress. **2** give moral support to.

buxom *adj* having a full bosom; plump.

buy *vt,vi* (bought) obtain in exchange for money; purchase. **buy up** buy all that is available of a particular commodity. ~*n* thing bought; purchase. **buyer** *n* person who buys, esp. one purchasing merchandise for resale.

buzz *n* **1** low continuous noise; hum. **2** *inf* telephone call; ring. **3** *sl* pleasant sensation caused by certain drugs, alcohol, etc. *vt,vi* **1** produce a low vibrating hum. **2** signal or call using a buzzer. **3** *inf* phone; ring. *vi* **1** move hurriedly from place to place. **2** produce an atmosphere of excitement. **buzz off** go away; leave. **buzzer** *n* electrical device producing a harsh continuous signal.

by *prep* **1** through the agency, means, or authorship of. **2** via; past. **3** beside; close to; near. **4** no later than. **5** to a greater or lesser extent than. **6** multiplied with. **7** with a second dimension of. **8** during; in the course of. **by and by** eventually; after a while. **by-election** *n* election held when a particular seat becomes vacant, as after the resignation or death of a Member of Parliament. **bylaw** *n* law made by a local authority and operational only within its own area. **bypass** *n* road constructed to direct the flow of traffic away from a town centre. *vt* **1** go round in order to avoid. **2** ignore (regulations, procedures, etc.) in order to proceed without delay.

C

cab *n* **1** driver's compartment of a lorry, bus, etc. **2** taxi.

cabaret ('kæbərei) *n* entertainment provided by a nightclub, restaurant, etc.

cabbage *n* vegetable with a short stalk and a head of green or purplish tightly packed leaves.

cabin *n* **1** small functional house, hut, or shelter. **2** living quarters on a ship; berth. **3** section of an aircraft for passengers or crew. **cabin cruiser** *n* motor boat with cabin accommodation.

cabinet *n* **1** piece of furniture for storing crockery, glassware, medicine, etc.; cupboard. **2** filing cabinet. **3** outer case of a radio or television set. **the Cabinet** body of Government ministers responsible for policy-making.

cable *n* **1** strong rope of twisted wire, hemp, etc. **2** set of insulated wires used for conducting electricity. **3** overseas telegram. **4** *also* **cable stitch** knitting stitch producing a twisted pattern. *vt,vi* send an overseas telegram (to).

cache (kæʃ) *n* hidden supply or store, esp. of weapons.

cackle *vi* **1** squawk like a hen. **2** laugh or shriek raucously. *n* **1** squawk. **2** raucous laugh or shriek.

cactus *n, pl* **cacti** ('kæktai) *or* **cactuses** plant adapted to grow in desert regions with tough spiny stems and bright showy flowers.

cadence *n* **1** sequence of chords marking the end of a musical phrase or section. **2** modulation of the voice; intonation.

cadet *n* young trainee, esp. in the armed forces or police force.

cadge *vt,vi* acquire or ask for without intending to pay; beg. **cadger** *n* person who cadges.

café *n* small restaurant serving snacks.

cafeteria *n* self-service restaurant or canteen.

caffeine *n* mild stimulant found in some plants, esp. coffee.

cage *n* **1** enclosure or box with bars used for confining animals or birds. **2** lift in a mine shaft. *vt* put or keep in a cage.

cajole *vt,vi* wheedle; coax; persuade by flattery.

cake *n* **1** sweet food made from flour, sugar, eggs, etc., and baked. **2** flattish compact mass, as of soap. **a piece of cake** *inf* something easily achieved or obtained. ~*vt* cover with a hard dry mass.

calamity *n* disaster; misfortune. **calamitous** *adj*.

calcium *n* silvery metallic element found in limestone, marble, and other rocks and in bones and teeth.

calculate *vt,vi* work out mathematically. *vt* **1** estimate; believe; suppose. **2** design; plan; intend. **calculating** *adj* ruthless; scheming. **calculation** *n*. **calculator** *n* electronic device used for mathematical calculation.

calendar *n* **1** system for determining the length of a year, order of months, etc. **2** chart showing the divisions of a year. **3** list or diary of events and engagements.

calf[1] *n, pl* **calves** **1** young of cattle. **2** young seal, whale, elephant, etc.

calf[2] *n* fleshy part of the back of the lower leg.

calibre *n* **1** diameter of a gun bore, bullet, etc. **2** worth; merit.

call *vt,vi* **1** shout out in order to summon, attract attention, etc. **2** telephone; ring. *vi also* **call on** visit. *vt* **1** name; christen. **2** describe as; label. **3** convene (a meeting). **call for 1** fetch; collect. **2** require; demand. **call in 1** drop by on a visit. **2** request the services of (a doctor, specialist, etc.). **call off 1** cancel or postpone. **2** order to stop attacking. **call on** appeal to; request. **call out 1** summon. **2** bring out on strike. **call to mind** recall. **call**

up 1 conscript. **2** reach by telephone. ~*n* **1** characteristic cry of a bird or animal. **2** shout. **3** visit. **4** telephone conversation. **5** duty; obligation. **6** demand; need. **on call** available for duty. **caller** *n*. **callbox** *n* public telephone box. **calling** *n* vocation. **call-up** *n* conscription.

callous *adj* cruelly indifferent to suffering. **callously** *adv*. **callousness** *n*.

calm *adj* **1** not excited or anxious; serene; untroubled. **2** peaceful. **3** still; hardly moving. *n also* **calmness** stillness; tranquillity; peace. *vt,vi also* **calm down** make or become calm(er); quieten; soothe. **calmly** *adv*.

calorie *n* unit of heat energy, used esp. for measuring the energy value of foods.

came *v pt* of **come.**

camel *n* long-legged largely domesticated mammal with one or two humps on its back, commonly found in desert areas of N Africa.

camera *n* **1** optical device for producing a photographic image. **2** *also* **television camera** device for converting optical images into electrical signals. **in camera** in private; not open.

camouflage *n* **1** use of certain materials as a disguise to prevent a person, military equipment, etc., from being seen by an enemy. **2** colour or markings of an animal that make it less conspicuous in a certain environment. *vt* make less noticeable by use of camouflage.

camp[1] *n* **1** site having tents, huts, etc., for use as temporary accommodation. **2** military base housing soldiers temporarily; encampment. **3** group of people with common political views. *vi also* **camp out** live in a tent or other temporary living accommodation. **camper** *n*. **camping** *n*.

camp[2] *adj* of a style that exaggerates or parodies what is thought to be appropriate homosexual behaviour. *n* exaggerated or effeminate style of behaviour.

campaign *n* **1** series of planned military operations. **2** technical activities designed to promote a political cause or candidate, commercial product, etc. *vi* mount a campaign; fight. **campaigner** *n*.

campus *n* area and buildings occupied by a university or college.

can[1] *v aux* (*pt* could) **1** be able or willing to; know how to. **2** have permission or opportunity to.

can[2] *n* metal container or tin. **carry the can** accept responsibility or blame. ~*vt* (-nn-) put or store in a can.

canal *n* **1** man-made waterway or channel for navigation, irrigation, etc. **2** passage or duct in the body.

canary *n* small yellow songbird of the finch family.

cancel *vt* (-ll-) **1** prevent (a planned event) from taking place; call off. **2** stop; discontinue. **3** make invalid by crossing through or stamping with a special mark. **cancel out** offset; compensate (for). **cancellation** *n*.

cancer *n* malignant growth or tumour in the body. **Cancer** fourth sign of the zodiac represented by the crab.

candid *adj* honest; frank; open; fair. **candidly** *adv*. **candour** *n*.

candidate *n* **1** person nominated or applying for a particular office, job, or position. **2** person sitting an examination.

candle *n* cylinder of wax with a central wick, which burns slowly when lit. **burn the candle at both ends** exhaust oneself by living strenuously.

cane *n* **1** pliant hollow stem of the bamboo or various palms, often used for making furniture. **2** sugar cane. **3** thorny stem of a raspberry or blackberry bush. **4** thin rod used as a walking stick or as an implement for inflicting punishment. *vt,vi* punish by beating with a cane.

canine *adj* **1** of the dog family. **2** like a dog.

canister *n* cylindrical metal storage container; can.

cannabis *n* **1** hemp plant. **2** marijuana.

cannibal *n* **1** person who eats human flesh. **2** animal that feeds on its own kind. **cannibalism** *n*. **cannibalize** *vt* take parts from (motor vehicles, etc.) to repair others.

cannon *n, pl* **cannons** *or* **cannon** heavy mounted gun that discharges large shells. *v* **cannon into** collide with; barge into.

cannot *v aux* **1** be unable or unwilling to. **2** be forbidden or have no opportunity to.

canoe *n* small narrow portable boat propelled with a paddle. *vi* travel or transport by canoe.

canon *n* **1** ecclesiastical law. **2** list of Christian saints. **3** priest attached to a cathedral or various religious orders. **4** moral principle; standard; criterion. **5** musical form in which the same melody is introduced at overlapping intervals by two or more voices. **canonical** *adj*. **canonize** *vt* recognize officially as a saint.

canopy *n* ornamental awning suspended above a throne, bed, etc.

canteen *n* **1** restaurant for the use of employees of a company, children at school, etc. **2** box of cutlery. **3** flask carried by soldiers, campers, etc.

canter *n* gait of a horse between a trot and a gallop. *vi,vt* move or take at a canter.

canvas *n* **1** hard-wearing waterproof material of flax or hemp. **2** piece of such material used for painting on in oils.

canvass *vi,vt* seek support or opinions from (potential voters, customers, etc.). **canvasser** *n*.

canyon *n* deep narrow valley or gorge; ravine.

cap *n* **1** flat closely fitting hat, sometimes with a peak. **2** small lid or cover. **3** natural or artificial covering of a tooth. **4** *also* **dutch cap** diaphragm used as a contraceptive device. *vt* (-pp-) **1** cover the top or surface of. **2** outdo; top. **to cap it all** in addition; on top; as a finishing touch.

capable *adj* **1** having the potential or capacity for. **2** able; competent. **capability** *n*. **capably** *adv*.

capacity *n* **1** power to contain a quantity. **2** amount that a container can hold; volume. **3** maximum number that can be accommodated. **4** ability to perform or behave in a particular way. **5** power or function of an office or rank.

cape[1] *n* short cloak.

cape[2] *n* headland.

capital *n* **1** city that is the seat of government of a country. **2** wealth or assets, esp. when used for investment or profit. **3** *also* **capital letter** large or upper case form of a written or printed letter of the alphabet. *adj* **1** *inf* excellent; first-class. **2** carrying the penalty of death. **capitalism** *n* economic system whereby private owners control the means of production and distribution. **capitalist** *adj,n*. **capitalize** *vt* **1** use, provide, or convert into capital. **2** write or print in capital letters. **capitalize on** exploit; take advantage of.

caprice (kəˈpriːs) *n* whim. **capricious** (kəˈpriʃəs) *adj* subject to or indicative of whim; changeable.

Capricorn *n* tenth sign of the zodiac, represented by the goat.

capsicum *n* tropical plant bearing edible fruit (peppers).

capsize *vi,vt* overturn; upset.

capsule *n* **1** soluble shell enclosing a dose of oral medicine. **2** pressurized compartment of a space vehicle. **3** closed structure containing seeds, spores, or fruits. **capsular** *adj*.

captain *n* **1** person in charge of a vessel or aircraft. **2** naval officer ranking above a commander and below a rear admiral. **3** army officer ranking above a lieutenant and below a major. **4** leader of a sports team. *vt* act as captain of. **captaincy** *n*.

caption *n* **1** brief description accompanying an illustration. **2** heading or title; headline; subtitle. *vt* provide with a caption.

capture *vt* **1** take prisoner. **2** gain control or possession of. *n* act of capturing. **captivate** *vt* fascinate; charm; enchant. **captivation** *n*. **captive** *n* prisoner. *adj* **1** imprisoned. **2** restrained; confined. **captivity** *n*.

car *n* **1** small wheeled vehicle for personal transport. **2** vehicle containing passengers, such as a railway carriage.

carafe (kəˈræf, ˈkærəf) *n* decorative bottle used for serving wine or water at the table.

caramel *n* **1** burnt sugar used for flavouring and colouring. **2** chewy kind of toffee.

carat *n* **1** measure of the purity of gold in an alloy. **2** measure of weight of precious stones, esp. diamonds.

caravan *n* **1** covered vehicle equipped for living in and capable of being drawn by a car, horse, etc. **2** company of travellers in desert regions. *vi* (-nn-) travel by caravan.

caraway *n* Eurasian plant whose aromatic fruits (caraway seeds) are used in cooking.

carbohydrate *n* organic compound, such as starch or sugar, containing carbon, hydrogen, and oxygen.

carbon *n* **1** widely distributed nonmetallic element occurring as diamond, graphite, or charcoal and forming many organic and inorganic compounds. **2** *also* **carbon paper** *n* paper coated on one side with a dark pigment, used to duplicate writing or typing. **carbon dioxide** *n* colourless incombustible gas present in the atmosphere, formed during respiration and the combustion of organic compounds.

carburettor *n* part of a petrol engine where the fuel is mixed with air.

carcass *n* dead body, esp. of an animal sold for food.

card *n* **1** piece of stiff paper used for filing, as proof of identity or membership, advertising, etc. **2** similar piece of paper, often illustrated, used for sending greetings, congratulations, etc. **3** any of a set of cardboard pieces, marked with symbols, used for playing games or telling fortunes. **a card up one's sleeve** thing or action kept in reserve to be used to gain an advantage. **on the cards** probable; likely. **put one's cards on the table** *or* **show one's cards** reveal one's intentions, plans, etc. **cardboard** *n* thin stiff board made of paper pulp.

cardigan *n* close-fitting woollen jacket.

cardinal *n* senior dignitary of the Roman Catholic Church, ranking next below the Pope. *adj* of prime importance; fundamental. **cardinal number** *n* number denoting quantity rather than order. **cardinal point** *n* one of the points of the compass, N, S, E, or W.

care *n* **1** solicitous attention. **2** caution. **3** supervision; charge; responsibility. **4** anxiety; trouble; worry. **care of** at the address of. ~*vi* feel interest or concern. **care for 1** feel affection for. **2** look after; tend. **3** wish for; want. **carefree** *adj* free from worry, anxiety, and responsibility. **careful** *adj* **1** cautious; wary. **2** meticulous; painstaking. **carefully** *adv*. **careless** *adj* **1** lacking sufficient thought or attention; negligent. **2** unconcerned; indifferent. **carelessly** *adv*. **carelessness** *n*. **caretaker** *n* person employed to look after and maintain a school, office, etc.

career *n* **1** pursuit of a profession or occupation. **2** course; progression. *vi* move rapidly, esp. in an uncontrolled way; hurtle.

caress *n* light gentle stroke of affection. *vt* stroke gently and affectionately; fondle.

cargo *n* goods carried in a ship or aircraft; freight; load.

caricature *n* satirical representation of a person that grossly exaggerates particular characteristics. *vt* represent as a caricature.

carnal *adj* sensual; not spiritual; of the flesh. **carnal knowledge** *n* sexual intercourse. **carnally** *adv*.

carnation *n* cultivated flower having fragrant pink, white, or red blooms.

carnival *n* public celebration, festivities, and revelry, esp. just before Lent.

carnivorous *adj* meat-eating. **carnivore** *n* meat-eating animal, esp. a mammal.

carol *n* joyous song, esp. to celebrate Christmas. *vi* (-ll-) sing joyfully.

carpenter *n* person skilled in using wood in building, making furniture, etc. *vi,vt* work as a carpenter. **carpentry** *n*.

carpet *n* **1** thick textile floor covering. **2** thick layer or covering. *vt* cover with or as if with a carpet.

carriage *n* **1** horse-drawn four-wheeled vehicle. **2** section of a train, often comprising several compartments. **3** movable gun-support. **4** part of a typewriter holding and moving paper. **5** deportment; bearing. **carriageway** *n* road, or part of a road, used by vehicles.

carrot *n* plant whose long orange root is eaten as a vegetable. **carroty** *adj* orange.

carry *vt,vi* take (something) from one place to another; transport; transmit; convey. *vt* **1** hold; bear; keep. **2** contain; include. **3** sustain; keep in operation. **4** influence. **carry oneself** conduct oneself; behave. **carry on** continue; persevere. **carrier** *n* **1** person or thing that carries. **2** *also* **carrier-bag** large paper or polythene bag with handles. **3** person or animal carrying disease.

cart *n* strong two-wheeled open vehicle used by farmers, tradesmen, etc. *vt,vi* **1** transport in a cart. **2** *inf* carry with difficulty.

cartilage *n* strong flexible tissue often developing into bone; gristle. **cartilaginous** *adj*.

carton *n* small light container, esp. of cardboard.

cartoon *n* **1** simple humorous or satirical drawing. **2** animated film. **3** sketch made in preparation for a painting, tapestry, etc. **cartoonist** *n*.

cartridge *n* **1** small cylindrical case containing explosives, a bullet, or shot. **2** large type of cassette for a tape recorder. **3** film cassette. **4** device fitted to the pickup arm on a gramophone that contains the stylus. **5** removable container filled with ink for a fountain pen. **cartridge paper** *n* strong white paper for drawing.

carve *vi,vt* **1** shape with a knife, chisel, etc. **2** cut (meat) into pieces or slices. **carve up 1** *inf* injure by an attack with a knife. **2** *sl* endanger by aggressive driving. **carver** *n*. **carving** *n* **1** act of carving. **2** artefact carved from wood, stone, etc.

cascade *n* **1** waterfall. **2** something that falls in folds or drapes. *vi* fall like a cascade.

case[1] *n* box, container, or protective outer covering.

case[2] **1** instance; circumstance; example. **2** instance of a medical condition. **3** legal suit, or grounds for suit. **4** patient or client dealt with by a doctor, social worker, lawyer, etc. **5** grammatical relationship of a noun, pronoun, or adjective to other parts of a sentence, sometimes shown by inflectional endings. **in case** in the event that. **in any case** whatever happens.

cash *n* money, esp. in the form of notes and coins. *vt* convert into cash. **cash in on** *inf* profit from; exploit.

cashier[1] *n* person employed to receive and pay out cash in a bank, shop, etc.

cashier[2] *vt* discharge dishonourably from the army.

cashmere *n* very fine soft woven hair of the Kashmir goat.

casino *n* building equipped for gambling.

casket *n* small box or case, esp. for jewels.

casserole *n* **1** heavy pan or dish for long slow cooking. **2** meal cooked in a casserole. *vt* cook in a casserole.

cassette *n* sealed container holding spools of film, magnetic tape, etc., for use in a camera, tape-recorder, etc.

cassock *n* long black tunic worn by various members of the clergy.

cast *vt* (cast) **1** throw; hurl; fling. **2** discard; shed; drop. **3** project; direct. **4** make (a vote). **5** allocate (parts) for a play. **6** make (shape of metal, glass, etc.) by pouring into a mould. **cast off** discard; throw away; reject. **castoff** *n* discarded thing or person. **cast on/off** form the first/last row of stitches of a piece of knitting. ~*n* **1** all the actors in a play. **2** throw, as of dice. **3** mould. **4** casing for a broken bone. **5** slight squint.

castanets *pl n* pair of hollow shells of hard wood or ivory held in the hand and clicked together to accompany music and dancing.

caste *n* **1** one of four hereditary social divisions in Hindu society. **2** social class.

castle *n* **1** large fortified building functioning as a fortress or stronghold. **2** (in chess) rook. **castellated** *adj* having battlements, turrets, etc., as a castle.

castrate *vt* remove the testicles of. **castration** *n*.

casual *adj* **1** accidental; not planned; chance. **2** informal. **3** not regular; temporary. **casually** *adv*.

casualty *n* victim of a serious accident, battle, etc.

cat *n* **1** small domestic animal, kept esp. as a pet. **2** feline mammal, such as the lion, tiger, or leopard. **cat's eye** *n* glass stud set into the road surface to mark traffic lanes as a guide to motorists at night.

catalogue *n* comprehensive orderly list of books in a library, goods for sale, etc. *vt* list or insert in a catalogue.

catapult *n* **1** device for hurling small rocks and stones. **2** equipment for launching aircraft from ships, etc. *vt* throw or hurl as from a catapult.

cataract *n* **1** powerful waterfall. **2** heavy rainstorm or flood. **3** eye disorder in which the lens becomes opaque.

catarrh *n* inflammation of a mucous membrane in the nose or throat, as during a cold.

catastrophe *n* major disaster; calamity. **catastrophic** *adj*. **catastrophically** *adv*.

catch *v* (caught) *vt* **1** grasp (something that has been thrown or is falling). **2** capture; seize. **3** discover by surprise; detect. **4** board or take (a train, bus, etc.). **5** hear or grasp the meaning of **6** contract (an infection or disease). **7** strike; hit. **8** portray accurately or convincingly. **9** make contact with; find. **10** deceive; swindle. *vi,vt* **1** ignite or become ignited by. **2** become tangled (with) or hooked up (on). **catch on** **1** learn or grasp. **2** become fashionable. **catch up** **1** reach or get level after following. **2** make up (arrears, a backlog, etc.). ~*n* **1** act of catching. **2** something caught. **3** device for fastening. **4** *inf* difficulty; snag. **5** *inf* highly eligible person. **6** ball game. **catchy** *adj inf* (esp. of a tune) easy to remember or imitate.

catechism *n* religious instruction, esp. in a dialogue form.

category *n* class; group; division. **categorical** *adj* absolutely; definite; explicit. **categorically** *adv*. **categorize** *vt* place in a category; classify.

cater *vi* provide food, entertainment, etc. **cater for** supply whatever is necessary. **caterer** *n*.

caterpillar *n* **1** larva of a moth, butterfly, etc. **2**

continuous band of steel plates fitted instead of wheels to a vehicle such as a tractor or tank.

cathedral *n* principal church in a diocese.

catholic *adj* widespread; liberal; of general interest. **Catholic** *adj, n* Roman Catholic. **Catholicism** *n.*

catkin *n* cluster of small flowers of the willow, hazel, etc., resembling a cat's tail.

cattle *pl n* cows, bulls, etc., collectively.

catty *adj inf* spiteful.

caught *v pt* and *pp* of **catch.**

cauliflower *n* variety of cabbage cultivated for its large edible white flower head.

cause *n* **1** something that produces an effect. **2** motive; grounds; reason. **3** general aim or set of ideals for which a person or group campaigns. *vt* be the cause of; bring about; make happen. **causal** *adj.* **causation** *or* **causality** *n.*

causeway *n* raised road or path over treacherous ground, water, etc.

caustic *adj* **1** burning or corrosive. **2** cutting; sarcastic. *n* substance that corrodes or burns. **caustic soda** *n* sodium hydroxide.

caution *n* **1** prudence; care; watchfulness. **2** warning. *vt* warn; advise caution. **cautionary** *adj* advising caution; intended as a warning. **cautious** *adj* careful; prudent; wary. **cautiously** *adv.*

cavalry *n* unit of troops, originally mounted on horseback but now equipped with armoured cars, tanks, etc.

cave hollow area in a rock or under a cliff. *vt* hollow out. **cave in** collapse; give way; subside. **cavern** *n* large underground cave. **cavernous** *adj.*

caviar *n* salted roe of the sturgeon, eaten as a delicacy.

cavity *n* **1** hollow space. **2** hollow part of a tooth caused by decay.

cayenne *n* hot red pepper produced from capsicum seeds.

cease *vt,vi* stop; end; discontinue; finish. *n* **without cease** endlessly; continuously. **ceasefire** *n* truce, esp. a temporary one. **ceaseless** *adj* incessant; endless.

cedar *n* large coniferous evergreen tree with hard sweet-smelling wood.

cede *vt,vi* concede or yield territory, rights, etc.

ceiling *n* **1** upper surface of a room. **2** upper limit of prices, wages, etc.

celebrate *vt* **1** mark or honour with festivity and rejoicing. **2** officiate at a religious or public ceremony. *vi* rejoice, make merry. **celebrated** *adj* famous. **celebrity** *n* **1** well-known or famous person. **2** fame; renown; notoriety.

celery *n* vegetable grown for its long greenish-white edible stalks.

celestial *adj* heavenly; of the sky.

celibate *adj* **1** unmarried. **2** abstaining from sexual intercourse. *n* person who is celibate, esp. one who has taken religious vows. **celibacy** *n.*

cell *n* **1** independent unit of an organism. **2** small room occupied by a monk, prisoner, etc. **3** device producing or storing electric current by chemical action. **4** small group working within a larger political or religious movement. **cellular** *adj.*

cellar *n* **1** underground room, used esp. for storage. **2** store of wine.

cello *n* musical instrument of the violin family, held between the knees when played. **cellist** *n.*

Cellophane *n Tdmk* thin transparent packaging material.

Celluloid *n Tdmk* inflammable material made from cellulose nitrate and camphor, used esp. as a coating for film.

cellulose *n* carbohydrate forming walls of plant cells.

cement *n* **1** substance made from limestone and clay mixed with water that hardens to form concrete. **2** substance used to fill cavities of the teeth. *vt* **1** join or spread with cement. **2** unite; bind together; strengthen.

cemetery *n* burial ground, esp. one not attached to a church.

censor *n* person authorized to examine and ban material in films, books, letters, etc., considered to be harmful, dangerous, or immoral. *vt* act as a censor of. **censorship** *n.* **censorious** *adj* critical; harsh.

censure *n* disapproval; blame; harsh criticism. *vt* reprimand; criticize; blame.

census *n* official population count.

cent *n* **1** US coin equivalent to one hundredth of a dollar. **2** coin of various other countries. **per cent** by the hundred; in a hundred. **hundred per cent** complete; absolute; total.

centenary *n* hundredth anniversary. *adj* relating to a period of a hundred years.

centigrade *adj* relating to a temperature scale

on which the freezing point of water is 0° and its boiling point 100°

centime *n* **1** French coin equivalent to one hundredth of a franc. **2** coin of various other countries.

centimetre *n* one hundredth of a metre.

centipede *n* small crawling animal having a body made up of several segments, each segment bearing a pair of legs.

central *adj* **1** of the centre. **2** principal; most important. **central heating** *n* system of heating a building with radiators, air vents, etc., connected to a central source. **centralize** *vt* **1** bring to a central point. **2** unite (several duties, powers, etc.) under one central authority. *vi* come to a central point. **centralization** *n*.

centre *n* **1** middle point of a circle, line, sphere, etc. **2** main point or focus of interest, attention, administration, importance, etc. *vt,vi* be concentrated (on); have a centre at or in. **centre-forward** *n* player in football, hockey, etc., positioned at the centre of the front line. **centre-half** *n, pl* **-halves** player in football, hockey, etc., positioned at the centre of the defence line.

century *n* **1** one hundred years. **2** one of the periods of a hundred years numbered before and since the birth of Christ. **3** score of a hundred runs in cricket.

ceramics *n* art of making pottery from clay, porcelain, etc. **ceramic** *adj,n*.

cereal *n* **1** crop yielding edible grain. **2** breakfast dish made from cereals.

ceremony *n* **1** formal or public act, religious rite, etc. **2** formal politeness. **stand (up)on ceremony** insist on exaggerated politeness or formality. **ceremonial** *adj* ritual; formal; pertaining to ceremony. *n* prescribed form of ceremonies; ritual. **ceremonially** *adv*. **ceremonious** *adj* elaborately correct, dignified, or precise. **ceremoniously** *adv*.

certain *adj* **1** sure; convinced; positive. **2** definite; inevitable. **3** indicating someone or something specific but unnamed. **certainly** *adv*. **certainty** *n*.

certificate *n* written declaration of a fact, such as success in an examination, ownership of shares, public status, etc. **certify** *vt* **1** declare; authorize; guarantee; endorse. **2** declare officially to be insane.

cervix *n, pl* **cervixes** *or* **cervices** ('sə:visi:z) **1** lower part of the uterus. **2** neck. **cervical** *adj*.

chafe *vt,vi* rub until sore or roughened. *n* soreness.

chaffinch *n* small European songbird of the finch family.

chain *n* **1** flexible line of connected metal links. **2** range of mountains. **3** series of connected events. *vt* fasten or restrict with or as with a chain. **chain reaction 1** chemical or nuclear process in which the product of each step initiates the next step. **2** series of rapid interconnected events. **chain-smoke** *vi* smoke continuously, esp. by lighting one cigarette from the stub of the last. **chain-smoker** *n*. **chain-store** *n* one of a number of shops owned and managed by the same organization.

chair *n* **1** movable seat usually with four legs and a back, for one person. **2** seat of dignity or authority. **3** chairmanship. **4** professorship. *vt* preside over; act as chairman of. **chairman** *n, pl* **-men 1** principal director of a company. **2** person presiding over a meeting, committee, etc. **chairmanship** *n*.

chalet *n* **1** wooden Swiss house with a steep overhanging roof. **2** house or bungalow built in this style, esp. for holidays.

chalk *n* **1** soft white rock consisting of calcium carbonate. **2** piece of chalk or similar material used for writing or drawing. *vt,vi* write or treat with chalk.

challenge *vt* **1** invite to a duel or other contest. **2** defy; dispute; call for an answer to. *n* **1** summons to a contest. **2** questioning of right; calling to account.

chamber *n* **1** room, esp a bedroom. **2** meeting hall. **3** enclosed cavity. **chambers** *pl* barrister's or judge's conference rooms. **chambermaid** *n* hotel maid in charge of bedrooms. **chamber music** *n* music written for a small ensemble of solo instruments.

chamberlain *n* **1** officer managing a royal household. **2** high-ranking Court official.

chameleon (kə'mi:liən) *n* type of lizard capable of changing its skin colour to match its surroundings.

champagne *n* type of sparkling French wine.

champion *n* **1** winner; victor; person excelling all others. **2** upholder of a cause. *adj* excellent. *vt* defend; stand up for. **championship** *n* **1**

competition or series of contests to find a champion. **2** status or conduct of a champion.

chance *n* **1** unexpected or inexplicable event. **2** risk. **3** possibility; opportunity. **by chance** accidentally; fortuitously. ~*adj* fortuitous; accidental. *vi,vt* **1** happen (to). **2** risk; dare.

chancel *n* eastern part of a church near the altar, reserved for the clergy and choir.

chancellor *n* **1** chief minister or other high official. **2** titular head of a university. **Chancellor of the Exchequer** *n* principal government finance minister.

chandelier *n* decorative branched fitting that hangs from a ceiling and supports a number of lights.

change *n* **1** substitution of one thing for another; alteration; variance. **2** money returned as balance for payment; coins of small value. *vt* **1** alter; substitute; make different. **2** give coins of smaller denomination in exchange for a larger coin or note. *vi* become different. *vt,vi* **1** put on (different clothes). **2** board (another train, bus, etc.). **changeable** *adj.*

channel *n* **1** navigable part of a harbour, river bed, etc. **2** comparatively narrow stretch of sea. **3** radio or television waveband. **4** tube; passage; groove. **5** means of communication, commerce, etc. *vt* (-ll-) **1** provide, use, or supply through a channel. **2** direct; find an outlet for.

chant *n* song, esp. intoned sacred music. *vt,vi* **1** sing, esp. in monotone. **2** recite.

chaos *n* disorder; confusion. **chaotic** *adj.*

chap[1] *vt,vi* (-pp-) (of skin) roughen and crack through excessive cold, etc.

chap[2] *n inf* man; fellow.

chapel *n* **1** small subordinate church often attached to a college, institution, etc. **2** small part of a larger church containing a separate altar. **3** association of printers or journalists.

chaplain *n* clergyman attached to a particular household, institution, unit of soldiers, etc.

chapter *n* **1** one of the principal divisions of a book. **2** governing body of a cathedral.

char[1] *vt,vi* (-rr-) scorch; singe; blacken; burn.

char[2] *n also* **charwoman** *or* **charlady** *inf* person employed to do housework. *vi* (-rr-) do rough housework.

character *n* **1** sum of particular qualities distinguishing an individual. **2** personality created by a writer. **3** distinguishing feature, mark, handwriting, etc. **4** eccentric or amusing person. **characteristic** *adj* distinctive; typical. *n* distinctive quality or trait. **characteristically** *adv.* **characterize** *vt* **1** distinguish (by); typify. **2** portray; describe. **characterization** *n.*

charcoal *n* carbon made from burnt wood, coal, etc.

charge *n* **1** price; liability to pay. **2** accusation. **3** responsibility; duty. **4** quantity, esp. of explosive, with which anything is loaded. **5** property of matter responsible for electrical phenomena and having two forms, positive and negative, which cause mutual attraction. **6** sudden attacking rush. **in charge of** with responsibility for. ~*vt,vi* **1** demand as a price. **2** rush aggressively towards. *vt* **1** accuse. **2** burden. **3** load; fill up. **4** supply (with electricity). **charge-hand** *n* workman or assistant in charge of others; foreman.

chariot *n* two-wheeled horse-drawn vehicle formerly used for races and battle. **charioteer** *n.*

charisma *n* spiritual quality inspiring great devotion and trust. **charismatic** *adj.*

charity *n* **1** quality of love, kindness, or generosity; compassion. **2** institution or organization founded for the benefit of others. **charitable** *adj* **1** kind; lenient; generous. **2** of a recognized charity.

charm *n* **1** ability to fascinate and delight by personal qualities. **2** magic spell, act, trinket, etc., thought to bring good fortune. *vt,vi* **1** attract; delight; enthrall. **2** enchant by magic. **charming** *adj* delightful.

chart *n* graph, plan, or map. *vt* record progress by means of a chart.

charter *n* document granting a right, establishing a university, etc. *vt* **1** establish by charter. **2** let or hire, esp. a ship or aircraft. **chartered** *adj* qualified according to established rules.

chase *vt* hunt; pursue; run after; drive away. *n* pursuit; hunt.

chasm (ˈkæzəm) *n* deep gulf or inlet; abyss.

chassis (ˈʃæsi) *n, pl* **chassis** basic frame, esp. of a motor car, on which other parts are mounted.

chaste *adj* pure or virtuous, esp. sexually. **chastity** *n.*

chastise *vt* punish, esp. by beating. **chastisement** *n.*

chat *vi* (-tt-) talk in a friendly informal way. *n*

easy informal conversation. **chatty** *adj inf* talkative.

chatter *vi* **1** talk rapidly and thoughtlessly. **2** (of monkeys, birds, etc.) make an excited rapid rattling noise. *n* **1** idle talk; gossip. **2** rattling noise. **chatterbox** *n inf* talkative person.

chauffeur ('ʃoufə) *n* person employed to drive another's car; driver. *vt* act as chauffeur for.

chauvinism ('ʃouvinizəm) *n* excessive aggressive patriotism. **male chauvinism** belief of men in their superiority over women. **chauvinist** *n,adj*.

cheap *adj* **1** inexpensive; low in price. **2** inferior; vulgar; shoddy. **cheaply** *adv*. **cheapness** *n*. **cheapen** *vt,vi* decrease in price or quality.

cheat *vt* defraud; swindle; trick. *vi* attempt to succeed by dishonest means. *n* person who cheats; fraud.

check *vt* **1** restrain; hinder; halt. **2** verify; test the truth of; inspect. *n* **1** obstruction; hindrance. **2** supervision; careful watch; verification. **3** move in chess threatening the opponent's King. **4** pattern of squares. **5** *US* bill; account; cheque. **checkmate** *n* stage in chess where a threat to the King cannot be countered. *vt* defeat at checkmate. **checkpoint** *n* place where traffic is halted and inspected by police, etc. **check-up** *n* careful detailed examination, esp. for medical purposes.

cheek *n* **1** side of the face below the eye. **2** *inf* impudence; rudeness; impertinence. *vt inf* speak impertinently to. **cheeky** *adj inf* impudent; saucy. **cheekily** *adv*. **cheekiness** *n*. **cheekbone** *n* bone of the face just below the eye.

cheer *n* **1** shout of approval or joy. **2** entertainment; comfort. **3** disposition; attitude. *vt* comfort; encourage. *vi,vt* shout with joy or approval. **cheer up** become more cheerful. **cheerful** *adj* happy; jovial; lively. **cheerfully** *adv*. **cheerfulness** *n*.

cheese *n* protein-rich food of many varieties made from the curd of milk.

cheetah *n* swift-running member of the cat family, resembling a leopard.

chef *n* master cook.

chemical *adj* pertaining to chemistry. *n* substance made by or used in chemical processes. **chemist** *n* **1** one qualified to sell drugs and medicine. **2** researcher or student of chemistry. **chemistry** *n* science concerned with the properties and interactions of elements and compounds.

cheque *n* signed order, written generally on a printed form, to a bank to pay out money from a customer's account.

chequer *n* pattern of squares. **chequered** *adj* **1** variegated; diversified in colour. **2** marked by fluctuations in fortune, nature, etc.

cherish *vt* protect; preserve; hold dear; nurture.

cherry *n* small red or yellow stone fruit.

cherub *n* one of the orders of angels, generally depicted as a plump winged child.

chess *n* game of skill for two players using thirty-two pieces (chessmen) on a board with sixty-four black and white squares.

chest *n* **1** upper front part of the body. **2** large strong box. **chest of drawers** *n* piece of furniture fitted with a set of drawers, used esp. for storing clothes or linen.

chestnut *n* **1** deciduous tree (sweet-chestnut, bearing edible nut, or horse-chestnut, bearing inedible nut). **2** fruit of these trees. **3** dark reddish-brown horse. *n,adj* dark reddish-brown.

chew *vt,vi* grind between the teeth. **chew over** wonder; ruminate. ~*n* act of chewing. **chewing gum** *n* sweetened flavoured preparation of resin or gum for chewing.

chick *n* **1** young bird, esp. a chicken. **2** *sl* girl.

chicken *n* **1** fowl reared for its eggs and meat. **2** *inf* young person. *adj sl* cowardly. **chickenpox** *n* mild infectious disease usually contracted by children, characterized by a blistery rash.

chicory *n* plant whose leaves are used in salads and whose root is ground to flavour coffee.

chief *adj* main; major; most important; principal. *n* **1** leader; superior head of a department, organization, etc. **2** *also* **chieftain** leader of a tribe or clan. **chiefly** *adv* mainly; principally.

chilblain *n* painful itchy red swelling on the hands and feet caused by extreme cold, bad circulation, etc.

child *n* **1** young person; infant; boy or girl. **2** son or daughter. **childbirth** *n* act of giving birth to a child. **childhood** *n* state or period of being a child. **childish** *adj* immature; foolish; naive. **childishly** *adv*. **childlike** *adj* trusting or innocent like a child.

chill *n* **1** coldness. **2** slight cold preceding fever. **3** discouraging influence. *vt,vi* make or become cold or cool. **chilly** *adj* **1** slightly cold; cool. **2** unfriendly.

chilli *n* pod of a capsicum, often dried and ground into the hot pungent spice, Cayenne pepper.

chime *n* melodious sound as of bells, esp. when ringing in sequence. *vt,vi* **1** ring musically. **2** agree; concur.

chimney *n* construction allowing smoke to escape from a fireplace, furnace, etc.

chimpanzee *n* small African ape.

chin *n* part of the face below the mouth.

china *n* crockery, esp. made of fine porcelain.

chink[1] *n* crevice; narrow opening; slit.

chink[2] *n* sharp clinking sound, as of coins or glasses struck together. *vi* clink; jingle.

chip *n* **1** small fragment or splinter of glass, wood, etc. **2** small oblong piece of deep-fried potato. **3** small crack or missing piece in china, glass, etc. **4** counter or token used in gambling games. **have a chip on one's shoulder** bear a grudge. ~*vt* (-pp-) **1** crack or break a small piece from. **2** cut (potatoes) into oblongs. **3** carve with a small tool. **chip in** contribute.

chiropody *n* treatment of minor foot disorders. **chiropodist** *n*.

chirp *vi* make the short shrill cry of a bird. *n* chirping sound. **chirpy** *adj inf* lively and cheerful.

chisel *n* steel cutting tool with wedge-shaped edge used in carpentry, masonry, etc. *vi,vt* (-ll-) cut or shape with a chisel.

chivalry *n* **1** courtesy or protectiveness, esp. as shown by men to women. **2** code of behaviour of medieval knights. **chivalrous** *adj*.

chive *n* small plant of the onion family whose leaves are used as a seasoning in cooking.

chlorine *n* greenish-yellow poisonous corrosive gaseous element, used as a disinfectant and bleach.

chlorophyll *n* green colouring matter present in plants, necessary for photosynthesis.

chocolate *n* preparation of cocoa mixed with sugar, milk, etc., eaten as a sweet, used for flavouring, etc. *adj,n* dark brown.

choice *n* **1** act of choosing. **2** variety to choose from. **3** thing chosen. *adj* of excellent quality; selected.

choir *n* **1** body of singers performing in public, esp. in a church. **2** part of a church or cathedral reserved for singers, above the nave and below the altar. **chorister** *n* member of a church choir.

choke *vt* **1** throttle or obstruct the breathing of; suffocate. **2** block; obstruct. *vi* **1** become choked. **2** become speechless through emotion. *n* **1** action or sound of choking. **2** valve controlling air supply, as in a carburettor.

cholera *n* highly infectious, often fatal disease characterized by feverish vomiting and diarrhoea.

choose *vt* select or take something in preference to something else. *vi* decide; determine.

chop[1] *vt* (-pp-) **1** cut with sharp blows. **2** cut into small pieces. *n* **1** act of chopping. **2** slice of pork or lamb containing part of a rib. **chopper** *n* axe or hatchet.

chop[2] *vi* (-pp-) make a sudden change of direction or attitude. **chop and change** change or alter repeatedly.

chopstick *n* one of a pair of small sticks used, esp. in the Far East, as an implement for eating.

choral *adj* written for or sung by a choir or chorus.

chord *n* **1** simultaneous sounding of several notes in music. **2** string of a musical instrument. **3** straight line linking two points on a curve.

chore *n* routine or repetitive task, esp. housework.

choreography *n* art of dance composition and notation. **choreographer** *n*.

chorus *n* **1** group of performers speaking, singing, or dancing together, esp. as separate from the action of a drama. **2** combined speech or song, esp. the refrain of a ballad, etc. *vt,vi* speak or sing as a group.

chose *v pt* of **choose.**

chosen *v pp* of **choose.**

Christ *n* title given to Jesus acknowledging him to be the Saviour foretold in the Old Testament.

christen *vt* give a name to, esp. at a Christian baptismal service. **christening** *n* ceremony of baptizing and naming a child in a church.

Christian *n* one professing to follow the teaching of Christ. *adj* **1** believing in Christ. **2** charitable; forgiving; unselfish. **3** of or pertaining to Christ. **Christian name** *n* personal name, esp. as given at a christening. **Christianity** *n* Christian faith, teaching, spirit, or way of life.

Christmas *n* celebration of the birth of Christ. **Christmas Day** December 25th.

chromatic *adj* **1** concerned with or having colours. **2** relating to a musical scale consisting of semitones.

chrome *n* chromium.

chromium *n* silvery-white metallic element used for highly polished coatings on other metals.

chromosome *n* small rod-like body found in living cells, responsible for the transmission of genetic information.

chronic *adj* **1** (esp. of a disease) of a long-standing or constantly recurring nature. **2** *inf* dreadful; tedious; objectionable. **chronically** *adv*.

chronological *adj* in order of time; according to time of occurrence. **chronologically** *adv*. **chronology** *n*.

chrysalis *n* pupa or insect larva, esp. enclosed in a sheath during its resting stage.

chrysanthemum *n* autumn-flowering garden plant with large blooms.

chubby *adj* plump and round-faced. **chubbiness** *n*.

chuck *vt,vi inf* **1** throw; toss. **2** give up. **chuck out 1** throw away or out. **2** eject forcibly.

chuckle *n* quiet burbling laugh. *vi* laugh quietly.

chunk *n* thick piece or portion. **chunky** *adj* thick and bulky.

church *n* **1** whole body of Christians or of one of the Christian denominations. **2** building used for Christian or other religious services. **3** the clergy. **churchyard** *n* burial ground surrounding a church.

churn *n* **1** vessel used for converting milk or cream into butter. **2** large cylindrical container used for transporting milk. *vt,vi* rotate or agitate vigorously, as in a churn. **churn out** produce rapidly and in great quantity.

chute *n* **1** sloping track or passage down which water, rubbish, laundry, etc., may be shot. **2** narrow waterfall.

chutney *n* sweet spicy relish made from pickled fruit and vegetables.

cider *n* drink made from pressed fermented apples.

cigar *n* roll of tobacco leaves for smoking.

cigarette *n* shredded tobacco leaves rolled in thin paper for smoking.

cinder *n* piece of burnt or charred wood, coal, etc.

cinecamera *n* camera used for taking motion pictures.

cinema *n* **1** the film industry. **2** building in which films are shown.

cinnamon *n* sweet pungent spice made from the bark of a type of laurel found largely in S and SE Asia.

circle *n* **1** plane figure bounded by an unbroken line, which is at every point the same distance from the centre. **2** ring. **3** group of people with a common interest. **4** gallery in a theatre. *vt,vi* move round in a circle.

circuit *n* **1** circular path; distance or way round. **2** journey taken regularly through a specific area, esp. by a judge or barrister in performance of professional duties. **3** path of an electric current. **circuitous** *adj* roundabout; long-winded; devious.

circular *adj* **1** relating to a circle. **2** round. **circulate** *vi,vt* move or pass around. **circulation** *n* **1** act of moving or passing around. **2** movement of blood through veins and arteries. **3** distribution or sale of newspapers, magazines, etc.

circumcise *vt* cut off the foreskin. **circumcision** *n*.

circumference *n* outer rim of a circle.

circumscribe *vt* **1** restrict or contain within certain limits. **2** draw a line around.

circumstance *n* incident; fact; detail. **circumstances** *n pl* **1** facts attendant on or relating to others; condition; state. **2** financial position. **circumstantial** *adj* **1** of or derived from circumstances. **2** fully detailed.

circus *n* **1** group of travelling entertainers, clowns, acrobats, performing animals, etc. **2** arena or amphitheatre. **3** place where several roads converge.

cistern *n* water tank, esp. supplying water to a lavatory.

cite *vt* **1** quote as an example or authority. **2** summon to appear in court. **citation** *n* **1** quotation. **2** summons. **3** mention, esp. for bravery, in military dispatches.

citizen *n* **1** resident of a city. **2** member of a state. **citizenship** *n*.

citrus *n* genus of fruit trees including orange, lemon, and lime.

city *n* large or important town, esp. containing a cathedral. **the City** financial centre of London.

civic *adj* of a city or local community. **civics** *pl* *n* science of government, esp. local government.

civil *adj* **1** courteous; polite. **2** of a citizen or the community. **3** not military. **4** (of legal proceedings, etc.) not criminal; disputed between ordinary citizens. **civil engineering** *n* branch of engineering concerned with designing and building roads, bridges, etc. **civil engineer** *n*. **civil service** *n* body of officials employed by the state in an administrative capacity. **civil servant** *n*. **civil war** *n* war between citizens of the same state.

civilian *n* one not in the employ of the armed forces.

civilization *n* **1** moral, social, intellectual, and artistic standards of a specific society. **2** advanced nonbarbaric condition or society. **civilize** *vt* bring out of a primitive condition; refine.

clad *adj* clothed; dressed.

claim *vt* **1** demand as a right. **2** ask or call for. *vt,vi* assert; maintain. *n* **1** demand or request by right. **2** that which is claimed or asserted. **3** right or title. **claimant** *n* person who makes a claim, esp. in law.

clam *n* edible bivalve shellfish. *v* **clam up** refuse to speak.

clamber *vi* climb, esp. with effort or difficulty. *n* awkward climb.

clammy *adj* damp and sticky.

clamour *n* raucous outcry; uproar. *vi* demand vociferously. **clamorous** *adj*. **clamorously** *adv*.

clamp *n* device used in carpentry, metalwork, surgery, etc., to hold things firmly in place. *vt* fasten or hold with a clamp. **clamp down on** *inf* suppress.

clan *n* large family or tribal group, esp. in Scotland. **clansman** *n*.

clandestine *adj* concealed; secret.

clang *n* resounding metallic sound, as of a large bell. *vt,vi* make or cause a clang. **clanger** *n* *inf* blunder.

clank *n* loud metallic sound, as of a heavy chain. *vt,vi* make or cause a clank.

clap *n* **1** sudden noise as of the palms of the hands brought sharply together. **2** sound of thunder. *vt,vi* (-pp-) **1** applaud with the hands. **2** place (down) suddenly. **3** throw (into prison, etc.). **clapper** *n* tongue suspended inside a bell. **like the clappers** very energetically or quickly.

claret *n* red wine from Bordeaux.

clarify *vt,vi* make or become clear. **clarification** *n*.

clarinet *n* musical wind instrument with a single reed. **clarinetist** *n*.

clarity *n* clearness.

clash *n* **1** loud banging noise, as of colliding metal objects. **2** opposition; dispute; conflict. *vt* bang noisily together. *vi* **1** strike against. **2** come into opposition; conflict. **3** (of colours) be displeasing or disharmonious when placed together.

clasp *n* **1** hinged or interlocking fastening. **2** embrace; grasp of the hand. *vt* **1** fasten with a clasp. **2** embrace; grasp with the hand.

class *n* **1** kind; sort; category. **2** social group defined according to occupation, position, wealth, birth, social status, etc. **3** group of students or pupils undergoing the same course of instruction. **4** division denoting standard of comfort in an aeroplane, train, etc. *vt* form into or place in a class.

classic *adj* widely recognized as standard, typical, or of great merit. *n* work of art, esp. literature, noted for its lasting excellence. **classical** *adj* **1** of ancient Greece or Rome, esp. in formalized literary or architectural style. **2** (of music) belonging to great serious European tradition, esp. if composed before 1800. **classics** *pl n* language, literature, and philosophy of ancient Greece and Rome. **classicist** *n* student of classics.

classify *vt* arrange in classes or categories; place in a class. **classification** *n*.

clatter *n* loud repetitive rattling noise. *vt,vi* make or cause a clatter.

clause *n* **1** part of a sentence with a subject, predicate, and finite verb. **2** subsection in a legal contract, will, agreement, etc.

claustrophobia *n* morbid dread of enclosed or confined places. **claustrophobic** *adj*.

claw *n* hard hooked nail of an animal or bird. *vt* seize or tear with claws or nails.

clay *n* heavy sticky fine-grained soil material, plastic when moist, and used in pottery, brick-making, etc.

clean *adj* free from dirt, marks, impurity, guilt, disease, etc. *adv* completely. *vt* make clean. **clean out** clean thoroughly; empty. **clean up** **1** tidy. **2** suppress crime, vice, etc. **3** gain a large profit, advantage, etc. **cleanliness** *n*.

cleanse *vt* clean (something) thoroughly; make pure. **cleanser** *n*.

clear *adj* **1** unclouded; bright; transparent. **2** obvious; distinct; straightforward. **3** net; after deductions. **4** without obstruction. *adv* completely. *vt* **1** clarify. **2** empty. **3** acquit; declare innocent. **4** pass without touching. **5** verify; justify. **6** receive (net). *vi* become clear. **clear off** *or* **out** leave hurriedly. **clear up 1** solve. **2** tidy. **3** become fine or sunny. **clearance** *n* **1** act of clearing. **2** space between moving and stationary objects. **3** certificate permitting passage through Customs, esp. of a ship. **clear-headed** *adj* lucid; intelligent; sensible. **clearing** *n* **1** act of making or becoming clear. **2** area free from trees, esp. in a forest.

clef *n* musical symbol denoting pitch of the notes written on the stave.

clench *vt* **1** grasp; grip; press (teeth, the fist, etc.) firmly together. **2** secure tightly; rivet.

clergy *n* priests and ordained ministers of a Christian church. **clergyman** *n, pl* **-men** priest, esp. in the Church of England.

clerical *adj* **1** of a clerk. **2** of a clergyman; religious.

clerk *n* **1** employee dealing with records, correspondence, etc., in an office. **2** person holding a particular administrative position in local government, the law, etc.

clever *adj* **1** intelligent; bright. **2** ingenious; cunning. **cleverly** *adv*. **cleverness** *n*.

cliché *n* hackneyed expression or phrase.

click *n* short sharp sound, as of a latch closing. *vi,vt* make a click.

client *n* customer; person employing another for business or professional purposes. **clientele** (kliːənˈtel) *n* clients.

cliff *n* steep high rock, esp. facing the sea.

climate *n* **1** general weather conditions of a region. **2** prevailing public attitude, economic situation, etc.

climax *n* **1** ultimate culmination of a series of events. **2** moment of supreme elation, terror, etc. **3** orgasm. **climactic** *adj*.

climb *vi,vt* **1** ascend or go up using hands and feet; scale. **2** rise; mount. *n* **1** distance or route to be climbed. **2** act of climbing. **climb down** admit to having been wrong; withdraw.

cling *vi* (clung) **1** adhere or stick to closely. **2** refuse to abandon a belief, idea, etc.

clinic *n* **1** hospital department or health centre for the diagnosis and treatment of specific disorders. **2** private nursing home. **clinical** *adj* **1** relating to a clinic. **2** of, used, or carried out in a hospital. **3** concerned with treatment of disease in the patient. **4** not biased or emotionally involved.

clink *n* **1** short ringing sound, as of metal, glass, etc., struck together. **2** *sl* prison. *vt,vi* make a clink.

clip[1] *n* **1** device for holding paper, etc., together. **2** hairgrip. *vt* (-pp-) fasten with a clip.

clip[2] *vt* (-pp-) **1** trim; cut closely; shorten. **2** smack; hit sharply. *n* **1** act of clipping. **2** piece clipped off. **3** sharp blow. **4** short extract from a film.

clitoris *n* female sexual organ similar to a rudimentary penis. **clitoral** *adj*.

cloak *n* long loose sleeveless garment fastening at the neck. *vt* disguise; mask. **cloakroom** *n* room in a public building, etc., where coats are left.

clock *n* instrument for telling or measuring time. *vt* **1** time (a runner). **2** *sl* hit; strike. **clock in** *or* **on/out** *or* **off** record the time of starting/finishing work. **clockwise** *adv* in the same direction as the hands of a clock. **clockwork** *n* mechanism of a clock or one working like that of a clock. **like clockwork** with perfect regularity and precision.

clog *n* heavy shoe with a sole and sometimes upper of wood. *vi* (-gg-) (of drains, pipes, etc.) become obstructed or blocked. *vt* block; obstruct.

cloister *n* **1** covered arcade surrounding a monastery quadrangle. **2** monastery, abbey, or nunnery. **cloistered** *adj* shut away; secluded.

close *adj* (klous) **1** nearby; near. **2** mean; stingy. **3** stuffy; sultry. **4** confined; restricted. **5** thorough. **6** intimate. *n* (klous for 1,2; klouz for 3) **1** alley; dead-end street or road; enclosure. **2** cathedral precinct. **3** end. *adv* (klous) tightly; leaving no space. **close-up** *n* (ˈklousʌp) film-shot or photograph giving a detailed view. ~*v* (klouz) *vt* **1** shut. **2** pull together; unite. **3** finish; end; complete. *vi* come to an end; terminate. **close in** surround and move in on. **close down** terminate; cease functioning. **close up** shut completely. **closed-shop** *n* factory employing only union members. **closure** *n*.

closet *n* **1** small private room. **2** cupboard. **3** lavatory. **closeted** *adj* shut away; kept secret.

clot *n* **1** small solidified mass of blood, mud, etc. **2** *sl* fool. *vt,vi* (-tt-) form into clots; congeal; coagulate.

cloth *n* **1** small piece of fabric used for polishing, mopping, covering, etc. **2** woven fabric from which clothing, curtains, etc., are cut and sewn.

clothe *vt* **1** provide with clothes; dress. **2** cover; disguise. **clothing** *n* clothes; garments in general. **clothes** *pl n* **1** garments; materials fashioned to be worn on the person; dress. **2** bed-coverings. **in plain clothes** (of a policeman, etc.) not wearing uniform.

cloud *n* **1** visible mass of small droplets of water floating in the sky, from which rain or snow falls. **2** mass of dust, smoke, etc., resembling a cloud. **3** anything depressing or threatening. *vt,vi* **1** fill or cover with clouds. **2** make or become murky or opaque. **3** fill or cover with gloom, doubt, etc. **cloudy** *adj* **1** covered or scattered with clouds. **2** opaque; not clear.

clove[1] *n* dried flower-bud of an aromatic tropical tree, used as a spice.

clove[2] *n* small bulb, esp. of garlic, that forms part of a larger one.

clover *n* small flowering plant with three-lobed leaves, often grown as cattle fodder.

clown *n* comic fool, esp. in a circus. *vi* play the fool.

club *n* **1** association of people with a common interest in a social, cultural, or sporting activity, etc. **2** the building, etc., used by such a group. **3** thick heavy stick. **4** stick used in golf. **clubs** *pl n* one of the four suits in cards. ~*vt* (-bb-) beat with a club. **club together** unite for a common end; contribute to a collection.

cluck *n* sound made by a hen. *vi* make such a sound.

clue *n* **1** hint or suggestion leading to the solution of a mystery. **2** information; idea. **clueless** *adj inf* stupid.

clump *n* **1** cluster of trees, bushes, etc. **2** heavy tread. *vi* **1** tread heavily. **2** group together.

clumsy *adj* **1** inclined to stumble, drop things, etc.; awkward. **2** tactless; gauche. **clumsily** *adv.* **clumsiness** *n.*

cluster *n* closely packed group, as of flowers, diamonds, stars, etc. *vi* grow or be gathered together.

clutch *vt* grasp or seize tightly. *n* **1** grasp; grip. **2** mechanical coupling device allowing gradual engagement of gears, etc. **3** number of eggs laid at one time.

clutter *n* confused jumble. *vt* crowd with a confused or untidy mass.

coach *n* **1** bus, esp. one used for long trips. **2** large horse-drawn carriage. **3** railway carriage. **4** tutor training people for exams, athletic events, etc. *vt* prepare for examination, contest, etc.; train.

coagulate *vi* solidify; clot; congeal. **coagulation** *n.*

coal *n* solid black mineral consisting of carbonized vegetation and mined for use as fuel. **coalmine** *n* workings from which coal is obtained, pit.

coalition *n* short-term alliance, esp. between political parties.

coarse *adj* **1** rough in texture; not fine. **2** vulgar; base; impolite. **coarsely** *adv.* **coarseness** *n.*

coast *n* land bordering the sea. *vi* sail or drift along. **coastal** *adj.* **coastguard** *n* person employed to watch the coast and sea for ships in danger, smuggling, etc. **coastline** *n* line of the shore, esp. as seen from the sea or air or as shown on a map.

coat *n* **1** outer garment with sleeves. **2** hair, fur, etc., covering an animal; pelt. **3** layer of paint, etc., on a surface. *vt* cover with a layer.

coax *vt* persuade, esp. by soothing or flattery; cajole.

cobble *n* rounded stone used for paving, road-making, etc. *vi,vt* mend or repair clumsily or shoddily.

cobbler *n* one who makes or mends shoes and boots.

cobra *n* poisonous hooded snake found in Asia and Africa.

cobweb *n* spider's web.

cock *n* **1** male bird, esp. of domestic fowl. **2** water-tap. **3** hammer of a gun. **4** *inf* chap; fellow. **5** *sl* penis. *vt* **1** tilt; turn to one side; set at a jaunty angle. **2** pull back the hammer of (a gun). **cocky** *adj* cheeky; self-assured; impudent. **cockiness** *n.*

cockle *n* edible bivalve mollusc with a heart-shaped shell.

Cockney *n* **1** Londoner, esp. one born within the sound of Bow Bells. **2** dialect of a Cockney.

cockpit *n* pilot's compartment in an aircraft.

cockroach *n* brown or black insect with long antennae.

cocktail *n* **1** drink made from a mixture of spirits and flavourings. **2** dish made from mixed fruit or prawns, etc.

cocoa *n* powder from the ground seeds of the cacao tree, used to make chocolate or to flavour drinks.

coconut *n* large fruit of a tropical palm-tree, with edible flesh, juice resembling milk, and a hard hairy husk.

cocoon *n* protective silky coating spun by various insect larvae before becoming pupae.

cod *n, pl* **cod** large edible sea fish.

coddle *vt* **1** boil lightly. **2** pamper; indulge; be protective towards.

code *n* **1** system of symbols for secret or esoteric communication. **2** system of regulations, laws, social customs, or moral principles. *vt* put into a code.

codeine *n* pain-killing drug obtained from opium.

coeducation *n* education of children of both sexes at the same school.

coerce (kouˈɔːs) *vt* persuade forcefully; compel. **coercion** *n.* **coercive** *adj.*

coexist *vi* exist at the same time, esp. in harmony. **coexistence** *n.*

coffee *n* drink made from the roasted ground seeds (beans) of the coffee tree. *adj,n* light brown.

coffin *n* wooden box in which a corpse is placed for burial.

cog *n* one of the teeth on the rim of a wheel. **cogwheel** *n* wheel fitted with cogs, used in engineering, etc., for transmitting movement; gearwheel.

cognac *n* French brandy.

cohabit *vi* live together as man and wife. **cohabitation** *n.*

cohere *vi* stick together; remain consistent. **coherence** *n.* **cohesion** *n.* **coherent** *adj* clear; comprehensible; articulate; consistent.

coil *vt,vi* wind in rings; twist. *n* **1** piece of rope, string, etc., coiled into rings. **2** coil of wire in an electrical circuit.

coin *n* stamped metal disc used as official currency. *vt* **1** form or stamp coins in a mint. **2** invent (an expression or phrase). **coinage** *n.*

coincide *vi* **1** occur at the same time or place. **2** agree; concur. **coincidence** *n* **1** act or state of coinciding. **2** striking accidental concurrence of events.

colander *n* large strainer for draining vegetables.

cold *adj* **1** not hot; chilly; low in temperature. **2** unfriendly; indifferent; unemotional. *n* **1** lack of heat. **2** acute nasal inflammation. **coldly** *adv.* **coldness** *n.* **cold-blooded** *adj* **1** having a blood temperature varying with that of the surrounding water or air. **2** unemotional; callous; ruthless. **cold-bloodedly** *adv.* **cold-bloodedness** *n.* **cold war** *n* period or state of political and military hostility between nations, involving no armed conflict.

collaborate *vi* **1** co-operate; work together. **2** co-operate with an enemy. **collaboration** *n.* **collaborator** *n.*

collapse *vi* **1** break or fall down; fail totally; give up. **2** fold away. *n* **1** breakdown; physical or mental exhaustion. **2** falling down of a structure. **collapsible** *adj.*

collar *n* **1** part of a garment encircling the neck. **2** leather strap worn round the neck by a dog, horse, etc. *vt inf* seize; tackle. **collarbone** *n* prominent frontal bone linking the ribs to the shoulder blades.

colleague *n* associate, esp. someone following the same profession as oneself.

collect *vt* **1** gather together; seek out and acquire. **2** solicit (money) for a cause. **3** fetch; pick up. **collection** *n* **1** group of objects collected together. **2** act of collecting, esp. for a charity, church, etc. **collective** *adj* taken as a whole. **collectively** *adv.*

college *n* **1** place of higher or specialized education. **2** autonomous group of people. **collegiate** *adj.*

collide *vi* **1** strike violently; crash into. **2** come into conflict. **collision** *n.*

colloquial *adj* of informal everyday speech. **colloquialism** *n* informal phrase; slang, idiom.

colon *n* punctuation mark (:) used to indicate a definite pause or division in a sentence.

colonel *n* military officer of a rank between lieutenant-colonel and brigadier.

colony *n* group of settlers from another country. **colonize** *vt* take over as a colony. **colonial** *adj* from or of a colony. *n* inhabitant of a colony.

colossal *adj* extremely large; enormous; gigantic; huge.

colour *n* **1** sense impression produced by light of different wavelengths, or the property of objects or light producing this. **2** pigment; hue. **3** skin pigmentation. **4** quality of vividness or distinction. **5** false quality. **colours** *pl* *n* **1** military flag or standard. **2** award for membership of a team. **off colour** unwell. ~*vt* **1** impart colour to. **2** give a false or biased impression of. *vi* take on a colour. **coloration** *n*. **colour-bar** *n* discrimination against people of coloured or dark-skinned races. **colour-blind** *adj* unable to distinguish or identify specific colours. **colour-blindness** *n*. **coloured** *adj* **1** having a colour. **2** (of a person) of a non-White race. **3** deceptive; biased. **colourful** *adj* **1** full of colour. **2** picturesque; vivid.

colt *n* young male horse.

column *n* **1** tall pillar, esp. one supporting a building. **2** row or line of people, figures, etc. **3** newspaper or magazine article or report. **columnist** *n* journalist providing regular articles for a newspaper or magazine.

coma *n* condition of very deep unconsciousness. **comatose** *adj* **1** drowsy. **2** in a coma.

comb *n* **1** small toothed instrument for separating and tidying hair, wool, etc. **2** group of wax cells made by bees. **3** crest of certain birds, esp. cocks. *vt* **1** untangle and tidy hair, wool, etc. **2** search thoroughly.

combat *vt,vi* fight against; oppose. *n* fight; struggle; battle. **combatant** *n*. **combative** *adj*.

combine *vt,vi* (kəm'bain) join together; unite; amalgamate. *n* ('kɔmbain) association of several similar companies, institutions, etc. **combine harvester** *n* mechanical corn harvester. **combination** *n* mixture; amalgamation.

combustion *n* process of burning. **combustible** *adj* capable of burning; flammable.

come *vi* (came; come) **1** arrive; be delivered; reach. **2** happen; occur. **3** originate; be caused by. **4** be available; be supplied. **come across** discover or meet by chance. **come back** return. **come off 1** become separated or broken. **2** be successfully completed. **come out 1** emerge. **2** be issued. **3** erupt. **come round 1** recover consciousness. **2** be persuaded. **come to 1** recover consciousness. **2** amount to. **come up** arise; appear. **come up with** suggest; think of; produce. **comeback** *n* **1** return or success after an absence or failure. **2** retort. **comedown** *n* **1** anticlimax. **2** reduction in status, quality, etc.

comedian *n* entertainer who performs comic songs or plays, tells jokes, etc.

comedy *n* humorous, amusing, or light-hearted play.

comet *n* heavenly body having a luminous head and a long tail, which always points away from the sun.

comfort *n* **1** encouragement; relief. **2** ease; peacefulness; lack of anxiety or pain. *vt* relieve; console; cheer. **comfortable** *adj* **1** providing or enjoying comfort. **2** fairly affluent. **comfortably** *adv*.

comic *adj* **1** funny; amusing. **2** relating to comedy. *n* **1** comic person; comedian. **2** children's paper consisting mainly of strip cartoons. **comical** *adj* ridiculous; absurd; laughable. **comically** *adv*.

comma *n* punctuation mark (,) used to indicate a slight pause, to separate clauses, etc.

command *vt* order; control; have authority or influence over; dominate. *n* order; rule; authority; control. **in command** in charge. **commander** *n* **1** someone who commands; leader. **2** naval officer ranking below a captain.

commandeer *vt* take over or seize arbitrarily or by force, esp. for military purposes.

commandment *n* order; command. **Ten Commandments** *pl n* laws given by God to Moses according to the Old Testament.

commando *n, pl* **commandos** *or* **commandoes** soldier specially trained to carry out dangerous raids.

commemorate *vt* celebrate the memory of; provide a memorial to. **commemoration** *n*.

commence *vt,vi* begin; start. **commencement** *n*.

commend *vt* **1** praise; recommend. **2** entrust. **commendable** *adj*. **commendation** *n*.

comment *n* brief, critical, or explanatory remark expressing an opinion, reaction, etc. *vi* make a comment. **commentary** *n* **1** series of comments, esp. analysing a book. **2** description of and comments on a sporting event, state occasion, etc., esp. when broadcast. **commentator** *n* one who provides a commentary, esp. on radio or television.

commerce *n* business; trade. **commercial** *adj* relating to commerce or business. **commercial traveller** *n* representative employed by a firm as a salesman.

commission *n* **1** document conferring authority, position, agency, etc. **2** body of people holding an enquiry and producing a report. **3**

piece of work, esp. a work of art, specifically ordered. **4** percentage payment taken by an agent, salesman, etc. *vt* **1** give authority to. **2** put in an order for. **commissioner** *n* one holding or appointed by a commission.

commit *vt* (-tt-) **1** entrust; charge with. **2** perform; do; perpetrate (a crime, etc.). **3** promise; pledge. **4** send to prison or for further trial. **commit oneself** take on an obligation or duty. **commitment** *n*.

committee *n* small group instructed by a larger organization to deal with specific matters.

commodity *n* particular type of goods, produce, or merchandise.

common *adj* **1** shared by or belonging to all or to many. **2** usual; frequent. **3** general; widespread. **4** relating to the public. **5** habitual. **6** ordinary; familiar; well-known. **7** coarse; vulgar; low. *n* piece of land belonging to the community and available for public use. **in common** in joint use; of mutual interest; shared. **commonly** *adv*. **commonness** *n*. **common law** unwritten law based on custom or tradition. **common sense** *n* practical sense; good judgment; normal mental capacity. **commonplace** *adj* ordinary; not remarkable. *n* trite remark; cliché. **commonwealth** *n* **1** people of a state or nation, esp. when viewed as a political entity. **2** federation of self-governing units or former colonies.

commotion *n* disturbance; public disorder; uproar

communal *adj* relating to or belonging to a commune or community; public; common.

commune[1] *vi* (kə'mju:n) converse or act intimately or spiritually. *n* ('kɔmju:n) intimate conversation; communion.

commune[2] ('kɔmju:n) *n* **1** smallest administrative division of some countries, such as France or Belgium. **2** group or small community organized to promote mutual interests and goals.

communicate *vt* **1** give or transmit; impart. **2** make known. *vi* **1** exchange thoughts or information in a way that may be easily understood. **2** be connected, as by a passage. *vt,vi* administer or receive the Eucharist. **communicant** *n,adj*. **communication** *n*.

communion *n* **1** participation; act of sharing. **2** fellowship. **3** intimate exchange of thoughts and feelings. **Communion** *also* **Holy Communion** the Eucharist or its celebration.

communism *n* belief or social system based on the doctrine that all goods, property, and means of production belong to the community or state. **communist** *adj,n*.

community *n* **1** group of people living in the same area or sharing a common culture. **2** joint possession or ownership.

commute *vi* travel regularly, usually over relatively long distances, from home to work. *vt* reduce (a prison sentence, penalty, etc.). *vt,vi* transform; substitute. **commuter** *n*.

compact[1] *adj* (kəm'pækt) **1** packed neatly and closely together. **2** concentrated; dense. **3** terse; pithy. *vt* (kəm'pækt) pack closely together; condense; compress. *n* ('kɔmpækt) small hinged container, usually with a mirror, for holding face powder. **compactly** *adv*. **compactness** *n*.

compact[2] ('kɔmpækt) *n* agreement or contract between parties.

companion *n* **1** mate; comrade. **2** person who accompanies another or shares the same experience. **3** something that matches another. **companionable** *adj*. **companionship** *n* fellowship; friendship.

company *n* **1** gathering of persons, as for social purposes; group. **2** guest or guests. **3** association for business. **4** officers and crew of a ship. **5** infantry unit of two or more platoons. **6** troupe of actors, dancers, or singers. **part company** end association or friendship (with).

compare *vt* notice or identify similarities; liken. *vi* be in relation to. **comparable** *adj* capable or worthy of being compared. **comparably** *adv*. **comparative** *adj* **1** relating to or involving comparison. **2** not absolute or positive; relative. **comparatively** *adv*. **comparison** *n*.

compartment *n* **1** part or parts into which an enclosed space is partitioned or divided off; section; division. **2** section of a railway carriage.

compass *n* **1** instrument for determining bearings, usually by means of a magnetized needle that always points north. **2** limit or scope. **compasses** *pl n* small instrument with two hinged arms, used for drawing circles, arcs, etc. *vt* encircle; surround.

compassion *n* deeply felt pity or sympathy. **compassionate** *adj*.

compatible *adj* **1** able to live or exist well or

harmoniously together. **2** consistent; not contradictory. **compatibility** *n.* **compatibly** *adv.*

compel *vt* (-ll-) **1** force or bring about by force. **2** subdue; overpower.

compensate *vt,vi* pay money (to) in acknowledgement of loss, damage, or injury; recompense. *vt* offset. *vi* modify or exaggerate one's behaviour to make up for a fault or shortcoming. **compensation** *n.*

compete *vi* strive against others. **competitor** *n.* **competition** *n* **1** competing; rivalry; opposition. **2** contest to show worth or ability, often with a prize for the winner. **competitive** *adj.* **competitively** *adv.*

competent *adj* **1** skilful; able; properly qualified. **2** sufficient; adequate. **competence** *or* **competency** *n.* **competently** *adv.*

compile *vt* assemble; make or put together (a book, its parts, etc.) from various materials or sources. **compilation** *n.* **compiler** *n.*

complacent *adj* self-satisfied. **complacency** *n.* **complacently** *adv.*

complain *vi* express unhappiness or lack of satisfaction; grumble; moan. **complaint** *n* **1** statement of a grievance, wrong, etc. **2** illness.

complement *n* **1** something that serves to complete or make whole or perfect. **2** full allowance, quantity, etc. **complementary** *adj.*

complete *adj* **1** whole; finished; full; perfect. **2** utter; absolute. *vt* finish; make whole, perfect, or full. **completely** *adv.* **completion** *n.*

complex *adj* **1** involved; intricate; complicated. **2** having many facets or parts. *n* **1** whole composed of many parts, often different or distinct. **2** set of mental attitudes, often subconscious, that affect personality. **complexity** *n.*

complexion *n* **1** texture, colour, and quality of the skin, esp. of the face. **2** aspect; appearance.

complicate *vt* make difficult, intricate, or involved. **complication** *n.*

compliment *n* ('kɔmplimənt) remark expressing praise, admiration, respect, etc. *vt* ('kɔmpliment) pay a compliment to; congratulate; praise. **complimentary** *adj* **1** expressing a compliment; flattering. **2** free of charge.

comply *vi* do as one is asked; consent; conform. **compliance** *n.* **compliant** *adj.*

component *n* essential or constituent part of something.

compose *vt* **1** create or write (a literary or musical work). **2** constitute; make up. **3** make of various parts or elements; fashion. **4** set type in lines. *vi* write music. **compose oneself** calm or settle oneself. **composer** *n* writer of music. **composite** *adj* made up of different parts. **composition** *n* **1** putting together of parts or elements to form a whole. **2** parts that form the whole; make-up. **3** piece of music. **4** artistic creation. **5** short essay, esp. one written at school. **composure** *n* calmness of mind; serenity.

compost *n* decomposed matter, manure, etc., used as fertilizer.

compound[1] *adj* ('kɔmpaund) composed of separate parts or substances. *vt* **1** (kəm'paund) assemble into a whole; combine. **2** complicate; increase. *n* ('kɔmpaund) **1** something formed by putting together separate substances, ingredients, or components. **2** chemical substance composed of atoms of two or more elements held together by chemical bonds.

compound[2] ('kɔmpaund) *n* enclosure containing houses or other buildings.

comprehend *vt,vi* **1** understand; grasp. **2** include. **comprehensible** *adj.* **comprehension** *n.* **comprehensive** *adj* **1** inclusive; covering everything; broad. **2** able to understand fully. *n also* **comprehensive school** state secondary school taking in pupils from a given area irrespective of ability.

compress *vt* (kəm'pres) **1** force or squeeze together. **2** make smaller in bulk, size, etc. *n* ('kɔmpres) pad or cloth for applying pressure, moisture, etc., to a bodily part. **compression** *n.*

comprise *vt* contain; include; consist of.

compromise *n* **1** settlement of a dispute or disagreement by giving up part of a claim. **2** something between two extremes, courses of action, etc. **3** exposure to jeopardy, suspicion, loss of reputation, etc. *vi* settle a dispute through a compromise. *vt* expose to jeopardy, etc.

compulsion *n* **1** impulse or urge that cannot be resisted. **2** act of compelling. **compulsive** *adj* acting on a sudden urge or impulse. **compulsively** *adv.* **compulsiveness** *n.* **compulsory** *adj* **1** obligatory; required. **2** compelling; employing compulsion. **compulsorily** *adv.*

computer *n* electronic apparatus that performs

calculations, processes data, etc., usually equipped with a memory and able to print out required information.

comrade *n* **1** close associate or companion; mate. **2** fellow member of a communist group or party. **comradeship** *n*.

concave *adj* curved inwards; being hollow and curved. *n* concave surface or part.

conceal *vt* **1** hide. **2** keep secret. **concealment** *n*.

concede *vt* admit having lost. *vt,vi* **1** acknowledge to be true. **2** yield.

conceit *n* excessive estimation of one's achievements, abilities, or worth; vanity. **conceited** *adj*.

conceive *vt,vi* **1** become pregnant with (a child). **2** form (an idea); imagine. **conceivable** *adj*.

concentrate *vt,vi* **1** direct (one's attention or energies) towards a particular objective. **2** make or become less diluted; condense. **3** place or be confined in a dense mass. *n* concentrated solution. **concentration** *n*. **concentration camp** *n* (esp. during World War II) place, such as a guarded compound, for the detention of political prisoners, racial minorities, etc.

concentric *adj* having a common centre.

concept *n* abstract notion; idea; thought. **conceptual** *adj*. **conception** *n* **1** fertilization; start of pregnancy. **2** idea; concept. **3** plan; design.

concern *vt* be of interest to; relate to; affect; worry. *n* **1** care; regard; anxiety; interest. **2** affair; matter. **3** business; firm; company. **concerning** *prep* about; regarding; relating to.

concert *n* (ˈkɔnsət) **1** public musical entertainment. **2** agreement; union; harmony. *vt* (kənˈsəːt) plan together; arrange by agreement. **concerted** *adj*.

concertina *n* musical instrument with bellows and button-like keys.

concerto (kənˈtʃɛətou) *n* musical piece for solo instrument and orchestra.

concession *n* **1** act of conceding or yielding. **2** that which is conceded or yielded. **3** franchise or privilege; grant. **concessionary** *adj*.

concise *adj* brief; terse; succinct. **concisely** *adv*.

conclude *vt,vi* bring or come to an end; finish. *vt* **1** settle; arrange or agree finally. **2** say or declare in ending or finishing. **conclusion** *n*. **conclusive** *adj*.

concoct *vt* **1** prepare with various ingredients; make a mixture of. **2** make up; devise; invent. **concoction** *n*.

concrete *adj* **1** real; not abstract. **2** relating to a specific object or case. *n* building material formed from sand, cement, water, etc., that hardens as it dries. *vt* cover over with concrete.

concur *vi* (-rr-) **1** agree; have the same opinion. **2** occur together; coincide. **concurrent** *adj*.

concussion *n* injury to the brain, caused by a blow, fall, etc., often causing loss of consciousness. **concuss** *vt* cause concussion in.

condemn *vt* **1** blame; find guilty. **2** pronounce judicial sentence against. **3** judge to be unfit for service or use. **condemnation** *n*.

condense *vt* **1** concentrate; make more solid, compact, or dense. **2** abridge; put into a few or fewer words. **3** change (a gas or vapour) to a liquid, esp. by cooling. *vi* become liquid or solid. **condensation** *n* anything condensed from a vapour, esp. fine droplets of water on a window, etc., condensed from the atmosphere.

condescend *vi* **1** lower oneself to the level of one's inferiors. **2** be gracious or patronizing. **condescension** *n*.

condition *n* **1** state or mode of existence. **2** state of health. **3** stipulation; restriction. **conditions** *pl n* **1** circumstances. **2** terms of an agreement, contract, etc. ~*vt* **1** accustom (someone) to. **2** affect; change. **conditional** *adj* tentative; not absolute; dependent on certain conditions. **conditionally** *adv*.

condolence *n* expression of sympathetic grief.

condone *vt* overlook; forgive; pardon.

conduct *v* (kənˈdʌkt) *vt,vi* **1** transmit (heat, electricity, etc.). **2** control (an orchestra) during a performance or rehearsal. *vt* **1** guide; lead. **2** direct; manage; control. *n* (ˈkɔndʌkt) **1** behaviour. **2** execution or handling of business. **conduction** *n* transfer of heat or electricity through a medium. **conductor** *n* **1** director of an orchestra, choir, etc. **2** leader; guide. **3** person who collects fares from passengers on public transport vehicles. **4** that which conducts electricity, heat, etc.

cone *n* **1** solid figure with a circular base and tapering to a point. **2** fruit of certain trees, such as the pine or fir. **3** anything shaped like or resembling a cone.

confectioner *n* person who makes or sells sweets, cakes, etc. **confectionery** *n* **1** sweets, chocolate, etc. **2** confectioner's trade or business.

confederate *adj* (kən'fedərit) united; allied. *n* (kən'fedərit) ally; accomplice. *vt,vi* (kən'fedəreit) unite in an alliance, conspiracy, etc. **confederation** *or* **confederacy** *n*.

confer *v* (-rr-) *vt* grant as a favour, gift, honour, etc. *vi* talk with; compare opinions.

conference *n* meeting for discussion.

confess *vt,vi* **1** admit or acknowledge (a crime, sin, etc.). **2** concede; agree. **confession** *n*. **confessor** *n* priest who gives absolution to those who confess their sins.

confetti *n* small bits of coloured paper for throwing at weddings, etc.

confide *vi also* **confide in** divulge information (to); disclose in secret. **confidence** *n* **1** feeling of trust, assurance, etc.; firm belief. **2** self-assurance. **confident** *adj*. **confidently** *adv*. **confidential** *adj* secret; private. **confidentially** *adv*.

confine *vt* (kən'fain) **1** imprison; shut in. **2** keep in bed or in the house. **3** limit; keep within limits. **confines** ('kɔnfainz) *pl n* limits; restrictions. **confinement** *n*.

confirm *vt* **1** verify; substantiate; make valid. **2** give a firm undertaking of. **3** administer confirmation to. **confirmation** *n* **1** verification. **2** rite by which baptized persons are admitted into full membership of the Church.

confiscate *vt* seize by authority; appropriate. **confiscation** *n*.

conflict *n* ('kɔnflikt) **1** struggle; trial of strength. **2** opposition or clash of interests, ideas, etc. *vi* (kən'flikt) be inconsistent or at odds with; clash.

conform *vi also* **conform to** comply (with); agree to certain standards, rules, etc.; fit in (with). **conformist** *n,adj*. **conformity** *n*.

confound *vt* **1** baffle; perplex. **2** mix up; confuse. **confounded** *adj* **1** astonished; utterly confused. **2** dreadful; irritating.

confront *vt* **1** face; present. **2** bring face to face with. **confrontation** *n*.

confuse *vt* **1** throw into disorder. **2** mix mentally; obscure. **3** bewilder; muddle. **confusion** *n*.

congeal *vt,vi* **1** solidify by freezing or cooling. **2** coagulate; stiffen. **congealment** *n*.

congenial *adj* **1** pleasing; agreeable. **2** similar in disposition; compatible. **congenially** *adv*.

congenital *adj* existing at birth.

congested *adj* **1** crowded; overcrowded; blocked. **2** (of an organ or part) excessively suffused with blood. **congestion** *n*.

congratulate *vt* acknowledge the good fortunes or achievements of; praise; compliment. **congratulation** *n*.

congregate *vi* assemble; flock together; gather. **congregation** *n* **1** act of congregating. **2** assembly of people, esp. those who gather in a church to worship.

congress *n* **1** assembly; conference. **2** legislative body. **congressional** *adj*.

conical *adj also* **conic** relating to or having the shape of a cone.

conifer *n* tree, such as the pine or fir, having evergreen needle-shaped leaves and bearing cones. **coniferous** *adj*.

conjugal *adj* marital; relating to husband and wife.

conjugate *vt* ('kɔndʒugeit) inflect (a verb) in its various forms. *adj* ('kɔndʒugit) joined together in pairs; coupled. **conjugation** *n*.

conjunction *n* **1** union; association. **2** simultaneous occurrences; combination of events. **3** part of speech joining words, phrases, etc. **conjunctive** *adj*.

conjure *vt also* **conjure up** **1** call or produce as if by magic. **2** imagine; evoke; recall. *vi* practice or perform tricks of illusion or magic. **conjurer** *n*.

connect *vt,vi* link; join; fasten together. *vt* associate in the mind. **connection** *n* **1** link; joining together. **2** association; relationship. **3** public transport, esp. a train, timed to meet another train for the transfer of passengers. **connections** *pl n* influential business or social contacts.

connoisseur *n* person who is an expert, esp. in matters of taste and art.

connotation *n* suggestion or implication of a word in addition to its chief meaning. **connotative** *adj*.

conquer *vt,vi* **1** overcome (an enemy) by force; defeat. **2** surmount. *vt* gain possession of by force; take over. **conqueror** *n*. **conquest** *n*.

conscience *n* **1** mental sense of right and wrong. **2** feeling of guilt. **conscientious** *adj* **1**

paying attention to conscience; scrupulous. **2** painstaking; hard-working. **conscientiously** *adv*.

conscious *adj* **1** aware of one's surroundings; awake. **2** sensitive to or recognizing some truth, fact, etc. **3** performed or registered with full awareness. **4** intended; deliberate. **consciously** *adv*. **consciousness** *n*.

conscript *vt* (kən'skript) enrol compulsorily into service, esp. in the armed forces; call up. *n* ('kɔnskript) person who has been conscripted. **conscription** *n*.

consecrate *vt* **1** make sacred or holy; sanctify. **2** devote; dedicate. **consecration** *n*.

consecutive *adj* in unbroken or logical order or succession. **consecutively** *adv*.

consent *vi* agree (to); give assent. *n* **1** permission. **2** agreement.

consequence *n* **1** effect or result; conclusion. **2** significance; importance. **in consequence** as a result. **consequent** *adj*.

conservative *adj* **1** opposed to change, as in social or political conditions; traditional. **2** moderate. *n* person who is conventional or opposed to change. **Conservative Party** *n* British political party which generally favours private enterprise. **conservatively** *adv*.

conservatory *n* glassed-in room for growing blooming or exotic plants, esp. one attached to an outside wall of a house.

conserve *vt* preserve; keep from decay, change, etc. *n* jam made with whole fruit. **conservation** *n* preservation, esp. of the natural environment.

consider *vt,vi* **1** think about; reflect on; contemplate; examine. **2** suppose; think to be; believe. **3** look upon with respect, sympathy, etc. **considerable** *adj* **1** somewhat large in amount, extent, or degree. **2** important; great. **considerably** *adv*. **considerate** *adj* thoughtful; kind. **consideration** *n* **1** thought; contemplation; reflection. **2** payment; financial reward. **3** thoughtfulness for others. **4** importance. **take into consideration** take into account; bear in mind. **considering** *prep* in view of.

consign *vt* **1** hand over formally; commit (to). **2** give over to another's custody; entrust. **consignment** *n*.

consist *vi* be composed or made up (of). **consistency** *n* **1** degree of solidity, density, or firmness. **2** agreement; correspondence; accordance; regularity. **consistent** *adj* harmonious; not contradictory; regular. **consistently** *adv*.

console *vt,vi* comfort in distress or grief; cheer. **consolation** *n*.

consolidate *vt,vi* **1** make or become firm or solid; strengthen. **2** combine; unite. **consolidation** *n*.

consonant *n* **1** speech sound made by constriction or stoppage of the breath stream. **2** letter or symbol representing this, such as *p, t,* or *s*.

conspicuous *adj* easily seen; noticeable; standing out. **conspicuously** *adv*.

conspire *vt,vi* plot (an evil or criminal act) in secret. *vi* act together; contribute in combination. **conspiracy** *n*. **conspirator** *or* **conspirer** *n*.

constable *n* police officer of the lowest rank. **constabulary** *n* local police force.

constant *adj* **1** always present, happening, or continuing. **2** unchanging; permanent. *n* quantity or value that does not vary. **constancy** *n*. **constantly** *adv*.

constellation *n* star group, esp. one with a given name.

consternation *n* dismay; anxiety.

constipation *n* difficulty or infrequency in evacuating the bowels.

constituency *n* body of electors or area served by a member of Parliament.

constituent *adj* **1** serving to make up a whole; component. **2** having power to elect. *n* **1** component or essential part. **2** elector; voter.

constitute *vt* **1** set up; establish. **2** be an element of; make up. **3** appoint; make into. **constitution** *n* **1** manner in which something is made up. **2** state of physical or mental health. **3** character; temperament; disposition. **4** principles or laws by which a state is governed. **constitutional** *adj*.

constrain *vt* **1** compel. **2** confine; restrain; restrict. **constraint** *n*.

constrict *vt* make narrower or tighter; compress. **constriction** *n*.

construct *vt* (kən'strʌkt) **1** put together; build; make. **2** devise; formulate; fabricate. *n* ('kɔnstrʌkt) something constructed; formulation. **construction** *n*. **constructive** *adj* useful; helpful.

consul *n* official state representative, residing and performing administrative duties in a foreign city. **consular** *adj*. **consulate** *n* **1** premises occupied by a consul. **2** period of office of a consul.

consult *vt* seek advice or information from; refer to. **consultant** *n* **1** person qualified to give expert professional advice. **2** medical or surgical specialist. **consultation** *n*.

consume *vt* **1** use up. **2** eat or drink up. **3** destroy as by burning or decomposition. **4** spend (time, money, etc.), esp. foolishly or wastefully. **5** engross; absorb. **consumer** *n* person who buys or uses a commodity or service. **consumption** *n*.

contact *n* **1** touching or being in touch. **2** connection; association. **3** person exposed to a contagious disease. **4** person who may be useful to one socially or for business purposes. *vt,vi* get in touch, be in contact, or communicate (with). **contact lenses** *pl n* optical lenses that fit directly on to the surface of the eye to correct visual defects.

contagious *adj* **1** (of an infectious disease) transmitted directly or indirectly from one person to another. **2** (of an infected person) able to spread disease to others. **3** tending to spread or influence; catching. **contagion** *n*.

contain *vt* **1** hold; enclose. **2** comprise; include; have room for. **contain oneself** control or restrain oneself. **container** *n* something able to hold a product, substance, etc.; receptacle.

contaminate *vt* **1** make impure by mixture or contact; pollute. **2** corrupt; spoil. **3** make dangerous or worthless by being exposed to radioactivity. **contamination** *n*.

contemplate *vt* **1** gaze upon, esp. thoughtfully. **2** meditate on. **3** intend; plan. *vi* consider carefully; meditate. **contemplation** *n*.

contemporary *adj* **1** of roughly the same date or age. **2** of the present; reflecting current styles, fashions, etc.; modern. *n* person of the same age or time as another. **contemporaneous** *adj*.

contempt *n* **1** scorn. **2** disrespect. **3** lack of regard for authority, esp. for the rules of a court or legal body. **contemptible** *adj*. **contemptuous** *adj*.

contend *vi* struggle; fight for; compete. *vt* assert; claim; maintain. **contention** *n*.

content[1] ('kɔntent) *n* **1** capacity. **2** proportion of a substance contained; subject matter. **contents** *pl n* **1** items placed in a container. **2** list of chapters or divisions in a book.

content[2] (kən'tent) *adj* **1** satisfied; happy. **2** willing; resigned. *vt* make content; please. *n also* **contentment** happiness; satisfaction.

contest *n* ('kɔntest) **1** competition; match. **2** conflict; struggle. *vt* (kən'test) fight for; dispute; struggle against. **contestant** *n* person who takes part in a contest; competitor.

context *n* **1** text or section preceding or following a particular passage, word, etc. **2** facts or circumstances relating to an event, situation, etc.; background. **contextual** *adj*.

continent *n* major land mass of the earth. **continental** *adj*. **Continental** *adj* relating to the mainland of Europe or to Europeans. *n* inhabitant of the mainland of Europe. **continental quilt** *n* duvet.

contingency *n* chance occurrence; unforeseen event or circumstance; possibility; eventuality. **contingent** *adj* dependent upon an uncertain event or condition; possible. *n* representative group in a body of people.

continue *vt,vi* **1** go on; carry on; proceed (with). **2** remain existing; persist. **3** resume; take up again. **continual** *adj* occurring at regular intervals; constant; persistent. **continually** *adv*. **continuation** *n* **1** extended or connected part or section. **2** prolonged action. **3** resumption; renewal. **continuity** *n* **1** continuous flow; logical sequence. **2** complete film scenario, script, etc. **continuous** *adj* without interruption; unbroken. **continuously** *adv*.

contour *n* outline or shape of a body or figure. *vt* form the outline or shape of. **contour line** *n* line on a map that passes through all points that have equal elevation.

contraband *n* **1** illegal importing or exporting. **2** smuggled goods.

contraception *n* prevention of conception; birth control. **contraceptive** *adj* serving to prevent conception. *n* agent or device that prevents conception.

contract *n* ('kɔntrækt) agreement, esp. legally binding, between two or more persons, groups, etc. *v* (kən'trækt) *vt,vi* **1** make or become smaller or more compressed **2** ('kɔntrækt) enter into or settle by agreement. **3** draw or be drawn together. *vt* **1** shorten by omitting parts, elements, etc. **2** acquire (a disease, liability, etc.). **contraction** *n*.

contradict *vt* **1** state the opposite of (a statement, etc.). **2** deny; refute. *vt,vi* be inconsistent (with). **contradiction** *n*. **contradictory** *adj*.

contralto *n* female alto voice.

contraption *n* strange or cumbersome invention, machine, etc.

contrary *adj* **1** opposite. **2** opposed in direction, tendency, or nature. **3** perverse. *n* exact opposite. *adv* in opposition.

contrast *vt,vi* (kən'tra:st) show or display dissimilarity. *n* ('kɔntra:st) striking difference or distinction.

contravene *vt* **1** infringe; conflict with; violate. **2** contradict; dispute. **contravention** *n*.

contribute *vt,vi* **1** pay with others to a common fund. **2** supply or give as one's share in a discussion, task, etc. **contribution** *n*. **contributor** *n*. **contributory** *adj*.

contrive *vt* **1** devise; design. **2** succeed in bringing about; manage. *vi,vt* plot; conspire. **contrivance** *n*. **contrived** *adj* unnatural; not spontaneous.

control *vt* (-ll-) **1** command; dominate. **2** check; curb; restrain. **3** verify or test by a standard comparison. *n* **1** domination; command. **2** restraint; check. **3** standard of comparison. **controls** *pl n* devices for regulating or guiding a machine, as an aircraft, car, etc.

controversy *n* debate; dispute; argument. **controversial** *adj*.

convalesce *vi* recover from illness. **convalescence** *n* period of recovery. **convalescent** *adj,n*.

convenience *n* **1** suitability; usefulness. **2** personal comfort; ease. **3** public lavatory. **convenient** *adj* **1** well adapted to one's purpose; suitable. **2** helpful; useful; handy. **conveniently** *adv*.

convent *n* **1** religious community, esp. of nuns. **2** buildings occupied by such a community.

convention *n* **1** large assembly, conference, or formal meeting. **2** traditionally observed custom or rule; norm. **conventional** *adj* conforming to accepted standards.

converge *vi* tend to meet or move towards the same point; approach. **convergence** *n*. **convergent** *adj*.

converse[1] (kən'və:s) *vi* talk or hold a conversation (with). **conversation** *n* talk; exchange of thoughts, opinions, etc.

converse[2] ('kɔnvə:s) *adj* opposite; reverse. *n* statement with the terms of another interchanged; opposite. **conversely** *adv*.

convert *vt* (kən'və:t) **1** modify or change into something different; adapt. **2** change in outlook, religion, opinion, etc. *n* ('kɔnvə:t) person who has been converted, esp. to a particular religion. **conversion** *n*. **convertible** *adj* capable of being converted. *n* car with a folding or removable roof.

convex *adj* curved outwards; bulging.

convey *vt* **1** carry; transport. **2** communicate. **conveyance** *n* **1** transfer of property from one person to another. **2** transportation. **conveyor belt** *n* endless flexible belt used to convey goods, esp. in a factory.

convict *vt* (kən'vikt) prove or declare guilty. *n* ('kɔnvikt) imprisoned criminal.

conviction *n* **1** firm belief; certainty. **2** verdict of guilt.

convince *vt* satisfy by argument or evidence; persuade.

convoy *n* **1** escort of naval vessels, armed forces, etc., provided for protection. **2** group of vehicles moving together.

cook *vt,vi* **1** prepare (food) by roasting, boiling, etc. **2** subject or be subjected to heat; burn. *n* person who prepares food, esp. professionally. **cooker** *n* oven; stove. **cookery** *n* art or practice of cooking.

cool *adj* **1** somewhat cold. **2** unexcited; calm. **3** lacking interest or friendliness. *vt,vi* make or become cool(er). *n* cool part, place, time, etc. **cool one's heels** be kept waiting. **coolly** *adv*. **coolness** *n*.

coop *n* pen or cage for poultry. *vt also* **coop up** confine in a small space.

cooperate *vi* work together; act jointly. **cooperation** *n*. **cooperative** *adj* helpful; willing to cooperate. *n* joint enterprise based on collective principles.

coordinate *vt* (kou'ɔ:dineit) bring into order as parts of a whole; combine harmoniously. *adj* (kou'ɔ:dinit) combined; harmonious. *n* (kou'ɔ:dinit) combination.

cope *vi* deal with; manage satisfactorily.

copper[1] *n* **1** soft reddish lustrous metal, used in electrical wiring, plumbing, etc. **2** coin made or formerly made of copper. *adj,n* red or reddish-gold.

copper[2] *n sl* policeman.

copulate *vi* have sexual intercourse. **copulation** *n*.

copy *n* **1** reproduction or imitation; duplicate. **2** single specimen of a book. **3** matter for printing. *vt,vi* **1** make a copy (of); duplicate. **2** imitate. **copyright** *n* exclusive legal right to produce or dispose of copies of a literary or artistic work over a given period of time. *vt* secure a copyright on.

coral *n* **1** hard red or white substance secreted by sea polyps, often forming reefs or islands. **2** polyps producing this. **3** ornament, etc., fashioned from coral.

cord *n* **1** thin rope or thick string. **2** ribbed fabric, such as corduroy. *vt* furnish or fasten with cord.

cordial *adj* sincere; warm; hearty. *n* concentrated fruit juice. **cordially** *adv.*

cordon *n* **1** ornamental cord or badge. **2** line of police, troops, etc., guarding an area.

corduroy *n* thick cotton fabric with a corded or ribbed surface.

core *n* **1** central or innermost part of anything. **2** middle part of an apple or other fleshy fruit, containing the seeds. *vt* remove the core of.

cork *n* **1** porous outer bark of a certain tree (cork oak), used for making bottle stoppers, floats, etc. **2** piece of cork used as a bottle stopper. *vt* stop up with a cork. **corkscrew** *n* device for extracting corks from bottles, usually consisting of a sharp pointed metal spiral.

corn[1] *n* **1** edible grain, esp. the small hard seeds of cereal plants. **2** *US* maize. **cornflakes** *n* breakfast cereal made from flakes of roasted maize. **cornflour** *n* finely ground flour from maize, used mainly to thicken gravies, sauces, etc. **cornflower** *n* blue flower commonly found growing in cornfields.

corn[2] *n* horny growth on the toe or foot, caused by friction of shoes.

corner *n* **1** angle or area formed when two sides, surfaces, or lines meet. **2** nook; secluded place. *vt* **1** force or drive into a difficult position. **2** establish a monopoly.

cornet *n* **1** brass musical instrument with three valves, similar to but smaller and more mellow than a trumpet. **2** cone-shaped wafer for ice cream.

coronation *n* ceremony of crowning a monarch.

coroner *n* public official in charge of an inquest in cases of suspicious death.

coronet *n* small crown.

corporal[1] *adj* relating to the body; physical.

corporal[2] *n* noncommissioned officer below a sergeant in the army or airforce.

corporation *n* **1** body of persons, usually in business, legally authorized to function as an individual. **2** municipal authority or council. **corporate** *adj.*

corporeal *adj* physical; material; not spiritual.

corps (kɔː) *n* **1** military unit comprising several divisions. **2** group of dancers, actors, etc. **3** body of officials, esp. diplomats.

corpse *n* dead human body.

corpuscle (ˈkɔːpʌsəl) *n* small free-floating cell present in the blood.

correct *vt* **1** set right. **2** point out faults or errors. **3** neutralize; counteract. *adj* **1** factual; true; accurate. **2** proper; conforming to a custom or standard. **correction** *n.* **correctly** *adv.*

correlate *vt,vi* have or bring into mutual relation. *n* either of two related things that imply each other. **correlation** *n.*

correspond *vi* **1** conform; match. **2** be similar or equivalent. **3** communicate by exchanging letters. **correspondence** *n* **1** agreement; conformity. **2** communication by letters. **correspondent** *n* **1** person who communicates by letters. **2** person employed by a newspaper, etc., to cover a special area or to report from a foreign country. *adj* similar.

corridor *n* long passageway connecting rooms, railway compartments, etc.

corrode *vt* eat away; eat into the surface of. **corrosion** *n.* **corrosive** *adj,n.*

corrupt *adj* **1** dishonest; open to bribery. **2** depraved; evil. **3** rotten; putrid; tainted. *vt* **1** cause to be dishonest. **2** pervert; debase. **3** taint. **corruptible** *adj.* **corruption** *n.*

corset *n* close-fitting stiffened undergarment that supports and shapes the stomach, worn esp. by women.

cosmetic *n* preparation to beautify the complexion or the hair. *adj* relating to cosmetics.

cosmic *adj* relating to or forming part of the universe.

cosmonaut *n* Soviet astronaut.

cosmopolitan *adj* **1** relating to all parts of the world; worldwide. **2** widely travelled; urbane. *n* person who is widely travelled or sophisticated.

cosmos *n* **1** universe. **2** harmonious system; order.

cost *n* **1** price of something. **2** loss; sacrifice; penalty. **3** expenditure of time, labour, money, etc. **at all costs** *or* **at any cost** regardless of the cost. ~*vt* (cost) **1** have as the price **2** result in a loss, sacrifice, or penalty. **3** determine or estimate the cost of. **costly** *adj*.

costume *n* style of dress, esp. one indicating a particular period, nationality, etc.

cosy *adj* snug; comfortable. *n* padded cover for keeping a teapot, boiled egg, etc., warm. **cosily** *adv*.

cot *n* **1** child's bed with high sides. **2** portable bed or hammock.

cottage *n* small house, esp. in the country.

cotton *n* **1** plant producing white downy fibres that cover its seeds. **2** thread or cloth produced from these fibres. *v* **cotton on** realize; grasp. **cotton-wool** *n* raw bleached cotton, esp. as used for surgical dressings.

couch *n* upholstered furniture that seats two or more persons. *vt* express in a particular style.

cough *vi* expel air from the lungs with effort and noise. **cough up** *sl* produce; hand over. ~*n* act or sound of coughing.

could *v pt* of **can.**

council *n* administrative or legislative body, esp. one elected to govern a town or district. **councillor** *n*.

counsel *n* **1** advice; guidance. **2** barrister. **3** consultation; debate. *vt* (-ll-) give advice to; recommend. **counsellor** *n* adviser.

count[1] *vt,vi* **1** enumerate, add; reckon up; calculate. **2** list or name numerals in sequence. *vt* take into account; consider. *vi* be of importance; matter. **count on** rely or depend on. **count out** exclude. ~*n* **1** reckoning; calculation. **2** total number. **countdown** *n* period immediately before firing a missile, launching a spacecraft, etc., timed by counting backwards to zero. **countless** *adj* innumerable.

count[2] *n* nobleman of certain European countries, corresponding to a British earl.

counter[1] *n* **1** table or other surface on which money is counted, business transacted, etc. **2** long narrow table at which food is served. **3** small disc used as a token. **under the counter 1** conducted in a secret or dishonest manner. **2** reserved for special persons, favoured clients, etc.

counter[2] *adv* in the opposite or reverse direction. *adj,n* opposite. *vt,vi* oppose; contradict.

counterattack *n* military attack launched just after an enemy attack. *vt,vi* make such an attack (on).

counterfeit *adj* not genuine; fake; forged. *vt* imitate with intent to deceive; forge. *n* something counterfeited.

counterfoil *n* stub of a cheque, receipt, etc., kept as a record.

counterpart *n* person or thing having an identical or equivalent function.

countess *n* **1** wife or widow of a count or earl. **2** woman of a rank equivalent to a count or earl.

country *n* **1** nation; territory; state. **2** population of a nation. **3** land of birth or residence. **4** rural area as opposed to a town.

county *n* major administrative, political, or judicial division of certain countries or states.

coup (ku:) *n* successful and often unexpected attack, stroke, etc.

couple *n* **1** pair. **2** two people in a relationship. **a couple of** a small number of; a few. ~*vt* **1** link or fasten together. **2** associate mentally. *vi* **1** associate in pairs. **2** unite sexually; copulate.

coupon *n* detachable slip or ticket used when ordering goods, claiming discount, etc.

courage *n* capacity to deal with danger; bravery; boldness. **courageous** *adj*. **courageously** *adv*.

courgette *n* small vegetable marrow.

courier *n* **1** special or express messenger. **2** person employed to take care of tourists and their travel arrangements.

course *n* **1** movement in space or time. **2** direction of movement; route. **3** type of action or conduct. **4** duration. **5** area or stretch of land over which a race is run, golf is played, etc. **6** series of lessons, sessions, etc. **7** any of the sequential parts of a meal. **in the course of** during. **of course** certainly; in fact. ~*vi* move or flow quickly.

court *n* **1** *also* **courtyard** space enclosed by buildings. **2** area marked off or enclosed for playing games, such as tennis or squash. **3** household or establishment of a sovereign. **4** body with judicial powers; tribunal. **5** building or room in which a trial or tribunal is held. **6** attention; homage. *vt,vi* **1** seek the affection of (a member of the opposite sex). **2** seek the approval or support of. **court card** *n* playing card that is a king, queen, or jack; face card. **court-martial** *n pl* **courts-martial** court of officers for trying naval, airforce, or army offences. **courtship** *n* courting of a woman.

courtesy *n* polite behaviour or disposition. **courteous** *adj*.

cousin *n* son or daughter of one's uncle or aunt.

cove *n* **1** small inlet; sheltered bay. **2** nook or recess.

covenant *n* **1** agreement; bargain. **2** sealed contract or one of its clauses. *vt,vi* agree to or enter into a covenant.

cover *vt* **1** place or spread over. **2** overlie. **3** shield or conceal. **4** include. **5** protect by insurance. **6** report (an event) for a newspaper, etc. *n* **1** anything that covers. **2** funds to meet possible liability or loss. **coverage** *n* extent, amount, or risk covered.

cow *n* **1** female of the ox family, esp. one kept by farmers for milk. **2** female of certain other animals, such as the elephant, whale, and seal. **cowboy** *n* herdsman in charge of cattle on the western plains of North America, esp. one on horseback.

coward *n* person given to fear. **cowardice** *n*. **cowardly** *adj*. **cower** *vi* crouch in fear or shame; tremble.

coy *adj* shy; modest; slow to respond, esp. deliberately. **coyly** *adv*. **coyness** *n*.

crab *n* **1** ten-legged shellfish. **2** flesh of the crab, used as food. **3** ill-tempered person. **4** species of small apple. *vi* (-bb-) criticize; find fault.

crack *vi,vt* **1** break into pieces; form fissures. **2** make or cause to make a sharp sound. **3** change suddenly in tone; become hoarse. *vt* **1** strike sharply. **2** *inf* open; break into. **3** *inf* find the solution to. **4** tell (a joke). *vi also* **crack up** have a physical or mental breakdown. *n* **1** sharp explosive noise. **2** split or fissure. **cracker 1** thin crisp biscuit. **2** exploding firework. **3** paper and cardboard Christmas toy that emits a bang when pulled apart. **crackle** *n* **1** sound of rapid repeated cracking. **2** network of fine cracks. *vi* emit a sharp cracking sound.

cradle *n* **1** infant's bed. **2** supporting frame. **3** origin or home. *vt* hold in or as if in a cradle.

craft *n* **1** skilled trade. **2** manual skill. **3** cunning. **4** boat; vessel. **craftsman** *n*. **craftsmanship** *n*. **crafty** *adj* cunning; artful. **craftily** *adv*.

crag *n* rugged projecting rock or rock mass.

cram *v* (-mm-) *vt* fill or pack tightly. *vt,vi* **1** study intensively, as just before an examination. **2** eat greedily.

cramp[1] *n* sudden painful involuntary contraction of a muscle.

cramp[2] *n* clamp for holding things together. *vt* **1** hold with a cramp. **2** hem in; keep within too narrow limits; hinder. **cramp someone's style** hinder someone from doing his best, etc.

crane *n* **1** large wading bird with long legs, neck, and bill. **2** machine for moving heavy objects. *vi* stretch the neck (for a better view).

crash *n* **1** violent noisy impact, fall, etc. **2** burst of mixed loud sound, such as thunder. **3** sudden downfall or collapse. *vi,vt* **1** make or cause to make a crash. **2** fall or strike with a crash. **3** involve or be involved in a collision.

crate *n* large packing case. *vt* pack in a crate.

crater *n* **1** bowl-shaped cavity or depression, such as one made by a meteorite on the earth or moon or by an exploding bomb. **2** mouth of a volcano. **cratered** *adj*.

crave *vt,vi* have a strong desire (for); yearn (for). **craving** *n*.

crawl *vi* **1** move along on the ground, etc., on the stomach or on the hands and knees. **2** move or progress very slowly. **3** creep or go stealthily or abjectly. **4** behave abjectly. *n* **1** act of crawling. **2** *also* **front crawl** fast swimming stroke.

crayfish *n* freshwater shellfish resembling a lobster.

crayon *n* stick of coloured chalk or wax used for drawing.

craze *n* **1** mania; tremendous liking. **2** temporary fashion. *vt* **1** impair mentally; drive insane. **2** make small cracks in. *vi* become insane. **crazy** *adj* **1** insane; mad. **2** eccentric; peculiar. **3** unsound; shaky. **4** *inf* wildly enthusiastic or excited (about). **crazily** *adv*. **craziness** *n*.

creak *vi* make a sharp squeaking or grating sound. *n* such a sound. **creaky** *adj*.

cream *n* **1** fatty part of milk. **2** dish or delicacy resembling or made of cream. **3** creamlike substance, esp. a cosmetic. **4** best part of anything. *n,adj* yellowish-white. *vt* **1** beat (a mixture, etc.) until light and smooth. **2** remove the cream from. **3** apply a cream to. **creamy** *adj*.

crease *n* **1** line made by folding. **2** wrinkle. *vt,vi* make or develop creases.

create *vt* **1** bring into being. **2** give rise to. **3** make; produce. **creation** *n* **1** act of creating or state of being created. **2** something created, esp. an original design, work of art, etc. **3** universe and all living creatures. **creative** *adj* having the ability to create; original; inventive. **creativity** *n*.

creature *n* **1** living being, esp. an animal. **2** contemptible or pitiful person.

crèche *n* **1** nursery for infants. **2** model of the Nativity scene.

credible *adj* believable; worthy of belief.

credit *n* **1** system of doing business without immediate receipt or payment of cash. **2** power to purchase items, services, etc., by deferred payment. **3** money at one's disposal in a bank, etc. **4** belief; trust. **5** source of honour, reputation, etc. **6** good name; reputation. **7** influence; respect; commendation. **8** acknowledgement of authorship, direction, performance, etc. *vt* **1** believe; trust; have faith in. **2** attribute; acknowledge. **3** give credit for. **credit card** *n* card that identifies and authorizes the holder to obtain goods or services on deferred payment. **creditor** *n* person, etc., to whom money is owed.

creep *vi* (crept) **1** move like a snake; crawl. **2** move stealthily, quietly, or very slowly. **3** feel a shrinking shivering sensation due to fear, repugnance, etc. *n* **1** creeping movement. **2** *sl* servile or unpleasant person. **creeps** *pl n* feeling of fear, repugnance, etc. **creeper** *n* plant, such as ivy, that trails over ground, etc., by means of roots, tendrils, etc., along its stem.

cremate *vt* dispose of (a corpse) by burning. **cremation** *n*. **crematorium** *n* place where corpses are cremated.

crept *v pt* or *pp* of creep.

crescent *n* **1** waxing or waning moon. **2** narrow curved and pointed figure or symbol. **3** curved row of houses.

cress *n* plant of the mustard family, whose leaves are used in salads or as a garnish.

crest *n* **1** comb or tuft on an animal's head. **2** plume on top of a helmet. **3** top of a wave, mountain ridge, etc. *vt* reach or lie on the top of. *vi* form or rise into a crest. **crestfallen** *adj* dejected.

crevice *n* fissure; narrow split or crack.

crew *n* persons that man a boat, ship, aircraft, etc.

crib *n* **1** child's cot. **2** barred rack for fodder. *vt,vi* (-bb-) *inf* copy unfairly; plagiarize.

cricket[1] *n* chirping leaping insect.

cricket[2] *n* **1** team game played on a grass pitch with bats, ball, and wickets. **2** *inf* fair play.

cried *v pt* or *pp* of **cry.**

crime *n* **1** serious violation of the law. **2** wicked act; sin; grave offence. **3** *inf* senseless or foolish act. **4** unlawful acts in general. **criminal** *n* person guilty or convicted of crime. *adj* **1** relating to or involving crime or its punishment; guilty of crime. **2** wicked; senseless.

crimson *n,adj* deep rich red.

cringe *vi* cower; crouch; shrink back. *n* act of cringing.

crinkle *vt,vi,n* **1** wrinkle; twist. **2** rustle.

cripple *n* lame or disabled person. *vt* **1** disable; maim; make a cripple of. **2** damage, esp. financially. **crippling** *adj* damaging.

crisis *n, pl* **crises** ('kraisi:z) **1** time of acute danger, stress, suspense, etc. **2** turning point; decisive moment.

crisp *adj* **1** brittle; dry; crackling. **2** brisk. **3** clear-cut; sharp; lively. **4** fresh. *n* fine slice of fried potato. **crisply** *adv*. **crispness** *n*.

criterion *n, pl* **criteria** (kraiˈtiəriə) standard of judgement or comparison; test.

critic *n* **1** person who passes judgment or criticizes. **2** expert in assessing the merits of works of art, literature, drama, etc. **critical** *adj* **1** given to judging, fault-finding, etc. **2** of great importance; decisive. **3** involving suspense or risk. **4** relating to critics or criticism. **critically** *adv*. **criticism** *n* **1** severe judgment; disapproval. **2** assessment; review; analysis; evaluation. **criticize** *vt,vi* **1** judge severely; censure. **2** examine critically; evaluate.

croak *n* deep hoarse cry or sound. *vi,vt* utter or speak with a croak. **croakily** *adv*. **croaky** *adj*.

crochet *n* type of knitting done with a single hooked needle. *vt,vi* do such work.

crockery *n* china or earthenware vessels.

crocodile *n* **1** large predatory amphibious reptile of the tropics, with armour-like skin, long tapering snout, and massive jaws. **2** long line of schoolchildren.

crocus *n* small bulbous plant with yellow, purple, or white flowers.

crook *n* **1** criminal; swindler. **2** hooked staff. **3** sharp turn or bend. *vt* bend; curve; make a crook in. **crooked** *adj* **1** bent; curved. **2** set at an angle; askew. **3** *inf* dishonest.

crop *n* **1** cultivated produce. **2** harvest of this. **3** group of things occurring together. **4** pouch in a bird's gullet. **5** stock of a whip. **6** hunting or riding whip. **7** closely cut head of hair. *vt* (-pp-) **1** clip; cut short; cut off. **2** raise or harvest produce. **crop up** *inf* occur, arise, etc., unexpectedly.

croquet *n* lawn game played with wooden balls and mallets and wire hoops.

cross *n* **1** upright stake with a transverse bar. **2** model, mark, or figure of a cross, esp. as a Christian emblem or symbol of Christianity. **3** sign of the Cross made with the hand. **4** intermixture of breeds, qualities, etc. **5** misfortune; trouble. **the Cross 1** cross on which Jesus died. **2** model or picture of this. ~*vt* **1** place so as to intersect. **2** make the sign of the Cross on or over. **3** pass across. **4** meet and pass. **5** mark with lines across. **6** oppose; thwart. **7** modify a breed of animals or plants by intermixture. *vi* **1** intersect. **2** pass over. *adj* **1** out of temper. **2** transverse. **3** intersecting. **4** contrary; adverse. **cross-examine** *vt* examine a witness already examined by the other side. **cross examination** *n*. **cross-eyed** *adj* having a squint. **cross-fire** *n* **1** sharp verbal exchange. **2** crossing of two or more lines of fire. **crossing** *n* **1** act of crossing. **2** intersection of roads, rails, etc. **3** special place for crossing easily, safely, etc. **cross-question** *vt* cross-examine. **cross-reference** *n* reference from one word, part, etc., in a book to another. *vt,vi also* **cross-refer** make a cross-reference. **crossword** *n* puzzle in which words are written horizontally and vertically in numbered spaces according to numbered clues.

crotchet *n* musical note or symbol equal to quarter of a semibreve. **crotchety** *adj inf* cross; quick-tempered.

crouch *vi* **1** huddle down close to the ground, floor, etc. **2** cringe; fawn. *n* crouching position.

crow[1] *n* large black bird with glossy feathers.

crow[2] *vi* **1** *inf* boast. **2** utter a shrill cry.

crowd *vi* flock together. *vt* **1** cram or pack. **2** fill with people. *n* large number; throng. **crowded** *adj*.

crown *n* **1** monarch's headdress. **2** wreath for the head. **3** royal power. **4** former coin. **5** top, as of the head. **6** completion; perfection. *vt* **1** put a crown on. **2** make a king or queen. **3** honour; reward; invest with dignity, etc. **4** bring to completion or perfection. **crown prince** *n* male next in line to the throne.

crucial *adj* decisive; critical.

crucifix *n* cross, esp. one with a figure of Jesus crucified on it. **crucifixion** *n* crucifying, esp. of Jesus. **crucify** *vt* **1** put to death by nailing or tying to a cross. **2** treat severely; torment.

crude *adj* **1** in the natural or raw state. **2** unfinished; rough. **3** without grace; unpolished. **4** blunt; vulgar. **crudely** *adv*. **crudeness** *or* **crudity** *n*. **crude oil** *n* petroleum before it is made into petrol or other products.

cruel *adj* **1** delighting in the pain or suffering of others; heartless. **2** enjoying the infliction of pain on others. **3** distressing; painful. **cruelty** *n*.

cruise *vi* **1** sail about, esp. for pleasure. **2** fly, drive, etc., at moderate speed. *n* act of cruising. **cruiser** *n* armed high-speed naval ship of light or medium displacement.

crumb *n* small particle; fragment, esp. of bread. *vt* break into or cover with crumbs.

crumble *vt,vi* **1** break into small fragments. **2** decay; fall to pieces. *n* baked fruit pudding with a crumbled cake-like topping.

crumple *vt,vi,n* crease; wrinkle.

crunch *vt,vi* crush, grind, or chew noisily. *n* **1** act or sound of crunching. **2** *sl* critical moment.

crusade *n* **1** *also* **Crusade** medieval Christian war to recover the Holy Land from the Turks. **2** campaign in favour of a cause. *vi* participate in a crusade.

crush *vt* **1** compress so as to break, bruise, or crumple. **2** break into small pieces. **3** defeat utterly. *n* **1** act of crushing. **2** crowded mass, esp. of people.

crust *n* **1** hard outer surface of bread. **2** any hard or firm outer part, deposit, or casing. **3** surface of the earth. *vt,vi* cover with or form a crust. **crusty** *adj* **1** having or like a crust. **2** ill-tempered. **crustily** *adv*.

crustacean *n* hard-shelled animal with antennae, usually living in water, such as a crab or lobster.

crutch *n* **1** support for a lame person that fits under the armpit. **2** something needed for moral or psychological support.

crux *n* **1** real issue. **2** hard problem.

cry *vi* **1** weep; shed tears. **2** cry out; shout. **3**

(esp. of animals) utter a characteristic sound. *vt* utter or implore loudly. **cry for** beg for. **cry off** break a promise; withdraw from an agreement. ~*n* **1** loud utterance. **2** call of an animal or bird. **3** fit of weeping. **a far cry 1** long way. **2** very different.

crypt *n* underground chamber or vault, esp. one beneath a church, used for burials, etc. **cryptic** *adj* secret; hidden; mysterious.

crystal *n* **1** transparent piece of mineral. **2** form of certain substances having a definite internal structure and external surfaces that intersect at characteristic angles. **3** very clear glass. **4** cut-glass vessels. **5** something made of or resembling crystal. **crystalline** *adj*. **crystallize** *vt,vi* **1** form into crystals. **2** become or cause to be definite or certain.

cub *n* **1** young of certain animals, such as lions or bears. **2** inexperienced person.

cube *n* **1** regular solid figure bounded by six equal squares. **2** cube-shaped or nearly cube-shaped block. **3** product obtained by multiplying a number by itself twice. **cubic** *adj* **1** having the shape of a cube. **2** relating to volume or volume measure. **3** having three dimensions.

cubicle *n* small room or walled-off space, as for sleeping, dressing, studying, etc.

cuckoo *n* widely distributed bird named from the sound of its call.

cucumber *n* long fleshy green edible fruit, commonly used in salads.

cuddle *vt* hug; fondle. *vi* lie close. *n* hug; affectionate embrace.

cue[1] *n* **1** words or actions used as a guide or signal. **2** hint.

cue[2] *n* long tapered rod with a soft tip used to strike the ball in billiards, etc.

cuff[1] *n* end of a sleeve; wrist-band. **off the cuff** without preparation; improvised.

cuff[2] *vt* hit with the open hand. *n* such a blow.

culinary *adj* relating to or used in cooking or the kitchen.

culprit *n* guilty person; offender.

cult *n* **1** system of religious worship. **2** devotion to or pursuit of some object.

cultivate *vt* **1** raise (crops) on land; grow. **2** develop; improve, refine. **cultivation** *n*.

culture *n* **1** intellectual, behavioural, and artistic ideas, beliefs, etc., of a particular group, time, or place. **2** particular form or stage of civilization. **3** development and training of the mind. **4** refinement of taste, manners, etc. **5** cultivation. **cultural** *adj*. **cultured** *adj* **1** refined. **2** grown in an artificial medium.

cumbersome *adj* **1** troublesome; vexatious. **2** clumsy; unwieldy.

cunning *n* **1** dexterity; skill. **2** skill in deceit or evasion. *adj* having such qualities or characteristics. **cunningly** *adv*.

cup *n* **1** drinking vessel, esp. one with a handle. **2** any cup-shaped formation, depression, cavity, etc. **3** prize in the shape of a cup. **4** fruit-flavoured wine, cider, etc. **one's cup of tea** what especially or particularly suits one; what one likes. ~*vt* (-pp-) form (one's hand) into a hollow shape.

cupboard *n* closed cabinet, usually with shelves.

curate *n* assistant to a parish priest or vicar.

curator *n* person in charge of a museum, a specific collection, etc.

curb *n* **1** check or means of restraint; control. **2** framework or border that encloses. *vt* restrain; control; check.

curd *n* substance obtained by coagulating milk, used as food or in cheese-making. **curdle** *vt vi* form into curd.

cure *vt* **1** heal; remedy. **2** preserve (fish, skins, etc.). *n* **1** remedy. **2** course of medical treatment. **3** restoration to health.

curfew *n* **1** restriction on movement after nightfall or a signal indicating that this is to be enforced. **2** time at which such a signal is given.

curiosity *n* **1** eagerness to know; inquisitiveness. **2** strange, rare, or odd object.

curious *adj* **1** eager to know; inquisitive. **2** prying; tending to meddle. **3** exciting interest. **4** odd; eccentric. **curiously** *adv*.

curl *vt,vi* bend into a curved shape or spiral. *n* **1** spiral lock of hair. **2** spiral or curved form, state, or motion. **curly** *adj*. **curling** *n* game played on ice with large rounded stones.

currant *n* small seedless raisin.

currency *n* **1** time during which anything is current. **2** state of being in use. **3** money.

current *adj* **1** in general use or circulation. **2** going on; not yet superseded. *n* **1** moving body of water or air. **2** flow of something, such as a river. **3** movement of electric charge through a conductor or the rate of its flow.

curry *n* **1** oriental dish flavoured with hot spices.

2 spicy seasoning. *vt* add curry to (food) while cooking.

curse *n* **1** obscene or profane utterance. **2** utterance designed to destroy or harm someone. **3** affliction; bane; scourge. *vi* swear. *vt* **1** abuse by uttering curses at. **2** call on supernatural powers to bring harm to (someone).

curt *adj* **1** short. **2** rudely brief. **curtly** *adv*. **curtness** *n*.

curtail *vt* cut short; end. **curtailment** *n*.

curtain *n* **1** cloth, etc., hung as a screen in front of a window or door. **2** screen between the audience and a stage. **3** end to an act or scene. *vt* provide or cover with a curtain.

curtsy *n* formal woman's bow made as a sign of respect, greeting, etc *vi* make such a bow.

curve *n* **1** line with no straight parts. **2** bend in a road, etc. **3** curved form or object. *vt,vi* bend in a curve. **curvature** *n*.

cushion *n* **1** bag or pad filled with soft stuffing or air, used to sit on, lean against, etc. **2** something that absorbs shocks, jolts, etc. *vt* provide or protect with a cushion.

custard *n* cooked dessert of flavoured eggs and milk.

custody *n* **1** safe-keeping; guardianship. **2** imprisonment. **custodian** *n* person having custody of someone or something.

custom *n* **1** established or habitual practice, usage, etc. **2** business patronage. **3** customers of a shop, business, etc. **customs** *pl n* **1** duties levied on certain imports. **2** area in an airport, etc., where such duties are collected. **customary** *adj* usual. **customer** *n* **1** buyer; patron. **2** *inf* fellow; chap.

cut *vt* (-tt-; cut) **1** sever; penetrate. **2** divide; separate. **3** detach, trim, or shape by cutting. **4** abridge; shorten. **5** ignore (someone). **6** strike (with a whip, sword, etc.). **cut down 1** reduce. **2** fell (trees). **3** *inf* kill. **cut it fine** leave very small margin of time, etc. **cut off 1** discontinue supply of (gas, etc.). **2** interrupt. **3** separate; isolate. **cut out 1** cut (pieces, etc.) from something. **2** remove. **3** suit or equip for. **4** cease to operate. **cut up 1** chop into small pieces. **2** *inf* upset; distress. ~*n* **1** act or result of cutting. **2** incision. **3** engraving. **4** piece cut off. **5** division. **a cut above** superior to. *adj* **cut and dried** settled. **cut-price** *adj* below the normally charged price. **cutting** *n* **1** act of cutting or thing cut off or out. **2** newspaper clipping. **3** piece cut from a plant for replanting.

cute *adj* **1** quaint; sweet. **2** clever; sharp. **cutely** *adv*. **cuteness** *n*.

cuticle *n* skin at the edges of the nails.

cutlery *n* **1** knives and other cutting implements. **2** eating implements.

cutlet *n* small piece of meat, esp. for frying or grilling.

cycle *n* **1** recurrent or complete series or period. **2** development following a course of stages. **3** series of poems, etc. **4** short for **bicycle.** *vi* **1** move in cycles. **2** ride a bicycle. **cyclic** *or* **cyclical** *adj*. **cyclist** *n* person who rides a bicycle.

cyclone *n* system of winds moving round a centre of low pressure.

cygnet *n* young swan.

cylinder *n* **1** tube-shaped figure, usually with a circular base. **2** piston chamber of an engine. **cylindrical** *adj*.

cymbal *n* saucer-shaped piece of brass used as a musical instrument of percussion.

cynic *n* sceptical or distrusting person. **cynical** *adj*. **cynicism** *n*.

cypress *n* coniferous tree having dark foliage and durable wood.

cyst *n* abnormal sac containing bodily secretions.

czar *n* tsar.

D

dab *vt,vi* (-bb-) touch gently; apply with a light touch. *n* **1** gentle blow. **2** small lump of soft substance.

dabble *vt,vi* move about in water or other liquid. *vi* engage in some activity in a superficial manner. **dabbler** *n*.

dad *n* *inf* father.

daffodil *n* variety of yellow narcissus.

daft *adj* silly; feeble-minded.

dagger *n* short stabbing weapon with a double-edged blade.

daily *adj* performed, occurring, etc., every day. *adv* every day. *n* **1** daily newspaper. **2** non-resident domestic help.

dainty *adj* **1** pretty; elegant. **2** fastidious; delicate. **daintily** *adv*. **daintiness** *n*.

dairy *n* place for keeping, processing, or supplying milk and milk products. **dairy farm** *n* farm producing milk and milk products.

daisy *n* small white-petalled flower with a yellow centre.

dam[1] *n* barrier to hold back water. *vt* (-mm-) obstruct or hold back with a dam.

dam[2] *n* female parent, esp. of an animal.

damage *vt,vi* injure; harm; impair; spoil. *n* harm; injury. **damages** *pl n* financial compensation awarded by law for loss or harm.

dame *n* lady, esp. a mistress of a household or school. **Dame** title of a female member of an order of knighthood.

damn *vt* **1** curse; doom; condemn to hell. **2** censure. *interj* expression of anger or annoyance. **damnable** *adj* **1** deserving condemnation. **2** wretched. **damnation** *n* state of being damned.

damp *adj* moist; slightly wet. *n* moisture. *vt also* **dampen 1** moisten. **2** depress; discourage.

damson *n* small purple fruit of the plum family.

dance *n* **1** sequence of rhythmical steps usually performed to music. **2** social gathering for dancing. *vt,vi* **1** perform (a dance). **2** move quickly, energetically, or gracefully. **dance attendance** (**on**) attend constantly. **dancer** *n*.

dandelion *n* plant with bright yellow flowers and leaves with jagged edges.

dandruff *n* flakes of scurf formed on the scalp.

danger *n* exposure to risk of harm; peril; risk. **dangerous** *adj*. **dangerously** *adv*.

dangle *vt,vi* swing loosely; hang freely.

dare *vt,vi* be brave enough (to do something). *vt* challenge; defy. *n* challenge to do something. **daring** *adj* bold; adventurous. *n* boldness; audacity.

dark *adj* **1** without light. **2** deeply tinted, brown or almost black. **3** mysterious; secret; evil. *n* **1** absence of light; night. **2** ignorance; secrecy. **darkness** *n*. **darken** *vt,vi* make or become dark(er).

darling *n* person greatly loved; favourite. *adj* greatly loved or desired.

darn *vt,vi* mend (a hole in fabric) by stitching over. *n* repair so made.

dart *n* **1** small pointed missile, such as a short arrow. **2** swift sudden movement. **3** short seam or tuck in a garment. *vi,vt* move swiftly and suddenly; shoot out. **darts** *n* game in which darts are thrown at a circular board (dartboard).

dash *vi* rush hastily. *vt* **1** hurl; thrust; knock violently. **2** discourage; ruin. *n* **1** sudden rush. **2** small quantity, esp. as a flavouring in food or drink. **3** punctuation mark (-) used to indicate a pause, change of subject, etc. **4** energy; vigour. **dashing** *adj* **1** showy; stylish. **2** impetuous; spirited. **dashboard** *n* instrument panel of a motor vehicle.

data *n s or pl* facts, figures, statistics, etc., used as a basis for discussion or calculation.

date[1] *n* **1** day on which an event occurs or a statement of this in days, months, and years. **2** *inf* appointment; rendezvous. **3** person with whom one has an appointment. *vt* **1** determine the date of. **2** *inf* make an appointment, esp. with a member of the opposite sex. **date from** originate from a certain date.

date[2] *n* sweet oblong single-stoned fruit of the date palm.

daughter *n* **1** female offspring, esp. in relation to her parents. **2** any female descendant. **daughter-in-law** *n, pl* **daughters-in-law** son's wife.

dawdle *vi* move slowly; loiter; fall or lag behind. **dawdler** *n*.

dawn *n* **1** period during which the sun rises; daybreak. **2** beginning. *vi* **1** begin to grow light. **2** begin to appear or develop. **dawn upon** become evident to.

day *n* **1** period between sunrise and sunset. **2** period of 24 hours beginning at midnight. **daybreak** *n* dawn. **daydream** *n* pleasant sequence of thoughts or musing while awake. *vi* have daydreams. **daylight** *n* light from the sun.

daze *vt* stupefy; bewilder; stun. *n* state of being dazed or stunned; drowsiness.

dazzle *vt* **1** blind temporarily with brilliant light. **2** confuse or surprise with brilliance, beauty, etc.

dead *adj* **1** without life; having died. **2** dull; numb; resembling death. **3** extinct; no longer active. **deaden** *vt* make insensible; numb; dull the vitality of. **deadline** *n* time by which some task must be completed. **deadlock** *n* complete standstill in which further progress is impossible. **deadly** *adj* **1** fatal; poisonous. **2** like death.

deaf *adj* **1** lacking or deficient in the sense of hearing. **2** unwilling to listen. **deafen** *vt* **1** make deaf. **2** make impervious to sound. **deafness** *n*.

deal *v* (dealt) *vt,vi* distribute, esp. playing cards to the players. *vt* inflict; deliver. *vi* do business; trade. **deal with** manage; settle. ~*n* **1** business transaction. **2** distribution of playing cards. **3** *inf* amount. **dealer** *n*.

dean *n* **1** head clergyman of a cathedral. **2** college or university official.

dear *adj* **1** much loved; precious. **2** expensive; costly. *n* someone much loved. *adv* at high cost. **dearly** *adv*. **dearness** *n*.

death *n* **1** end of life; state of being dead. **2** dying. **3** cause of death. **deathly** *adj* resembling death; lifeless; pale.

debase *vt* undervalue; lower in value; degrade.

debate *n* **1** formal public discussion. **2** argument; controversy. *vt,vi* discuss; argue (about). **debatable** *adj* open to discussion; questionable.

debit *n* **1** record in an account of money owed. **2** debt; something owed. *vt* record as money owing; charge.

debris *n* wreckage; fragments.

debt *n* **1** something owed. **2** obligation. **in debt** **1** owing money. **2** having an obligation. **debtor** *n* person who is in debt to another.

decade *n* period of ten years.

decadent *adj* **1** declining or deteriorating, esp. morally. **2** corrupted. **decadence** *n*.

decant *vt* pour liquid gently from one vessel to another. **decanter** *n* glass vessel for serving wine.

decapitate *vt* sever or chop off the head of. **decapitation** *n*.

decay *vi* **1** decompose; rot. **2** deteriorate; decline. *n* **1** decomposition. **2** deterioration; decline.

decease *n* death. *vi* die.

deceive *vt,vi* mislead deliberately; delude; cheat. **deceit** *n*. **deceitful** *adj*. **deceitfully** *adv*.

December *n* twelfth month of the year

decent *adj* **1** respectable; proper; modest. **2** *inf* fairly good; adequate. **decency** *n*. **decently** *adv*.

deceptive *adj* tending to deceive or give a false impression. **deception** *n*.

decibel *n* unit for measuring intensities of sounds.

decide *vt* give judgment on; settle. *vi* make up one's mind; conclude. **decided** *adj* **1** certain; definite. **2** resolute. **decidedly** *adv*.

deciduous *adj* **1** (of leaves, teeth, etc.) shed periodically. **2** (of trees) shedding leaves annually.

decimal *adj* based on the number ten; numbered or proceeding by tens. *n also* **decimal fraction** fraction having a denominator that is a power of ten, written with a dot in front of the numerator.

decipher *vt* **1** decode. **2** make out the meaning of.

decision *n* **1** judgment; settlement; conclusion. **2** firmness; determination. **decisive** *adj* **1** conclusive; deciding. **2** resolute; firm. **decisively** *adv*.

deck *n* **1** horizontal platform forming the floor of a ship, bus, etc. **2** pack of cards. *vt* adorn; decorate. **deckchair** *n* portable folding chair with a canvas back.

declare *vt,vi* **1** announce formally; proclaim; assert. **2** state that one has an income, goods, etc., on which duty or tax must be paid. **3** close an innings in cricket before all the wickets have fallen. **declaration** *n*.

declension *n* **1** change in form of a noun, pronoun, or adjective depending on its case. **2** decline; deterioration.

decline *vt,vi* **1** slope downwards. **2** deteriorate; decay. **3** refuse. *n* gradual deterioration; loss of strength, vigour, etc.

decode *vt* interpret from a code; decipher.

decompose *vt,vi* putrefy; rot; decay. **decomposition** *n*.

decorate *vt* **1** embellish; adorn. **2** restore with new paint, wallpaper, etc. **3** invest with a medal, badge, etc. **decoration** *n*. **decorative** *adj*. **decorator** *n*.

decoy *n* something used to attract others into a trap; lure.

decrease *vt,vi* diminish; make or grow less; reduce. *n* process of or amount of lessening; reduction.

decree *n* official decision, judgment, or law. *vt,vi* command; judge; order.

decrepit *adj* worn out; old and useless.

dedicate *vt* **1** devote solemnly or wholly. **2** set apart for a special purpose. **3** inscribe or address as a compliment. **dedication** *n*.

deduce *vt* draw as a conclusion from given facts; infer. **deduct** *vt* take away; subtract. **deduction** *n* **1** act of deducting. **2** amount deducted. **3** logical reasoning from given facts. **4** the conclusion reached.

deed *n* **1** something done; action; exploit. **2**

legal document stating terms of a contract, rights, etc.

deep *adj* **1** extending far down, in, or across. **2** at or of a specified distance down or in. **3** profound; intense; serious. **4** absorbed; engrossed. **5** low-pitched. **6** dark-coloured. *adv also* **deeply** so as to be deep. *n* deep place, esp. in the sea. **deepness** *n*. **deepen** *vt,vi* make or become deep(er). **deep-freeze** *n* refrigerator to keep food fresh for long periods. **deeply** *adv* strongly; profoundly; extremely. **deep-seated** *adj* firmly established; not superficial.

deer *n, pl* **deer** ruminant, the male of which has deciduous antlers.

deface *vt* spoil the appearance or surface of; disfigure. **defacement** *n*.

defame *vt* injure the good name or reputation of, as by libel, slander, etc. **defamation** *n*. **defamatory** *adj*.

default *n* **1** absence; want. **2** failure to act or appear. *vi* fail to act or appear as required. **defaulter** *n*.

defeat *vt* conquer; vanquish; overcome; beat. *n* act of being beaten or conquered.

defect *n* ('di:fekt) failing; blemish; imperfection; fault; flaw. *vi* (di'fekt) desert one's country, duty, etc.; switch allegiance. **defection** *n*. **defector** *n*. **defective** *adj* imperfect; faulty; deficient.

defend *vt,vi* **1** protect against attack. **2** justify, as in answer to a legal charge. **defence** *n*. **defences** *pl n* **1** fortifications. **2** self-protective attitudes. **defensive** *adj* protective; resisting attack. **defensively** *adv*.

defer[1] *vt,vi* (-rr-) postpone; put off.

defer[2] *vi* (-rr-) make concessions; submit (to). **deference** *n* respectful submission to another's will. **deferential** *adj*.

defiant *adj* stubbornly or aggressively hostile; insolent. **defiance** *n*. **defiantly** *adv*.

deficient *adj* incomplete; defective; lacking. **deficiency** *n*.

deficit *n* lack or shortage, esp. of money.

define *vt* **1** mark out; show the limits of. **2** describe exactly; give the meaning of.

definite *adj* **1** certain; fixed; exact. **2** clear; distinct. **definite article** *n* the word 'the'. **definitely** *adv*.

definition *n* **1** act of defining. **2** brief description or explanation, esp. of a word or phrase. **3** quality of distinctness or clarity.

deflate *vt,vi* **1** release air from or lose air. **2** reduce economic inflation. **3** lessen the dignity or conceit of. **deflation** *n*. **deflationary** *adj*.

deflect *vt,vi* turn or move at an angle. **deflection** *n*.

deform *vt* spoil the shape of; make ugly; disfigure. **deformation** *n*. **deformity** *n*.

defraud *vt* cheat; swindle; deprive by fraud.

defrost *vt* remove ice from.

deft *adj* skilful; nimble. **deftly** *adv*. **deftness** *n*.

defunct *adj* obsolete; no longer used.

defy *vt* **1** challenge; resist stubbornly. **2** disobey.

degenerate *vi* (di'dʒenəreit) decline in standard or qualities; deteriorate. *adj* (di'dʒenərət) degraded; depraved. *n* (di'dʒenərət) degenerate person. **degeneration** *or* **degeneracy** *n*.

degrade *vt,vi* **1** reduce in grade or rank. **2** lower in character; debase; humiliate. **degradation** *n*.

degree *n* **1** grade; stage; relative position; extent. **2** academic rank awarded for proficiency or as an honour. **3** unit of measurement in temperature scales. **4** unit of angular measure; 1/360th part of a complete turn.

dehydrate *vt* remove water from. **dehydration** *n*.

deity *n* god or goddess.

dejected *adj* depressed; despondent; sad; miserable.

delay *vt* cause to be late; postpone. *vi* be late; linger. *n* act of delaying; fact or period of being delayed; postponement.

delegate *vt* ('deligeit) **1** send or elect as a representative. **2** entrust to as a deputy. *n* ('deligət) representative; deputy; agent. **delegation** *n* **1** number of delegates in a group. **2** act of delegating.

delete *vt* strike out; erase; remove. **deletion** *n*.

deliberate *vi* (di'libəreit) reflect; consider carefully. *adj* (di'libərət) **1** intentional; purposeful. **2** slow in deciding; cautious. **deliberately** *adv*. **deliberation** *n*.

delicate *adj* **1** finely made or prepared; pleasing. **2** sensitive; easily hurt or damaged. **3** refined; fastidious. **delicacy** *n* **1** sensitivity; tact. **2** refinement; gracefulness. **3** attractive and tasty food. **delicately** *adv*.

delicatessen *n* shop specializing in foreign food, cooked meats, delicacies, etc. *pl n* the foods sold.

delicious *adj* **1** pleasing, esp. to the senses of taste or smell. **2** delightful.

delight *vt* give great pleasure to. **delight in** take pleasure in. ~*n* intense pleasure or joy or a cause of this. **delightful** *adj.* **delightfully** *adv.*

delinquency *n* neglect of duty; wrongdoing; petty crime. **delinquent** *n,adj.*

deliver *vt* **1** set free; liberate. **2** hand over or distribute (mail, goods, etc.). **3** give forth; discharge. **4** pronounce; utter. **5** assist at the birth of. **deliverance** *n* liberation; rescue. **delivery** *n* **1** delivering of mail, goods, a speech, etc. **2** childbirth.

delta *n* fan-shaped area of land at the mouth of a river.

delude *vt* deceive; mislead. **delusion** *n.* **delusive** *adj.*

deluge *n* violent flood. *vt* rush upon or at, as a flood; inundate.

delve *vt,vi* **1** dig. **2** *also* **delve into** research deeply (into).

demand *vt* **1** ask for; claim; request urgently. **2** require; need. *n* pressing request or requirement.

democracy *n* **1** government by the people, esp. by majority vote; equality of rights. **2** state or community so governed. **democrat** *n.* **democratic** *adj.*

demolish *vt* destroy; pull down. **demolition** *n.*

demon *n* **1** devil; evil spirit. **2** cruel or wicked person. **demonic** *adj.*

demonstrate *vt* show by reasoning or practical example; prove; explain. *vi* manifest opposition or sympathy in public; make a protest. **demonstrable** *adj.* **demonstration** *n.* **demonstrator** *n.*

demoralize *vt* **1** lower the morale of; cause to lose courage. **2** harm morally; corrupt.

demure *adj* modest; reserved; sedate. **demurely** *adv.*

den *n* **1** wild animal's retreat or resting place. **2** hiding-place of thieves. **3** private room for work.

denial *n* **1** contradiction. **2** refutation; rejection. **3** refusal of a request.

denim *n* strong cotton fabric.

denomination *n* **1** name or designation. **2** class of units in money, weights, etc. **3** name of a group of people, esp. a religious sect.

denominator *n* lower number in a fraction; divisor. **common denominator** *n* something possessed in common by all members of a group.

denote *vt* **1** mark out; distinguish. **2** stand for; indicate. **denotation** *n.*

denounce *vt* **1** condemn strongly or publicly. **2** inform against. **3** repudiate.

dense *adj* **1** thick; closely packed. **2** opaque. **3** *inf* stupid. **density** *n* **1** thickness. **2** mass per unit volume.

dent *n* small hollow left by a blow or by pressure. *vt,vi* make a dent in or become marked by a dent.

dental *adj* of or relating to the teeth. **dentist** *n* person who treats decayed teeth, fits false teeth, etc. **dentistry** *n.* **denture** *n* set of false teeth.

deny *vt* **1** declare to be untrue; contradict. **2** reject; repudiate. **3** refuse. **deny oneself** abstain from.

deodorant *n* substance that counteracts offensive smells.

depart *vi* **1** go away; leave. **2** die. **departure** *n.*

department *n* **1** subdivision; branch; separate section of an organization. **2** field of activity special concern.

depend *v* **depend (up)on** **1** be conditional or contingent on. **2** rely on; trust. **dependable** *adj* reliable. **dependant** *n* person relying upon another for maintenance or support. **dependent** *adj.* **dependence** *n.*

depict *vt* represent in words or pictures; portray; describe. **depiction** *n.*

deplete *vt* exhaust; empty; reduce. **depletion** *n.*

deplore *vt* **1** regret deeply; lament. **2** disapprove of. **deplorable** *adj.*

deport *vt* expel from a country; banish. **deportation** *n.*

deportment *n* manner of standing, walking, etc.; bearing.

depose *vt* remove from office, esp. from a high position. *vi* bear witness; testify. **deposition** *n.*

deposit *vt* **1** set down. **2** put aside for safekeeping or as a pledge of faith. *n* **1** money entrusted to a bank, etc., or as part-payment of a transaction. **2** layer of ore or sediment in the earth. **depository** *n* place for safekeeping, esp. a store for goods.

depot *n* **1** store or military headquarters. **2** central garage for buses.

deprave *vt* corrupt morally; pervert. **depravity** *n*.

deprecate *vt* express disapproval of.

depreciate *vt,vi* **1** lower or fall in price or value. **2** disparage. **depreciation** *n*.

depress *vt* **1** press down; lower. **2** lessen the activity of. **3** make humble or gloomy. **depression** *n* **1** lowered surface; hollow. **2** low spirits; dejection. **3** state or period of reduced economic activity; slump. **4** region of low barometric pressure in the atmosphere.

deprive *vt* prevent from possessing or using; take away from. **deprivation** *n*.

depth *n* **1** distance downwards; deepness. **2** intensity or extent, as of emotion. **3** profundity of thought or explanation. **4** lowness of pitch. **5** most extreme or intense point. **out of one's depth** unable to understand or cope with a subject, situation, etc. **the depths** *pl n* **1** deepest part. **2** condition of low spirits or dejection.

deputize *vi,vt* act or appoint as an agent or representative. **deputation** *n* body of persons sent to represent others. **deputy** *n* assistant; representative; delegate.

derail *vt* cause (a train) to leave the rails. **derailment** *n*.

derelict *adj* abandoned; in a poor condition; dilapidated. *n* something abandoned. **dereliction** *n* neglect, esp. of duty.

deride *vt* mock at; scorn. **derision** *n*. **derisive** *adj*.

derive *vt* obtain or receive from. *vi* originate (from); be descended (from). **derivation** *n*. **derivative** *n,adj*.

derogatory *adj* insulting; not complimentary; damaging.

descend *vt,vi* move, come, or bring down. *vi* **1** move or slope downwards. **2** originate (from). **descendant** *n* person descended from another; offspring. **descent** *n* **1** descending; going down. **2** downward slope or path. **3** ancestry; transmission by inheritance.

describe *vt* **1** give a detailed account of, esp. in words. **2** trace or mark out. **description** *n*. **descriptive** *adj*.

desert[1] (ˈdezət) *n* waterless and uninhabited region. *adj* barren; lonely.

desert[2] (diˈzəːt) *vt* abandon; leave. *vi* leave service, esp. the army, without permission. **deserter** *n*. **desertion** *n*.

desert[3] (diˈzəːt) *n* something deserved, as a reward or punishment.

deserve *vt* be entitled to by conduct or qualities; merit. *vi* be worthy.

design *vt* **1** plan; make sketches for. **2** intend. *n* **1** plan; scheme; project. **2** art of making designs or patterns. **designer** *n*.

designate *vt* (ˈdezigneit) **1** indicate; point out; name. **2** appoint to office. *adj* (ˈdezignət) appointed to but not yet holding office. **designation** *n*.

desire *vt* **1** wish for greatly; yearn for; want. **2** request. *n* **1** longing; craving; urge; appetite. **2** request. **3** thing or person desired. **desirable** *adj*.

desist *vi* refrain; cease; stop.

desk *n* table with a flat or sloping writing surface.

desolate *adj* (ˈdesələt) **1** abandoned; lonely. **2** dreary; gloomy. *vt* (ˈdesəleit) **1** lay waste; destroy. **2** make unhappy. **desolation** *n*.

despair *n* loss of hope; hopelessness; despondency. *vi* lose hope.

desperate *adj* **1** very serious or dangerous; beyond hope. **2** reckless; violent; careless of risk. **desperation** *n*.

despise *vt* feel contempt for; scorn. **despicable** *adj*.

despite *prep* in spite of.

despondent *adj* dejected; lacking hope or courage. **despondency** *n*.

despot *n* tyrant; cruel ruler or master. **despotic** *adj*.

dessert *n* fruit, confectionery, etc., served as the final course of a meal. **dessertspoon** *n* spoon of a size between a tablespoon and a teaspoon.

destine *vt* **1** determine the future of; doom. **2** set apart for a special purpose; intend. **destination** *n* place towards which a person travels or a thing is sent; end of a journey. **destiny** *n* **1** fate; supernatural or divine power. **2** that which is destined to happen.

destitute *adj* in extreme poverty; penniless. **destitution** *n*.

destroy *vt* demolish; annihilate; ruin. **destruction** *n*. **destructive** *adj*.

detach *vt* separate; disconnect. **detached** *adj* **1** disconnected. **2** aloof; impartial. **detachment** *n*.

detail *n* small part of a whole; item; fact; piece of information. **in detail** thoroughly; fully.

~*vt* **1** give particulars of. **2** appoint for special duty.

detain *vt* **1** keep waiting; prevent from leaving; delay. **2** keep possession of; withhold. **3** hold in custody. **detainee** *n*. **detention** *n*.

detect *vt* **1** notice; see. **2** find out; discover. **detection** *n*. **detective** *n* person, esp. a policeman, who investigates crimes.

deter *vt* (-rr-) discourage or dissuade from action, esp. by fear of consequences. **deterrent** *n,adj*.

detergent *n* cleansing substance. *adj* cleansing.

deteriorate *vt,vi* make or become worse; degenerate. **deterioration** *n*.

determine *vt* **1** be the cause of or deciding factor in. **2** set limits to; fix. *vi* resolve; decide. **determination** *n*.

detest *vt* dislike intensely; loathe; hate. **detestable** *adj*.

detonate *vt,vi* explode. **detonation** *n*. **detonator** *n* detonating device.

detour *n* diversion; deviation from a usual route.

detract *vt* disparage. **detract from** diminish; spoil.

devalue *vt* reduce the value of. **devaluation** *n*.

devastate *vt* destroy wholly; demolish. **devastation** *n*.

develop *vi* evolve; grow; open out. *vt* **1** bring to a more advanced stage. **2** bring forth; reveal. **3** treat (photographic film) to make the image visible. **development** *n*.

deviate *vi* diverge; turn away from what is normal or expected. **deviant** *adj,n*.

device *n* **1** mechanical contrivance; apparatus, appliance, or machine. **2** plot; scheme.

devil *n* **1** demon; wicked fiend. **2** *sl* lively or energetic person; rascal. **the Devil** personification of evil; Satan. **devilish** *adj*.

devious *adj* **1** roundabout; winding; erratic. **2** deceitful.

devise *vt* **1** invent; contrive. **2** bequeath.

devoid *adj* **devoid of** empty (of); lacking in.

devolve *vt* to delegate or transfer (power, responsibility, etc.). *vi* to be transferred. **devolution** *n* the act of devolving, esp. the transfer of government from a central to a regional organisation.

devote *vt* give up wholly, esp. to some cause or person; dedicate. **devotion** *n* **1** great loyalty; dedication. **2** religious worship. **devotee** *n*.

devour *vt* **1** eat greedily; consume. **2** absorb mentally with great eagerness.

devout *adj* **1** pious. **2** earnest; solemn.

dew *n* droplets of moisture deposited on ground surfaces at night.

dexterous *adj* skilful; deft; clever. **dexterity** *n*.

diabetes (daiə'bi:tis) *n* disease of the pancreas, characterized by allergy to sugar and abnormal discharge of urine. **diabetic** *n,adj*.

diagonal *adj* joining two opposite corners; slanting; oblique. *n* diagonal line. **diagonally** *adv*.

diagram *n* sketch, drawing, or plan, used esp. to illustrate or demonstrate something. **diagrammatic** *adj*.

dial *n* **1** graduated face or disc on a watch, compass, or other instrument. **2** numbered disc on a telephone. *vt* (-ll-) call using a telephone dial.

dialect *n* regional variation of a language.

dialogue *n* **1** conversation. **2** passage of written work in conversational form.

diameter *n* **1** straight line across a circle passing through the centre. **2** length of this line; thickness.

diamond *n* **1** very hard precious stone of pure carbon. **2** equilateral parallelogram. **3** playing card of the suit marked with a red diamond-shaped pip, or the symbol itself.

diaphragm *n* **1** muscular membrane between the chest and the abdomen. **2** thin vibrating disc in certain instruments. **3** contraceptive device inserted over the mouth of the cervix to act as a barrier to sperm.

diarrhoea (daiə'riə) *n* abnormal looseness of the bowels.

diary *n* daily record of events, or book in which such a record is kept.

dice *n pl or s* small cube with faces marked with between one and six spots, used in games of chance. *vt* cut into small cubes. **dice with** gamble with; deal with recklessly.

dictate *vt* (dik'teit) **1** say or read for another to write down. **2** prescribe; command. *n* ('dikteit) authoritative command. **dictation** *n* act of dictating for another to write down or the matter so dictated. **dictator** *n* absolute ruler. **dictatorial** *adj* of or resembling a dictator; autocratic. **dictatorship** *n* **1** office of or government by a dictator. **2** country so ruled.

dictionary *n* **1** book containing an alphabetical list of words and their meanings, pronunciation, etc. **2** reference book relating to a particular subject, with items listed in alphabetical order.

did *v pt* of **do.**

die *vi* (dying) cease to live; perish. **die down** gradually diminish or become less forceful.

diesel *n* internal-combustion engine fuelled by oil or a vehicle driven by this.

diet *n* **1** regulated allowance of food, esp. one prescribed for slimming or medical reasons. **2** the food a person normally eats. *vi* to eat a special diet.

differ *vi* be unlike; disagree. **difference** *n* degree of differing or point in which things differ; disagreement. **different** *adj*. **differently** *adv*. **differentiate** *vi* **1** constitute a difference between. **2** become unlike; diverge. *vt* distinguish between. **differentiation** *n*.

difficult *adj* not easy; hard to do or understand. **difficulty** *n*.

dig *v* (-gg-; dug) *vt,vi* cut into or remove earth, esp. with a spade; excavate. *vt* poke or prod. *n* **1** prod. **2** sarcastic remark. **3** archaeological excavation.

digest *vt* (di'dʒest) **1** dissolve (food) in the stomach for bodily absorption. **2** classify or summarize to aid mental assimilation. **3** reflect on; absorb. *n* ('daidʒest) **1** summary. **2** publication containing condensed versions of other articles, books, etc. **digestion** *n* natural assimilation of food into the bodily system.

digit *n* **1** any number from nought to nine. **2** finger or toe.

dignified *adj* stately; exalted; noble.

dignity *n* **1** stateliness; gravity; distinction of mind or character. **2** high office or title.

digress *vi* stray from the main point or theme of a story, argument, etc. **digression** *n*.

dike *n,vt* dyke.

dilapidated *adj* decayed; neglected; in ruins. **dilapidation** *n*.

dilemma *n* situation in which alternative choices are equally unattractive; difficult predicament.

diligent *adj* industrious; conscientious. **diligence** *n*.

dilute *vt* reduce the strength of by adding water; water down. **dilution** *n*.

dim *adj* **1** not bright; indistinct; obscure. **2** *also* **dim-witted** *inf* stupid, not intelligent. *vt,vi* (-mm-) make or become dim(mer).

dimension *n* measurement of length, breadth, height, etc.; extent; size.

diminish *vt,vi* make or become smaller or less; lessen; reduce. **diminutive** *adj* extremely small.

dimple *n* small hollow, esp. in the surface of the skin on the face.

din *n* loud continuous noise. *vt* (-nn-) **1** subject to din. **2** repeat (facts, opinions, etc.) insistently.

dine *vi* eat dinner. *vt* entertain at dinner.

dinghy *n* small open boat.

dingy *adj* **1** shabby; dirty. **2** badly lit; gloomy. **dinginess** *n*.

dinner *n* **1** chief meal of the day. **2** formal banquet.

dinosaur *n* large extinct reptile.

diocese ('daiəsis) *n* district under a bishop's jurisdiction. **diocesan** (dai'ɔsizən) *adj*.

dip *vt* (-pp-) **1** submerge briefly in liquid; immerse. **2** lower. *vi* **1** sink briefly under the surface of a liquid. **2** slope downwards. *n* **1** act of dipping. **2** downward slope. **3** bathe.

diphthong *n* union of two vowel sounds in one syllable.

diploma *n* document conferring some privilege, title, or qualification.

diplomacy *n* **1** management of international relations. **2** tact or skill in dealing with others. **diplomat** *n* person engaged in international diplomacy. **diplomatic** *adj*.

direct *vt* **1** give orders; manage; control. **2** give directions to; point; indicate a route to. *adj* straight; straightforward; immediate. **direct object** *n* word in a sentence receiving the direct action of the main verb. **direction** *n* **1** instruction; command. **2** course to which anything moves, faces, etc. **director** *n* **1** person who directs, esp. the production of a film or play. **2** member of a board controlling a company or organization. **directory** *n* book listing names with addresses, telephone numbers, etc.

dirt *n* **1** any unclean substance; filth. **2** soil; earth. **dirty** *adj*.

disable *vt* incapacitate; cripple. **disability** *n*. **disabled** *adj*.

disadvantage *n* unfavourable circumstance or situation; handicap.

disagree *vi* **1** differ in opinion; dissent. **2** be incompatible. **disagreeable** *adj*. **disagreement** *n*.

disappear *vi* vanish; go out of sight. **disappearance** *n*.

disappoint *vt* fail to fulfil the desires or expectations of; frustrate. **disappointment** *n*.

disapprove *vt,vi* fail to approve; have an unfavourable opinion (of). **disapproval** *n*.

disarm *vt* **1** deprive of weapons; make defenceless. **2** win over; conciliate. *vi* lay down weapons; reduce national military forces. **disarmament** *n*.

disaster *n* extreme misfortune; calamity. **disastrous** *adj*.

disc *n* **1** thin flat circular plate. **2** *inf* gramophone record. **disc jockey** *n* person who plays recorded music on the radio, at parties, etc.

discard *vt,vi* throw out; cast off; reject.

discern *vt* see clearly; detect; distinguish. **discerning** *adj* having good taste; discriminating. **discernment** *n*.

discharge *vt* (dis'tʃɑːdʒ) **1** release; send forth. **2** dismiss. **3** unload. *n* ('distʃɑːdʒ) **1** matter discharged. **2** state of being discharged; release.

disciple *n* follower; loyal pupil.

discipline *n* **1** obedience and orderliness; self-control. **2** training or system of rules that produces such conduct. *vt* **1** subject to strict rules of conduct; train. **2** punish.

disclose *vt* reveal; make known. **disclosure** *n*.

disconcert *vt* upset; take aback; dismay.

disconnect *vt* break connection between; separate.

disconsolate *adj* unhappy; lacking hope or comfort.

discontinue *vt,vi* cease to continue; leave off.

discord *n* lack of harmony; disagreement; strife.

discotheque *n* public place for dancing to recorded pop music.

discount *n* ('diskaunt) reduction in the price of anything. *vt* (dis'kaunt) **1** reduce the value or price of. **2** leave out of consideration; ignore.

discourage *vt* **1** lessen the courage or confidence of; dishearten. **2** oppose by expressing disapproval; deter. **discouragement** *n*.

discover *vt* **1** find out; learn about. **2** uncover; reveal. **discoverer** *n*. **discovery** *n*.

discreet *adj* careful; prudent; tactful.

discrepancy *n* difference; inconsistency; variance.

discrete *adj* separate; distinct.

discretion *n* **1** prudence; tact. **2** freedom to act or choose as one likes.

discriminate *vt,vi* **1** make or see distinctions; distinguish. **2** treat persons, groups, etc., as different from others. **discrimination** *n*.

discus *n* heavy disc thrown in athletic contests.

discuss *vt* argue or write about in detail; debate. **discussion** *n*.

disease *n* illness; condition of impaired health.

disembark *vt,vi* set or go ashore from a ship; land.

disfigure *vt* spoil the appearance of; deform. **disfigurement** *n*.

disgrace *n* shame; dishonour. *vt* bring shame or discredit on; humiliate.

disgruntled *adj* discontented; sulky.

disguise *vt* conceal the true nature or appearance of; misrepresent. *n* clothing, make-up, etc., worn to give a false appearance.

disgust *n* extreme dislike; loathing; repugnance. *vt* cause disgust in; offend greatly.

dish *n* **1** shallow vessel or basin for food. **2** particular variety or preparation of food.

dishearten *vt* discourage; make despondent.

dishevelled *adj* untidy; scruffy; bedraggled.

dishonest *adj* not honest; insincere; deceitful. **dishonesty** *n*.

dishonour *n* **1** state of shame or disgrace. **2** cause of this. *vt* **1** bring shame or discredit on; disgrace. **2** treat with disrespect. **3** fail to pay (a debt, etc.). **dishonourable** *adj*.

disillusion *vt* cause to lose illusions; disenchant. **disillusionment** *n*.

disinfect *vt* free from infection; remove infectious germs from; sterilize. **disinfection** *n*. **disinfectant** *n* substance that prevents or removes infection.

disinherit *vt* deprive of inheritance. **disinheritance** *n*.

disintegrate *vt,vi* break into fragments; crumble. **disintegration** *n*.

disinterested *adj* impartial; objective; free from selfish or private motives.

disjointed *adj* **1** disconnected. **2** incoherent.

dislike *vt* feel aversion to; disapprove of. *n* aversion; disapproval.

dislocate *vt* put out of joint; displace. **dislocation** *n*.

disloyal *adj* not loyal; unfaithful. **disloyalty** *n*.

dismal *adj* gloomy; depressing; dreary. **dismally** *adv*.

dismantle *vt* take apart, esp. carefully or piece by piece.

dismay *vt* fill with alarm or fear. *n* apprehension; anxiety.

dismiss *vt* **1** send away; discharge from a job. **2** give only brief consideration to. **dismissal** *n*.

disobey *vt* refuse or fail to obey. **disobedience** *n*. **disobedient** *adj*.

disorder *n* **1** lack of order or organization; confusion. **2** breach of the peace; riot. **3** illness; ailment. **disordered** *adj* upset; disturbed; badly arranged. **disorderly** *adj* unruly; badly organized.

disown *vt* refuse to acknowledge; repudiate.

disparage *vt* speak scornfully of; belittle. **disparagement** *n*.

dispassionate *adj* without emotion or prejudice; objective.

dispatch *vt* **1** send off. **2** finish off. *n* **1** sending off. **2** speed; promptness. **3** official message or report.

dispel *vt* (-ll-) clear away; make disappear; scatter.

dispense *vt* **1** deal out; administer. **2** make up (medicines). **dispense with** do without; get rid of. **dispensary** *n* place where medicines are made up.

disperse *vt,vi* scatter; spread widely. **dispersal** *n*.

displace *vt* **1** move out of place. **2** remove from office. **3** take the place of. **displacement** *n*.

display *vt* exhibit; show; expose to view. *n* **1** exhibition. **2** ostentatious show.

dispose *vt* **1** arrange; set in order. **2** make willing or inclined. **dispose of** get rid of; deal with. **disposal** *n*. **disposition** *n* **1** arrangement. **2** inclination; tendency. **3** temperament.

dispossess *vt* deprive of rights, possessions, etc.

disprove *vt* prove false; refute.

dispute *v* (di'spju:t) *vi,vt* argue, debate, or disagree. *vt* **1** doubt or question the truth of. **2** compete to win (something). *n* ('dispju:t) argument; quarrel.

disqualify *vt* **1** make ineligible or unsuitable. **2** ban from competing in sports, etc., for a breach of the rules. **3** deprive of legal or other rights, etc. **disqualification** *n*.

disregard *vt* **1** take no notice of; ignore. **2** treat with no respect. *n* lack of respect.

disrepute *n* ill repute. **disreputable** **1** discreditable. **2** shabby.

disrespect *vt* have or show no respect for. *n* lack of respect or courtesy. **disrespectful** *adj*.

disrupt *vt* **1** cause chaos or disorder. **2** interrupt the continuity of. **disruption** *n*. **disruptive** *adj*.

dissect *vt* **1** cut up and examine (an animal or plant). **2** analyse in detail. **dissection** *n*.

dissent *vi* **1** disagree. **2** express views opposing established or orthodox doctrines, esp. of a church. **dissension** *n*. **dissenter** *n*.

dissimilar *adj* not similar; different. **dissimilarity** *n*.

dissolve *vi,vt* **1** disperse or cause to disperse into a solution. **2** dismiss (a company, organization, etc.). *vi* vanish. **dissolution** *n*.

dissuade *vt* discourage from an intention by persuasion.

distance *n* length of a space between two points. **keep (someone) at a distance** refuse to allow someone to become friendly. **keep one's distance** behave in a reserved or formal way. **distant** *adj* **1** far away. **2** remote. **3** reserved.

distaste *n* dislike. **distasteful** *adj* unpleasant; objectionable.

distil *v* (-ll-) *vt* **1** boil (a liquid) and condense the vapour. **2** purify by this process. **3** obtain the essential part of something. *vi* undergo distillation. **distillation** *n*. **distillate** *n* product of distillation. **distillery** *n* place where alcoholic spirits are produced.

distinct *adj* **1** easily understood; clear. **2** noticeable. **distinct from** different; not the same as. **distinction** *n* **1** act of distinguishing things as different or distinct. **2** mark of difference. **3** mark of superiority or excellence. **distinctive** *adj* of distinguishing characteristic.

distinguish *vt* **1** be able to see a difference; discriminate. **2** characterize. **3** recognize; perceive. **distinguish oneself** do something with distinction.

distort *vt* **1** twist; deform. **2** give an untrue impression of. **distortion** *n*.

distract *vt* **1** divert the attention of. **2** confuse; disturb. **3** entertain or amuse. **distraction** *n*. **distractive** *adj*.

distraught *adj* **1** agitated or bewildered. **2** frantic.

distress *vt* cause acute mental or physical discomfort. *n* **1** state of acute anxiety or anguish. **2** state of danger, extreme discomfort, etc.

distribute *vt* **1** give out in shares; allot. **2** spread; scatter. **3** divide into groups or categories. **distribution** *n*.

district *n* geographical, political, or administrative region.

distrust *vt* have no trust in; suspect. *n* lack of trust.

disturb *vt* **1** interrupt; disrupt. **2** cause disorder; disarrange. **3** cause worry or anxiety. **disturbance** *n* **1** act of disturbing or being disturbed. **2** disturbing of the public peace.

ditch *n* narrow trench dug for drainage purposes. *vi* repair or dig ditches. *vt inf* throw away; abandon.

ditto *n* the same as above; used in accounts, lists, etc., to save repetition.

divan *n* **1** low backless cushioned couch set against a wall. **2** *also* **divan bed** type of bed with an enclosed base and no visible frame.

dive *vi* **1** jump into water headfirst or in a controlled fashion. **2** throw oneself forward headlong. **3** (of a submarine) submerge. *vi,vt* **1** move in a steep downward path through the air. *n* **1** act of diving. **2** *inf* shabby disreputable café, pub, etc. **diver** *n*.

diverge *vi* **1** turn off and go in different directions; move apart. **2** differ. **divergence** *n*.

diverse *adj* varied; different. **diversify** *vt,vi* make or become diverse. **diversification** *n*.

divert *vt,vi* turn (a person or thing) from a previously intended course. *vt* distract. **diversion** *n* **1** act of diverting. **2** temporary detour caused by repairs, etc., on a road. **3** distraction; amusement.

divide *vt,vi* **1** separate or split into two or more parts. **2** distribute. **3** find out how many times a number is contained in another. *vt* cause a disagreement (between).

dividend *n* **1** money paid to shareholders as interest, profit, etc. **2** number to be divided by another.

divine *adj* **1** relating to God, a god, or theology. **2** sacred; religious; heavenly. *vt,vi* guess or discover intuitively. **divinely** *adv*. **divinity** *n* **1** state or quality of being divine. **2** god; deity. **3** theology.

divisible *adj* able to be divided.

division *n* **1** act of dividing. **2** part of a unit or whole. **3** administrative or legislative body. **4** military unit larger than a regiment.

divorce *n* **1** legal termination of a marriage. **2** total or radical separation. *vt,vi* obtain a divorce (from). *vt* separate. **divorcé(e)** *n* man (woman) who is divorced.

divulge *vt* reveal; disclose; let out (a secret, etc.).

dizzy *adj* **1** experiencing a sensation of confusion, being unsteady, or whirling; giddy. **2** causing such a sensation. **dizzily** *adv*. **dizziness** *n*.

do *v* (does; did; done) *vt* **1** perform; act. **2** deal with; complete. **3** serve; provide. **4** fix; arrange. **5** have as a job or occupation. **6** *inf* swindle; defraud. *vi* **1** suffice; be accepted. **2** manage; cope. **3** make progress. *v aux* used in certain interrogative, negative, or emphatic statements. **do in** *sl* kill; murder. **do up 1** tie; fasten. **2** make smart. **make do (with)** manage with what is available. ~*n inf* function; social event.

docile *adj* willing to be trained; tame; gentle; obedient.

dock[1] *n* area or wharf for mooring, loading, repairing ships, etc. *vt,vi* bring or come in to dock; moor. **docker** *n* person employed to load and unload cargo. **dockyard** *n* enclosure with docks for repairing, equipping, or building ships.

dock[2] *n* **1** solid part of an animal's tail. **2** stump remaining after clipping a tail. *vt* **1** cut (an animal's tail). **2** deduct from.

dock[3] *n* section in a lawcourt where the accused is seated.

doctor *n* **1** person qualified to practise medicine. **2** person holding the highest diploma or degree of a university. *vt* **1** treat medically. **2** falsify; adulterate.

doctrine *n* **1** teaching of a school, church, political group, etc. **2** dogma; belief.

document *n* ('dɔkjumənt) printed or written evidence or information. *vt* ('dɔkjument) furnish with evidence, references, etc. **documentation** *n*. **documentary** *adj* relating to a document. *n* detailed factual film.

dodge *vi,vt* move quickly, so as to avoid; evade. *n* clever plan or move.

does *v* 3rd person singular of **do** in the present tense.

dog *n* domesticated or wild four-footed animal of various breeds. *vt* (-gg-) pursue steadily; tail; hound. **dog-collar** *n inf* clergyman's collar. **dogged** ('dɔgid) *adj* persistent; stubborn; tenacious.

dogma *n* system of beliefs, such as those of a church; doctrine. **dogmatic** *adj* **1** relating to dogma. **2** asserting beliefs or opinions with persistent arrogance. **dogmatically** *adv*.

dole *n* money or food given charitably or for maintenance. **on the dole** receiving unemployment benefit. *v* **dole out** give or share out; distribute.

doll *n* **1** child's toy in the image of a person. **2** *sl* attractive girl or young woman. *v* **doll up** dress up in fine clothes.

dollar *n* unit of currency of the US and various other countries, comprising 100 cents.

dolphin *n* sea mammal resembling but larger than a porpoise.

domain *n* **1** territory ruled over, as by a sovereign. **2** field of interest, influence, etc., province.

dome *n* large high rounded roof.

domestic *adj* **1** relating to the home or household matters. **2** not foreign. **3** (of animals) tame. **domestic science** *n* study or art of cooking, needlework, household management, etc. **domesticate** *vt* tame; train for domestic purposes. **domesticity** *n* home life; matters concerning the home or a household.

dominate *vt,vi* **1** rule; control; govern. **2** be the most important or conspicuous feature (of). **domination** *n*. **dominant** *adj* **1** prevailing; having power, authority, or priority. **2** prominent; most important. **dominance** *n*. **domineer** *vi* behave in an overbearing or arrogant manner. **dominion** *n* **1** sovereignty governing authority; rule. **2** land controlled by a government; domain. **3** name formerly given to the self-governing countries of the Commonwealth of Nations.

domino *n, pl* **dominoes** small rectangular brick marked with various combinations of spots for use in various games.

donate *vt* give. **donation** *n* gift, esp. for charity. **donor** *n* person making a donation.

done *v pp* of **do.**

donkey *n* **1** long-eared member of the horse family, used esp. as a beast of burden; ass. **2** *sl* fool.

doodle *vi,vt* draw or scribble casually, esp. while attending to some other matter. *n* scribbled drawing or shape. **doodler** *n*.

doom *n* **1** fate; destiny. **2** unfavourable judicial sentence; condemnation. *vt* **1** sentence; condemn. **2** destine to an unhappy end or fate.

door *n* **1** hinged or sliding structure fitted across a passage or entrance. **2** *also* **doorway** entrance to a building, room, etc.

dope *n* **1** kind of varnish used for waterproofing. **2** drug, esp. a narcotic. **3** *sl* information. **4** *sl* stupid person; dunce. *vt,vi* drug or take drugs. **dopey** *adj also* **dopy** **1** drugged; drowsy. **2** stupid.

dormant *adj* inactive.

dormitory *n* large room containing a number of beds.

dormouse *n, pl* **dormice** hibernating rodent similar to but smaller than a squirrel.

dorsal *adj* relating to or on the back.

dose *n* **1** amount of a medicine, etc., to be given or taken at one time. **2** bout; spell. *vt* give medicine or doses (to). **dosage** *n* **1** giving of medicine in doses. **2** amount of medicine to be given.

dot *n* small point or spot; speck. *vt* (-tt-) **1** mark with dots; spot. **2** place a dot over a letter, after a musical note, etc.

dote *vi* be silly or mentally weak. **dote on** be excessively fond of. **dotage** *n* silliness or childishness in old age; feeble-mindedness.

double *adj* **1** two of a kind together; of two kinds. **2** twice as much. **3** having two functions, uses, etc. **4** suitable for two. **5** having extra weight, thickness, width, etc. **6** ambiguous. *adv* **1** twice. **2** in pairs. *n* **1** something or someone exactly like another. **2** quantity that is twice that of another. **3** sharp backward turn or bend. **4** evasion; trick; shift. *vt,vi* **1** make or become twice as great. **2** multiply by two. **3** fold in half. **4** turn sharply. **double up** be contorted with pain, laughter, etc. **double bass** *n* largest instrument of the violin family. **double-cross** *vt* betray. *n* betrayal. **double-dutch** *n inf* nonsense; gibberish. **doubly** *adv* to twice the extent.

doubt *vt* **1** hesitate to accept; fail to believe immediately. **2** suspect. *n* uncertainty; lack of conviction or belief. **no doubt** probably; presumably. **doubtful** *adj*. **doubtless** *adv,adj*.

dough *n* flour or meal mixed with water and kneaded before baking. **doughnut** *n* small round cake made of dough and sugar and fried in deep fat.

douse *vt,vi also* **dowse** plunge into water; immerse; drench. *vt* extinguish (a light).

dove *n* bird belonging to the pigeon family.

dowdy *adj* drab; shabby.

down[1] *adv* **1** from a higher to a lower place or

position. **2** to or at the bottom; towards or on the ground. **3** below the horizon. **4** from an earlier to a later time. **5** into a worse physical or mental condition. *prep* **1** towards, at, in, or near a lower place, rank, condition, etc. **2** in the same direction as; with. *adj* dejected; miserable; depressed.

down^2 *n* **1** fine soft feathers of young ducks or other birds. **2** fine hair.

downcast *adj* **1** looking or directed downwards. **2** dejected.

downfall *n* **1** ruin; destruction. **2** cause of overthrow or destruction. **3** falling, as of rain or snow.

downhearted *adj* dejected in spirits; depressed.

downhill *adv* down a hill; downwards. *adj* descending; sloping.

downpour *n* heavy fall of rain.

downright *adj* in plain terms; straightforward. *adv* absolutely; thoroughly.

downstairs *adv* **1** down the stairs. **2** towards or on a lower floor. *adj* relating to or situated on a lower floor. *n* lower floor.

downstream *adv* down or in the direction of flow of a stream. *adj* farther down or moving with the current.

downtrodden *adj* trodden or trampled down; oppressed.

downward *adj* moving or extending from a higher to a lower place. **downwards** *adv* from a higher place to a lower; in a descending course.

dowry *n* money, goods, or property that a woman brings to her husband at marriage.

dowse *vt,vi* douse.

doze *vi* sleep lightly or for a short time. *n* light or brief sleep.

dozen *n* group of twelve. **dozens** *pl n* many.

drab *adj* **1** of a dull colour. **2** monotonous; not exciting.

draft *n* **1** first or rough copy, outline, sketch, etc. **2** detachment of soldiers. **3** conscription. **4** written order for money. *vt* **1** prepare a first or rough copy of. **2** send or select (a detachment of soldiers). **3** conscript; recruit.

drag *v* (-gg-) *vt,vi* **1** pull; draw or be drawn along. **2** trail. **3** search or sweep with a net, hook, etc. *vi* move slowly; lag. **drag out** prolong, esp. unnecessarily. ~*n* **1** device used for dragging. **2** something that slows movement or progress. **3** *sl* something or someone that is tedious or a waste of time. **4** *inf* puff or inhaling of a cigarette. **in drag** (of a man) wearing women's clothing.

dragon *n* **1** fire-breathing monster usually depicted as a winged reptile. **2** *inf* fierce or fiery person, esp. a woman; tyrant. **dragonfly** *n* long-bodied insect with large delicate wings.

drain *vt* **1** draw off (liquid) so as to empty or leave dry. **2** exhaust; consume utterly; empty. *vi* **1** flow out or away. **2** become dry or empty. *n* **1** pipe, channel, or ditch for drawing off water, sewage, etc. **2** steady depletion or expenditure. **drainage** *n* **1** act or process of draining. **2** system of pipes or channels for draining. **3** substance drained. **draining board** *n* sloping surface beside a sink on which wet dishes, etc., are placed to dry. **drainpipe** *n* pipe channelling water, sewage, etc.

drake *n* male bird of the duck family.

dram *n* **1** unit of weight, equal to one sixteenth of an ounce. **2** small amount of alcoholic drink; tot.

drama *n* **1** story performed by actors; play. **2** plays collectively. **3** compelling event or series of events. **dramatic** *adj* **1** relating to or resembling drama. **2** vivid; forceful. **dramatically** *adv*. **dramatics** *pl n* acting by an amateur company. **dramatist** *n* person who writes drama, playwright. **dramatize** *vt* **1** act out or put into the form of a drama. **2** express vividly or forcefully or in an exaggerated manner.

drank *v pt* of **drink.**

drape *vt* cover, esp. with cloth or fabric. *vt,vi* hang in folds (about). *n* arrangement of folds. **draper** *n* person who deals in cloth, linen, etc. **drapery** *n* **1** cloth or other fabrics. **2** business of a draper.

draught *n* **1** current of air, esp. in an enclosed space. **2** act of pulling or that which is pulled. **3** quantity drunk in one go. **4** drawing of beer, wine, etc., from a barrel or cask. **5** dose of medicine. **draughts** *n* game played with round flat pieces on a board marked off in squares. **draughtsman** *n, pl* **-men 1** person skilled in mechanical drawing. **2** *also* **draught** piece used in draughts.

draw *v* (drew; drawn) *vt,vi* **1** pull; haul; drag. **2** bring or come nearer; approach. **3** portray in lines; sketch. *vt* **1** pull out; extract; withdraw; take. **2** inhale. **3** infer; deduce. **4** describe. **5** obtain by lot. **6** attract. *vi* **1** finish a game with an equal score for both sides, tie. **2** permit the circulation of air. **draw on 1** use as a resource. **2** approach. **draw up** draft (a will, contract, etc.). ~*n* **1** attraction. **2** raffle; lottery. **3** game ending in a tie. **drawback** *n* disadvantage. **drawbridge** *n* bridge that can be raised.

drawer *n* sliding compartment in a desk, chest, etc. **drawers** *pl n inf* underpants or knickers.

drawing *n* **1** art or practice of portraying in lines; sketching. **2** image or sketch so done. **drawing pin** *n* short pin with a flat head, fixed by pushing with the thumb. **drawing room** *n* room for the reception or entertaining of guests; living room.

drawl *vt,vi* speak slowly, esp. with elongated vowel sounds. *n* such speech.

dread *vt* anticipate with great fear or apprehension. *n* great apprehension or fear; terror. **dreadful** *adj* **1** causing dread. **2** *inf* unpleasant; bad. **dreadfully** *adv inf* terribly; awfully; very.

dream *n* **1** sequence of thoughts or images during sleep. **2** something hoped for. **3** vision. *vi,vt* (dreamt *or* dreamed) have dreams (of).

dreary *adj* gloomy; not exciting; dull. **dreariness** *n*.

dredge *n* device for bringing up mud and other material from the bottom of a river, etc. *vt* bring up, clean, etc., with a dredge.

dregs *pl n* sediment.

drench *vt* wet completely; soak.

dress *vt,vi* put clothes on. *vt* arrange for show; decorate; adorn. **3** prepare (meat, fish, etc.) by trimming, gutting, etc. **4** treat (a wound, etc.) by applying a dressing. *n* **1** clothing. **2** female outer garment consisting of a bodice and skirt. **3** formal evening wear. **dress circle** *n* first gallery above the floor in a theatre or cinema. **dressmaker** *n* person skilled in making dresses. **dress rehearsal** *n* final rehearsal of a stage production, in which the actors appear in full costume.

dresser[1] *n* kitchen sideboard.

dresser[2] *n* person assisting an actor with costume changes.

dressing *n* **1** sauce applied to various foods. **2** stuffing. **3** something applied to a wound to aid healing. **dressing-gown** *n* loosely fitting robe or gown, usually worn over night attire. **dressing-room** *n* special room, esp. in a theatre, where one dresses. **dressing-table** *n* small table, usually with a mirror, for cosmetics etc.

drew *v pt of* **draw.**

dribble *vi,vt* **1** flow or allow to flow in small drops; trickle. **2** propel (a ball) with a series of small kicks. *n* drop; trickle.

drier *n* appliance for drying clothes, hair, etc.

drift *n* **1** snow, sand, etc., piled up by the wind. **2** general meaning. **3** deviation from a plan, course, etc. **4** general movement, progress, etc. *vi* **1** be carried, as by air or water currents. **2** move without purpose or direction. **driftwood** *n* wood carried ashore by water.

drill[1] *n* **1** tool or device for boring holes. **2** routine exercises or training. *vt,vi* **1** bore (a hole) in. **2** exercise, esp. by repetition.

drill[2] *n* **1** small trench for seed. **2** machine or device for sowing seed in drills.

drink *v* (drank, drunk); *vt,vi* swallow (liquid). *vt* **1** absorb; take in. **2** consume (alcoholic drinks). *n* **1** amount of liquid suitable for consumption; beverage. **2** alcohol.

drip *vi,vt* (-pp-) fall or let fall in drops. *n* process of dripping or that which falls by dripping. **drip-dry** *adj* (of clothing, etc.) drying without creases if hung up when wet. **dripping** *n* fat that drips from a roasting joint.

drive *vt,vi* (drove; driven) **1** move by force, power, etc. **2** urge onward; compel. **3** control or steer (an animal, vehicle, etc.). **4** transport or be transported in a vehicle. **5** move or fix by striking, hitting, etc. *n* **1** act of driving. **2** trip in a vehicle. **3** road, esp. a private one leading to a house. **4** energy; force; motivation. **driver** *n*.

drivel *vi* (-ll-) **1** let secretions flow from the mouth or nose; dribble. **2** talk or act foolishly. *n* nonsense; silly talk.

drizzle *vi* rain lightly. *n* fine rain.

droll *adj* witty; satirical; wry.

dromedary *n* camel with one hump.

drone *n* **1** male bee. **2** idle person. **3** deep buzz or hum. **4** monotonous voice, tone, etc. *vi* **1** buzz or hum continuously. **2** speak in a low monotonous voice.

drool *vi* **1** gloat; gush. **2** drivel; dribble.

droop *vi,vt* bend or hang down limply; sag. *vi* become disheartened; languish. *n* drooping state or condition.

drop *n* **1** small spherical amount of liquid; globule. **2** very small amount of anything. **3** steep descent; fall. **4** distance through which something falls. **5** round sweet. *v* (-pp-) *vt,vi* **1** fall or permit to fall. **2** lower; decrease; sink. *vt* **1** cease to consider or discuss. **2** mention casually. **3** allow (passengers, goods, etc.) to disembark or be unloaded. **4** omit; cease to make use of. **drop in** make a casual visit. **drop off 1** fall asleep. **2** decline; decrease. **drop out** cease to compete, complete one's education, etc. **dropout** *n* person who rejects society's norms, fails to complete an educational course, etc.

drought *n* prolonged period during which no rain falls.

drove¹ *v pt* of **drive.**

drove² *n* herd or flock, esp. when on the move.

drown *vt,vi* kill or die by suffocating in water. *vt* **1** overpower; extinguish; destroy. **2** cover completely; flood. **3** shut out (sound); muffle.

drowse *vi,vt* be or make sleepy. *n* condition of being sleepy or half asleep. **drowsy** *adj* **1** sleepy or sluggish. **2** inducing sleep; soporific. **drowsily** *adv.* **drowsiness** *n.*

drudge *vi* work hard; slave. *n* person doing menial work. **drudgery** *n* hard menial work; toil.

drug *n* substance, esp. a narcotic. *vt* (-gg-) **1** mix a drug or drugs with (food, drink, etc.) **2** administer a drug (to).

drum *n* **1** percussion instrument having skin, etc., stretched tightly over a hollow chamber. **2** large cylindrical container for oil, water, etc. *vt,vi* (-mm-) **1** beat or play (a drum). **2** beat, tap, or strike continuously. *vt* instil by insistent repetition. **drummer** *n.*

drunk *adj* **1** *also* **drunken** intoxicated; inebriated. **2** emotionally overcome. *n also* **drunkard** person who is drunk, esp. habitually.

dry *adj* **1** not wet or moist. **2** having little or no rainfall; arid. **3** thirsty or causing thirst. **4** not yielding milk, water, etc. **5** not stimulating; dull. **6** caustically clever or witty. **7** not permitting the legal sale or consumption of alcohol. *vt,vi* make or become dry(er). **dry-clean** *vt* clean with chemical solvents rather than water.

dual *adj* **1** relating to two or a pair. **2** having two parts; double. **dual carriageway** *n* major road with opposite lanes separated by a barrier, area of grass, etc. **duality** *n.* **dually** *adv.*

dubious *adj* causing doubt; suspicious; questionable.

ducal *adj* relating to a duke or duchy.

duchess *n* **1** wife or widow of a duke. **2** woman holding a rank equivalent to that of a duke. **duchy** *n* territory ruled by a duke or duchess.

duck¹ *n* wild or tame edible bird with webbed feet. **duckling** *n* young duck.

duck² *vi* **1** bend down or lower suddenly; bob. **2** plunge temporarily under water. **3** avoid; dodge.

duct *n* channel or tube for conveying liquid, secretions, etc. **ductile** *adj* **1** (of gold, copper, etc.) capable of being drawn out into wire or hammered very thin. **2** flexible; pliant.

due *adj* **1** payable at once. **2** fitting; usual; proper; adequate. **3** expected to arrive or be ready. **due to** attributed or ascribed to. ~*n* fair share. **dues** *pl n* fee; charges.

duel *n* **1** fight with pistols, swords, etc., between two persons. **2** contest between two parties. *vi* (-ll-) fight a duel.

duet *n* composition for two musicians or performers.

dug *v pt* and *pp* of **dig.**

duke *n* **1** nobleman ranking next below a prince. **2** ruler of a small state (duchy).

dulcimer *n* percussion instrument having a set of strings, which are struck with hammers.

dull *adj* **1** lacking intelligence; stupid. **2** having no feelings; insensible. **3** not clear or sharp. **4** tedious. **5** moving slowly; sluggish. **6** overcast. **7** blunt. *vt,vi* make or become dull. **dullness** *n.* **dully** *adv.*

duly *adv* as expected; properly; in a fitting manner.

dumb *adj* **1** incapable of uttering speech sounds. **2** temporarily unable to speak. **3** silent. **4** *sl* stupid. **dumbfound** *vt* amaze into silence; astound. **dumbly** *adv.* **dumbness** *n.*

dummy *n* **1** model of a human being used esp. for displaying clothes. **2** imitation; copy. **3** *inf* inactive or silent person. **4** rubber teat sucked by a baby.

dump *vt* **1** throw down in a pile or heap. **2** unload; dispose of. *n* **1** place where rubbish is dumped; tip. **2** *inf* messy, dirty, or ugly place, room, etc. **down in the dumps** depressed; dejected; miserable. **dumpling** *n* ball of dough cooked in a stew, etc. **dumpy** *adj* short and fat; plump.

dunce *n* person who is slow to learn or mentally dull.

dune *n* ridge or hill of sand.

dung *n* excrement; manure.

dungeon *n* underground cell or prison, esp. in a castle.

duplicate *adj* (ˈdju:plikət) **1** resembling or exactly like another. **2** occurring in pairs; double. *n* (ˈdju:plikət) exact copy. *vt* (ˈdju:plikeit) reproduce exactly; copy. **duplication** *n*. **duplicator** *n* machine for producing stencilled copies.

durable *adj* resisting decay or wear; lasting. **durability** *n*.

duration *n* period of time that something lasts.

during *prep* **1** throughout the period, existence, or activity of. **2** in the course of.

dusk *n* period of the evening before darkness falls; twilight. **dusky** *adj* **1** dark-skinned. **2** dim; shadowy.

dust *n* dry fine particles of earth, mineral deposits, etc. *vt,vi* wipe the dust (from). *vt* sprinkle; powder. **dusty** *adj*. **dustbin** *n* container for refuse, ashes, etc. **duster** *n* cloth used to wipe dust from furniture, etc. **dustman** *n, pl* **-men** person employed to remove refuse, empty dustbins, etc.

duty *n* **1** obligation, esp. of a moral or legal nature. **2** allocated work or task. **3** tax on imported or exported goods; tariff. **on/off duty** at work/not at work, esp. as a nurse, doctor, soldier, etc. **duty-free** *adj* requiring no duty to be paid. **dutiful** *adj* respectful; obedient. **dutifully** *adv*.

duvet (ˈdu:vei) *n* quilt for a bed, padded with feathers, down, etc.; continental quilt.

dwarf *n, pl* **dwarfs** *or* **dwarves** **1** person of exceptionally small stature or size. **2** plant or animal of a smaller type than average. **3** supernatural being in the form of a small ugly man. *vt* **1** restrict the growth of. **2** cause to appear relatively small, insignificant, etc., by comparison.

dwell *vi* (dwelt *or* dwelled) reside as a permanent occupant; live (in). **dwell (up)on** emphasize; concentrate on. **dwelling** *n* place where someone lives; abode; house.

dwindle *vi* grow gradually less in size, number, etc.; decrease.

dye *n* substance used for colouring fabric, the hair, etc. *v* (dyeing; dyed) *vt* colour (fabric, hair, etc.) with a dye. *vi* become coloured with a dye.

dying *v pres p* of **die. dying to/for** having a strong desire to/for.

dyke *n also* **dike** **1** embankment for holding back sea or river water. **2** ditch; trench. *vt* hold back or drain with a dyke.

dynamic *adj* **1** relating to force or energy; not static. **2** forceful; ambitious. **dynamically** *adv*. **dynamics** *n* branch of science concerned with forces and their effects on motion.

dynamite *n* high explosive of nitroglycerine and other substances.

dynamo device that converts mechanical energy into electrical energy.

dynasty *n* **1** unbroken line of hereditary rulers of the same family. **2** period of their rule.

dysentery *n* disease of the intestines.

dyslexia *n* condition leading to impaired reading ability. **dyslexic** *adj,n*.

E

each *adj,pron,adv* every separate one considered individually.

eager *adj* **1** strongly desirous. **2** keen; willing. **eagerly** *adv*. **eagerness** *n*.

eagle *n* large bird of prey having very keen eyesight.

ear[1] *n* **1** one of two organs of hearing, situated on either side of the head. **2** sense of hearing or appreciation of sound, esp. music. **3** attention. **be all ears** be listening attentively. **eardrum** *n* membrane in the inner part of the ear that vibrates when struck by sound waves. **earmark** *vt* designate for a special purpose. **earphone** *n* small loudspeaker placed in or over the ear for listening to a radio or telephone communication. **earring** *n* jewellery worn on or hanging from the ear lobe.

ear[2] *n* spike of a cereal plant containing the seed.

earl *n* British nobleman ranking next above a viscount.

early *adj,adv* **1** before the expected or appointed time. **2** at or near the beginning of a period or season. **earliness** *n*.

earn *vt,vi* gain (money, etc.) by working. *vt* deserve. **earnings** *pl n* wages or salary.

earnest *adj* **1** sincere; serious. **2** zealous; determined. **earnestly** *adv*.

earth *n* **1** third planet from the sun, lying between Venus and Mars and orbited by the moon, on which life has developed; world. **2** surface of this planet. **3** soil; ground. **4** home of a fox, etc. **5** connection of an electrical apparatus to the ground, assumed to be at zero voltage. **down-to-earth** sensible; realistic. **earthenware** *n* domestic pottery of coarse baked clay. **earthly** *adj* **1** of the earth or world. **2** likely; conceivable. **earthquake** *n* violent natural movement of the earth's crust; tremor. **earthworm** *n* worm that lives in and eats soil. **earthy** *adj* coarse; basic; crude.

earwig *n* small insect having pincers on the tail.

ease *n* **1** freedom from work, pain, or exertion; comfort; relaxation. **2** lack of difficulty (in doing something). *vt,vi* make or become less painful, difficult, etc.

easel *n* frame for supporting a blackboard or artist's canvas.

east *n* **1** one of the four cardinal points of the compass situated to the front of a person facing the sunrise. **2** part of a country, area, etc., lying towards the east. *adj also* **eastern** of, in, or facing the east. *adv,adj also* **easterly** **1** towards the east. **2** (of winds) from the east. **easterner** *n*. **eastward** *adj* facing or moving towards the east. **eastwards** *adv* in the direction of the east.

Easter *n* annual Christian festival in the spring, celebrating Christ's resurrection.

easy *adj* **1** requiring little effort; not difficult. **2** relaxed; comfortable. **3** tolerant; casual. **easily** *adv*. **easiness** *n*. **easygoing** *adj* tolerant; relaxed.

eat *v* (ate; eaten) *vt,vi* consume (food) through the mouth; have (a meal). *vt* **1** corrode; wear away. **2** use up in great quantities.

eavesdrop *vi* (-pp-) listen secretly to a private conversation. **eavesdropper** *n*.

ebb *n* **1** tidal falling back of the sea away from land. **2** decline; decay. *vi* **1** flow back from the land. **2** decline; diminish; wane.

ebony *n* hard almost black wood, obtained from a tropical or subtropical tree.

ebullient *adj* fervent; enthusiastic; full of life. **ebullience** *n*.

eccentric *adj* **1** not having the same centre; having a noncentral axis. **2** unconventional; odd. *n* eccentric person. **eccentricity** *n*.

ecclesiastic *adj also* **ecclesiastical** of or relating to the Church or clergymen. *n* clergyman.

echo *n, pl* **echoes** **1** sound like or repeating a first sound, caused by reflection of sound waves by a solid object. **2** anything that repeats or mimics. *vt,vi* reverberate; repeat; imitate.

éclair *n* cake made of light pastry and filled with cream.

eclipse *n* phenomenon in which light from one heavenly body is blocked by another, esp. a **solar eclipse,** where the moon moves between the earth and the sun. *vt* **1** cause an eclipse of. **2** throw into obscurity; surpass.

ecology *n* **1** relationship between natural things and their surroundings, and the effect of technology on this. **2** study of this. **ecological** *adj*. **ecologist** *n*.

economic *adj* **1** of or relating to economics. **2** worth doing; profitable. **3** economical. **economical** *adj* **1** frugal; thrifty. **2** not wasteful; giving value for money. **economically** *adv*. **economics** *n* study of the causes of and relationships between production, exchange, distribution, and consumption. **economize** *vt,vi* reduce expenditure or consumption to save money. **economy** *n* **1** arrangement or condition of trade, production, and commerce of an area. **2** thrift; frugality.

ecstasy *n* **1** intense joy; bliss. **2** state of extreme religious fervour. **ecstatic** *adj*.

edge *n* **1** outer side or margin. **2** cutting side of a blade. **3** keenness; sharpness. **4** slight advantage. **on edge** tense. ~*vt* **1** sharpen. **2** be or provide the border of. *vi,vt* move gradually; inch. **edgy** *adj* tense.

edible *adj* that may be eaten; not poisonous; not disgusting to the palate.

edit *vt* **1** prepare (a manuscript) for publication. **2** prepare the final form of (a film).

edition *n* set of books, newspapers, etc., printed at the same time. **editor** *n* **1** person who edits. **2** person who directs content and coverage of a newspaper, etc. **editorial** *adj* of or relating to the task of an editor. *n* newspaper article containing the opinions of its editor.

educate *vt* **1** give teaching to; instruct. **2** bring up; raise. **3** refine; improve. **education** *n* **1** process of gaining knowledge; training; schooling. **2** state of being educated. **3** upbringing. **educational** *adj*.

eel *n* snakelike fish.

eerie *adj* frighteningly strange; weird; ghostly. **eerily** *adv*. **eeriness** *n*.

effect *n* **1** change produced by an action; result. **2** impression on the mind, eyes, etc. **in effect**

actually; virtually. **take effect** start; become operative. ~*vt* bring about; cause. **effective** *adj* **1** producing a result, esp. a considerable one. **2** causing a pleasant or striking effect or impression. **3** taking effect. **effectively** *adv*.

effeminate *adj* (of a man) like a woman; not masculine or virile.

effervesce *vi* (of a liquid) give off bubbles of gas; fizz. **effervescent** *adj* **1** bubbling; fizzy. **2** merry; lively. **effervescence** *n*.

efficient *adj* producing the desired effect without waste; competent; effective. **efficiency** *n*. **efficiently** *adv*.

effigy *n* model or solid representation of a person.

effort *n* **1** exertion of energy. **2** attempt; try. **effortless** *adj* needing or using little effort; easy. **effortlessly** *adv*.

egg[1] *n* **1** oval object consisting of the embryo of birds, reptiles, etc., within a protective shell. **2** egg of certain birds, esp. hens, eaten as food.

egg[2] *v* **egg on** encourage or incite; urge; persuade.

ego *n* **1** the self; part of the mind that is conscious of itself. **2** self-centredness; conceit. **egocentric** *adj* self-centred; conceited. **egoism** *n* characteristic of thinking only of oneself; self-centredness. **egoist** *n*. **egoistic** *adj*. **egotism** *n* characteristic of talking only or too much about oneself; arrogance; conceit. **egotist** *n*. **egotistic** *or* **egotistical** *adj*.

eiderdown *n* **1** fine down from the eider duck. **2** bed cover or quilt filled with down, feathers, etc.

eight *n* **1** number equal to one plus seven. **2** group of eight things or people. **3** *also* **eight o'clock** eight hours after noon or midnight. *adj* amounting to eight. **eighth** *adj* **1** coming between seventh and ninth in sequence. *n* **1** eighth person, object, etc. **2** one of eight equal parts; one divided by eight. *adv* after the seventh.

eighteen *n* **1** number that is eight more than ten. **2** eighteen things or people. *adj* amounting to eighteen. **eighteenth** *adj,adv,n*.

eighty *n* **1** number equal to eight times ten. **2** eighty things or people. *adj* amounting to eighty. **eightieth** *adj,adv,n*.

either *adj,pron* one or each of two. *conj* used to introduce a choice between alternatives. *adv* (after negatives) as well; furthermore; anyway.

ejaculate *vt,vi* **1** say (something) suddenly; exclaim. **2** discharge; eject. **ejaculation** *n*.

eject *vt* throw out; expel; send forth; discharge. **ejection** *n*.

eke *v* **eke out** cause to last; supplement; draw out.

elaborate *adj* (i'læbərət) complicated; intricate; detailed. *vt,vi* (i'læbəreit) make more detailed; give further explanation of. **elaborately** *adv*. **elaboration** *n*.

elapse *vi* (of time) pass; go by.

elastic *adj* easily stretched; flexible; able to return to its original shape after being distorted, etc. *n* material made elastic by interwoven strips of rubber, used in clothes. **elasticity** *n*.

elated *adj* very happy and excited; overjoyed; high-spirited. **elatedly** *adv*. **elation** *n*.

elbow *n* **1** joint between the forearm and upper arm. **2** part of a coat, etc., covering this. **elbow grease** *n inf* hard work. ~*vt* push (one's way) through, towards, etc.

elder[1] *adj* older of two, esp. two brothers or sisters; senior. *n* **1** older person. **2** official in some churches. **elderly** *adj* old; aged.

elder[2] *n* bush or small tree with whitish flowers and purple or black berries.

eldest *adj* oldest of three or more people.

elect *vt* appoint or choose by voting. *vi* choose; decide. **elector** *n*. **election** *n* process of choosing and voting for candidates for office, esp. for Parliament.

electric *adj* **1** *also* **electrical** of, relating to, or worked by electricity. **2** charged with emotion; tense. **electrically** *adv*.

electrician *n* person whose job is to install or mend electrical equipment.

electricity *n* **1** phenomenon caused by motion of electrons or by excess of electric charge. **2** electric current; electric charge.

electrify *vt* **1** supply with or adapt to work by electric power. **2** startle; shock; thrill. **electrification** *n*.

electrocute *vt* kill by passing an electric charge through the body. **electrocution** *n*.

electrode *n* metal plate or wire by which an electric current enters or leaves a device.

electron *n* elementary particle with negative electric charge that moves round the nucleus of an atom.

electronic *adj* relating to or operated by the conduction of electrons through a vacuum, gas, or semiconductor **electronics** *n* **1** *s* study and technology of electronic equipment. **2** *pl* circuits in electronic equipment.

elegant *adj* tasteful; refined; graceful **elegance** *n* **elegantly** *adv*

element *n* **1** constituent part. **2** chemical substance that cannot be broken down into simpler substances by chemical reactions. **3** small amount; suggestion. **elements** *pl n* **1** weather; rain, wind, etc. **2** basic ideas **elemental** *adj*.

elementary *adj* **1** easy; simple; basic. **2** relating to the earliest stages of teaching or development

elephant *n* largest land mammal, found in India and Africa, having a trunk and two tusks of ivory **elephantine** *adj* enormous

elevate *vt* **1** make higher in physical position, raise, lift up. **2** promote in rank. **3** make more refined or cultured **elevation** *n* **1** act of elevating or state of being elevated. **2** altitude; height. **elevator** *n US* **lift** (def 2).

eleven *n* **1** number that is one greater than ten **2** eleven things or people. *adj* amounting to eleven **eleventh** *adj adv,n*

elf *n, pl* **elves** small magical being in human form, fairy **elfin** *adj*.

eligible *adj* having the necessary qualities or qualifications to be chosen, suitable

eliminate *vt* get rid of; remove. **elimination** *n*

elite *n* select group of people

ellipse *n* geometric figure having an oval shape **elliptical** *adj also* **elliptic** oval-shaped

elm *n* tall deciduous tree

elope *vi* run away with one's lover to get married secretly **elopement** *n*

eloquent *adj* speaking persuasively or expressively **eloquence** *n* **eloquently** *adv*

else *adv* **1** other, different **2** more **or else** otherwise, if not **elsewhere** *adv* to, in, or at another place

elucidate *vi* explain the meaning of, clarify **elucidation** *n*

elude *vt* **1** escape from, avoid capture **2** escape (a person's mind or memory). **elusive** *adj* **1** hard to find catch, or see **2** evasive

emaciated *adj* very thin, esp through starvation or illness **emaciation** *n*

emanate *vi* come from originate from **emanation** *n*

emancipate *vt* free from slavery or legal or social restraint, esp. by giving the right to vote. **emancipation** *n*.

embalm *vt* preserve (a corpse) by removing internal organs and applying chemicals, etc

embankment *n* artificial mound or ridge piled up to carry a railway, etc., or hold back water, as along a river

embargo *n, pl* **embargoes** order prohibiting ships from entering or leaving port; veto, prohibition (esp. on trade).

embark *vi,vt* go or put on board a ship, aircraft, etc. **embark on** begin; start. **embarkation** *n*

embarrass *vt* **1** cause awkwardness or shyness in; disconcert. **2** hinder; hamper **embarrassment** *n*

embassy *n* **1** ambassador's official residence. **2** staff of an ambassador. **3** mission or message of an ambassador

embellish *vt* **1** make more beautiful; decorate, adorn **2** add greater detail or description to. **embellishment** *n*

ember *n* piece of wood or coal in a dying fire. glowing cinder

embezzle *vt* misuse or misappropriate (money in one's care), defraud **embezzlement** *n* **embezzler** *n*

embitter *vt* cause to feel bitterness or rancour

emblem *n* sign or symbol representing an idea, principle, etc **emblematic** *adj*.

embody *vt* **1** represent in physical form **2** include, comprise **embodiment** *n* person or thing representing a quality, etc. personification

emboss *vt* impress (a raised design, lettering, etc.) on (a surface)

embrace *n* clasp, hug *vt,vi* hug, as to show affection or welcome *vt* **1** take up (a religion etc.), adopt **2** include, cover

embroider *vt,vi* sew (a pattern) on to (fabric) using coloured silks and fancy stitches *vt* add untrue details to **embroidery** *n*

embryo *n* **1** unborn young of animals during early stages of development **2** early stage of development **embryonic** *adj*

emerald *n* bright green precious stone *n,adj* bright green

emerge *vi* **1** come into view, as from concealment appear **2** become revealed or known **emergence** *n* **emergent** *adj* beginning to develop

emergency *n* unforeseen and dangerous situation requiring immediate action, crisis

emigrate *vi* leave a country to live permanently in another. **emigrant** *n,adj*. **emigration** *n*.

eminent *adj* **1** famous and respected; distinguished; high; exalted. **2** outstanding or obvious. **eminence** *or* **eminency** *n*. **eminently** *adv*.

emit *vt* (-tt-) give forth; make (sounds, etc.). **emission** *n*.

emotion *n* feeling, esp. strong feeling; anger, hate, love, etc. **emotional** *adj* given to strong or changeable emotion. **emotionally** *adv*. **emotive** *adj* arousing emotion; provocative.

empathy *n* ability to imagine and share the feelings of another person.

emperor *n* ruler of an empire.

emphasis *n* **1** calling of special attention to an important fact, etc.; stress. **2** accent on a particular or important word, phrase in music, etc. **emphasize** *vt* represent as important; give emphasis to; lay stress on. **emphatic** *adj* **1** stressed; accented. **2** sure; decided. **emphatically** *adv*.

empire *n* group of territories or countries ruled by one person or government.

empirical *adj* based on experience or experiment; not theoretical. **empirically** *adv*.

employ *vt* **1** hire (a person) to work for money; provide work for. **2** make use of. **3** occupy; use. **employment** *n*. **employee** *n* person hired to work for money. **employer** *n* person, firm, etc., employing people.

empower *vt* invest with the power (to); authorize.

empress *n* **1** female ruler of an empire. **2** wife or widow of an emperor.

empty *adj* **1** containing nothing; unoccupied. **2** lacking significance or feeling; meaningless; dull. **3** lacking force or substantiation. *vt,vi* discharge; vacate; leave empty; evacuate. **emptiness** *n*. **empty-handed** *adj* **1** carrying nothing. **2** having won or gained nothing. **empty-headed** *adj* not thinking deeply about important matters; silly.

emu *n* large flightless Australian bird.

emulate *vt* imitate (a person or thing admired or envied); try to equal. **emulation** *n*.

emulsion *n* **1** mixture in which one liquid is suspended in the form of tiny droplets in another. **2** household paint consisting of an emulsion of oil paint in water. **3** light-sensitive coating on photographic film or plates. **emulsify** *vt,vi* make into or become an emulsion.

enable *vt* make able (to); make possible for (a person) to do something.

enact *vt* **1** make into a law or statute. **2** represent on or as if on a stage; perform. **enactment** *n*.

enamel *n* **1** opaque glossy substance applied by fusion to metal for protection or decoration. **2** glossy paint. **3** protective outer layer of the teeth. *vt* (-ll-) coat or decorate with enamel.

enchant *vt* **1** cast a magic spell on; charm. **2** be delightful or fascinating to; bewitch. **enchantment** *n*.

encircle *vt* **1** make a circle round; surround. **2** pass round (the waist, etc.).

enclose *vt* **1** place within a surround, wall, etc., shut in. **2** put in an envelope for posting, esp. as an additional item. **enclosure** *n* **1** act of enclosing or something enclosed. **2** fencing off of land, esp. common land. **3** area of a sports ground, etc., reserved for spectators, officials, or others.

encore *interj* call from an audience to a performer to repeat a piece of music, etc., or perform an additional item. *n* song or item so performed.

encounter *vt* **1** meet unexpectedly; come across. **2** be faced or confronted with. *n* meeting or confrontation.

encourage *vt* cause to feel more hopeful or confident. **encouragement** *n*.

encroach *vi* overstep the proper limits; intrude on (another's property, area of responsibility, etc.).

encumber *vt* **1** weigh down; be a burden to. **2** hamper; impede. **encumbrance** *n*.

encyclopedia *n* reference book or books giving information on a wide range of topics or on one particular subject. **encyclopedic** *adj*.

end *n* **1** final or last part; furthest point. **2** conclusion or completion. **3** aim; object. **4** death. **at a loose end** having nothing to do. **in the end** finally; at last. ~*vi,vt* come or bring to an end; finish; conclude. **endless** *adj* without end; never ceasing. **endlessly** *adv*.

endanger *vt* bring into danger; put at risk.

endeavour *vt,vi* try hard (to do something); attempt. *n* act of trying; attempt.

endemic *adj* always present in a particular country or area.

endorse *vt* **1** sign the back of (a cheque, etc.). **2** enter a motoring offence in (a driving licence). **3** support; uphold. **endorsement** *n*.

endow *vt* **1** give money or property to (a college, etc.). **2** bestow (beauty, kindness, etc.) upon; bless with. **endowment** *n*.

endure *vi* last; continue in existence. *vt* tolerate; bear. **endurance** *n*. **endurable** *adj* bearable. **enduring** *adj* longlasting.

enemy *n* **1** person hostile to or hated by one; foe; opponent; antagonist. **2** nation with which one is at war.

energy *n* **1** capacity to do work. **2** physical strength; vitality; force. **energetic** *adj*. **energetically** *adv*.

enfold *vt* fold in; hold tightly; embrace.

enforce *vt* **1** force (a law) to be carried out or obeyed. **2** force; compel. **enforcement** *n*.

engage *vt* **1** hire; employ. **2** promise; pledge, esp. to marry someone. **3** occupy. **4** begin fighting against; attack. *vt,vi* (of gears, etc.) lock in position; mesh. **engagement** *n* **1** state of being engaged; act of engaging. **2** appointment to meet; date. **3** military encounter; battle.

engine *n* **1** machine able to convert energy into mechanical work. **2** railway locomotive. **3** any mechanical apparatus or device. **engineer** *n* **1** person skilled in a branch of engineering. **2** someone in charge of engines, esp. on a ship. **3** planner or organizer. *vt* **1** plan, supervise, or construct as an engineer. **2** plan or arrange skilfully; contrive. **engineering** *n* **1** practical application of scientific knowledge in the design, construction, or management of machinery, roads, bridges, buildings, etc. **2** planning or contrivance.

engrave *vt* **1** cut (letters, designs, etc.) into a hard surface. **2** print from an engraved and inked surface. **3** make a deep impression on. **engraver** *n*. **engraving** *n* **1** print made from an engraved surface. **2** engraved surface. **3** art of engraving.

engross *vt* occupy the attention of; absorb.

engulf *vt* swallow up. **engulfment** *n*.

enhance *vt* raise in importance or prominence; heighten; intensify. **enhancement** *n*.

enigma *n* **1** puzzle; riddle. **2** baffling or perplexing person, situation, etc. **enigmatic** *or* **enigmatical** *adj*. **enigmatically** *adv*.

enjoy *vt* **1** take pleasure in. **2** have the use or benefit of; possess. **enjoy oneself** feel pleasure, amusement, satisfaction, etc. **enjoyable** *adj*. **enjoyment** *n*.

enlarge *vt,vi* make or become larger; increase in size, scope, extent, etc. **enlarge on** *or* **upon** treat more fully. **enlargement** *n*.

enlighten *vt* impart knowledge or information to, esp. to free from ignorance, superstition, etc. **enlightenment** *n*.

enlist *vt,vi* **1** enrol in some branch of the armed forces. **2** secure or join in support of a person, cause, etc. **enlistment** *n*.

enmity *n* hatred between enemies; hostility; animosity.

enormous *adj* very great; huge; gigantic. **enormity** *n*. **enormously** *adv*.

enough *adj* adequate for the purpose; sufficient. *n* adequate amount; sufficiency. *adv* **1** sufficiently; adequately; tolerably. **2** fully.

enquire *vt,vi* **1** ask questions or seek information (about). **2** inquire. **enquiry** *n* **1** act of enquiring. **2** question. **3** inquiry.

enrage *vt* fill with rage; anger.

enrich *vt* **1** make wealthy or wealthier. **2** make more splendid in appearance; adorn **3** increase the value or quality of.

enrol *v* (-ll-) *vt* place (a name) or write the name of (a person) on a list, register, etc. *vt,vi* make or become a member; enlist. **enrolment** *n*.

ensemble (ɑːn'sɑːmbəl) *n* **1** collection of parts. **2** group of performers. **3** outfit; set of matching clothes and accessories.

ensign *n* **1** flag of a nation, regiment, etc. **2** badge or emblem of office.

enslave *vt* make a slave of. **enslavement** *n*

ensue *vi* come about or follow, esp as a consequence.

ensure *vt* **1** make sure or certain. **2** make safe; secure.

entail *vi* have as a consequence; inevitably involve. **entailment** *n*.

entangle *vt* **1** catch or snare in a mesh, net, etc. **2** make tangled. **3** involve in difficulties, complications, etc. **entanglement** *n*.

enter *vt,vi* **1** come or go in(to). **2** penetrate; pierce. **3** be or cause to be admitted (to). *vt* **1** put into; insert. **2** become a member of. **3** write down in a record, list, etc. **4** begin upon. **enter into** take part in; become a party to. **enter upon 1** begin; set out on. **2** come into enjoyment or possession of.

enterprise *n* **1** undertaking or project, esp. an important one. **2** boldness, daring, or adventurousness; initiative. **3** commercial undertaking; business.

entertain *vt,vi* **1** divert, amuse, or interest. **2**

give hospitality (to); receive (guests). *vt* consider; cherish. **entertainment** *n*.

enthral *vt* (-ll-) captivate; enchant. **enthralment** *n*.

enthusiasm *n* intense interest, admiration, approval, etc.; zeal; fervour. **enthusiast** *n*. **enthusiastic** *adj*. **enthusiastically** *adv*. **enthuse** *vi* display enthusiasm.

entice *vt* lure or attract by exciting hope of reward, gratification, etc.; tempt. **enticement** *n*. **enticingly** *adv*.

entire *adj* **1** whole; complete; undivided; unbroken; intact. **entirely** *adv*. **entirety** *n*.

entitle *vt* **1** give a particular title or name to. **2** give a right, claim, or legal title to. **entitlement** *n*.

entity *n* **1** something that has real existence; thing; object. **2** being; existence.

entrails *pl n* **1** internal organs of an animal, esp. the intestines. **2** internal parts of anything.

entrance[1] ('entrəns) *n* **1** act of entering. **2** place of entry, such as a doorway, passage, etc. **3** admission. **4** act or instance of an actor coming on stage.

entrance[2] (en'trɑ:ns) *vt* delight; charm; captivate; enthral.

entreat *vt,vi* beseech; implore; beg. **entreaty** *n*.

entrench *vt* **1** fortify or defend by digging trenches. **2** establish firmly and securely. **entrenchment** *n*.

entrepreneur (ɑ:ntrəprə'nə:) *n* someone who sets up and organizes business enterprises.

entrust *vt* give into the care of; trust with; invest or charge with a duty, etc.

entry *n* **1** act or instance of entering. **2** place for entering, esp. a passageway or hall; entrance. **3** access or admission. **4** entering of an item in a record, ledger, etc., or the item entered. **5** contestant in a race, competition, etc.

entwine *vt,vi* twist or tangle together; interweave (with).

enumerate *vt* **1** mention or specify one by one, as in a list; itemize. **2** count. **enumeration** *n*.

enunciate *vt,vi* say or pronounce (a word or words). *vt* state, declare, or proclaim, esp. clearly and carefully. **enunciation** *n*.

envelop (en'veləp) *vt* **1** wrap or cover up. **2** surround, enclose, or engulf. **3** obscure; conceal. **envelopment** *n*.

envelope ('envəloup) *n* **1** covering or container for a letter. **2** any enclosing structure, etc.

environment *n* all the external influences, surroundings, conditions, etc., immediately affecting a person or other organism. **environmental** *adj*.

envisage *vt* contemplate as actual or real; visualize.

envoy *n* **1** diplomatic representative ranking just below an ambassador. **2** any messenger or agent.

envy *n* **1** feeling of discontent caused by the possessions, status, etc., of someone else. **2** desire to have or enjoy an advantage, possession, etc., of another. **3** object of such feelings. *vt* view with envy. **enviable** *adj*. **envious** *adj*. **enviously** *n*.

enzyme *n* any of numerous organic substances that are produced in living cells and act as catalysts for biochemical changes.

epaulet *n also* **epaulette** decorative shoulder piece, esp. as worn on military uniforms.

ephemeral *adj* lasting only for a short time; transitory; fleeting.

epic *n* **1** long narrative poem in formalized style relating the exploits of a hero or heroes. **2** film, novel, etc., resembling this in style or content.

epidemic *adj* spreading rapidly among people in a certain area. *n* widespread occurrence of a disease, etc.

epilepsy *n* disorder of the nervous system characterized by convulsions and, usually, loss of consciousness. **epileptic** *adj,n*.

epilogue *n* **1** speech made to an audience at the end of a play by one of the actors. **2** concluding part of a novel, television or radio broadcast, etc.

episcopal *adj* **1** of or relating to a bishop. **2** governed by bishops.

episode *n* **1** incident or occurrence in the course of a series of events. **2** digression in a narrative, piece of music, etc. **3** instalment of a book, play, etc., serialized on television or radio. **episodic** *adj*.

epitaph *n* **1** inscription on a tomb or other monument. **2** anything serving as a memorial.

epitome (i'pitəmi) *n* **1** summary; abstract. **2** representative or typical characteristic. **epitomize** *vt* **1** summarize; abstract. **2** typify.

epoch *n* **1** period of time, esp. one considered as distinctive; era. **2** beginning of an important era in the history of anything.

equable *adj* **1** uniform or steady in effect,

operation, motion, etc.; unvarying. **2** tranquil; even; serene.

equal *adj* **1** as great as another in extent, size, degree, etc.; equivalent. **2** having the same rank, value, quality, etc., as another. **3** evenly proportioned. **4** uniform; equable. **5** adequate in quantity, powers, ability, etc. **6** smooth; even; level. *n* someone or something equal to another. *vt* (-ll-) be equal to or the same as. **equality** *n*. **equalize** *vt* make equal. *vi* reach a score equal to an opponent's.

equate *vt* **1** treat or regard as equal or equivalent. **2** put in the form of an equation. **equation** *n* **1** mathematical expression of the equality of two quantities. **2** representation in symbols of a chemical reaction.

equator *n* circle round the earth dividing the Northern hemisphere from the Southern hemisphere. **equatorial** *adj*.

equestrian *adj* **1** of or relating to horses, horsemen, or the skill of riding. **2** on horseback. *n* rider on horseback, esp. an entertainer or competitor.

equilateral *adj* having all sides equal.

equilibrium *n* **1** state of poise or balance prevailing when equal and opposing forces, influences, etc., counter each other in effect. **2** mental composure or stability.

equinox *n* either of the two dates in the year, at the beginning of spring and auntumn, when day and night are of equal length.

equip *vt* (-pp-) provide with necessary equipment, skills, etc. **equipment** *n* **1** equipping or being equipped. **2** collection of tools, implements, resources, etc., necessary for a task or undertaking.

equity *n* **1** fairness; impartiality. **2** system of law co-existing with and supplementing Common Law. **3** total ordinary shares of a limited company. **equitable** *adj*.

equivalent *adj* **1** equal in value, significance, force, etc. **2** corresponding in meaning, function, etc. *n* something equivalent. **equivalence** *n*.

equivocal *adj* **1** uncertain; ambivalent. **2** ambiguous; debatable.

era *n* **1** period of time with its own distinctive flavour, trends, characteristics, etc.; age; epoch. **2** system of dating from a particular event, etc., in the past.

eradicate *vt* wipe out; destroy; obliterate. **eradication** *n*.

erase *vt* **1** rub or scratch out (something written). **2** remove all trace of; wipe out. **eraser** *n*.

erect *adj* **1** upright; vertical. **2** raised or directed upwards. **3** stiff or firm. *vt* **1** build, construct, or elevate. **2** set up; establish. **erection** *n*.

ermine *n* **1** stoat with a brown summer coat and white winter fur. **2** white fur of the animal used to trim judges' robes, etc. **3** rank or functions of a judge.

erode *vt* wear or eat away by gradual action. **erosion** *n*.

erotic *adj* of, relating to, or exciting sexual desire. **eroticism** *n*.

err *vi* **1** be mistaken; make an error. **2** deviate from a moral code; sin.

errand *n* short task entrusted to someone, esp. a short journey to deliver or fetch something.

erratic *adj* **1** irregular; random. **2** irresponsible; unpredictable.

error *n* **1** something incorrect; mistake. **2** sin.

erudite *adj* learned; having great knowledge or wisdom. **erudition** *n*.

erupt *vi* **1** (of a volcano) emit lava, etc. **2** burst out; emit suddenly. **eruption** *n*.

escalate *vt,vi* increase by stages or in intensity. **escalator** *n* moving staircase consisting of steps in an endless belt.

escape *vt,vi* **1** free oneself from; get away (from). **2** avoid (harm, punishment, etc.). *vi* become free; leak out. *vt* be forgotten by; elude. *n* **1** act of escaping or means by which this occurs. **2** sport, pastime, or other release from pressure or reality. **escapism** *n* avoidance of unpleasant reality by fantasy, etc. **escapist** *adj,n*.

escort *n* ('eskɔ:t) **1** person or group acting as guard or protection for others on a journey. **2** man accompanying a woman to a social function. *vt* (e'skɔ:t) accompany as an escort.

esoteric *adj* **1** restricted to a specialized group. **2** difficult to understand; obscure in meaning.

especial *adj* **1** outstanding; notable; special. **2** particular. **especially** *adv*.

espionage *n* spying; obtaining secret information.

esplanade *n* wide level road or walk, esp. one constructed along the shore.

essay *n* **1** ('esei) short prose composition. **2** (e'sei) attempt; try; test. *vt,vi* (e'sei) attempt; try; test.

essence *n* **1** characteristic fundamental feature

or nature of something. **2** oil or other constituent of a plant, extracted as a perfume, flavouring, etc. **essential** *adj* **1** highly important; indispensable; necessary. **2** constituting the essence; fundamental. **3** absolute; perfect. *n* something that is essential.

establish *vt* **1** make secure or permanent. **2** found; bring about. **3** set up in a position, business, etc. **4** cause to be accepted. **establishment** *n* **1** act or an instance of establishing something. **2** permanent large business or government organization. **3** institution. **4** small business premises, club, hotel, etc. **5** large private household. **the Establishment** *n* group of people and institutions thought of as holding the power in a country.

estate *n* **1** country property with extensive land. **2** new building development for housing or light industry. **3** person's collective assets and liabilities. **4** position in society; social standing. **estate agent** *n* person whose business is the management, lease, and sale of houses and land. **estate car** *n* car with a long body and rear doors, designed to carry goods as well as passengers.

esteem *vt* **1** think highly of; respect. **2** consider; regard. *n* judgment or opinion, esp. a favourable one.

estimable *adj* **1** deserving respect; worthy. **2** able to be estimated; calculable.

estimate *vt* ('estimeit) **1** calculate roughly; gauge. **2** judge. *n* ('estimət) **1** approximation. **2** judgment. **estimation** *n* **1** act or result of estimating. **2** regard; esteem.

estuary *n* tidal mouth of a river.

etch *vt* **1** produce (a design, picture, etc.) on a metal plate by cutting into a wax coating and removing exposed metal with acid. **2** eat away by chemical action. **etching** *n* etched plate or a print made from this.

eternity *n* **1** endless time. **2** time after death. **eternal** *adj* **1** lasting for ever; timeless; without end. **2** continual; incessant. **eternally** *adv*.

ether ('i:θə) **1** volatile highly flammable liquid formerly used as an anaesthetic. **2** hypothetical weightless substance once thought to permeate all space. **ethereal** (i'θiəriəl) *adj* **1** light and airy. **2** spiritual; heavenly.

ethics *n* **1** *s* branch of philosophy concerned with moral conduct, right and wrong, etc. **2** *pl* moral principles; rules or standards of conduct. **ethical** *adj*. **ethically** *adv*.

ethnic *adj* **1** relating to a group of people of a particular culture, religion, language, etc. **2** relating to the racial classification of man.

etiquette *n* customs and rules determining good behaviour; manners.

etymology *n* study of the derivation of words and changes in their meaning and form. **etymological** *adj*. **etymologist** *n*.

eucalyptus *n* tree native to Australasia yielding an aromatic oil, which is used medicinally.

Eucharist *n* **1** Christian sacrament of communion, commemorating the Last Supper. **2** consecrated bread or wine offered at communion.

eunuch *n* male who has been castrated.

euphemism *n* **1** socially acceptable word or phrase used in place of one considered offensive or impolite. **2** practice of using euphemisms. **euphemistic** *adj*.

euphoria *n* feeling of bliss or elation. **euphoric** *adj*.

euthanasia *n* act of killing a person, esp. one experiencing intense pain or suffering; mercy killing.

evacuate *vi,vt* leave or remove from (an unsafe place). *vt* empty; discharge; vacate. **evacuation** *n*.

evade *vt* avoid; escape; elude.

evaluate *vt* **1** determine the quantity or worth of. **2** judge critically; appraise. **evaluation** *n*.

evangelist *n* preacher, esp. one not attached to a particular church. **Evangelist** any one of the four writers of the Gospels. **evangelical** *adj* **1** relating to the Gospels. **2** relating to certain Protestant groups that stress the importance of personal religious experiences and missionary work.

evaporate *vt,vi* **1** change from a solid or liquid state to a vapour. **2** lose or cause to lose some liquid, leaving a concentrated residue. **3** disappear; vanish. **evaporation** *n*.

eve *n* **1** evening or day before a holiday, festival, etc. **2** period immediately preceding an event.

even *adj* **1** level; flat; plane. **2** uniform; regular. **3** calm; placid. **4** equally balanced; fair. **5** (of numbers) divisible by two. **6** exact. *adv* **1** still; yet. **2** used to emphasize comparative forms. **3** used when the content of a phrase or sentence is unexpected. **4** used to modify a statement or add precision to it. *vt,vi* make or become even;

balance. **evenly** *adv*. **even-tempered** *adj* calm; not easily upset or angered.

evening *n* **1** latter part of the day or early night. **2** concluding or final period.

event *n* **1** anything that takes place; occurrence. **2** outcome; result. **3** sports contest.

eventual *adj* final; ultimate; last. **eventually** *adv*.

ever *adv* **1** at any time. **2** by any possibility. **3** always. **evergreen** *adj* (of trees, shrubs, etc.) having foliage that remains green throughout the year. *n* evergreen tree or shrub. **everlasting** *adj* **1** endless; unending. **2** perpetual; of long duration. **evermore** *adv* always; forever; constantly.

every *adj* **1** each. **2** all possible. **every other** every second or alternate. **everybody** *pron* each person; everyone. **everyday** *adj* **1** daily. **2** commonplace; ordinary. **3** suitable for normal days; not special. **everyone** *pron* each person; everybody. **everything** *pron* **1** each thing, aspect, factor, etc. **2** a great deal; something very important. **everywhere** *adv* towards or in all places, parts, etc.

evict *vt* eject or expel (a person) from a house, building, etc. **eviction** *n*.

evidence *n* proof; ground for belief. **evident** *adj* apparent; obvious; plain. **evidently** *adv*.

evil *adj* **1** wicked; sinful. **2** harmful; malicious. **3** offensive; vile. *n* wickedness; sin; depravity.

evoke *vt* **1** summon; call forth. **2** excite; provoke. **evocation** *n*.

evolution *n* **1** natural process of very gradual continuous change in all plants and animals. **2** development; unfolding. **evolutionary** *adj*.

evolve *vt,vi* develop; unroll. *vi* undergo evolution.

ewe *n* female sheep.

exacerbate *vt* **1** aggravate; heighten. **2** exasperate; irritate; provoke. **exacerbation** *n*.

exact *adj* **1** completely correct. **2** precise. **3** very same; particular. **4** rigorous; strict. *vt* **1** extort. **2** demand; require authoritatively. **exactly** *adv*.

exaggerate *vt,vi* represent (something) as being greater or more than it really is. *vt* make more noticeable. **exaggeration** *n*.

exalt *vt* **1** raise; elevate. **2** praise. **exaltation** *n*.

examine *vt* **1** inspect; observe. **2** investigate; study. **3** test (a person's skill, knowledge, etc.). **examiner** *n*. **examination** *n* **1** act of being examined. **2** questions or tasks intended to test skill or knowledge. **3** medical inspection of the body.

example *n* **1** specimen; sample. **2** someone or something worthy of emulation. **3** precedent.

exasperate *vt* irritate; provoke; incense. **exasperation** *n*.

excavate *vt,vi* **1** dig out. **2** hollow out. **3** expose (buried objects) by digging. **excavation** *n*. **excavator** *n* machine for digging and moving soil, gravel, etc.

exceed *vt,vi* be greater than (another). *vt* overstep the limit of. **exceedingly** *adv* very; greatly.

excel *v* (-ll-) *vt,vi* surpass; be superior to. *vi* do extremely well (in).

excellency *n* term of address used for ambassadors, governors, high-ranking government officials, etc.

excellent *adj* of the best quality; thoroughly good and praiseworthy. **excellence** *n*.

except *prep* with the exception of; save. *vt* exclude; omit. **exception** *n* **1** act of being excepted. **2** instance to be excepted; unusual situation, person, thing, etc. **exceptional** *adj* **1** relating to an exception; irregular. **2** having higher than average intelligence, skill, talent, etc. **exceptionally** *adv*.

excerpt *n* selected passage from a book; extract.

excess *n* (ek'ses) **1** surplus. **2** amount, degree, etc., by which something is exceeded by another. *adj* ('ekses) over and above what is normal, necessary, or required. **excessive** *adj*. **excessively** *adv*.

exchange *vt* **1** barter; trade for something. **2** interchange; trade (information). **3** replace; substitute. *n* **1** act of exchanging. **2** anything that substitutes for or replaces something offered. **3** argument. **4** central office or station. **5** place where brokers, dealers, etc., buy and sell securities and certain commodities.

exchequer *n* **1** department of the treasury dealing with accounting. **2** treasury or government department of a country, state, etc., controlling financial matters.

excise *n* ('eksaiz) **1** tax levied on certain commodities or for certain licences. **2** branch of the civil service responsible for collecting such taxes. *vt* (ek'saiz) impose excise on; tax; levy.

excite *vt* **1** arouse; awaken; provoke. **2** stir up;

instigate. **3** disturb; agitate. **excitable** *adj*. **excitement** *n*.

exclaim *vt* cry out; shout. **exclamation** *n* **1** act of exclaiming; outcry. **2** interjection; emphatic word, phrase, or sentence. **exclamation mark** *n* punctuation mark (!) used after an exclamation.

exclude *vt* **1** keep out; bar. **2** deny inclusion or consideration of. **exclusion** *n*. **exclusive** *adj* **1** barring or excluding everything else. **2** sole; not shared; individual. **3** fashionable; select. **exclusively** *adv*.

excommunicate *vt* bar (someone) from church membership or receiving certain sacraments. **excommunication** *n*.

excrete *vt* (of an animal) discharge (waste, such as urine, sweat, etc.) from the body. **excrement** *n* waste matter, esp. solid, discharged from the body. **excreta** *pl n* waste matter discharged from the body.

excruciating *adj* agonizing; tortuous; intensely painful.

excursion *n* **1** short journey, pleasure trip, or outing. **2** group or party taking an excursion.

excuse *vt* (ik'skju:z) **1** pardon; forgive. **2** justify or make allowances for. **3** exempt or release (from). *n* (ik'skju:s) **1** justification; reason. **2** explanation offered to explain bad behaviour, rudeness, etc. **3** pretext; pretence. **excusable** *adj*.

execute *vt* **1** kill, esp. following a legal decision; put to death. **2** perform; achieve; carry out. **3** administer; enforce. **execution** *n*. **executive** *adj* relating to administration, the execution of a duty, etc. *n* person or group running or administrating a company, project, etc. **executor** (ig'zekjutə) *n* person who carries out a duty, esp. someone responsible for dealing with the provisions of a will.

exempt *vt* release or excuse from a duty, obligation, etc. *adj* released from a duty, obligation, etc. **exemption** *n*.

exercise *n* **1** physical exertion, esp. for the purpose of training or to maintain health. **2** task undertaken to improve one's skill or competence. **3** operation or use of one's power, right, etc. *vt,vi* give exercise to or take exercise. *vt* **1** use; employ. **2** put into action; carry out. **3** exert; wield.

exert *vt* use the power of (strength, influence, etc.); exercise. **exert oneself** make an effort; strive. **exertion** *n*.

exhale *vi,vt* breathe out; force (air) out of the lungs. **exhalation** *n*.

exhaust *vt* **1** drain; empty; consume completely. **2** use, discuss, etc., to the full. *n* **1** gases that are expelled from an engine as waste. **2** expulsion of such gases. **exhaustion** *n*. **exhaustive** *adj*. **exhaustively** *adv*.

exhibit *vt* **1** present for viewing or inspection. **2** indicate; disclose; demonstrate. *n* something presented for public viewing. **exhibitor** *n*. **exhibition** *n* **1** act of exhibiting. **2** public show or display. **exhibitionism** *n* practice of or tendency towards showing off or drawing undue attention to oneself in public. **exhibitionist** *adj,n*.

exhilarate *vt* enliven; animate; stimulate. **exhilaration** *n*.

exhume *vt* dig up (a corpse) after burial.

exile *n* **1** banishment; ostracism. **2** banished person; outcast. *vt* banish; expel (from a country).

exist *vi* **1** be; have reality. **2** endure; continue. **3** be present in a particular place or situation. **existence** *n* life; state of being. **existent** *adj*.

exit *n* **1** way out. **2** departure; withdrawal. *vi* go out or away; depart.

exonerate *vt* **1** absolve; acquit. **2** release; exempt. **exoneration** *n*.

exorbitant *adj* excessive; extravagant; enormous. **exorbitantly** *adv*.

exorcize *vt* deliver from evil spirits, demons, etc. **exorcism** *n*. **exorcist** *n*.

exotic *adj* unusual; foreign; not native.

expand *vt,vi* **1** make or become greater in size, range, scope, etc. **2** swell; fill out; extend. **3** develop (a theme, story, etc.). **expansion** *n*. **expansive** *adj*. **expanse** *n* continuous surface that extends or spreads; stretch.

expatriate *vt* (eks'peitrieit) **1** banish; exile. **2** move (oneself) away from one's own country. *adj* (eks'peitriit) expatriated. *n* (eks'peitriit) expatriated person. **expatriation** *n*.

expect *vt* **1** consider as probable. **2** await; look forward to. **3** rely on; require; want. *vt,vi* be pregnant (with). *vi* suppose; anticipate. **expectant** *adj*. **expectation** *n* **1** act of expecting. **2** goal; aim; hope. **3** something expected or anticipated.

expedient *adj* **1** proper; suitable. **2** advantageous; profitable. **expediency** *n*.

expedition *n* **1** organized journey for exploration, hunting, etc. **2** group or party on such a journey.

expel *vt* (-ll-) eject; drive out; ban.

expend *vt* use up; spend; consume. **expenditure** *n* money spent; outgoings.

expense *n* **1** cost; charge; outlay. **2** something costing a great deal. **expensive** *adj* costly; high-priced; dear.

experience *n* **1** direct personal observation, knowledge, practice, etc. **2** specific situation that one has undergone. **3** process of gaining knowledge, esp. when not through study. **4** acquired knowledge. *vt* **1** undergo; encounter. **2** feel; be moved by. **experienced** *adj* fully trained or qualified; expert.

experiment *n* **1** trial, test, or examination to discover something by observation. **2** original or new attempt. *vi* perform an experiment. **experimental** *adj*. **experimentation** *n*. **experimenter** *n*.

expert *n* person having great knowledge, experience, skill, etc., in a particular subject. *adj* **1** relating to an expert. **2** knowledgeable; specialist; skilled. **expertise** *n* specialist skill or knowledge.

expiate *vt* atone for; redeem. **expiation** *n*.

expire *vi* **1** end; terminate; conclude. **2** exhale. **3** die. **expiry** *n* termination; lapsing; end.

explain *vt,vi* **1** make clear or understandable. **2** interpret; expound. **3** account for; justify. **explanation** *n*. **explanatory** *adj*. **explicable** *adj*.

expletive *n* exclamation; swearword or curse.

explicit *adj* **1** clear; precise; definite. **2** open; unreserved. **explicitly** *adv*.

explode *vt,vi* **1** burst; blow up. **2** destroy or be destroyed by bursting. *vi* suddenly or violently display anger, rage, etc. **explosion** *n* **1** act of exploding. **2** any rapid or very large increase, as in population. **explosive** *adj* **1** characterized by or capable of explosion. **2** potentially violent, turbulent, or dangerous. *n* substance or device capable of exploding. **explosively** *adv*.

exploit *n* ('eksplɔit) heroic act, deed, or feat. *vt* (ik'splɔit) **1** take unjust advantage of. **2** utilize fully. **exploitation** *n*. **exploitative** *adj*.

explore *vt* investigate thoroughly and methodically. *vt,vi* go to or into (distant lands, areas, etc.) to investigate. **exploration** *n*. **explorer** *n*.

exponent *n* person or thing that functions as an example, representation, or symbol.

export *vt,vi* (ik'spɔ:t) sell or send (goods) out of a country for foreign sale. *n* ('ekspɔ:t) commodity sold or sent to a foreign country. **exporter** *n*.

expose *vt* **1** uncover; disclose; lay open. **2** subject; make liable. **3** make familiar with. **4** subject (camera films, etc.) to light. **exposure** *n* **1** act of exposing. **2** direction in which the main wall of a house or building faces. **3** frame of photographic film that has been exposed to light.

expound *vt* explain in detail.

express *vt* **1** utter; verbalize; speak. **2** represent or symbolize as in a painting, piece of music, etc. *adj* **1** clear; plain; definite. **2** special; particular. *n* train, bus, etc., stopping only at major stations. **expression** *n* **1** verbal communication. **2** manifestation; representation. **3** saying; phrase; term. **4** look on the face that expresses a particular emotion. **expressionless** *adj*. **expressive** *adj*. conveying emotion. **expressly** *adv* particularly; especially; explicitly.

exquisite *adj* delicate; refined; excellent; rare. **exquisitely** *adv*.

extend *vt,vi* **1** stretch; reach out; spread. **2** prolong or last (for). *vt* **1** offer; give. **2** expand; broaden. **extension** *n* **1** act of extending. **2** additional room(s) built on to a house, etc. **3** additional telephone apparatus connected to a central switchboard or having the same number as another. **4** delay or additional period. **extensive** *adj* **1** wide; large. **2** comprehensive; far-reaching. **extensively** *adv*. **extent** *n* degree to which something extends; range; scope.

exterior *n* outside; outward appearance. *adj* outer; outside; external.

exterminate *vt* annihilate; destroy or kill. **extermination** *n*.

external *adj* **1** situated at or coming from the outside; outer. **2** foreign; alien. **3** (of medicines, etc.) not to be taken internally. **externally** *adv*.

extinct *adj* **1** (of plants, animals, etc.) no longer existing. **2** obsolete; out-of-date. **3** (of volcanoes) inactive; incapable of further eruption. **extinction** *n*.

extinguish *vt* **1** put out or suppress (fire, lights, etc.). **2** destroy completely. **extinguisher** *n*.

extort *vt* obtain by force or threats. **extortion** *n*.

extra *adj* additional; supplementary. *n* **1** something additional. **2** special edition of a newspaper. **3** actor taking part in crowd scenes, etc.

extract *vt* (ik'strækt) **1** draw or pull out; remove. **2** derive or develop (an idea, theory, etc.). **3** select (from a written work). *n* ('ekstrækt) **1** quotation; excerpt. **2** essence; vital principle or substance. **extraction** *n*.

extramural *adj* related to but not under direct control of an academic institution.

extraneous (ik'streiniəs) *adj* not strictly necessary or central; external; extra.

extraordinary *adj* remarkable; unusual; amazing. **extraordinarily** *adv*.

extravagant *adj* **1** wasteful. **2** free or generous. **3** excessive; inordinate; exorbitant. **3** ornate; fussy. **extravagance** *n*. **extravagantly** *adv*.

extreme *adj* **1** greatest; highest; most intense. **2** immoderate; unreasonable. **3** drastic; radical. **4** most distant or remote; utmost. *n* **1** highest or greatest degree. **2** upper or lower limit of a scale, range, etc. **extremely** *adv*. **extremity** *n* **1** utmost or farthest point or degree. **2** end part of a limb; hand or finger or foot or toe.

extricate *vt* disengage; clear; set free (from). **extrication** *n*.

extrovert *n* gregarious outgoing person. *adj also* **extroverted** gregarious; outgoing; not shy.

exuberant *adj* **1** joyful; vigorous; lively. **2** lavish; prolific; abundant. **exuberance** *n*. **exuberantly** *adv*.

exude *vt,vi* emit; ooze; gush.

eye *n* **1** organ of sight. **2** *also* **eyesight** sight; vision. **3** gaze; look; glance. **4** ability to inspect, judge, or observe. **5** aperture in a camera, etc., through which light can pass. **6** small hole in a needle, etc. **7** calm centre of a hurricane, tornado, etc. **8** bud on a potato, etc. *vt* inspect carefully; scrutinize. **eyeball** *n* round ball-shaped part of the eye. **eyebrow** *n* **1** fringe of hair growing on the ridge above the eye. **2** ridge above the eye; brow. **eye-catching** *adj* stunning; attracting attention. **eyelash** *n* short hair growing out of the edge of the eyelid. **eyelid** *n* fold of skin that can be closed over the eyeball. **eye-opener** *n* revelation; startling occurrence. **eye shadow** *n* cosmetic applied to colour the eyelids and draw attention to the eyes. **eyesore** *n* extremely ugly or offending building, object, etc. **eyestrain** *n* fatigue and tiredness of the eye. **eye-witness** *n* someone who has been present at and has observed a particular event.

F

fable *n* **1** tale with a moral, whose characters are often animals. **2** fictional story or account.

fabric *n* **1** woven or knitted cloth. **2** structure or basis, as of society, personality, etc. **fabricate** *vt* **1** manufacture or construct, esp. by putting together components. **2** invent; give a false account of. **fabrication** *n*.

fabulous *adj* **1** wonderful; marvellous. **2** almost impossible; unbelievable. **3** mythical. **fabulously** *adv*.

facade (fə'sɑːd) *n* **1** front of a building, esp. when considered for its artistic merit. **2** image that a person presents, esp. when misleading.

face *n* **1** front part of the head, including the mouth, nose, eyes, etc. **2** particular expression of the face. **3** outward attitude or pose, as of self-confidence. **4** any outward appearance. **5** most prominent or front part, as of a cliff, building, etc. **6** dial of a clock or watch. **7** flat surface of something, such as a coin, crystal, etc. **save/lose face** maintain/lose one's dignity or prestige. ~*vt,vi* position or be positioned to point in a particular direction. *vt* **1** come into contact with; meet. **2** confront; challenge. **3** apply to or cover (a surface). **face up to** accept and deal with realistically. **faceless** *adj* anonymous. **facelift** *n* **1** surgical operation to tighten the skin on the face and improve the appearance. **2** any improvement in appearance, as by decoration; renovation. **facepack** *n* cream or paste applied to the face to improve the skin. **face value** *n* **1** stated monetary value. **2** apparent value or meaning of something. **facial** *adj* relating to the face. *n* cosmetic treatment for the face.

facet *n* **1** flat surface of a polished gem. **2** aspect of a situation, subject, or personality.

facetious (fə'siːʃəs) *adj* meant or attempting to be amusing, sometimes inappropriately. **facetiously** *adv*.

facile *adj* **1** easy; simple. **2** glib; superficial; too easy.

facility *n* **1** ease or skill. **2** equipment or means enabling execution of an action. **facilitate** *vt* make easier or simpler.

facsimile (fæk'simili) *n* exact copy; reproduction.

fact *n* something that actually happened, existed, or exists; provable statement. **in fact** *or* **as a matter of fact** really; truly. **factual** *adj* true or truthful; actual.

faction *n* dissenting group within a larger group.

factor *n* **1** something that contributes towards a result. **2** number that can be divided into another number evenly.

factory *n* building equipped with manufacturing machinery.

faculty *n* **1** ability or power, as the senses, etc. **2** department of a university or its staff.

fade *vt,vi* make or become pale, less clear, etc. **fade out** disappear gradually.

fag *n* **1** difficult chore. **2** *sl* cigarette. *vt,vi* (-gg-) *also* **fag out** make or become tired through arduous work; exhaust.

Fahrenheit *adj* relating to a temperature scale on which the freezing point of water is 32° and its boiling point 212°.

fail *vi,vt* have no success (at). *vi* **1** become inoperative; break down. **2** be inadequate or insufficient. **3** omit; forget. *vt* **1** judge to have failed. **2** disappoint; let down. *n* instance of failing. **without fail** certainly; definitely. **failing** *n* inadequacy; fault. **failure** *n* person or thing that fails.

faint *adj* **1** lacking in clarity, contrast, etc. **2** without conviction; weak; feeble. **3** feeling as though one is going to lose consciousness. **4** cowardly; timid. *vi* lose consciousness for a short time. *n* short period of loss of consciousness. **faint-hearted** *adj* cowardly; timid.

fair[1] *adj* **1** impartial; just; without bias. **2** conforming to regulations. **3** (of a person) having light colouring. **4** beautiful or unblemished. **5** acceptable; good. **6** sunny; cloudless. **fair and square** legitimate; correct. **fairness** *n*. **fairly** *adv* **1** moderately; rather. **2** justly; deservingly. **fair-minded** *adj* just; impartial.

fair[2] *n* **1** event, usually out of doors, with various entertainments and sideshows. **2** cattle market. **3** gathering of people dealing in similar products for trade purposes. **fairground** *n* place where a fair is held.

fairy *n* imaginary being having small human form and supernatural or magical powers. **fairytale** *n* a story containing imaginary or supernatural characters, usually intended for children.

faith *n* **1** belief; trust. **2** any religion. **faithful** *adj* **1** loyal; true. **2** remaining close to the original. **faithfully** *adv*. **faith-healing** *n* healing by means of supernatural or religious powers.

fake *vt,vi* forge; pretend. *n* counterfeit; forgery. *adj* not real; counterfeit.

falcon *n* bird of prey, which is sometimes trained for sport.

fall *vi* (fell; fallen) **1** descend quickly; drop. **2** collapse from an upright position. **3** decrease; decline. **4** diminish in tone. **5** extend towards a lower level; hang down. **6** be defeated or overthrown; submit. **7** pass into sleep or a similar condition. **8** occur at a specified time. **9** be transferred. **10** be classified into. **fall back on** have recourse to for support. **fall for** *inf* **1** be deceived by. **2** develop a deep affection for. **fall in with 1** become acquainted with. **2** agree to. **fall on one's feet** emerge successfully from a precarious situation. **fall out** quarrel; disagree. ~*n* **1** act or instance of falling or dropping. **2** lowering; decline. **3** distance over or through which something falls. **4** capture or decline of a city, civilization, etc. **falls** *pl n* waterfall; cataract. **fallout** *n* descent of particles of radioactive substances, which contaminate the air after a nuclear explosion.

fallacy *n* incorrect opinion or belief; deceptive notion. **fallacious** *adj*.

fallible *adj* **1** liable to make mistakes or be deceived. **2** likely to contain errors.

fallow *adj* (of land) left uncultivated for one or more seasons.

false *adj* **1** untrue; incorrect. **2** unfaithful; given to deceit. **3** synthetic; not genuine, artificial. **falsehood** *n* lie or fallacy. **false pretences** *pl n* forgeries and misrepresentations for illegally obtaining money, property, etc. **falsify** *vt* **1** make false or incorrect, esp. to mislead. **2** prove incorrect; disprove.

falsetto *n* male voice pitched within a range that is higher than normal. *adj,adv* using such a voice.

falter *vi* hesitate; waver; stumble. *vt* say with hesitation; stammer.

fame *n* state of being well known; reputation. **famed** *adj* acknowledged; recognized.

familiar *adj* **1** well-known or easily recognizable. **2** often used or frequented; customary. **familiar with** well acquainted with. **familiarize** *vt* make knowledgeable about a subject, place, etc.

family *n* **1** group consisting of parents and their children. **2** group of related people. **3** any interrelated group of things.

famine *n* widespread shortage of food, esp. because of drought or crop failure.

famished *adj* extremely hungry; starved.

famous *adj* **1** well-known; celebrated. **2** *inf* fantastic; splendid.

fan[1] *n* **1** device for causing a flow of air for cooling, such as a folding wedge-shaped device held in the hand. **2** anything shaped like a fan. *vt,vi* (-nn-) **1** cool by means of a fan. **2** *also* **fan out** spread or move in the shape of a fan; separate.

fan[2] *n* enthusiastic admirer of a pop star, actor, etc.

fanatic *n* **1** person with extreme and irrational dedication to a cause. **2** *inf* person dedicated to a particular pastime. **fanatical** *adj*.

fancy *adj* **1** elaborate, decorated, or ornamental. **2** high in quality. **3** coming from the imagination. *n* **1** whim; pleasure. **2** poetic imagery. *vt* **1** imagine; picture in the mind. **2** like; be attracted by. **fancy dress** *n* costume worn for a masquerade. **fanciful** *adj* **1** not factual; imaginary. **2** produced creatively or imaginatively.

fanfare *n* short musical piece played on trumpets.

fang *n* long pointed tooth, as of a snake or dog.

fantasy *n* **1** unrestrained imagination. **2** something imagined, esp. when bizarre. **3** imagined sequence that fulfils some unsatisfied need; daydream. **4** hallucination. **5** notion that is not based on fact. **fantastic** *adj* **1** strange or eccentric in design, appearance, etc. **2** exaggerated or incredible. **3** *inf* very large or great. **4** *inf* fabulous; splendid.

far *adv* **1** at, to, or from a long way or great distance. **2** at or to a distant time. **3** very much. **as far as** to the point that. **by far** by a great deal. **far and near** *or* **far and wide** everywhere; over a great distance or area. **far gone 1** in an advanced condition. **2** mad; crazy. **3** *inf* drunk. **far out** *sl* strange; unconventional. **in so far as** to the extent that. ~*adj* **1** long way away. **2** extending or protruding a great distance. **3** remote; isolated. **far-away** *adj* **1** distant; removed. **2** preoccupied; daydreaming. **far-fetched** *adj* improbable; exaggerated. **far-off** *adj* distant; remote. **far-reaching** *adj* having extensive effects or importance.

farce *n* **1** form of drama in which characters, plot, etc., are presented as highly comical or ridiculous. **2** absurdly silly event or situation. **farcical** *adj*.

fare *n* **1** amount of money paid for a journey, etc. **2** menu; type of food.

farewell *interj,n* goodbye.

farinaceous *adj* made of or containing flour or grain.

farm *n* tract of land, with buildings, used for the rearing of livestock or cultivation of crops. *vi,vt* rear livestock or cultivate (land) for a living. **farm out** distribute. **farmer** *n*. **farmyard** *n* enclosed area adjacent to farm buildings.

farther *adv* **1** to or at a distant place or time; further. **2** in addition (to). **farthest** *adv* to or at the most distant place or time; furthest. *adj* most remote in place or time.

fascinate *vt* make curious or interested; captivate. **fascination** *n*.

fascism *n* ideology or government that is authoritarian and undemocratic. **fascist** *adj,n*.

fashion *n* **1** style of dress, makeup, etc. **2** custom; behaviour. **3** kind; type. *vt* make or form. **fashionable** *adj* relating to a current trend, style, or fashion.

fast[1] *adj* **1** moving or able to move rapidly; quick. **2** lasting only a short period. **3** (of a timepiece) indicating a more advanced time than is accurate. **4** promiscuous. **5** retaining colour; not prone to fading. *adv* **1** quickly; rapidly; swiftly. **2** securely; tightly. **3** soundly.

fast[2] *vi* abstain from food, esp. for religious reasons or as a protest. *n also* **fasting** abstinence from food.

fasten *vt,vi* attach; secure; tie.

fastidious *adj* difficult to please; fussy.

fat *n* **1** greasy semi-solid chemical substance. **2** animal tissue containing such substances. *adj* **1** overweight; obese. **2** containing fat. **3** thick. **4** rewarding or promising. **fatten** *vt,vi* make or become fat(ter). **fatty** *adj*.

fatal *adj* **1** leading to death. **2** disastrous; tragic. **fatality** *n* **1** accident that has resulted in death. **2** person so killed. **3** condition causing death.

fate *n* **1** force or power that determines events. **2** fortune; destiny. **fated** *adj* determined by fate. **fateful** *adj* awful; dreadful.

father *n* **1** male parent. **2** person who has founded a field of study, movement, etc. *vt* be the father (of). **father-in-law** *n, pl* **fathers-in-law** father of one's husband or wife. **fatherland** *n* person's native country or that of his ancestors.

fathom *n* unit used to measure depth of water, equal to 6 feet. *vt* **1** measure the depth of (water). **2** probe into (a problem, situation, etc.) and discover its meaning.

fatigue *n* **1** tiredness; weariness. **2** strain, esp. in fibres, metals, etc. *vt* make tired or weak.

fatuous *adj* silly; foolish.

fault *n* **1** flaw; defect. **2** mistake. **3** misdemeanour; wrong. **4** accountability for a mistake or error. **at fault** to blame. **find fault** criticize; find a mistake in. **to a fault** excessively. ~*vt* find a mistake in. **faulty** *adj*.

fauna *n, pl* **faunas** *or* **faunae** ('fɔ:ni:) all animal life of a particular time or region.

favour *n* **1** kind gesture of good will. **2** good will. **3** partiality. **4** token or gift. **in favour of** **1** commending. **2** to the advantage of. *vt* **1** prefer. **2** advocate or endorse. **favourable** *adj* advantageous; encouraging. **favourably** *adv*. **favourite** *adj* given preference to over others; best liked. *n* someone or something regarded preferentially.

fawn[1] *n* young deer. *adj,n* greyish or yellowish brown.

fawn[2] *vi* seek attention or favour servilely.

fear *n* **1** feeling of alarm or terror. **2** something causing this. **3** reverence. **4** anxiety; apprehension. **for fear of** so as to avoid. ~*vt,vi* feel fear (of). **fearless** *adj*. **fearful** *adj* **1** afraid. **2** *inf* very great.

feasible *adj* **1** able to be done. **2** suitable or likely. **feasibility** *n*.

feast *n* **1** lavish meal; banquet. **2** periodic religious celebration. **3** something lavishly pleasing. *vi* **1** eat at a feast. **2** take extreme pleasure in. *vt* **1** provide with a feast. **2** please; delight.

feat *n* deed or action, esp. when noteworthy.

feather *n* one of the external structures that form a bird's outer covering. *vt* cover or fill with feathers. **feathery** *adj*.

featherweight *n* **1** boxer of a weight under 126 lbs. **2** something extremely lightweight or of little consequence.

feature *n* **1** part of the face, such as mouth, eyes, etc. **2** characteristic or quality. **3** full-length cinema film. **4** particular article in a periodical. *vi* be a distinctive characteristic of. *vt* offer as or make a feature; give main importance to.

February *n* second month of the year.

feckless *adj* weak; ineffectual.

federal *adj* **1** relating to a league of nations or states. **2** relating to a system of government in which states retain a degree of autonomy under a central government. **federally** *adv*. **federate** *vi,vt* join in a federation or league. **federation** *n*.

fee *n* amount of money due for a service, right of entrance, etc.

feeble *adj* **1** weak or exhausted, either physically or mentally. **2** deficient in strength or force. **feeble-minded** *adj* lacking in intelligence.

feed *v* (fed) *vt* **1** offer food or other essential materials to. **2** offer as food. *vi* eat. *n* **1** food, esp. as for infants, livestock, etc. **2** amount of food or material allowed. **fed up** disgruntled with a particular situation.

feel *v* (felt) *vt* **1** sense or examine by touching. **2** experience (an emotional or physical sensation). **3** have an emotional or physical reaction to. *vi* produce a sensation as specified. **feel for** sympathize with. **feel like** want. **feel up to** be well enough to. ~*n* **1** instance of feeling. **2** nature of something as perceived by touch or by intuition. **feeler** *n* organ in some animals especially adapted for touch. **feeling** **1** ability to experience a sensation or a sensation itself. **2** mood; attitude; emotion. **3** impression; premonition. *adj* **1** sensitive; sympathetic. **2** showing emotion.

feet *n pl* of **foot.**

feign *vt* pretend; invent; imitate.

feint *n* deceptive movement, action, etc. *vi* make such a movement.

feline *adj* **1** of the cat family. **2** like a cat. *n* animal in the cat family.

fell[1] *v pt* of **fall.**

fell[2] *vt* bring down or cause to fall.

fellow *n* **1** man; boy **2** companion; colleague. **3**

member of the same class, kind, etc. **4** member of a learned society. **fellowship** *n* **1** sharing of interests, activities, etc. **2** group sharing such things; brotherhood. **3** position of being a fellow, esp. in a learned society, university, etc. **4** religious communion.

felon *n* criminal. **felony** *n*.

felt[1] *v pt* and *pp* of **feel.**

felt[2] *n* fabric whose fibres have not been woven but joined together by pressure.

female *n* person or animal of the sex that conceives and gives birth. *adj* designating a female. **feminine** *adj* **1** considered suitable to or representative of women or girls. **2** of a grammatical gender normally denoting females. **feminism** *n* **1** ideology or movement that advocates the equality of women. **feminist** *n,adj*.

fence *n* **1** structure enclosing an area or forming a barrier. **2** *inf* distributor of illegally obtained goods. **on the fence** indecisive; neutral. ~*vt* build a fence around or on. *vi* **1** participate in the sport of fencing. **2** evade questions or arguments. **fencing** *n* sport or activity of fighting with swords.

fend *v* **fend off** ward off (something). **fend for** provide for; support.

ferment *vt,vi* (fə'ment) undergo or cause fermentation. *n* ('fə:ment) **1** agent, such as yeast, that causes fermentation. **2** tumult; commotion. **fermentation** *n* chemical reaction in which sugar is changed into alcohol by action of microorganisms.

fern *n* plant with green feathery leaves that forms spores.

ferocious *adj* fierce; savage.

ferret *n* weasel-like animal used for hunting rabbits and rats. *vt* **1** drive out from cover. **2** *also* **ferret out** find; search out; seek.

ferry *n* boat or service used for transportation across a body of water. *vt,vi* transport or travel over water.

fertile *adj* **1** able to produce young. **2** capable of sustaining vegetation. **fertility** *n*. **fertilize** *vt* **1** cause the union of (a female reproductive cell) with sperm or a male reproductive cell. **2** make fertile. **fertilizer** *n* substance added to soil to increase crop yield.

fervour *n* ardour; zeal; passion. **fervent** *adj*.

fester *vi* **1** form pus. **2** become gradually resentful, bitter, etc.

festival *n* **1** celebration or feast. **2** series of cultural performances. **festivity** *n* **1** gaiety; merry-making. **2** feast or celebration.

festoon *n* **1** decorative chain of flowers, foliage, etc.; garland. **2** something that resembles a festoon. *vt,vi* decorate with or form festoons.

fetch *vt* **1** go and get; bring. **2** cost or sell for. **fetching** *adj* becoming or charming.

fete (feit) *n* **1** festival or celebration, esp. in aid of charity. **2** holiday. *vt* **1** entertain. **2** celebrate with a fete.

fetid *adj* smelling stale or rotten.

fetish *n* **1** object believed to have magic powers in certain cultures. **2** object or activity to which one is blindly devoted.

fetlock *n* part of a horse's leg above the hoof.

fetter *n* chain fastened to the ankle; shackle. *vt* restrain with fetters; shackle.

feud *n* long bitter hostility between two families, factions, etc. *vi* participate in a feud.

feudal *adj* of a social system based on land ownership and on ties between lords and vassals. **feudalism** *n*.

fever *n* **1** abnormally high body temperature. **2** disease characterized by fever. **3** extreme excitement. **feverish** *adj*.

few *adj* not many; small number of. *n* small number. **quite a few** large number.

fiancé *n* engaged man. **fiancée** *f n*.

fiasco *n* disaster; absolute failure.

fib *inf n* harmless lie. *vi* (-bb-) tell fibs. **fibber** *n*.

fibre *n* **1** yarn or cloth or the filaments from which they are made. **2** thread; filament. **3** structure or substance. **4** character; nature. **fibreglass** *n* **1** fabric made from pressed or woven glass fibres. **2** material made by binding glass fibres with synthetic resin.

fickle *adj* not faithful; changeable.

fiction *n* **1** literary works not based on fact. **2** falsehood; lie. **3** act of lying. **fictional** *adj*. **fictitious** *adj* not genuine; false.

fiddle *n* **1** *inf* violin. **2** *inf* illegal or fraudulent dealing or arrangement. *vi* **1** play on a fiddle. **2** fidget or tamper with. *vt* do something deceptively or illegally.

fidelity *n* **1** faithfulness or devotion to duty, a cause, person, etc.; loyalty. **2** truthfulness. **3** faithfulness of reproduction in sound recording.

fidget *vi* **1** be restless or uneasy. **2** play with or handle something in a restless manner. **fidgety** *adj*.

field *n* **1** open plot of land, esp. one for pasture

or crops. **2** tract of land on which sports are played; pitch. **3** battleground. **4** area rich in minerals, etc. **5** area of knowledge, study, etc. **6** area away from normal working quarters where new data or material can be collected. **7** the side that is not batting in a game of cricket. *vt* stop or recover (the ball) in cricket. **fieldwork** *n* work done away from normal working quarters for purposes of research, investigation, etc.

fiend *n* **1** evil spirit. **2** wicked or cruel person. **3** *inf* fanatic; addict. **fiendish** *adj* cruel; wicked.

fierce *adj* savage; wild; ferocious.

fiery *adj* **1** of or like fire. **2** emotional; passionate. **3** causing a feeling of burning.

fifteen *n* **1** number that is five more than ten. **2** fifteen things or people. *adj* amounting to fifteen. **fifteenth** *adj,adv,n*.

fifth *adj* coming between fourth and sixth in a sequence. *n* **1** one of five equal parts; one divided by five. **2** fifth person, object, etc. *adv* after the fourth.

fifty *n* **1** number equal to five times ten. **2** fifty things or people. *adj* amounting to fifty. **fiftieth** *adj,adv,n*.

fig *n* plant bearing sweet fleshy fruit, which is sometimes dried.

fight *n* **1** battle; combat. **2** quarrel; conflict. **3** boxing contest. *vt,vi* (fought) **1** struggle against (a person) in physical combat. **2** contend with (a person, situation, etc.). **3** support or campaign (for). **4** box. **fighter** *n*.

figment *n* invention; fiction.

figurative *adj* not literal; metaphorical.

figure *n* **1** symbol for a number. **2** amount; number. **3** shape; form. **4** person. **5** pattern; design. *vt,vi* **1** calculate. **2** mark with a pattern, diagram, etc. *vi* be important; feature. **figure out** *inf* solve; think out. **figurehead** *n* person who is an apparent leader, but with no real power.

filament *n* **1** thin wire inside a light bulb. **2** single strand of fibre.

file¹ *n* **1** holder for the orderly storage of documents. **2** correspondence or information on a particular subject, person, etc. **3** row or line. **on file** in a file; recorded. ~*vt* **1** keep or put in a file. **2** institute (a legal suit). *vi* proceed in a row. **filing cabinet** *n* cabinet designed for orderly storage of documents.

file² *n* **1** hand tool with a blade that has small cutting teeth. **2** nailfile.

filial *adj* of or suitable to a son or daughter.

fill *vt* **1** make full to capacity. **2** extend; permeate. **3** insert material into (an opening). **4** fulfil (a requirement). **5** cover, as with writing, etc. **6** do or perform the duties of (a job). **7** hire or elect for. **fill in 1** supply information on a form. **2** be a substitute for. **3** insert. **4** fill up (a hole, gap, etc.). **fill out** become or make fuller. *n* **one's fill** enough; one's limit.

fillet *n* piece of boneless meat or boned fish. *vt* remove the bones from (meat or fish).

filly *n* female horse or pony of under four years.

film *n* **1** cellulose that has been specially treated for making photographs, negatives, etc. **2** sequence of pictures projected onto a screen in a cinema or transmitted on television, etc. **3** thin layer or coating. *vt* take moving pictures with a cinecamera. *vt,vi* cover or be covered with a film.

filter *n* **1** substance or device through which fluid is passed to remove particles, impurities, etc. **2** device which allows only certain signals, kinds of light, etc., to pass through. *vt,vi* pass through a filter. *vi* become known or occur slowly.

filth *n* **1** dirt, squalor, or pollution. **2** obscenity. **filthy** *adj*.

fin *n* wing-like organ of a fish, used for locomotion.

final *adj* **1** last; ultimate. **2** decisive; conclusive. **finally** *adv*. **finalize** *vt* conclude or arrange.

finance (fiˈnæns, ˈfainæns) *n* study or system of public revenue and expenditure. *vt* provide funds for. **finances** *pl n* monetary affairs, resources, etc. **financial** *adj*. **financially** *adv*. **financier** *n* person engaged in finance, esp. on a large scale.

finch *n* small bird that feeds mainly on seeds.

find *vt* (found) **1** discover or come upon. **2** become aware of. **3** regard or consider as being. **4** determine; arrive at (a conclusion). **5** provide. *n* lucky discovery, bargain, etc.

fine¹ *adj* **1** superior in quality, skill, or ability. **2** pleasurable. **3** minute, powdered, or thin. **4** (of weather) clear and dry. **5** in good health or condition. **6** subtle or acute. **7** refined; well-mannered. *adv inf* very well; in good health. **finely** *adv*. **fine arts** *pl n* painting, sculpture, architecture, etc.

fine² *n* amount of money paid as a penalty for a crime, offence, etc. *vt* impose a fine on.

finery *n* showy or elaborate dress, jewellery, etc.

finesse (fi'nes) *n* delicate or subtle skill.

finger *n* any of the five appendages attached to the hand. *vt* handle; touch with the fingers. **fingermark** *n* smudge made by a finger. **fingerprint** *n* impression of the pattern on the underside of the end joint of a finger.

finish *vt,vi* end; complete; conclude; terminate. *vt* **1** use up; consume. **2** perfect. **3** put a finish on. *n* **1** final stage; completion; conclusion; end. **2** surface or texture of a material or a preparation used to produce this. **3** refinement; elegance.

finite *adj* bounded or limited.

fiord *n also* **fjord** narrow inlet of the sea between high cliffs.

fir *n* coniferous tree with needle-like leaves.

fire *n* **1** state of burning or combustion. **2** mass of burning material. **3** any device for heating a room. **4** something that resembles a fire. **5** discharge of a firearm. **6** passion or enthusiasm. **7** liveliness or brilliance. *vt,vi* (of a firearm or explosive) discharge or be discharged. *vt* **1** *inf* terminate (someone's) employment. **2** expose to heat, as clay in a kiln. **3** provide the fuel for. **firearm** *n* weapon from which a bullet, etc., is propelled by means of an explosion. **fire brigade** *n* group of persons trained in fire-fighting. **fire drill** *n* practice of emergency measures to be taken in case of fire. **fire engine** *n* motor vehicle equipped with fire-fighting apparatus. **fire-escape** *n* staircase or other means of escape in the event of a fire. **fireman** *n, pl* **-men** man specially trained in fire-fighting. **fireplace** *n* recess in a wall for a fire. **fire station** *n* building where fire engines are housed and where firemen are stationed. **firework** *n* device made from combustible material that is lit for entertainment. **firing squad** *n* group of men who carry out a death sentence by shooting.

firm[1] *adj* **1** hard; solid. **2** stationary; secured. **3** settled; established. **4** steadfast; resolute. **firmly** *adv*. **firmness** *n*.

firm[2] *n* business concern; company.

first *adj* coming before all others. *adv* **1** before any other. **2** for the first time. *n* **1** beginning. **2** highest honours degree. **first aid** *n* emergency medical aid administered before professional help is available. **first-class** *adj* best or most expensive; belonging to the highest grade. *adv* by first-class means. **first-hand** *adj,adv* from the original source. **first person** *n* form of a pronoun or verb when the speaker is the subject. **first-rate** *adj* of the best kind or class.

fiscal *adj* relating to state finances.

fish *n, pl* **fish** *or* **fishes** **1** any of a large group of aquatic animals, usually having gills and fins. **2** flesh of this animal used for food. *vi* **1** catch or attempt to catch fish. **2** *also* **fish out** obtain from an inaccessible place. **3** draw out, as by hinting or questioning. *vt* fish in (a particular body of water). **fisherman** *n, pl* **-men** man who catches fish for a living. **fishmonger** *n* person who sells fish.

fission *n* **1** breaking into parts or bits. **2** *also* **nuclear fission** splitting of the nucleus of atoms, used in atom bombs and as a source of energy.

fist *n* closed or clenched hand.

fit[1] *vt,vi* (-tt-) **1** make or be suitable or well adapted for. **2** be proper or correct for. **3** adjust to make (something) appropriate. **4** qualify or make competent. **5** alter (clothing) for a particular person. *adj* **1** suitable or well adapted. **2** competent. **3** healthy; well. **4** worthy. **5** ready or inclined to. *n* **1** way in which something fits. **2** something that fits. **3** process of fitting. **fitting** *adj* appropriate; suitable.

fit[2] *n* **1** attack; seizure; convulsion. **2** period or spell of emotion, activity, etc. **fitful** *adj* coming on in or characterized by sudden irregular spells.

five *n* **1** number equal to one plus four. **2** group of five persons, things, etc. **3** *also* **five o'clock** five hours after noon or midnight. *adj* amounting to five.

fix *vt,vi* fasten; secure; attach. *vt* **1** settle; determine. **2** assign; allot. **3** repair; mend; correct. *n* **1** *inf* predicament; dilemma. **2** *sl* injection of a narcotic. **fixation** *n* compulsive preoccupation with or concentration on (a particular object, idea, etc.). **fixture** *n* **1** household appliance that is firmly or permanently attached. **2** person regarded as being permanently installed in a particular place, position, etc. **3** scheduled football match, sports meeting, etc.

fizz *vi* bubble; effervesce. *n* **1** hiss. **2** effervescence. **3** drink containing soda water or sparkling wine.

fizzle *vi* **1** hiss; make bubbling sounds. **2** *inf also* **fizzle out** die out after an energetic start.

fjord *n* fiord.

flabbergasted *adj* amazed; astonished.

flabby *adj* **1** without firmness; soft. **2** having limp flesh. **3** lacking vitality; listless. **flabbiness** *n*.

flag[1] *n* piece of cloth decorated with an emblem or symbol. *vt* (-gg-) **1** decorate with flags. **2** signal with flags.

flag[2] *vi* (-gg-) become limp or weak; tire.

flagon *n* vessel for holding liquids.

flagrant *adj* blatant; glaring.

flair *n* **1** ability or aptitude. **2** style; elegance.

flake *n* thin layer or piece. *vt,vi* **1** peel off in flakes or chips. **2** cover with flakes. **flaky** *adj*.

flamboyant *adj* showy; ostentatious; extravagant. **flamboyance** *n*.

flame *n* **1** blaze or fire. **2** ardour; passion. *vt,vi* burn. *vi* flash; be inflamed.

flamingo *n, pl* **flamingos** *or* **flamingoes** large wading bird with bright pinkish red plumage and long legs.

flammable *adj* capable of burning; inflammable.

flan *n* open tart, either savoury or sweet.

flank *n* **1** part of the body of man or animals between the ribs and hip. **2** cut of beef from this area. **3** either side of a body of armed troops, ships, etc. *vt,vi* **1** place or be next to. **2** go round the flank of (an enemy).

flannel *n* **1** light fabric with a short nap. **2** piece of cloth used for washing the body. **3** *inf* evasive speech, explanation, etc. *vt* (-ll-) clean or polish with a flannel.

flap *v* (-pp-) *vt,vi* swing or flutter. *vi* panic; become agitated or upset. *n* **1** action or sound made by flapping. **2** flat sheet attached at one end, used to cover an opening, etc. **3** *inf* state of panic or distress.

flare *vt,vi* **1** burn with an unsteady or sudden flame. **2** spread outwards in a wedge shape. *vi* develop quickly; break out. **flare up** suffer a sudden outburst of anger, violence, etc. ~*n* **1** sudden burst of flame, sometimes used as a signal. **2** spreading or tapering section. **3** sudden burst of emotion, etc.

flash *n* **1** flame; flare. **2** outburst. **3** instant; moment. **4** display. *adj also* **flashy** **1** ostentatious or gaudy. **2** counterfeit; false. *vi* **1** move quickly; race. **2** occur suddenly. **3** send out a sudden intermittent bright light. *vt* **1** send a signal or message by means of a flash. **2** *inf* display ostentatiously. **flashback** *n* abrupt change of scene to one earlier in time in a play, film, etc. **flashbulb** *n* bulb producing a bright flash used to take photographs. **flashlight** *n* **1** source of intermittent or flashing light. **2** electric torch.

flask *n* bottle or similar container for liquids.

flat[1] *adj* **1** horizontal; level; even or smooth. **2** low; prostrate. **3** collapsed or deflated. **4** unqualified; outright. **5** dull; lifeless. **6** insipid; stale. **7** pointless. **8** having a pitch below the true pitch; half a semitone below a specified note. *adv* **1** horizontally. **2** absolutely; definitely. *n* **1** flat surface, piece of land, etc. **2** deflated tyre. **3** flat musical note. **flatfish** *n, pl* **-fish** fish that swims horizontally and has both eyes on the uppermost side of the body, such as plaice, sole, etc. **flat-footed** *adj* having feet with flattened arches. **flatten** *vt,vi* make or become flat.

flat[2] *n* room or set of rooms in a building, used as a self-contained dwelling.

flatter *vt,vi* **1** praise insincerely or immoderately. **2** show to advantage. **3** please by paying compliments or attention to. **flattery** *n*.

flaunt *vt,vi* **1** show off. **2** wave or flutter.

flautist *n* person who plays the flute.

flavour *n* **1** taste. **2** seasoning or extract. **3** essence; characteristic quality. **4** smell; aroma. *vt* give a flavour to. **flavouring** *n* seasoning.

flaw *n* defect; imperfection; blemish. **flawless** *adj*.

flax *n* plant producing fibres used in the manufacture of linen, paper, etc.

flea *n* small blood-sucking insect, a parasite on mammals and birds, noted for its ability to leap.

fleck *n* speck; spot.

flee *vt,vi* (fled) run away (from).

fleece *n* **1** woollen coat of a sheep, etc. **2** something resembling this. *vt* **1** shear (a sheep). **2** swindle.

fleet[1] *n* **1** large number of warships functioning as a unit. **2** nation's navy. **3** group of aeroplanes, motor vehicles, ships, etc., operated by the same company.

fleet[2] *adj* moving quickly; fast. **fleeting** *adj* passing quickly; transitory.

flesh *n* **1** soft body tissue of animals or man. **2** skin; body surface. **3** thick pulpy part of a fruit or vegetable. **4** man's physical nature, as opposed to his spiritual side. **5** one's family. **fleshy** *adj*.

flew *v pt* of **fly**[1].

flex *vt,vi* bend. *n* insulated cable for connecting an appliance with a source of electricity. **flexible** *adj* **1** pliable; supple. **2** adaptable or yielding. **flexibility** *n*.

flick *n* sudden light stroke. *vt* strike, move, or remove with a sudden jerky movement. **the flicks** *pl n inf* cinema.

flicker *vi,n* **1** flash; glimmer. **2** flutter; flap.

flight[1] *n* **1** act, ability, or manner of flying. **2** route taken by an airborne animal or object. **3** trip or journey of or on an aircraft or spacecraft. **4** soaring mental digression. **5** fin fitted to a dart, arrow, etc., to stabilize its flight. **6** set of steps or stairs. **flighty** *adj* irresponsible; frivolous or erratic.

flight[2] *n* act of fleeing, as from danger.

flimsy *adj* **1** weak or insubstantial. **2** (of paper, fabrics, etc.) thin.

flinch *vi* **1** withdraw suddenly, as if from pain or shock; wince. **2** avoid; shirk.

fling *v* (flung) *vt* **1** toss or hurl; throw forcefully. **2** cast aside; abandon. *vi* move quickly and violently. *n* **1** instance of flinging. **2** period of unrestrained or irresponsible behaviour. **3** any of several lively Scottish dances.

flint *n* **1** hard dark grey stone. **2** small piece of this stone used for striking fires.

flip *v* (-pp-) *vt* toss lightly or carelessly. *vt,vi* move with a jerky motion; flick. *n* **1** tap; flick. **2** alcoholic drink containing egg. **flipper** *n* **1** broad flat limb of certain aquatic animals, used for swimming. **2** paddle-like device worn on the feet for use in swimming.

flippant *adj* impertinent or impudent. **flippancy** *n*.

flirt *vi* **1** behave as if one is amorously attracted to another person. **2** trifle or toy (with an idea, situation, etc.). **flirtation** *n*. **flirtatious** *adj*.

flit *vi* (-tt-) **1** dart; skim along; flutter. **2** pass or pass away quickly. *n* rapid movement; flutter.

float *vt,vi* **1** suspend or be suspended on the surface of a liquid. **2** move lightly through the air or through a liquid. **3** come or bring to mind vaguely. *vt* **1** circulate (a rumour, idea, etc.). **2** offer (stocks, bonds, etc.) for sale on the market. *n* **1** something that floats. **2** small floating object attached to a fishing line. **3** light electrically powered vehicle, as for delivering milk, etc.

flock[1] *n* **1** group of sheep, goats, birds, etc., that keep or are kept together. **2** crowd of people. *vi* **1** gather or cluster together. **2** go or attend in large numbers.

flock[2] *n* **1** tuft of wool, cotton, etc. **2** wool remnants used for mattress stuffing, etc.

flog *vt* (-gg-) **1** beat or whip. **2** *sl* sell.

flood *n* **1** overflowing of water on usually dry ground. **2** great outpouring or gush. **3** rising tide. *vt,vi* **1** cover or be covered in quantities of water. **2** overflow or cause to overflow. **3** overwhelm or be overwhelmed with a great quantity of something. **4** cover or fill completely; saturate. *vi* flow copiously; gush. **floodlight** *n* artificial light that illuminates an area evenly. *vt* illuminate with or as if with a floodlight.

floor *n* **1** lowest horizontal surface of a room, compartment, etc. **2** storey. **3** bottom of a river, ocean, cave, etc. **4** area used for a particular purpose. *vt,vi* cover with or make a floor. *vt* **1** knock over or down. **2** defeat or confound. **floorboard** *n* board in a wooden floor.

flop *v* (-pp-) *vi,vt* **1** fall or drop quickly or clumsily. **2** flap; flutter clumsily. *vi inf* fail. *n* failure.

flora *n, pl* **floras** *or* **florae** ('flɔːriː) **1** plant life of a particular area or time period. **2** catalogue of such plant life. **floral** *adj* of flowers. **florist** *n* person who sells flowers or plants.

flounce[1] *vi* move or go with angry or jerky movements. *n* instance of flouncing.

flounce[2] *n* ruffle used to ornament a garment, etc.

flounder[1] *vi* stumble or plod; move or act with difficulty.

flounder[2] *n* common marine flatfish.

flour *n* powdered wheat or other grain, used in baking and cooking. *vt* **1** make into flour or a fine powder. **2** sprinkle or cover with flour.

flourish *vi* **1** thrive; prosper. **2** make a display; show off. *vt* wave in the air. *n* **1** ostentation; show. **2** embellishment. **3** showy musical passage.

flout *vt,vi* mock; show contempt (for).

flow *vi* **1** (of liquids) move in a stream; circulate. **2** move or proceed as if in a stream. **3** hang loosely. **4** abound. *n* **1** act or rate of flowing. **2** current; stream. **3** continuity. **4** amount that flows. **5** outpouring; flood; overflowing.

flower *n* **1** blossom or a plant that bears a blossom. **2** finest period, part, example, etc. **3** ornament or embellishment. *vi* **1** bear flowers; blossom. **2** mature; develop fully. *vt* cover or adorn with flowers. **flowery** *adj* **1** covered with flowers. **2** ornate; highly embellished.

flown *v pp* of **fly**[1].

fluctuate *vi* waver; change; vary. **fluctuation** *n*.

flue *n* pipe or passage conducting hot gases, air, etc., from a fireplace or boiler.

fluent *adj* **1** speaking or writing a foreign language well. **2** spoken or written well and with ease. **3** flowing, smooth, or graceful. **fluency** *n*. **fluently** *adv*.

fluff *n* light downy particles or material. *vt,vi* make or become fluffy or like fluff. **fluffy** *adj*.

fluid *n* **1** liquid substance. **2** (in physics) liquid or a gas. *adj* **1** capable of flowing. **2** changing; not stable.

flung *v pt* and *pp* of **fling.**

fluorescent *adj* giving off light by the influence of radiation, electrons, etc.; luminous. **fluorescence** *n*.

fluoride *n* **1** chemical compound of fluorine. **2** sodium fluoride added to the water supply to reduce tooth decay.

fluorine *n* yellow poisonous corrosive gaseous element.

flush[1] *vt,vi* **1** blush or make blush; glow. **2** flow or cause to flow with water, etc. *vt* excite; exhilarate. *n* **1** blush; rosy colour; ruddiness. **2** emotion; exhilaration. **3** hot feeling; fever.

flush[2] *adj,adv* level; even. *adj* **1** *inf* affluent. **2** *inf* plentiful; easily obtainable. **3** vigorous. **4** full; almost overflowing.

fluster *vt,vi* make or become nervous or confused. *n* state of nervousness or confusion.

flute *n* **1** musical wind instrument made of wood or metal. **2** narrow rounded channel or groove, as in pillars, etc. *vt* cut flutes in.

flutter *vt,vi* **1** wave or flap. **2** make or be nervous; fluster. *vi* **1** fall or move with irregular motion. **2** move uneasily or aimlessly. *n* **1** flap; wave. **2** state of nervousness. **3** excitement; sensation. **4** distortion of higher frequencies in record-players, radios, etc. **5** *inf* gamble; wager.

flux *n* **1** flow. **2** continuous change.

fly[1] *v* (flew; flown) *vi* **1** move through the air; take wing; soar. **2** move quickly or rapidly. **3** vanish; disappear. *vt,vi* **1** travel in or operate (an aircraft). **2** float; glide; flutter. **3** transport or be transported by aircraft. *n* strip of fabric concealing the zip on trousers. **flyover** *n* road intersection having a bridge that passes over another road.

fly[2] *n* any of certain two-winged insects, such as the housefly.

foal *n* horse, ass, etc., less than one year old. *vt,vi* (of horses, etc.) give birth (to).

foam *n* **1** mass of tiny bubbles, as soap suds. **2** sweat of a horse. **3** frothy saliva. **4** lightweight porous substance made from rubber, plastic, etc. *vi,vt* produce foam; froth; lather.

focus *n, pl* **focuses** *or* **foci** ('fousai) **1** point to which light converges or from which it appears to diverge by the action of a lens or curved mirror. **2** central point, as of attraction or interest. *vt,vi* **1** bring or come to a focus. **2** concentrate (on). **focal** *adj*.

fodder *n* feed for livestock.

foe *n* enemy; opponent.

foetus *n* young of an animal or person while still developing in the womb.

fog *n* **1** cloudlike mass of water vapour near the ground. **2** bewilderment; confusion. *vt,vi* (-gg-) **1** surround or be surrounded with fog. **2** blur; confuse; obscure. **foggy** *adj*. **foghorn** *n* loud horn used to signal warning to ships, etc., in foggy weather.

foible *n* slight weakness or fault; failing.

foil[1] *vt* frustrate; thwart.

foil[2] *n* thin flexible metal sheet.

foil[3] *n* light flexible sword used in fencing.

foist *vt* impose or force (unwanted or inferior goods, etc.).

fold[1] *vt,vi* bend or double (paper, etc.) over itself. *vt* **1** position (the arms) with one round the other. **2** wrap up. **3** wind; bend; enclose. *vi inf* fail; flop. *n* **1** section or mark made by folding. **2** act of folding.

fold[2] *n* enclosure for livestock, esp. sheep.

foliage *n* leaves of a plant.

folk *n* **1** people in general. **2** family; relatives. **folkdance** *n* traditional dance having common or popular origins. **folklore** *n* traditional legends, proverbs, etc., of a people. **folksong** *n* **1** song whose words and music have been passed down through the common people. **2** composition imitating such a song. **folktale** *n* traditional legend or tale.

follicle *n* small cavity or gland, such as that from which a hair grows.

follow *vt,vi* **1** go or come after. **2** result from; ensue. **3** comprehend or understand. **4** watch closely; monitor. *vt* **1** accompany. **2** keep to (a path, road, etc.); trace. **3** comply with; observe; conform to. **4** be interested in. **follower** *n*.

folly *n* **1** foolishness. **2** elaborate nonfunctional building erected to satisfy a whim, fancy, etc.

fond *adj* **1** affectionate; loving. **2** doting; indulgent. **be fond of** have a liking for; be pleased by. **fondness** *n*.

fondant *n* creamy sugary paste, used for sweets, icing, etc.

fondle *vt* touch or handle tenderly or with affection.

font *n* receptacle for baptismal water in a church.

food *n* **1** substance, esp. when solid, eaten for nourishment. **2** something that provides nourishment or stimulation.

fool *n* **1** senseless, silly, or stupid person. **2** jester; buffoon. *vt* deceive; trick; take in. *vi* act like a fool; joke or tease. **fool (around) with** behave stupidly or irresponsibly with. **foolish** *adj* **1** silly; senseless. **2** unwise; thoughtless. **foolishly** *adv*.

foot *n, pl* **feet 1** part of the end of the leg below the ankle. **2** similar part in animals. **3** unit of length equal to 12 inches (30.48 centimetres). **4** anything resembling a foot in form or purpose. **5** bottom or base. **6** way of walking. **on foot** walking or running. **football** *n* any of various team games in which a ball is kicked towards a goal. **footballer** *n*. **footbridge** *n* bridge for pedestrians. **foothold** *n* **1** place capable of providing support for a foot. **2** secure situation or position. **footing** *n* **1** foothold. **2** foundation or base. **3** status or level. **footlights** *pl n* row of lights along the front of the stage floor in a theatre. **footnote** *n* note printed on the bottom of a page giving additional information to the main text. **footprint** *n* mark made by a foot. **footwear** *n* articles worn on the feet, as shoes, boots, etc.

for *prep* **1** with the intention of. **2** intended to belong to. **3** towards. **4** over or across. **5** in support of. **6** to obtain. **7** suited to. **8** over a particular period or length of time. **9** instead of. **10** because of. **11** with regard to a norm. **12** as. **13** at a particular time. **14** to join in. **15** in spite of. *conj* because.

forage *n* **1** fodder. **2** search for food. *vt,vi* search for food, etc.

forbear *vt,vi* (-bore; -borne) abstain or refrain (from).

forbid *vt* (-dd-; -bad *or* -bade; -bidden) **1** prohibit. **2** hinder.

force *n* **1** strength; intensity; energy. **2** power or might. **3** power to affect; influence. **4** organized military group. **5** group of people organized for a particular purpose. **6** violence; coercion. **7** effectiveness; potency. **8** influence producing motion or strain in an object or material. *vt* **1** compel or oblige. **2** obtain through effort or by overpowering. **3** propel or drive. **4** break down or open; overpower. **5** impose; urge upon. **6** strain; labour. **forceful** *adj*. **forcefully** *adv*. **forcible** *adj* having or done through force. **forcibly** *adv*.

forceps *pl n* surgical pincers.

ford *n* area of a river, etc., shallow enough to be crossed on foot, horseback, etc. *vt* cross (a river, etc.) in this manner.

fore *adj* at or towards the front. *n* front section or area. *adv* at or towards the bow of a ship or boat.

forearm[1] ('fɔ:rɑ:m) *n* part of the arm between the elbow and wrist.

forearm[2] (fɔ:r'ɑ:m) *vt* arm beforehand.

forebear *n* ancestor.

forecast *vt,vi* predict; foretell. *vt* herald; anticipate. *n* prediction; estimate.

forecourt *n* court in front of a building, petrol station, etc.

forefather *n* ancestor; forebear.

forefinger *n* finger next to the thumb; index finger.

forefront *n* most outstanding or advanced position.

foreground *n* nearest part of a scene or view.

forehand *adj* **1** made or relating to the right side of a right-handed person or the left side of a left-handed person. **2** foremost; most important. *n* forehand stroke in tennis, squash, etc.

forehead *n* part of the face between the hairline and eyebrows.

foreign *adj* **1** in, from, dealing with, or relating to another country, people, or culture. **2** not familiar; alien. **3** not coming from or belonging to the place where found. **4** not pertinent or applicable; inappropriate. **foreigner** *n*.

foreleg *n* one of the front legs of a four-legged animal.

forelock *n* lock of hair growing above the forehead.

foreman *n, pl* **-men** person who supervises workers.

foremost *adj,adv* first in order, prominence, etc.

forensic *adj* relating to courts of law.

forerunner *n* **1** predecessor; forebear. **2** herald.

foresee *vt* (-saw; -seen) see or realize beforehand; anticipate.

foresight *n* **1** prudence, forethought, or precaution. **2** forecast.

forest *n* **1** large tree-covered tract of land. **2** anything resembling this in appearance, density, etc.

forestall *vt* **1** thwart or foil beforehand. **2** anticipate; consider in advance.

foretaste *n,vt* sample or taste in advance.

foretell *vt* (-told) predict; prophesy.

forethought *n* foresight; anticipation.

forfeit *n* **1** fine or penalty. **2** something lost in order to pay a fine or penalty. *vt* surrender or lose (something) as a forfeit. **forfeiture** *n*.

forge[1] *n* **1** place or furnace where metal is heated and worked. **2** device for hammering heated metal into shape. *vt* **1** hammer (heated metal) into a form. **2** make or produce. **3** invent or make up (a story, etc.). **4** duplicate or copy (a signature, money, etc.) **forgery** *n* act or result of illegally duplicating (a signature, money, etc.).

forge[2] *vi* move ahead or make progress, esp. slowly and with difficulty.

forget *v* (-got; -gotten) *vt,vi* fail to remember or recall. *vt* **1** neglect or ignore. **2** leave behind unintentionally. **forget oneself** **1** behave improperly. **2** forget one's position or station.

forgive *vt,vi* (-gave; -given) **1** pardon; excuse, acquit. **2** cease to blame or harbour ill will (for). **forgiveness** *n*.

forgo *vt* (-went; -gone) do without; deny oneself.

fork *n* **1** pronged instrument for holding and lifting, esp. one used at table or for gardening. **2** branching or dividing of a road, river, etc. **3** tuning fork. *vi,vt* divide as or with a fork.

forlorn *adj* **1** abandoned; deserted; forsaken. **2** desolate; miserable.

form *n* **1** shape; structure. **2** variety; type. **3** nature. **4** printed document with blank spaces to be filled in. **5** long backless bench. **6** class in a school. **7** conventional social behaviour. **8** formula; conventional procedure. **9** fitness or level of performance, as in a sport. *vt,vi* **1** make into or assume a particular shape, arrangement, or condition. **2** develop. **3** constitute; make up. **formation** *n*.

formal *adj* **1** relating or adhering to set conventions, rituals, behaviour, etc. **2** precise or symmetrical in form. **formally** *adv*. **formality** *n* **1** something done solely for the sake of custom or appearance. **2** state of being formal. **3** rigorous observation of ceremony, protocol, etc.

formation *n* **1** forming. **2** arrangement, as of a group of soldiers, aircraft, etc.

formative *adj* **1** relating to growth or development. **2** giving form.

former *adj* previous. *n* first of two things mentioned. **formerly** *adv*.

formidable *adj* **1** fearful; threatening; menacing. **2** difficult to resolve, conquer, etc. **3** awe-inspiring.

formula *n, pl* **formulas** *or* **formulae** ('fɔːmjuliː) **1** standard procedure or method for doing or expressing something. **2** mathematical relationship expressed, esp. in the form of an equation. **3** representation of the chemical structure of something. **formulaic** *adj*. **formulate** *vt* express in exact form or formula. **formulation** *n*.

forsake *vt* (-sook; -saken) **1** leave; desert; abandon. **2** renounce; forgo.

fort *n also* **fortress** fortified building or enclosure. **hold the fort** maintain or control during the absence of those usually in charge.

forte (fɔːt, 'fɔːtei) *n* person's strong point or particular ability.

forth *adv* **1** forwards; onwards. **2** out or away from. **forthcoming** *adj* **1** happening soon; imminent. **2** willing to talk; open; forward.

fortify *vt* strengthen or enrich. **fortification** *n*.

fortnight *n* two weeks; fourteen days. **fortnightly** *adv* every two weeks.

fortress *n* fort.

fortune *n* **1** amount of great wealth; bounty. **2** fate; destiny. **3** good luck. **fortunate** *adj* lucky; happy; favourable. **fortunately** *adv*. **fortune-teller** *n* person who predicts future events.

forty *n* **1** number equal to four times ten. **2** forty things or people. *adj* amounting to forty. **fortieth** *adj,adv,n*.

forum *n, pl* **forums** *or* **fora** ('fɔːrə) **1** meeting for discussion. **2** court or tribunal.

forward *adv* **1** onward; ahead; in advance. **2** out or forth. *adj* **1** well-advanced; ahead. **2** ready; prompt; eager. **3** bold; impertinent. **4** radical; progressive. **5** early; premature. *n* an attacking player in certain team games. *vt* send (a letter) on to a new address. **forwards** *adv* **1** towards the front; ahead. **2** into the future.

forwent *v pt* of **forgo.**

fossil *n* **1** remains or impression of a plant or animal of an earlier geological age. **2** *inf* old-fashioned person or thing. **fossilize** *vt,vi* make into or become a fossil.

foster *vt* **1** promote; encourage; further. **2** bring up; rear; nourish. **3** cherish; care for. **foster-parent** *n* person who takes care of another's child.

fought *v pt* and *pp* of **fight.**

foul *adj* **1** offensive; disgusting; repulsive. **2** filthy; squalid; polluted. **3** stormy; tempestuous. **4** wicked; shameful; infamous. **5** obscene; smutty; profane. **6** unfair; dishonourable; underhanded. *n* breaking of the rules (of a sport, game, etc.). *vt* **1** soil; defile; stain. **2** commit a foul on. *vt,vi* entangle or clog. *adv* unfairly. **foul play** *n* unfair or underhanded goings-on or behaviour.

found[1] *v pt* and *pp* of **find.**

found[2] *vt* set up; establish; organize. *vt,vi* base (on). **founder** *n.* **foundation** *n* **1** base or basis. **2** supporting base of a building, structure, etc. **3** organization or institution supported by an endowment. **4** cosmetic used to cover the skin.

founder *vt,vi* sink; fill with water. *vi* **1** break down or collapse. **2** stumble or fail.

foundry *n* place where metal is cast.

fountain *n* **1** jet or gush of water. **2** decorative structure producing jets of water. **fountain pen** *n* pen with a built-in ink reservoir or cartridge.

four *n* **1** number equal to one plus three. **2** group of four persons, things, etc. **3** *also* **four o'clock** four hours after noon or midnight. *adj* amounting to four. **fourth** *adj* coming between third and fifth in sequence. *adv* after the third. **four-poster** *n* bed having a post at each corner and sometimes a canopy. **foursome** *n* group of four.

fourteen *n* **1** number that is four more than ten. **2** fourteen people or things. *adj* amounting to fourteen. **fourteenth** *adj,adv,n.*

fowl *n* **1** hen or cock; chicken. **2** any bird that is hunted as game or used or bred for food. **3** flesh of these birds.

fox *n* **1** undomesticated doglike mammal having pointed ears and muzzle and a bushy tail. **2** fur of this animal. **3** sly or crafty person. *vt inf* trick or perplex. **foxhound** *n* hound trained and kept for foxhunting. **foxhunting** *n* sport in which people on horseback pursue a fox that is being chased by a pack of hounds.

foxglove *n* wild flower having trumpet-like purple or white flowers.

foyer ('fɔijei) *n* lobby or entrance hall.

fraction *n* **1** small part of something. **2** quantity that is not a whole number, often expressed as one number divided by another. **fractional** *adj* being a part, esp. a small part.

fracture *n* act of breaking or something broken, esp. a bone. *vt,vi* break.

fragile *adj* easily broken, marred, or damaged; frail. **fragility** *n.*

fragment *n* ('frægmənt) **1** broken-off part; chip. **2** incomplete portion or part. *vt,vi* (fræg'ment) break into fragments or bits. **fragmentation** *n.*

fragrant *adj* perfumed; sweet-smelling; aromatic. **fragrance** *n*

frail *adj* **1** weak; delicate; feeble. **2** fragile; breakable; brittle. **frailty** *n.*

frame *n* **1** supporting structure of anything. **2** form; basis. **3** surrounding structure, such as a border around a picture or mirror. **4** small glass structure for growing plants. **5** single picture in a film or television transmission. *vt* **1** surround with a frame. **2** support with a frame. **3** form the basic outlines of (a plan, theory, etc.). **4** *sl* incriminate (someone) by falsifying evidence. **framework** *n* **1** basis or outline. **2** structure that supports or sustains.

franc *n* monetary unit of France, Belgium, Switzerland, and several other countries.

franchise *n* **1** rights of citizenship, esp. the right to vote. **2** privilege granted by the government. **3** permission to market a product in a specified area.

frank *adj* **1** straightforward; honest; candid. **2** blunt; unrestrained; outright. **3** undisguised; avowed. *vt* mark (mail) so as to authorize for free delivery.

frankfurter *n* thin smoked sausage made of

beef or pork that is served hot, usually in a roll.

frantic *adj* agitated; frenzied; raving. **frantically** *adv*.

fraternal *adj* **1** of or relating to a brother. **2** brotherly; showing affection or support. **fraternally** *adv*. **fraternity** *n* **1** group of people with common interests or goals. **2** brotherhood; brotherly consideration and affection. **fraternize** *vi* associate or be friendly (with). **fraternization** *n*.

fraud *n* **1** deceit; trickery; deception. **2** something false or forged; counterfeit. **3** person who practises fraud. **fraudulent** *adj*.

fraught *adj* abounding in; full of.

fray[1] *n* noisy argument or brawl.

fray[2] *vt,vi* **1** unravel or wear away. **2** strain; vex; annoy. **3** rub or rub against.

freak *n* **1** deformed person, animal, or plant. **2** abnormal or odd thing, event, etc. **3** *sl* person deeply interested in something.

freckle *n* small brownish spot on the skin. *vt,vi* cover or be covered with freckles.

free *adj* **1** at liberty; independent; unfettered. **2** not restricted or regulated. **3** clear, immune, or exempt. **4** easy; firm or unimpeded. **5** loose; unattached. **6** available; unoccupied. **7** costing nothing; without charge. **8** frank or open. **9** liberal; generous. *vt* (freed) **1** liberate; set free; release. **2** exempt. **3** rid; clear. *adv* **1** *also* **freely** in a free manner. **2** without cost. **freedom** *n* **1** state or quality of being free; liberty. **2** immunity or privilege. **3** ease; facility. **4** frankness. **5** familiarity; lack of formality. **freehand** *adj* done by hand without the use of other aids. **freehold** *n* absolute ownership of land, property, etc. **freeholder** *n*. **freelance** *n also* **freelancer** self-employed writer, artist, etc. *adj* relating to a freelance. *adv* in the manner of a freelance. **free will** *n* doctrine that people have free choice and that their actions are not predetermined.

freeze *v* (froze; frozen) *vt,vi* **1** change into a solid by a drop in temperature. **2** cover, be, or become covered or blocked with ice. **3** attach (to). **4** be or cause to be motionless through terror, fear, surprise, etc. **5** be or make very cold. *vt* **1** preserve (food) by subjecting to extreme cold. **2** stabilize and prevent increases in (prices, incomes, etc.). *n* fixing of levels of prices, incomes, etc. **freezer** *n* refrigerator in which food can be deep-frozen; deep freeze.

freezing point *n* temperature at which a liquid freezes.

freight *n* **1** cargo; shipment; load. **2** transportation of goods.

French bean *n* thin green seed pod used as a vegetable.

French dressing *n* salad dressing made from oil and vinegar and usually seasoned.

French horn *n* coiled brass instrument with a mellow tone.

French window *n* door made of glass and wood that opens outwards.

frenzy *n* wild excitement or enthusiasm; rage. *vt* make very excited; enrage. **frenzied** *adj*.

frequent *adj* (ˈfriːkwənt) **1** occurring often and at short intervals. **2** habitual; usual. *vt* (friˈkwent) visit regularly or repeatedly. **frequently** *adv*. **frequency 1** state of being frequent. **2** rate of occurrence. **3** rate of repetition of a periodic process per unit time.

fresco *n, pl* **frescoes** *or* **frescos** technique or example of wall-painting in which pigments are applied to the plaster before it has dried.

fresh *adj* **1** new; recent. **2** additional; more. **3** (of food) not preserved in any way. **4** (of water) not salt. *adv* in a fresh manner. **freshly** *adv*. **freshness** *n*. **freshen** *vt,vi* make or become fresh. **freshwater** *adj* relating or indigenous to fresh water.

fret[1] *vt,vi* (-tt-) **1** worry; irritate; vex. **2** wear away; erode. *n* **1** annoyance; irritation; vexation. **2** erosion; eating away. **fretful** *adj*.

fret[2] *n* ornamental geometric pattern. *vt* (-tt-) adorn with such a pattern. **fretsaw** *n* fine narrow saw with a curved frame used for cutting designs. **fretwork** *n* interlacing geometric designs cut in thin wood.

friar *n* male member of a religious order supported by alms.

friction *n* **1** resistance met when two surfaces are rubbed together. **2** discord; conflict.

Friday *n* sixth day of the week.

fridge *n inf* refrigerator.

friend *n* **1** companion; intimate. **2** acquaintance; colleague. **3** ally. **friendly** *adj* **1** relating or fitting to a friend. **2** amicable or helpful. **friendliness** *n*. **friendship** *n* **1** being friends or a friend. **2** goodwill; benevolence.

frieze *n* ornamental band or border on a column, wall, etc.

fright *n* scare; alarm; dismay. **look a fright** look terrible or grotesque. **frighten** *vt* **1** scare;

terrify. **2** cause to worry or feel apprehensive about something. **frightful** *adj* dreadful; terrible. **frightfully** *adv* **1** dreadfully; terribly. **2** *inf* very.

frigid *adj* cold in manner, feeling, temperature, etc. **frigidity** *n*.

frill *n* **1** decorative ruffle. **2** trimming; ornamentation. *vt* decorate with frills.

fringe *n* **1** border or edging having hanging thread, tassels, flaps, etc. **2** section of hair cut short to hang over the forehead. **3** outer region; margin. *vt* provide with a fringe. *adj* additional; supplementary.

frisk *vi,vt* move about playfully. *vt inf* search or rob (a person) by examination of clothing. **frisky** *adj*.

fritter[1] *vt* waste (money, time, etc.).

fritter[2] *n* type of pancake dipped in batter and deep-fried.

frivolity *n* gaiety; revelry; merriment. **frivolous** *adj* **1** unimportant; trifling; petty. **2** idle; silly; foolish.

frizz *vt,vi* make or become tightly curled or kinky. **frizzy** *adj*.

frizzle[1] *vt,vi* frizz. *n* tight wiry curl.

frizzle[2] *vi* emit a hiss or sizzling noise. *vt* cook (meat, etc.) until crisp and dry.

fro *adv* from or back. **to and fro** back and forth.

frock *n* **1** dress. **2** monk's cloak. *vt* install (a cleric) in office.

frog *n* smooth-skinned web-footed amphibian. **have a frog in one's throat** speak hoarsely. **frogman** *n, pl* **-men** underwater diver.

frolic *n* gaiety or merry occasion. *vi* (-ck-) act in a lively playful manner. **frolicsome** *adj*.

from *prep* **1** indicating the original place or circumstance. **2** starting at. **3** indicating a distance between (two places). **3** indicating removal or restraint.

front *n* **1** forward position or side that is usually closest to a viewer or user. **2** beginning or opening part or section. **3** leading position. **4** separating area between two different masses of air. **5** *inf* cover; outward appearance. **6** alliance; coalition. *vt,vi* face (on). **frontal** *adj*. **frontally** *adv*.

frontier *n* **1** unexplored or unsettled area. **2** boundary.

frost *n* **1** (formation of) ice particles that are white in appearance. **2** below-freezing temperature. **3** *inf* coldness of attitude, manner, etc. *vt,vi* coat or be coated with frost or something similar. **frostbite** *n* injury to the body caused by exposure to extreme cold. **frostbitten** *adj*. **frosty** *adj*.

froth *n,vi,vt* foam.

frown *vi,n* scowl. **frown on** disapprove of.

froze *v pt* of **freeze. frozen** *v pp* of **freeze.**

frugal *adj* economical; thrifty. **frugality** *n*. **frugally** *adv*.

fruit *n* **1** produce of a plant, usually eaten raw or cooked as a sweet. **2** result; product. *vi* bear fruit. **fruit machine** *n* gambling machine with pictures of fruits as variables. **fruitful** *adj* prolific; fertile; productive. **fruitfully** *adv*. **fruitfulness** *n*. **fruitless** *adj* **1** yielding nothing; useless. **2** barren; sterile. **fruitlessly** *adv*. **fruition** (fruːˈiʃən) *n* **1** fulfilment or maturity. **2** bearing of fruit.

frustrate *vt* baffle; disconcert; foil. **frustration** *n*.

fry *vt,vi* cook in oil or fat.

fuchsia (ˈfjuːʃə) *n* ornamental plant or shrub yielding hanging red, purple, or white flowers.

fudge *n* thick sweet made of butter, sugar, cream, and flavouring.

fuel *n* substance that can be used to supply energy. *vt,vi* (-ll-) provide with or receive fuel.

fugitive *n* person who flees or hides.

fulcrum *n, pl* **fulcrums** *or* **fulcra** (ˈfulkrə) **1** pivot. **2** support; prop.

fulfil *vt* (-ll-) **1** carry out; complete. **2** perform; do; obey. **3** satisfy; gratify. **4** complete; terminate. **fulfilment** *n*.

full *adj* **1** filled to capacity. **2** having eaten as much as one can. **3** entire; complete. **4** enjoying all rights and privileges. **5** ample or plump. **full of** preoccupied with. ~*adv also* **fully** entirely; exactly. *n* **in full** in entirety. **to the full** to capacity. **full-length** *adj* **1** relating to the complete length; unabridged. **2** (of dresses and skirts) reaching the floor. **full stop** *n* punctuation mark (.) used to mark the end of a sentence. **full-time** *adj,adv* relating to or lasting normal working hours.

fumble *vi* **1** handle something clumsily. **2** grope; find one's way clumsily. *vi,vt* utter (something) in an awkward manner. **fumbler** *n*.

fume *vi* storm; rage. *vt,vi* smoke; give off (smoke). *n* smoke; vapour.

fun *n* enjoyment; pleasure; amusement. **make fun of** ridicule; tease. **funfair** *n* fair; amusement park.

function *n* **1** purpose; special or natural activity.

2 formal gathering. **3** variable factor. *vi* perform (as). **functional** *adj* **1** relating to a function. **2** useful rather than decorative or ornamental. **functionally** *adv*.

fund *n* store or reserve, esp. of money, resources, etc. *vt* supply with a fund or funds.

fundamental *adj* **1** basic; underlying; principal. **2** original; first. *n* principle; rule. **fundamentally** *adv*.

funeral *n* burial ceremony.

fungus *n, pl* **fungi** ('fʌndʒai) plant lacking chlorophyll, such as a mould, mushroom, etc.

funnel *n* **1** hollow tapering apparatus for transferring a substance to a more narrow-necked container. **2** something shaped like a funnel. *vt,vi* (-ll-) **1** pour through a funnel. **2** direct or channel. **3** fix attention or focus (on).

funny *adj* amusing; comical; humorous. **funnily** *adv*.

fur *n* **1** dense coat of an animal. **2** *inf* sediment caused by hard water. *v* (-rr-) *vt* decorate with fur. *vi,vt inf* cover or be covered with sediment.

furious *adj* raging; angry; violent. **furiously** *adv*.

furnace *n* apparatus equipped to produce steam, etc., by burning fuel.

furnish *vt* **1** provide furniture, carpets, etc., for. **2** equip or supply (with).

furniture *n* movable items such as tables, chairs, or beds, found in a house, office, etc.

furrow *n* **1** trench. **2** groove or line, esp. in the forehead. *vt,vi* make or become wrinkled or lined.

further *adv* **1** *also* **furthermore** moreover. **2** to a greater degree or distance. *adj* more. *vt* assist; help along. **furthest** *adv* to the most extreme degree or place. *adj* most.

furtive *adj* secret; sly. **furtively** *adv*.

fury *n* **1** passion; anger; frenzy. **2** violence; turbulence.

fuse[1] *vi,vt* **1** melt. **2** combine; blend. *n* safety device in plugs, electric wiring, etc. **fusion** *n* act of fusing; coming together.

fuse[2] *n* combustible wire or device leading to and capable of setting off an explosive. *vt* provide with a fuse.

fuselage *n* body of an aeroplane.

fuss *n* activity; ado; bustle. *vi* worry; be unduly preoccupied with. **fussy** *adj* **1** fussing; worrying. **2** preoccupied with petty details. **3** particular.

futile *adj* **1** ineffective; useless; unsuccessful. **2** trivial; frivolous. **futility** *n*.

future *n* **1** time that is yet to come. **2** prospects. *adj* yet to come.

fuzz *n* **1** fluffy or curly hairy mass. **2** blur. *vt,vi* make or become like fuzz. **fuzzy** *adj*.

G

gabble *vi,vt* speak rapidly and inarticulately. *n* rapid inarticulate speech.

gable *n* triangular part of a wall immediately below that part of a pitched roof that juts out.

gadget *n* ingenious, novel, or useful tool, device, or appliance. **gadgetry** *n* gadgets collectively.

gag[1] *n* something placed in or over the mouth in order to silence or control. *vt* (-gg-) place a gag on.

gag[2] *n inf* comedian's joke.

gaiety *n* jollity; light-heartedness; merriment.

gaily *adv* in a gay manner; light-heartedly.

gain *vt* **1** obtain; acquire; win; earn. **2** reach; attain. *vi* **1** increase; gather speed. **2** profit. *n* **1** advantage; win; profit. **2** increase; advancement. **gainful** *adj* profitable.

gait *n* manner of walking.

gala *n* special performance or display; festival.

galaxy *n* **1** large grouping of stars, such as the Milky Way. **2** impressive group of famous people. **galactic** *adj*.

gale *n* strong wind.

gallant *adj* ('gælənt) **1** dashing and brave; courageous. **2** ('gælənt, gə'lænt) chivalrous. *n* ('gælənt) **1** brave knight or nobleman. **2** attentive suitor. **gallantly** *adv*. **gallantry** *n*.

galleon *n* large sailing ship originally used by Spain.

gallery *n* **1** building or room(s) exhibiting works of art. **2** block of seats above the circle in a theatre. **3** upper floor or section opening out on to the interior of a hall, church, etc.

galley *n* **1** ship's kitchen. **2** warship propelled by oars. **3** long tray for holding metal type.

gallon *n* measure of liquid equal to approx. 4.5 litres (8 pints).

gallop *n* **1** the fastest gait of a horse or similar animal. **2** rapid movement or course. *vi,vt* ride at a gallop. *vi* race; move rapidly.

gallows *s n* wooden structure used for execution by hanging.

galore *adv* in abundance.

galvanism *n* process of producing electricity by chemical action. **galvanize** *vt* **1** coat with a metal by galvanism. **2** stimulate into action. **galvanic** *adj*.

gamble *vi,vt* **1** place a bet (on); stake. **2** risk; hazard; speculate. *vi* play at games of chance, esp. in order to win money. *n* risk; something of uncertain outcome; chance. **gambler** *n*.

game *n* **1** something played for amusement or sport. **2** match; contest. **3** certain wild animals that are hunted for sport or food. *vi* take part in games of chance such as roulette. *adj* willing; plucky. **gamekeeper** *n* person employed to take care of animals, fish, etc., on an estate, to prevent poaching, etc.

gammon *n* lower end of a side of bacon.

gander *n* male goose.

gang *n* **1** group of people, esp. one engaged in unlawful activity. **2** band of workers. *v* **gang up** (**on**) band together in order to attack. **gangster** *n* armed criminal, usually operating in a gang.

gangrene *n* death and putrefaction of part of a living organism caused by lack of blood supply.

gangway *n* **1** aisle or passageway separating blocks of seats. **2** movable bridge placed between a ship and the quay.

gaol *n,vt* jail. **gaoler** *n*.

gap *n* **1** opening; hole or space between two things. **2** interval; pause.

gape *vi* **1** stare in a stupid way, with astonishment, etc. **2** be wide open. *n* **1** open-mouthed stare. **2** split; hole; breach.

garage *n* **1** small building or shelter for a vehicle, esp. a car. **2** commercial premises selling petrol, repairing motor vehicles, etc.; service station.

garble *vt* give a muddled or misleading account of.

garden *n* **1** plot of land adjoining a house, where flowers, vegetables, etc., are cultivated. **2** small park. *vi* engage on work in a garden. **gardener** *n*. **gardening** *n*.

gargle *vi* rinse out the mouth and throat with liquid, which is kept moving by the action of air drawn up from the lungs. *n* mouthwash; rinse.

gargoyle *n* carved stone face, usually of a grotesque form and often functioning as a waterspout.

garish (ˈgɛəriʃ) *adj* gaudy; vulgar in taste, colour, etc.

garland *n* flowers, leaves, etc., woven into a ring and worn for decoration round the neck or on the head. *vt* decorate with a garland.

garlic *n* plant with a pungent bulbous root, which is used as a seasoning.

garment *n* item of clothing.

garnish *vt* add extra decoration, seasoning, etc., to (food). *n* trimmings or seasoning used to decorate or enhance the flavour of food.

garrison *n* military establishment where troops are stationed. *vt* station (troops, etc.) in a garrison.

garter *n* elasticated band worn round the leg to hold up a stocking or sock.

gas *n* **1** substance, such as nitrogen, oxygen, or carbon dioxide, that has no fixed volume or shape. **2** fuel in the form of gas. *vt* (-ss-) poison or asphyxiate with gas. **gaseous** (ˈgæsiəs, ˈgeiʃəs) *adj*.

gash *n* deep cut, wound, or tear. *vt* cut deeply; slash.

gasket *n* asbestos sheet used as a seal in an engine cylinder.

gasp *vi* **1** struggle to breathe; pant. **2** catch one's breath in surprise, shock, etc. **3** *inf* crave; long (for). *n* **1** sudden sharp intake of air. **2** strangled cry of surprise, etc.

gastric *adj* relating to the stomach.

gastronomic *adj* relating to the art of good eating. **gastronomy** *n*.

gate *n* wooden or metal structure forming a barrier across an opening in a fence, wall, etc. **gatecrash** *vt,vi* force one's way into (a party, meeting, etc.) as an uninvited guest. **gatecrasher** *n*.

gâteau *n, pl* **gâteaus** *or* **gâteaux** (ˈgætou) rich cake decorated with cream, fruit, nuts, etc.

gather *vi,vt* **1** collect together in a crowd or group; assemble; congregate. **2** increase in speed, intensity, etc. **3** draw thread through material to form pleats or folds. *vt* **1** amass; accumulate; collect. **2** pick or pluck (flowers, berries, etc.). **3** assume; understand; believe. **gathering** *n* assembly of people; congregation.

gauche (gouʃ) *adj* awkward; clumsy; ill at ease. **gaucheness** *n*.

gaudy *adj* brightly coloured; showy; garish. **gaudiness** *n*.

gauge (geidʒ) *n* **1** instrument for measuring

speed, temperature, pressure, etc. **2** standard or criterion. **3** thickness of metal. **4** width of a railway track. *vt* **1** measure or estimate the measurement of. **2** assess; judge.

gaunt *adj* thin and bony; haggard; angular.

gauze *n* thin loosely woven fabric used for surgical dressings, curtains, etc.

gave *v pt* of **give.**

gay *adj* **1** cheerful; bright; light-hearted; merry. **2** vivid; of a bright colour. *adj,n sl* homosexual.

gaze *vi* stare fixedly or for a considerable time. *n* fixed or long look or stare.

gazelle *n* small antelope of Africa and Asia.

gear *n* **1** mechanism consisting of a set of toothed wheels, such as that on a motor vehicle used for transmitting motion from the engine to the road wheels. **2** the engaging of a particular gear. **3** *inf* equipment or apparatus required for a particular activity. *vt* set up or arrange one thing to fit in with another.

geese *n pl* of **goose.**

gelatine *n also* **gelatin** yellowish protein obtained by boiling animal bones and skin, used in the manufacture of glue, jellies, etc. **gelatinous** *adj.*

gelignite *n* type of dynamite.

gem *n also* **gemstone** jewel created from a polished stone.

Gemini *n* third sign of the zodiac, represented by the Twins.

gender *n* **1** category, such as masculine, feminine, or neuter, into which nouns may be placed in some languages. **2** sexual identity.

gene *n* part of a chromosome carrying hereditary information.

genealogy *n* **1** descent through a line of ancestors; lineage. **2** family tree. **genealogical** *adj.*

general *adj* **1** not specific or particular; broad. **2** common; widespread; usual. **3** vague; indefinite. *n* military officer of a rank below that of field marshal. **general election** *n* nationwide election held to elect parliamentary representatives. **generalize** *vi,vt* come to a general conclusion from particular statements or facts. **generalization** *n.* **generally** *adv* **1** usually. **2** widely; commonly. **general practitioner** *n* doctor dealing with a wide range of cases rather than specializing in any particular area of medicine.

generate *vt* **1** create. **2** produce (electricity). **generation** *n* **1** production; creation. **2** whole range of people within the same general age group. **3** particular genealogical stage. **4** span of about 30 years. **generator** *n* machine producing electrical energy.

generic *adj* **1** relating to a genus. **2** representing a whole group or class.

generous *adj* **1** unselfish; not mean; kind. **2** tolerant; liberal. **3** ample; lavish. **generosity** *n.* **generously** *adv.*

genetic *adj* relating to genes or genetics. **genetics** *n* study of heredity.

genial *adj* amiable; friendly; warm. **geniality** *n.*

genitals *pl n* male or female sexual organs. **genital** *adj.*

genius *n* **1** person of exceptionally high intelligence or talent. **2** remarkable talent or ability.

genteel *adj* displaying extremely refined manners or taste.

gentile *n* non-Jewish person, esp. a Christian. *adj* non-Jewish.

gentle *adj* **1** not rough or violent. **2** mild. **3** docile; tame. **4** gradual. **gentleness** *n.* **gently** *adv.* **gentleman** *n, pl* **-men** **1** man who is cultured and well-mannered. **2** aristocrat or nobleman.

genuine *adj* **1** real; authentic; not false or artificial. **2** sincere. **genuinely** *adv.*

genus (ˈdʒenəs, ˈdʒiːnəs) *n, pl* **genera** (ˈdʒenərə) biological subdivision containing one or more species.

geography *n* **1** study of the features of the earth's surface. **2** physical features of a region. **geographer** *n.* **geographical** *adj.*

geology *n* study of the composition and evolution of the earth. **geological** *adj.* **geologist** *n.*

geometry *n* branch of mathematics concerned with the properties of figures in space. **geometric** *or* **geometrical** *adj.*

geranium *n* garden or house plant having pink, scarlet, or white flowers and roundish leaves.

germ *n* any microbe that causes disease.

German measles *n* contagious disease characterized by a rash and swelling of the glands.

germinate *vi,vt* **1** develop through warmth and moisture from a seed into a plant. **2** create; spring up. **germination** *n.*

gesticulate *vi* make wild or broad gestures. **gesticulation** *n.*

gesture *n* **1** movement of the arms or head. **2**

act of friendship, sympathy, etc. *vi,vt* express by means of gestures.

get *v* (-tt-; got) *vt* **1** obtain; acquire; gain possession of. **2** fetch. **3** cause to happen or be done. **4** *inf* grasp; understand. **5** make; force; persuade. *vi* **1** become; grow. **2** start. **3** go; proceed. **get about** *or* **around 1** be active. **2** move about; circulate. **get across** communicate so as to be understood. **get ahead** progress; continue. **get along 1** manage; cope. **2** succeed. **get at 1** reach. **2** intend; imply. **get away** escape. **get away with** remain undetected or unpunished. **get by** just about manage to cope adequately. **get down 1** descend. **2** depress; make unhappy. **get down to** begin to concentrate on. **get off 1** dismount or disembark. **2** be permitted to leave. **3** escape punishment. **get on 1** board (a bus, train, etc.). **2** mount (a horse, etc.). **3** make successful progress. **4** have a friendly relationship (with). **get over** recover from; come to terms with. **get round 1** cajole; persuade; bribe. **2** solve or resolve (a difficulty, problem, etc.) by using a different technique or approach. **get round to** find time for. **get through** (**to**) **1** contact by telephone. **2** make (someone) understand or listen. **get up 1** stand up. **2** get out of bed. **3** organize; arrange. **get up to** engage in, esp. when not being watched or controlled. **getaway** *n* escape.

geyser *n* **1** natural hot spring. **2** gas-fuelled water heater.

ghastly *adj* dreadful; shocking; gruesome; horrific.

gherkin *n* small cucumber used for pickling.

ghetto *n, pl* **ghettos** *or* **ghettoes 1** poor district or quarter in a city; slum area. **2** (formerly) poor Jewish quarter in a city.

ghost *n* supernatural being believed to be a dead person's soul, which returns to haunt the living; spirit. *vt,vi* write (a book) for another person, who is then acknowledged as the author.

giant *n* **1** abnormally tall person. **2** prominent or powerful person. **3** one of a race of huge mythological people with superhuman powers. *adj* huge; enormous.

gibberish *n* nonsense; gabbling speech.

gibbon *n* small long-armed ape.

giddy *adj* **1** dizzy. **2** frivolous. **giddiness** *n*.

gift *n* **1** present; donation. **2** talent. **gifted** *adj* talented.

gigantic *adj* very large; huge.

giggle *vi* laugh in a silly or uncontrolled manner. *n* silly laugh; chuckle.

gild *vt* (gilded *or* gilt) coat with gold, gold paint, etc.

gill[1] (gil) *n* respiratory organ of aquatic animals.

gill[2] (dʒil) *n* liquid measure equal to one quarter of a pint.

gimmick *n* device or method used to gain publicity, promote sales, etc.

gin *n* alcoholic drink made by distilling barley or rye and flavoured with juniper berries.

ginger *n* plant whose pungent root is used as a flavouring for drinks, confectionery, etc. *n,adj* reddish-orange; auburn. *v* **ginger up** *inf* enliven; give energy to.

gingerly *adv* cautiously; warily; uncertainly.

gingham *n* cotton fabric patterned with coloured checks or stripes.

Gipsy *n* Gypsy.

giraffe *n* African mammal with a mottled hide and very long neck.

girder *n* iron or steel beam; joist.

girdle *n* **1** cord or thin belt worn round the waist. **2** light corset. **3** band or circle. *vt* **1** fasten with a girdle. **2** encircle.

girl *n* **1** female child; young woman. **girlish** *adj*. **girlhood** *n*. **Girl Guide** *n* female member of an organization with aims similar to those of the Scouts.

giro *n* banking system whereby transfers between accounts may be made by special cheques.

girth *n* **1** leather strap secured under a horse's belly to hold a saddle in position. **2** measurement of circumference. *vt* secure with a girth.

give *v* (gave; given) *vt* **1** present as a gift; donate. **2** place into the hands of; offer; hand. **3** provide; supply. **4** be the cause of. **5** transmit or transfer. **6** yield; produce. **7** *also* **give out** emit or radiate. **8** grant; award; confer. **9** pay; offer to buy for. **10** set aside; allow; spare. **11** act as the host for (a party, meal, etc.). **12** administer (drugs, a punishment, etc.). **13** communicate; make known; tell. **14** inflict; cause to suffer. **15** utter. *vi* **1** donate. **2** be flexible or elastic. **3** *also* **give way** collapse or break under strain or pressure. **give away 1** dispose of; offer for no payment. **2** reveal; disclose. **give in** submit;

surrender. **give up** abandon; cease to do, study, care for, etc. ~*n* elasticity; flexibility.

glacier *n* mass of ice extending over a large area. **glacial** *adj*.

glad *adj* happy; pleased. **gladly** *adv*. **gladness** *n*. **gladden** *vt,vi* make or become glad; cheer.

gladiolus *n, pl* **gladioli** (glædi'oulai) *or* **gladioluses** plant with long narrow leaves and one stem bearing a brightly coloured flower.

glamour *n* attraction or attractiveness; allure; glittering charm. **glamorous** *adj*. **glamorize** *vt* make attractive or glamorous; exaggerate the charms of; idealize.

glance *vi* **1** take a brief look. **2** flash; shine. **glance off** bounce off sharply. ~*n* **1** brief look; glimpse. **2** quick movement of the eyes. **3** flash; spark.

gland *n* one of various organs in the body that secrete different substances. **glandular** *adj*.

glare *vi* **1** shine fiercely or dazzlingly. **2** stare angrily; glower; scowl. *n* **1** harsh blinding light; dazzle. **2** angry look.

glass *n* **1** hard brittle transparent material used in windows, vessels, etc. **2** drinking vessel made of glass. **3** mirror. **4** telescope. *vt* glaze. **glasses** *pl n* **1** spectacles. **2** binoculars. **glasshouse** *n* greenhouse or conservatory. **glassy** *adj* of or like glass.

glaze *vt,vi* **1** fit with glass. **2** apply or have a thin glassy coating. *n* shiny coating, esp. on ceramics.

gleam *n* beam of light; glow. *vi* shine; beam; glow.

glean *vt,vi* **1** gather (remnants of corn) after reaping. **2** collect painstakingly.

glee *n* mirth; cheerfulness; joy. **gleeful** *adj*. **gleefully** *adv*.

glen *n* (in Scotland) narrow valley.

glib *adj* smooth but insincere in manner. **glibly** *adv*. **glibness** *n*.

glide *vi,vt* move smoothly and noiselessly. *n* smooth flowing movement. **glider** *n* aircraft without an engine that moves according to air currents.

glimmer *vi* shine dimly or faintly. *n* **1** faint light. **2** slight hint or suggestion of hope, intelligence, etc.

glimpse *n* fleeting look; glance; brief view. *vt* see very briefly; get a partial view of.

glint *n* flash; sparkle; gleam. *vi* sparkle; glitter.

glisten *vi* sparkle; shine brightly.

glitter *vi* shine brilliantly; flash; twinkle. *n* sparkle; twinkle.

gloat *vi* take malicious pleasure in one's own greed, another's misfortune, etc.

globe *n* **1** the earth. **2** model of the earth. **3** spherical object; ball. **global** *adj*. **globule** *n* small drop, particle, or bubble.

gloom *n* **1** dim light; semi-darkness; shadow. **2** pessimism; cynicism; despondency; depression. **gloomy** *adj*. **gloomily** *adv*.

glory *n* **1** state of being highly honoured, revered, etc.; exaltation. **2** magnificence; splendour. **3** fame; renown. **glorify** *vt* exalt; treat with great reverence; worship or admire. **glorification** *n*. **glorious** *adj* **1** overwhelmingly beautiful; magnificent. **2** stunning. **3** highly distinguished; great. **gloriously** *adv*.

gloss *n* **1** bright or reflective surface or appearance; sheen; lustre. **2** *also* **gloss paint** type of paint giving a smooth shiny finish. *vt* polish; shine. **gloss over** try to hide; cover up mistakes, etc. **glossy** *adj* shiny.

glossary *n* explanatory list of specialist or technical terms or words.

glove *n* covering for the hand with individual sections for each finger and the thumb. *vt* cover with a glove.

glow *vi* **1** burn with a steady light; shine warmly or brightly. **2** radiate excitement, pride, enthusiasm, etc. *n* steady bright light; blaze. **glow-worm** *n* small beetle, the female of which possesses organs that give off a luminous greenish light.

glower ('glauə) *vi* scowl; frown; stare angrily. *n* angry stare; scowl.

glucose *n* type of sugar obtained from grapes and other fruits.

glue *n* substance used as an adhesive, made from gelatine, resin, etc. *vt* **1** stick with glue. **2** attach firmly.

glum *adj* disconsolate; unhappy; gloomy; sullen. **glumly** *adv*. **glumness** *n*.

glut *n* surfeit; excess. *vt* (-tt-) supply with an excess amount; provide with too much. *vi* gorge; overeat. **glutton** *n* **1** excessively greedy person; one who habitually overeats. **2** fanatic. **gluttony** *n*.

gnarled *adj* twisted and knotty; misshapen; lumpy.

gnash *vt* grind or clench (the teeth); grate. *n* grinding action or sound.

gnat *n* small mosquito.

gnaw *vt,vi* **1** bite continuously (on); chew. **2** corrode; wear away. **3** torment persistently. *n* act of gnawing.

gnome *n* mythological being living underground and having a dwarflike appearance.

go *v* (went; gone) *vi* **1** move; proceed. **2** function; work; operate. **3** depart; leave. **4** make a trip or take a walk with a particular purpose. **5** vanish; disappear. **6** extend as far as; reach. **7** become. **8** be put; belong. **9** be ordered; have as a sequence. **10** be used for. **11** fail; break down; collapse. **12** attend; be a member of. **13** be decided (by). **14** be able to fit. **15** be applicable or relevant. **16** be awarded. **17** be allowed to escape. *vt* **1** take or follow (a route, path, etc.). **2** travel (a specified distance). **go against** defy; infringe. **go down 1** descend. **2** be reduced. **3** deflate. **4** be received or appreciated by an audience. **go for 1** aim at. **2** attack suddenly. **go in for** take up as a hobby, career, etc. **go off 1** explode. **2** cease to be interested in. **3** happen. **4** (of food) turn bad. **go on 1** proceed; continue. **2** criticize or nag incessantly. **3** appear (on stage, TV, etc.). **4** take place; occur. **go out 1** be extinguished. **2** cease to be fashionable. **3** attend a social function. **go over 1** repeat; re-examine. **2** cross. **3** be communicated. **go slow** work slowly to enforce one's demands for more pay, etc. **go through 1** suffer; have to bear; experience. **2** make a search of. **3** inspect. **go under** succumb; sink. ~*n* **1** turn. **2** *inf* energy; drive. **go-between** *n* person acting as a messenger between parties; intermediary.

goad *n* **1** sharp pointed stick used for driving cattle. **2** provocation; stimulus. *vt* **1** drive or prod with a goad. **2** urge; incite; provoke.

goal *n* **1** area between two posts through which a ball must pass in games such as football or hockey in order to score. **2** winning post on a race track. **3** point scored by getting a ball through the goal. **4** aim; object; target. **goalkeeper** *n* player who guards the goal area.

goat *n* brownish-grey mammal often domesticated for its milk or wool. **get one's goat** irritate; annoy.

gobble[1] *vt,vi* eat quickly or greedily; gulp; bolt.

gobble[2] *vi* (of a turkey cock) make a harsh gurgling sound. *n* harsh gurgling sound.

goblet *n* drinking vessel with a long stem.

goblin *n* mythological being that is malevolent or mischievous; demon.

god *n* **1** supernatural being having power over mankind who is worshipped and revered; deity. **2** any object of worship or idolatry. **God** *n* spiritual being who is the creator and ruler of mankind. *interj* exclamation of disgust, horror, surprise, etc. **the gods** highest gallery in a theatre. **godchild** *n, pl* **-children** child for whom a godparent acts. **goddaughter** *n* female godchild. **godfather** *n* male godparent. **godfearing** *adj* intensely religious; pious. **godless** *adj* **1** having no religious beliefs. **2** wicked; evil. **godmother** *n* female godparent. **godparent** *n* person who acts as a sponsor for a child at baptism. **godsend** *n* timely and fortunate event or gift. **godson** *n* male godchild.

goddess *n* **1** female god. **2** extremely beautiful woman.

goggle *vi* **1** stare stupidly; gape. **2** roll the eyes. **goggles** *pl n* protective covering worn over the eyes.

going *n* **1** departure; leaving. **2** manner of travelling. *adj* thriving. **going to** intending to.

gold *n* **1** valuable yellow metal used for coins, jewellery, etc. **2** coins of this metal. **3** wealth; money; riches. *adj,n* bright yellowish-orange. **golden** *adj* **1** made of gold. **2** of the colour of gold. **3** valuable; precious. **golden syrup** *n* kind of treacle of a pale golden colour. **goldfinch** *n* European finch with gold and black plumage. **goldfish** *n* reddish-gold freshwater fish. **goldmine** *n* **1** place where gold ore is mined. **2** source of great wealth. **goldsmith** *n* craftsman who works with gold.

golf *n* sport played on a grass course with the aim of driving a small ball into a succession of holes with a long club. **golfer** *n*.

gondola *n* long narrow open boat traditionally used on the canals in Venice. **gondolier** *n* person who makes a living by transporting passengers in a gondola.

gone *v pp* of **go.**

gong *n* percussion instrument consisting of a large metal disc, which is struck with a hammer.

gonorrhoea (gɔnə'riə) *n* type of venereal disease.

good *adj* **1** of a high quality; not bad. **2** obedient; not naughty. **3** pleasing; attractive. **4** virtuous. **5** efficient; suitable. **6** kind;

benevolent. **7** beneficial. **8** correct; accurate. **9** able; competent. **10** fitting; apt. **11** considerable. **12** safe; not harmful. **13** full; complete. *n* **1** use; point. **2** benefit; advantage. **3** virtue. **for good** for ever; definitely and finally. **Good Friday** *n* Friday before Easter when Christ's Crucifixion is commemorated. **good-humoured** *adj* affable; in a good mood. **good-looking** *adj* handsome; attractive. **good-natured** *adj* kind; genial; easygoing. **goods** *pl n* **1** merchandise; products. **2** items; articles. **3** possessions; property. **good will** *n* **1** generosity; kindness. **2** assets, such as clientele, reputation, etc., taken into consideration when a business is bought or sold.

goose *n, pl* **geese** **1** web-footed bird that is similar to but larger than a duck. **2** foolish or timid person.

gooseberry *n* small edible green berry that grows on a bush with thorny stems.

gore[1] *n* blood that flows from a wound.

gore[2] *vt* stab and wound by ramming with horns or tusks.

gorge *n* **1** steep-sided river valley; ravine. **2** lavish feast. *vi,vt* stuff (oneself) with food; overeat; glut.

gorgeous *adj* very beautiful; magnificent; wonderful.

gorilla *n* large African ape.

gorse *n* prickly evergreen shrub with bright yellow flowers.

gory *adj* **1** covered with blood. **2** bloodthirsty; involving bloodshed. **3** horrifying.

gosh *interj* exclamation of surprise.

gosling *n* young goose.

gospel *n* something taken as the truth; doctrine. **Gospel** *n* one of the first four books of the New Testament, namely Matthew, Mark, Luke, and John.

gossip *vi* talk, esp. in a way that spreads scandal, rumours, etc. *n* **1** act of gossiping. **2** casual or malicious talk; news; scandal. **3** person who gossips.

got *v pt* and *pp* of **get. have got** possess; hold; own. **have got to** must.

gouge *vt* **1** carve a deep hole in with a sharp instrument. **2** tear or scoop out.

goulash *n* stew seasoned with paprika that is a traditional Hungarian dish.

gourd *n* large fruit of various plants, having a tough outer skin and a large number of seeds.

gourmand *n* glutton.

gourmet *n* connoisseur of good food and wine.

govern *vt,vi* **1** rule; reign (over); control. **2** participate in a government. *vt* **1** check; restrain. **2** determine; influence completely. **governess** *n* woman employed as a tutor in a private household. **government** *n* **1** control; rule. **2** body of representatives who govern a country, state, etc. **governor** *n* **1** ruler, esp. of a colony, province, etc. **2** person in charge of a prison. **3** chief controller of a state in the US. **4** *inf* boss. **governorship** *n*.

gown *n* **1** woman's dress, esp. for evening wear. **2** loose light garment, often signifying academic or official status; robe.

grab *vt,vi* (-bb-) **1** take hold of hastily, clumsily, or greedily; seize; snatch. **2** take possession of by force; confiscate. *n* **1** act of grabbing. **2** mechanical device for gripping large objects.

grace *n* **1** elegance, beauty, or charm of movement, style, etc. **2** good will; magnanimity; mercy. **3** short prayer of thanks offered before or after a meal. *vt* serve to add elegance or beauty to; adorn. **graceful** *adj*. **gracefully** *adv*. **gracious** *adj* **1** elegant; dignified. **2** benevolent; courteous; kind. *interj also* **good gracious!** expression of surprise or alarm.

grade *n* **1** position on a scale or in a category. **2** mark or score awarded in an examination, test, etc. *vt* **1** place in a category according to size, quality, etc. **2** award a mark or score to. **gradation** *n* **1** step or stage within a system or on a scale. **2** gradual progression or transition.

gradient *n* slope of a road, railway, etc., measured by the increase in height per distance travelled.

gradual *adj* **1** slowly changing. **2** not steep. **gradually** *adv*.

graduate *vi* ('grædju:eit) **1** receive a degree or diploma from a university, college, etc. **2** change gradually; move along a scale. **3** progress. *n* ('grædju:it) person holding a degree, diploma, etc. **graduation** *n*.

graffiti *pl n* scribbled messages or drawings on walls, public buildings, etc.

graft *n* **1** small plant shoot that is united with another plant in order to produce a new plant. **2** transplanted bone or skin tissue. *vt,vi* **1** propagate by means of a graft. **2** transplant or be transplanted.

grain *n* **1** fruit or seed of a cereal plant. **2** cereal crops. **3** small particle or granule of sand, sugar, etc. **4** pattern, texture, or arrangement of layers of a piece of timber, rock, etc. **5** minute quantity or proportion.

gram *n also* **gramme** metric unit of weight equivalent to approx. 0.035 ozs.

grammar *n* **1** system of rules governing the correct use of a language. **2** branch of linguistics concerned mainly with syntax and word formation. **grammar school** *n* (in Britain) state secondary school that selects pupils at the age of eleven by means of examination. **grammatical** *adj* relating or conforming to the rules of grammar. **grammatically** *adv*.

gramophone *n* machine for playing records, having a turntable, amplifier, and pick-up arm fitted with a stylus; record player.

granary *n* storage place for grain.

grand *adj* **1** impressively large; magnificent; tremendous. **2** haughty; elegant. **3** marvellous; great. **4** admirable; worthy. **5** final and complete. *n also* **grand piano** large piano whose strings are arranged horizontally rather than vertically. **grandeur** *n*. **grandly** *adv*. **grandchild** *n* grandson or granddaughter. **granddaughter** *n* daughter of one's son or daughter. **grandfather** *n* father of one's father or mother. **grandmother** *n* mother of one's father or mother. **grandparent** *n* grandfather or grandmother. **grandson** *n* son of one's son or daughter. **grandstand** *n* covered block of seats for spectators at a race meeting, football match, etc.

granite *n* hard greyish-white crystalline rock.

granny *n inf* grandmother.

grant *vt* **1** give as a favour. **2** admit; concede. **3** give (a sum of money). *n* sum of money given for research, education, etc.

granule *n* small grain. **granular** *adj*.

grape *n* small sweet green or purple fruit that is eaten raw, dried, or pressed to make wine. **grapevine** *n* **1** vine producing grapes. **2** informal or underground information network.

grapefruit *n* large round citrus fruit with a yellow peel.

graph *n* chart or diagram for depicting the relationship between variables, particular sets, quantities, etc. **graphic** *adj* **1** clearly or imaginatively expressed. **2** relating to writing or drawing. **3** in graph form.

graphite *n* soft black carbon, used in pencils, electrodes, etc.

grapple *vi* struggle physically; wrestle; tussle. **grapple with** attempt to deal with (a problem, difficult situation, etc.). ~*n* **1** iron hook. **2** grip in wrestling; hold.

grasp *vt,vi* **1** take hold (of) firmly in the hands; grip; clasp. *vt* understand; comprehend. *n* **1** firm grip. **2** knowledge; understanding. **3** power to dominate.

grass *n* **1** plant with green spiky blades. **2** lawn, field, or pasture of such plants. **3** *sl* marijuana. *vt,vi* sow with grass. *vi sl* act as an informer, esp. to the police. **grassy** *adj*. **grasshopper** *n* greenish-brown insect renowned for its characteristic chirping sound produced by friction of the hind legs against the wings. **grass roots** *pl n* **1** section of the population regarded as representing true political or public opinions at a local level. **2** underlying or essential principles.

grate[1] *vt* cut or shred (cheese, vegetables, etc.) by rubbing against a rough surface. *vt,vi* **1** produce a harsh squeak by scraping. **2** annoy; jar. *n* harsh squeak.

grate[2] *n* iron structure or rack placed in a fireplace to hold fuel and allowing air to circulate underneath.

grateful *adj* thankful; appreciative of kindness, a gift, opportunity, etc. **gratefully** *adv*.

gratify *vt* **1** seek or obtain satisfaction of (one's desires); indulge. **2** please; make happy. **gratification** *n*.

grating *n* cover or guard made of a network of metal bars; grille.

gratitude *n* feeling or expression of appreciation; thankfulness.

gratuity *n* gift of money; tip. **gratuitous** *adj* **1** free of charge. **2** not asked for or solicited; unjustified.

grave[1] *n* trench or hole dug in the ground for a coffin. **have one foot in the grave** be feeble or near to death.

grave[2] *adj* **1** serious; solemn. **2** dangerous; bad. **gravely** *adv*.

gravel *n* coarse mixture of fragments of rock.

gravity *n* **1** force of attraction between objects with mass, exerted by the earth, moon, etc., to pull objects towards their centre. **2** seriousness; solemn importance. **gravitate** *vi* **1** be drawn by the force of gravity. **2** be attracted to a certain place. **gravitation** *n*.

gravy *n* stock or juice produced by cooking meat, often thickened for a sauce.

graze[1] *vi,vt* feed or allow to feed on grass or other vegetation in a pasture.

graze[2] *vt,vi* touch lightly; scrape. *vt* produce a scratch or cut on the skin by scraping. *n* abrasion; scratch.

grease *n* **1** melted animal fat. **2** lubricant; oil. *vt* **1** cover or smear with grease. **2** lubricate. **greasy** *adj*. **greasepaint** *n* waxy substance used by actors as make-up for the stage.

great *adj* **1** large; big; huge; vast; tremendous. **2** excellent. **3** famous. **4** important; significant. **5** impressive; grand. **greatly** *adv*. **greatness** *n*.

greed *n* **1** desire to overeat; gluttony. **2** desire to take more than one's fair share of wealth, power, etc. **greedy** *adj*. **greedily** *adv*.

green *n* **1** colour of grass; spectral colour. **2** grass pitch or field. *adj* **1** of the colour green. **2** inexperienced; naive. **3** jealous; envious. **4** unripe. **greenery** *n* green vegetation; foliage. **greenfly** *n* green aphid. **greengage** *n* fruit of the plum family with a yellowish-green skin. **greengrocer** *n* person who sells fruit and vegetables. **greengrocery** *n*. **greenhouse** *n* shed with walls and roof mainly of glass, used for housing and cultivating plants. **greens** *pl n* leaves of green vegetables, such as cabbage or spinach.

greet *vt* **1** welcome. **2** send good wishes to. **3** be present at the arrival of; meet. **greeting** *n* statement or act of welcome, good wishes, etc.

gregarious *adj* enjoying other people's company; sociable.

grenade *n* small explosive shell thrown by hand or fired from a gun.

grey *n* colour between black and white, having no hue. *adj* **1** of a grey colour. **2** having grey hair. **3** dull; gloomy. **greyish** *adj*. **greyhound** *n* breed of smooth-haired dog with a slender body and pointed muzzle, often used for racing.

grid *n* **1** network of squares printed or placed over a map or drawing. **2** network of electricity cables, water pipes, etc.

grief *n* sorrow; distress; remorse. **grief-stricken** *adj* suffering intense grief; heart-broken. **grievance** *n* complaint; feeling of being hurt or offended. **grieve** *vi,vt* feel or cause great sorrow or distress.

grill *n* rack or section of an oven on or under which food is cooked. *vt,vi* cook on or under a grill. *vt inf* interrogate; cross-question.

grille *n* framework of metal bars forming an ornamental screen or grating.

grim *adj* **1** bleak; unpleasant; formidable. **2** stern; unbending; severe. **grimly** *adv*.

grimace *n* facial expression of disgust, hatred, etc. *vi* screw up the face in a grimace.

grime *n* **1** soot. **2** dirt. **grimy** *adj*.

grin *n* broad happy smile. *vi,vt* (-nn-) smile with the lips widely parted.

grind *vt,vi* (ground) **1** crush or pound into powder or small particles. **2** sharpen (a blade) or smooth by friction. **3** oppress; enslave. **4** grate or gnash (the teeth). *n* hard toil; repetitious routine. **grinder** *n* appliance for grinding coffee beans, etc.

grip *n* **1** firm hold or clasp; grasp. **2** strength of the fingers. **3** handle of a racquet or bat. **4** understanding; comprehension. **5** holdall; bag. **get** *or* **come to grips with** learn to control; master; tackle. ~*vt,vi* (-pp-) **1** hold firmly; clasp. **2** mesmerize; enthrall.

gripe *vi* moan; nag; complain. *vi,vt* feel or cause sudden pain.

gristle *n* cartilage, esp. when present in meat.

grit *n* **1** small pieces of gravel, sand, etc. **2** *inf* courage; stamina. *v* **grit one's teeth** (-tt-) **1** clench the teeth. **2** bear suffering bravely and without complaint.

groan *n* **1** low cry of pain, distress, disappointment, etc. **2** harsh noise made by the wind. **3** complaint; grumble. *vi,vt* **1** utter or sound like a groan. **2** complain; moan.

grocer *n* shopkeeper selling food, household articles, etc. **grocery** *n* trade or business of a grocer. **groceries** *pl n* items purchased from a grocer.

groin *n* part of the body where the legs join the abdomen.

groom *n* **1** person employed to look after horses. **2** bridegroom. *vt* **1** rub down (a horse). **2** keep (hair, clothes, etc.) clean and neat. **3** train or instruct for a particular role.

groove *n* **1** narrow channel cut into the surface of something; rut; furrow. **2** monotonous routine. *vt* cut a groove (into).

grope *vi* **1** search by touch; handle uncertainly; fumble. **2** seek (a solution) with difficulty. *n* fumbling touch.

gross *adj* **1** offensively fat. **2** vulgar; crude. **3** excessive; extreme. **4** before deductions. *n* **1**

pl **gross** quantity of 144 (12 dozen). **2** majority; bulk. *vt* earn before deductions. **grossly** *adv*.

grotesque *adj* extremely ugly; bizarre.

grotto *n* small cave; cavern.

ground[1] *n* **1** surface of the earth; land; soil. **2** enclosure or pitch. **3** area of knowledge; field. **down to the ground** perfectly; entirely. ~*vt* **1** prevent the take-off of (an aircraft). **2** give basic but thorough instructions to. **grounds** *pl n* **1** justification; valid reasons. **2** land attached to a large house, castle, etc. **3** coffee dregs. **groundsheet** *n* waterproof sheet used when camping in a tent. **groundsman** *n, pl* **-men** caretaker or gardener employed on an estate, park, sports ground, etc. **groundwork** *n* basic preparation for a job or project.

ground[2] *v pt* and *pp* of **grind.**

group *n* number of people or things placed or classed together; set. *vt,vi* form into a group or set; assemble.

grouse[1] *n* game bird with reddish-brown or black plumage.

grouse[2] *vi* grumble; nag; complain. *n* complaint; grievance.

grove *n* area of trees; plantation.

grovel *vi* (-ll-) **1** humiliate oneself; behave in a servile manner. **2** crawl in an undignified manner.

grow *v* (grew; grown) *vi* **1** become larger, taller etc.; mature. **2** increase in size or number. **3** develop; arise; become. *vt* produce; bring forth; yield. **grow up** become adult. **grown-up** *n* adult person. *adj* mature; adult. **growth** *n* **1** process of growing. **2** amount by which something grows. **3** increase; development. **4** cancer or tumour.

growl *vt,vi* **1** (esp. of an animal such as a dog) utter a low warning or hostile sound. **2** say in a low angry voice. *vi* rumble; grumble. *n* low hostile sound.

grub *n* **1** larva of certain insects, esp. a beetle. **2** *sl* food. *vt,vi* (-bb-) dig or root (in).

grubby *adj* dirty; grimy; soiled. **grubbiness** *n*.

grudge *n* grievance; feeling of resentment. *vt* resent; feel grieved about; begrudge. **grudgingly** *adv*.

gruelling *adj* extremely strenuous; exhausting; taxing; rigorous.

gruesome *adj* ghastly; horrible; spine-chilling.

gruff *adj* rough in manner or voice; rough. **gruffly** *adv*.

grumble *vt,vi* express dissatisfaction; groan; complain. *vi* rumble. *n* **1** expression of discontent; groan. **2** rumble.

grumpy *adj* inclined to grumble; cross; bad-tempered. **grumpiness** *n*.

grunt *vi,vt* **1** (esp. of a pig) snort. **2** say in a low incoherent manner. *n* **1** snort. **2** low incoherent noise.

guarantee *n* **1** statement that goods supplied conform to a certain standard or that they will be repaired or replaced. **2** formal undertaking to honour another's debts. **3** assurance that something is right or will happen. *vt* give a guarantee of; assure; undertake. **guarantor** *n* person giving a guarantee.

guard *vt,vi* **1** keep watch (over) in order to defend, protect, or prevent entry or escape. **2** shield; protect. *vt* restrain; control. **guard against** take precautions to avoid. ~*n* **1** person who guards, esp. a warder. **2** military or police escort. **3** sentry; keeper. **4** person officially in charge of a train. **5** safety device fitted to a machine, fire, etc. **6** safeguard; precaution. **on/off one's guard** alert or watchful/unwary. **guarded** *adj* cautious. **guardian** *n* **1** person having custody of another, esp. a minor. **2** defender; protector; keeper.

guerrilla *n also* **guerilla** member of a group of fighters waging war against regular military forces, using tactics of ambush, sabotage, etc.

guess *vt,vi* **1** attempt to judge or find an answer or solution (to) without having sufficient information; estimate. **2** give the right answer (to); discover correctly. *n* attempt at solving; estimate. **guesswork** *n* **1** process of guessing. **2** conclusion reached by guessing.

guest *n* **1** person invited as a visitor. **2** person whom one entertains or treats to a meal. **3** person staying at a hotel. **guesthouse** *n* small private hotel or boarding house.

guide *vt* **1** lead; show the way to; conduct. **2** influence; direct. **3** steer; control the movement of. *n* **1** person who guides, esp. one who conducts tourists or sightseers round places of interest. **2** *also* **guidebook** book giving information on places of interest. **3** book containing practical information on a subject; manual. **4** *also* **guideline** suggested principle or standard. **5** Girl Guide. **guidance** *n*.

guild *n* **1** society of craftsmen or merchants of the Middle Ages. **2** association; society.

guile *n* cunning; slyness; deceit. **guileless** *adj*.

guillotine *n* **1** execution device used to behead people. **2** machine fitted with a sharp blade for cutting and trimming paper, metal, etc. *vt* use a guillotine on.

guilt *n* **1** fact of having committed a criminal or other offence. **2** deep feeling of shame or remorse at having been responsible for a crime, error, omission, etc. **guiltless** *adj*. **guilty** *adj*. **guiltily** *adv*.

guinea *n* former British gold coin worth 21 shillings (£1.05).

guinea pig *n* **1** small tailless rodent often kept as a pet or used for experiments. **2** person used as the subject of experiment.

guitar *n* long-necked musical instrument, usually with six strings, which are plucked. **guitarist** *n*.

gulf *n* **1** large bay or inlet of the sea. **2** chasm or abyss. **3** great discrepancy; irreconcilable difference. *vt* engulf.

gull *n* seabird with white or grey plumage and webbed feet.

gullet *n* **1** oesophagus. **2** throat.

gullible *adj* easily cheated or taken in. **gullibility** *n*.

gulp *vt,vi* **1** swallow (food) quickly and noisily; bolt. **2** inhale noisily; choke; gasp. *n* act of gulping.

gum[1] *n* **1** sticky substance produced by various plants and used as an adhesive. **2** chewing gum. *v* (-mm-) *vt* stick with gum. *vt,vi also* **gum up** smear or become smeared with gum; clog.

gum[2] *n* pink fleshy tissue in which the teeth are rooted.

gun *n* any type of weapon capable of discharging bullets or shells from a barrel. **jump the gun** begin too soon or without adequate preparation. **stick to one's guns** keep to one's opinions or principles; persevere. ~*vt* (-nn-) *also* **gun down** shoot at with a gun. **gun for** pursue with determination. **gunman** *n, pl* **-men** person who uses a gun to commit a crime. **gunpowder** *n* explosive mixture of sulphur, charcoal, and saltpetre. **gunrunning** *n* smuggling of firearms. **gunrunner** *n*.

gurgle *vi* **1** (esp. of flowing water) make a bubbling or rushing sound. **2** produce a throaty chuckle; bubble. *n* gurgling sound.

guru *n* Hindu or Sikh religious teacher.

gush *vt,vi* **1** pour out with great force; flow; stream. **2** utter with exaggerated enthusiasm or sentiment. *n* sudden stream or flow.

gust *n* blast of wind, smoke, etc.

gut *n* **1** alimentary canal or any part of it. **2** strong type of thread made from an animal's intestines. *vt* (-tt-) **1** remove the entrails of (fish). **2** reduce to a shell; destroy. **guts** *pl n* **1** intestines or bowels. **2** courage; tenacity; determination. **3** essential part; core.

gutter *n* drainage channel at the side of a road or attached to the eaves of a roof.

guy[1] *n* **1** *inf* man. **2** effigy of Guy Fawkes that is burnt on Nov. 5th.

guy[2] *n* rope or chain used to keep a tent, mast, etc., in position.

guzzle *vt,vi* eat or drink greedily or noisily.

gymkhana (dʒim'kɑ:nə) *n* horseriding event in which competitors are judged for their skill or speed in various contests.

gymnasium *n, pl* **gymnasiums** *or* **gymnasia** (dʒim'neiziə) building or hall equipped with gymnastic apparatus and also used for various indoor sports. **gymnastics** *n* method of physical training that includes exercises in balance, vaulting, etc. **gymnast** *n*. **gymnastic** *adj*.

gynaecology *n* branch of medicine concerned with diseases peculiar to women. **gynaecological** *adj*. **gynaecologist** *n*.

gypsum *n* white mineral consisting of calcium sulphate, used to make plaster of Paris.

Gypsy *n also* **Gipsy** member of a nomadic race living in many parts of Europe and N America.

gyrate (dʒai'reit) *vi* rotate. **gyration** *n*.

H

haberdasher *n* shop or shopkeeper selling pins, thread, lace, etc. **haberdashery** *n*.

habit *n* **1** custom; usual practice or way of behaving. **2** type of garment worn by monks, nuns, etc. **habit-forming** *adj* causing addiction. **habitual** *adj* **1** usual; customary. **2** having a specified habit or addiction. **habitually** *adv*.

habitable *adj* fit to be lived in.

hack[1] *vi,vt* cut, chop, or strike roughly or clumsily. *vi inf* cough dryly and spasmodically. *n* rough cut or blow. **hacksaw** *n* saw for cutting metal, consisting of a narrow blade in a U-shaped frame.

hack[2] *n* **1** horse that can be hired. **2** old overworked horse. **3** writer or journalist who produces poor work fast and for little money. **hackneyed** *adj* unoriginal; said too often; trite.

had *v pt* and *pp* of **have.**

haddock *n, pl* **haddock** common N Atlantic food fish, related to the cod.

haemorrhage *n* profuse bleeding. *vi* to bleed profusely.

hag *n* ugly old woman; witch.

haggard *adj* looking ill, tired, or pale; gaunt.

haggis *n* Scottish dish of sheep's offal and oatmeal boiled in a sheep's stomach.

haggle *vi* dispute noisily (over) a price, etc.; wrangle.

hail[1] *n* **1** *also* **hailstones** pellets of frozen rain. **2** shower of hail. **3** profusion or shower of insults, abuse, or bullets. *vi* fall as hail.

hail[2] *vt* **1** greet or salute. **2** call out to; attract the attention of. **hail from** be a native of. *n* shout; greeting.

hair *n* **1** threadlike growth on or from the skin of mammals. **2** mass of hairs, esp. that on the human head. **hair's breadth** very short distance or margin. **keep your hair on!** keep calm! **let one's hair down** act informally and without reserve. **not turn a hair** show no fear or surprise. **split hairs** make petty unimportant distinctions. **hairy** *adj*. **hairdo** *n* arrangement of a woman's hair, esp. by a hairdresser. **hairdresser** *n* **1** person who cuts and arranges hair. **2** shop employing such persons. **hairdressing** *n*. **hairgrip** *n also* **hairpin** clip for securing women's hair. **hairpiece** *n* false hair worn to hide baldness, etc. **hair-raising** *adj* frightening; terrifying.

half *n, pl* **halves 1** amount obtained by dividing a whole into two equal or nearly equal parts. **2** either of the parts. **3** half a pint, esp. of beer. **better half** one's wife or husband. **go halves** share equally. ~*adv* **1** to the extent of a half. **2** partially; nearly. *adj* amounting to a half in number. *pron* amount of half in number. **half-and-half** *adj* neither one thing nor the other. **half-back** *n* player or position in rugby, soccer, etc., behind the forwards. **half-baked** *adj* foolish; not properly thought out. **half-breed** *n* **1** person having parents of different races; half-caste. **2** domestic animal having parents of different breeds. *adj* relating to a half-breed. **half-brother** *n* brother related through only one parent. **half-caste** *n,adj* half-breed. **half-hearted** *adj* not enthusiastic. **half-heartedly** *adv*. **half-sister** *n* sister related through only one parent. **half-term** *n* point or holiday in the middle of a scholastic term. **half-time** *n* point or interval in the middle of a football match, etc. **halfway** *adv,adj* equally far from two points. **halfwit** *n* **1** idiot; cretin. **2** stupid or foolish person. **halfwitted** *adj*.

halibut *n, pl* **halibut** large N Atlantic flat fish, important as a food fish.

hall *n* **1** large room for dining, lectures, etc. **2** public building for dances, meetings, etc. **3** *also* **hallway** passage or room leading from an entrance to other rooms. **4** large country house. **5** students' residence, hostel, or college.

hallelujah *interj,n, also* **alleluia** cry of praise to God.

hallmark *n* **1** stamp of an official body on a silver or gold article, indicating its purity. **2** typical characteristic proving authenticity; distinguishing feature.

hallowed *adj* **1** holy; consecrated. **2** revered; respected.

Hallowe'en *n* Oct 31st, eve of All Saints Day, when witches are supposed to ride at night and graves give up their dead.

hallucination *n* **1** alleged but imaginary perception of an object, sound, etc., because of illness or through taking certain drugs. **2** act of such perception. **hallucinate** *vi* experience hallucinations.

halo *n* **1** circle of light around the head of Christ, an angel, saint, etc., as shown in paintings. **2** circle of light around the sun or moon, caused by refraction by ice particles.

halt *vi,vt* stop. *n* **1** act of stopping; stop. **2** place, as on a train or bus route, at which it stops briefly.

halter *n* **1** rope by which horses, etc., can be led or tethered. **2** *also* **halterneck** neckline of a woman's dress that leaves the back bare.

halve *vt* **1** divide in half; share equally. **2** cut by half.

ham *n* **1** salted, sometimes smoked meat from the thigh of a pig. **2** back of the thigh; thigh and buttocks. **3** actor who overacts. **4** amateur radio operator. **ham-fisted** *adj* clumsy.

hamburger *n* fried cake of seasoned minced beef often served in a bread roll.

hammer *n* **1** tool with a head fitted at right angles to a handle for driving in nails, beating metal, etc. **2** any device for striking, knocking, etc. **3** heavy metal sphere with a flexible wire handle, thrown by athletes. **go at it hammer and tongs** argue or fight fiercely. ~*vt,vi* strike or pound with a hammer. *vt* **1** strike violently. **2** defeat conclusively. **3** criticize severely. **hammer away at** work hard to do or produce. **hammer in(to)** teach by repetition. **hammer out** settle or work out after much discussion or dispute.

hammock *n* bed of canvas, rope, etc., suspended between two supports.

hamper[1] *vt* prevent from moving or working easily; hinder; impede.

hamper[2] *n* basket or case in which food and other things can be packed.

hamster *n* tailless ratlike animal with pouched cheeks, kept as a pet.

hand *n* **1** part of the arm below the wrist. **2** help; assistance; role. **3** manual worker; labourer. **4** indicator, esp. on a clock. **5** single game at cards or the cards so dealt. **6** position or direction. **change hands** pass to another owner. **a free hand** complete freedom. **from hand to mouth** precariously; in poverty. **hand and foot** completely. **hand in glove** in close cooperation. **in good hands** well cared for. **in/out of hand** under/beyond control. **on/at/to hand** near; close by. **on the other hand** in contrast. **take in hand** discipline; control. **wash one's hands of** disclaim responsibility. **win hands down** win easily. ~*vt* **1** pass to; give. **2** *also* **hand on, hand down** pass on; transmit. **handbag** *n* small bag for carrying personal items, etc. **handbook** *n* book of useful hints or information; manual; guide. **handbrake** *n* manual brake on cars, etc. **handful** *n* **1** small amount or number. **2** person that is difficult to control. **handmade** *adj* made by a person rather than a machine. **hand-pick** *vt* select very carefully. **handstand** *n* vertical upside-down position maintained by balancing on one's hands. **handwriting** *n* **1** writing done by hand. **2** individual's style of handwriting. **handwritten** *adj.*

handicap *n* **1** something that hinders; disadvantage; defect; drawback. **2** mental or physical defect or disability. **3** disadvantage given to certain sports competitors to equalize everybody's chances. *vt* (-pp-) be a disadvantage to. **handicapped** *adj.*

handicraft *n* skilled manual work, often artistic, such as pottery.

handiwork *n* **1** skilled or artistic manual work. **2** result of someone's actions or plans.

handkerchief *n* piece of absorbent material on which to blow or wipe one's nose.

handle *n* part of a tool, machine, case, etc., by which to hold, carry, or control it. **fly off the handle** lose one's temper. ~*vt* **1** hold or feel with one's hands. **2** control or use (a machine, etc.). **3** deal with; cope with; manage. **handlebars** *pl n* metal crosspiece by which a bicycle, etc., is steered.

handsome *adj* **1** good-looking. **2** generous or ample. **handsomely** *adv.*

handy *adj* **1** useful; easy or convenient to use. **2** capable of doing manual jobs well. **3** easily accessible. **handyman** *n, pl* **-men** person adept at odd jobs.

hang *vi,vt* (hung *or for def. 2* hanged *or* hung). **1** suspend or be suspended from above. **2** execute or be executed by strangling with a noose. *vt* **1** suspend by a hook; attach, fix or stick in position. **2** keep (meat, esp. game) suspended until ready for eating. **hang around** *or* **about** linger; loiter; wait without purpose. **hang back** hesitate. **hang on** wait; persevere; cling to. **hang out 1** live; frequent. **2** display; hang outside. **hang up** replace (telephone receiver). *n* **get the hang of** understand or begin to be able to do. **hanger** *n* coathanger. **hangover** *n* after-effects of excessive drinking, esp. a headache.

hanker *vi* desire persistently; yearn (for). **hankering** *n* lingering desire or wish.

haphazard *adj* happening or arranged without planning, by chance, or at random. *adv also* **haphazardly** by chance; at random.

happen *vi* occur; take place, esp. by chance. **happen to (one)** befall; affect. **happen to** chance to (be, do, know, etc.). **happening** *n* occurrence; event, esp. a social one characterized by spontaneity.

happy *adj* **1** feeling, indicating, or causing contentment, pleasure, or joy. **2** fortunate. **3** willing (to). **4** suitable; apt. **5** mildly drunk. **happily** *adv.* **happiness** *n.*

harass *vt* annoy, pester, or pursue (someone)

continually. **harassed** *adj* nervous; irritated; bothered. **harassment** *n*.

harbour *n* **1** sheltered coastal area providing safe anchorage for ships, etc. **2** place for shelter or safety. *vt* **1** give refuge to (a hunted criminal, etc.); shelter. **2** cherish or maintain secretly. *vi* take shelter (in).

hard *adj* **1** not easily cut, dented, etc.; rigid. **2** difficult to do or understand. **3** violent or strenuous; arduous. **4** unfair; harsh or strict; severe; distressing. **5** unfeeling or insensitive. **6** (of water) impairing the lathering of soap. **hard and fast** strict; rigid. **hard cash** paper money and coins rather than cheques, etc. **hard to come by** difficult to obtain. **hard drugs** addictive drugs. **hard of hearing** deaf or slightly deaf. **hard up** having little money. ~*adv* **1** with force; violently. **2** with effort or vigour. **3** closely; with careful scrutiny. **hard at it** working strenuously. **hard put to** finding difficulty in. **harden** *vt,vi* **1** make or become hard(er). **2** make or become insensitive or accustomed to pain or suffering.

hardback *n* book with stiff cardboard covers.

hardboard *n* sheeting formed from compressed sawdust and woodchips, used as a building material, etc.

hard-boiled *adj* **1** (of eggs) boiled until the whole inside is solid. **2** cynical; callous.

hard-headed *adj* practical or shrewd, esp. in business. **hard-headedness** *n*.

hard-hearted *adj* not feeling or showing sympathy for the sufferings of others; cruel. **hard-heartedly** *adv*. **hard-heartedness** *n*.

hardly *adv* scarcely; not quite; barely.

hardship *n* lack of material comforts; deprivation; suffering.

hardware *n* **1** household utensils, tools, etc., ironmongery. **2** computer equipment.

hardy *adj* **1** able to tolerate difficult physical conditions; tough; robust. **2** (of plants) able to survive outdoors all year round.

hare *n* animal resembling a rabbit but having longer legs and ears. *vi* rush (about, after, etc.), esp. in a confused manner. **harebrained** *adj* stupid; rash; foolish.

hark *vi* listen (to). **hark back** revert (to a previous question or topic).

harm *n* damage or injury. *vt* cause damage or injury to. **harmful** *adj*.

harmonic *adj* relating to or characterized by harmony. *n* component of a musical note whose frequency is a multiple of the note's pitch. **harmonically** *adv* with or in harmony. **harmonics** *n* study of musical sounds.

harmonica *n* small musical instrument played by blowing into a small case in which metal reeds are set; mouth-organ.

harmony *n* **1** pleasant relationship of musical sounds. **2** friendly agreement in personal relationships. **3** pleasant arrangement, as of colours. **harmonious** *adj*. **harmoniously** *adv*. **harmonize** *vt,vi* come or bring into harmony; reconcile. *vi* sing or play in harmony (with). **harmonization** *n*.

harness *n* **1** complete set of straps and other parts fitted to a working horse. **2** fitment for a baby, etc., used for controlling, guiding, etc. *vt* **1** put a harness on (a horse). **2** gain control over (a form of energy, etc.).

harp *n* triangular musical instrument played by plucking or drawing the fingers over strings. *v* **harp on** talk repeatedly about.

harpoon *n* spear with a line attached that is fired or thrown when hunting whales, etc. *vt,vi* catch (whales, etc.) using a harpoon.

harpsichord *n* pianolike musical instrument.

harsh *adj* **1** not soft; coarse; rough. **2** severe; cruel; unkind. **3** jarring on the senses; strident; too bright or loud. **harshly** *adv*. **harshness** *n*.

harvest *n* **1** act of cutting and gathering ripe crops. **2** the crop itself. **3** result; product. *vt,vi* **1** gather in ripe crops. **2** get the benefit from.

has *v* 3rd person singular of **have** in the present tense.

hashish *n also* **hash** intoxicating drug prepared from dried leaves, flower tops, etc., of Indian hemp.

hasten *vi,vt* hurry or cause to hurry; rush. **haste** *n* **1** speed; hurry; urgency. **2** rashness. **hastily** *adv*. **hasty** *adj*.

hat *n* shaped covering for the head. **keep (something) under one's hat** keep secret. **old hat** old-fashioned; no longer novel.

hatch[1] *vi,vt* to emerge or cause to emerge from an egg. *vt also* **hatch up** think up (a plot, surprise, or idea).

hatch[2] *n* **1** small door covering an opening in a wall, esp. between two rooms. **2** cover for an opening on the deck of a boat or ship providing access below decks.

hatchet *n* small axe. **bury the hatchet** make peace after a quarrel.

hate *vt,vi* dislike fiercely; abhor. *n* **1** *also* **hatred** feeling of strong dislike or abhorrence. **2** person or thing so disliked. **hateful** *adj* loathsome.

haughty *adj* proud and arrogant; condescending; supercilious. **haughtily** *adv*. **haughtiness** *n*.

haul *vt,vi* pull or drag along with great effort; transport. *n* **1** something hauled. **2** act of hauling or the effort involved. **3** distance hauled or travelled. **4** result or amount obtained from an enterprise.

haunch *n* part of the body from the hip to the thigh.

haunt *vt,vi* visit as or be visited by a ghost. *vt* **1** go to habitually; frequent. **2** be continually in the thoughts of; obsess. **3** pester. **4** pervade. *n* place one frequents.

have *v* (*3rd person s present* has; *pp and pt* had) *vt*. **1** be characterized by. **2** own, possess. **3** hold; keep. **4** experience or undergo. **5** bear (children or young). **6** eat or drink (something). **7** take or receive. **8** must; be forced (to). **9** cause to happen or be done. **10** tolerate; put up with; allow. **11** cheat or deceive. *v aux* (used to form the perfect and pluperfect tenses). **have had it** be near death, no longer usable, tolerable, etc. **have on 1** wear. **2** fool; hoax.

haven *n* **1** place of shelter; refuge. **2** harbour.

haversack *n* canvas bag carried on the back or over the shoulder while hiking, etc.

havoc *n* disorder or confusion.

hawk *n* type of small long-tailed bird of prey.

hawthorn *n* thorny tree or bush with white, pink, or red flowers.

hay *n* dried grass used as fodder. **hayfever** *n* allergic reaction to inhaled pollen or dust, causing sneezing, runny eyes, etc. **haystack** *n* pile of hay in a field. **haywire** *adj*. **go haywire** go badly wrong; become disorganized.

hazard *n* **1** danger; peril; risk. **2** something causing danger or risk; obstacle. *vt* **1** risk; gamble. **2** venture (an opinion, etc.). **hazardous** *adj*.

haze *n* **1** light mist that impairs visibility. **2** vague or confused state of mind. **hazy** *adj* **1** slightly misty. **2** dimly or imperfectly remembered or remembering. **hazily** *adv*. **haziness** *n*.

hazel *n* small tree producing edible nuts. *adj,n* light to medium brown.

he *pron* male person or animal.

head *n* **1** part of the body above the neck. **2** intelligence; mental power. **3** chief person; commander; ruler. **4** highest or foremost point or part; top. **5** *pl* **head** person or animal considered as a unit in a group. **6** short for **headmaster** or **headmistress. bite someone's head off** rebuke sharply. **come to a head** reach a critical point. **give someone his head** allow greater freedom. **go to one's head** make proud, rash, etc. **head over heels (in love)** madly in love. **keep/lose one's head** keep calm/become flustered. **not make head nor tail of** completely fail to understand. **off one's head** crazy. **over someone's head** to someone of greater authority. ~*vt,vi* be, form, or put at the head of. *vt* hit (a football) with one's head. **head for** be directed towards (a place, trouble, etc.). **heady** *adj* intoxicating; affecting the mind or senses.

headache *n* **1** pain in the head. **2** troublesome person or thing.

headgear *n* any covering for the head.

heading *n* title at the beginning of an article, chapter of a book, etc.

headland *n* area of land jutting out to sea; cape.

headlight *n also* **headlamp** powerful light on the front of a car, etc.

headline *n* words in large or heavy type at the top of a newspaper article.

headlong *adv also* **headfirst 1** with the head foremost. **2** rashly; impetuously.

headmaster *n* chief male teacher in a school. **headmistress** *f n*.

headphones *pl n* pair of receivers fitted over the ears for communications purposes.

headquarters *pl n* chief office of a military force or other organization.

headstrong *adj* **1** obstinate, wilful. **2** rash; impetuous.

headway *n* **1** movement forward by a vessel. **2** progress, as in a struggle or problem.

heal *vt* cure; restore to health. *vi* (of a wound) close up.

health *n* **1** person's general bodily condition. **2** condition of being well; freedom from illness. **3** general condition of a business, country, etc. **healthy** *adj* **1** in good health. **2** conducive to good health. **3** promising or encouraging. **healthily** *adv*.

heap *n* **1** jumbled mass; pile; mound. **2** *also* **heaps** great deal. **3** something no longer useful. *vt* place (things) in a heap.

hear (heard) *vt,vi* **1** perceive (sound) with the ears. **2** become informed (about news). *vt* listen to. **hear from** receive news, etc., from. **hear of 1** obtain news or information about. **2** allow the possibility of. **hear out** allow (a person) to finish what he is saying. **hear, hear!** exclamation of agreement, approval, etc. **hearing** *n* **1** sense by which one hears; ability to hear. **2** range in which a person may be heard. **3** chance or opportunity to be heard.

hearse *n* car or carriage for carrying a corpse to burial or cremation.

heart *n* **1** muscular internal organ that pumps blood round the body. **2** symbolic seat of love, sympathy, or courage; these feelings themselves. **3** soul; inner thoughts. **4** centre; core. **5** heart-shaped symbol. **6** playing card marked with one or more red hearts. **hearts** *pl or s n* suit of cards each marked thus. **after someone's own heart** exactly of the type someone likes or approves of. **break someone's heart** upset or disappoint someone, esp. in love. **by heart** from memory. **heart of hearts** inmost feelings. **heart to heart** (discussion that is) intimate. **set one's heart on** want very much. **take to heart** be greatly influenced by. **wear one's heart on one's sleeve** make one's feelings, esp. of love, very obvious. **with all one's heart 1** with deep love. **2** willingly.

heart attack *n* sudden very painful, often fatal, malfunction of the heart.

heartbeat *n* single pulsation of the heart.

heartbroken *adj* very unhappy, disappointed, etc.

hearth *n* **1** place where a domestic fire is lit. **2** the whole fireplace. **3** the home.

heartless *adj* cruel; unfeeling; unsympathetic. **heartlessly** *adv*.

hearty *adj* **1** jovial; cheerful. **2** cordial; sincere. **3** in good health; vigorous. *n* fellow; comrade. **heartily** *adv*.

heat *n* **1** form of energy resulting from the motion of atoms and molecules in an object, etc. **2** degree of hotness, esp. when great. **3** hot weather. **4** strong or deep feeling; anger; enthusiasm. **5** pressure; intensity. **6** period of sexual excitement in female animals. **7** preliminary race or contest. *vt,vi* make or become hot. *vi* become agitated or nervous. **heated** *adj*. **heater** *n* domestic appliance for heating rooms, water, etc. **heatwave** *n* period of very hot weather.

heath *n* **1** area of open uncultivated ground. **2** heather.

heathen *adj* **1** not believing in the same god or religion as oneself; pagan. **2** uncivilized; barbaric. *n* person who is heathen.

heather *n also* **heath** small evergreen plant having small purplish or white bell-shaped flowers. **heathery** *adj*.

heave *vt,vi* pull or drag (something heavy); haul. *vt* **1** throw with great effort. **2** give out (a sigh, etc.). *vi* **1** move up and down rhythmically. **2** retch. *n* act of heaving.

heaven *n* **1** abode of God, the angels, and the good after death. **2** great happiness; intense pleasure. **3** place or state that induces this. **4** *also* **heavens** sky. **move heaven and earth** do everything possible to effect. **heavenly** *adj*.

heavy *adj* **1** of great or considerable weight. **2** difficult to move or lift because of weight. **3** serious; weighty; considerable. **4** difficult to bear, fulfil, digest, read, etc. **5** violent; of great force. *n* **1** role of a villain in a play or film. **2** actor playing this. **heavily** *adv*. **heaviness** *n*. **heavyweight** *n* boxer who weighs 175 pounds or more.

Hebrew *n* **1** language of the ancient Jews and modern Israel. **2** Jew; Israelite.

heckle *vt,vi* try to disconcert a public speaker by continual taunts. **heckler** *n*.

hectic *adj* **1** very busy or active. **2** hurried and confused; agitated. **hectically** *adv*.

hedge *n* **1** closely planted row of bushes and small trees forming a fence, etc. **2** barrier. *vt* **1** provide or surround with a hedge. **2** give an answer that does not reveal one's true thoughts. **hedge one's bets** make a safe bet, investment, etc., to protect oneself. **hedgehog** *n* small animal with long prickles on its back.

heed *vt,vi* take careful notice of. *n* **1** attention; notice. **2** caution; care. **take heed!** be careful!

heel[1] *n* **1** back part of a the foot. **2** part of a sock, stocking, etc., that covers the heel. **3** part of a shoe or boot beneath the heel. **4** despicable man. **Achilles' heel** person's only weak point. **down at heel** shabbily dressed. **cool one's heels** be kept waiting. **take to one's heels** run away. **to heel** under control. ~*vt* repair the heel of (a shoe).

heel[2] *vi also* **heel over 1** tilt to one side; list. **2** fall to the ground.

hefty *adj* **1** strong and muscular. **2** forceful.

height *n* **1** distance from bottom to top. **2** altitude. **3** most successful point; culmination. **4** most extreme or exaggerated form. **heights** high place or point. **heighten** *vt,vi* **1** make or become higher. **2** accentuate; be increased.

heir *n* **1** male person who inherits the wealth, rank, etc., of another when the latter dies. **2** successor, as to a tradition. **heiress** *f n*. **heirloom** *n* object passed down to succeeding generations in a family.

held *v pt* and *pp* of **hold.**

helicopter *n* aircraft powered by large overhead horizontally rotating blades.

helium *n* light inert rare gaseous element.

hell *n* **1** abode of Satan; place of eternal damnation for the wicked after death. **2** extreme suffering; torture; difficulty. **3** place or situation causing this. **a hell of a** very much of a. **for the hell of it** for fun. **give someone hell 1** cause much trouble to. **2** scold severely. **like hell 1** very much, fast, etc. **2** certainly not.

hello *interj* exclamation of greeting, surprise, etc.

helm *n* **1** steering device on a boat; tiller or steering-wheel. **2** position of control or authority. **helmsman** *n*.

helmet *n* **1** soldier's protective metal headgear worn during battle. **2** protective headgear worn by miners, firemen, motorcyclists, etc.

help *vt,vi* **1** give assistance (to); aid. **2** cause improvement in. *vt* **1** be of use in (doing). **2** avoid (doing); prevent oneself from. **3** serve with food or drink. **it can't be helped** it cannot be avoided or rectified. **help oneself (to) 1** take without permission, payment, etc. **2** serve oneself. **help out** give assistance to, esp. in time of need. ~*n* **1** assistance; aid; cooperation. **2** domestic servant. **helper** *n*. **helpful** *adj*. **helpfully** *adv*. **helpless** *adj* **1** weak; dependent. **2** powerless.

hem *n* edge of a piece of cloth or clothing turned over and sewn. *vt* (-mm-) sew a hem on. **hem in** surround; encircle.

hemisphere *n* **1** half a sphere. **2** half of the earth. **hemispherical** *adj*.

hemp *n* **1** tough-fibred Asian plant from which the drug cannabis is obtained. **2** cannabis. **3** rope or coarse cloth made from the fibres.

hen *n* **1** female bird, esp. a chicken. **2** old woman. **hen party** *n* gathering for women only.

hence *adv* **1** and so; therefore; for this reason. **2** from this time forward. **3** from this place.

henna *n* reddish dye for hair, etc., obtained from an Asiatic shrub.

her *adj* belonging to a female person. *pron* that particular woman or girl. **herself** *r pron* **1** her own self. **2** her normal self.

herald *n* **1** official who makes public or ceremonial announcements. **2** person or thing that indicates the approach of something. *vt* usher in; proclaim.

heraldry *n* practice and rules governing official coats of arms, etc. **heraldic** *adv*.

herb *n* plant, such as parsley, that can be used as a flavouring in cooking, as a medicine, etc. **herbal** *adj*. **herbaceous** *adj* relating to plants with fleshy stems that die down after flowering. **herbivore** *n* animal feeding on plants. **herbivorous** *adj*.

herd *n* **1** large group of wild or domestic animals that live and feed together. **2** mass of people; rabble. *vt,vi* **1** gather or be gathered into a herd. **2** drive or be driven (forward or back). **herdsman** *n* man who tends a herd.

here *adv* **1** in or to this place. **2** at this point in time or space. **here and there 1** in or to several places. **2** scattered around. **be neither here nor there** be irrelevant or unimportant. ~*n* this place.

heredity *n* **1** biological process by which characteristics, etc., are transmitted from parents to children in the genes. **2** characteristics so transmitted. **hereditary** *adj*.

heresy *n* belief or doctrine, esp. religious, that is contrary to established order. **heretic** *n* person originating or believing a heresy. **heretical** *adj*. **heretically** *adv*.

heritage *n* **1** culture or tradition passed on to successive generations. **2** something inherited at birth, esp. property or family characteristics.

hermit *n* **1** person living completely alone to pray or undergo mystic experiences. **2** person who lives a solitary life; recluse. **hermitage** *n* dwelling of a hermit.

hero *n, pl* **heroes** **1** man admired for his courage, nobleness, or fortitude. **2** central male character in a book, play, or film. **3** person who suffers much without complaint. **heroic** *adj.* **heroically** *adv.* **heroine** *f n.* **heroism** *n.*

heroin *n* addictive narcotic drug obtained from morphine.

heron *n* long-legged wading bird.

herring *n, pl* **herring** *or* **herrings** marine food fish. **red herring** misleading fact or argument.

hers *pron* belonging to her. **herself** *r pron* her own self; her normal self.

hesitate *vi* pause through doubt; waver; falter; be unwilling (to). **hesitancy** *n.* **hesitant** *adj.* **hesitation** *n.*

heterosexual *n* person sexually attracted to members of the opposite sex. **heterosexuality** *n.*

hexagon *n* six-sided geometric figure. **hexagonal** *adj.*

hibernate *vi* (of animals) spend the winter in a sleeplike state. **hibernation** *n.*

hiccup *n also* **hiccough** one of a series of sudden involuntary coughlike noises. *vi* (-pp-) *also* **hiccough** experience such a spasm; make such a noise.

hide[1] *vt* (hid; hidden) **1** keep from sight; conceal. **2** keep secret. *vi* conceal oneself. *n* place where someone is concealed, esp. for observing birds.

hide[2] *n* skin of some large animals, usually hairless, esp. when tanned. **tan someone's hide** beat or flog someone.

hideous *adj* **1** extremely ugly. **2** morally repulsive. **3** of an extreme nature. **hideously** *adv.*

hiding[1] *n* act or place of concealment.

hiding[2] *n* **1** beating or thrashing. **2** conclusive defeat in a contest.

hierarchy *n* strictly graded structure, as of society or some other system. **hierarchical** *adj.*

high *adj* **1** having or being at a considerable or specified height. **2** being at a peak; considerable; relatively great in value or amount. **3** important; exalted. **4** main; chief. **5** noble; lofty; admirable. **6** slightly intoxicated by liquor or drugs. **high and dry** stranded; abandoned. **high and low** in every place possible. **high time** the correct or appropriate time. *~adv* **1** at or to a high point or place. **2** for considerable gambling stakes. *n* **1** high point; peak. **2** high place. **highly** *adv* greatly; considerably.

highbrow *adj* relating to very intellectual tastes in music, literature, art, etc. *n* person having such tastes.

high-fidelity *adj* reproducing sounds electronically without distortion.

high jump *n* athletic event in which competitors leap over a high, continuously elevated bar. **be for the high jump** be in trouble. **high-jumper** *n.*

highland *n also* **highlands** hilly or mountainous region, esp. in Scotland.

highlight *n* **1** small concentration of light on something shiny. **2** best or most impressive or enjoyable part. *vt* **1** put highlights in. **2** put emphasis on; accentuate.

highness *n* **1** condition of being high. **2** honorary address to a royal person.

highway *n* public road, esp. a main road.

hijack *vt* **1** board and capture (an aeroplane, etc.) and threaten to destroy it or kill its passengers unless one's demands are met. **2** steal (a lorry, etc.) with its load. *n* instance of hijacking. **hijacker** *n.*

hike *n* long walk or walking holiday in the country; ramble. *vi* go for a hike. **hiker** *n.*

hilarious *adj* very funny; causing much amusement. **hilariously** *adv.* **hilarity** *n.*

hill *n* **1** elevated area of ground; small mountain. **2** slope, as in a road. **hilly** *adj.*

him *pron* that particular man or boy. **himself** *r pron* **1** his own self. **2** his normal self.

hind *adj* in or at the back or rear; posterior. **hindsight** *n* ability to guess or act correctly when looking back on an event.

hinder *vt* cause obstruction or delay to; impede. **hindrance** *n* **1** obstruction; delay. **2** person or thing causing this.

hinge *n* **1** joint by which a door, lid, etc., is attached to a frame, container, etc., so that it can open and close. **2** central fact or argument on which all else depends. *vi* **hinge on** depend on.

hint *n* suggestion; piece of helpful advice. *vt,vi* make suggestions (about).

hip *n* side of the body from the upper thigh to the waist.

hippopotamus *n, pl* **hippopotamuses** *or* **hippopotami** (hipə'pɔtəmai) very large thick-skinned African mammal living in and around rivers.

hire *vt* obtain the temporary use or services of, for payment. *n* **1** act of hiring. **2** charge of hiring.

his *pron* belonging to him.

hiss *vi* **1** produce a whistling sound like a prolonged *s*. *vt,vi* display scorn or disapproval (for) by making such a noise. *n* such a noise.

history *n* **1** development and past events of a country, etc. **2** study concerned with this. **3** book, play, or other chronological account about past events. **make history** do something important or influential. **historian** *n* scholar or student of history. **historic** *adj* **1** important or memorable in history. **2** *also* **historical** relating to history.

hit *vt,vi* (-tt-; hit) **1** give a blow to; knock; strike. **2** reach (a target, etc.). *vt* **1** come upon by chance; find. **2** wound; injure. **hit it off with** get on well (with somebody). **hit on** *or* **upon** guess or find (an answer, etc.) by chance. **hit out** (**at** *or* **against**) speak angrily or critically (about). ~*n* **1** blow or knock. **2** act of reaching a target. **3** great success.

hitch *vt* pull up roughly. *vt,vi* **1** fasten or become fastened (on to); become entangled or caught. **2** procure (a lift) from a driver. *n* **1** abrupt pull. **2** unexpected difficulty or obstacle causing a delay. **3** type of knot. **hitched** *adj* married. **hitch-hike** *vi* **1** procure free travel in a motor vehicle. **2** travel around by such means. **hitch-hiker** *n*.

hive *n* **1** structure in which bees are kept. **2** bees kept in a hive. **3** very busy or industrious place. *vt* gather (bees) into a hive.

hoard *n* **1** accumulated store, often hidden or secret. **2** hidden or buried treasure. **3** *also* **hoards** great quantity (of). *vt,vi* amass (a hoard). **hoarder** *n*.

hoarding *n* **1** temporary wooden fence on which advertising posters are often stuck. **2** structure intended for posters, etc.

hoarse *adj* **1** coarse and husky; raucous. **2** having a harsh voice, esp. from shouting or due to a cold. **hoarsely** *adv*.

hoax *n* mischievous deception; practical joke. *vt,vi* play a hoax on.

hobble *vi* walk lamely or clumsily; limp. *vt* tie together two legs of a horse, etc., to prevent it from straying. *n* clumsy or lame walk.

hobby *n* favourite leisure occupation; pastime.

hockey *n* **1** team game in which a ball is hit with curved wooden sticks into opposing goals. **2** ice hockey.

hoe *n* long-handled horticultural tool with transversely set blade, used to weed, break up ground, etc. *vt,vi* weed, break up, etc., with a hoe.

hoist *vt* raise or lift, esp. using a mechanical device. *n* **1** act of hoisting. **2** device for doing this.

hold[1] (held) *vt* **1** grasp, grip, or support. **2** reserve or keep; maintain; control. **3** have; occupy; use. **4** contain. **5** cause to take place; conduct. **6** think that; consider. *vi* **1** withstand. **2** remain in a certain attitude or condition; remain valid. **3** maintain beliefs, etc. **4** refrain; forbear. **hold back** restrain; hesitate. **hold down** keep a job, esp. when difficult. **hold forth** talk at length or pompously. **hold good** remain valid. **hold off** **1** keep or stay at a distance. **2** stay aloof. **hold on** **1** cling to. **2** wait. **hold one's own** maintain one's position, as in an argument. **hold one's tongue** say nothing. **hold out** **1** resist successfully; remain firm. **2** last; be sufficient. **hold up** **1** cause delay in. **2** rob while threatening with a gun. **holdup** *n* **1** delay. **2** armed robbery. **hold water** remain true or logical under analysis. **hold with** agree with out of principle. ~*n* **1** act or method of holding. **2** something to grasp. **3** control or influence. **get hold of** **1** grasp. **2** get in contact with. **holdall** *n* large bag or case.

hold[2] *n* cargo storage area below the deck of a vessel.

hole *n* **1** empty or hollow space in something; cavity; gap; opening; rupture or tear. **2** animal's burrow. **3** squalid or dingy room or house. **4** dull place. **5** predicament; difficulty. **make a hole in** use up a large part. **pick holes in** find faults with. ~*vt,vi* produce a hole in.

holiday *n* **1** time or period of rest from work, esp. when spent away from home. **2** day of rest or recreation, esp. a public one. **3** day for celebrating a religious event; festival. *vi* spend a holiday.

hollow *adj* **1** having an empty interior or a cavity inside. **2** having a depression in it; sunken. **3** insincere; flattering. **4** without substance; unreal. **5** dull or muffled. **6** hungry. *n* **1** hollow part of something. **2** sunken place; depression; cavity. **3** shallow valley. *vt* *also*

hollow out scoop out a hollow in. *adv* in a hollow way. **beat hollow** defeat completely. **hollowness** *n*.

holly *n* evergreen tree or shrub having shiny prickly leaves and red berries.

hollyhock *n* tall garden plant having large showy open flowers.

holster *n* leather case for a pistol.

holy *adj* **1** of God or a religion; sacred. **2** worshipped as sacred; sanctified. **3** saintly; pious. **holiness** *n* condition of being holy. **Holiness** title or term of address of the Pope.

homage *n* **1** loyalty; allegiance; reverence. **2** act of respect or reverence rendered to someone.

home *n* **1** place where a person lives; family residence. **2** place where something originated or is situated. **3** native country or town. **4** institution for the old or infirm. **at home** feeling comfortable. **at home with** familiar with. ~*adv* **1** at or towards home. **2** to a required point, target, etc. **come/bring home to** realize/cause to realize fully. **homely** *adj* plain; simple; unpretentious. **homeliness** *n*. **homesick** *adj* feeling great longing or nostalgia for one's home or native country. **homework** *n* pupil's work that is to be done outside school hours.

homosexual *n* person sexually attracted to members of his or her own sex. *adj* relating to such people. **homosexuality** *n*.

honest *adj* **1** not lying, deceiving, or cheating. **2** not given to stealing or other criminal activities. **3** sincere; open; frank. **4** trustworthy or conscientious. **honestly** *adv*. **honesty** *n*.

honey *n* **1** sweet liquid made from nectar by bees. **2** something sweet, soothing, flattering, etc. **honeycomb** *n* **1** waxy structure of hexagonal cells in which bees store their honey and eggs. **2** intricate system of passages and tunnels. **honeymoon** *n* holiday of a newly married couple. *vi* spend one's honeymoon (in). **honeysuckle** *n* sweet-smelling climbing shrub.

honorary *adj* **1** given or conferred as an honour. **2** acting or done without pay.

honour *n* **1** good reputation; public esteem; integrity; respect. **2** person or thing bringing honour. **3** mark of respect, etc. **4** act of courtesy. **5** title or address, esp. of a judge. **do the honours** act as host. ~*vt* **1** treat with honour; show respect or courtesy for. **2** confer an honour on. **3** keep a promise or bargain. **4** accept as valid. **honourable** *adj*. **honourably** *adv*.

hood *n* **1** loose covering for the head and neck. **2** collapsible or removable cover for a car or pram. **3** hood-shaped structure. **hooded** *adj* (of the eyes) half closed.

hoof *n* horny part of the foot of horses, cows, etc.

hook *n* **1** small implement curved or bent at one end, by which something is hung, pulled, fastened, etc. **2** something shaped like a hook. **3** swerving blow or stroke. **off the hook** out of trouble or difficulty. ~*vt* **1** connect, hang, fasten, catch, etc., with a hook. **2** put in the shape of a hook; crook. **hooked on** addicted to.

hooligan *n* wild, violent, or destructive person; vandal. **hooliganism** *n*.

hoop *n* circular band or ring, used as a binding, toy, etc. *vt* bind with a hoop.

hoot *vi* **1** make or give out a hollow noise like the cry of an owl. **2** laugh noisily. **3** express derision with a hoot. *n* **1** such a noise. **2** cause of great amusement. **hooter** *n* **1** mechanical device giving out a hoot as a time signal **2** *inf* nose.

hop[1] *vi* (-pp-) **1** jump on one leg. **2** move by hopping or jumping. **hop it!** go away! ~*n* **1** act of hopping. **2** short distance or journey. **3** small dance. **on the hop** unprepared.

hop[2] *n* climbing plant whose flowers are used in flavouring beer.

hope *n* **1** desire; expectation. **2** person or thing expected to bring desired success, etc. *vt,vi* wish (for); expect or trust (that). **hopeful** *adj*. **hopefully** *adv*.

horde *n* large number or group; throng; gang. *vi* gather together in a horde.

horizon *n* **1** line where the sea or land appears to meet the sky. **2** limit of a person's hopes, intellect, or ambition. **horizontal** *adj* parallel to the horizon; lying flat; level. **horizontally** *adv*.

hormone *n* biochemical substance produced in certain glands and secreted into the blood to trigger or stimulate certain processes. **hormonal** *adj*.

horn *n* **1** hard pointed growth projecting from the head of certain animals. **2** drinking vessel made from a hollowed horn. **3** curved projection. **4** metal musical wind instrument. **5** siren or hooter on a car, etc. **draw in one's**

horns reduce one's expenditure. ~*vt* injure with a horn.

hornet *n* large wasp.

horoscope *n* astrological prediction.

horrible *adj* **1** causing horror or great fear. **2** horrid. **horribly** *adv*.

horrid *adj* **1** unpleasant; nasty; cruel. **2** shocking; repulsive. **horridly** *adv*.

horrify *vt* cause to feel horror; shock. **horrific** *adj*.

horror *n* **1** great fear; disgust. **2** thing causing such feeling. **3** ugly thing. **4** annoying or disagreeable person. **horror-struck** *adj* overwhelmed with horror.

hors d'oeuvres *n* (ɔːˈdəːv) course before the main course of a meal, esp. a light savoury or appetizing fruit dish.

horse *n* **1** large hoofed domestic animal that may be ridden or used as a draught animal. **2** wooden frame for drying or airing clothes. **3** large wooden box over which gymnasts vault. **dark horse** person with hidden or unknown merit. **flog a dead horse** work at or revive a lost or hopeless cause. *vi* **horse about** act noisily or foolishly. **horsy** *adj* **1** relating to a horse. **2** interested in horses and riding. **horsebox** *n* large trailer or van for transporting horses. **horse chestnut** *n* large tree with clusters of white or red flowers and shiny brown nuts enclosed in a prickly case. **horsepower** *n* unit of power, as of a car engine. **horseradish** *n* plant whose pungent root is made into a thick sauce.

horticulture *n* growing of flowers, fruit, and vegetables; gardening. **horticultural** *adj*. **horticulturist** *n*.

hose *n* long narrow flexible pipe for transporting liquids, directing water, etc. *vt* direct water at.

hospitable *adj* offering a friendly welcome to guests; sociable. **hospitably** *adv*. **hospitality** *n*.

hospital *n* institution where the sick or injured are cared for or treated by doctors, nurses, etc.

host[1] *n* **1** person who receives and entertains guests. **2** person who runs an inn, hotel, etc. **3** animal or plant on which parasites live.

host[2] *n also* **hosts** large number of people, such as an army.

hostage *n* person seized and kept under threat until his captors' demands are fulfilled.

hostel *n* residential house or hall for students, hikers, or workers.

hostess *n* **1** female host. **2** female attendant on an aeroplane, etc.

hostile *adj* showing enmity or opposition; aggressive; unfriendly. **hostility** *n*.

hot *adj* **1** having a high temperature; very warm. **2** highly spiced; pungent. **3** violent; passionate. **4** recently occurring, produced, etc.; following closely. **hot air** meaningless or boastful talk. **hot stuff** person or thing exciting or excellent. **hot water** trouble. ~*adv* in a hot manner; hotly. **blow hot and cold** repeatedly enthuse then hesitate. *vt,vi* (-tt-) **hot up** make or become more exciting, powerful, etc. **hotly** *adv* with ardour or deep feeling. **hot-blooded** *adj* passionate. **hot dog** *n* hot sausage in a bread roll or sandwich. **hothouse** *n* artificially heated greenhouse. **hot-tempered** *adj* losing one's temper easily.

hotel *n* building offering accommodation and service to travellers, etc.

hound *n* **1** dog that hunts by following the scent of its quarry. **2** despised person. *vt* pursue or persecute ruthlessly.

hour *n* **1** unit or period of time; sixty minutes. **2** correct or appointed time. **3** destined time, as of a person's death. **hours** *pl n* **1** normal time of operation, as of a shop. **2** long time. **the eleventh hour** the last possible moment. **hourly** *adj* **1** occurring or done every hour. **2** measured by the hour.

house *n* (haus) **1** building designed for living in; residence; home. **2** building used for a special purpose. **3** household. **4** important or noble family. **5** part of a school. **6** business firm. **7** legislative assembly. **8** theatre audience. **bring the house down** cause great merriment or applause. **get on like a house on fire** get on very well. **on the house** free. **safe as houses** very safe. ~*vt* (hauz) **1** contain; enclose. **2** put in a house; provide shelter for.

housebound *adj* unable to leave the house.

household *n* those living together in a house. **household word** *or* **name** very well-known name, as of a product.

housekeeper *n* **1** woman hired to cook and look after someone else's house. **2** woman servant in charge of other servants in a large household. **housekeeping** *n* **1** domestic management. **2** money allowed or required for this.

houseman *n, pl* **-men** junior resident doctor in a hospital.

House of Commons *n* lower house of the British legislative assembly consisting of representatives elected by the people; parliament.

House of Lords *n* upper house of the British legislative assembly consisting of non-elected hereditary peers and life peers and acting also as the supreme court of judicial appeal.

housewife *n, pl* **-wives** married woman who stays at home to run the house instead of working.

housing *n* **1** houses collectively. **2** provision of houses by the government, etc.

hover *vi* **1** remain suspended in air, almost motionless. **2** remain close, as to help or protect. **hovercraft** *n* passenger craft that moves above a water or land surface on a cushion of air.

how *adv* **1** in what way or manner; by what method or means. **2** in what condition. **3** to what extent or degree. **4** why; for what reason. **5** to what a great degree or amount. **however** *conj* nevertheless; in spite of this. *adv* in any way; by whatever means.

howl *vi* **1** make a prolonged mournful cry. **2** cry loudly. **3** laugh uncontrollably. *n* **1** loud or mournful cry. **2** loud laugh. **howler** *n* ridiculous or amusing mistake.

hub *n* **1** centre of a wheel from which the spokes radiate. **2** central point, as of activity.

huddle *vi,vt* crowd or be crowded together, as for warmth or protection. *n* confused heap. **in/into a huddle** in/into a private discussion.

hue *n* **1** attribute of colour that enables different colours, red, yellow, blue, etc., to be distinguished. **2** colour; shade. **hue and cry** public outcry.

huff *n* angry, offended, or sulky fit of temper. **huffish** *or* **huffy** *adj.*

hug *v* (-gg-) *vt,vi* clasp affectionately; cuddle. *vt* keep close to. *n* affectionate clasp; cuddle.

huge *adj* extremely large; vast; immense. **hugely** *adv* very much.

hulk *n* **1** old, useless, abandoned, or partially dismantled ship. **2** large clumsy person. **hulking** *adj* large and clumsy.

hull *n* basic frame of a ship, without masts, etc.

hum *v* (-mm-) *vi* **1** make a continuous musical sound like singing but with the mouth shut. **2** make a prolonged low buzzing noise. **3** be alive with activity, rumour, etc. *vt* sing (a tune, etc.) by humming. *n* **1** sound like a prolonged 'm'. **2** low buzz or drone. **3** sound of great activity.

human *adj* **1** relating to man or mankind. **2** having or appealing to human kindness, weakness, etc. *n also* **human being** person; man or woman. **humane** *adj* sympathetic; merciful; kind; compassionate. **humanely** *adv.* **humanity** *n* **1** mankind. **2** compassion for others.

humble *adj* **1** not proud or conceited; modest. **2** unimportant or lowly; subjected; submissive. *vt* **1** cause to feel humble; shame. **2** make humble or lowly. **eat humble pie** apologize in a humble way. **humbly** *adv.*

humdrum *adj* commonplace; dull; monotonous.

humid *adj* damp; moist. **humidity** *n.*

humiliate *vt* cause to feel humble, foolish, or ashamed. **humiliation** *n.*

humility *n* condition of being humble; meekness; modesty.

humour *n* **1** ability to see or appreciate what is funny. **2** humorous or amusing quality. **3** temper; mood. *vt* indulge someone's whims or ideas. **humorous** *adj* causing laughter; funny; amusing; droll; witty. **humorously** *adv.*

hump *n* **1** natural lump on the backs of camels. **2** rounded deformity on the back of humans. **3** any curved protuberance, such as a small hill. *vt* lift clumsily. *vt,vi* arch.

hunch *n* suspicion; intuitive guess. *vt* **1** draw (one's shoulders) up, as when sitting. **2** thrust out or arch (one's back). **hunchback** *n* **1** lumplike deformity on the back. **2** person with such a deformity.

hundred *n* **1** number equal to ten times ten. **2** hundred things or people. **hundreds** very many. *adj* consisting of or amounting to a hundred or about a hundred. **hundredth** *adj,adv,n.* **hundredweight** *n* measure of weight equal to 112 pounds; one twentieth of a ton.

hung *v pt* and *pp* of **hang.**

hunger *n* **1** sensation that one needs or desires to eat. **2** lack of food; famine. **3** deep desire or need; craving. *vi* **1** feel hungry. **2** lack food. **hunger for** *or* **after** desire or crave. **hunger-strike** *n* refusal to eat, as when in prison, as a protest. **hungry** *adj.*

hunt *vt,vi* **1** chase or pursue wild animals to kill them for food or sport. **2** search (for); seek. *vt* chase or pursue a criminal, etc. **hunt down**

capture after pursuing ruthlessly. ~*n* **1** practice or instance of hunting animals. **2** group of people and working animals so involved. **3** search; pursuit. **hunter** *n*.

hurdle *n* **1** light frame used as a temporary fence. **2** framelike barrier over which an athlete (**hurdler**), show jumper, etc., must leap. **3** problem to be overcome; obstacle. *vi,vt* jump over (hurdles) in a race.

hurl *vt* **1** throw with great effort or force. **2** shout; yell.

hurrah *interj,n also* **hurray** exclamation of pleasure or applause.

hurricane *n* **1** very strong wind. **2** violent storm; tropical cyclone.

hurry *vi,vt* **1** move or cause to move more quickly or with haste. **2** do quickly. *n* **1** haste; bustle. **2** need for haste; urgency.

hurt *vt,vi* (hurt) **1** cause physical pain or injury (to). **2** offend; distress. **3** affect adversely; damage. *n* **1** pain; injury; wound. **2** harm; damage. *adj* **1** injured. **2** offended.

hurtle *vi* rush violently; move very fast.

husband *n* man to whom a woman is married.

hush *vt,vi* **1** make or become quiet or silent. **2** make or become soothed. **hush up** keep secret; suppress. ~*n* quiet; silence. *interj* be quiet!

husk *n* dry outer covering of some seeds. *vt* remove the husk from.

husky *adj* hoarse or whispery. **huskily** *adv*.

hustle *vt,vi* hurry along or be hurried along roughly. *vi* act quickly and efficiently. *n* rush of activity; bustle; jostling.

hut *n* small wooden building, esp. a temporary or ramshackle one.

hutch *n* small wooden cage for pet rabbits, etc.

hyacinth *n* plant that grows from a bulb and produces a spike of white, pink, or blue fragrant flowers in spring.

hybrid *n* **1** plant or animal that is a cross between two different species or varieties. **2** blend of two dissimilar things.

hydraulic *adj* **1** worked by the flow or pressure of fluids, esp. water. **2** relating to fluids and their use in engineering. **hydraulics** *n* study of fluid flow.

hydrocarbon *n* organic compound containing only carbon and hydrogen.

hydro-electric *adj* relating to the generation of electricity by the force of falling water. **hydro-electricity** *n*.

hydrogen *n* inflammable gas that is the lightest element and occurs in water and most organic compounds.

hyena *n* doglike carnivorous animal.

hygiene *n* **1** cleanliness; healthy practices. **2** science of preserving health. **hygienic** *adj*.

hymn *n* religious song; song of praise to God.

hyphen *n* mark (-) in writing or printing used to compound two words or syllables or when a word is split at the end of a line. **hyphenate** *vt* insert a hyphen in. **hyphenation** *n*.

hypnosis *n* **1** induced relaxed state of semiconsciousness during which a person will obey suggestions or commands made to him. **2** hypnotism. **hypnotic** *adj* **1** having the power to hold the attention; fascinating. **2** of or like hypnosis; lulling or trancelike. **hypnotism** *n* induction of hypnosis. **hypnotist** *n*. **hypnotize** *vt* **1** induce hypnosis in. **2** fascinate; dominate the will or mind of.

hypochondria *n* obsessive concern with one's own health. **hypochondriac** *adj,n*.

hypocrisy *n* **1** feigning of beliefs or feelings one does not have; insincerity. **2** false virtue. **hypocrite** *n*. **hypocritical** *adj*. **hypocritically** *adv*.

hypodermic *n* **1** syringe or needle used to administer injections below the skin. **2** such an injection. *adj* relating to the tissue area below the skin.

hypothesis *n* idea or suggestion put forward for discussion or verification; proposition. **hypothetic** *or* **hypothetical** *adj* not based on facts. **hypothetically** *adv*.

hysterectomy *n* surgical removal of the womb or part of the womb or uterus.

hysteria *n* **1** neurotic uncontrollable outbursts of panic or other emotions. **2** any uncontrollable emotion. **hysterical** *adj* **1** relating to hysteria. **2** extremely funny. **hysterically** *adv*.

I

I *pron* used as the subject to refer to oneself.

ice *n* **1** water frozen until solid. **2** ice-cream. *vt* **1** produce ice in; freeze. **2** put icing on (a cake). **3** chill (a drink) with ice. **iceberg** *n* large floating mass of ice in the sea. **ice-cream** *n* dessert made of flavoured frozen cream, custard, etc. **ice lolly** *n* confectionery consisting of flavoured ice on a short stick. **ice**

hockey *n* team game similar to hockey, played on ice. **ice rink** *n* an area of ice for skating, esp. one kept frozen artificially. **ice-skate** *vi* skate on ice. *n* **1** shoe fitted with a narrow metal runner for skating on ice. **2** such a runner.

icicle *n* thin tapering piece of hanging ice.

icing *n* mixture of fine sugar (icing sugar) and water, egg whites, etc., spread over cakes as a decoration.

icon *n* sacred image of Christ, saints, angels, etc.

icy *adj* **1** so cold as to cause ice. **2** relating to ice. **3** (of roads) slippery. **4** unfriendly; aloof; distant. **icily** *adv*. **iciness** *n*.

idea *n* **1** mental concept; anything thought of in the mind. **2** opinion; belief. **3** plan or suggestion. **4** impression of what something is like.

ideal *adj* **1** of the best that could be imagined; perfect. **2** conforming to a notion of excellence or purity. *n* **1** standard of excellence or complete perfection. **2** principle or aim that is pure or noble. **3** concept of perfection in a person, object, etc. **ideally** *adv*. **idealistic** *adj* **1** having or cherishing ideals or high-minded principles. **2** relating to such principles. **idealist** *n,adj*. **idealism** *n*. **idealize** *vt* **1** consider that (a person or thing) conforms to an ideal or standard of excellence. **2** present or write about (a person or thing) as if ideal. **idealization** *n*.

identical *adj* exactly the same. **identically** *adv*. **identify** *vt* recognize or prove the identity of. **identify with** associate oneself or give support to (a group, person, etc.). **identity** *n* **1** fact of being who one is or what something is. **2** exact sameness.

ideology *n* body of related ideas or doctrines of a religious, political, or economic system. **ideological** *adj*. **ideologically** *adv*.

idiom *n* **1** phrase or expression meaning something other or more than its literal meaning. **2** language restricted to a particular type of speaker, period, group, etc. **idiomatic** *adj*. **idiomatically** *adv*.

idiosyncrasy *n* individual and unusual tendency or characteristic. **idiosyncratic** *adj*.

idiot *n* **1** foolish or stupid person. **2** mentally subnormal person. **idiotic** *adj* foolish; silly. **idiotically** *adv*.

idle *adj* **1** not doing anything; inactive. **2** (of a machine) not in use. **3** lazy. **4** vain or ineffectual; useless. **5** frivolous. *vi,vt* waste (time) doing nothing. *vi* (of an engine) turn over gently while not providing drive. **idleness** *n*. **idly** *adv*.

idol *n* **1** image, esp. a sculpture, of a god or something that is worshipped as a god. **2** god of another religion from one's own. **3** very popular or admired person or thing, esp. a pop star or film star. **idolatry** *n* **1** worship of idols. **2** excessive admiration. **idolater** *n*. **idolatrous** *adj*. **idolize** *vt* treat or worship as an idol.

idyllic *adj* charmingly simple, peaceful, or poetic. **idyllically** *adv*.

if *conj* **1** in case that; supposing that. **2** whether. **3** even though; allowing that.

igloo *n* Eskimo's dome-shaped hut made of blocks of hard snow.

ignite *vt,vi* **1** set or be set on fire; kindle. **2** cause or reach a temperature at which combustion takes place. **3** arouse the passion of or be so aroused. **ignition** *n* **1** act or fact of igniting. **2** starting system in an internal-combustion engine.

ignorant *adj* **1** lacking knowledge. **2** lacking education or upbringing. **ignorance** *n*.

ignore *vt* **1** fail to notice or take into account; disregard. **2** refuse to acknowledge or greet.

ill *adj* **1** in bad health; sick. **2** bad; wicked. **3** hostile; malicious. **4** rude. **5** unfavourable; indicating misfortune. **ill at ease** embarrassed; uneasy. ~*adv* badly. *n* misfortune; harm. **ill-bred** *adj* lacking good manners or refinement; badly brought up. **illness** *n* **1** state of being ill; sickness; ill health. **2** specific complaint or disease. **ill-treat** *vt* treat cruelly or carelessly; abuse. **ill-treatment** *n*. **ill will** *n* feeling of dislike, jealousy, or hatred; malice.

illegal *adj* not in accordance with the law; unlawful. **illegally** *adv*.

illegible *adj* not able to be read; badly written; partially obliterated.

illegitimate *adj* **1** born of parents who are not married to each other. **2** contrary to the law; unlawful. **illegitimacy** *n*.

illicit *adj* not permitted or authorized; unlawful. **illicitly** *adv*.

illiterate *adj* **1** unable to read or write. **2** ignorant, uneducated, or uncultured. **illiteracy** *n*.

illogical *adj* **1** contrary to logic; irrational. **2** not thinking logically. **illogically** *adv.*

illuminate *vt* **1** light up; provide light for. **2** clarify. **3** decorate with bright gay lights or floodlighting. **4** decorate (a manuscript) by adding painted ornamentation. **illumination** *n.*

illusion *n* **1** something that is falsely or mistakenly thought to exist or be so. **2** deception; delusion; hallucination. **3** conjuring trick. **illusionist** *n* conjurer. **illusory** *adj* based on illusion; not real; deceptive.

illustrate *vt* **1** provide pictures for (a book, talk, etc.). **2** provide examples for; clarify. **illustration** *n.*

illustrious *adj* eminent.

image *n* **1** representation or likeness of a person or thing. **2** exact likeness. **3** view of an object as seen in a mirror, lens, etc. **4** mental concept; idea. **5** figure of speech, esp. a metaphor or simile in poetry, etc. **6** way the personality or character of a person, company, etc., is presented to others, esp. the general public. **7** symbol; emblem. **imagery** *n* **1** metaphorical language. **2** repetition or use of certain symbols, as in a cultural tradition.

imagine *vt,vi* **1** form a mental image or idea (of). **2** suppose; believe. **imaginary** *adj* created by the imagination; not real. **imagination** *n* **1** power or ability to create mental concepts or images. **2** act of imagining. **3** baseless or fanciful belief or idea. **imaginative** *adj* **1** having considerable powers of creative imagination. **2** relating to or characterized by imagination. **imaginatively** *adv.*

imbecile *n* idiot.

imitate *vt* **1** copy the behaviour, appearance, etc., of; take as a model. **2** impersonate or mimic. **3** be or look like. **imitation** *n* **1** act of imitating. **2** impersonation or copy. *adj* made of a synthetic material.

immaculate *adj* **1** completely free from dirtiness or untidiness. **2** free from sin; pure. **immaculately** *adv.*

immature *adj* **1** not yet fully grown or developed. **2** lacking adult judgment or stability. **immaturity** *n.*

immediate *adj* **1** without delay; instant. **2** very close or near. **3** without another intervening; next. **immediacy** *n.* **immediately** *adv.*

immense *adj* **1** very large; vast; huge. **2** very great in number, quantity, etc. **immensely** *adv* **1** to an immense degree. **2** very greatly; very much. **immensity** *n.*

immerse *vt* **1** put into water or other liquid; plunge or steep. **2** absorb or engross. **3** involve (someone) in an affair; entangle. **4** baptize (a person) by plunging him in a river, special bath, etc. **immersion** *n.*

immigrate *vi* come to a country other than one's own in order to take up permanent residence. **immigration** *n.* **immigrant** *n* person who immigrates.

imminent *adj* likely to happen very soon. **imminence** *n.* **imminently** *adv.*

immobile *adj* **1** not moving; still or fixed. **2** not capable of moving or being moved. **immobility** *n.* **immobilize** *vt* make incapable of moving. **immobilization** *n.*

immoral *adj* not in accordance with morals; against moral laws. **immorality** *n.*

immortal *adj* **1** never dying or ceasing. **2** never forgotten. **immortality** *n.*

immovable *adj* unable to be moved or altered; rigid. **immovably** *adv.*

immune *adj* **1** protected from a disease, etc., esp. because of previous exposure or inoculation. **2** not affected or moved emotionally (by). **3** free or safe (from). **immunity** *n.* **immunize** *vt* render immune to a disease. **immunization** *n.* **immunology** *n* science dealing with immunity to disease.

imp *n* **1** mischievous small fairy; sprite; goblin. **2** naughty, impudent, or mischievous child. **impish** *adj.*

impact *n* ('impækt) **1** act of one object colliding with another. **2** force with which an object collides with something. **3** effect or impression. *vt* (im'pækt) press forcefully into something or together.

impair *vt* reduce the effectiveness, value, or strength of. **impairment** *n.*

impart *vt* give (information, news, enthusiasm, etc.) to.

impartial *adj* not favouring either side; fair; disinterested; not biased. **impartiality** *n.* **impartially** *adv.*

impatient *adj* **1** not willing to wait or delay. **2** irritated; vexed. **3** intolerant (of). **impatience** *n.* **impatiently** *adv.*

impeach *vt* **1** charge with (a crime, esp. of treason). **2** cast doubt on; call in question. **3** accuse or try to discredit. **impeachment** *n.*

impeccable *adj* without fault; perfect. **impeccably** *adv*.
impediment *n* **1** something that prevents something happening or working properly; obstacle. **2** speech defect, such as a stammer or lisp.
imperative *adj* **1** urgent or necessary; essential. **2** commanding; authoritative. **3** designating that form of a verb used in commands. *n* **1** command. **2** form of a verb used in commands.
imperfect *adj* not perfect; defective, faulty, or incomplete. **imperfection** *n* defect or flaw.
imperial *adj* **1** relating to an emperor or empire. **2** commanding in manner; majestic. **imperialism** *n* form of government in which one state establishes and extends its rule over foreign lands and people. **imperialist** *n,adj*.
impermeable *adj* impervious.
impersonal *adj* **1** not personal; formal; unfriendly. **2** (of verbs) limited in use to the third person singular form with *it* as the subject. **3** (of pronouns) not specifying; indefinite. **impersonally** *adv*.
impersonate *vt* pretend to be (another person). **impersonation** *n*.
impertinent *adj* rude; cheeky; impudent. **impertinence** *n*. **impertinently** *adv*.
impervious *adj* **1** not absorbing liquid; watertight. **2** not affected by criticism, etc.; insensitive.
impetuous *adj* done or acting without due consideration; rash. **impetuosity** *n*. **impetuously** *adv*.
impetus *n* **1** driving force or momentum. **2** incentive.
impinge *vi* come into contact or collision (with). **impinge (up)on 1** have an effect or bearing on. **2** encroach or infringe on. **impingement** *n*.
implement ('impləmənt) *n* tool; instrument. *vt* ('impləment) put (a law, etc.) into force. **implementation** *n*.
implicit *adj* **1** implied though not expressly stated. **2** unquestioning; unqualified; absolute. **implicitly** *adv*.
implore *vt* beg or plead.
imply *vt* **1** state or show in an indirect way. **2** insinuate; suggest; hint at. **3** indicate as a logical consequence. **implication** *n*.
import *vt* (im'pɔ:t) **1** bring (goods) into a country from another for resale, etc. **2** mean; signify. *n* ('impɔ:t) **1** imported commodity. **2** act or practice of importing. **3** importance. **4** meaning; consequence. **importer** *n*.
important *adj* **1** of significance or consequence; notable. **2** wielding power or influence. **3** pompous; self-satisfied. **importance** *n*. **importantly** *adv*.
impose *vt* **1** force to comply with. **2** force to pay (a tax). **3** take advantage of. **4** foist (one's company) on. **imposition** *n*. **imposing** *adj* of grand or impressive appearance or nature.
impossible *adj* **1** not possible; unable to be done. **2** difficult to deal with; annoying. **impossibility** *n*. **impossibly** *adv*.
impostor *n* person who pretends to be someone else in order to cheat or defraud.
impotent *adj* **1** not able to act; powerless or helpless. **2** (of men) not able to have an erection of the penis. **impotence** *or* **impotency** *n*. **impotently** *adv*.
impound *vt* **1** take legal possession of; confiscate. **2** confine; enclose.
impress *vt* **1** have a great effect or influence on the mind or feelings of. **2** cause to remember. **3** press a mark into; stamp. **impressive** *adj* producing a great or lasting effect; remarkable. **impressively** *adv*.
impression *n* **1** effect on the mind or feelings. **2** idea or memory, esp. when vague or general. **3** mark or stamp left when something is pressed on something. **4** imitation or impersonation. **5** printing of a book, esp. a subsequent one with no amendments. **impressionable** *adj* easily impressed. **impressionism** *n* late 19th-century movement in the arts, using effects of light, sound, form, etc., to give a general impression of the subject.
imprint *vt* (im'print) **1** stamp or print on to. **2** make a lasting impression on. *n* ('imprint) **1** mark or print on something. **2** publisher's or printer's mark, as on the title page of a book.
improbable *adj* unlikely; not very probable. **improbability** *n*.
impromptu *adj,adv* made or done without preparation, rehearsal, or consideration. *n* short piece of music.
improper *adj* **1** not proper; not conforming to rules of etiquette, morality, etc. **2** unsuitable; inappropriate. **improperly** *adv*.
improve *vi,vt* become or make better or more valuable. **improvement** *n*.
improvise *vt,vi* **1** make or do (something)

without preparation or proper materials. **2** play (music) without rehearsal or with the addition of one's own embellishments. **improvisation** *n*.

impudent *adj* rude; cheeky; insolent; impertinent. **impudence** *n*. **impudently** *adv*.

impulse *n* **1** sudden desire for something; whim. **2** thing that drives or forces something to happen. **3** electrical signal in certain machines. **impulsive** *adj* done or acting on impulse. **impulsively** *adv*.

impure *adj* **1** not pure; mixed with other substances. **2** not chaste; indecent. **impurely** *adv*. **impurity** *n*.

in *prep* **1** on the inside of; within. **2** at or to (a place). **3** during. **4** according to. **5** involved with. **6** through the medium of; using. **7** made of. **8** wearing. *adv* **1** inside; on the interior. **2** at home. **3** so as to have power. **4** so as to be fashionable. **5** accepted as a friend. **in for** going to receive or experience. **in on** knowing about. *n* **ins and outs** complicated details.

inability *n* lack of ability, power, or means.

inaccurate *adj* not accurate; wrong; incorrect. **inaccuracy** *n*. **inaccurately** *adv*.

inadequate *adj* **1** not adequate; insufficient. **2** not able to cope or deal with a task, etc. **inadequacy** *n*. **inadequately** *adv*.

inadvertent *adj* **1** done, said, etc., by accident. **2** not paying attention; careless; heedless. **inadvertently** *adv*.

inane *adj* **1** having no sense; silly. **2** having no content; empty; void. **inanely** *adv*. **inaneness** *or* **inanity** *n*.

inarticulate *adj* **1** not able to voice one's thoughts or feelings fluently. **2** not clearly said or expressed. **inarticulately** *adv*.

inasmuch *adv* **inasmuch as** since; because.

inaugurate *vt* **1** declare open or in use with ceremony. **2** install in office ceremonially. **inaugural** *adj*. **inauguration** *n*.

incapable *adj* **1** not able (to). **2** not capable; lacking the necessary powers. **incapacity** *n*. **incapacitate** *vt* render incapable or unfit; disable.

incendiary *adj* **1** relating to fires, esp. intentional fires. **2** stirring up strong feelings, esp. of revolt against authority. *n* **1** person who illegally sets fire to buildings, etc. **2** person who stirs up revolt, violence, etc. **3** type of bomb causing fires.

incense[1] *n* ('insens) substance that gives off sweet or aromatic smells when burnt.

incense[2] *vt* (in'sens) enrage.

incessant *adj* never-ending; constant; ceaseless. **incessantly** *adv*.

incest *n* illicit sexual intercourse between closely related members of the same family. **incestuous** *adj*.

inch *n* unit of length equal to one twelfth of a foot or 2.54 centimetres. *vi* move forward very slowly.

incident *n* event or occurrence. **incidence** *n* degree or scope of occurrence of something. **incidental** *adj* **1** happening at the same time as or as a natural part of. **2** not specially planned; chance; casual. **3** less important or significant. **incidentally** *adv* **1** in an incidental manner. **2** by the way.

incisor *n* tooth adapted for cutting.

incite *vt* stir up in; inflame; urge on. **incitement** *n*.

incline *v* (in'klain) *vt,vi* **1** slope or slant. **2** tend or cause to tend towards. *vt* **1** bend or bow (the head, etc.). **2** influence (someone) towards; dispose. *n* ('inklain, in'klain) slope; gradient. **inclination** *n*.

include *vt* **1** contain as a part or member; comprise. **2** regard as a part of a category, class, etc. **inclusion** *n*. **inclusive** *adj*.

incognito *adj,adv* in disguise; under an assumed identity.

incoherent *adj* not easy to understand because of being rambling, inconsistent, or illogical. **incoherently** *adv*.

income *n* money gained, esp. regularly, from work done, investments, etc.

incompatible *adj* **1** not able to agree or remain on friendly terms together. **2** not capable of or suitable for existing, working, etc. (with or together). **incompatibility** *n*.

incompetent *adj* **1** lacking the necessary skill or knowledge. **2** not capable or able; inefficient. *n* person who is incapable or inefficient. **incompetence** *or* **incompetency** *n*. **incompetently** *adv*.

incongruous *adj* out of place; irrelevant; not suitable. **incongruously** *adv*.

inconsistent *adj* **1** not consistent. **2** changing one's opinions often. **3** not agreeing or compatible. **inconsistency** *n*. **inconsistently** *adv*.

inconvenient *adj* not convenient; causing

trouble or difficulty. **inconvenience** *n.* **inconveniently** *adv.*

incorporate *vt,vi* unite, blend, or mix into another body or thing. **incorporation** *n.*

increase *vt,vi* (in'kri:s) make or become more, larger, or greater; multiply; enlarge. *n* ('inkri:s) **1** act or fact of increasing. **2** amount increased by. **increasingly** *adv* more and more.

incredible *adj* **1** not able to be believed; unlikely or amazing. **2** very surprising; extraordinary. **incredibly** *adv.*

incubate *vt* (of birds, reptiles, etc.) sit on eggs to hatch them. *vi* **1** (of eggs) hatch. **2** undergo incubation. **incubation** *n* **1** hatching of eggs. **2** stage of a disease between infection and the appearance of symptoms. **incubator** *n* **1** heated apparatus in which delicate or premature new-born babies are protected. **2** similar device for hatching eggs, growing bacteria, etc.

incur *vt* (-rr-) bring upon oneself; become liable or responsible for.

indecent *adj* **1** shameful; immodest. **2** improper or unseemly. **indecency** *n.* **indecently** *adv.*

indeed *adv* **1** certainly. **2** in fact. *interj* really!

indefinite *adj* **1** not clearly or exactly stated, limited, or defined. **2** not precise or fixed; vague; unsure. **3** (of pronouns) impersonal. **indefinite article** *n* 'a' or 'an'. **indefinitely** *adv* **1** in an indefinite manner. **2** for an unknown, esp. a long, period of time.

indent *vt* **1** put or cut notches or regular recesses in. **2** set lines (such as the first line of a paragraph) in printed or written matter further from the margin than the rest. **indentation** *n* **1** act of indenting. **2** notched portion as formed. **3** series of such notches or recesses.

independent *adj* **1** not under the control or authority of someone or something else; free; self-governing. **2** not relying or dependent on other people or things; self-sufficient. **3** without any connection (with) or reference (to). **independence** *n.* **independently** *adv.*

index *n, pl* **index** *or* **indices** ('indisi:z) **1** alphabetical list of names, subjects, etc., at the end of a book, indicating where or on what page they are mentioned. **2** pointer on a dial, etc. **3** indication; sign. *vt* provide an index for (a book). **index finger** *n* finger next to the thumb.

indicate *vt* **1** show, as by sign or gesture; point out. **2** imply; mean. **indication** *n.* **indicative** *adj* suggestive (of); meaning or implying (that). *adj,n* (of or designating) grammatical mood of verbs expressing simple statements, not wishes, etc. **indicator** *n* **1** person or thing that indicates, esp. a directional signal on a car. **2** chemical substance that changes colour when certain reactions take place.

indifferent *adj* **1** not caring (about); not interested (in). **2** mediocre. **indifference** *n.* **indifferently** *adv.*

indigenous *adj* originally belonging (to); native.

indigestion *n* **1** inability to digest food or difficulty in digesting. **2** pain in the stomach caused by this. **indigestible** *adj* not easy to digest.

indignant *adj* righteously angry, as at something one considers justifies anger. **indignantly** *adv.* **indignation** *n.*

indirect *adj* not direct, straightforward, or explicit. **indirectly** *adv.*

individual *adj* of, for, or characteristic of one particular person or thing. *n* **1** single person, as distinguished from a group. **2** any person. **individuality** *n.* **individually** *adv.*

indoctrinate *vt* teach (someone) rigidly so that he does not question or think for himself. **indoctrination** *n.*

indolent *adj* lazy; idle. **indolence** *n.* **indolently** *adv.*

indoor *adj* done or suitable for inside a house or other building. **indoors** *adv* in, into, or inside a house or other building.

induce *vt* **1** have the effect of; cause; produce. **2** persuade or influence. **inducement** *n.*

indulge *vi,vt* yield to or satisfy (a desire, whim, etc.). *vt* pamper; spoil. **indulgence** *n.* **indulgent** *adj.*

industry *n* **1** system of manufacturing goods using mechanization. **2** particular branch of this; trade. **3** hard work or diligent application. **industrial** *adj* relating to industry. **industrially** *adv.* **industrialism** *n.* **industrialist** *n.* **industrialize** *vt* bring industry, factories, etc., to. **industrialization** *n.*

inebriate *vt* intoxicate.

inept *adj* **1** not suitable or appropriate. **2** stupid; slow, as to learn. **ineptly** *adv.* **ineptness** *n.* **ineptitude** *n* **1** ineptness. **2** inept remark, etc.

inequality *n* state or instance of a person or

thing being unequal, esp. in having fewer rights or advantages.

inert *adj* **1** not showing movement, activity, or change; sluggish. **2** not chemically active. **inertly** *adv*. **inertia** *n* lack of activity or movement.

inevitable *adj* unavoidable; certain to happen. **inevitability** *n*. **inevitably** *adv*.

inextricable *adj* unable to be separated, parted, or solved. **inextricably** *adv*.

infallible *adj* **1** never failing; always successful, correct, or effective. **2** certain; inevitable. **infallibility** *n*. **infallibly** *adv*.

infamous ('infəməs) *adj* **1** notorious; disreputable. **2** shocking; scandalous. **infamy** *n*.

infant *n* **1** small child. **2** person under eighteen and therefore not legally independent or responsible; minor. **infancy** *n* **1** period of being an infant. **2** early stages of development. **infantile** *adj* childishly immature.

infantry *n* foot soldiers.

infatuated *adj* wildly or foolishly in love or obsessed, esp. temporarily. **infatuation** *n*.

infect *vt* **1** transmit a disease or germs to. **2** communicate a feeling to. **3** pollute; contaminate. **infectious** *adj*. **infection** *n* **1** act of infecting or state of being infected. **2** disease or organism causing disease.

infer *vt* (-rr-) deduce; conclude. **inference** *n*.

inferior *adj* lower in position, rank, value, or quality. *n* person lower in rank or authority; subordinate. **inferiority** *n*.

infernal *adj* **1** of, like, or found in hell or the underworld. **2** wicked; diabolical. **3** annoying; confounded. **infernally** *adv*.

infest *vt* (of vermin, pests, etc.) swarm over or into; overrun. **infestation** *n*.

infidelity *n* **1** unfaithful or disloyal act or behaviour. **2** adultery.

infiltrate *vt* enter (a country, political group, etc.) gradually and stealthily as to subvert it. **infiltration** *n*. **infiltrator** *n*.

infinite *adj* without end or limit; boundless or countless. **infinity** *n*. **infinitely** *adv* **1** without limit or end. **2** extremely; very.

infinitive *n* grammatical form of verbs, usually preceded by *to*, and not indicating tense, person, or subject.

infirm *adj* **1** in poor health; ill or weak. **2** not resolute; uncertain. **infirmity** *n*.

inflame *vt* **1** cause a part of the body, etc., to become red and swollen, as when hit or infected. **2** anger or excite. **3** make more intense or worse. **inflammable** *adj* **1** likely to ignite; easy to burn. **2** excitable. **inflammation** *n* **1** act of inflaming or state of being inflamed. **2** swelling or redness.

inflate *vt,vi* **1** fill with gas; blow or swell up. **2** raise (prices) or increase in price. **inflation** *n* persistent fall in the value of money leading to continuously rising prices. **inflationary** *adj*.

inflection *n* **1** modulation of tone and stress in speech. **2** alteration in the form of a word to denote a grammatical change, as in the tense, number, case, etc.

inflict *vt* make (a person) suffer, undergo, or endure (something unpleasant); impose. **infliction** *n*.

influence *vt* have an impression on; affect; persuade, often indirectly. *n* **1** power to influence others. **2** person or thing that influences. **influential** *adj*.

influenza *n also inf* **flu** contagious viral disease characterized by fever, breathing difficulties, and muscular aches and pains.

influx *n* sudden abundant flow or large increase.

inform *vt* **1** tell; instruct; impart knowledge (to). **2** give character to; inspire. **inform on** reveal a person's activities, esp. secret or discreditable ones, to a higher authority. **informer** *n* person who informs on others. **information** *n* knowledge acquired from another source; news; relevant facts. **informative** *adj*.

informal *adj* casual; easy-going; not formal. **informality** *n*. **informally** *adv*.

infringe *vi* go beyond the limits or boundaries of. *vt* break or disobey (a law or rule). **infringement** *n*.

infuriate *vt* annoy or irritate intensely.

infuse *vt* impart; inspire. *vt,vi* soak or steep in a liquid, esp. to extract flavour. **infusion** *n*.

ingenious *adj* inventive; cleverly contrived; resourceful; cunning. **ingenuity** *n*.

ingenuous *adj* innocent or naive; not sophisticated.

ingredient *n* constituent; something that forms part of a mixture.

inhabit *vt* live or reside in. **inhabitable** *adj*. **inhabitant** *n* person living in a place; occupier.

inhale *vt,vi* draw into the lungs; breathe in.

inherent *adj* existing as an essential part (of). **inherently** *adv*.

inherit *vt,vi* have as a legacy; become heir (to).

vt possess (a family trait); derive from one's family. **inheritance** *n*.

inhibit *vt* prevent; restrain; hold back. **inhibition** *n*.

inhuman *adj* cruel; barbarous; unfeeling. **inhumanity** *n*.

initial *adj* existing at the beginning or outset; early; first. *n* first letter of a name. *vt* (-ll-) sign one's initials on.

initiate *vt* (ɪˈnɪʃɪeɪt) **1** begin; originate. **2** introduce; admit. *n* (ɪˈnɪʃɪɪt) initiated person. **initiation** *n*.

initiative *n* **1** capacity to be enterprising and efficient. **2** first step; introductory move.

inject *vt* **1** drive (liquid) into living tissue using a syringe. **2** introduce vigorously. **injection** *n*.

injure *vt* hurt; harm; damage. **injury** *n* **1** damage. **2** wound. **3** something causing damage or offence.

injustice *n* **1** lack of fairness; practice of being biased or unjust. **2** wrong; unjust act.

ink *n* coloured liquid used in writing, printing, etc.

inkling *n* hint; vague idea; notion.

inland *adj* **1** situated in the interior of a country or region; away from the coast. **2** operating inside a country; domestic. *adv* towards an inland area. *n* interior of a country or region. **Inland Revenue** *n* **1** money obtained by taxes and duties levied within a country and on residents living abroad. **2** government body that collects and administers this money.

inmate *n* **1** person confined to an institution. **2** occupant.

inn *n* public house, esp. one that serves meals and offers lodgings.

innate *adj* inherent in one's nature. **innately** *adv*.

inner *adj* **1** situated or occurring further in, inside, or within. **2** not superficial; hidden.

innings *n pl or s* turn of a batsman or team of batsmen in cricket.

innocent *adj* **1** ignorant of evil; uncorrupted; naive; unsophisticated. **2** not guilty. **3** not harmful. *n* innocent person. **innocence** *n*. **innocently** *adv*.

innocuous *adj* totally harmless.

innovation *n* a newly introduced device, procedure, method, or change. **innovate** *vt,vi* make an innovation.

innuendo *n, pl* **innuendoes** malicious or obscene implication or reference.

innumerable *adj* too many to be calculated; countless.

inoculate *vt,vi* introduce a vaccine into the body to immunize against a specific disease. **inoculation** *n*.

input *n* amount, material, or data put into or supplied to a machine, factory, project, etc.

inquest *n* **1** judicial inquiry, esp. one into an unnatural death. **2** any official investigation.

inquire *vi* investigate; request information. *vt,vi* enquire. **inquiry** *n* **1** investigation; official examination of the facts. **2** enquiry.

inquisition *n* lengthy, thorough, and painful investigation or interrogation. **The Inquisition** tribunal set up by the Roman Catholic Church to abolish heresy. **inquisitor** *n*.

inquisitive *adj* **1** fond of inquiring into other people's affairs; curious. **2** eager to learn. **inquisitively** *adv*. **inquisitiveness** *n*.

insane *adj* **1** mentally ill or out of control; mad; crazy. **2** dangerously foolish. **insanely** *adv*. **insanity** *n*.

insatiable *adj* unable to be satisfied; voracious; greedy.

inscribe *vt* write, engrave, or mark (names, words, etc.). **inscription** *n*.

insect *n* **1** invertebrate animal or class of animals with six legs, a segmented body, and wings, such as beetles, butterflies, flies, and ants. **2** *inf* any similar animal, such as a spider. **insecticide** *n* substance used to kill insects.

insecure *adj* **1** not balanced; wobbly; unsafe. **2** lacking confidence or stability. **insecurely** *adv*. **insecurity** *n*.

inseminate *vt* implant semen into (a female). **insemination** *n*.

insensible *adj* **1** insensitive; indifferent. **2** unconscious; unable to experience sensations.

insensitive *adj* **1** thick-skinned; not sensitive. **2** heartless; cruel; ruthless.

insert *vt* put or place in, among, or between; introduce into. **insertion** *n*.

inside *n* **1** inner area, surface, or side; interior. **2** *inf* stomach. *adj* relating to the inside. *adv* **1** on or in the inside; indoors. **2** *inf* in prison. *prep also* **inside of** within; on the inside of.

insidious *adj* **1** secretly spreading; tending to corrupt or destroy. **2** intended to trap; treacherous. **insidiously** *adv*. **insidiousness** *n*.

insight *n* **1** perception; discernment; sympathetic understanding. **2** sudden revealing glimpse.

insinuate *vt* **1** imply or hint (something unpleasant). **2** introduce covertly or gradually. **insinuation** *n*.

insist *vt,vi* **1** declare or assert emphatically or repeatedly. **2** demand strongly; persist in urging. **insistence** *n*. **insistent** *adj* persistent; demanding attention.

insolent *adj* insulting; impertinent; rude. **insolence** *n*. **insolently** *adv*.

insoluble *adj* **1** not soluble. **2** unable to be solved.

insolvent *adj* unable to meet debts; bankrupt. *n* insolvent person. **insolvency** *n*.

insomnia *n* inability to get to sleep. **insomniac** *n* person suffering from insomnia.

inspect *vt* examine; scrutinize; look into; investigate. **inspection** *n*. **inspector** *n* **1** person, esp. an official, who inspects. **2** police officer inferior in rank to a superintendent and superior to a sergeant.

inspire *vt* **1** stimulate; fill with creative or intellectual urges or impulses. **2** arouse; excite. **3** communicate or produce by superhuman influence. **inspiration** *n* **1** artistic genius or impulse. **2** sudden bright idea.

instability *n* lack of stability, esp. in mood or character.

install *vt* **1** fix (apparatus) in position ready for use. **2** place in office. **3** settle; set (oneself) down. **installation** *n*.

instalment *n* one portion of something that appears, is sent, or paid in parts at regular intervals or over a period of time.

instance *n* example; illustration of a general statement or truth. **for instance** for example. **in the first instance** to begin with; firstly.

instant *adj* **1** occurring immediately or at once; immediate; urgent. **2** requiring little or no preparation. *n* **1** precise moment. **2** brief time. **instantaneous** *adj* occurring or done immediately or with little delay. **instantaneously** *adv*. **instantly** *adv* immediately; at once.

instead *adv* as an alternative. **instead of** in place of; rather than.

instep *n* **1** top part of the foot between the toes and ankle. **2** part of a shoe, etc., that covers the instep.

instigate *vt* stir up; urge; incite; bring about. **instigation** *n*. **instigator** *n*.

instil *vt* (-ll-) gradually introduce (ideas, values, etc.) into the mind. **instillation** *n*.

instinct *n* **1** innate impulse or feeling. **2** mode of behaviour that is innate and not learned or acquired through experience. **instinctive** *adj*. **instinctively** *adv*.

institute *vt* establish; start up. *n* society or establishment, esp. for promoting the arts or sciences or for education. **institution** *n* **1** act of instituting. **2** established law, procedure, custom, or practice. **3** establishment set up for educational, medical, social, or corrective purposes. **institutional** *adj*.

instruct *vt* teach; direct; order. **instruction** *n* **1** act of instructing. **2** information. **instructions** *pl n* directions as to use, etc.; orders. **instructive** *adj* informative.

instrument *n* **1** implement; tool; mechanical device. **2** object played to produce music. **3** person exploited by another as a means to an end. **instrumental** *adj*. **instrumentalist** *n* person who plays a musical instrument. **instrumentation** *n* arrangement of music for instruments; orchestration.

insubordinate *adj* disobedient; rebelling against authority. *n* insubordinate person. **insubordination** *n*.

insular *adj* **1** inward-looking; narrow-minded; remote; aloof. **2** relating to an island. **insularity** *n*.

insulate *vt* **1** protect against heat or sound loss or the passage of electric current by means of nonconducting material. **2** isolate or separate by means of a barrier. **insulation** *n*.

insulin *n* hormone secreted by the pancreas to control blood sugar levels.

insult *vt* (in'sʌlt) speak or act in order to hurt a person's pride or dignity; abuse. *n* ('insʌlt) insulting remark or action.

insure *vt* **1** safeguard against loss, damage, illness, etc., by paying insurance. **2** ensure. **insurance** *n* **1** act, system, or business of insuring. **2** state of being insured. **3** money paid to provide financial compensation in the event of illness, injury, loss of or damage to property, etc. **4** financial protection so obtained.

intact *adj* **1** whole; complete. **2** unharmed; untouched.

intake *n* amount or number taken in, admitted, or consumed.

integer ('intidʒə) *n* whole number.

integral *adj* **1** being an essential part (of). **2** complete; entire.

integrate *vt* combine or mix parts to make a whole; coordinate; unify. **integration** *n*.

integrity *n* **1** uprightness; honesty; soundness of character. **2** unity; wholeness.

intellect *n* **1** ability to absorb knowledge and think rationally; intelligence. **2** person of great intelligence; brilliant mind. **intellectual** *adj* **1** relating to the intellect. **2** having or revealing great powers of mind. *n* person of high intellect and cultural tastes, esp. one interested in ideas.

intelligence *n* **1** ability to learn, to reason, and to use the mental faculties. **2** information, esp. secret information about an enemy. **intelligent** *adj* possessing or showing intelligence; clever. **intelligently** *adv*. **intelligible** *adj* comprehensible; capable of being easily understood.

intend *vt* have as a purpose; mean.

intense *adj* **1** extreme. **2** strenuous; strong. **3** violent; deeply felt; passionate. **4** unable to relax; tense. **intensely** *adv*. **intensify** *vt,vi* make or become stronger, greater, brighter, or more extreme. **intensification** *n*. **intensity** *n* **1** quality or state of being intense. **2** strength; power; concentration. **intensive** *adj* **1** thorough and organized; exhaustive; concentrated. **2** requiring and using large amounts of labour or capital. **intensively** *adv*.

intent *adj* **1** determined; resolved; having in mind. **2** concentrating (on). *n* purpose; motive. **to all intents and purposes** as good as; more or less; pretty well. **intention** *n* aim; purpose; plan of action; design; motive. **intentional** *adj* meant; on purpose. **intentionally** *adv*.

inter (in'tə:) *vt* (-rr-) bury.

interact *vi* have an effect upon other things; influence. **interaction** *n*.

intercept *vt* stop or seize during transit; interrupt the progress of. **interception** *n*.

interchange *vt,vi* **1** exchange; switch. **2** substitute; alternate. *n* **1** exchange; alternation. **2** motorway junction of interconnecting roads and bridges. **interchangeable** *adj*.

intercourse *n* **1** dealings; interchange of ideas, benefits, etc. **2** *also* **sexual intercourse** copulation.

interest *n* **1** curiosity; concern; involvement. **2** cause of such a feeling. **3** pursuit; pastime; hobby. **4** personal advantage. **5** right, share, or claim, as in a business. **6** charge or payment for a financial loan. *vt* arouse the curiosity of; take an interest in. **interested** *adj* **1** having or showing interest. **2** personally involved.

interfere *vi* meddle; concern oneself with others' affairs. **interfere with** have a bad effect on; impede; hinder; molest. **interference** *n* **1** act of interfering. **2** interruption of broadcast signals by atmospheric conditions, etc.

interim *n* time between; time that has elapsed; meantime. *adj* temporary.

interior *n* **1** inside, esp. of a house or room. **2** inland regions of a country. *adj* of, on, or in the interior.

interjection *n* exclamation; sudden interrupting remark. **interject** *vt* interpose; interrupt with.

interlock *vi,vt* lock together; join firmly or inextricably.

interlude *n* **1** intermission; interval. **2** intervening period or episode of contrasting activity.

intermediary *n* go-between; mediator. *adj* **1** acting as an intermediary. **2** intermediate.

intermediate *adj* coming or existing between; in between.

intermission *n* **1** short interval; pause between the parts of a performance, film show, etc. **2** respite; rest.

intermittent *adj* occurring at intervals; sporadic; periodic. **intermittently** *adv*.

intern *vt* confine to a particular area, camp, or prison, esp. during wartime. **internee** *n*.

internal *adj* **1** concerning the interior workings or inside of something. **2** domestic; within a country. **3** essential; intrinsic. **internally** *adv*.

international *adj* of, between, or shared by a number of countries. *n* **1** member of a national team. **2** international match or contest.

interpose *vt,vi* **1** put in or between; interrupt (with). **2** intervene; mediate.

interpret *vt,vi* **1** translate. **2** reveal the meaning or significance of. **3** take to mean; understand. **interpretation** *n*. **interpreter** *n* person who makes an immediate verbal translation of speech.

interrogate *vt* ask (a prisoner or suspect) a series of questions; cross-examine; cross-question. **interrogation** *n*. **interrogator** *n*. **interrogative** *adj* **1** questioning; in the form of a query. **2** describing a word, such as *who* or *which*, used in or forming a question. *n* interrogative word.

interrupt *vt,vi* **1** stop the flow, passage, or progress (of). **2** break in (on); disturb. *vt* obstruct. **interruption** *n*.

intersect *vt,vi* divide by crossing; cut across; cross. **intersection** *n* **1** act of intersecting. **2** place or point where two things cross.

interval *n* **1** period of time between two events, acts, or parts; intermission. **2** intervening space.

intervene *vi* **1** occur or come between. **2** interfere or step in in order to prevent, hinder, or protest. **intervention** *n*.

interview *n* **1** formal meeting or discussion. **2** conversation between a journalist and a newsworthy person. **3** article resulting from this. *vt* have an interview with. **interviewer** *n*.

intestines *pl n* portion of the digestive tract between the stomach and anus. **intestinal** *adj*.

intimate[1] ('intimit) *adj* **1** close; dear; being a good friend. **2** deep; profound; private. **3** sexual; having sexual relations. *n* close friend. **intimacy** *n*.

intimate[2] ('intimeit) *vi* hint; imply.

intimidate *vt* **1** frighten; make nervous or timid; bully. **2** discourage by threats. **intimidation** *n*.

into *prep* **1** in; to the inside of. **2** to; from one point or condition to another.

intolerable *adj* **1** unbearable; unendurable. **2** extremely annoying. **intolerably** *adv*.

intolerant *adj* not tolerant; narrow-minded; bigoted. **intolerance** *n*.

intonation *n* **1** variation of pitch in the speaking voice. **2** correct pitching of musical notes.

intoxicate *vt* **1** make drunk; inebriate. **2** excite; inflame; exhilarate. **intoxication** *n*.

intransitive *adj* describing a verb that does not take or need a direct object.

intricate *adj* complex; complicated; difficult to work out or solve. **intricacy** *n*. **intricately** *adv*.

intrigue *n* ('intri:g) **1** plot; conspiracy; secret plan. **2** illicit love affair. *v* (in'tri:g) *vt* fascinate; stimulate the curiosity or wonder of. *vi* plot; conspire.

intrinsic *adj* real; fundamental; essential. **intrinsically** *adv*.

introduce *vt* **1** bring in; put forward. **2** bring into use; first establish. **3** present and identify (a stranger) to another or others; make acquainted. **4** insert. **introduction** *n* **1** act of introducing. **2** something introduced. **3** preface; foreword; opening. **4** preliminary guide; basic handbook. **introductory** *adj*.

introspective *adj* mentally inward-looking; aware of and critical of one's mental processes.

introvert *n* withdrawn or introspective person.

intrude *vt,vi* force (one's presence, etc.) uninvited. **intruder** *n*. **intrusion** *n*. **intrusive** *adj*.

intuition *n* **1** ability to perceive and understand things instinctively. **2** knowledge acquired through this ability; hunch. **intuitive** *adj* using or revealing powers of intuition rather than logic or rationality. **intuitively** *adv*.

inundate *vt* flood; overwhelm; swamp. **inundation** *n*.

invade *vt,vi* attack or forcibly enter (another's country or territory). *vt* violate; intrude or encroach on. **invader** *n*. **invasion** *n*.

invalid[1] ('invəli:d) *n* sick, disabled, or permanently bedridden person. *vt also* **invalid out** send home or retire (military personnel) because of ill health or injury.

invalid[2] (in'vælid) *adj* not valid; not legally justifiable or effective. **invalidate** *vt* render invalid. **invalidation** *n*.

invaluable *adj* of great worth or usefulness; priceless.

invariable *adj* constant; unvarying; not changing; usual. **invariably** *adv* always; constantly.

invent *vt* **1** think up (something untrue or imaginary). **2** design or devise (something new or original). **inventor** *n*. **invention** *n* **1** act of inventing. **2** thing invented. **3** ability to invent; ingenuity. **inventive** *adj* good at thinking up or creating new ideas or things; ingenious.

invert *vt* turn upside down; put back to front; reverse. **inverse** *adj* inverted; back to front; contrary. **inversion** *n*.

invertebrate *adj* having no backbone. *n* invertebrate animal.

invest *vt,vi* put in (money, capital, time, effort, etc.) in order to make a profit. *vt* **1** endow; provide. **2** confer a rank or office upon with ceremony. **investor** *n*. **investiture** *n* ceremonial conferring of office. **investment** *n* **1** act of investing. **2** thing invested.

investigate *vt* make enquiries about; look into; examine; inquire into. **investigation** *n*. **investigator** *n*.

invincible *adj* unconquerable.

invisible *adj* **1** incapable of being seen. **2** hard to see; not conspicuous. **invisibility** *n*.

invite *vt* **1** request (a person) to be present or take part. **2** ask for (comments, questions, etc.). **3** court; provoke. **invitation** *n* **1** act of inviting. **2** spoken or written request for a person's presence.

invoice *n* bill listing goods sold or services rendered with prices charged. *vt* present with or make an invoice of.

invoke *vt* summon the powers of; appeal or call for. **invocation** *n*.

involve *vt* **1** include. **2** embroil; entangle. **3** engross. **4** entail; mean. **involvement** *n*.

inward *adj* **1** inner. **2** existing in the mind or emotions; situated within. **inwardly** *adv* inside; deep down. **inwards** *adv* towards the inside or middle.

iodine *n* chemical element found in seawater and seaweed and used in photography and the manufacture of antiseptics and dyes.

ion *n* positively or negatively charged atom or group of atoms. **ionize** *vt,vi* convert into ions.

iridescent *adj* shimmering with rainbow colours. **iridescence** *n*.

iris *n* **1** circular coloured area around the pupil of the eye. **2** garden plant with narrow leaves and purple or yellow flowers.

iron *n* **1** malleable magnetic metallic element that is easily corroded and widely used in alloyed form, esp. steel. **2** heated appliance for removing creases from clothes, etc. **3** iron or steel tool, usually heated. **4** great hardness, strength, or resolution. **5** golf club with a metal head. *vt,vi* remove creases from (clothes, etc.) with a hot iron. **iron out** settle; put right. **Iron Curtain** *n* the ideological, cultural, and social barrier that exists between the Soviet dominated countries of Eastern Europe and most of Western Europe. **ironmonger** *n* person selling hardware, tools, etc. **ironmongery** *n* **1** hardware, tools, etc. **2** shop or business of an ironmonger.

irony *n* **1** subtle use of words to imply a meaning opposite to the literal one. **2** incongruous usually unfortunate situation or sequence of events. **ironic** *or* **ironical** *adj*. **ironically** *adv*.

irrational *adj* not rational or consistent; illogical. **irrationality** *n*. **irrationally** *adv*.

irreconcilable *adj* not capable of being reconciled or made compatible. **irreconcilably** *adv*.

irregular *adj* **1** not occurring regularly. **2** not symmetrical; uneven; not uniform. **3** contravening customs, rules, or laws. **4** not following the usual grammatical pattern. **irregularity** *n*. **irregularly** *adv*.

irrelevant *adj* not relevant or applicable. **irrelevance** *n*.

irresistible *adj* **1** impossible to resist. **2** extremely delightful or charming; fascinating. **irresistibly** *adv*.

irrespective *adv* **irrespective of** not taking into consideration; regardless of.

irresponsible *adj* not behaving in a responsible manner; unreliable. **irresponsibly** *adv*.

irrevocable (i'revəkəbəl) *adj* unable to be reversed; unalterable. **irrevocably** *adv*.

irrigate *vt* keep (land) constantly supplied with water using ditches, pipes, etc. **irrigation** *n*.

irritate *vt* **1** annoy; exasperate. **2** sore; itch; chafe. **irritation** *n*. **irritable** *adj* easily annoyed.

is *v* 3rd person singular form of **be** in the present tense.

Islam *n* **1** Muslim faith based on a belief in one God, Allah, and on the teachings of his prophet, Mohammed, set down in the Koran. **2** Muslim culture; Muslim world. **Islamic** *adj*.

island *n* **1** area of land surrounded by water. **2** anything resembling an island in being isolated from its surroundings. **islander** *n*. **isle** *n* small island.

isolate *vt* **1** set apart or keep separate. **2** put in quarantine. **isolation** *n*.

issue *vi* **1** emerge; come, go, or pour out. **2** result; be derived. *vt* **1** give out; offer; distribute. **2** publish. *n* **1** something issued at one time, such as stamps or copies of a magazine or journal. **2** outflow; discharge. **3** disputed point; question; topic. **4** result. **5** offspring. **at issue** in dispute; under discussion. **take issue** disagree; dispute.

it *pron* **1** that or this thing, animal, group, etc., when not specified or identified precisely or when previously mentioned. **2** used as the subject with impersonal verbs such as 'rain', 'snow', etc. **3** used as the subject or object when referring to a following clause or phrase.

italic *adj* in or denoting a style of type with letters sloping to the right. *n also* **italics** italic type, sometimes used to isolate or emphasize a word or phrase.

itch *n* **1** irritating sensation of the skin causing a desire to scratch. **2** constant craving; restless desire. *vi* have or feel an itch. **itchy** *adj*.

item *n* **1** one unit or object from a list or collection. **2** piece of news or information. **itemize** *vt* list.

itinerary *n* **1** detailed plan of a journey; route. **2** account of a journey. **itinerant** *adj* travelling from place to place. *n* itinerant worker.

its *adj* belonging to it. **itself** *r pron* of its own self.

ivory *n* hard smooth cream-coloured highly prized material forming the tusks of the elephant, walrus, etc.

ivy *n* trailing evergreen plant with shiny leaves.

J

jab *vt,vi* (-bb-) poke; thrust; stab. *n* **1** sharp thrust or poke. **2** *inf* injection.

jack *n* **1** tool used for raising heavy objects, esp. a vehicle. **2** lowest court card in a pack; knave. *vt,vi also* **jack up** raise by using a jack. **jackpot** *n* accumulated sum of money given as a prize.

jackal *n* wild animal of the dog family.

jackdaw *n* large black bird of the crow family.

jacket *n* **1** short coat. **2** *also* **dust jacket** detachable paper cover of a book. **3** skin of a baked potato.

jade *n* semiprecious hard stone of a green or whitish colour, valued as a gemstone.

jaded *adj* worn out or stale; weary.

jagged ('dʒægid) *adj* having rough sharp points or edges.

jaguar *n* wild animal of the cat family resembling the leopard.

jail *or* **gaol** *n* prison. *vt* imprison. **jailer** *n*.

jam[1] *v* (-mm-) *vt* **1** crush or squeeze into a confined space; cram; clog. **2** *also* **jam on** apply (brakes) suddenly and forcefully. *vt,vi* stick or become stuck; wedge. *n* congestion or blockage, esp. of a number of vehicles on the road.

jam[2] *n* preserve made by boiling fruit and sugar together.

jangle *vi,vt* produce a harsh or discordant metallic ringing sound. *n* harsh metallic ringing sound.

janitor *n* caretaker; porter; warden.

January *n* first month of the year.

jar[1] *n* glass or earthenware vessel used for preserves, pickles, etc.

jar[2] *vi,vt* (-rr-) **1** vibrate with an unpleasant grating sound. **2** grate (on the nerves). *n* jolt; grating vibration.

jargon *n* **1** idiomatic or specialized language developed by a particular group, trade, or profession. **2** any talk or writing difficult to understand.

jasmine *n* shrub of the olive family having sweet-scented yellow, red, or white flowers.

jaundice *n* disease caused by excessive bile pigment in the blood, characterized by a yellowing of the skin. **jaundiced** *adj* affected or distorted by prejudice, jealousy, etc.

jaunt *n* **1** short trip or excursion. **2** spree; carefree adventure.

jaunty *adj* sprightly; brisk; lively. **jauntily** *adv*.

javelin *n* long slender spear thrown as a field event in athletics.

jaw *n* bony structure forming the bottom of the face or head in which the teeth are set. **jaws** *pl n* gripping part of a machine, tool, etc. ~*vi inf* gossip; chatter. **jawbone** *n* either of the two bones of the jaw.

jazz *n* popular music of Negro origin, often improvised and making use of syncopation.

jealous *adj* experiencing strong feelings of resentment or envy, esp. towards a rival in love. **jealously** *adv*. **jealousy** *n*.

jeans *pl n* trousers of a strong cotton or denim material.

jeep *n* open-sided motor truck used esp. by military personnel.

jeer *vi* shout insults; scorn; scoff; mock. *n* mocking remark or shout; taunt.

jelly *n* **1** type of confectionery made from gelatin, sugar, and fruit flavouring. **2** gelatinous substance produced when meat is boiled. **jellyfish** *n* small marine creature with tentacles and a soft gelatinous body.

jeopardize *vt* place at risk; endanger. **jeopardy** *n*.

jerk *vt* pull or push sharply; tug. *vi* move quickly

and suddenly; jolt. *n* **1** sharp tug. **2** spasm. **jerky** *adj*. **jerkily** *adv*. **jerkiness** *n*.

jersey *n* **1** woollen jumper. **2** type of knitted fabric. **Jersey** breed of dairy cattle.

jest *n* witty or amusing joke or trick. *vi* joke light-heartedly. **jester** *n* **1** clown or fool formerly employed at the court of a king or nobleman. **2** joker in a pack of cards.

Jesuit ('dʒezjuit) *n* member of a religious order (Society of Jesus) founded by Ignatius Loyola.

Jesus *n also* **Jesus Christ** founder of Christianity.

jet[1] *n* **1** fast stream of water, gas, etc., forced by pressure through a nozzle. **2** aircraft propelled by a jet of gas.

jet[2] *n* type of hard black coal used for jewellery. **jet black** *adj,n* deep glossy black.

jetty *n* small pier.

Jew *n* person belonging to or following the religion of the race which is descended from the ancient Israelites. **Jewish** *adj*.

jewel *n* precious stone worn or used for adornment; gem. **jewellery** items such as necklaces, rings, or brooches; jewels. **jeweller** *n*.

jig[1] *n* **1** lively folk-dance. **2** music for such a dance, usually in triple time. *vi,vt* (-gg-) **1** dance or play (a jig). **2** bounce or jog up and down.

jig[2] *n* cutting tool or a guide for such a tool. **jigsaw** *n also* **jigsaw puzzle** puzzle consisting of a number of specially shaped pieces of cardboard or wood, which interlock to make up a complete picture.

jiggle *vt,vi* jerk or shake up and down; rattle.

jilt *vt* forsake (a lover, intended husband or wife, etc.).

jingle *vt,vi* produce a light ringing sound; tinkle. *n* **1** light metallic sound. **2** catchy tune or song.

job *n* **1** employment; occupation; work. **2** specific task; assignment. **a good job** a fortunate thing or occurrence.

jockey *n* professional rider of racehorses. *vt,vi also* **jockey for** jostle; manoeuvre.

jocular *adj* given to joking; jolly. **jocularity** *n*.

jodhpurs ('dʒɔdpəz) *pl n* type of close-fitting trousers worn when riding a horse.

jog *v* (-gg-) *vi* **1** knock or push lightly; nudge; jerk. **2** move slowly but steadily; trot or plod. *vt* stimulate (the memory). *n* nudge; light blow.

joggle *vt,vi* jolt; jerk; jiggle; shake; jog. *n* slight shake or jolt.

join *vt,vi* **1** bring or come together; fasten; connect. **2** become a member (of). **3** *also* **join up** enlist (in). *vt also* **join in** accompany; take part in with. *n* seam. **joinery** *n* craft of making wooden doors, window frames, etc. **joiner** *n*.

joint *n* **1** connection of two parts or components. **2** junction at which two bones connect. **3** large piece of meat including a bone. **4** *inf* marijuana cigarette. **5** *inf* bar or club. **6** *inf* place. *adj* shared; combined. *vt* cut up (meat) into joints. **jointly** *adv*.

joist *n* steel or timber beam or girder.

joke *n* something done or said to cause amusement or laughter; jest. *vi* speak or act amusingly or wittily. **joker** *n* **1** person who jokes. **2** one of two extra cards in a pack with a picture of a clown or jester..

jolly *adj* cheerful; funny; jovial. *adv* very. **jollity** *n*.

jolt *vt,vi* shake or bump sharply; lurch; jerk. *n* **1** sudden sharp jerk. **2** shock.

jostle *vi,vt* push or move so as to gain more room or a better position. *n* rough push.

journal *n* **1** periodical; newspaper or magazine. **2** diary or logbook recording daily events. **journalism** *n* art or practice of writing for the press. **journalist** *n*.

journey *n* process of travelling or distance travelled; trip; voyage; excursion. *vi* travel; take a trip.

jovial *adj* hearty; jolly; good-humoured.

joy *n* delight; pleasure; gladness. **joyful** *or* **joyous** *adj*. **joyfully** *adv*.

jubilant *adj* joyful; rejoicing; triumphant. **jubilance** *or* **jubilation** *n*.

jubilee *n* celebration of a particularly significant anniversary.

Judaism *n* Jewish religion or tradition.

judge *n* **1** person presiding over a trial in a court of law. **2** person who chooses the winner(s) of a competition; adjudicator. **3** critic; assessor. *vt,vi* act as a judge (for). **judgment** *or* **judgement** *n*. **judicial** *adj* relating to a judge, court of law, or justice. **judiciary** *adj* relating to judgment. *n* **1** method or administration of justice. **2** judges collectively. **judicious** *adj* wise; well-judged; sensible. **judiciously** *adv*.

judo *n* Japanese sport embracing certain principles of self-defence by unarmed combat.

jug *n* vessel with a handle and spout or lip, used for holding or serving liquids.

juggernaut *n* large articulated lorry.

juggle *vi,vt* **1** perform tricks (with) by tossing and catching (various objects). **2** manipulate or rearrange, esp. in order to deceive. **juggler** *n*.

juice *n* liquid from fruit, vegetables, etc. **juicy** *adj* **1** containing plenty of juice. **2** suggesting scandal. **juiciness** *n*.

jukebox *n* coin-operated record-player found mainly on commercial premises.

July *n* seventh month of the year.

jumble *vt,vi* mix up; place or be out of sequence. *n* muddled heap or mixture. **jumble sale** *n* sale of second-hand articles, which have been donated, esp. in aid of charity.

jump *vi* **1** leap into the air, spring. **2** move involuntarily, esp. in reaction to a noise, shock, etc. **3** jerk. **4** increase, rise, or switch suddenly. *vt* leap over or across; clear. **jump at** take advantage of or seize (an opportunity) eagerly. ~*n* **1** leap; spring. **2** obstacle to be cleared by jumping. **3** spasm; jerk. **4** sudden increase, rise, or switch. **jumpy** *adj* nervous; tense.

jumper *n* garment fitting the upper part of the body, often made of wool; sweater.

junction *n* **1** joining place or point of intersection. **2** place where railway lines converge or intersect. **3** point of contact between different electrical circuits.

juncture *n* **1** critical point in time. **2** junction; connection.

June *n* sixth month of the year.

jungle *n* **1** area of land in tropical regions, having thick dense vegetation and undergrowth. **2** situation or environment characterized by ruthless competition, lack of law and order, etc.

junior *adj* of a lower rank or status; not senior. *n* person who is younger or of a lower rank or status; subordinate. **junior school** *n* school for children after primary but before secondary levels.

juniper *n* conifer producing pungent purple cones, which are used in medicines, distilling, etc.

junk[1] *n* discarded articles regarded as worthless; rubbish; trash. **junkie** *n also* **junky** *sl* drug addict.

junk[2] *n* flat-bottomed square-sailed ship of Chinese origin.

junta *n* **1** self-appointed group that seizes political power. **2** administrative council in some parts of Latin America.

Jupiter *n* largest of the planets, orbiting between Mars and Saturn.

jurisdiction *n* legal power, authority, or administration.

jury *n* **1** body of persons required to hear evidence and deliver a verdict at a trial. **2** panel of judges. **juror** *n* member of a jury.

just *adj* **1** fair in the administration of justice; impartial; unbiased. **2** deserved; proper. *adv* **1** a moment earlier; recently. **2** exactly; precisely. **3** barely; hardly. **4** at the same time (as). **5** merely; only. **justly** *adv*.

justice *n* moral or legal correctness; fairness; lawfulness. **do justice to** treat according to merit.

justify *vt* give sufficient or valid reasons for; uphold; defend. **justifiable** *adj*. **justification** *n*.

jut *vi* (-tt-) *also* **jut out** stick out; extend beyond a particular point; protrude.

jute *n* strong natural fibre used for ropes or sacking.

juvenile *adj* **1** immature; young; childish. **2** intended for young people. *n* young person; child or adolescent. **juvenile delinquency** *n* criminal behaviour by young offenders. **juvenile delinquent** *n*.

juxtapose *vt* place immediately next to. **juxtaposition** *n*.

K

kaftan *n also* **caftan** traditional loose full-length tunic of the Near East.

Kaiser *n* (formerly) German emperor.

kaleidoscope (kə'laidəskoup) *n* sealed tube containing at one end pieces of coloured glass whose reflections produce patterns when the tube is turned or shaken.

kangaroo *n* Australian marsupial with powerful hind limbs and a broad tail.

karate (kə'rɑːti) *n* Oriental system of self-defence by unarmed combat employing smashes, chops, or kicks with the hands, elbows, head, or feet.

kebab *n* Middle Eastern dish of small cubes of

meat and vegetables cooked on a skewer over a charcoal grill.

keel *n* timber or plate running along the length of the bottom of a ship's hull. **on an even keel** maintaining a steady course; stable. *v* **keel over** capsize; overturn.

keen *adj* **1** enthusiastically willing or interested. **2** anxious; eager. **3** perceptive; observant; shrewd. **4** having a sharp cutting edge. **5** bitingly cold. **6** intense; strong. **keen on** very interested in. **keenly** *adv*. **keenness** *n*.

keep *v* (kept) *vt* **1** hold in one's possession; retain. **2** detain. **3** maintain in a particular state or condition. **4** own and look after or care for. **5** abide by; observe; comply with. **6** store; have in stock. **7** restrain; deter; prevent. **8** provide for; earn money for. **9** make a record in. *vi* **1** remain; stay. **2** carry on; continue to. **3** stay fresh. **keep on 1** continue to employ. **2** nag; persist. **3** proceed. **keep to** proceed as planned; stick or adhere to. **keep up** (**with**) maintain the same rate of progress (as). *~n* **1** cost of maintaining. **2** fortified central tower of a castle. **keeper** *n* **1** person in charge of animals in a zoo. **2** museum or gallery attendant. **3** warder; jailer. **keeping** *n* **in keeping with** in accordance with; conforming or appropriate to. **keepsake** *n* memento; token gift or souvenir.

keg *n* small barrel.

kennel *n* **1** small shed for housing a dog. **2** *also* **kennels** establishment breeding and caring for dogs.

kerb *n* edge of a pavement.

kernel *n* edible central part of a nut or fruit stone.

kestrel *n* small falcon.

kettle *n* metal vessel with a lid, spout, and handle, used for boiling water. **kettledrum** *n* large percussion instrument having a hollow body with a skin stretched tightly over the top.

key *n* **1** metal instrument cut and shaped to fit a particular lock. **2** lever on a typewriter. **3** lever on a piano and certain woodwind instruments. **4** set of notes in a musical scale. **5** crucial piece of information, component, etc. **6** guide to coded information or symbols used. *adj* most important or vital. **keyed up** tense with anticipation. **keyboard** *n* set of levers or keys on a piano, typewriter, etc.

khaki ('kɑːki) *adj,n* yellowish-brown, often used as the colour for military uniforms.

kibbutz (kiˈbuts) *n, pl* **kibbutzim** (kibutˈsiːm) collective farm in Israel.

kick *vt,vi* strike or aim (at) with the foot. *vi* raise or shake the feet or legs. **kick up** create (a fuss, trouble, etc.). *~n* **1** blow or jerky movement of the foot. **2** *inf* thrill. **kick-off** *n* start of play in football.

kid[1] *n* **1** young goat. **2** *inf* child; young person. **3** soft goatskin.

kid[2] *vt,vi* (-dd-) *inf* deceive by teasing; hoax.

kidnap *vt* (-pp-) seize and carry off (a person), esp. in order to obtain ransom. **kidnapper** *n*.

kidney *n* one of a pair of bodily organs that filters the blood and removes waste products, which are discharged to the bladder as urine. **kidney bean** *n* reddish-brown kidney-shaped bean.

kill *vt,vi* **1** cause the death (of). **2** destroy completely. **3** *inf* cause pain, suffering, etc., to; exhaust. **kill time** find something to do whilst waiting. *~n* act of killing, esp. a hunted animal or prey. **killer** *n*.

kiln *n* large oven used for baking clay, bricks, etc.

kilogram *n also* **kilogramme** *or* **kilo** one thousand grams (approx. 2.2 lbs.).

kilometre ('kiləmiːtə, kiˈlɔmitə) *n* one thousand metres (approx. 0.6 miles).

kilowatt *n* one thousand watts.

kilt *n* pleated tartan skirt, traditionally worn by Highland Scotsmen.

kimono *n* full-length wide-sleeved dress with a wide sash, traditionally worn by Japanese women.

kin *n also* **kindred** one's relatives.

kind[1] *adj* **1** *also* **kind-hearted** friendly; generous; helpful; considerate. **2** mild; not harmful. **kindness** *n*. **kindly** *adj* sympathetic; warm-hearted. *adv* **1** in a kind manner; sympathetically. **2** please.

kind[2] *n* sort; type; class.

kindergarten *n* nursery group or school for children under primary school age.

kindle *vt* **1** set light to. **2** arouse or excite (interest, passion, etc.). *vi* catch fire.

kindred *adj* **1** of one's kin. **2** compatible, in sympathy. *n* kin.

kinetic *adj* relating to motion.

king *n* **1** male monarch or sovereign. **2** most influential or prominent person or thing. **3** highest court card ranking above a queen and often below an ace. **4** key chess piece, able to move one square at a time in any direction. **kingdom** *n* **1** nation ruled by a king or queen; realm. **2** one of three major divisions into which animals, plants, or minerals may be classified. **kingfisher** *n* fish-eating river bird having bright blue and orange plumage. **king-size** *adj also* **king-sized** of a larger than average size.

kink *n* **1** twist, loop, or curl in a piece of rope, string, hair, etc. **2** *inf* perversion. *vi,vt* form into kinks; bend; curl. **kinky** *adj sl* sexually deviant; perverted.

kiosk *n* **1** public telephone booth. **2** small open-fronted shop selling newspapers, cigarettes, etc.

kipper *n* herring or similar fish that has been salted and smoked.

kiss *vt,vi* caress or touch with lips as a token of love, affection, reverence, etc. *n* act of kissing.

kit *n* **1** items of clothing and equipment issued to a member of the armed forces. **2** equipment or tools used by a workman, sportsman, etc. **3** collection of parts sold for assembly by the purchaser. *vt* (-tt-) *also* **kit out** supply or issue with a kit.

kitchen *n* room equipped for cooking. **kitchen garden** *n* garden where vegetables, herbs, etc., are grown.

kite *n* **1** light framework of wood, paper, etc., that can be flown in the air at the end of a long string. **2** type of hawk.

kitten *n* young cat.

kitty *n* pooled sum of money; fund.

kiwi *n* large bird native to New Zealand that is unable to fly.

kleptomania *n* compulsion to steal. **kleptomaniac** *n,adj.*

knack *n* skilful or intuitive ability; aptitude; flair.

knave *n* **1** jack in a pack of cards. **2** rogue; scoundrel.

knead *vt* shape and mould (dough, clay, etc.) with the hands.

knee *n* joint connecting the upper and lower leg. **kneecap** *n* flat bone at the front of the knee. **kneedeep/kneehigh** *adj* so deep/high as to reach the knees.

kneel *vi* (knelt *or* kneeled) rest or bend with the knees on the ground.

knickers *pl n* woman's undergarment covering the lower half of the body.

knife *n, pl* **knives** cutting implement consisting of a sharpened blade set into a handle. *vt* stab or wound with a knife. **on a knife-edge** in a state of extreme tension or anxious anticipation.

knight *n* **1** medieval nobleman of high military rank. **2** person honoured by the sovereign with a non-hereditary rank below that of the nobility. **3** chess piece usually in the shape of a horse's head. **knighthood** *n* rank of a knight.

knit *vi,vt* (-tt-; knitted *or* knit) **1** make (a garment, fabric, etc.) by winding and looping wool or yarn round two or more long needles in a particular way. **2** join together; mesh; interlock. **knitwear** *n* knitted garments.

knob *n* **1** rounded handle on a door, drawer, etc. **2** round switch on a radio, TV set, etc. **3** lump; swelling. **knobbly** *adj also* **knobby** lumpy; bumpy; having knobs.

knock *n* **1** blow; bang; tap. **2** tapping noise. *vt,vi* **1** tap; bang; hit; strike. **2** produce a tapping sound; rattle. **3** *inf* criticize; find fault (with). **knock about** *or* **around 1** travel around. **2** be in a group (with). **3** beat; batter. **knock down 1** hit and push over. **2** sell in an auction. **3** reduce in price. **knock off** *sl* **1** finish work. **2** pilfer; steal. **3** complete hurriedly. **4** deduct. **knock out 1** cause to lose consciousness. **2** exhaust; tire. **knockout** *n* **1** blow that renders (someone) unconscious. **2** contest in which competitors are eliminated by heats. **3** person of stunningly attractive appearance. **4** overwhelming experience. **knock up 1** assemble quickly. **2** rouse; waken. **knocker** *n* hinged metal bar attached to a door and used for knocking.

knot *n* **1** tight loop tied in a piece of rope, string, ribbon, etc. **2** small bunch of people. **3** irregular lump in a piece of wood. **4** unit used to measure the speed of a ship or aircraft equal to one nautical mile per hour. *vt,vi* (-tt-) form into a knot; tangle; tie.

know *v* (knew; known) *vt,vi* **1** be aware or certain of (a fact). **2** understand; have experience (of). *vt* **1** be acquainted or familiar with. **2** have a grasp of or skill in. **3** be able to distinguish. **know how** be able (to); have the skill (to). **knowhow** *n inf* skill; ability. **knowing** *adj* **1** shrewd; aware. **2** intentional; deliberate. **knowingly** *adv.* **knowledge** *n* **1** information or facts. **2** experience; awareness; consciousness. **3** familiarity; understanding. **4**

learning; wisdom. **knowledgeable** *adj* well-informed. **knowledgeably** *adv*.

knuckle *n* joint of the finger. *v* **knuckle down** get on with a task. **knuckle under** submit to authority or pressure.

kosher *adj* conforming to the requirements for the preparation of food under Jewish law.

kung fu *n* Chinese system of self-defence combining the principles of both karate and judo.

L

label *n* **1** slip of paper, card, etc., affixed to luggage, a parcel, etc., for identification; tag. **2** name or description. *vt* (-ll-) **1** affix a label to. **2** describe as; name.

laboratory *n* room or building equipped for scientific experiments, manufacture of drugs, etc.

laborious *adj* **1** requiring great effort or hard work. **2** painstaking; hardworking. **laboriously** *adv*.

labour *n* **1** work; toil; task. **2** period of childbirth. **3** body of people available for employment; workers. *vi* **1** work hard; toil. **2** move with difficulty; struggle. *vt* go into excessive detail about. **labourer** *n* unskilled manual worker. **Labour Party** *n* British political party representing the interests of the working class and trade unions.

labrador *n* breed of dog with a golden or black coat.

laburnum *n* small tree bearing clusters of drooping yellow flowers.

labyrinth *n* **1** complex network of paths, tunnels, caves, etc. **2** complicated system, situation, etc.

lace *n* **1** delicate fabric woven from cotton, silk, etc. **2** cord for fastening a shoe or boot. *vt* **1** *also* **lace up** tie (footwear) with a lace. **2** add a dash of alcohol to. **lacy** *adj*.

lack *n* deficiency, absence, shortage. *vt,vi* be without or short (of).

lacquer *n* **1** resinous substance for varnishing wood. **2** hairspray. *vt,vi* coat or spray with lacquer.

lad *n inf* boy or young man.

ladder *n* **1** framework for climbing consisting of two uprights fitted with horizontal bars or rungs. **2** flaw in knitting where vertical threads have unravelled. **3** means of moving within a social structure. *vt* produce a ladder in (stockings, tights, etc.).

laden *adj* **1** loaded; weighed down. **2** overburdened.

ladle *n* spoon with a long handle and deep bowl for serving soups, stews, etc. *vt also* **ladle out** serve by using a ladle.

lady *n* woman, esp. one who is wealthy or noted for her good manners. **Lady** title, rank, or form of address of certain female members of the nobility. **ladylike** *adj* refined and well-mannered as befits a lady. **Your/Her Ladyship** *n* form of address used to/of certain women with the rank of Lady.

ladybird *n* small beetle having a red back with black spots.

lag[1] *vi* (-gg-) fall behind. *n* interval; lapse.

lag[2] *vt* (-gg-) protect (pipes, etc.) with insulating material.

lager *n* type of beer stored in a cool place and served chilled.

laid *v pt* and *pp* of **lay**.

lain *v pp* of **lie**.

laity *n* persons who are not members of the clergy; laymen.

lake *n* inland expanse of water.

lamb *n* young sheep or its meat.

lame *adj* **1** unable to walk properly; crippled or limping. **2** feeble; unconvincing. *vt* make lame; cripple. **lame duck** *n* liability, worthless cause, etc.

lament (lə'ment) *vi,vt* express great sorrow or grief (for); mourn. *n* song or poem expressing grief or mourning. **lamentable** ('læməntəbəl) *adj* deplorable.

lamp *n* device producing light by electricity, oil, etc., usually having a shade for protection.

lance *n* **1** long spear. **2** *also* **lancet** sharp surgical knife. *vt* pierce with a lance. **lance corporal** *n* noncommissioned officer of the lowest rank in the British Army.

land *n* **1** solid mass forming the earth's surface. **2** country, nation. **3** soil; ground. **4** domain, sphere. *vi* **1** arrive on the shore or ground after a journey by ship or aircraft; disembark. **2** come to the ground after falling or jumping. *vt* **1** bring (a ship) to shore or (an aircraft) to the ground. **2** catch (a fish). **3** obtain (a job, contract, etc.). *vt,vi* place or be in a difficult situation. **landing** *n* **1** flat area at the top of a flight of stairs. **2** act of bringing a ship or aircraft to land. **landlady** *n* **1** woman who rents out rooms to tenants or guests. **2** female owner or manager of a public house. **landlord** *n* **1** person who owns and rents out property, land, rooms, etc. **2** male owner or manager of a public house. **landmark** *n* **1** prominent feature of the landscape. **2** significant historical event or achievement. **landscape** *n* **1** scenery of an area. **2** painting, drawing, etc., depicting this. *vt,vi* design and lay out (a park, garden, etc.).

lane *n* **1** narrow road, esp. in the country. **2** marked division of a motorway, racing track, etc. **3** prescribed route for shipping or aircraft.

language *n* **1** structured system of speech sounds used by a community. **2** written form of such a system. **3** any system of communication. **4** style of expression of speech or writing.

languid *adj* lacking energy; weakened; listless; inert. **languish** *vi* become languid; lose strength through neglect, deprivation, etc. **languor** *n*.

lanky *adj* tall and thin.

lantern *n* lamp with a light enclosed in a glass case.

lap[1] *n* **1** part formed by the area from the waist to the thighs when a person is sitting down. **2** comfortable or safe place.

lap[2] *vt,vi* (-pp-) **1** drink by licking up with the tongue. **2** wash gently against with a soft slapping sound. **lap up** take in (information) greedily. ~*n* gentle slapping movement or sound.

lap[3] *n* one circuit of a racing track. *vt* (-pp-) **1** wrap round; overlap; envelop. **2** overtake so as to be one or more laps ahead.

lapel *n* front part of a garment that folds back to join the collar.

lapse *n* **1** error; deviation; aberration; fault. **2** decline to a lower standard. **3** interval or passing of time. *vi* **1** decline; fall into disuse. **2** cease to subscribe to or be a member of a club, organization, religion, etc. **3** elapse; pass slowly. *vt* cancel the subscription of.

larceny *n* theft.

larch *n* type of deciduous conifer.

lard *n* pig fat melted down for use in cooking. *vt* **1** smear with lard. **2** embellish (a speech, story, etc.).

larder *n* room used for storing food; pantry.

large *adj* **1** of considerable size, weight, extent, etc.; great; big. **at large 1** free; unchecked. **2** on the whole; generally. **largely** *adv* mostly; to a great extent.

lark[1] *n* small songbird; skylark.

lark[2] *n* piece of fun or mischief; prank; spree. *v* **lark about** act mischievously.

larva *n, pl* **larvae** ('lɑ:vi:) immature form of an insect such as the butterfly or an animal such as the frog. **larval** *adj*.

larynx *n* organ containing the vocal cords, situated at the base of the tongue. **laryngitis** *n* inflammation of the larynx resulting in temporary loss of voice.

lascivious (lə'siviəs) *adj* lewd; lustful; lecherous.

laser *n* electronic device for producing a narrow parallel very intense beam of light of a single wavelength.

lash[1] *n* **1** whip, esp. the flexible part or thong. **2** stroke of a whip. **3** cutting remark. **4** beating or impact of waves, rain, etc. **5** eyelash. *vt* **1** whip; thrash. **2** scold; criticize sharply. **3** strike forcefully and repeatedly. **4** move like a whip. **lash out 1** attack wildly. **2** spend extravagantly.

lash[2] *vt* bind with ropes.

lass *n inf* girl or young woman.

lasso *n, pl* **lassoes** *or* **lassos** long rope with a noose for catching horses, etc. *vt* catch with a lasso.

last[1] *adj* **1** coming at the end; final. **2** most recent; latest. **3** one remaining. **4** ultimate; most conclusive. *adv* **1** at the end; after the rest. **2** most recently. *n* person or thing at the end. **at last** finally; eventually. **lastly** *adv* as a conclusion.

last[2] *vi* **1** exist or continue for a specified time. **2** endure; remain useful or in good condition; keep. **lasting** *adj* permanent; continuing.

latch *n* bar or lever for securing a door or gate. *vt* fasten with a latch. **latch on (to)** *inf* **1** attach oneself to. **2** grasp; come to understand.

late *adj* **1** not punctual. **2** happening or continuing after the normal or expected time. **3** occurring towards the end of a period, stage, etc. **4** former; recent. **5** deceased. *adv* **1** after the expected time. **2** at an advanced stage. **lately** *adv also* **of late** recently.

latent *adj* present but not yet developed or apparent; potential. **latency** *n*.

lateral *adj* directed to or coming from the side.

lathe *n* machine for holding and shaping or cutting wood, metal, etc.

lather *n* **1** foam produced by soap or detergent; suds. **2** frothy sweat, esp. of a horse. *vi,vt* produce lather; foam; froth.

latitude *n* angular distance north or south of the equator.

latrine *n* lavatory, esp. a temporary one for use at a camp site, barracks, etc.

latter *adj* **1** relating to the second of two things. **2** occurring in the second half. **latterly** *adv* lately.

lattice *n* network of strips of wood, metal, etc., arranged to form a pattern of squares, diamonds, etc.

laudable *adj* praiseworthy; commendable.

laugh *vi,vt* utter a sound of amusement, scorn, etc. **laugh at** make fun of; mock. *n* **1** single sound uttered in amusement, scorn, etc. **2** *inf* something that is fun to do or watch. **laughable** *adj* ridiculous. **laughter** *n* act or sound of laughing.

launch[1] *vt* **1** send (a ship) into the water for the first time. **2** send (a rocket) into space. **3** propel; hurl. **4** start off on a new course or enterprise. **launch into** start without hesitation or introduction.

launch[2] *n* small open motorboat.

launder *vt,vi* wash and press or iron (clothes, sheets, etc.). **Launderette** *n Tdmk* public laundry equipped with coin-operated machines. **laundry** *n* **1** place where clothes, sheets, etc., are laundered. **2** items to be laundered.

laurel *n* evergreen tree with smooth broad aromatic leaves; bay. **laurels** *pl n* honours; credit for achievement. **rest on one's laurels** cease to strive after having attained victory or success.

lava *n* molten rock from an erupting volcano.

lavatory *n* water-closet or the room where it is situated; toilet.

lavender *n* bush bearing fragrant mauve flowers. *n,adj* mauve.

lavish *adj* done on a generous scale; abundant; lush. *vt* bestow; spend generously. **lavishly** *adv*.

law *n* **1** binding regulation laid down by a government, council, or sovereign. **2** scientific rule or principle. **3** code of behaviour. **the law 1** legal profession. **2** body of legal regulations. **3** *inf* police. **lay down the law** behave domineeringly, dogmatically, or tyrannically. **law-abiding** *adj* obedient according to the law. **lawful** *adj* permitted by law; legal; legitimate. **lawsuit** *n* instance of bringing a case before a court of law; action. **lawyer** *n* practising member of the legal profession.

lawn *n* area of grass laid out in a garden or park. **lawn-mower** *n* machine for cutting grass.

lax *adj* **1** not strict. **2** loose; slack. **3** having open or loose bowels. **laxative** *n* medicine taken to relieve constipation.

lay[1] *v* (laid) *vt* **1** place gently on the ground or a surface; rest; deposit. **2** set (a table) for a meal. **3** fit (a carpet). **4** place a bet on; stake. **5** *tab* copulate with. *vt,vi* produce (eggs). **lay down** surrender; sacrifice; relinquish. **lay off 1** dismiss (workers) temporarily. **2** *sl* stop; desist. **lay on** provide; organize. **lay out 1** spread out; arrange for display. **2** prepare (a body) for burial. **3** spend. **lay up** incapacitate. **layabout** *n* lazy person. **layby** *n* parking space at the side of a road. **layout** *n* arrangement of material for a book, newspaper, etc.

lay[2] *v pt of* **lie** .

lay[3] *adj* relating to people, duties, etc., concerned with the laity. **layman** *n, pl* **-men 1** person who is not a member of the clergy. **2** person who has an amateur rather than a professional knowledge of something.

layer *n* **1** coating spread over a surface. **2** stratum; band. **3** strip placed over or resting on another. **4** shoot of a plant pegged underground so that it will produce its own roots. *vi,vt* form or place in layers. *vt* propagate by means of a layer.

lazy *adj* not inclined to work; idle; inactive. **lazily** *adv*. **laziness** *n*. **laze** *vi,vt* be lazy; spend (time) idly.

lead[1] (led) *n* **1** tough malleable bluish-grey metal, used for pipes, as a roofing material, etc. **2** graphite used for pencils. **leaden** *adj* **1** made of lead. **2** heavy or sluggish.

lead[2] (li:d) *v* (led) *vi,vt* **1** show the way (to); guide; conduct. **2** act as the leader or head (of); control. **3** be in or take first place; be ahead (of). *vi* **1** be a means of reaching. **2** follow a particular direction. *vt* live; follow (a particular way of life). **lead astray** persuade to do wrong; corrupt. **lead on** entice; provoke. **lead up to** move towards; prepare for; approach. ~*n* **1** clue; hint; guideline. **2** position in front or ahead of others. **3** main role in a play, film, etc. **4** flex, cord, or cable for an electrical appliance. **5** leash. **leader** *n* **1** person in charge; head of a political party, movement, etc. **2** person in a winning position. **3** principal violinist in an orchestra. **4** editorial in a newspaper. **leadership** *n*. **leading** *adj* main; principal; chief.

leaf *n, pl* **leaves 1** flat photosynthetic organ of a plant. **2** page of a book. **turn over a new leaf** make a fresh start by reforming one's behaviour. ~*vi* produce leaves. **leaf through** glance through (a book, papers, etc.) by turning the pages quickly. **leaflet** *n* **1** advertisement or notice printed on a single sheet of paper. **2** small undeveloped leaf.

league *n* **1** political alliance; coalition. **2** association of sports teams. **in league (with)** conspiring (with); allied (to). ~*vt,vi* bring or come together in a league.

leak *n* **1** crack or hole through which liquid, gas, etc., escapes. **2** disclosure of confidential information. *vi,vt* **1** escape or allow to escape through a leak. **2** divulge; disclose. **leaky** *adj*. **leakage** *n* process of leaking or the amount leaked.

lean[1] *vt,vi* (leaned *or* leant) place or be in a sloping position; tilt; incline. **lean on 1** rest against; use for support. **2** rely or depend on. **3** *sl* threaten; intimidate. **lean towards** favour; have a bias towards. **leaning** *n* tendency; bias; inclination.

lean[2] *adj* **1** (of meat) having very little fat. **2** thin; skinny. **3** not productive; barren; of a poor quality or standard. **leanness** *n*.

leap *vi,vt* (leapt *or* leaped) **1** jump or spring high into the air; bound. **2** increase sharply. *n* **1** high or sudden jump. **2** abrupt change of position. **leap at** take advantage of eagerly. **leapfrog** *n* game in which one person bends over for another to leap or vault over him. *vi* (-gg-) **1** play leapfrog. **2** move erratically. **leap year** *n* year having one day (i.e. Feb. 29th) more than the usual 365.

learn *vi,vt* (learned *or* learnt) **1** acquire knowledge (of) or skill by studying or being taught. **2** experience. **3** obtain information (of); hear (about). **learned** ('lɜːnid) *adj* scholarly; wise; having great learning. **learning** *n* academic knowledge or study; scholarship.

lease *n* contract drawn up between a landlord and tenant. *vt* grant or take possession of by lease. **leasehold** *adj* held by lease. *n* tenure by lease. **leaseholder** *n*.

leash *n* strap for attaching to a dog's collar as a means of control; lead. *vt* attach a leash to.

least *adj* smallest in amount or importance. *n* smallest amount. **at least 1** as a minimum. **2** even if nothing else. **not in the least** not at all; not in the slightest; not to any extent. ~*adv* of the lowest amount.

leather *n* strong material made from the cured hide of certain animals. **leathery** *adj* of or resembling leather.

leave[1] *v* (left) *vt,vi* **1** go away or depart (from). **2** cease to attend. **3** cease to be a member (of) or participant (in). *vt* **1** forget to take; lose. **2** deposit; place. **3** result in. **4** cause a visible sign (of). **5** bequeath. **6** cause to remain. **7** fail to complete; postpone. **8** keep open, free, or vacant. **9** abandon; forsake. **leave out** omit, fail to consider.

leave[2] *n* **1** permission. **2** time off from duty or work. **take one's leave (of)** depart (from); say goodbye (to).

leaves *n pl* of **leaf.**

lecherous *adj* lewd; lascivious; lustful. **lecher** *n*. **lechery** *n*.

lectern *n* stand for the Bible in a church.

lecture *n* **1** formal talk given to instruct an audience, esp. as part of a university course. **2** rebuke; reproof; scolding; reprimand. *vt,vi* deliver a lecture (to). **lecturer** *n*. **lectureship** *n*.

ledge *n* narrow horizontal shelf projecting from a wall, window, cliff, etc.

ledger *n* book in which credits and debits of an account are recorded.

leech *n* **1** blood-sucking wormlike animal living usually in water. **2** person who lives off another's efforts.

leek *n* vegetable related to the onion, having a long edible greenish-white bulb.

leer *vi* stare lustfully, mockingly, or slyly. *n* lascivious, mocking, or sly look. **leery** *adj*.

left[1] *v pt* and *pp* of **leave .**

left[2] *adj* of or on the side of a person or thing that is turned towards the west when facing north. *adv* towards the left side. *n* direction, location, or part that is on the left side. **the Left** party or political group following radical or socialist policies. **left-hand** *adj* on the side towards the left. **left-handed** *adj* using the left hand for writing, etc. **left wing** *n* the Left. *adj* **left-wing** relating to the left wing.

leg *n* **1** limb used for walking, standing, running, etc. **2** upright support of a chair, table, etc. **3** part of a garment covering the leg. **4** particular stage of a journey, race, or competition. **not have a leg to stand on** be unable to defend oneself; have no justifiable case. **on its/one's last legs** about to disintegrate or collapse; worn out. **pull someone's leg** hoax; tease; deceive jokingly. *v* **leg it** (-gg-) walk; go on foot.

legacy *n* gift of property left by will; bequest.

legal *adj* **1** relating to law. **2** authorized or required by law; legitimate; lawful. **legality** *n*. **legally** *adv*. **legalize** *vt* make legal; sanction by law. **legalization** *n*.

legend *n* traditional story popularly believed to concern actual people or events. **legendary** *adj* known from legend; renowned.

legible *adj* written so as to be clear to read; easily deciphered.

legion *n* **1** military unit of Ancient Rome comprising several thousand soldiers. **2** vast number; multitude.

legislate *vi,vt* formulate officially and pass laws (about). **legislation** *n*. **legislative** *adj*. **legislator** *n*. **legislature** *n* body of statesmen who pass laws; parliament.

legitimate *adj* **1** permitted by law; legal. **2** conforming to rules; allowable; permissible. **3** logical; justifiable. **4** born of parents who are legally married. **legitimacy** *n*. **legitimately** *adv*.

leisure *n* period outside working hours; free time. **at leisure** when free; at a convenient time. **leisurely** *adj* without haste; unhurried. *adv* at an easy or unhurried rate or pace.

lemon *n* sharp-tasting citrus fruit with a bright yellow skin. *n,adj* bright light yellow.

lend *vt* (lent) **1** give with the expectation of repayment or return; loan. **2** add to the quality or character of; impart. **lend a hand** help; cooperate; assist. **lender** *n*.

length *n* **1** measurement of something from one end to another. **2** time taken from beginning to end; duration. **3** piece of cloth, rope, wire, etc. **at arm's length** at a distance; apart. **at length 1** in great detail; for a long time. **2** eventually. **lengthen** *vt,vi* make or become longer. **lengthways** *adj,adv also* **lengthwise** measured from one end to another. **lengthy** *adj* long and detailed.

lenient *adj* not strict; inclined not to punish severely. **leniency** *n*. **leniently** *adv*.

lens *n* piece of transparent material with curved surfaces for converging or diverging a beam of light.

Lent *n* period of forty days before Easter, traditionally observed by Christians as a time for fasting and penitence.

lentil *n* plant producing brownish-orange seeds, which are eaten as a vegetable, used to thicken soups, etc.

Leo *n* fifth sign of the zodiac, represented by the Lion.

leopard *n* large animal of the cat family having a yellowish coat with black markings.

leprosy *n* infectious disease characterized by skin inflammation and disfigurement. **leper** *n* person suffering from leprosy.

lesbian *n* woman who has a sexual relationship with someone of her own sex; female homosexual. **lesbianism** *n*.

less *adj,adv* not as much; to a smaller extent; not as often. *prep* minus. *pron* a smaller amount. **lessen** *vt,vi* make or become less; reduce; decrease. **lesser** *adj* smaller; less important.

lesson *n* **1** period of time spent learning or teaching. **2** something that is learned or taught. **3** short reading from the Bible given during a service.

lest *conj* in case; for fear that; so as to avoid.

let *vt* (-tt-; let) **1** allow; permit. **2** rent or hire (accommodation, etc.). **let alone 1** leave alone. **2** not to mention; apart from. **let down 1** lower; take down. **2** deflate. **3** disappoint; fail to keep a promise. **let (someone) know** inform; tell. **let off 1** excuse; pardon; refrain from punishing. **2** cause to explode. **3** release; allow to escape. **let on** divulge; tell; reveal. **let out 1** allow to leave. **2** divulge; leak. **3** alter (a garment) so as to be larger. **4** utter; emit. **let up** cease; become less persistent. **let-down** *n* disappointment; anticlimax.

lethal *adj* likely to cause death; highly dangerous.

lethargy ('leθədʒi) *n* extreme lack of energy or vitality; inertia; sleepiness; idleness; sluggishness. **lethargic** (le'θɑːdʒik) *adj*.

letter *n* **1** written message or account that is

sent to someone. **2** written or printed alphabetical symbol or character. **letter of the law** the law when interpreted literally. **lettering** *n* art or practice of inscribing letters.

lettuce *n* vegetable with broad green leaves used in salads.

leukaemia *n* disease in which an excessive number of white corpuscles in the blood is produced.

level *adj* **1** having an even surface or plane; horizontal. **2** not tilted or sloping. **3** equal; even. **4** *also* **level-headed** calm and sensible; not inclined to panic. *n* **1** measured height or altitude. **2** flat even surface or area. **3** standard or status; grade. **4** instrument or device for measuring or checking that something is horizontal or level. **5** layer; stratum. **on the level** *inf* honest; straightforward. ~*vt* (-ll-) **1** make level or horizontal; line up. **2** equalize; bring to the same standard or status; even up. **3** raze; demolish. **4** take aim with; point. **5** direct (a remark, gaze, etc.). **levelly** *adv*. **levelness** *n*. **level crossing** *n* intersection of a road and railway track.

lever *n* **1** bar or rod used to move a heavy object, set machinery in motion, etc. **2** means of persuasion or coercion. *vt,vi* use a lever (on); prise. **leverage** *n* **1** force or action of a lever. **2** means of exerting power or influence.

levy *n* tax; duty; toll. *vt,vi* impose a levy (on).

lewd *adj* **1** lecherous; lustful. **2** vulgar; crude; obscene; indecent.

liable *adj* **1** obliged by law; subject (to). **2** likely; apt; inclined. **liability** *n* **1** legal obligation. **2** likelihood; probability. **3** tendency; inclination. **4** responsibility; burden; disadvantage; drawback.

liaison *n* **1** close working relationship; association; cooperation. **2** illicit sexual relationship. **liaise** *vi* work together; cooperate.

liar *n* person who tells lies.

libel *n* **1** written defamatory statement. **2** crime of publishing such a statement. *vt* (-ll-) publish libel about. **libellous** *adj*.

liberal *adj* **1** tolerant, esp. on political or religious matters. **2** progressive; enlightened. **3** generous; free. **Liberal** *n* member or supporter of the Liberal Party. **Liberal Party** *n* British political party advocating individual freedom and occupying a position to the right of the Labour Party but to the left of the Conservative Party.

liberate *vt* set free; release; emancipate. **liberation** *n*.

liberty *n* freedom from restraint, restriction, or control. **take liberties (with)** take unfair advantage (of).

Libra *n* seventh sign of the zodiac, represented by the Scales.

library *n* **1** room or building housing a collection of books. **2** collection of films, documents, etc. **librarian** *n* person working in a library. **librarianship** *n*.

libretto *n* text of an opera, operetta, etc.

lice *n pl* of **louse.**

licence *n* **1** official document or certificate of authorization. **2** permission granted by an authority. **3** misuse of freedom; lack of self-control. **4** allowable deviation from a particular convention, esp. in art or literature. **license** *vt* grant or authorize a licence (for). **licensee** *n* person holding a licence, esp. to sell alcoholic drinks.

lichen ('laikən, 'litʃən) *n* moss-like plant that grows on tree-trunks, rocks, etc.

lick *vt,vi* **1** touch or stroke with the tongue. **2** *inf* beat or defeat soundly. **3** *inf* thrash; flog. **lick into shape** improve or groom by special training or instruction. ~*n* **1** stroke of the tongue. **2** *inf* pace; rate; speed.

lid *n* **1** cover for a container. **2** eyelid.

lie[1] *n* untrue statement, esp. one deliberately intended to deceive. *vi* (lying) tell a lie or lies.

lie[2] *vi* (lying; lay; lain) **1** be stretched out or placed in a horizontal position; rest. **2** be situated. **3** be buried. **4** be the responsibility (of). **lie in** remain in bed for longer than usual. **lie low** remain in hiding.

lieu (lu:) *n* **in lieu of** instead of; in place of.

lieutenant (lef'tenənt) *n* **1** military officer of a rank below that of captain. **2** naval officer of a rank below that of lieutenant commander. **lieutenant colonel** *n* military officer of a rank below that of colonel. **lieutenant commander** *n* naval officer of a rank below that of commander.

life *n, pl* **lives** **1** condition of existing or being alive; being. **2** *also* **lifetime** period of existence; length of time lived. **3** all living things. **4** biographical account. **5** liveliness; vivacity; vitality. **6** way of living; mode of existence. **7** maximum prison sentence that can be awarded. **come to life 1** recover consciousness; be revived. **2** become lively or animated. **lifeboat** *n* boat used for searching for those in distress at sea or one carried by a ship in case of emergency. **lifeguard** *n* person who patrols the shore, attends a swimming pool, etc., for the safety of swimmers. **lifelike** *adj* resembling something real. **lifeless** *adj* **1** dead. **2** motionless; seemingly dead. **3** dull; uninspired. **lifeline** *n* **1** rope used in life-saving. **2** something that ensures survival. **lifelong** *adj* lasting throughout one's life; permanent. **life-saving** *n* practice or method of rescuing someone in distress, esp. at sea. *adj* able to save life.

lift *vt* **1** take or carry upwards; pull up; haul; raise. **2** turn or direct upwards. **3** put into a happy or cheerful mood; gladden. **4** exalt; elevate. **5** revoke or cancel (a ban, restriction, etc.). **6** *inf* steal; shoplift. **7** *inf* copy or borrow (an idea, piece of text, etc.). **8** dig up (plants). *vi* **1** move upwards; rise. **2** (of fog, mist, etc.) clear; disperse. *n* **1** act of lifting or raising. **2** boxlike compartment driven hydraulically, mechanically, or by electricity that moves vertically between floors of a building. **3** free ride in someone else's vehicle. **4** something that gives one energy or makes one cheerful or happy. **lift-off** *n* launching of a rocket; blast-off.

light[1] *n* **1** brightness emitted by the sun, a lamp, etc. **2** daylight. **3** source of illumination. **4** match, etc., that produces a flame. **5** aspect; context; view. **6** enlightenment; knowledge. **7** small window pane. **bring/come to light** make/become known or apparent. **in the light of** taking into account; with the knowledge of. **set light to** ignite or kindle. **shed** *or* **throw light on** clarify; explain. ~*adj* **1** not dark; illuminated. **2** of a pale or pastel shade or colour. **3** fair-haired. *vt,vi* (lit *or* lighted) **1** set light to; ignite. **2** provide with light or illumination. **light up 1** illuminate; make bright. **2** apply a match to. **3** cause to sparkle or shine; brighten. **light bulb** *n* glass bulb containing a metal filament, which lights up when an electrical current is passed through it. **lighten** *vt,vi* brighten; make or become light(er). **lighter** *n* device producing a flame for lighting cigarettes, etc. **lighthouse** *n* tower situated on or near the coast that sends out a powerful light as a guide or warning to shipping.

light[2] *adj* **1** not heavy; weighing little. **2** not forceful; gentle; not hard. **3** of a small amount; slight. **4** not overpowering; subtle. **5** buoyant. **6** *also* **light-headed** giddy; faint; dizzy. **7** *also* **light-hearted** cheerful; not serious; happy. **8** not severe or strict; lenient. **9** airy; spongy; porous. **10** not classical or highbrow. **11** nimble; graceful or quick. **12** not arduous; simple or easy. **make light of** treat as unimportant; make no fuss about. ~*adv* without being weighed down; comfortably. *vi* (lighted *or* lit) settle or perch; alight. **light (up)on** come across by chance; discover. **lightly** *adv*. **lightness** *n*. **lighten** *vt,vi* **1** make or become less heavy. **2** make or become more cheerful, optimistic, etc.; lift. **lightweight** *adj* **1** light in weight. **2** not intellectually demanding; superficial. *n* boxer whose weight is between 126 lbs and 135 lbs.

lightning *n* electricity discharged in the atmosphere producing a flash of light and usually accompanied by thunder. **like lightning** with tremendous speed.

like[1] *prep* **1** very similar to; in the manner of; the same as. **2** for example; such as. **3** as though; as if. **feel like 1** desire; want; be tempted or inclined to. **2** have the sensation of; resemble; feel similar to. **like-minded** *adj* having the same or similar views or opinions. **liken** *vt* compare; draw an analogy or find a resemblance (between). **likeness** *n* **1** resemblance; similarity. **2** representation in a painting, photograph, etc. **likewise** *adv* **1** similarly; in the same way. **2** moreover; furthermore; also.

like[2] *vt* be fond of; find pleasing, attractive, agreeable, etc. *vi,vt* wish; prefer; choose.

likely *adj* probable; to be expected; liable. *adv* probably; possibly. **likelihood** *n*.

lilac *n* hardy shrub having fragrant purple, mauve, or white flowers.

lilt *n* **1** rhythmic or melodious quality in speech or music. **2** tune or song with such a quality. *vi,vt* sing, speak, or sound with a lilt.

lily *n* bulb producing large white, purple, yellow, or orange flowers. **lily-of-the-valley** *n* small plant having fragrant white bell-shaped flowers and broad leaves.

limb *n* **1** part of the body attached to the trunk,

such as an arm or leg. **2** branch; bough. **(out) on a limb** isolated and vulnerable.

limbo *n* **1** supposed state of those who have died without being baptized. **2** state of being unwanted, cast aside, or without a proper place.

lime[1] *n* **1** *also* **quicklime** calcium oxide; white substance made from limestone. **2** *also* **slaked lime** calcium hydroxide; white substance produced by adding water to quicklime. *vt* treat with lime. **limelight** *n* **in the limelight** attracting a great deal of public notice or acclaim. **limestone** *n* whitish rock composed of calcium carbonate.

lime[2] *n* green-skinned citrus fruit similar to a lemon.

limerick *n* humorous five-lined poem.

limit *n* **1** extent to which something is possible or permissible. **2** most acceptable amount; minimum or maximum. **3** boundary. *vt* place a restriction on. **limitation** *n* restriction; limiting circumstance.

limp[1] *vi* walk in an abnormal way because of injury or disablement; be lame. *n* act of limping.

limp[2] *adj* **1** sagging; not rigid; floppy. **2** feeble; weak.

limpet *n* marine mollusc having a conical shell that clings to rocks, etc.

line[1] *n* **1** mark drawn in pencil, paint, etc., across a surface. **2** groove; crease; furrow. **3** row; column. **4** outline; edge. **5** boundary; limit. **6** cable, rope, cord, or string used for a particular purpose. **7** means of transport; route. **8** railway track. **9** policy; method or system. **10** direction taken by a missile. **11** field of research; area of interest. **12** single horizontal row of written or printed words. *vt* **1** draw lines on. **2** produce grooves or furrows in. **3** form a row along; border. **line up 1** set in a straight or orderly row or line. **2** provide; organize.

line[2] *vt* provide with an inside covering or layer of material.

lineage *n* line of descent from a common ancestor.

linear ('liniə) *adj* **1** relating to a line. **2** made up of lines. **3** of one dimension only.

linen *n* **1** strong fabric of woven flax. **2** sheets, tablecloths, etc., made esp. of linen.

liner *n* ship designed to carry a large number of passengers.

linger *vi* **1** be reluctant to hurry away; stay behind; loiter. **2** remain or persist, esp. as a memory.

lingerie ('lɑːnʒəri) *n* women's underwear and nightwear.

linguist *n* **1** person who is able to speak one or more foreign languages skilfully. **2** student of linguistics. **linguistic** *adj* relating to language, linguistics, or speech. **linguistics** *n* study of the structure or history of language.

lining *n* material used to line a coat, curtain, etc.

link *n* **1** single loop forming part of a chain. **2** connecting part or piece in a mechanism. **3** connection or relationship between people, different places, times, etc. *vt,vi* form a link (between); connect; relate.

linoleum *n* *also* **lino** material having a canvas backing coated with linseed oil, cork, etc., used as a floor covering.

linseed *n* seed of flax from which oil is extracted.

lion *n* **1** large mammal of the cat family, the male of which has a shaggy mane. **2** powerful or strong person. **lioness** *f n*.

lip *n* **1** one of two fleshy parts surrounding the opening of the mouth. **2** that part of the rim of a jug, etc., that channels liquid being poured out. **3** *sl* impudent remark. **lip-read** *vi,vt* (-read) interpret (speech) by following a person's lip movements. **lipstick** *n* cosmetic used to add colour to the lips.

liqueur *n* sweet alcoholic drink generally taken after a meal.

liquid *n* substance that can flow but cannot easily be compressed. *adj* **1** relating to a liquid; capable of flowing. **2** harmonious; flowing. **3** (of assets) readily convertible into cash. **liquidate** *vt* **1** settle (debts). **2** dissolve (a company) by realizing assets in order to pay off creditors, shareholders, etc. **3** dispose of (an enemy, spy, etc.) by violent means. **liquidize** *vt,vi* *also* **liquefy** make or become liquid.

liquor *n* any alcoholic drink, esp. a spirit.

liquorice *n* black substance extracted from the root of a shrub for use in medicines, confectionery, etc.

lira ('liərə) *n, pl* **lire** ('liəri) *or* **liras** standard monetary unit of Italy.

lisp *n* manner of pronunciation in which *s* and *z* sound like *th* (θ and ð). *vt,vi* pronounce or speak with a lisp.

list[1] *n* record or statement placing a number of items one after the other. *vt* place on a list; make a list of.

list[2] *vi* (of a ship) lean to one side. *n* leaning to one side.

listen *vi* **1** pay attention or concentrate in order to hear. **2** take notice; heed. **listener** *n*.

listless *adj* not energetic; lethargic; weary.

lit *v* a *pt* and *pp* of **light**[1] and **light**[2].

literal *adj* **1** not metaphorical. **2** interpreted or translated word for word. **literally** *adv*.

literary *adj* concerning literature, authorship, or scholarship.

literate *adj* able to read and write. **literacy** *n*.

literature *n* body of written material, such as novels, poetry, or drama.

lithe *adj* supple; moving easily or gracefully.

litmus *n* type of vegetable dye that turns red in acids and blue in alkalis.

litre *n* unit of volume equal to one thousand cubic centimetres.

litter *n* **1** rubbish or refuse that is dropped or left lying about, esp. in a public place. **2** set of offspring produced by a sow, bitch, etc., at one birth. *vt* **1** cover or make untidy with litter. **2** scatter or be scattered untidily on.

little *adj* **1** small; tiny; not big or tall. **2** not important; trivial. **3** brief; not lasting long. *pron* not much. *adv* not often; hardly at all. **a little** *pron* a small number or quantity. *adv* to a small extent. **little by little** gradually.

live[1] (liv) *vi* **1** exist; be alive; have life. **2** have one's home (in); reside; stay. **3** continue; flourish. **4** make a living. *vt* **1** spend (one's life). **2** have as a fundamental part of one's life. **live up to** match (required standards or expectations).

live[2] (laiv) *adj* **1** alive; not dead; living. **2** stimulating; interesting. **3** (of a shell, cartridge, etc.) not yet exploded. **4** broadcast directly without being previously recorded. **5** carrying electric current. **livestock** *n s or pl* animals kept or reared on a farm, such as cattle, pigs, or poultry.

livelihood *n* means of earning a living.

lively *adj* **1** active; having energy; vigorous. **2** busy; fully occupied. **3** alert; quick. **4** bright; cheerful. **liveliness** *n*.

liver *n* reddish-brown organ situated below the diaphragm in the body that secretes bile, neutralizes toxic substances, etc.

livid *adj* **1** extremely angry; furious. **2** discoloured, as when bruised.

living *adj* still alive; not yet dead or extinct. *n* **1** livelihood. **2** way of life. **living room** *n* room in a house used for recreation, receiving guests, etc.

lizard *n* reptile having four limbs, a long tail, and a scaly body.

llama *n* mammal related to but smaller than a camel, valued for its fleece.

load *n* **1** something carried or transported. **2** cargo. **3** burden; weight of responsibility, etc. **4** *inf* large amount; lot; heap. *vt,vi* **1** place a load on or in (a lorry, ship, etc.). **2** burden. **3** put ammunition in (a gun).

loaf[1] *n, pl* **loaves** baked bread in a particular shape.

loaf[2] *vi* pass time idly; lounge; loiter.

loan *n* something lent, such as a sum of money or a book from a library. **on loan** borrowed. ~*vt,vi* lend.

loathe *vt* hate; detest; abhor. **loathsome** *adj* detestable; abhorrent.

lob *vt,vi* (-bb-) hit or bowl (a ball) so as to form a high arc. *n* ball hit or bowled in such a way.

lobby *n* **1** entrance hall, waiting room, or corridor. **2** group seeking to persuade officials, members of parliament, etc., to support or oppose a particular policy or piece of legislation. *vt,vi* seek to influence as a lobby.

lobe *n* **1** lower fleshy part of the ear. **2** subdivision of certain organs such as the lung or brain.

lobster *n* large edible crustacean with long claws or pincers.

local *adj* **1** belonging to or concerning a particular district or locality. **2** affecting a particular part of the body. *n* **1** person belonging to the locality. **2** *inf* public house nearest to one's home or place of work. **locality** *n* neighbourhood; vicinity; district. **localize** *vt* **1** limit to a particular part of the body. **2** make local.

locate *vt* **1** look for and find the position of. **2** situate; place; position. **location** *n* **1** place; site; position. **2** act of locating or finding. **3** place other than a studio, where a film is shot.

loch *n* (in Scotland) lake or narrow sea inlet.

lock[1] *n* **1** device for securely fastening a door, drawer, box, etc., operated usually by means of a key. **2** section of a canal or river enclosed within a barrier or gate, which can be opened or shut to control the water level. **3** wrestling hold in which a limb or the head is unable to move. *vt,vi* **1** fasten or become secure with a lock. **2** jam; fix so as to be unable to move. **3** interlock.

lock[2] *n* length or curl of hair from or on the head.

locker *n* cupboard provided esp. in a public building, used for storing personal property, clothes, etc.

locket *n* small case containing a portrait, memento, etc., attached to a chain and worn as a necklace.

locomotion *n* power of motion. **locomotive** *n* engine driven by steam, electricity, or diesel power, used to draw a train along a railway track.

locust *n* insect of the grasshopper family that travels in swarms stripping vegetation over a wide area.

lodge *vt,vi* **1** provide or be provided with accommodation, esp. in a private household. **2** embed or become embedded (in); wedge. *vt* **1** make (a formal complaint). **2** deposit for safekeeping *n* **1** small house located near or at the gate of a park, estate, etc. **2** cabin or house used by hunters, skiers, etc. **lodger** *n* person lodging in a private household. **lodgings** *pl n* accommodation, such as rented rooms in a private household.

loft *n* **1** room or space immediately below the roof of a house. **2** upper floor of a barn, stable, etc., where hay is stored. **3** building constructed as a shelter for racing pigeons. **lofty** *adj* **1** high and imposing. **2** idealistic; noble. **3** haughty; arrogant.

log *n* **1** section of a felled branch or tree trunk. **2** regular or daily record kept during a voyage, flight, etc. *vt* (-gg-) **1** fell or saw (logs). **2** record as a log. **logbook** *n* book in which records or logs are kept.

logarithm *n* power to which a base number, usually 10, is raised to give a specified number, tabulated as an aid to calculation. **logarithmic** *adj*.

logic *n* **1** branch of philosophy concerned with determining the validity of particular statements according to certain principles of reasoning. **2** consistency of method or practice; validity of reasoning. **logical** *adj*. **logically** *adv*.

loins *pl n* lower part of the back and sides of the body.

loiter *vi* lurk; linger; move about aimlessly. **loiterer** *n*.

loll *vi* laze; lounge. *vt,vi* droop; sag; hang loosely.

lollipop *n* **1** boiled sweet on a small stick. **2** ice lolly.

lonely *adj* **1** without friends; isolated; alone. **2** remote; desolate. **loneliness** *n*. **lone** *adj* solitary; single.

long[1] *adj* **1** of considerable extent from one end to another; not short. **2** lasting for a considerable time. **3** of a particular length or duration. **4** having a large number of entries, parts, etc. **in the long run** over a long period. *adv* for a particular time. **as long as** on condition that; provided that. *n* **before long** after a short time; soon. **for long** for a long time. **no/any longer** no/any more. **long-sighted** *adj* **1** able to see clearly at a distance. **2** having imagination or foresight. **long-standing** *adj* having been in effect over a long period. **longwinded** *adj* using an excessive number of words; tediously long.

long[2] *v* **long for** crave; yearn for; desire. **longing** *n*.

longevity *n* relatively long life span or state of living to a great age.

longitude *n* angular distance east or west of a standard meridian (through Greenwich)

loo *n inf* lavatory or toilet.

look *vi* **1** *also* **look at** direct the eyes (towards) in order to see. **2** *also* **look at** begin to examine; attend (to). **3** seem; appear; be likely to be. **4** face; overlook. **5** *also* **look for** search (for); seek. **6** *also* **look through** read; glance at; scan. *vt* **1** direct one's gaze at; stare or glance at. **2** have the appearance of being, correspond to. **look after** take care of; tend, be in charge of. **look down on** regard as inferior or worthy of contempt. **look forward (to)** anticipate with pleasure. **look out** be cautious; heed. **look up** begin to improve. **look up to** admire; respect. ~*n* **1** act of looking. **2** appearance; impression. **lookout** *n* **1** person placed on guard, to watch out for danger, etc. **2** *inf* matter for personal concern; affair. **looks** *pl n* physical appearance.

loom[1] *n* machine for weaving by hand or mechanically.

loom[2] *vi* **1** approach or appear menacingly. **2** give an impression of greatness; dominate.

loop *n* shape of a circle, oval, spiral, etc.,

formed by string, wire, etc.; coil. *vt,vi* form a loop.

loophole *n* flaw or ambiguity in a law, contract, etc., that enables one to evade obligations, penalties, etc.

loose *adj* **1** not tight; slack. **2** not fastened or fitted securely. **3** not put in a bundle or tied together. **4** free; not confined. **5** not compact. **6** approximate; rough. **7** promiscuous. **8** not careful; sloppy. **9** not controlled. **at a loose end** having nothing in particular to do; not occupied. ~*adv also* **loosely** in a loose manner. *vt* **1** liberate; set free; allow to escape. **2** loosen; slacken. **loosen** *vt,vi* make or become loose(r); slacken; unfasten.

loot *n* money, property, etc., stolen or seized, esp. during a battle or riot. *vt,vi* steal; plunder. **looter** *n*.

lop *vt* (-pp-) chop or sever (branches, a limb, etc.) swiftly and in one movement.

lopsided *adj* tilted to one side; uneven or crooked; not symmetrical.

lord *n* nobleman. **Lord 1** title, rank, or form of address of certain male members of the nobility. **2** title of certain high officials in the Church or of the law. **the Lord 1** God. **2** Jesus Christ. **the Lords** House of Lords. *v* **lord (it) over** be master of; dominate. **lordship** *n* rank of a lord. **Your/His Lordship** form of address used to/of certain men with the rank of Lord and also bishops and judges of the high court.

lorry *n* motor vehicle for carrying heavy loads, transporting goods, etc.; truck.

lose *v* (lost) *vt* **1** drop or leave (something) and be unable to find it again. **2** decrease in power, speed, etc. **3** be deprived of as through death, accident, etc. **4** be unable to maintain (a particular state, belief, etc.). **5** fail to take advantage of or use. *vt,vi* **1** fail to win; suffer defeat (in). **2** (of a watch, clock, etc.) be slow (by). **loser** *n*. **loss** *n* act of losing or that which is lost. **at a loss** helpless; incapable.

lot *pron* **a lot** a large number or quantity; much or many; a great deal. *n* **1** group; collection; bunch. **2** assigned task. **3** article or set of items in an auction. **draw lots** select at random by using tickets, slips, etc. *adv* **a lot 1** to a great extent. **2** often; regularly.

lotion *n* liquid preparation used as a skin cleanser, antiseptic, etc.

lottery *n* **1** system of raising money by selling tickets, one or more of which are drawn at random to entitle the holder to a prize. **2** situation governed by luck or chance.

lotus *n* **1** mythical fruit that induces laziness or forgetfulness. **2** variety of tropical water lily.

loud *adj* **1** of a relatively high volume of sound; not quiet. **2** of a vulgar style; garish. *adv also* **loudly** in a loud manner. **out loud** aloud. **loudness** *n*. **loud-mouthed** *adj* rude; abusive; brash. **loudspeaker** *n* device for converting electrical signals into sound that can be heard over a wide area.

lounge *n* **1** sitting room. **2** room or area at an airport, hotel, etc., where one may sit or wait. **3** *also* **lounge bar** saloon bar. *vi* laze; move or sit idly.

louse *n, pl* **lice** wingless bloodsucking insect that is a parasite of mammals. **lousy** *adj* **1** infested with lice. **2** *inf* very bad; awful.

lout *n* uncouth person.

love *n* **1** feeling of deep passion, desire, affection, or fondness. **2** score of nil in tennis, squash, etc. **make love (to)** have sexual intercourse (with). ~*vt,vi* feel love (for). **lover** *n*. **lovesick** *adj* pining; suffering through love.

lovely *adj* **1** giving pleasure; nice; highly enjoyable. **2** beautiful; attractive. **loveliness** *n*.

low[1] *adj* **1** not tall or high; relatively close to the ground. **2** close to the bottom of a particular scale, grade, etc.; poor. **3** inferior; below average. **4** mean; despicable. **5** depressed or ill. **6** almost empty; having only a small amount left. **7** deep and quiet. *adv* towards or into a low position, state, or condition. **lie low** remain hidden, esp. to avoid capture. **lowness** *n*. **lowbrow** *adj* relating to a style or taste, esp. in the arts, that is not very sophisticated or intellectual; not highbrow. **lower** *vt,vi* **1** decrease; reduce. **2** move downwards. **lower case** *n* printed letters of the alphabet that are not capitals. **lowland** *n* region or area that is relatively flat. **lowlander** *n*.

low[2] *vt,vi,n* (of cattle) moo.

loyal *adj* faithful; maintaining allegiance; patriotic. **loyally** *adv*. **loyalty** *n*.

lozenge *n* **1** small tablet eaten as a sweet for medicinal purposes. **2** diamond-shaped equilateral figure.

LSD *n* **lysergic acid diethylamide:** synthetic hallucinatory drug.

lubricate *vt* apply oil or grease to. **lubrication** *n*. **lubricant** *n* lubricating substance; oil. *adj* serving to lubricate.

lucid *adj* **1** expressed in a way that is easily understood; clear. **2** shining; bright. **lucidity** *n*.

luck *n* **1** state of affairs, event, etc., apparently occurring at random; chance; fortune. **2** good fortune. **lucky** *adj* having or bringing good luck; fortunate. **luckily** *adv* fortunately.

lucrative *adj* profitable.

ludicrous *adj* absurd; ridiculous.

lug *vt* (-gg-) pull or carry with effort; drag.

luggage *n* suitcases, bags, etc., carried on a journey; baggage.

lukewarm *adj* **1** tepid; moderately warm. **2** not enthusiastic.

lull *vt* soothe; make calm or drowsy. *n* brief respite or period of tranquillity. **lullaby** *n* soothing song intended to lull a child to sleep.

lumbago *n* backache.

lumber[1] *n* **1** (esp. in North America) timber or logs. **2** large unwanted furniture or other household articles. *vt* **1** store or fill with household lumber. **2** *inf* burden with an unpleasant duty, boring person, etc. **lumberjack** *n* (esp. in North America) person who fells trees and cuts timber.

lumber[2] *vi* move clumsily and heavily.

luminous *adj* reflecting light.

lump *n* **1** solid mass, usually irregular in shape. **2** swelling; bump. *vt also* **lump together** place in or consider to be one group or mass. **lumpy** *adj* having many lumps; bumpy.

lunar *adj* relating to the moon.

lunatic *n* insane person. **lunacy** *n* madness; insanity.

lunch *n also* **luncheon** midday meal. *vi* eat lunch.

lung *n* one of a pair of respiratory organs situated in the thorax that oxygenates the blood.

lunge *n* **1** thrust of a sword in fencing. **2** sudden forward movement. *vi* make or move with a lunge.

lupin *n* plant with a tall stem bearing bright flowers of various colours.

lurch[1] *vi* stagger; sway; jerk or jog violently. *n* sudden violent jerk or stagger.

lurch[2] *n* **leave in the lurch** abandon at a critical time; forsake.

lure *vt* entice in order to trap; tempt.

lurid *adj* **1** sensational; shocking; scandalous. **2** having strange bright colours.

lurk *vi* loiter; lie in wait; remain hidden.

luscious *adj* **1** gorgeous; delightful. **2** having a rich flavour; succulent.

lush *adj* **1** characterized by rich dense growth; luxuriant; abundant. **2** luxurious.

lust *n* **1** strong sexual desire. **2** craving; passion; greed. **lustful** *adj* consumed with lust. **lusty** *adj* robust; hearty; vigorous.

lustre *n* brightness or gloss of a surface; sheen; shine; radiance. **lustrous** *adj*.

lute *n* pear-shaped stringed instrument of the 14th–17th centuries, related to the guitar. **lutenist** *n*.

luxury *n* **1** condition of having all that one needs to gratify one's desires. **2** item not regarded as a necessity. **luxuriant** *adj* abundant; lush. **luxurious** *adj* providing luxury. **luxuriously** *adv*.

lynch *vt* (of a mob) hunt down and kill without legal trial.

lynx *n* long-eared wild cat inhabiting forest regions in parts of Europe, North America, and Africa.

lyre *n* stringed instrument of ancient Greece, resembling a small harp.

lyric *adj* relating to a style of poetry expressing personal feelings, originally recited to a lyre accompaniment. **lyrical** *adj* **1** expressive of the emotions of love, sorrow, etc. **2** enthusiastically eloquent. **lyrics** *pl n* words of a song.

M

mac *n* short for **mackintosh.**

macabre (mə'kɑːbrə) *adj* suggesting or associated with death; frightening.

macaroni *n* type of pasta shaped into thin tubes.

mace[1] *n* **1** hammer-like medieval weapon with a spiked metal head. **2** ceremonial staff that is a symbol of office.

mace[2] *n* spice produced from nutmeg.

machine *n* **1** apparatus that performs useful work using applied forces. **2** mechanism, such as a car or aeroplane. **3** highly organized controlling body. *vt,vi* use a machine to shape, cut, or work on something. **machine gun** *n* automatically loaded and repeatedly firing gun. **machine-gun** *vt* (-nn-) shoot at with a machine gun. **machinery** *n* **1** machines or machine parts. **2** system or way of organization. **machinist** *n* person who makes or works on machines.

mackerel *n, pl* **mackerel** *or* **mackerels** marine food fish with a silvery belly and green stripes on its back.

mackintosh *n* light coat worn esp. as protection from rain; raincoat.

mad *adj* **1** mentally disturbed; insane. **2** eccentric; crazy. **3** *inf* extremely pleased, angry, enthusiastic, noisy, etc. **drive** *or* **make someone mad** annoy. **go mad** become very excited, angry, pleased, etc. **madly** *adv.* **madness** *n.* **madden** *vt,vi* anger, excite, irritate.

madam *n* polite form of address to a woman.

made *v pt* and *pp* of **make.**

Madonna *n* Virgin Mary, esp. when painted or a statue.

madrigal *n* **1** love poem or song. **2** part song performed usually by six or seven voices without musical accompaniment.

magazine *n* **1** paper-covered periodical containing contributions from various writers and usually illustrated. **2** place where arms, explosives, etc., are stored. **3** replaceable metal containers for cartridges inserted into some automatic guns or rifles.

maggot larva of a housefly, etc., often breeding in decaying matter.

magic *n* **1** art of producing certain effects with the help of supernatural forces; witchcraft. **2** art of producing seemingly inexplicable results by means of tricks. **3** mysterious power or agency. *adj* **1** relating to magic. **2** *also* **magical** as if by magic; miraculous; enchanting. **magician** *n* person who is skilled in tricks or in spells.

magistrate *n* person who officiates in a lower court of law; justice of the peace. **magisterial** *adj* **1** relating to a magistrate. **2** dictatorial; authoritative.

magnanimous *adj* generous; noble; not petty. **magnanimity** *n.* **magnanimously** *adv.*

magnate *n* wealthy highly influential person, esp. in industry.

magnet *n* piece of iron or steel that can attract iron or steel objects and point north when suspended. **magnetic** *adj* **1** relating to a magnet or magnetism. **2** attractive, alluring. **magnetism** *n* **1** science or attractive properties of magnets. **2** charm; attractiveness. **magnetize** *vt* **1** make magnetic. **2** attract.

magnificent *adj* remarkable; splendid. **magnificence** *n.* **magnificently** *adv.*

magnify *vt* **1** make apparently larger, esp. by means of a lens or microscope. **2** exaggerate. **magnification** *n.*

magnitude *n* **1** size; extent. **2** importance; significance.

magnolia *n* shrub or tree with large, usually sweet-smelling creamy-pink flowers.

magpie *n* bird with a long tail, black-and-white plumage, and a chattering call.

mahogany *n* tropical American tree, the hard reddish-brown wood of which is used for furniture.

maid *n* **1** girl. **2** female servant. **old maid** old unmarried woman, spinster. **maiden** *n* young single woman. **maiden aunt** *n* unmarried aunt. **maiden name** *n* family name before a woman marries. **maiden speech** *n* first speech.

mail *n* **1** letters, parcels, etc., sent or received by post. **2** postal service. **mailing list** *n* list of names and addresses of persons to whom specific information is regularly sent. **mail order** *n* order and delivery of goods by post.

maim *vt* disable, cripple.

main *adj* chief, principal, most important. *n also* **mains** principal pipe or cable for gas, water, or electricity supply. **mainly** *adv.* **mainland** *n* land mass, such as a country or continent, excluding its islands. **mainspring** *n* **1** chief spring of a clockwork mechanism. **2** driving force; chief motivation. **mainstream** *n* leading trend.

maintain *vt* **1** keep going; keep in fair condition; support. **2** assert. **maintenance** *n* **1** act or way of keeping or supporting a person or thing. **2** financial support, as after a divorce.

maize *n* tall annual grass grown for its yellow grain, used as food and fodder, and for its oil.

majesty *n* grandness, splendour, stateliness. **Majesty** term of address for a queen or king or the spouse or widow of a sovereign. **majestic** *adj* stately, dignified.

major *adj* **1** of greater importance, extent, size, etc. **2** of or relating to a musical scale in which the third and fourth and the seventh and eighth notes are a semitone apart. *n* military officer ranking below a lieutenant colonel and above a captain. **major general** *n* military officer ranking above a brigadier.

majority *n* **1** greater number, part, etc.; more than half. **2** number by which a winning vote in an election, etc., exceeds the runner-up. **3** state or time of reaching full legal age.

make *v* (made) *vt* **1** create; produce; construct, form; prepare; establish. **2** cause to be, become, or seem. **3** cause; force. **4** amount to; constitute. **5** earn; acquire. **6** develop into. **7** do; perform. **8** appoint. *vt,vi* cause to become or become (happy, sad, merry, etc.). *n* brand; style; way things are made. **on the make** *inf* seeking an easy profit or conquest. **make do (with)** be content with; improvise with. **make for** go towards. **make good 1** repair. **2** be successful in. **make it** achieve or reach a goal. **make off (with)** go or run off (with). **make out 1** understand. **2** see; discern. **3** write out or fill in (a cheque, etc.). **4** attempt to establish; represent as. **make up 1** complete; form. **2** invent; compose; fabricate. **3** reconcile or become reconciled. **4** apply cosmetics to the face, esp. for theatrical effect. **make-up** *n* **1** cosmetics. **2** person's constitution or personality. **make up for** compensate or atone for. **make up one's mind** decide; resolve.

make-believe *n* pretence; fantasy.

makeshift *adj* provisional; acting as a substitute. *n* makeshift object, method, etc.

maladjusted *adj* not adjusted or adapted properly to personal environment. **maladjustment** *n*.

malaria *n* infectious tropical disease transferred by mosquitoes and characterized by chills and high fever.

male *adj* **1** of or related to the sex that produces young by fertilizing the female; masculine. **2** composed of or for men or boys. *n* male person or animal.

malevolent *adj* harmful; evil; spiteful; malicious. **malevolence** *n*. **malevolently** *adv*.

malfunction *vi* fail to function properly. *n* failure to function properly.

malice *n* intention to inflict harm on another; spite. **malicious** *adj*. **maliciously** *adv*.

malignant *adj* **1** inclined to cause suffering; showing ill will. **2** (of disease) likely to cause death if not treated successfully. **malign** *vt* insult; slander. *adj* evil. **malignancy** *n*.

malleable *adj* (esp. of metal) easily shaped or treated.

mallet *n* hammer-shaped tool, usually with a wooden head.

malnutrition *n* defective or inadequate nutrition.

malt *n* grain, often barley, soaked then dried for use in brewing beers or distilling spirits.

maltreat *vt* treat in an abusive or cruel manner. **maltreatment** *n*.

mammal *n* any of the class of warm-blooded animals whose offspring are fed by mother's milk. **mammalian** *adj*.

mammoth *n* huge extinct elephant. *adj* huge; immense.

man *n, pl* **men 1** human male adult. **2** individual; person. **3** mankind. **4** husband or lover. **5** workman; male employee. **6** piece in draughts, chess, etc. **man in the street** *n* person considered as representative of an average member of society. **to a man 1** unanimously. **2** completely; utterly. ~*vt* (-nn-) supply with people for a specific purpose. **manly** *adj* denoting conduct and qualities expected of a man. **manliness** *n*.

manage *vt,vi* control; be in charge (of); handle. *vt* succeed in; be successful in. *vi* cope. **manageable** *adj*. **management** *n* **1** managing techniques. **2** body of persons in charge of a business. **3** administration. **manager** *n* person managing or controlling a business, etc. **manageress** *f n*. **managerial** *adj*.

mandarin *n* **1** high-ranking official in imperial China. **2** high-ranking or pompous official. **3** small orange-like fruit. **Mandarin** *n* official Chinese dialect.

mandate *n* **1** authorization; official command. **2** sanction or support given to a government by the electorate. **mandatary** ('mændətəri) *n* person, body, or state holding a mandate. **mandatory** ('mændətəri) *adj* **1** having the nature or command of a mandate. **2** compulsory.

mandolin *n* musical instrument of the lute family with eight strings tuned and plucked in pairs.

mane *n* long growth of hair on the back of the neck of a horse, lion, etc.

mange *n* contagious skin disease of domestic animals, esp. dogs. **mangy** *adj* **1** having mange. **2** scruffy.

mangle[1] *vt* **1** disfigure as by severe cuts, etc; mutilate. **2** spoil by errors.

mangle[2] *n* machine with two rollers used for removing water from and smoothing clothes, etc. *vt* put through a mangle.

mango *n, pl* **mangos** *or* **mangoes** pear-shaped tropical fruit with sweet yellowish flesh, borne on an evergreen tree.

manhandle *vt* **1** treat roughly; use physical violence on. **2** use physical rather than mechanical force.

manhole *n* hole, covered by a lid, that serves as an access to a sewer, pipe, etc.

mania *n* **1** excessive excitement. **2** obsession or excessive liking for something. **3** condition characterized by abnormal excitement and often manifestations of violence. **maniac** *n* **1** person showing excessive enthusiasm for something; fanatic. **2** mad person; lunatic. **manic** *adj* relating to mania.

manicure *n* care or treatment of hands and fingernails. *vt* treat (fingernails) by cutting, varnishing, etc.

manifest *adj* quite apparent and obvious; visible. *vt* reveal clearly. **manifest itself** show itself; appear. **manifestation** *n*. **manifestly** *adv*.

manifesto *n* written declaration by a sovereign or body of people proclaiming certain principles or rights.

manifold *adj* of many parts, aspects, or uses; varied. **manifoldly** *adv*.

manipulate *vt* **1** operate skilfully; use; handle. **2** exercise shrewd control over; influence cleverly. **3** exercise treatment on. **manipulation** *n*. **manipulator** *n*.

mankind *n* human race.

man-made *adj* artificially produced.

manner *n* **1** way something happens or is done. **2** style. **3** particular way a person behaves towards others. **4** kind; sort. **manners** *pl n* social conduct. **mannerism** *n* gesture, speech habit, etc., particular to an individual.

manoeuvre (mə'nuːvə) *n* planned, calculated, or strategic movement, as in a war; clever plan. *vt,vi* **1** make or perform manoeuvres. **2** move or cause to move into a desired direction or position.

manor *n* **1** feudal territorial unit occupied and worked by serfs paying rent in crops and service to their lord. **2** *also* **manor house** residence of the lord with its grounds. **3** mansion on an estate.

manpower *n* number of people needed or supplied for something.

mansion *n* large stately residence; manor house.

manslaughter *n* unlawful but unintentional killing of a person.

mantelpiece *n* structure above and around a fireplace, often incorporating a shelf.

mantle *n* **1** loose sleeveless cloak. **2** something covering or concealing. **3** net-like luminous cover over a gas lamp. *vt* cover with or in a mantle.

manual *adj* of the hands; done or operated by hand; not mechanical. *n* book containing fundamentals of a subject; textbook; handbook. **manually** *adv*.

manufacture *n* **1** commercial production or processing of goods, usually on a large scale. **2** manufactured product. *vt,vi* make (goods); produce; process. *vt* fabricate; concoct. **manufacturer** *n*.

manure *n* animal excrement used for fertilizing soil. *vt* apply manure to (soil).

manuscript *n* author's original piece of writing or document before its printing.

many *adj* much more than few; numerous. *n,pron* large number of people or things.

map *n* two-dimensional representation of a geographical area. *vt* (-pp-) produce a map of.

maple *n* deciduous tree or shrub with hard close-grained wood, used for furniture, etc.

mar *vt* (-rr-) spoil; ruin.

marathon *n* **1** long-distance race run over a distance of 42 km. **2** any long and trying task or contest.

marble *n* **1** hard, usually veined, limestone rock, used in a polished form, esp. in architecture. **2** small glass ball. **marbles** *n* game played with such balls.

march *vi* **1** walk with regular steps in an orderly military fashion. **2** proceed steadily. *vt* force to go or march. *n* **1** act or instance of marching. **2** distance or route marched. **3** piece of music composed for marching.

March *n* third month of the year.

marchioness *n* (mɑːʃə'nes) wife or widow of a marquess.

mare *n* female horse.

margarine *n* food product, similar to butter, usually made from vegetable fats.

margin *n* **1** border. **2** empty space on the sides

of a text. **3** vertical line bordering this. **4** limit of something. **5** tolerable excess. **marginal** *adj* **1** relating to a margin. **2** close to a limit. **3** insignificant. **marginally** *adv*.

marguerite *n* garden plant resembling a large daisy.

marigold *n* plant having orange or yellow flowers.

marijuana (mæri'wɑːnə) *n* dried hemp leaves or flowers smoked for euphoric effect.

marinade *n* **1** seasoned mixture of vinegar or wine with oil in which meat, vegetables, etc., are steeped before cooking. **2** food thus steeped. **marinate** *vt,vi also* **marinade** soak (meat, fish, etc.) in marinade.

marine *adj* **1** of or relating to the sea and sea life. **2** of navigation and shipping or the navy. *n* **1** soldier trained to serve both on land and the sea. **2** sea vessels collectively.

marital *adj* relating to marriage.

maritime *adj* **1** relating to the sea, shipping, or navigation. **2** of a place or area by the sea.

marjoram *n* plant with sweet-scented leaves, which are used in cooking.

mark[1] *n* **1** visible trace on a surface, such as a stain, dot, scratch, etc. **2** sign or symbol indicating or distinguishing something. **3** figure or letter evaluating a piece of work, examination, etc. **4** distinguishing quality. **5** target. *vt* **1** put a mark on. **2** distinguish, characterize, indicate, or show, as by a mark. **3** select; designate. *vt,vi* **1** stain; scratch. **2** evaluate and correct (an examination paper, essay, etc.). **marked** *adj* **1** noticeable; evident. **2** watched with suspicion; singled out. **markedly** *adv*. **marksman** *n, pl* **-men** a person who shoots a gun skilfully and accurately.

mark[2] *n* German monetary unit.

market *n* **1** place, usually with outdoor stands, where food, clothes, etc., are sold. **2** area of trade in certain goods. **3** demand for goods. *vt,vi* offer for sale. **market garden** *n* establishment where fruit and vegetables are grown for sale. **market research** *n* research into consumers' needs and preferences.

marmalade *n* jelly-like preserve usually made from oranges.

maroon[1] *n,adj* brownish-red.

maroon[2] *vt* abandon or isolate on an island, etc., without resources.

marquee *n* large tent used for exhibitions, etc.

marquess *n also* **marquis** ('mɑːkwis) nobleman ranking below a duke and above an earl or count. **marquise** (mɑː'kiːz) *n* wife of a marquess.

marriage *n* **1** relationship or legal bond between a man and woman, making them husband and wife. **2** harmonious union of two things.

marrow *n* **1** soft nutritious tissue inside bones that is vital for production of certain blood cells. **2** *also* **vegetable marrow** plant with a long, rounded, and usually green striped fruit, eaten as a cooked vegetable. **marrowbone** *n* bone containing marrow used in cooking, esp. for making stock.

marry *vi* become husband and wife. *vt* **1** make (a person) one's spouse; join or take in marriage. **2** unite.

Mars *n* fourth planet from the sun, lying between earth and Jupiter. **Martian** *adj*.

Marseillaise (mɑːsə'leiz) *n* French national anthem.

marsh *n* low, poorly drained, and usually very wet ground. **marshy** *adj*.

marshal *n* **1** highest military rank in certain countries. **2** official in charge of ceremonies, parades, etc. *vt* (-ll-) **1** arrange in proper order. **2** assemble. **3** conduct.

marshmallow *n* sweet with a soft spongy texture.

marsupial *n* any of the group of mammals, including the kangaroo, whose young are carried in and complete their development in a pouch.

martial *adj* relating to war.

martin *n* kind of swallow.

martini *n* drink made of gin and vermouth.

martyr *n* person who endures suffering out of religious or some other conviction. *vt* kill, torture, or persecute as a martyr. **martyrdom** *n*.

marvel *n* something wonderful. *vi,vt* (-ll-) feel wonder or surprise (at). **marvellous** *adj* wonderful; excellent. **marvellously** *adv*.

Marxism *n* political theory describing the historical change of capitalism into a classless society as the outcome of the struggle of the working classes against their exploitation. **Marxist** *n,adj*.

marzipan *n* sweet paste of ground almonds and sugar, moulded into small fruits or used in cakes, etc.

mascara *n* cosmetic for painting eyelashes.

mascot *n* object believed to bring luck.

masculine *adj* **1** relating to or characteristic of a man. **2** of a grammatical gender normally denoting males. **masculinity** *n*.

mash *n* **1** mixture of warm water and crushed grain, etc., used as fodder, in brewing, etc. **2** mashed potatoes. *vt* crush into a soft pasty mass.

mask *n* **1** facial covering, worn, esp. as a disguise. **2** pretence; disguise. *vt* **1** put a mask on. **2** disguise; hide.

masochism *n* condition in which a person suffers voluntarily in order to experience pleasure, esp. sexual. **masochist** *n*. **masochistic** *adj*.

mason *n* person who works with building stone. **masonry** *n* profession or work of a mason.

masquerade *n* **1** ball, etc., where people wear masks, costumes, and other disguises. **2** pretence; false show. *vi* wear a disguise.

mass[1] *n* **1** bulk of matter that is not particularly shaped. **2** large number or quantity of something. **3** measure of the amount of matter in a body. *vt,vi* form or gather into a large crowd. **mass media** *pl n* newspapers, television, radio, etc., informing and influencing the public. **mass-produce** *vt* manufacture on a very large scale. **mass production** *n*.

mass[2] *n* **1** *also* **Mass** celebration of the Eucharist, esp. in the Roman Catholic Church. **2** music composed for this occasion.

massacre *n* ruthless killing, esp. of innocent people; slaughter. *vt* kill indiscriminately.

massage *n* treatment of muscles in order to relax them by rubbing and kneading. *vt* give a massage to. **masseur** *n* person who practises massage. **masseuse** *f n*.

massive *adj* **1** large and solid. **2** considerable.

mast *n* **1** vertical pole for supporting a vessel's sails and rigging. **2** any high upright pole.

mastectomy *n* surgical removal of a breast.

master *n* **1** person who controls others. **2** expert in a special field. **3** employer of servants. **4** male teacher. **5** form or mould for making duplicates; original. *vt* **1** become highly skilled in. **2** gain control over; overcome. **masterful** *adj* **1** highly capable; skilful. **2** showing authority; dominant. **mastermind** *n* person who creates or plans a major project or activity. *vt* plan with great skill. **masterpiece** *n* great work of art; example of excellence or skill.

masturbate *vi,vt* excite oneself or another to orgasm by manipulation or rubbing of the genitals. **masturbation** *n*.

mat[1] *n* **1** piece of fabric, used to cover floors, stand or sit on, wipe shoes on, etc. **2** piece of material placed under vases, plates, etc. **3** tangled mass. *vi* (-tt-) become tangled.

mat[2] *adj* matt.

matador *n* man who kills the bull in bullfights.

match[1] *n* slender strip of wood with a coated head that bursts into flame when rubbed.

match[2] *n* **1** person or thing that resembles or corresponds to another. **2** contest; team game. **3** marriage or person eligible for marriage. *vt* **1** equal or be equal to. **2** be the match of. **3** make to fit or correspond; adapt. *vi* correspond in shape, size, colour, etc.; harmonize. **matchless** *adj* incomparable; having no equal.

mate *n* **1** one of a couple or pair, esp. a pair of breeding animals. **2** husband or wife. **3** friend; one's equal; fellow worker. **4** officer of a merchant ship ranking below a captain. *vt,vi* **1** join or pair. **2** (of animals) unite in order to produce young.

material *n* **1** stuff or substance of which anything is made. **2** raw data; facts. **3** cloth; fabric. **materials** *pl n* elements or tools required to make or perform something. ~*adj* **1** composed of matter; not spiritual; relating to physical well-being or wealth. **2** essential; important. **materialist** *n* person who values possessions and physical well-being more than ideas or spiritual beliefs. **materialism** *n*. **materialistic** *adj*. **materialize** *vi,vt* appear or cause to appear out of nothing. *vi* assume solid, material, or bodily form; become fact.

maternal *adj* **1** relating to a mother or mothers; motherly. **2** related through a mother. **maternalistic** *adj*.

maternity *n* state of being a mother. *adj* relating to mothers or the period of their pregnancy.

mathematics *n* science concerned with the logical study of space, numbers, relationships, etc., using various forms of analysis and special symbols. **mathematical** *adj*. **mathematician** *n*.

matinée *n* afternoon or first evening performance at a theatre, cinema, etc.

matrimony *n* state of being married. **matrimonial** *adj*.

matrix *n, pl* **matrices** ('meitrisi:z) **1** mould for casting or shaping objects. **2** anything that encloses or gives form to something.

matron *n* **1** married woman, esp. one of at least middle age. **2** woman in charge of nurses or domestic arrangements in a school, hospital, or other institution. **matronly** *adj* of or like a matron; dignified.

matt *adj also* **matte, mat** dull; without lustre; not shiny.

matter *n* **1** stuff or substance of which the physical universe is composed. **2** any physical or bodily substance. **3** topic or issue; thing; concern. **4** difficulty or trouble. **5** content of a book, etc. *vi* be of significance or importance.

mattress *n* flat case filled with soft or firm supporting material, used as a bed or placed on a bed frame.

mature *adj* **1** fully developed; ripe. **2** complete in growth; grown-up. **3** characteristic of an adult; mentally developed; sensible. **4** perfected; complete. *vi,vt* become or make mature. **maturity** *n*.

maudlin *adj* over-sentimental; tearfully drunk.

maul *vt* treat roughly; attack savagely; injure badly.

mausoleum *n* **1** stately building used as a tomb or housing tombs. **2** large depressing building.

mauve *n,adj* pale bluish purple.

maxim *n* condensed general truth or principle of conduct.

maximum *adj* greatest; highest. *n, pl* **maximums** *or* **maxima** ('mæksimə) greatest or highest amount, extent, degree, etc. **maximize** *vt* **1** increase to a maximum. **2** make the most of.

may *v aux* (*pt* might) **1** be able or permitted to. **2** be likely or probable that. **maybe** *adv* perhaps; possibly.

May *n* fifth month of the year. **May Day** *n* first day of May, celebrated with various festivities, parades, etc. **maypole** *n* decorated pole around which persons dance on May Day.

mayonnaise *n* thick dressing for salads, etc., consisting usually of egg yolk, oil, and vinegar.

mayor *n* official head of a town corporation. **mayoress** *f n*.

maze *n* **1** intricate network of interconnecting paths, passages, etc. **2** confused state.

me *pron* form of **I** when used as the object.

meadow *n* grassland, often used for grazing or growing hay.

meagre *adj* lacking quality or quantity; insufficient; scanty; thin.

meal[1] *n* **1** food, esp. when eaten at regular times during the day. **2** occasion or time of eating.

meal[2] *n* coarsely ground grain, used esp. as fodder.

mean[1] *vt,vi* (meant) **1** signify; intend; intend to express; denote. **2** be resolved to; be serious about.

mean[2] *adj* **1** stingy; petty; not generous. **2** low in quality, character, rank, or performance. **3** not important; having little consequence. **4** offensive; nasty. **meanly** *adv*. **meanness** *n*.

mean[3] *adj* **1** halfway between two extremes, values, numbers, etc.; intermediate. **2** average. *n* anything intermediate or between two extremes, values, etc.; average.

meander (mi'ændə) *vi* wander; move about aimlessly; follow a winding course. *n* winding course of a river or stream.

meaning *n* **1** significance; import. **2** sense of a word, phrase, etc.; definition. **meaningful** *adj*. **meaningless** *adj*.

means *pl n* **1** method for achieving a purpose or function. **2** financial or material resources. **by all means** certainly; without fail or hesitation. **by no means** most definitely not; on no account; not at all.

meantime *n* intervening time. *adv also* **meanwhile** during or in an intervening time; at the same time.

measles *n* **1** infectious viral disease producing a red rash, common in childhood. **2** German measles.

measure *n* **1** size, quantity, extent, etc., of something, determined by comparing it with a standard. **2** unit of size, quantity, etc. **3** criterion. **4** vessel or instrument for determining size, quantity, etc. **5** certain amount, extent, or degree. **6** regular beat or movement in music, poetry, etc.; rhythm. **for good measure** as something extra; as an addition. **take measures** do things to achieve some goal or purpose. ~*vt* determine the size or quantity of; judge; estimate. *vi* have a specified measure. **made to measure** (of clothes) fitted to the individual. **measure up** live up to expectations; be adequate for. **measurement** *n*.

meat *n* **1** flesh of animals used as food, often excepting fish and poultry. **2** edible part of anything. **3** main principle of something; essence.

mechanical *adj* **1** relating to machinery. **2** operated or produced by machines; automatic. **3** not requiring thought; spontaneous. **mechanic** *n* person skilled in repairing, building, or using machinery. **mechanics 1** *s n* study of the action of forces on physical bodies and the motions they produce. **2** *pl n* technical aspects or workings of something.

mechanism *n* **1** machine or its structure or parts. **2** means by which a machine works. **3** way in which anything works or operates.

mechanize *vt* **1** make mechanical. **2** substitute mechanical power as a source of production or energy. **3** operate by machines or machinery. **mechanization** *n*.

medal *n* flat piece of metal, usually round, with a design or inscription to commemorate an event or given as an award. **medallion** *n* **1** large medal. **2** circular decorative design or panel.

meddle *vi* **1** *also* **meddle in** concern oneself with things that are not one's business. **2** *also* **meddle with** interfere; tamper.

media *pl n* newspapers, radio, and television; collective means of communication.

medial *adj also* **median** relating to or situated in the middle. **median** *n* middle point, part, value, etc.; dividing line or plane.

mediate *vt* **1** settle; reconcile. **2** serve as the medium for communicating, conveying, etc. *vt,vi* intervene to bring about a reconciliation or compromise. **mediation** *n*.

medicine *n* **1** practice and profession of preserving or restoring health. **2** drugs or other agents used to treat bodily diseases or disorders. **medicinal** *adj*. **medical** *adj* **1** relating to medicine. **2** relating to treatment that does not require surgery. *n* physical examination by a doctor. **medication** *n* **1** use of medicine or medical agents. **2** drug or other medical agent.

medieval *adj* **1** relating to the Middle Ages. **2** *inf* primitive; crude.

mediocre *adj* between good and bad; of only average quality or excellence; ordinary. **mediocrity** *n*.

meditate *vi* engage in deep mental reflection; contemplate. *vt* think about doing; plan. **meditation** *n*. **meditative** *adj*.

medium *n* **1** means; agency. **2** middle degree or quality; mean. **3** substance through or in which something is transmitted, conveyed, or effected. **4** material used by an artist. **5** environment. **6** person claiming to be able to communicate with spirits. **7** *pl* **media** means of mass communication, such as the press, radio, or television. *adj* average; intermediate.

meek *adj* humble; submissive; lacking in spirit; mild. **meekly** *adv*.

meet *v* (met) *vt* **1** encounter; come across. **2** be present at the arrival point of. **3** satisfy; handle; cope with. *vi* come together; come into contact; join. *vt,vi* **1** be introduced (to). **2** gather for a meeting, etc. (with). **3** fight; confront. *n* assembly of people and animals prior to a hunt. **meeting** *n* **1** coming together; encounter. **2** gathering; assembly of persons, esp. for a common cause. **3** joining of things.

megaphone *n* instrument shaped like a funnel, used to amplify the voice or direct sound.

melancholy *n* depression; sadness; tendency to be morose. *adj* depressing; sad; gloomy. **melancholic** *adj*.

mellow *adj* **1** not harsh; rich and full. **2** genial; warm. **3** rendered receptive and friendly, as through advancing years, alcoholic drink, etc. *vt,vi* make or become mellow.

melodrama *n* **1** play or drama displaying violent or exaggerated emotions. **2** over-emotional language or behaviour. **melodramatic** *adj*.

melody *n* **1** agreeable or pleasing music or tune. **2** recognizable sequence of musical notes. **melodic** *adj* relating to melody. **melodious** *adj* pleasing to listen to; tuneful.

melon *n* plant of the gourd family, the edible fruit of which has a hard rind and juicy flesh.

melt *vi,vt* **1** liquefy by heat; thaw; pass or convert from solid to liquid. **2** soften; dissolve. **3** disappear; disperse. **4** blend; merge. *n* act of melting or state of being melted. **melting point** *n* temperature at which a solid becomes liquefied.

member *n* **1** person who belongs to a group, society, or organization. **2** distinct part of a whole. **3** limb or other bodily organ. **membership** *n* **1** state of being part of a group or society. **2** total number of persons who are part of a group, etc.

membrane *n* thin pliable sheet of tissue that lines, connects, or covers an organ or part.

memento *n, pl* **mementoes** *or* **mementos** reminder; souvenir; keepsake.

memoir *n* record of facts or events written from experience or gathered through research. **memoirs** *pl n* biography or autobiography; published reminiscences.

memorable *adj* easily or worthy to be remembered.

memorandum *n, pl* **memorandums** *or* **memoranda** (memə'rændə); *also* **memo 1** note to aid the memory. **2** short informal communication to colleagues, business firms, clients, etc.

memorial *n* object or custom in memory of a person, event, etc.; monument. *adj* preserving the memory of a person or event; commemorative.

memory *n* **1** faculty of recalling to mind or recollecting. **2** something remembered. **3** capacity to remember. **4** commemoration. **5** part of a computer where information is stored. **memorize** *vt* commit to memory.

men *n pl* of **man.**

menace *n* something that threatens or constitutes a threat. *vt* threaten; intimidate.

menagerie *n* exhibition of caged animals.

mend *vt* **1** repair; make whole; put right. **2** make better; improve; correct. *vi* improve in health. *n* improvement; repair. **on the mend** recovering; improving in health.

menial *adj* lowly; servile. *n* servile person; domestic servant.

menopause *n* time of life during which women cease to menstruate, usually between the ages of 45 and 50.

menstrual *adj* relating to the monthly discharge from the womb of blood and cellular material in women. **menstruate** *vi* produce menstrual discharge. **menstruation** *n.*

mental *adj* **1** relating to the mind or intellect; done or existing in the mind. **2** *sl* insane; mad; crazy. **mental hospital** *n* institution for treating persons with disorders of the mind. **mentality** *n* mental or intellectual capacity; mind.

menthol *n* substance obtained from peppermint oil, used esp. as a flavouring.

mention *vt* speak of; refer to. *n* remark about or reference to a person or thing.

menu *n* **1** list of dishes available to be served, with their prices. **2** dishes served.

mercantile *adj* **1** relating to merchants or commerce; commercial. **2** engaged in commerce or trade.

mercenary *adj* working simply for reward or gain. *n* professional soldier serving a foreign country.

merchandise *n* **1** goods or commodities bought and sold in commerce or trade. **2** stock of a store. *vt,vi* buy and sell; promote the sale (of).

merchant *n* wholesale trader, esp. with foreign countries. **merchant bank** *n* bank chiefly involved in foreign commerce. **merchant navy** *n* **1** ships of a nation engaged in commerce. **2** officers and crews of merchant ships.

mercury *n* heavy silvery toxic metallic element, normally liquid, used in thermometers, barometers, etc. **Mercury** nearest planet to the sun. **mercurial** *adj* lively; changeable.

mercy *n* **1** compassion; kindness; pity. **2** forgiveness of an injustice, transgression, or injury by someone with the power to inflict punishment. **3** act of compassion, kindness, etc. **at the mercy of** completely in the power of; defenceless. **merciful** *adj* compassionate. **mercifully** *adv.* **merciless** without mercy; cruel. **mercilessly** *adv.*

mere *adj* nothing more than; only. **merely** *adv.*

merge *vt,vi* **1** blend; mingle. **2** combine; unite. **merger** *n* commercial combination of two or more companies.

meridian *n* **1** position of the sun at noon. **2** highest point or period of development of something. **3** imaginary circle encompassing the earth and passing through both poles. *adj* **1** relating to a meridian. **2** relating to or at noon.

meringue (mə'ræŋ) *n* **1** mixture of sugar and beaten egg whites, slightly browned, used as an icing, etc. **2** small cream-filled cake of meringue.

merit *n* **1** worth; excellence. **2** commendable quality. *vt* be worthy of. **meritorious** *adj.*

mermaid *n* mythical sea creature with the head, arms, and torso of a woman and the tail of a fish.

merry *adj* **1** joyous; cheerful; festive; happy; gay. **2** slightly drunk. **merry-go-round** *n* fairground amusement consisting of a rotating platform fitted with models of animals, cars, etc., on which one may ride; roundabout **merrily** *adv.* **merriment** *or* **merriness** *n.*

mesh *n* net; network. *vt* catch in a mesh. *vi* **1**

(of gearwheels) engage. **2** merge; blend; harmonize.

mesmerize *vt* **1** hypnotize. **2** fascinate greatly.

mess *n* **1** untidy state or condition. **2** state of confusion or disorder. **3** difficult or embarrassing situation. **4** place where military personnel, etc., take their meals. **5** meals taken by military personnel, etc. **6** *inf* person who is untidy, sloppy, or dirty. *vt also* **mess up** make dirty or untidy. **mess around** *or* **about** busy oneself in an ineffective or aimless manner.

message *n* **1** spoken or written communication. **2** moral conveyed in a literary or artistic work. **messenger** *n* person who conveys a message, does errands, etc.

metabolism *n* sum of the chemical changes in an animal or plant that result in growth, production and use of energy, etc. **metabolic** *adj*.

metal *n* **1** chemical element, such as iron, tin, or silver, that is usually lustrous, easily worked, and often a good conductor of heat and electricity. **2** alloy. **metallic** *adj*. **metallurgy** *n* study and technology of metals. **metallurgical** *adj*. **metallurgist** *n*.

metamorphosis *n* **1** complete change in form. **2** marked change in character, etc. **3** relatively rapid transformation of certain larvae into adult form, as tadpole to frog. **metamorphic** *adj*.

metaphor *n* figure of speech in which a word is applied to something for which it does not literally stand. **metaphorical** *adj*.

meteor *n* small body from space that burns up in the earth's atmosphere producing a bright streak. **meteoric** *adj* **1** relating to meteors. **2** rapid; transient. **meteorite** *n* larger body able to reach earth.

meteorology *n* study of the earth's atmosphere, climate, and weather. **meteorological** *adj*. **meteorologist** *n*.

meter *n* measuring or recording instrument or device. *vt* measure with a meter.

methane *n* inflammable gas occurring in natural gas and used as a fuel and in chemical manufacture.

method *n* **1** way of doing something. **2** systematic or orderly procedure. **methodical** *adj* systematic; orderly.

Methodist *n* adherent of the Christian beliefs and tenets (Methodism) of a Protestant nonconformist denomination founded by John Wesley. *adj* relating to Methodists or Methodism.

meticulous *adj* extremely careful about small details.

metre *n* **1** unit of length equal to 1.09 yards. **2** rhythmic arrangement of syllables in verse. **metric** *adj*. **metric system** *n* system of scientific units based on the metre, the kilogram or gram, and the second. **metrication** *n* conversion to the metric system.

metropolitan *adj* **1** relating to or characteristic of the capital or any large city. **2** relating to the characteristics or attitudes of a city dweller; sophisticated. **metropolis** *n* chief or major city; capital.

miaow *n* sound a cat makes. *vi* make such a sound.

mice *n pl* of **mouse.**

microbe *n* microorganism, esp. one causing disease; germ.

microorganism *n* microscopic animal or plant, such as a bacterium or virus.

microphone *n* instrument for converting sound waves into electrical currents or voltages that can then be amplified.

microscope *n* instrument for magnifying very small objects, usually consisting of at least two lenses mounted in a tube. **microscopic** *adj* visible only under a microscope; tiny.

midday *n* noon.

middle *adj* **1** equidistant from two extremes; intermediate; mean. **2** central. *n* **1** something intermediate or equidistant from two extremes. **2** central area of the body; waist. **middle-aged** *adj* relating to the age between youth and old age; aged about 40 to 65. **Middle Ages** *n* historical period now usually regarded as being from about the fifth to the late fifteenth century. **middle class** *n* generally well-educated class of people in commerce, the professions, etc., who often hold conformist views. **middle-class** *adj* relating to the middle class.

midget *n* **1** very small person. **2** anything unusually small of its kind.

midnight *n* middle of the night; 12 o'clock at night.

midst *n* middle; central part, stage, or point. **in the midst of** surrounded by; among.

midwife *n, pl* **-wives** woman who assists others in childbirth. **midwifery** *n*.

might[1] *v pt* of **may.** *v aux* used to express likelihood or possibility.

might[2] *n* strength; power. **mighty** *adj.*

migraine *n* severe headache.

migrate *vi* **1** leave one country, region, etc., to settle or work in another. **2** (of certain birds, animals, etc.) move seasonally from one region to another. **migrant** *n.* **migration** *n.* **migratory** *adj.*

mike *n sl* microphone.

mild *adj* **1** moderate; gentle; not harsh or drastic. **2** not having a sharp taste. **mildly** *adv.*

mildew *n* destructive fungus or fungal disease that attacks plants or objects exposed to damp.

mile *n* **1** unit of length equal to 1760 yards or 1.61 kilometres. **2** *also* **miles** great distance. **mileage** *n* **1** total number of miles travelled. **2** distance in miles between two points. **3** travel expenses based on a given sum per mile. **mileometer** *n* device for measuring and recording the number of miles travelled. **milestone** *n* **1** roadside stone showing number of miles to the next large city or town. **2** important event or turning point in history, a person's life, etc.

militant *adj* **1** aggressive; forceful. **2** engaged in warfare. *n* aggressive person. **militancy** *n.*

military *adj* relating to the armed forces, soldiers, or warfare. *n* soldiers collectively; armed forces.

milk *n* **1** whitish liquid produced in the mammary glands of female mammals, used to feed their young. **2** cow's or goat's milk, used as food. **3** whitish juice of various plants or fruits. **cry over spilt milk** regret or complain about something that cannot be undone or remedied. ~*vt* **1** extract milk from the udder of. **2** draw off from. **milkman** *n, pl* **-men** person who sells or delivers milk. **Milky Way** *n* faint band of light in the night sky that consists of millions of stars and is part of our galaxy.

mill *n* **1** machinery for grinding grain into flour. **2** machinery for manufacturing paper, textiles, steel, etc. **3** building containing such machinery. **4** small machine for grinding pepper corns, coffee beans, etc. *vt* grind, work, or shape in or as if in a mill. **millstone** *n* **1** either of two large round slabs of stone between which grain, etc., is ground. **2** heavy emotional burden.

millennium *n, pl* **millenniums** *or* **millennia** (mi'leniə) thousand years.

millet *n* cereal grass cultivated for its small seeds or grain.

milligram *n* one thousandth of a gram.

millimetre *n* one thousandth of a metre.

million *n* **1** number or numeral, 1 000 000, equal to 1000 multiplied by 1000. **2** *also* **millions** extremely large number or amount. **3** million units of money, etc. *adj* amounting to a million. **millionth** *adj,n.* **millionaire** *n* **1** person worth a million pounds, dollars, etc. **2** very rich person.

mime *n* **1** art or practice of wordless acting. **2** person who performs wordless acting. *vt,vi* act or express in mime.

mimic *n* person or animal that imitates or copies others. *vt* (-ck-) imitate in action, speech, etc.; copy; caricature. **mimicry** *n.*

minaret *n* slender tower of a mosque, from which the faithful are called to prayer.

mince *vt* **1** cut or chop into small pieces. **2** utter with affected carefulness. *vi* speak or act in an affected way. *n* minced meat.

mind *n* **1** thinking faculties or consciousness. **2** intellect. **3** memory. **4** person of great intelligence. **5** sanity; reason. **6** way of thinking; opinion; temper. **7** attention. **bear in mind** continue to remember. **be of one mind** be in total agreement with. **be of two minds** be undecided. **make up one's mind** decide. **out of one's mind** mad; highly agitated; confused. **take (someone's) mind off** help (someone) stop worrying about something; distract. ~*vt,vi* **1** object (to); be upset or concerned (about). **2** pay attention (to). **3** be careful (about). *vt* attend to; look after. **mind out** be careful; watch.

mine[1] *pron* that belonging to me.

mine[2] *n* **1** deep hole or shaft in the ground for extracting coal, metals, etc. **2** associated buildings, etc. **3** underground or surface deposit of minerals. **4** rich source of something. **5** explosive device, detonated on impact. *vt,vi* **1** dig or extract (minerals) from a mine. **2** make a mine in or under.

mineral *n* **1** inorganic substance that occurs in the earth and has a definite chemical composition. **2** nonliving matter. **mineralogy** *n* study of minerals. **mineral water** *n* **1** water containing dissolved minerals or gases. **2** fizzy nonalcoholic drink.

minestrone (mini'strouni) *n* Italian soup containing vegetables, etc.

mingle *vt,vi* **1** blend; mix; combine. **2** mix in company.

miniature *n* **1** very small painting, esp. a portrait. **2** model, copy, etc., greatly reduced in size. *adj* small-scale; reduced; tiny.

minim *n* musical note half the length of a semibreve.

minimum *n* least possible or lowest quantity, number, degree, etc. **minimal** *adj.* **minimize** *vt* **1** reduce to or estimate at a minimum. **2** belittle; underestimate.

mining *n* act, process, or industry of extracting minerals, coal, etc., from mines.

minister *n* **1** person authorized to conduct religious services; clergyman. **2** person in charge of a government department. **3** diplomatic representative. *vi* give aid or service (to). **ministerial** *adj.*

ministry *n* **1** functions or profession of a clergyman or clergymen. **2** profession or department of a government minister. **3** building in which government offices are located. **4** act of giving service.

mink *n* **1** animal of the weasel family with highly valued brownish fur. **2** garment made of mink fur.

minor *adj* **1** lesser in size, extent, significance, etc. **2** of or relating to a musical scale in which the second and third and the fifth and sixth notes are a semitone apart. *n* **1** person under full legal age. **2** person or thing of inferior importance, rank, etc. **minority** *n* **1** smaller number, part, etc.; less than half. **2** group whose race, religion, etc., is different from most others in the same country or community. **3** state or period of being under full legal age.

minstrel *n* medieval musician or singer.

mint[1] *n* **1** aromatic herb. **2** sweet with a peppermint or similar flavouring.

mint[2] *n* **1** place where money is officially minted. **2** large amount, esp. of money. *vt,vi* make (coins and paper money) under government authority. **mint condition** perfect condition.

minuet *n* **1** slow stately dance in triple time. **2** music in the rhythm of this dance.

minus *prep* **1** less by the deduction of; decreased by. **2** without; lacking. *adj* **1** indicating deduction or subtraction. **2** negative. **3** lacking. *n also* **minus sign** symbol denoting subtraction.

minute[1] ('minit) *n* **1** one sixtieth of an hour; 60 seconds. **2** short time. **3** one sixtieth of a degree of angular measure. **4** memorandum. **up to the minute** current; very latest; modern. **minutes** *pl n* summary of a meeting.

minute[2] (mai'nju:t) *adj* **1** very small. **2** insignificant; trivial. **3** precise; detailed. **minutely** *adv.*

miracle *n* **1** supernatural event. **2** something wonderful; marvel. **miraculous** *adj.*

mirage *n* **1** optical illusion caused by intense heat, etc. **2** something unreal or illusory.

mirror *n* **1** polished surface that reflects images of objects, esp. glass backed with metal. **2** any reflecting surface, as of water. **3** something that gives a true representation or portrayal. *vt* reflect or represent faithfully.

mirth *n* merriment; festive or joyous gaiety.

misbehave *vi* behave badly. **misbehaviour** *n.*

miscarriage *n* **1** expulsion of a foetus from the womb before it is capable of living independently. **2** failure to carry out or attain a desired result. **miscarry** *vi* **1** undergo a miscarriage. **2** fail; go wrong.

miscellaneous *adj* **1** varied; mixed; assorted. **2** having various qualities or aspects; many-sided. **miscellany** *n* miscellaneous collection.

mischance *n* bad luck; misfortune; unlucky accident.

mischief *n* **1** teasing or annoying conduct. **2** source of annoyance or harm. **mischievous** *adj.* **mischievously** *adv.*

misconceive *vt,vi* misunderstand; interpret incorrectly. **misconception** *n.*

misconduct *n* improper conduct.

misdeed *n* evil or criminal deed.

miser *n* person who hoards money. **miserly** *adj.*

miserable *adj* **1** extremely unhappy or uncomfortable. **2** causing misery. **3** characterized by wretched poverty and neglect. **4** pitiable. **miserably** *adv.* **misery** *n* condition or cause of great suffering or distress.

misfire *vi* **1** fail to fire correctly or on time. **2** fail to be successful or have a desired effect. *n* failure to fire.

misfit *n* **1** person who does not fit in socially

with others. **2** something that does not fit properly.

misfortune *n* bad luck; calamity.

misgiving *n* feeling of fear, doubt, or mistrust.

misguided *adj* mistaken; misled.

mishap *n* unlucky or unfortunate accident.

mislay *vt* (-laid) put something in a place later forgotten.

mislead *vt* (-led) lead astray; deceive, esp. by giving incorrect or inadequate information or advice.

misplace *vt* **1** lose; put in the wrong place. **2** place or bestow unwisely or improperly.

misprint *n* mistake in printing.

miss[1] *vt* **1** fail to hit, find, reach, notice, catch, etc. **2** *also* **miss out** omit; pass over. **3** notice or regret the absence of. **4** fail. **5** escape; avoid. *vi* **1** (of an engine) fail to fire. **2** fail to hit or attain something. **miss the boat** fail to take advantage of an opportunity. *~n* failure.

miss[2] *n* girl; young woman. **Miss** form of address for an unmarried young woman or girl.

missile *n* object or weapon that can be thrown or fired, esp. a rocket-propelled weapon.

mission *n* **1** group of persons sent to a foreign country as envoys or missionaries. **2** official business or task of an envoy or missionary. **3** aim or calling in life. **4** military operation against an enemy. **5** any duty, esp. one that has been assigned. **missionary** *n* person sent to convert natives or primitive peoples to his religion, educate them, etc.

mist *n* **1** water vapour in fine drops; thin fog. **2** something that blurs or dims. *vt,vi* be, become, or make dim or blurred. **misty** *adj.*

mistake *n* error in thought or action. *vt* (-took; -taken) **1** form a wrong opinion about; misunderstand. **2** take (a person or thing) for another; confuse.

Mister *n* form of address for an adult male: normally written *Mr.*

mistletoe *n* evergreen plant with white berries that grows as a partial parasite on other trees.

mistress *n* **1** woman teacher. **2** woman who employs others. **3** woman with whom a man has a continuing sexual relationship outside marriage.

mistrust *n* lack of trust. *vt* regard with lack of trust; distrust.

misunderstand *vt,vi* (misunderstood) fail to understand correctly or properly. **misunderstanding** *n* **1** failure to understand. **2** slight quarrel.

misuse *n* (mis'ju:s) wrong or improper use. *vt* (mis'ju:z) **1** use wrongly. **2** treat badly.

mitre *n* **1** bishop's tall pointed hat. **2** corner joint formed by two pieces of wood, etc., that meet at equal angles. *vt* join so as to form a mitre joint.

mitten *n* glove with one compartment for the four fingers and a separate one for the thumb.

mix *vt,vi* combine; blend. *vi* associate with others freely or easily. *vt* form by blending. **mix up 1** confuse. **2** blend. **mixture** *n* **1** product of mixing. **2** combination of two or more ingredients, elements, types, qualities, etc. **mix-up** *n* confusion; muddle.

moan *n* low sound, usually indicating pain or suffering. *vi,vt* **1** utter or say with a moan. **2** grumble; complain.

moat *n* deep wide ditch, originally filled with water, round a castle or town.

mob *n* disorderly crowd of people. *vt* (-bb-) crowd round; attack in a crowd.

mobile *adj* **1** capable of movement. **2** easily moved. **3** expressive. *n* ornament consisting of a delicate hanging construction of balanced parts, which move with the air current. **mobility** *n.* **mobilize** *vt* **1** prepare (armed forces) for active service. **2** organize for a task. **3** put into motion or use. *vi* be ready or assembled for battle.

mock *vt,vi* make fun of by imitating; scoff or jeer (at). **mockery** *n* **1** ridicule. **2** derisive action or imitation.

mode *n* manner; style; method; fashion.

model *n* **1** representation of an object made to scale. **2** pattern to be followed; design; style. **3** person or object worthy of imitation. **4** person who poses for an artist, etc. **5** person who wears and displays clothing for potential customers. *v* (-ll-) *vt,vi* **1** make a model (of). **2** form or work (clay, etc.). **3** wear and display (clothing) for potential customers. *vi* pose for an artist, etc.

moderate *adj* ('mɔdərit) **1** not going to extremes. **2** of medium quantity, quality, or extent; not excessive. *n* ('mɔdərit) person of moderate views. *vt,vi* ('mɔdəreit) make or become less violent or excessive. **moderately** *adv.*

modern *adj* relating to or characteristic of

present and recent time. **modernize** *vt* make modern; bring up to date. **modernization** *n*.

modest *adj* **1** unassuming; shy; not vain. **2** free from pretension; not showy. **3** moderate. **modestly** *adv*. **modesty** *n*.

modify *vt* **1** make small changes in. **2** tone down. **3** qualify. **4** make less severe. **modification** *n*.

modulate *vt* **1** vary the tone, pitch, or volume of. **2** regulate; adjust; soften. *vi* change from one musical key to another. **modulation** *n*.

module *n* **1** separable compartment of a space vehicle. **2** standard or unit of measurement. **3** removable framework or assembly.

mohair *n* yarn or fabric made from the soft silky hair of the Angora goat or made to resemble it.

moist *adj* damp; slightly wet. **moistly** *adv*. **moisten** *vt,vi* make or become moist. **moisture** *n* **1** water or other liquid diffused as a vapour or condensed on a surface. **2** dampness. **moisturize** *vt* give or restore moisture to.

mole[1] *n* small dark birthmark on the skin.

mole[2] *n* small nocturnal burrowing animal with a smooth silky pelt.

molecule *n* simplest unit of a chemical compound, consisting of two or more atoms. **molecular** *adj*.

molest *vt* **1** disturb or annoy by interfering with. **2** interfere with improperly, esp. sexually.

mollusc *n* soft-bodied invertebrate, such as the snail, oyster, or octopus, usually with a hard shell.

molten *adj* liquefied by intense heat.

moment *n* **1** very short space of time. **2** appropriate time. **at the moment** now. **in a moment 1** soon; shortly. **2** quickly; instantly. **momentary** *adj* lasting a moment. **momentarily** *adv*. **momentous** *adj* important.

momentum *n* **1** mass multiplied by velocity of a moving body. **2** impetus; driving strength.

monarch *n* sovereign head of a country; king or queen. **monarchic** *or* **monarchical** *adj*. **monarchy** *n* **1** form of government in which authority is vested, constitutionally or traditionally, in the monarch. **2** country of a monarch.

monastery *n* house occupied by a community of monks. **monastic** *adj* relating to monks or their way of life.

Monday *n* second day of the week.

money *n* **1** official medium of exchange of a country, consisting of coins and paper currency of various denominations. **2** amount or sum of money; income. **3** funds; assets. **monetary** *adj* relating to money.

mongrel *n* dog of mixed breeds.

monitor *n* **1** pupil appointed to special duties in a school. **2** person who warns or advises. **3** control or checking device on a machine or system. **4** person who officially listens to and records foreign broadcasts. *vt* listen to in order to record or check.

monk *n* member of a male community, having taken final religious vows.

monkey *n* **1** long-tailed primate usually living in forests. **2** mischievous child. *vi also* **monkey around** *or* **about** play or fool (with).

monochrome *n* something of one colour or in black and white.

monogamy *n* custom or state of being married to only one person at a time. **monogamous** *adj*.

monologue *n* **1** prolonged talk by a single speaker. **2** dramatic work or part to be performed by one speaker.

monopoly *n* exclusive control or possession of a trade, privilege, etc. **monopolize** *vt* obtain or exercise sole control or possession of.

monosyllable *n* word of one syllable. **monosyllabic** *adj*.

monotone *n* sound, note, or voice of an unvaried pitch. **monotonous** *adj* lacking variation; dull; tedious. **monotonously** *adv*. **monotony** *n*.

monsoon *n* **1** seasonal wind of S Asia and the Indian Ocean, blowing from the southwest in summer. **2** rainy season that accompanies the wind from this direction.

monster *n* **1** legendary animal of a combination of forms. **2** grossly deformed animal or plant. **3** evil person. **4** something huge. **monstrous** *adj* **1** very great; huge. **2** ugly; hideous. **3** outrageous; revolting.

month *n* any of the 12 periods into which a year is divided. **monthly** *adj* **1** occurring, done, etc., once a month. **2** lasting a month. *adv* once a month.

monument *n* **1** something, esp. a statue, that commemorates. **2** statue, structure, etc., of historical importance. **3** written record. **monumental** *adj* **1** colossal; massive; stupendous. **2** relating to or serving as a monument.

moo *n* sound a cow makes. *vi* make a sound like a cow.

mood[1] *n* **1** state of mind and feelings. **2** depressed or sulky state of mind. **moody** *adj* changeable in mood.

mood[2] *n* form of a verb that indicates a particular function, such as the imperative, subjunctive, conditional, etc.

moon *n* **1** cratered and mountainous body that revolves around the earth in about 27.3 days, changing in apparent shape. **2** apparent shape of the moon; phase. *vi also* **moon around** *or* **about** go about idly, dreamily, listlessly, etc. **moonlight** *n* light from the sun reflected from the moon to the earth.

moor[1] *n also* **moorland** tract of open waste land, often hilly and covered with heather. **moorhen** *n* black red-billed water bird living on rivers etc.

moor[2] *vt,vi* secure or fasten (a ship, etc.) with cables or ropes or be secured so. **mooring** *n* place for securing a vessel. **moorings** *pl n* ropes, etc., used in securing a vessel.

mop *n* sponge or bundle of yarn, cloth, etc., fastened to the end of a handle for cleaning floors, etc. *vt* (-pp-) *also* **mop up** clean or wipe with a mop.

mope *vi* be depressed. **mope about** *or* **around** act aimlessly. **mopes** *pl n* dejected state.

moped *n* motorized bicycle.

moral *adj* **1** relating to or concerned with right and wrong conduct; ethical. **2** of good conduct; virtuous; honest. *n* practical lesson, esp. one taught by a fable or other story. **morally** *adv*. **morale** (mə'rɑːl) *n* discipline and spirit of a group of persons. **morality** *n* **1** virtuous conduct. **2** moral principles. **moralize** *vt* interpret or explain in a moral sense; derive a moral from. *vi* make moral reflections; talk about morality. **morals** *pl n* personal conduct, or principles.

morbid *adj* **1** gloomy; unpleasant. **2** unhealthy. **morbidly** *adv*.

more *adj* **1** greater in quantity, number, or degree. **2** additional; extra. *n* additional quantity, number, or degree. *adv* to a greater extent; in addition. **more or less** approximately; roughly. **moreover** *adv* besides; further.

morgue *n* room or building where dead bodies are taken to await identification before burial.

morning *n* early part of the day, usually up to noon or lunchtime.

moron *n* **1** mentally deficient person. **2** foolish person. **moronic** *adj*.

morose *adj* sullen; gloomy; unsociable.

morphine *n* drug to relieve severe pain.

Morse Code *n* signalling system in which numbers and letters are represented by combinations of dots and dashes.

mortal *adj* subject to or causing death. *n* human being. **mortality** *n* **1** condition of being subject to death. **2** large loss of life. **3** frequency of death; death rate.

mortar *n* **1** mixture of lime, sand, and water for holding bricks and stones together. **2** vessel in which substances are pounded or ground. **3** short cannon for throwing shells at high angles. *vt* fix or plaster with mortar.

mortgage *n* conveyance of property pledged as security for a debt until the loan is repaid. *vt* pledge (property) by mortgage.

mortify *vt* **1** humiliate. **2** subdue by self-denial. **mortification** *n*.

mortuary *n* place where dead bodies are temporarily kept before burial.

mosaic *n* picture or pattern made of small pieces of coloured stone, glass, etc.

Moslem *n,adj* Muslim.

mosque *n* Muslim place of worship.

mosquito *n, pl* **mosquitoes** *or* **mosquitos** blood-sucking insect that can transmit a disease such as malaria.

moss *n* small plant that grows in dense clumps on moist surfaces. **mossy** *adj*.

most *adj* greatest in size, number, or degree; nearly all. *n* greatest amount or degree. **at (the) most** not over; at maximum. **make the most of** use to the greatest advantage. ~*adv* in the greatest degree. **mostly** *adv* mainly; almost entirely; usually.

motel *n* roadside hotel, often consisting of private cabins with parking space in front.

moth *n* usually nocturnal insect similar to the butterfly. **motheaten** *adj* decrepit; damaged; filled with holes.

mother *n* **1** female parent. **2** head of a religious community of women. *vt* care for or protect as a mother. **motherhood** *n* state or qualities of being a mother. **mother-in-law** *n, pl* **mothers-in-law** mother of one's husband or wife. **mother superior** *n* head of a religious community of women.

motion *n* **1** movement. **2** manner or power of movement. **3** formal proposal at a meeting. **in motion** in operation, functioning. ~*vi* make a gesture, as with the hand. *vt* direct or guide by a gesture. **motionless** *adj* not moving; still.

motive *n* **1** reason; cause; intention; incentive. **2** chief idea in a work of art. *adj* causing motion or action. **motivate** *vt* provide with a motive. **motivation** *n*.

motor *n* **1** engine. **2** machine that transforms electrical into mechanical energy to produce motion. *vi* travel by car. **motorboat** boat powered by a motor. **motor car** *n* car. **motorcycle** *n* *also* **motorbike** two-wheeled road vehicle, heavier and more powerful than a moped. **motorist** *n* person who drives a (motor) car. **motorway** *n* main road with separate carriageways of several lanes and limited access.

motto *n, pl* **mottoes** *or* **mottos** **1** saying adopted as a rule of conduct. **2** short phrase or sentence inscribed on a coat of arms, etc.

mould[1] *n* **1** hollow form or container in which molten metal, plastic, etc., is cast or shaped. **2** anything cast or shaped in a mould. **3** character; type. *vt* form; shape; model.

mould[2] *n* fungal growth caused by dampness; mildew. **mouldy** *adj*.

moult *vi,vt* shed (feathers, skin, fur, etc.). *n* act or process of moulting.

mound *n* **1** pile, as of earth or stones; heap. **2** small hill. *vt* form into a mound.

mount[1] *vt,vi* **1** go up; ascend; climb. **2** get up on (a horse, platform, etc.). *vt* **1** set at a height or elevation. **2** provide with or place on a horse. **3** fix in a setting, backing, or support. *vi* rise; increase. *n* **1** act of mounting. **2** something mounted. **3** setting, backing, or support on which something is mounted.

mount[2] *n* mountain; hill.

mountain *n* **1** natural and usually very high and steep elevation of the earth's surface. **2** large pile or heap. **mountainous** *adj*. **mountaineer** *n* person who climbs mountains. *vi* climb mountains.

mourn *vi* feel sorrow. *vt* grieve for.

mouse *n, pl* **mice** small long-tailed rodent. **mousy** *adj* **1** like or suggestive of a mouse. **2** (of hair) fair but not blond(e).

mousse *n* dish made with whipped cream, beaten eggs, etc.

moustache *n* hair growing on the upper lip.

mouth *n* (mauθ) **1** cavity between the lips and the throat, containing the teeth, tongue, etc., in which food is chewed and speech sounds are formed. **2** opening into anything hollow. **3** entrance to something. **4** part of a river where its waters empty into a sea, lake, etc. *v* (mauð) *vt* form (words) with the lips without speaking. *vi* declaim. **mouthpiece** *n* **1** end of something intended to be put between or near the lips. **2** person who speaks for others. **mouth-watering** *adj* appetizing.

move *vt,vi* **1** change the place or position (of). **2** stir. *vt* **1** propose. **2** affect with emotion. *vi* **1** change one's place of residence. **2** make progress; advance. *n* act of moving; movement. **get a move on** *inf* hurry up. **movable** *adj* capable of being moved; not fixed. **movement** *n* **1** process or act of moving. **2** moving parts of a mechanism, as of a watch. **3** main division of a musical work, esp. of a symphony. **4** group engaged in or activities directed towards some goal or end. **5** trend.

mow *vt,vi* (mowed; mown *or* mowed) cut or cut down (grass, grain, etc.). **mower** *n*.

Mr abbreviation for **Mister.**

Mrs abbreviation for **mistress**; used as a form of address for a married woman.

much *adj* in great quantity or degree. *n* **1** large amount. **2** notable or important matter or thing. *adv* in or to a great degree. **as much** exactly that. **make much of** **1** make sense of. **2** give importance to. **not much of** not really. **not think much of** have a poor opinion of.

muck *n* **1** manure. **2** filth; dirt. *vt* make dirty. **muck about** *sl* mess or fool about. **muck in** *sl* join in to achieve something. **muck out** clean out; remove muck from. **muck up** *sl* ruin; spoil. **mucky** *adj*.

mud *n* wet soft earth. **mudguard** *n* guard over a wheel to protect against mud. **mudslinging** *n* reckless accusations or abuse. **muddy** *adj* **1** covered with or abounding in mud. **2** mudlike in colour or texture. **3** vague; obscure; not clear. *vt,vi* make or become muddy.

muddle *vt* **1** confuse; bewilder. **2** mismanage; mix up in a cónfused way. **muddle through** succeed in spite of inadequate planning, etc. ~*n* muddled state or condition; mess.

muffle *vt* **1** wrap or cover up with something

warm. **2** wrap up to deaden sound. **3** deaden (sound). **4** conceal. *n* something that muffles.

mug *n* **1** large drinking cup with a handle. **2** *sl* face or mouth. **3** fool; gullible person. *vt,vi* (-gg-) *sl* attack and rob. **mug up** obtain (information) or study during a short intensive period. **mugger** *n sl* person who assaults and robs someone.

mulberry *n* tree that bears dark red edible berries.

mule[1] *n* sterile offspring of a mare and a donkey. **mulish** *adj* stubborn.

mule[2] *n* slipper with an exposed heel.

multiple *adj* have many parts, elements, etc. *n* quantity that contains another quantity an exact number of times.

multiply *vt,vi* **1** find the mathematical product of two or more numbers or quantities. **2** increase or cause to increase in number or amount. **multiplication** *n*.

multitude *n* **1** great number of persons; crowd; throng. **2** the common people.

mum *n inf* mother.

mumble *vt,vi* speak or utter indistinctly. *n* indistinct talk or sound.

mummy[1] *n* dead body preserved by embalming or other techniques. **mummify** *vt* preserve as a mummy.

mummy[2] *n inf* mother.

mumps *n* contagious viral disease, esp. of children, marked by a swelling of the glands in the neck.

munch *vt,vi* chew vigorously and often noisily.

mundane *adj* ordinary; everyday; common.

municipal *adj* relating to the local government of a city or town. **municipality** *n* city or town with local self-government.

mural *n* painting executed on a wall.

murder *n* **1** unlawful and deliberate killing of a human being. **2** *inf* difficult or unpleasant task. *vt* **1** kill. **2** *inf* ruin; destroy. *vi* commit murder. **murderer** *n*. **murderess** *f n*.

murmur *n* **1** low and continuous sound. **2** grumble; complaint. *vt* utter in a low voice. *vi* **1** make a murmur. **2** complain.

muscle *n* **1** specialized body tissue that produces movement by contracting. **2** strength; brawn. **muscular** *adj*.

muse *vi* ponder; meditate; be lost in thought.

museum *n* building housing objects or illustrations of art, science, history, etc., for observation and study.

mushroom *n* fungus, esp. an edible variety, having a cap on the end of a stem. *vi* **1** increase, grow, or expand rapidly. **2** gather mushrooms.

music *n* **1** organization of vocal or instrumental sounds into a pleasing or stirring rhythm or harmony. **2** sequence of pleasing sounds. **3** art of producing music. **4** record of notes for reproducing music. **musical** *adj* **1** relating to music. **2** liking or skilled in music. *n* light stage or film entertainment with songs and dancing. **musician** *n* composer or performer of music.

Muslim *n also* **Moslem** adherent of Islam. *adj also* **Moslem** relating to the religion or culture of Islam.

muslin *n* fine cotton fabric.

mussel *n* mollusc with a dark elongated hinged shell.

must *v aux* be obliged to; be certain to; be resolved to. *n* something imperative.

mustard *n* strong-flavoured yellowish or brownish paste or powder prepared from the seeds of the mustard plant, used as a condiment and seasoning.

mute *adj* **1** silent; soundless. **2** dumb; not capable of speech. *n* person unable to speak. *vt* deaden the sound of; soften.

mutilate *vt* injure, disfigure, or make imperfect, as by damaging parts, removing a limb, etc. **mutilation** *n*.

mutiny *n* revolt or rebellion against authority, esp. by soldiers or sailors. *vi* engage in mutiny. **mutinous** *adj*.

mutter *vt,vi* utter indistinctly or in a low tone; mumble. *n* muttered sound; complaint.

mutton *n* flesh of mature sheep, used as food.

mutual *adj* done, felt, possessed, etc., by each of two with respect to the other; common to both or all. **mutually** *adv*.

muzzle *n* **1** open end of the barrel of a firearm. **2** projecting nose and mouth of an animal. **3** device placed over the mouth of an animal to prevent it from biting. *vt* **1** put a muzzle on. **2** prevent from speaking.

my *pron* belonging to or associated with me. **myself** *pron* reflexive or emphatic form of **me** or **I**.

myrrh (mə:) *n* aromatic gum exuded from certain shrubs, used as perfume, incense, etc.

mystery *n* secret, puzzling, or obscure thing. **mysterious** *adj*. **mysteriously** *adv*.

mystic *n* person who claims spiritual knowledge or insight, as by following mysticism. **mystical** *adj also* **mystic 1** of hidden, spiritual, or occult nature or significance. **2** mysterious. **3** relating to mysticism. **mysticism** *n* belief in direct communion with God and awareness of divine truth by means of contemplation and love alone.

mystify *vt* **1** bewilder; confuse; perplex. **2** make obscure or mysterious. **mystification** *n*.

mystique *n* atmosphere of mystery associated with or investing certain activities, doctrines, arts, etc.

myth *n* **1** ancient story or legend, usually with supernatural characters or events. **2** imaginary or fictitious event, person, or thing. **mythical** *adj*. **mythology** *n* **1** collection of myths. **2** study of myths. **mythological** *adj*.

N

nag *vt,vi* (-gg-) annoy, pester, or be troubled with constant complaints, reminders, worries, or pain.

nail *n* **1** narrow flat-headed piece of metal hammered in as a means of joining or for use as a peg. **2** hard horny covering on the tip of a finger or toe. **as hard as nails** cold; ruthless; tough. **hit the nail on the head** describe exactly; pinpoint (a problem, situation, etc.). ~*vt* **1** join or fasten with a nail. **2** *inf* get hold of (a person); catch. **nail down** make (a person) declare his aims or opinions. **nailfile** *n* small metal file for shaping fingernails.

naive *adj* **1** unsophisticated; ingenuous. **2** credulous; gullible. **naively** *adv*. **naiveté** *or* **naivety** *n*.

naked *adj* without clothes or protection; bare. **nakedly** *adv*. **nakedness** *n*.

name *n* **1** word or words by which a person or thing is known or identified. **2** reputation. **3** *inf* celebrity. *vt* **1** give a name to; identify. **2** declare (a price, terms, etc.). **namely** *adv* that is to say. **namesake** *n* person or thing having the same name as another.

nanny *n* **1** woman employed to look after children, esp. in a private household. **2** *inf* grandmother.

nap[1] *n* short period of sleep, esp. during the day. *vi* (-pp-) sleep for a short period.

nap[2] *n* surface fibres on cloth.

napalm *n* jellied mixture of petrol and acids used in bombs, etc.

nape *n* back of the neck.

napkin *n* square of cloth or paper used for protecting clothes and wiping the mouth and fingers during meals.

nappy *n* square of cloth or disposable pad worn by a baby to absorb excreta.

narcissus *n, pl* **narcissi** (nɑːˈsisai) bulb producing yellow or white flowers.

narcotic *n* addictive drug, such as morphine, that induces sleep and dulls the senses. *adj* inducing sleep or insensibility.

narrate *vt* relate or tell (a story). **narration** *n*. **narrator** *n*. **narrative** *n* story; account. *adj* consisting of or relating to a narrative.

narrow *adj* **1** measuring little across. **2** strict; accurate. **3** bigoted; not liberal. **4** limited; restricted. *vt,vi* make or become narrow or narrower. **narrowly** *adv*. **narrowness** *n*. **narrow-minded** *adj* having rigid and narrow views.

nasal *adj* **1** relating to the nose. **2** (of sounds) formed by breathing through the nose.

nasturtium *n* garden plant having orange, yellow, or red flowers and roundish leaves.

nasty *adj* **1** unpleasant. **2** spiteful. **3** offensive; disgusting. **nastily** *adv*. **nastiness** *n*.

nation *n* **1** country; land. **2** large group of people having a common cultural background, history, and language. **nationwide** *adj,adv* throughout the country.

national *adj* **1** relating to a country as a whole. **2** typical of a particular country. **3** controlled by the government. **nationally** *adv*. **national anthem** *n* country's official song. **national insurance** *n* state scheme to provide financial aid during unemployment, sickness, widowhood, etc. **national service** *n* compulsory military training. **nationalism** *n* patriotism; belief in national unity. **nationalist** *n,adj*. **nationality** *n* citizenship of a particular country. **nationalize** *vt* transfer (an industry or property) to public ownership and control. **nationalization** *n*.

native *adj* **1** relating to the place of birth or origin. **2** innate. **3** indigenous. **4** relating to the indigenous population. *n* **1** person born or living in or animal found in a certain country or area. **2** person belonging to a race of original inhabitants of a country. **nativity** *n* **1**

birth. **2** *also* **nativity play** play or artistic representation of the birth of Christ.

natural *adj* **1** produced by, present in, or relating to the physical world; not artificial. **2** innate. **3** normal; to be expected; automatic. **4** unaffected. **5** not domesticated or civilized. *n* **1** *inf* person naturally equipped for a particular skill or job. **2** musical note or key that is neither sharp nor flat. **naturally** *adv.* **natural gas** *n* gas formed like oil in natural deposits and burned for cooking, heating, etc. **natural history** *n* study of animals and plants. **natural science** *n* science, such as chemistry or zoology, that is concerned with laws and processes of the external physical world. **naturalize** *vt,vi* **1** confer or adopt citizenship of a country. **2** introduce or adapt to another country or area. **naturalization** *n.*

nature *n* **1** external physical world and its laws, plants, and animals. **2** character or temperament; characteristics. **3** kind or sort.

naughty *adj* **1** mischievous. **2** indecent; suggestive. **naughtily** *adv.* **naughtiness** *n.*

nausea *n* **1** feeling of sickness; desire to vomit. **2** absolute disgust. **nauseous** *adj.* **nauseate** *vt* **1** induce a feeling of sickness. **2** disgust; repel.

nautical *adj* relating to ships, seamen, or navigation.

naval *adj* relating to the equipment, personnel, or activities of a navy.

nave *n* central seating area of a church up to the chancel.

navel *n* small pit in the abdomen left by the severed umbilical cord.

navigate *vt,vi* direct or plan the course or route of (a ship, car, etc.). *vt* **1** follow the course of (a river). **2** sail across. **navigator** *n.* **navigable** *adj* **1** (of water) deep enough to admit ships. **2** able to be navigated. **navigation** *n* **1** theory and practice of navigating. **2** shipping.

navy *n* **1** fleet of warships with sea aircraft. **2** personnel of the fleet. **navy blue** *n,adj* dark blue.

near *prep* at or within a short time or distance. *adj* **1** close in position or time. **2** intimate; dear. **3** only just avoided; narrow. *adv* close (to). **nearness** *n.* **nearby** *adv,adj* close by; not far away. **nearly** *adv* almost. **nearside** *n* the side of a car, traffic lane, etc., nearest to the kerb. **near-sighted** *adj* short-sighted.

neat *adj* **1** tidy; carefully arranged. **2** skilful; deft. **3** well-planned; clever. **4** precise. **5** undiluted. **neatly** *adv.* **neatness** *n.* **neaten** *vt* make neat; tidy up.

necessary *adj* **1** essential; needed. **2** logical. **necessarily** *adv.* **necessity** *n* **1** essential requirement. **2** pressing need. **3** logical consequence.

neck *n* **1** part of the body connecting the head and shoulders. **2** *also* **neckline** part of a garment round the neck and shoulders. **3** long narrowed portion of land, slender part of a bottle, etc. **neck and neck** abreast in a race or contest. **stick one's neck out** act defiantly and risk censure. ~*vi inf* kiss and cuddle lengthily (with). **necklace** *n* neck ornament.

nectar *n* **1** sweet liquid that bees obtain from certain flowers for making honey. **2** very sweet, soothing drink.

née (nei) *adj* having a maiden name of; born.

need *vt* require; lack. *vi* be obliged to; be necessary to. *v aux* **need I, you, he?, etc.** must I, you, he?, etc. **I, you, he, etc., need not** I, you, he, etc., do/does not have to. ~*n* **1** circumstances in which something is needed. **2** misfortune; poverty. **3** requirement. **needy** *adj* poor.

needle *n* **1** sharp pointed sliver of steel with a hole at one end to take thread for sewing. **2** plastic or metal rod for knitting. **3** gramophone stylus. **4** indicator arrow on a compass, dial, etc. **5** pointed part of a hypodermic syringe. **6** sharply pointed leaf of a conifer. **needlework** *n* hand-sewing.

negate *vt* **1** deny. **2** cancel out; make void. **negation** *n.*

negative *adj* **1** indicating *no;* not affirmative. **2** not productive or positive. **3** indicating opposition or disapproval. **4** denoting numbers less than zero. **5** with light and dark areas reversed. **6** designating the electrical charge carried by an electron. *n* **1** word(s) indicating a denial or refusal. **2** negative number. **3** negative photographic plate.

neglect *vt* **1** fail to care for. **2** omit; overlook. *n* act or result of neglecting. **negligent** *adj* careless; not paying proper attention. **negligence** *n.* **negligently** *adv.* **negligible** *adj* so minor as to be not worth considering. **negligibly** *adv.*

négligé ('negliʒei) *n* woman's dressing gown, usually of a light or flimsy material.

negotiate *vi* reach an agreement through discussion. *vt* **1** settle through discussion. **2** successfully come through or deal with (an obstacle). **3** obtain cash settlement for. **negotiation** *n*. **negotiator** *n*.

Negro *n, pl* **Negroes** black-skinned person of African descent.

neigh *vi* (of a horse) produce a braying sound. *n* cry of a horse; bray.

neighbour *n* **1** person living nextdoor or nearby. **2** thing situated near or adjacent to another. *v* **neighbour on** border on; adjoin. **neighbourhood** *n* (people living in) the vicinity; surrounding area.

neither *adj,pron* not either (one). *conj* nor yet.

neon *n* gaseous element used in strip lighting and advertising display.

nephew *n* son of one's brother or sister, or of one's husband's or wife's brother or sister.

nepotism *n* favouritism shown to relatives in unfairly procuring positions or promotion for them. **nepotist** *n*.

Neptune *n* outer giant planet lying beyond Uranus.

nerve *n* **1** bundle of fibres that connects the central nervous system with all parts of the body transmitting sensory and motor impulses. **2** courage; confidence. **3** *sl* impudence; cheek. **nerves** *pl n* anxiety; hysteria; irritability. **get on one's nerves** irritate. **nervy** *adj* anxious; tense. **nerve-racking** *adj* causing emotional strain; worrying.

nervous *adj* **1** tense; excitable. **2** timid; anxious. **3** vigorous; spirited. **4** relating to the nerves. **nervous breakdown** *n* severe mental and emotional collapse. **nervous system** *n* body mechanism coordinating internal functions and external impulses.

nest *n* **1** shelter made of twigs, grass, etc., where birds, reptiles, mice, etc., lay eggs or give birth. **2** protective or comfortable place in which young animals are reared. *vi* **1** make a nest. **2** look for nests. **nest egg** *n* savings.

nestle *vi* cuddle; settle comfortably.

net[1] *n* **1** *also* **netting** open mesh of knotted string, wire, etc., used for catching fish, birds, etc., or to protect against birds, insects, etc. **2** mesh barrier dividing playing areas in tennis and other games or to enclose a goal area. *vt,vi* (-tt-) **1** catch or cover with nets. **2** snare. **3** construct a net. **netball** *n* sport in which goals are scored by throwing a ball into a net. **network** *n* **1** complex connected pattern or system of wires, roads, etc. **2** series of linked radio or television stations.

net[2] *adj* remaining after deductions. *vt* (-tt-) earn as net profit or income.

nettle *n* plant with toothed leaves and stinging hairs. *vt* irritate.

neurosis *n* nervous disorder involving irrational anxiety, obsessions, or other abnormal behaviour. **neurotic** *adj* **1** relating to a neurosis or to the nerves. **2** prone to anxiety or hysteria. *n* neurotic person.

neuter *adj* **1** of neither masculine nor feminine gender. **2** sexually underdeveloped. **3** deprived of sexual organs. *n* neuter word, animal, plant, etc. *vt* make neuter.

neutral *adj* **1** impartial; not taking sides. **2** belonging to neither side. **3** having no definite characteristics. **4** neuter. **5** neither alkali nor acid. **6** neither positive nor negative. **7** (of gears) not engaged. *n* **1** person, country, etc., who favours no side or who does not take part in an argument, war, etc. **2** (of gears) state of being not engaged. **neutrality** *n*. **neutralize** *vt* **1** make neutral. **2** render powerless; deaden.

neutron *n* minute uncharged particle occurring in the nuclei of all atoms except hydrogen.

never *adv* **1** at no time. **2** not at all. **never mind!** don't worry! **well I never!** how surprising!

nevertheless *adv* even so; in spite of that.

new *adj* **1** of recent origin or existence; not old; freshly produced. **2** recently acquired or discovered. **3** modern; novel; different. **4** another. **new at** *or* **to** unaccustomed to; unfamiliar with. ~*adv also* **newly** freshly; recently. **newcomer** *n* recently arrived person; beginner. **New Year** *n* **1** coming year. **2** first or first few days of January.

news *s n* **1** current information about recent events. **2** broadcast information about local, national, and international events. **newsagent** *n* shopkeeper who sells newspapers, journals, etc. **newspaper** *n* daily or weekly publication containing news, features, specialist information, and advertisements. **newsreel** *n* filmed report of current events.

newt *n* small lizard-like amphibian.

next *adj* **1** following; subsequent. **2** adjacent; neighbouring. **3** closest. *adv* after this or that.

nib *n* pointed writing end of a pen.

nibble *n* **1** small bite. **2** morsel. *vt,vi* take a nibble (at); eat in nibbles.

nice *adj* **1** pleasant; attractive. **2** good; virtuous. **3** refined. **4** precise; subtle; delicate. **nicely** *adv*.

niche *n* **1** alcove or recess, often used for shrines or statues. **2** suitable or comfortable place or position.

nick *n* tiny notch. **the nick** *sl* jail. **in the nick of time** just in time. ~*vt* **1** make a nick in. **2** *sl* steal; pinch.

nickel *n* **1** hard silvery metal used for plating and coin-making. **2** *US* five-cent coin.

nickname *n* name by which a person is known affectionately or mockingly. *vt* give a nickname to.

nicotine *n* narcotic found in tobacco.

niece *n* daughter of one's brother or sister, or of one's husband's or wife's brother or sister.

nigger *n abusive* Negro.

night *n* period of time between evening and morning; darkness. **nightclub** *n* place of entertainment open at night providing food and drink. **nightdress** *n also* **nightgown** woman's sleeping garment. **nightly** *adv* **1** during the night. **2** every night. **nightmare** *n* **1** terrifying dream. **2** frightening experience; trauma. **night-time** *n* period of darkness between sunset and sunrise. **night watchman** *n* person employed to guard premises at night.

nightingale *n* red-brown European songbird noted for its nocturnal trilling song.

nil *n* nothing.

nimble *adj* agile; deft; quick. **nimbly** *adv*.

nine *n* **1** number equal to one plus eight. **2** group of nine persons, things, etc. **3** *also* **nine o'clock** nine hours after noon or midnight. *adj* amounting to nine. **nine days wonder** something that causes short-lived excitement or admiration. **ninth** *adj* coming between eighth and tenth in sequence. *n* **1** ninth person, object, etc. **2** one of nine equal portions; one divided by nine. *adv* after the eighth.

nineteen *n* **1** number that is nine more than ten. **2** nineteen things or people. **talk nineteen to the dozen** talk fast and unceasingly. ~*adj* amounting to nineteen. **nineteenth** *n,adj,adv*.

ninety *n* **1** number equal to nine times ten. **2** ninety things or people. *adj* amounting to ninety. **ninetieth** *adj,adv,n*.

nip *vt,vi* (-pp-) **1** catch, pinch, or bite sharply. **2** check the growth (of). *vi inf* go quickly; pop. *n* **1** small bite or pinch. **2** touch of frost. **nippy** *adj* cold; sharp; frosty.

nipple *n* **1** suckling teat of a breast or bottle. **2** device similar in shape or function to a nipple.

nit *n* **1** egg of a head louse or other parasite. **2** *sl* fool.

nitrogen *n* colourless gas forming 78 per cent of the air and used esp. in the manufacture of fertilizers.

nitroglycerine *n* unstable chemical used in dynamite and other explosives.

no *adv* **1** not any; not one. **2** not in any way; not at all. **3** not. **4** expressing denial, refusal, etc. *n* statement of denial, refusal, etc.; negative.

noble *adj* **1** courageous; worthy; high-minded. **2** aristocratic. **3** stately; splendid. *n also* **nobleman** member of the nobility; aristocrat; peer. **nobility** *n* **1** hereditary class of the highest status; aristocracy. **2** moral courage, worthiness, or endurance.

nobody *pron* **1** no-one. **2** person of no importance or of low birth.

nocturnal *adj* of, occurring in, or active during the night. **nocturnally** *adv*.

nod *vt,vi* (-dd-) bend (the head) forward to indicate (agreement or approval). *vi* doze. *n* nodding motion.

noise *n* sound. **noisy** *adj* loud. **noisily** *adv*. **noisiness** *n*.

nomad *n* **1** member of a tribe constantly on the move in search of new pasture. **2** habitual wanderer; roamer. **nomadic** *adj*.

nominal *adj* **1** not actual; existing in name only. **2** very small; token. **nominally** *adv*.

nominate *vt* **1** propose as a candidate. **2** appoint. **nomination** *n*. **nominee** *n* person who is nominated.

non- *prefix* indicating negation, absence, etc.

nonchalant *adj* coolly casual; offhand. **nonchalance** *n*. **nonchalantly** *adv*.

nondescript *adj* having no distinguishing characteristics; dull.

none *pron* **1** not any (of them or it). **2** no part or section. **3** no such person. *adv* not at all; in no way.

nonentity *n* **1** insignificant person or thing. **2** non-existent thing.

nonsense *n* **1** meaningless or foolish words or ideas. **2** trifle. **nonsensical** *adj*.

noodle *n* thin strip of pasta.

nook *n* secret or sheltered corner or hiding place.

noon *n* midday; 12 o'clock in the daytime.

no-one *pron* no person at all; nobody.

noose *n* loop of rope with a slipknot to tighten it, used esp. for execution by hanging.

nor *conj* also not; not either.

norm *n* **1** usual or recognized standard or pattern. **2** expected or potential output.

normal *adj* **1** usual; ordinary; average. **2** not physically or mentally handicapped. **normality** *n*. **normally** *adv*.

north *n* **1** one of the four cardinal points of the compass situated to the left of a person facing the sunrise. **2** part of a country, area, etc., lying towards the north. *adj also* **northern** of, in, or facing the north. *adv,adj also* **northerly** **1** towards the north. **2** (of winds) from the north. **northerner** *n*. **northeast** *n* point situated midway between the north and east. *adj also* **northeastern** of, in, or facing the northeast. *adv,adj also* **northeasterly** **1** towards the northeast. **2** (of winds) from the northeast. **northward** *adj* facing or moving towards the north. **northwards** *adv* in the direction of the north. **northwest** *n* point situated midway between north and west. *adj also* **northwestern** of, in, or facing the northwest. *adv,adj also* **northwesterly** **1** towards the northwest. **2** (of winds) from the northwest.

nose *n* **1** central projection in the face used for breathing and smelling. **2** ability to smell out or discover. **be led by the nose** follow blindly. **keep one's nose to the grindstone** work persistently. **pay through the nose** pay too much. **poke one's nose into** interfere in. **turn one's nose up (at)** reject contemptuously. **under one's (very) nose** in one's presence; in full view. ~*vt,vi* smell or sniff (at).

nostalgia *n* **1** sentimental longing for things past. **2** homesickness. **nostalgic** *adj*.

nostril *n* one of the two openings of the nose.

nosy *adj* unpleasantly inquisitive. **nosiness** *n*.

not *adv* expressing negation, denial, refusal, etc.

notable *adj* important; remarkable; conspicuous. *n* important person. **notably** *adv*.

notation *n* **1** act or process of organizing a scheme of signs that represent scientific, musical, or other concepts. **2** such a scheme or method.

notch *n* V-shaped cut in a piece of wood, etc. *vt* cut a notch in, esp. as a way of keeping count. **notch up** score.

note *n* **1** short written record, summary, or comment. **2** short letter. **3** piece of paper money. **4** written promise to pay. **5** (symbol indicating) a musical sound of a certain pitch. **6** distinction; fame; importance. **7** notice; attention. **8** certain quality. *vt* **1** make a note of. **2** take note of; observe. **noteworthy** *adj* **1** deserving attention; worth noting. **2** remarkable.

nothing *n* **1** not anything; no thing. **2** no part. **3** something of no importance or value. **4** something requiring no effort. **5** zero; nought. **for nothing** **1** free of charge. **2** with no purpose. **think nothing of** do without hesitation. ~*adv* not in any way.

notice *vt,vi* **1** observe; take note of. **2** comment on, esp. favourably. *n* **1** attention; observation. **2** piece of displayed written information. **3** public announcement. **4** warning. **5** official announcement or notification of the termination of employment. **6** critical review. **at short notice** with little warning or preparation time. **noticeable** *adj*.

notify *vt* let (a person) know; inform officially. **notification** *n*.

notion *n* impression; view; idea; concept. **notional** *adj* **1** expressing a concept; not based on fact. **2** nominal.

notorious *adj* infamous; having a bad reputation. **notoriety** *n*. **notoriously** *adv*.

notwithstanding *adv* nevertheless. *prep,conj* in spite of.

nougat *n* chewy white sweet containing nuts.

nought *n* zero; nothing. **noughts and crosses** *n* game played on a criss-cross grid in which the object is to get three noughts or crosses in a row.

noun *n* word used to denote a thing, person, concept, act, etc.

nourish *vt* **1** give food to. **2** encourage or harbour (feeling). **nourishment** *n* food.

novel[1] *adj* new and different. **novelty** *n* **1** quality of being novel. **2** cheap often gaudy small article for sale.

novel[2] *n* sustained work of prose fiction longer than a short story. **novelist** *n*.

November *n* eleventh month of the year.

novice *n* **1** beginner; learner. **2** nun or monk who has not yet taken final vows.

now *adv* **1** at present. **2** immediately; this minute. **3** recently. **4** presently. **5** at this point; currently. **6** consequently. **now and then** every so often; occasionally. ~*conj also* **now that** since; as a consequence of. **nowadays** *adv* these days; in modern times.

nowhere *adv* not in any place; not anywhere. **get nowhere** be unsuccessful; fail to achieve something.

noxious *adj* poisonous.

nozzle *n* tube or spout through which liquid or gas is let out.

nuance *n* subtle variation in meaning, shade, etc.

nuclear *adj* **1** of, forming, or relating to a nucleus or central core. **2** relating to the structure or splitting of atoms. **nuclear fission/fusion** *n* splitting of a heavy atom/fusion of light atoms attended by enormous release of energy. **nuclear physics** *n* science relating to the behaviour of atoms. **nuclear reactor** *n* device for generating power from nuclear fission. **nuclear weapon** *n* bomb or missile using energy from nuclear fission or fusion.

nucleus *n, pl* **nuclei** ('nju:kliai) *or* **nucleuses 1** central or most active part of a movement, organization, etc. **2** positively charged central mass of an atom consisting of protons and neutrons.

nude *adj* naked. *n* naked figure, esp. one depicted in a painting, sculpture, etc. **in the nude** naked. **nudity** *n*.

nudge *n* deliberate slight push with the elbow; prod. *vt* give a nudge (to).

nugget *n* **1** small hard irregularly shaped lump, esp. of gold. **2** small valuable piece.

nuisance *n* thing or person causing annoyance, trouble, or offence.

null *adj* **1** without value or feeling. **2** having no legal force. **null and void** legally invalid. **nullity** *n*. **nullify** *vt* make null. **nullification** *n*.

numb *adj* without feeling, sensation, or emotion. *vt* make numb or insensitive. **numbness** *n*.

number *n* **1** mathematical concept of quantity, each unit of which has a unique value, enabling them to be used in counting. **2** numeral. **3** sum; quantity; aggregate. **4** one of a series; issue. **5** short musical piece. **6** exclusive article. **a number of** several. **number one** oneself. **without** *or* **beyond number** too many to be counted. ~*vt* **1** assign a number to. **2** add up to. **3** enumerate; list. **numberless** *adj* countless; innumerable.

numeral *n* symbol or group of symbols, such as 6 or VI, denoting a number.

numerate *adj* ('nju:mərət) able to understand and use mathematical concepts. *vt* ('nju:məreit) number; count. **numeracy** *n*.

numerical *adj* relating to or consisting of numbers. **numerically** *adv*.

numerous *adj* great in number; abundant.

nun *n* woman who has taken final vows in a religious order. **nunnery** *n* community of nuns; convent.

nurse *n* **1** person trained and employed to care for the sick under the direction of doctors. **2** woman employed to look after very small children. *vt,vi* **1** act as a nurse (to). **2** suckle. *vt* cherish; foster; nurture; encourage. **nursing home** *n* small privately run hospital for convalescent, aged, or chronically ill patients.

nursery *n* **1** playroom. **2** place for growing or stocking plants. **nursery rhyme** *n* traditional children's song or verse. **nursery school** *n* school for children under five; kindergarten.

nurture *vt* foster; rear; feed. *n* upbringing; education.

nut *n* **1** hard shelled fruit with a single sometimes edible kernel. **2** small regularly shaped metal block with a central threaded hole used for securing bolts. **3** *sl* fanatic; enthusiast. **4** *sl* insane or peculiar person. **nuts** *sl adj* crazy. **nutcracker** *n also* **nutcrackers** device having pincers for cracking nutshells. **nutmeg** *n* seed of an East Indian tree, ground as a spice. **nutshell** *n* woody covering of a nut kernel. **in a nutshell** precisely; concisely expressed.

nutrient *n* nourishing substance taken in, esp. by a plant.

nutrition *n* **1** digestion and assimilation of food. **2** feeding; nourishment. **nutritious** *adj* nourishing; health-giving.

nuzzle *vt,vi* rub or push (against) with the nose.

nylon *n* synthetic plastic fibre or material made from it. **nylons** *pl n* woman's stockings.

nymph *n* **1** minor Greek or Roman goddess inhabiting and guarding trees, rivers, etc. **2** beautiful young girl.

O

oak *n* deciduous acorn-bearing tree with hard wood and jagged leaves.

oar *n* wooden pole with one end flattened into a blade, used to propel a boat through water. **put one's oar in** interfere. **oarsman** *n pl* **-men** one who rows with an oar.

oasis *n, pl* **oases** (ou'eisi:z) fertile area in a desert.

oath *n* **1** solemn binding declaration of the truth of one's statement. **2** casual use of a solemn word or name in anger or irritation; swear-word. **on** *or* **under oath** sworn to tell the truth.

oats *pl n* grains of a hardy cereal plant, widely used as human and animal food. **sow one's wild oats** indulge in pleasures, esp. irresponsible sexual relationships, while young. **oatmeal** *n* coarse flour made from oats used for porridge, biscuits, etc.

obese *adj* extremely fat; gross. **obesity** *n*.

obey *vt,vi* do what is commanded by a person, law, instinct, etc. **obedient** *adj* ready and willing to obey; dutiful. **obedience** *n*. **obediently** *adv*.

obituary *n* notice of death, esp. in a newspaper, often including a short biography.

object *n* ('ɔbdʒekt) **1** thing discernible by the senses. **2** aim, goal, or intention. *vt,vi* (əb'dʒekt) oppose, disapprove, or protest against. **objection** *n* **1** act of or reason for objecting. **2** feeling or statement of dislike or disapproval. **objective** *adj* **1** separate; detached. **2** impartial; viewed fairly and dispassionately. *n* point or situation to be aimed at; goal. **objectively** *adv*. **objectivity** *n*.

oblige *vt* **1** allow no choice; insist or force. **2** do a favour for. **3** make indebted to. **obligation** *n* duty enforceable by law, morality, a contract, promise, etc. **obligatory** (ɔ'bligətəri) *adj* necessary and binding.

oblique **1** slanting away from the horizontal or vertical. **2** indirect; devious; not straightforward. **obliquely** *adv*.

obliterate *vt* leave no trace of; destroy; blot out. **obliteration** *n*.

oblivion *n* state of forgetfulness or lack of awareness. **oblivious** *adj* **1** absent-minded; unaware. **2** unaffected by; impervious to. **obliviously** *adv*.

oblong *n* figure, esp. a rectangle, longer than it is broad. *adj* shaped like an oblong.

obnoxious *adj* **1** repulsive; causing disgust. **2** extremely rude or insulting.

oboe *n* woodwind instrument having a mouthpiece fitted with a double reed. **oboist** *n*.

obscene *adj* offending against decency or morality; vulgar; lewd. **obscenely** *adv*. **obscenity** *n*.

obscure *adj* **1** vague; enigmatic; not easily understood. **2** dim; gloomy; indistinct. **3** not famous or well-known. **obscurely** *adv*. **obscurity** *n*.

observe *vt,vi* **1** see, notice, or watch. **2** keep to the rules of a custom, law, religion, etc. **3** remark or comment. **observer** *n*. **observance** *n* adherence to the rules of law, religion, custom, etc. **observant** *adj* attentive; taking notice. **observation** *n* **1** careful watching; recognizing and noting. **2** comment or remark. **observatory** *n* building used for astronomical observation.

obsess *vt* be an obsession of; preoccupy. **obsessive** *adj*. **obsession** *n* fixed idea or addiction that fascinates and preoccupies the mind to an exaggerated or dangerous extent.

obsolete *adj* out-of-date; antiquated; disused. **obsolescent** *adj* becoming obsolete. **obsolescence** *n*.

obstacle *n* any snag or obstruction hindering progress or action.

obstinate *adj* stubborn; hard to persuade; unyielding. **obstinacy** *n*. **obstinately** *adv*.

obstruct *vt,vi* **1** block off; prevent access or progress. **2** impede or delay any action. **obstruction** *n*.

obtain *vt,vi* gain possession (of); get; secure or acquire. **obtainable** *adj*.

obtrusive *adj* interfering; impertinent. **obtrusion** *n*.

obtuse *adj* dull; blunt; not sharp or acute. **obtuse angle** *n* angle greater than 90° but less than 180°.

obvious *adj* evident; clear; apparent. **obviously** *adv*.

occasion *n* **1** particular time of an event, ceremony, etc. **2** suitable opportunity or chance. **3** reason; need. **rise to the occasion** display the necessary or suitable qualities. ~*vt* give rise to; bring about or cause. **occasional** *adj* infrequent; sporadic. **occasionally** *adv*.

Occident *n* the West, esp. W. Europe and America. **Occidental** *adj,n*.

occult *adj* supernatural; magical; mysterious. **the occult** *n* supernatural or magical knowledge or experience.

occupy *vt* **1** take or hold possession of (a country, building, etc.). **2** employ. **occupant** *n* one who possesses or lives in a particular place. **occupancy** *n*. **occupation** *n* **1** employment; pastime; job. **2** state or act of occupying or being occupied.

occur *vi* (-rr-) **1** happen; take place. **2** exist; be found at. **3** come into the mind. **occurrence** *n*.

ocean *n* one of the five vast areas of sea surrounding the continents of the globe. **oceanic** *adj*.

octagon *n* geometric figure, design, building, etc., having eight sides. **octagonal** *adj*.

octane *n* inflammable hydrocarbon present in petrol. **high-octane** *adj* denoting a superior grade of petrol.

octave *n* **1** range of eight notes in a musical scale. **2** set of eight.

October *n* tenth month of the year.

octopus *n, pl* **octopuses** *or* **octopi** ('ɔktəpai) eight-armed mollusc.

odd *adj* **1** strange; bizarre; peculiar. **2** uneven; irregular. **3** (of a number) not divisible by two. **odd man out** one remaining when others have formed a pair, class, group, etc. **oddly** *adv*. **oddity** *n* **1** strangeness; peculiarity. **2** remarkable or unlikely event, person, object, etc. **oddment** *n* scrap; remnant; leftover. **odds** *pl n* **1** chances; possibilities. **2** ratio between two stakes in a wager. **at odds** in disagreement. **odds and ends** small miscellaneous scraps.

ode *n* poem addressed to a particular person or object.

odious *adj* hateful; loathsome. **odium** *n*.

odour *n* smell; fragrance.

oesophagus (iː'sɔfəgəs) *n, pl* **oesophagi** (iː'sɔfəgai) tube running from the pharynx to the stomach; gullet.

oestrogen *n* female sex hormone.

oestrus *n* period of sexual receptiveness in most female mammals.

of *prep* **1** belonging to. **2** originating from. **3** created or produced by. **4** from the period relating to. **5** made with. **6** containing; holding. **7** towards or away from a specified place. **8** that is the same as. **9** for. **10** separated from.

off *prep* **1** so as to be away or distant from. **2** not present at or attending to. **3** removed or deducted from. **4** no longer interested in. **5** by the means of. *adv* **1** distant; away. **2** so as to be removed or rid of. **3** so as to stop or disengage. *adj* **1** cancelled or postponed. **2** not attached. **3** not working or turned on. **on the off chance** with the possibility or hope.

offal *n* edible internal organs or parts of an animal.

offend *vt* cause displeasure or pain to. *vi* sin; do wrong. **offence** *n* **1** crime or infringement of the law. **2** any cause of anger, grievance, or pain. **to take/give offence** to be/cause hurt. **offensive** *adj* aggressive; repellent; obnoxious. *n* attack.

offer *vt* give; present or hold out for acceptance. *vi* volunteer; be available or on hand. *n* **1** act of offering. **2** something offered.

offhand *adj* **1** impromptu; unprepared. **2** casual; impolite.

office *n* **1** position of authority, esp. public or governmental. **2** place of business. **3** government department. **4** rite or religious service. **officer 1** person holding a responsible position in a government, club, organization, etc. **2** holder of a commission in the armed forces. **3** policeman. **official** *n* one who holds an office. *adj* **1** authorized or vouched for. **2** relating to an office. **officially** *adv*. **officious** *adj* bossy; interfering.

offing *n* **in the offing** in view; near; likely to happen.

off-licence *n* shop licensed to sell alcoholic drink for consumption off the premises.

off-peak *adj,adv* at a less popular or less busy time.

off-putting *adj* discouraging; repelling.

offset *vt* (-tt-; -set) compensate for; balance out.

offshore *adj,adv* from or far from the shore or land.

offside *adj* in a part of a football field, etc., between the ball and the opponents' goal, where it is not allowable to kick the ball. *n* the right-hand side of a vehicle, horse, etc.

offspring 1 child or children. **2** any issue or result.

offstage *adj,adv* not visible to the audience in a theatre.

often *adv* frequently; repeatedly.

ogre *n* **1** monstrous man-eating giant of fairy tales and folklore. **2** cruel person; tyrant.

oil *n* viscous liquid obtained from many mineral and vegetable sources, lighter than and insoluble in water. **burn the midnight oil** work or study until late at night. ~*vt* apply oil to. **oily** *adj*. **oil painting** *n* **1** picture painted in oil-based paints (oils). **2** art or practice of painting such pictures. **oilskin** *n* cloth or clothing treated with oil to make it waterproof.

ointment *n* soothing or medicated cream applied to the skin.

old *adj* **1** aged; having existed for many years. **2** out-of-date; obsolete; belonging to an earlier age; stale. **old age** *n* last years of life. **old-fashioned** *adj* out-of-date; obsolete; quaint. **old hand** *n* experienced person.

olive *n* small oily Mediterranean fruit eaten either unripe (green olive) or ripe (black olive). *n,adj also* **olive green** brownish green.

omelette *n* eggs beaten together, fried, and flavoured with herbs, vegetables, cheese, etc.

omen *n* sign supposedly prophesying a future event.

ominous *adj* threatening; suggesting future trouble.

omit *vt* (-tt-) leave out; fail to do. **omission** *n*.

omnibus *n* bus. *adj* containing several assorted ingredients, items, etc.

omnipotent *adj* all-powerful. **omnipotence** *n*.

on *prep* **1** placed or being in contact with the top or surface of. **2** supported by or attached to. **3** during a particular day. **4** close to or by the side of; along. **5** being broadcast by or performed at. **6** at the time or occasion of. **7** with the support of. **8** concerning; about. **9** by means of. *adv* **1** so as to work or function. **2** so as to be covered with. **3** ahead. **on and off** sporadically. **on and on** repeatedly; continuously. ~*adj* **1** taking place; planned. **2** attached. **3** working; functioning; performing.

once *adv* **1** on a single occasion. **2** in the past. **at once 1** immediately. **2** simultaneously. **once and for all** finally.

one *adj* **1** single; individual. **2** only. **3** being a united entity. *n* **1** the smallest whole number represented by the symbol 1 or I. **2** particular or specified single person, thing, example, etc. **3** *also* **one o'clock** the first hour after noon or midnight. *pron* **1** a person; any person; each person. **2** *formal* I or me. **one another** each other; one to or with the other. **oneself** *r pron* **1** a or any person's own self. **2** yourself. **be/feel oneself** be/feel normal, natural, etc. **one-sided** *adj* unfairly biased. **one-way** *adj* **1** allowing traffic in one direction only. **2** not reciprocal.

onion *n* vegetable whose rounded pungent bulb is used in cooking.

onlooker *n* spectator; observer.

only *adj* being a single one or one of few; sole. *adv* **1** exclusively; solely. **2** merely; just. *conj* but; however.

onset *n* beginning; start; attack.

onslaught *n* violent assault.

onus *n* responsibility; duty; burden.

onward *adj* moving forwards. **onwards** *adv* forwards; towards the front.

onyx ('ɔniks) *n* quartz having bands or layers of different colours.

ooze *vi,vt* seep; leak; flow gradually.

opal *n* quartz-like mineral characterized by iridescent colours, often used as a gemstone.

opaque *adj* obscure; transmitting no light. **opacity** *n*.

open *adj* **1** not closed or sealed. **2** allowing access. **3** ready or available for business or trade. **4** free from obstruction. **5** vacant; unoccupied; free. **6** not yet settled or decided. **7** candid; honest; not prejudiced. **8** vulnerable; liable. *vt,vi* **1** make or become open. **2** undo; unfold. **3** start; give an introduction (to). *vt* **1** disclose; reveal. **2** declare officially to be open to the public. *n also* **the open air** outdoors; outside. **in the open** so as to be known or made public. **openly** *adv*. **openness** *n*. **open-ended** *adj* limitless. **opener** *n* gadget for opening tins, bottles, etc. **open-handed** *adj* generous. **open-hearted** *adj* frank; sincere. **opening** *n* **1** gap; space. **2** start; beginning. **3** opportunity; chance. **open-minded** *adj* not biased or prejudiced; liberal. **open-mouthed** *adj* astonished; aghast. **open-plan** *adj* having few or no internal walls to separate rooms.

opera *n* musical drama, largely or wholly sung. **operatic** *adj*.

operate *vi,vt* **1** work or function. **2** perform surgery (on). **operative** *adj*. **operator** *n*. **operation** *n* **1** working; action; function; effect. **2** instance of surgery. **operational** *adj*.

operetta *n* short, light, or comic opera.

ophthalmology *n* branch of medicine dealing with eye disorders. **ophthalmologist** *n*.

opinion *n* judgment; view; belief. **opinionated** *adj* dogmatic; stubborn. **opinion poll** *n* organized questioning to determine public opinion on a particular issue.

opium *n* narcotic, sedative, or stimulant drug prepared from juice of certain poppies. **opiate** *n* drug containing opium. *adj* made from opium; inducing sleep.

opponent *n* antagonist; one who opposes. *adj* opposing; adverse.

opportunity *n* favourable chance or occasion. **opportune** *adj* lucky; well-timed.

oppose *vt* set against; resist; obstruct or contest. **opposite** *adj* **1** facing; in front of. **2** opposed or contrary (to). *n* opposite person or thing; antithesis. *adv,prep* in an opposite position, direction, etc. **opposite number** *n* person holding a similar or equivalent position in another country, company, etc. **opposition** *n* **1** resistance; hostility. **2** state or position of being opposite. **3** most distant positioning of two stars or planets. **the Opposition** major political party not in office.

oppress *vt* **1** weigh down or overwhelm. **2** persecute severely. **oppression** *n*. **oppressive** *adj* **1** harsh; cruel. **2** (of weather) sultry.

opt *vt* choose; settle for; decide between. **option** *n* **1** choice; alternative. **2** right, freedom, or opportunity to purchase. **optional** *adj* not obligatory.

optical *adj* relating to the eyes; visual. **optician** *n* person who makes or sells glasses, lenses, etc.

optimism *n* feeling or belief that the best will happen; hopefulness. **optimist** *n*. **optimistic** *adj*.

opulent *adj* rich; lavish; sumptuous. **opulence** *n*.

or *conj* **1** with the alternative of. **2** and also; as well as.

oral *adj* **1** spoken. **2** relating to the mouth.

orange *n* round juicy citrus fruit with reddish-yellow peel. *n,adj* reddish-yellow. **orangeade** *n* orange-flavoured fizzy drink.

oration *n* eloquent public speech or address. **orator** *n*. **oratory** *n*.

orbit *n* **1** path followed around a planet or star by a satellite. **2** sphere of influence. **3** eye socket. **orbital** *adj*.

orchard *n* enclosed area of fruit trees.

orchestra *n* **1** company of instrumental musicians. **2** *also* **orchestra pit** semicircle between the stage and seats in a theatre. **orchestra stalls** *pl n* front seats in a theatre. **orchestral** *adj*. **orchestrate** *vt* arrange (music) for an orchestra. **orchestration** *n*.

orchid *n* one of a family of perennial plants with complicated specialized, often exotic, flowers.

ordain *vt* **1** decree; order. **2** appoint as a priest or minister. **ordination** *n*.

ordeal *n* severe trial of stamina or endurance.

order *n* **1** arrangement; sequence. **2** command; rule. **3** tidiness. **4** class or group. **5** religious body. **in order 1** in a proper state or condition. **2** correct or appropriate. **in order to** so as to; with the intention or purpose of. ~*vt* **1** command; instruct. **2** arrange; organize. **3** send for. **orderly** *adj* methodical; tidy; well-controlled. *n* **1** soldier serving an officer. **2** attendant in a hospital.

ordinal number *n* number, such as first, second, etc., that denotes order, quantity, or rank in a group.

ordinary *adj* usual; common; familiar; plain. *n* **out of the ordinary** unusual; exceptional. **ordinarily** *adv*.

ore *n* mineral from which metal may be obtained.

organ *n* **1** differentiated part of an animal or plant performing a particular function. **2** large musical wind instrument with a keyboard and pipes, often used in churches. **3** means or method of communication. **organist** *n*.

organic *adj* **1** relating to or derived from plants or animals. **2** inherent; structural. **3** (of food) grown without application of any non-organic fertilizer, pesticide, etc. **4** relating to chemical compounds of carbon. **organically** *adv*.

organism *n* any animal, plant, bacterium, or virus.

organize *vt* arrange, group, classify, or prepare. *vi* form a political group, union, etc. **organization** *n* **1** organized group, system, company, etc. **2** act of organizing.

orgasm *n* culmination of a sexual act, characterized by ejaculation in the male and vaginal contractions in the female.

orgy *n* drunken riotous revelry. **orgiastic** *adj*.

Orient *n* the East or the countries of Asia. **Oriental** *adj,n*.

orientate *vt* find the bearings of in relation to surroundings, conditions, etc. **orientation** *n*.

origin *n* source; beginning; starting point. **original** *adj* **1** existing since the beginning. **2** new; not copied; novel; creative. *n* the source from which copies, translations, etc., are made. **originate** *vt,vi* start or initiate; have as a source. **origination** *n*.

Orlon *n Tdmk* lightweight synthetic fibre used for clothing, etc.

ornament *n* ('ɔːnəmənt) **1** decoration; adornment. **2** item or article used for show. *vt* ('ɔːnəment) embellish; decorate. **ornamentation** *n*. **ornamental** *adj* decorative.

ornate *adj* elaborately or flamboyantly decorative.

ornithology *n* study of birds. **ornithologist** *n*.

orphan *n* child whose parents have died. *adj* bereaved of parents. *vt* leave bereaved of parents. **orphanage** *n* institution for bringing up orphans.

orthodox *adj* having sound, correct, or established views, esp. in religion. **orthodoxy** *n*.

orthopaedic *adj* intended to cure deformity.

oscillate *vi* **1** move from side to side as a pendulum. **2** waver; fluctuate. **oscillation** *n*.

ostensible *adj* apparent; seeming. **ostensibly** *adv*.

ostentatious *adj* showy; flamboyant; vulgar. **ostentation** *n*.

osteopath *n* one who manipulates the bones and muscles in order to cure diseases. **osteopathy** *n*.

ostracize *vt* isolate, shun, or bar from society. **ostracism** *n*.

ostrich *n* large fast-running long-necked bird that is native to Africa.

other *adj* alternative; remaining; different; additional. **on the other hand** alternatively. **the other day** recently. *~pron* second or additional person or thing. *adv* **other than 1** in addition to; apart from. **2** in a different way from. **others** *pl pron* remaining, different, or additional ones. **otherwise** *conj* or else. *adv* in a different way; in other respects. *adj* different.

otter *n* fish-catching aquatic mammal having a smooth coat and webbed feet.

ought *v aux* **1** have an obligation or duty. **2** need; will be wise or advised. **3** will be likely or liable. **4** will be pleased.

ounce *n* unit of weight equal to one sixteenth of a pound (approx. 28 grams).

our *adj* belonging to us. **ours** *pron* something or someone belonging to us. **ourselves** *r pron* **1** our own selves. **2** our normal selves.

oust *vt* eject or dispossess; usurp or replace.

out *adv* **1** away; towards the outside. **2** not present. **3** no longer in power. **4** on strike. **5** not accurate. **6** available to the public. **7** not alight or switched on. **8** no longer in fashion. **9** so as to eliminate or omit. **10** so as to project or protrude. **11** so as to appear. **12** acting with the intention of. **13** into a state of unconsciousness. *prep* away through. **out-of-date** *adj,adv* old-fashioned; obsolete.

outboard motor *n* engine that can be attached to the exterior of a small boat.

outbreak *n* eruption, epidemic, or sudden appearance.

outburst *n* sudden or violent expression of feelings.

outcast *n* one rejected by society; exile.

outcome *n* result; consequence.

outcry *n* eruption of public protest.

outdo *vt* (-does; -did; -done) excel or surpass.

outdoor *adj* used or existing outdoors. **outdoors** *adv* in the open air; outside any building.

outer *adj* external; further out. **outermost** *adj* furthest out or away. **outer space** *n* vast untravelled area beyond the known planets.

outfit *n* **1** complete equipment, such as a suit of clothes, for a specific purpose. **2** *inf* gang; group of people. **outfitter** *n* shop or dealer selling men's clothes.

outgoing *adj* **1** resigning; retiring; departing. **2** extrovert; gregarious. *n* expenditure.

outgrow *vt* (-grew; -grown) **1** grow larger or taller than. **2** grow too large for. **outgrowth** *n* something growing from a main stem, part, etc.

outhouse *n* shed; small building separate from larger one.

outing *n* excursion; pleasure trip.

outlandish *adj* extraordinary; eccentric; bizarre.

outlaw *n* fugitive from justice; bandit. *vt* ban; prohibit.

outlay *n* expenditure. *vt* (-laid) spend; expend.

outlet *n* **1** means of escape, expression, etc. **2** market or shop handling a particular commodity.

outline *n* **1** rough sketch or draft. **2** silhouette.

vt **1** produce an outline of. **2** give a preliminary account of.

outlive *vt* live longer than; survive.

outlook *n* **1** mental attitude; point of view. **2** prospect; forecast.

outlying *adj* remote; on the outside; far away.

outnumber *vt* surpass in number; be more than.

outpatient *n* non-resident patient who visits hospital for treatment.

outpost *n* position or station far away from headquarters.

output *n* quantity or amount produced by a factory, industry, person, etc.

outrage *n* **1** atrocity; intolerable act. **2** indignation or anger over such an act. *vt* shock; scandalize. **outrageous** *adj* **1** monstrous; appalling; horrifying. **2** absurdly ridiculous. **outrageously** *adv*.

outright *adj* **1** direct; thorough. **2** blatant; total. *adv* at once; completely.

outshine *vt* (-shone) be more successful than; surpass; overshadow.

outside *n* outer surface or side. *adj* exterior; on the outside. *adv* out of doors; not inside. *prep* beyond. **outsider** *n* **1** one not belonging to a particular group, society, party, etc. **2** competitor in a race, etc., considered to have very little chance of winning.

outsize *adj* larger than average.

outskirts *pl n* outer surrounding area or district; suburbs.

outspoken *adj* exceedingly frank and candid; forthright.

outstanding *adj* **1** prominent; conspicuous; exceptional. **2** not yet paid.

outstrip *vt* (-pp-) **1** do better than; surpass. **2** run faster than.

outward *adj* **1** towards the outside. **2** superficial; apparent; external. *adj,adv* away from home. **outwardly** *adv* ostensibly; apparently; on the surface. **outwards** *adv* out; away from the centre.

outweigh *vt* be more important, valuable, or heavy than.

outwit *vt* (-tt-) defeat by superior cunning or ingenuity.

oval *adj* egg-shaped. *n* something that is oval.

ovary *n* **1** one of the two female reproductive organs producing eggs. **2** part of a flower containing ovules.

ovation *n* enthusiastic applause.

oven *n* compartment enclosed by metal, brick, etc., and heated for baking, roasting, etc.; kiln; furnace.

over *prep* **1** above; higher than. **2** on the top or surface of; so as to cover. **3** across; on the other side of. **4** during. **5** in excess of; more than. **6** throughout. **7** about; concerning. **8** recovered from; finished with. **9** better than. **10** superior in rank to. **11** by means of. **12** whilst occupied with. *adv* **1** across. **2** throughout; during. **3** from start to finish. **4** so as to fall or bend. **5** so as to remain. **6** so as to be finished. **over and over** (**again**) repeatedly. ~*n* series of six balls bowled in cricket.

overall *adj,adv* including or considering everything. *n* light coat or apron worn to protect clothes from dirt. **overalls** *pl n* hard-wearing trousers with a high front and straps over the shoulders.

overbearing *adj* domineering; bossy.

overboard *adv* over the side of a boat or ship. **go overboard** enthuse.

overcast *adj* cloudy; gloomy.

overcharge *vt,vi* charge too much money.

overcoat *n* heavy coat.

overcome *vt* (-came; -come) **1** conquer; vanquish; get the better of. **2** overwhelm; affect totally.

overdo *vt* (-does; -did; -done) **1** do something to excess; exaggerate. **2** cook for too long.

overdose *n* too large a dose.

overdraw *vt,vi* (-drew; -drawn) draw from a bank more money than exists to one's credit. **overdraft** *n* amount by which debit exceeds credit in a bank account.

overdue *adj* late; past the time when due.

overeat *vi* (-ate; -eaten) eat excessively; gorge.

overestimate *vt* value too highly.

overfill *vt* flood; fill too full.

overflow *vt* (-flowed; -flown) flow over the edge of; reach beyond the limits of; be excessively full of. *n* **1** flood or profusion. **2** outlet for excess water.

overgrown *adj* covered with vegetation, weeds, etc.

overhang *vt,vi* (-hung) jut over. *n* jutting ledge.

overhaul *vt* **1** check thoroughly for faults. **2** repair; renovate; restore. *n* check-up; service.

overhead *adv,adj* above the head; in the sky. **overheads** *pl n* regular unavoidable expenses of administration.

overhear *vt* (-heard) eavesdrop; hear words intended for others by accident or design.
overjoyed *adj* ecstatic; thrilled; delighted.
overland *adj,adv* mainly or entirely by land.
overlap *vt,vi* (-pp-) **1** extend partly beyond the edge of. **2** coincide partly. *n* overlapping part or area.
overlay *vt* (-laid) **1** cover the surface of. **2** cover; disguise with. *n* something laid over as a cover, decoration, etc.
overleaf *adv* on the other side of the page.
overload *vt* load, fill, or weigh down excessively.
overlook *vt* **1** view from a higher place. **2** disregard or take no notice of; choose to ignore.
overnight *adv,adj* **1** during the night. **2** all night. **3** lasting for one night.
overpower *vt* **1** conquer by superior strength, weight, etc. **2** subdue; overwhelm; overcome.
overrate *vt* overestimate.
overreach *vt* **1** reach or extend too far for comfort. **2** outwit.
overrule *vt* rule against or annul by virtue of greater authority.
overrun *vt* (-nn-; -ran; -run) **1** swarm over and take possession of; infest. **2** extend beyond.
overseas *adv,adj* abroad; across the sea.
overshadow *vt* **1** cast a shadow over. **2** outshine.
overshoot *vt* (-shot) shoot or go over or beyond.
oversight *n* **1** omission; mistake; failure to take into account. **2** supervision.
oversleep *vi* (-slept) sleep longer than intended.
overspill *n* surplus, esp. of the population of a town.
overstep *vt* (-pp-) exceed; go beyond (a limit, constraint, etc.).
overt *adj* openly done; public; not concealed. **overtly** *adv*.
overtake *vt* (-took; -taken) **1** catch up with and pass. **2** come up on suddenly.
overthrow *vt* (-threw; -thrown) **1** defeat utterly **2** overturn; demolish. *n* defeat; ruin.
overtime *n* time worked beyond usual working hours or payment for this.
overtone *n* implication; suggestion.
overture *n* **1** instrumental prelude to an opera, ballet, etc. **2** opening negotiations or approach.
overturn *vt* upset, overthrow, or abolish.
overweight *adj* heavier than permissible or normal. *n* excess weight.
overwhelm *vt* **1** conquer by superior might. **2** overpower emotionally. **overwhelmingly** *adv*.
overwork *vt,vi* work or cause to work too hard. *n* excess work.
overwrought *adj* over-excited; in a state of nervous agitation.
ovulate *vi* produce and discharge an egg from an ovary. **ovulation** *n*.
ovule *n* part of a plant that contains the egg cell, which develops into a seed after fertilization.
owe *vt* be indebted for; be under an obligation. **owing to** because of.
owl *n* nocturnal bird of prey with a large head and eyes, small hooked beak, and a hooting cry.
own *adj* relating to oneself, itself, etc. **get one's own back** take revenge. **hold one's own** succeed in keeping one's position; acquit oneself well. **on one's own** by oneself; independently. ~*vt* possess; have. **own up** confess. **owner** *n*. **ownership** *n*.
ox *n pl* **oxen** castrated male of domestic cattle. **oxtail** *n* tail of an ox used esp. in soups and stews.
oxygen *n* colourless tasteless gaseous element present in air, water, and most minerals. **oxygenate** *vt,vi also* **oxygenize** fill with oxygen.
oyster *n* edible marine bivalve mollusc.

P

pace *n* **1** single step or its approximate length. **2** speed, esp. of walking or running. **put through one's paces** test (someone) for speed, talent, etc. ~*vi* walk with a regular step. *vt* measure out (distance) by pacing.
pacifism *n* opposition to or nonparticipation in warfare or violence. **pacifist** *n,adj*. **pacify** *vt* calm, soothe; placate; appease.
pack *n* **1** bundle; load; heap. **2** container; small package, as of cigarettes. **3** set of playing cards. **4** group of wolves, hounds, etc. **5** gang of people. **6** forwards in a Rugby team. **pack of lies** false story. ~*vt,vi* arrange (clothes, etc.) in a case, etc. *vt* **1** form into a bundle; roll up; put away. **2** crowd into; press

together; cram. **3** make compact. **pack off** send away. **send packing** send away abruptly; dismiss. **packhorse** *n* horse used to carry supplies, goods, etc.

package *n* **1** parcel; object or objects in a container, wrapping, etc. **2** group of separate items, services, ideas, etc., offered for sale or acceptance as a single unit. *vt* make a package of or for; wrap. **packaging** *n* materials or containers and wrappings used to package goods.

packet *n* **1** small package. **2** *sl* large sum of money.

pact *n* agreement; treaty; contract.

pad[1] *n* **1** piece of material used to fill out, cushion, or protect. **2** fleshy cushion on the underside of an animal's paw or foot. **3** covering or guard to protect part of the body. **4** sheets of writing paper fastened together. **5** *sl* flat or residence, esp. a small one. *vt* (-dd-) **1** stuff, fill, or protect with soft cushion-like material. **2** expand or extend with irrelevant or unnecessary information. **padding** *n*.

pad[2] *vt,vi* (-dd-) traverse on foot; trudge. *n* soft dull sound.

paddle[1] *n* **1** short oar flattened at one or both ends used without rowlocks in small boats, canoes, etc. **2** structure or implement shaped like a paddle. **3** spell of paddling. *vt,vi* move on water using a paddle.

paddle[2] *vi* dabble one's feet or hands in shallow water. *n* act or instance of paddling.

paddock *n* **1** small field used for grazing horses. **2** enclosure where racehorses assemble before a race.

paddyfield *n also* **paddy** field used for growing rice.

padlock *n* detachable lock having a hinged loop released by a key. *vt* secure with a padlock.

paediatrics *n* branch of medicine dealing with children and childhood diseases. **paediatric** *adj*. **paediatrician** *n*.

pagan *adj* heathen; relating to a religion other than Christianity, Judaism, or Islam. *n* pagan person.

page[1] *n* one side of a leaf of a book, newspaper, etc.

page[2] *n* **1** attendant in a hotel, etc. **2** junior servant of a king or nobleman. **3** boy attendant at a wedding. *vt* summon by calling out a name over a public address system.

pageant *n* lavish public spectacle, procession, or play, esp. of historical significance. **pageantry** *n*.

pagoda *n* Oriental temple with a tower of concave sloping roofs.

paid *v pt* and *pp* of **pay.**

pain *n* **1** physical or mental distress or discomfort. **2** *sl also* **pain in the neck** irritating or annoying person or thing. *vt* hurt; cause to feel physical or mental distress. **painful** *adj*. **painfully** *adv*.

painstaking *adj* careful; meticulous. **painstakingly** *adv*.

paint *n* colouring or covering matter on or for a surface. *vt* **1** apply paint or liquid to. **2** represent or depict in words. *vt,vi* portray or design using paint. **painter** *n*. **painting** *n* **1** picture; artist's representation in paint. **2** art or procedure of applying paint to a canvas.

pair *n* **1** two matched objects designed to be used or worn together. **2** two persons, animals, things, etc., normally found together. **3** single object consisting of two similar interdependent parts. *vt,vi* arrange in twos; make a pair.

pal *n inf* friend; mate; chum. *v* (-ll-) **pal up** *inf* become friends.

palace *n* present or former residence of a royal family, bishop, or archbishop. **palatial** *adj*.

palate *n* **1** roof of the mouth. **2** sensitive or refined sense of taste, esp. for wine. **palatable** *adj* **1** agreeable to the taste. **2** acceptable to the mind.

pale *adj* **1** light in shade; lacking in colour. **2** faint; dim. *vi* lose importance or significance (before). **paleness** *n*.

palette *n* **1** flat board used by artists for mixing colours. **2** range of colours used by a particular artist or school of painters.

pallid *adj* pale; sickly looking. **pallor** *n*.

palm[1] *n* cushioned underside of the hand between the fingers and wrist. *v* **palm off** (**on**) pass to or impose by trickery; get rid of.

palm[2] *n* tropical and subtropical tree with a straight branchless trunk and a crest of large fan-shaped leaves at the top. **Palm Sunday** *n* Church festival on the Sunday before Easter commemorating Christ's triumphal entry into Jerusalem.

palmistry *n* practice or skill of foretelling the future by inspecting lines on the palm of the hand. **palmist** *n*.

pamper *vt* spoil; over-indulge.

pamphlet *n* leaflet or short publication containing information of current interest.

pan *n* **1** metal or earthenware vessel in which food is cooked or served. **2** container resembling such a vessel. *vt,vi* (-nn-) wash (sand, gravel, etc.) in a pan to separate out any gold, silver, etc. **pancake** *n* thin round cake of batter that is fried on both sides.

pancreas *n* gland situated near the stomach that secretes insulin.

panda *n* large black and white bearlike mammal that is native to China.

pander *v* **pander to** minister to or gratify vices, weakness, etc.

pane *n* sheet of glass cut to fit a window or door.

panel *n* **1** section of a wall, door, etc., when framed, raised, or sunk. **2** vertical strip of material in a dress, skirt, etc. **3** small group of persons meeting for a specific purpose. *vt* (-ll-) cover with or provide panels for.

pang *n* sharp stabbing pain.

panic *n* fear or terror, often resulting in rash ill-considered behaviour. *vi,vt* (-ck-) feel or cause to feel panic. **panic-stricken** *adj*.

panorama *n* uninterrupted view of a landscape spread over a wide area. **panoramic** *adj*.

pansy *n* **1** garden plant with white, yellow, purple, or red flowers. **2** *sl* homosexual.

pant *vi,vt* gasp for breath. *vi* long or yearn (for). *n* gasping noise.

panther *n* leopard, esp. a black leopard.

pantomime *n* traditional English Christmas entertainment for children.

pantry *n* room adjoining a kitchen with shelves for storing provisions, etc.

pants *pl n* undergarment covering area of the body from the waist to the thighs.

papal *adj* relating to the Pope or his official function.

paper *n* **1** material produced by processing wood, rags, etc., used for books, packaging, etc. **2** examination; essay; report. **3** newspaper. *vt* cover with paper or wallpaper. **paperback** *n* book in a cheap edition with a paper cover. **paperclip** *n* piece of twisted wire used to fasten single sheets of paper together. **paperwork** *n* routine clerical work.

papier-mâché *n* pulped paper used in making models, masks, etc.

papist *n abusive* follower of the Pope and the Roman Catholic faith.

paprika *n* powdered sweet red pepper.

par *n* **1** equality; equal or even footing; average or usual value or level. **2** (in golf) standard score. **at par** (of shares, etc.) at face value. **on a par with** equal or equivalent to.

parable *n* story designed to illustrate a moral or philosophical point; allegory.

parachute *n* device that assumes an umbrella shape to slow down the descent of a person jumping from an aircraft, etc. *vi,vt* descend or land by parachute.

parade *n* **1** procession; march. **2** show; ostentatious display. **3** promenade. *vi* walk or march (through) in or as in a procession. *vt* flaunt; exhibit openly.

paradise *n* heaven; state of bliss.

paradox *n* **1** statement that appears selfcontradictory or absurd. **2** person or thing having self-contradictory qualities. **paradoxical** *adj*. **paradoxically** *adv*.

paraffin *n* light oil distilled from petroleum, used for domestic heating and as aircraft fuel.

paragraph *n* subdivision of the printed page containing several sense-connected sentences and indicated by indentation of the first word.

parallel *adj* **1** remaining equidistant to infinity. **2** similar; analogous. *n* **1** comparable situation. **2** circle marking a degree of latitude. *vt* (-ll-) compare with; correspond to.

paralyse *vt* **1** immobilize or cripple through damage to or destruction of a nerve function. **2** transfix; make immobile. **paralysis** *n, pl* **paralyses** (pəˈrælisiːz) pathological condition of crippling due to loss of muscle control. **paralytic** *adj,n*.

paramount *adj* chief; supreme; most important.

paranoia *n* mental disorder characterized by delusions of grandeur, persecution, etc. **paranoid** *adj,n*.

parapet *n* low protective wall built along the edge of a balcony, bridge, etc.

paraphernalia *n* **1** equipment; assorted personal possessions. **2** complicated procedure; rigmarole.

paraphrase *vt* express the sense of a passage by using other words. *n* passage thus reworded.

parasite *n* **1** animal or plant depending on another for sustenance. **2** person who lives off others. **parasitic** *adj*.

paratrooper *n* member of an army unit trained in parachute jumping.

parcel *n* wrapped object, esp. in paper. *vt* (-ll-) **1** make a parcel of. **2** divide (up); apportion.

parch *vt,vi* dry up. *vt* make thirsty.

parchment *n* **1** skin of a sheep or goat processed for use as paper. **2** old document.

pardon *vt* **1** forgive; excuse. **2** waive legal consequences of an offence for (a prisoner). *n* **1** forgiveness. **2** waiver of a penalty.

pare *vt* peel; skin; trim. **pare down** make smaller or more compact.

parent *n* **1** mother or father. **2** animal or plant that has produced one of its kind. **parental** *adj*. **parenthood** *n* state of being a parent.

parenthesis *n, pl* **parentheses** (pə'renθisi:z) either of a pair of characters used to separate or enclose matter in a written or printed text.

parish *n* ecclesiastical subdivision of a county with its own church and clergyman.

park *n* large enclosed area of land laid out for ornamental or recreational purposes. *vt,vi* position or leave (a car, etc.) in a place temporarily. *vt inf* put or leave.

parliament *n* democratic assembly of elected representatives constitutionally empowered to govern by legislation following free discussion. **parliamentary** *adj*.

parlour *n* sitting room or lounge.

parochial *adj* **1** relating to a parish. **2** provincial; limited; narrow.

parody *n* **1** imitation of a work or of an author or musician's style with comic or satirical intent. **2** poor imitation; travesty. *vt* imitate; mock.

parole *n* **1** early or temporary release from prison on condition of good behaviour. **2** period of such release. *vt* grant parole to.

parrot *n* brightly coloured tropical bird capable of imitating human speech.

parsley *n* mildly aromatic herb with curly green leaves.

parsnip *n* white tapering root vegetable.

parson *n* clergyman; minister. **parsonage** *n* residence of a clergyman.

part *n* **1** portion; piece; segment; component. **2** role; responsibility; duty. **3** actor's role. **4** melodic line in choral or orchestral music. **5** *also* **parts** region; area. **take part in** become involved in; join in. ~*vt,vi* **1** divide; separate; come, break, or take apart. **2** leave or stop seeing one another; keep apart. **part with** give up; relinquish. ~*adv* partially; in part. **partly** *adv*. **parting** *n* **1** leave-taking; separation. **2** division; splitting up. **3** line between two sections of hair that have been combed in opposite directions. **part-time** *adj,adv* for or during less than normal working time.

partake *vi* (-took; -taken) **1** participate. **2** have or receive a share or portion.

partial *adj* **1** incomplete; relating to a part. **2** biased; unfair. **3** having a liking for; fond of. **partially** *adv*.

participate *vi* take part (in); share (in). **participant** *n*. **participation** *n*.

participle *n* adjective derived from various verb forms, e.g. *laughing, loving, given,* or *written*.

particle *n* **1** tiniest visible portion; speck. **2** microscopic body of matter.

particular *adj* **1** relating to a single person, object, etc. **2** extraordinary; notable. **3** careful; fastidious; exact. **particulars** *pl n* details; features. **particularly** *adv*.

partisan *n* **1** supporter of a party, cause, etc. **2** guerrilla fighter in enemy-occupied territory.

partition *n* **1** division; separation into parts. **2** structure erected to separate rooms, areas, etc. *vt* divide into parts; separate.

partner *n* **1** associate; colleague; member of a partnership. **2** one of a pair in dancing, cards, etc. *vt* join with someone, esp. in a game or dance. **partnership** *n* legal relationship between two or more persons operating a joint business venture.

partridge *n* small European game bird.

party *n* **1** group united by a common belief or purpose, esp. political. **2** social gathering. **3** person or persons involved in a legal action.

pass *vt,vi* **1** go by or through; move ahead or on; proceed. **2** move or cause to move. **3** exchange or be exchanged. **4** undergo (an exam, trial, etc.) with favourable results. **5** elapse or allow to elapse. *vt* **1** hand over; transfer; throw. **2** surpass; exceed. **3** pronounce; utter. **4** adopt; approve (legislation, etc.). *vi* happen; occur; come to an end. **pass out** faint. ~*n* **1** favourable examination result, without honours. **2** ticket, authorization, etc., to enter or leave at will, without charge, etc. **3** critical position. **4** narrow passage between mountains. **5** amorous advance. **passable** *adj* **1** able to be crossed, passed, etc. **2** mediocre; fairly good. **password** *n* prearranged word used as a code for entry, etc.

passage *n* **1** corridor; channel; route. **2** state of transit; voyage; journey. **3** section of a book, etc **passenger** *n* **1** person travelling in but not controlling a motor vehicle, boat, etc. **2** *sl* person in a team, etc., who does not do his share of the work.

passion *n* **1** intense or ardent emotion. **2** strong liking or enthusiasm. **3** object of such liking. **passionate** *adj*. **passionately** *adv*.

passive *adj* **1** inactive, inert; not participating. **2** submissive; yielding. **3** denoting a sentence or construction in which the logical subject of a verb is the recipient of the action. **passively** *adv*.

Passover *n* Jewish festival commemorating the deliverance of the Hebrews from Egypt.

passport *n* official document issued by a country that identifies the bearer, permits his travel abroad, and requests safe passage while there.

past *adj* **1** relating to an earlier time; gone by; just over; finished. **2** previous; former. **3** relating to a verb tense used to express an action or condition occurring in the past. *n* **1** period prior to the present; past time. **2** person's past life, career, activities, etc. *prep* beyond. *adv* by; ago. **past participle** *n* verb form functioning as an adjective or used with an auxiliary verb to denote past or completed action, e.g. *grown, written,* or *spoken*.

pasta *n* food, such as spaghetti, macaroni, etc., made from a flour and water dough and boiled.

paste *n* **1** pliable, malleable, or sticky mess. **2** preparation of meat, fish, etc., mashed to a spreadable consistency. **3** glue; adhesive. *vt* stick, fix or cover with paste.

pastel *n* **1** crayon made from colour pigments and gum. **2** drawing made with these crayons. *adj* pale, light.

pasteurize *vt* partially sterilize (milk, beer, etc.) by heating in order to kill bacteria, limit fermentation, etc. **pasteurization** *n*.

pastime *n* recreation, amusement, hobby.

pastoral *adj* **1** of the country, rural. **2** (of land) used for grazing. **3** peaceful, idyllic. **4** relating to a clergyman or his duties.

pastry *n* **1** flour paste used for pies, tarts, etc. **2** baked foods.

pasture *n* **1** grass, etc., suitable for grazing cattle. **2** meadow, field. *vt* put to pasture.

pasty[1] ('peisti) *adj* **1** relating to paste. **2** (of a person's appearance) pale, unhealthy, white-skinned.

pasty[2] ('pæsti) *n* small pie filled with meat, vegetables, etc.

pat[1] *vt* (-tt-) **1** tap; touch lightly. **2** stroke softly; caress. **3** flatten by beating gently. *n* light blow; slap; tap.

pat[2] *adj* **1** apt; perfect. **2** presumptuous; glib. *adv* **1** exactly; perfectly. **2** aptly.

patch *n* **1** piece of material used to repair something. **2** irregular or small area, piece, plot of land, etc. **3** protective covering for an eye, etc. *vt* repair; mend. **patchwork** *n* **1** patches of material stitched together to form a pattern. **2** something made of different parts, pieces, etc.

pâté *n* paste or spread made from liver, meat, fish, etc.

patent ('pætn̩t) *n* **1** government permit granting sole rights for an invention, process, etc., for a set period of time. **2** something under such a permit. *adj* ('peitn̩t) obvious, evident. **patent leather** *n* leather treated to produce a hard lacquered appearance. ~*vt* obtain a patent for.

paternal *adj* **1** fatherly, characteristic of a father. **2** pertaining to a father or a father's side of a family. **paternally** *adv*. **paternity** *n* **1** fatherhood. **2** descent from a father.

path *n* **1** *also* **pathway** track worn by pedestrians, animals, etc. **2** walk in a park, garden, etc. **3** means, procedure, course of action.

pathetic *adj* **1** pitiful, evoking sadness. **2** *inf* poor, of low quality. **pathetically** *adv*.

pathology *n* study of diseases. **pathological** *adj*. **pathologist** *n*.

patience *n* ability to persevere or endure without complaint.

patient *n* person under the care of a doctor, dentist, etc. *adj* marked by or exhibiting patience. **patiently** *adv*.

patio *n* paved area adjoining a house.

patriarch *n* **1** male head of a family, tribe, etc. **2** elder, senior member of a community. **3** any of several Old Testament personages regarded as a father of the human race. **4** bishop of the Eastern Orthodox Church. **patriarchal** *adj*.

patriot *n* person who loves his country intensely. **patriotic** *adj*. **patriotism** *n*.

patrol *n* **1** regular inspection of an area or building to ensure security, orderliness, etc. **2** person or persons carrying out this inspection.

3 military detachment with the duty of reconnaissance. *vt,vi* (-ll-) take part in a patrol (of).

patron *n* **1** regular customer of a shop, etc. **2** one who offers financial support to a cultural or educational enterprise. **patronage** *n* **1** support given by a patron. **2** trade given a business by its customers. **3** power to bestow political favours, make appointments, etc. **patronize** *vt* **1** visit regularly; support **2** behave condescendingly (towards someone). **3** be a benefactor of; sponsor.

patter[1] *n* **1** glib inconsequential speech. **2** rapidly delivered lines of a salesman, comedian, etc. **3** *inf* jargon; expressions used by a clique *vi,vt* talk glibly, rapidly, etc.

patter[2] *vi* **1** make a sound like tapping. **2** walk with a patter. *n* light tapping sound.

pattern *n* **1** design; arrangement. **2** example; model; plan. **3** usual way of doing something. *vt* model after a pattern; imitate.

pause *n* temporary stop or break. *vi* **1** stop temporarily. **2** hesitate; linger.

pave *vt* **1** cover (a road, etc.) with a hard surface. **2** prepare; facilitate. **pavement** *n* paved path for pedestrians alongside a road.

pavilion *n* **1** building on a sportsground housing changing rooms, etc. **2** large tent erected temporarily at fairs, weddings, etc. **3** summerhouse; light ornamental building or structure.

paw *n* foot of certain mammals, esp. cats and dogs. *vi,vt* touch or strike with a paw or leg. *vt inf* caress clumsily; grope.

pawn[1] *vt* leave (an article) as security in exchange for a loan until repayment is made. **pawnbroker** *n* person who lends money on security of personal possessions.

pawn[2] *n* **1** chessman of least value whose second and subsequent moves are limited to one square in a forward direction. **2** manipulated person.

pay *v* (paid) *vt,vi* **1** give (money, etc.) to for, or in return for; recompense. **2** discharge (a debt, etc.). **3** *also* **pay off** be profitable or worthwhile; benefit. *vt* **1** bestow; give. **2** make (a visit, etc.). **pay back 1** repay (a loan, etc.). **2** retaliate against. **pay for** suffer or be punished because of. **pay off 1** pay wages of and discharge. **2** pay in total. ~*n* **1** money paid for work; salary; wages. **2** paid employment. **payment** *n* **1** act of paying. **2** sum of money paid. **3** due reward. **payoff** *n* **1** *inf* outcome; climax of events. **2** full payment. **payroll** *n* **1** list of employees to be paid and their salaries or wages. **2** total of or amount equal to a company's salary or wage expenditure.

pea *n* annual climbing plant whose round green seeds are eaten as a vegetable.

peace *n* **1** state of amity; absence of war. **2** tranquillity; period of rest or quiet. **peaceful** *adj*. **peacefully** *adv*.

peach *n* tree yielding a round juicy yellowish fruit with down-covered skin. *n,adj* bright pinkish-yellow.

peacock *n* brightly coloured male of a large pheasant with a crested head and a tail which can fan out to display bright blue and green markings. **peahen** *f n*.

peak *n* **1** any pointed edge or projection. **2** top of a mountain; summit. **3** projecting brim of a cap. **4** sharp increase or the highest point or value reached. *vi* reach the highest point or value. **peaked** *adj*.

peal *n* loud resounding sound, such as bells ringing, laughter, or thunder. *vt,vi* sound with a peal; ring out.

peanut *n* edible seed rich in food value and yielding oil.

pear *n* tree yielding a sweet juicy fruit whose shape is rounded and tapers towards the stalk.

pearl *n* **1** smooth lustrous creamy precious gem formed on the inside of a clam or oyster shell or synthesized. **2** highly valued person or thing. **pearly** *adj*.

peasant *n* **1** agricultural labourer; countryman; rustic. **2** *inf* uncultured and unsophisticated person. **peasantry** *n*.

peat *n* solid partially carbonized and decomposed vegetable matter used as a garden fertilizer and a fuel. **peaty** *adj*.

pebble *n* small rounded stone. *vt,vi* pave or cover with pebbles. **pebbly** *adj*.

peck *vt* **1** strike with the beak or something sharp. **2** *inf* kiss quickly on the cheek. *n* **1** quick strike or blow. **2** *inf* quick kiss on the cheek.

peckish *adj inf* hungry.

peculiar *adj* strange; odd; unusual. **peculiar to** special or specific to. **peculiarity** *n*. **peculiarly** *adv*.

pedal *n* foot lever of a machine, bicycle, piano, etc. *vt,vi* (-ll-) **1** operate by using pedals. **2** ride a bicycle.

peddle *vt,vi* sell from door to door; hawk. **pedlar** *n*.

pedestal *n* **1** plinth or base supporting an upright object. **2** position of superiority or eminence.

pedestrian *n* person who goes about on foot. *adj* plodding; dull; unimaginative.

pedigree *n* **1** record of an animal's ancestors, kept esp. for animals of good breeding. **2** animal of pedigree stock. **3** ancestral line. **pedigreed** *adj*.

peel *n* rind; outer layer of fruit, vegetables, etc. *vt,vi* strip or whittle (off) an outer skin or surface.

peep *vi* **1** look quickly or furtively. **2** appear briefly or partially. *n* quick look or glance.

peer[1] *n* **1** member of the nobility. **2** person equal in rank or social standing. **peerage** *n* **1** nobility as a group. **2** position, rank, or title of a peer.

peer[2] *vi* **1** look closely or intently (at). **2** appear partially; peep.

peevish *adj* irritable; bad-tempered. **peevishly** *adv*. **peevishness** *n*.

peg *n* **1** small piece of wood or metal used for hanging or fastening things. **2** pin or stake pushed into the ground, a scoreboard, or other surface. **3** pin on a guitar, violin, etc., used for tuning the strings. **4** hinged or grooved pin for hanging clothes on a line. **take down a peg** teach a lesson; humble. **off the peg** (of clothes) ready-made. ~*vt* (-gg-) **1** pierce with or insert a peg. **2** secure with a peg.

pejorative *adj* deprecatory; uncomplimentary.

pelican *n* water bird with white plumage and a large beak with a pouch used for catching fish.

pellet *n* **1** small ball of something solid. **2** piece of shot.

pelmet *n* wood or fabric used to conceal a curtain rail.

pelt[1] *n* skin or hide of a fur-bearing animal.

pelt[2] *vt* assail with a shower of missiles, blows, abuse, etc. *n* blow; knock; stroke.

pelvis *n* cavity or structure found in the lower part of the trunk in most vertebrates. **pelvic** *adj*.

pen[1] *n* instrument with a pointed nib used for writing with ink. **penfriend** *n* person, often living in a different country, with whom one corresponds. **penknife** *n* small folding knife usually carried in the pocket.

pen[2] *n* small enclosure for farm animals. *vt* (-nn-) enclose in a pen; confine.

penal *adj* relating to punishment, esp. for breaking a law. **penal code** *n* body of criminal law. **penalize** *vt* **1** punish; subject to penalty. **2** handicap; disadvantage. **3** award a point or points to an opposing team. **penalization** *n*. **penalty** *n* **1** punishment; price exacted as a punishment. **2** loss; suffering. **3** free kick at goal afforded to one football team because of a breach of rules by the other. **penance** *n* **1** self-imposed punishment. **2** regret; sorrow.

pence *n pl of* **penny** (def. 3).

penchant ('pɑːnʃɑːn) *n* liking; strong inclination.

pencil *n* writing instrument consisting of a thin rod of graphite encased in wood. *vt* (-ll-) write or draw with a pencil.

pendant *n* **1** hanging ornament, esp. on a necklace. **2** hanging lamp or chandelier.

pending *adj* about to be decided, confirmed, completed, etc. *prep* while waiting for.

pendulum *n* suspended weight that swings back and forth under the influence of gravity.

penetrate *vt,vi* **1** pass into or through. **2** enter or permeate. *vt* **1** see through. **2** unravel; understand. *vi* be understood. **penetrable** *adj*. **penetration** *n*.

penguin *n* large flightless black and white aquatic bird of Antarctica.

penicillin *n* antibiotic drug produced from a mould and capable of preventing the growth of certain bacteria.

peninsula *n* strip of land jutting into the sea. **peninsular** *adj*.

penis *n* male organ of copulation.

penitent *adj* repentent; remorseful. *n* penitent person. **penitence** *n*. **penitently** *adv*.

penniless *adj* having no money; very poor; destitute.

penny *n* **1** *also* **new penny** bronze coin worth one-hundredth of a pound sterling. **2** former bronze coin worth one-twelfth of a shilling. **3** *pl* **pence** unit of currency of such a value. **not worth a penny** worthless. **spend a penny** *inf* urinate.

pension *n* periodical payment by state or employer to the retired, disabled, widowed, etc. *vt* grant a pension to. **pensioner** *n* person receiving a pension.

pensive *adj* engaged in serious or sad thought. **pensively** *adv*.

pentagon *n* five-sided figure. **pentagonal** *adj*.

penthouse *n* subsidiary structure attached to the main part of a building, often a small house or flat on the roof.

penury *n* poverty; destitution.

people *pl n* **1** human beings in general. **2** racial group. **3** one's family. *vt* populate; fill as with people.

pepper *n* **1** pungent condiment made from the dried berries of a pepper plant. **2** red or green slightly pungent fruit of other types of pepper plant. *vt* flavour with pepper. **peppercorn** *n* dried berry of the pepper plant. **peppermill** *n* instrument for grinding peppercorns. **peppermint** *n* **1** aromatic and pungent herb of the mint family. **2** lozenge flavoured with oil from this mint.

per *prep* **1** for each. **2** by means of.

perambulator *n formal* pram.

perceive *vt* **1** see; discern. **2** be or become aware of. **3** understand. **perceivable** *adj*.

per cent *adv* in each hundred.

percentage *n* **1** number forming a proportion in each hundred. **2** interest paid per hundred.

perception *n* **1** process or power of becoming aware of something. **2** insight; discernment. **perceptible** *adj* noticeable; discernible. **perceptive** *adj* **1** able or quick to notice. **2** intelligent. **perceptively** *adv*.

perch[1] *n, pl* **perch** edible spiny-finned freshwater fish.

perch[2] *n* **1** pole, bar, or branch for birds to roost or sit on. **2** secure seat in a high position. *vi,vt* sit or place on a perch.

percolate *vt,vi* filter or trickle (through). *vi* gradually become known. **percolator** *n* apparatus for percolating water through coffee grounds.

percussion *n* **1** impact; collision. **2** production of noise by striking or tapping. **3** musical instruments, such as the drum, that are struck to produce a note.

perennial *adj* **1** continuing through the year or from year to year. **2** (of plants) living more than two years. **3** perpetual. **perennially** *adv*.

perfect *adj* ('pəːfikt) faultless; complete; functioning correctly; exact. *vt* (pə'fekt) make perfect or complete; finish. **perfection** *n*. **perfectly** *adv*.

perforate *vt,vi* make a hole or holes through, often in a line for easy separation. **perforation** *n*.

perform *vt,vi* **1** do; carry out; complete. **2** act. **performer** *n*. **performance** *n* **1** act of performing; carrying out of something. **2** piece of work; exhibition or entertainment. **3** manner or achievement in working.

perfume *n* **1** sweet-smelling substance applied to the body. **2** pleasant odour; fragrance. *vt* impart fragrance to.

perhaps *adv* maybe; possibly.

peril *n* danger; risk. **perilous** *adj*. **perilously** *adv*.

perimeter *n* circumference; boundary; length of outline of a plane figure.

period *n* **1** stretch of time; phase; era. **2** interval between recurrent phases. **3** full stop. **4** *inf* menstruation. **periodic** *adj*. **periodical** *adj* periodic; issued or occurring at roughly regular intervals. *n* magazine published at stated intervals of more than one day. **periodically** *adv*.

peripheral *adj* **1** of or on the circumference, boundary, or outskirts. **2** of less than central importance. **periphery** *n*.

periscope *n* tube with mirrors for viewing objects above eye level.

perish *vt* destroy; ruin; cause to decay. *vi* **1** die; decay; be ruined or destroyed. **2** distress with hunger and cold. **perishable** *adj*.

perjure *vt* **perjure oneself** lie deliberately under oath. **perjurer** *n*. **perjury** *n*.

perk *v* **perk up 1** look up jauntily. **2** make (oneself) smarter. **3** recover spirits or energy. *n inf* legitimate extra gain attached to a job, not included in wages.

permanent *adj* lasting or intended to last indefinitely. *n also inf* **perm** artificially induced and long-lasting waving of the hair. **permanently** *adv*.

permeate *vt,vi* spread through, pervade, or be pervaded. **permeation** *n*.

permission *n* act of permitting; allowing; consent. **permissible** *adj*. **permissive** *adj* granting permission or liberty; lenient; tolerant. **permissively** *adv*. **permissiveness** *n*.

permit *vt,vi* (pə'mit) (-tt-) grant leave; allow; concede; make possible. *n* ('pəːmit) written permission; warrant; licence.

permutation *n* **1** changing of the order of a set of objects. **2** each arrangement of these objects.

peroxide *n* **1** oxide containing more oxygen than normal oxide. **2** *inf* hydrogen peroxide, an antiseptic and bleach.

perpendicular *adj* upright; vertical; at right angles (to). *n* vertical position; perpendicular line. **perpendicularly** *adv*.

perpetual *adj* **1** never ceasing; not temporary. **2** continuously blooming through the growing season. **3** applicable or valid for ever or for an indefinite time. **perpetually** *adv*. **perpetuate** *vt* **1** make perpetual. **2** prolong indefinitely. **3** preserve from extinction or oblivion. **perpetuity** *n* quality or condition of lasting indefinitely.

perplex *vt* confuse; present difficulties or intricacies to bewilder; tease with suspense or doubt. **perplexity** *n*.

persecute *vt* **1** harass; treat cruelly; persistently attack. **persecution** *n*.

persevere *vi* continue in spite of obstacles; keep on striving. **perseverance** *n*.

persist *vi* **1** continue firmly or obstinately, esp. against opposition. **2** continue to exist; remain. **persistence** *n*. **persistent** *adj*. **persistently** *adv*.

person *n* **1** human being. **2** body of a person. **in person** physically present or active. **personal** *adj* **1** one's own; individual; of private concern. **2** relating to bodily appearance. **3** offensive to an individual; insulting. **personally** *adv*. **personality** *n* **1** state of having an identity. **2** celebrity. **3** total intellectual, emotional, or physical qualities of an individual, esp. as presented to others. **personify** *vt* **1** regard as a person. **2** embody; symbolize in human form. **personification** *n*.

personnel *n* persons engaged together in some work; work force.

perspective *n* **1** method of portraying relative size and distance of objects on a plane surface. **2** relative importance and true relationship of facts, ideas, etc.

perspex *n* tough transparent unsplinterable plastic material.

perspire *vi,vt* exude moisture through skin pores; sweat. **perspiration** *n*.

persuade *vt* induce by argument; cause to believe; convince. **persuasion** *n*. **persuasive** *adj*. **persuasively** *adv*.

pert *adj* **1** forward; saucy; cheeky. **2** open; brisk; flourishing. **pertly** *adv*.

pertain *vi* **1** belong as part of; be connected with. **2** have reference or relevance to. **3** be suitable for or appropriate to. **pertinent** *adj*. **pertinently** *adv*.

perturb *vt* disturb greatly; cause alarm or anxiety to. **perturbation** *n*.

pervade *vt* penetrate; diffuse through the whole of; permeate. **pervasion** *n*. **pervasive** *adj*.

perverse *adj* obstinately turning aside from right or truth; unreasonably contradictory. **perversely** *adv*. **perversion** *n*. **pervert** *vt,vi* (pəˈvəːt) turn from proper use or sense; corrupt or be corrupted. *n* (ˈpəːvəːt) one who is thought to deviate in sexual desires or practice. **perversion** *n*.

peseta *n* monetary unit of Spain.

peso *n* monetary unit of Argentina, Mexico, the Philippines, and various other countries.

pessimism *n* tendency to look on the worst side of things; despondency. **pessimist** *n*. **pessimistic** *adj*.

pest *n* **1** troublesome or destructive person, etc. **2** insect, fungus, etc., destructive of cultivated plants. **pesticide** *n* chemical for destroying pests.

pester *vt* cause slight but repeated annoyance to.

pet[1] *n* **1** tame animal kept as a companion, etc. **2** favourite; dearly loved and pampered person, esp. a child; darling. *v* (-tt-) *vt* treat as a pet; pamper; fondle. *vi* indulge in amorous caressing.

pet[2] *n* childish fit of aggrieved sulkiness; huff. *vi* (-tt-) be peevish; sulk.

petal *n* leaflike part, sometimes brightly coloured, of a flower.

peter *v* **peter out** gradually diminish to nothing; fade away.

petition *n* **1** humble or solemn entreaty. **2** formal request to an authority often signed by a number of persons. *vt,vi* make or receive a humble or formal request.

petrify *vt,vi* **1** turn into or become like stone; fossilize. **2** fix in amazement or horror.

petrol *n* inflammable liquid from refined petroleum, used esp. as fuel in motor-vehicle engines.

petroleum *n* dark thick oily mixture of hydrocarbons, other organic compounds, etc., found in rock deposits.

petticoat *n* woman's underskirt.

petty *adj* **1** unimportant; trivial; insignificant. **2** contemptible, spiteful, or mean over small matters. **petty cash** *n* cash fund in an office for small items of receipt or expenditure. **petty officer** *n* noncommissioned naval officer. **pettiness** *n*.

petulant *adj* peevishly impatient, irritated, or capricious. **petulance** *n*. **petulantly** *adv*.

pew *n* enclosed compartment or fixed bench with a back and sides, as in a church.

pewter *n* **1** alloy of tin and lead and sometimes other metals. **2** vessel, plate, or utensil made of pewter.

pfennig *n, pl* **pfennigs** *or* **pfennige** ('pfenigə) West German copper coin equal to one hundredth of a mark.

phallus *n* **1** male sexual organ; penis. **2** representation of the penis. **phallic** *adj*.

phantom *n* **1** supernatural apparition; ghost; immaterial form. **2** visual illusion.

pharmacy *n* **1** art or practice of preparing and dispensing medicines. **2** chemist's dispensary. **pharmacist** *n*. **pharmaceutical** *adj* relating to medical drugs.

pharynx *n* cavity behind nose and mouth forming the upper part of the gullet and the opening into the larynx.

phase *n* **1** transitory stage in a cycle. **2** appearance of a moon or planet at a particular stage of its orbit. **3** aspect or appearance of anything at any stage. *vt* separate into stages of activity or development. **phase out** bring to terminal stage; extinguish gradually; discontinue.

pheasant *n* **1** long-tailed game bird, brightly coloured in the male. **2** flesh of this bird as food.

phenomenon *n, pl* **phenomena** (fə'nominə) **1** anything perceived by the senses; observed event. **2** anything striking or exceptional. **phenomenal** *adj* of or like a phenomenon; extraordinary; exceptional; remarkable. **phenomenally** *adv*.

philanthropy *n* benevolence; active generosity in social action; love of mankind. **philanthropic** *adj*. **philanthropist** *n*.

philately *n* study and collection of postage and revenue stamps. **philatelist** *n*.

philosophy *n* **1** study of the ultimate nature of existence. **2** any specified system of thought in this. **3** general mental and moral outlook on life; reasoning. **philosopher** *n*. **philosophical** *adj* **1** relating to philosophy or philosophers. **2** calmly reasonable; wise. **3** stoical; bearing misfortune well.

phlegm (flem) *n* **1** thick slimy fluid secreted in the throat and chest and discharged by coughing. **2** apathy; sluggish indifference. **phlegmatic** (fleg'mætik) *adj* **1** not easily excited or perturbed; placid. **2** sluggish; apathetic; stolid. **phlegmatically** *adv*.

phobia *n* fear, often irrational; dread; dislike.

phoenix *n* bird fabled to burn itself to death every 500 years and be reincarnated from its own ashes.

phone *n,vt,vi* short for **telephone.**

phonetic *adj* relating to the sounds of spoken language. **phonetically** *adv*. **phonetics** *n* study of speech sounds.

phoney *adj* counterfeit; unreal; insincere.

phosphate *n* chemical salt containing phosphorus, used in fertilizers.

phosphorescent *adj* emitting a faint light, similar to fluorescence, esp. after bombardment by radiation. **phosphorescence** *n*.

phosphorus *n* nonmetallic chemical element having an unreactive red form and a toxic inflammable phosphorescent white form, used in matches.

photo *n* short for **photograph.**

photocopy *vt* reproduce an exact copy of by a photographic process. *n* copy produced in this way.

photogenic *adj* suitable for and making a pleasing photograph.

photograph *n* image of something produced by the action of light on chemically sensitized surfaces. *vt* make a photographic image of. **photographer** *n*. **photography** *n* art or process of producing photographs. **photographical** *adj*.

phrase *n* **1** group of words forming a subdivision of a sentence. **2** idiomatic expression. *vt* choose fitting words to express. **phrasebook** *n* collection of idioms and commonly used phrases of a language.

physical *adj* **1** pertaining to the natural world of matter and energy or its study. **2** relating to the body. **physically** *adv*. **physical education** *n* promotion of bodily fitness by exercising the body.

physician *n* doctor; person legally qualified to treat disease by medicines but not surgery.

physics *n* study of the properties of matter and energy. **physicist** *n*.

physiology *n* study of physical processes in living beings. **physiological** *adj*. **physiologist** *n*.

physiotherapy *n* treatment of disease, weakness, or disability by exercise, massage, heat, etc. **physiotherapist** *n*.

physique *n* bodily appearance and constitution.

pi *n* ratio of the circumference of a circle to its diameter, equal to about 3.142.

piano *n* keyboard instrument with strings struck by hammers. **pianist** *n*.

piccolo *n* small high-pitched woodwind instrument of the flute family.

pick[1] *vt,vi* **1** choose; select carefully. **2** gather (fruit, etc.). *vt* **1** poke at with the fingers. **2** provoke. **3** steal from (a pocket, etc.). **pick and choose** select with excessive care. **pick at** nibble at food, esp. due to loss of appetite. **pick on** select, esp. to blame or be unpleasant to. **pick out 1** select. **2** recognize; distinguish; make obvious. **pick up 1** lift or gather in the hands. **2** improve. **3** take on (passengers, etc.). **4** learn gradually and casually. **5** *inf* meet casually and get acquainted. **6** *inf* arrest. ~*n* **1** choice; selection. **2** best choice. **pickpocket** *n* one who steals from others' pockets. **pick-up** *n* **1** device for converting vibrations, as of a record-player stylus, into electric current. **2** recovery. **3** act of picking up or one picked up.

pick[2] *n* **1** *also* **pickaxe** tool having a long cross-bar with sharp or pointed ends, used for breaking up stone, etc. **2** any sharp or pointed instrument for picking.

picket *n* **1** striker or group of strikers outside their workplace to dissuade other workers from working. **2** vigil in a public place by a person or group expressing political or social protest. *vt,vi* surround with or act as a picket.

pickle *n* **1** brine or vinegar solution in which food is preserved. **2** vegetable so preserved. **3** *inf* plight. *vt* preserve in pickle. **pickled** *adj sl* drunk.

picnic *vi* (picnicking; picnicked) take a casual meal outdoors for pleasure. *n* **1** meal so eaten. **2** outing for such a purpose.

pictorial *adj* **1** having or expressed by pictures. **2** relating to painting or drawing. *n* magazine comprising mainly pictures. **pictorially** *adv*.

picture *n* **1** two-dimensional arrangement of lines and colours intended to have aesthetic value. **2** embodiment; representation; mental image. **3** impressive sight. **4** film shown at a cinema. **5** vivid verbal description. **in the picture** well-informed; in possession of the facts. **the pictures** *pl n* cinema. ~*vt* depict or represent in a picture, the mind, or in words.

picturesque *adj* suitable for a picture; graphic; quaint.

pidgin *n* trade language or jargon having elements from two or more languages.

pie *n* dish of meat, fish, vegetables, or fruit baked with a pastry covering. **easy as pie** very easy.

piece *n* **1** part or item of a whole; bit; portion. **2** example; specimen. **3** musical, artistic, or literary composition. **4** small object, as used in board games. **go to pieces 1** lose one's self-control. **2** disintegrate. **piecemeal** *adv* bit by bit; in pieces. **piecework** *n* work paid according to the amount done rather than the time taken. *v* **piece together** assemble; fit together; mend.

pier *n* **1** jetty; landing stage; breakwater. **2** column supporting an arch or bridge. **3** load-bearing brickwork between windows or doors.

pierce *vt* **1** penetrate; make a hole in; enter or force a way into. **2** be seen, heard, or felt through. **3** afflict; touch or move deeply.

piety *n* willing and devout observance of religious duties; devotion to God.

pig *n* **1** domesticated mammal with thick bristly skin and a long snout, bred for its meat. **2** coarse, dirty, or greedy person. **pig in a poke** something bought without examination. **pig-headed** *adj* stupidly stubborn; obstinate. **pigheadedly** *adv*. **pig-iron** *n* iron in rough bars as first extracted from its ore. **piglet** *n* young pig. **pigsty** *n* **1** pen in which pigs are kept. **2** very untidy or dirty house or room. **pigtail** *n* hair twisted into a bunch to form a plait or hang loose.

pigeon *n* widely distributed bird of the dove family. **pigeonhole** *n* **1** small compartment for storing or classifying papers. **2** compartment of the mind. **3** entrance to a dovecote or pigeon's nest. *vt* **1** put in a pigeonhole. **2** put aside; defer considering. **3** classify methodically.

piggyback *n* ride astride someone's back or shoulders. *adv* on someone's back or shoulders.

pigment *n* paint; any colouring matter; substance giving colour to living tissue. **pigmentation** *n* coloration by pigments.

pike *n, pl* **pike** large voracious freshwater fish with a pointed snout.

pilchard *n* small food fish, similar to the herring.

pile[1] *n* **1** heap of objects. **2** *inf* large sum or amount of money, work, etc. *vt,vi also* **pile up.** heap up; collect into a mound. *vi* move quickly and haphazardly as in a group. **pile-up** *n inf* accumulation of things, esp. of cars as a result of a multiple crash, traffic jam, etc.

pile[2] *n* post driven into the ground to support a structure. **piledriver** *n* **1** machine for driving piles into the ground. **2** (in games) powerful stroke; kick.

pile[3] *n* **1** fine soft hair; down. **2** raised yarn on cloth such as velvet or towelling.

pilfer *vt,vi* steal petty articles in small quantities.

pilgrim *n* **1** person journeying to a shrine for religious reasons. **2** wanderer. **pilgrimage** *n* journey to a sacred or revered place. **Pilgrim Fathers** *pl n* original settlers of New England.

pill *n* oral medicine formed into or contained in a small ball, capsule, etc. **bitter pill** something disagreeable that has to be accepted. **the pill** contraceptive pill.

pillar *n* **1** column supporting a structure or standing alone as a monument. **2** person who is a prominent supporter. **pillar-box** *n* short hollow red pillar in which letters are posted; letter box.

pillion *n* seat for a second person on a horse or motorcycle behind the rider or driver. *adv* on a pillion.

pillow *n* soft cushion to support a sleeper's head; padded support. *vt* rest one's head; serve as a pillow for. **pillowcase** *n* washable cover for a pillow.

pilot *n* **1** person qualified to conduct ships in harbours, channels, etc. **2** person qualified to operate flying controls of an aircraft. **3** person steering a ship. *vt* steer; navigate; guide. **pilot scheme** preliminary, experimental, or trial approach or procedure.

pimento *n* red pepper used for stuffing olives, in salads, and as a vegetable.

pimple *n* small swelling on the skin. **pimply** *adj.*

pin *n* **1** short stiff pointed piece of wire with a rounded or flat head. **2** anything resembling a pin in form or function. **3** brooch; badge. *vt* (-nn-) **1** fasten, attach, or secure by a pin. **2** hold or fix in position; immobilize. **pin down** **1** force to keep a promise, agreement, etc. **2** define exactly. **pin on** attribute to; blame. **pinpoint** *n* **1** point of a pin. **2** anything very tiny or minute. *vt* locate; define very exactly. **pinstripes** *n* repeated narrow stripes in a material pattern, etc. **pin-up** *n* **1** picture of a nude or seminude girl pinned up on wall. **2** one whose picture is thus displayed.

pinafore *n* apron. **pinafore dress** *n* sleeveless dress worn over a jumper, etc.

pincers *pl n* **1** gripping tool with jaws and handles on a pivot. **2** pair of grasping clawlike parts, as in a crab. **pincer movement** *n* attack by two converging forces.

pinch *vt,vi* **1** squeeze sharply between finger and thumb or be squeezed between two hard objects. **2** inconvenience or be inconvenienced by a lack (of something). *vt* **1** *sl* steal. **2** *sl* arrest. *n* **1** squeeze. **2** emergency. **3** small amount. **at a pinch** if absolutely necessary.

pine[1] *n* coniferous tree with evergreen needle-shaped leaves.

pine[2] *vi* **1** become feeble from mental or physical suffering. **2** languish with longing; yearn (for).

pineapple *n* tropical plant yielding a large edible fruit having yellow flesh and a tuft of leaves on top.

Ping-Pong *n Tdmk* table-tennis.

pinion *n* small wheel with teeth engaging with a larger wheel or rack, one imparting motion to the other.

pink *adj,n* pale red; light rose. *n* garden plant resembling the carnation.

pinnacle *n* **1** small ornamental turret or spire. **2** slender mountain peak. **3** highest point or degree. *vt* **1** set on a pinnacle. **2** adorn with pinnacles.

pint *n* **1** measure of liquid capacity equal to an eighth of a gallon (0.57 litre). **2** *inf* this amount of beer.

pioneer *n* one of the first to attempt, explore, research, or colonize; one who takes the lead. *vt,vi* be or act as a pioneer.

pious *adj* devout; faithful in religious duties. **piously** *adv.*

pip[1] *n* small seed of fleshy fruits.

pip[2] *n* shrill note repeated as a signal in broadcasting or telephoning.

pip[3] *n* spot on a playing card, domino, or die.

pipe *n* **1** tube for conveying water, etc. **2** vessel for smoking loose tobacco. **3** simple wind instrument. **4** note of a bird; shrill voice. **pipes** *pl n* bagpipes. ~*vt* **1** convey by pipe. **2** provide pipes or piping for. **3** play on a pipe. **pipe down** make less noise. **pipe up** begin to speak unexpectedly. **pipedream** *n* wishful daydream; futile hope or plan. **pipeline** *n* **1** long line of pipes conveying water or oil. **2** direct communication line. **in the pipeline** on the way.

piquant *adj* **1** pleasantly pungent; tasty. **2** rousing keen interest. **piquancy** *n*.

pique *n* ill-feeling; resentment; anger. *vt* **1** annoy; offend. **2** arouse (interest, etc.).

pirate *n* **1** one who attempts robbery or unlawful capture of ships at sea. **2** privately owned radio transmitter or operator without a licence. **3** one who infringes copyright or trading rights. *vt* infringe copyright or trading laws. **piracy** *n*.

pirouette *n* act of spinning on tiptoe, esp. in dancing. *vi* spin thus.

Pisces *n* twelfth sign of the zodiac, represented by the Fishes.

pistol *n* small hand gun.

piston *n* short cylinder moving to and fro in a cylindrical tube as part of an engine or pump.

pit *n* **1** hole; sunken area; depression. **2** mine shaft. **3** sunken area for an orchestra in front of a stage. **4** area near a race track in which cars are serviced or refuelled. **pit of the stomach** hollow below the breastbone. ~*vt,vi* (-tt-) make a hole in or become marked with hollows. **pit against** set to fight against; match against. **pitfall** *n* hidden danger or unexpected difficulty.

pitch[1] *vt,vi* **1** throw; fling. **2** set up (camp); erect (a tent). *vt* **1** set the slope or level of. **2** give a particular slant or character to. **3** sing or play (a note, etc.) accurately. *vi* toss up and down, as by waves. *n* **1** slope; gradient. **2** playing field. **3** frequency of a musical note. **4** *inf* persuasive sales talk. **pitchfork** *n* long-handled two-pronged fork for pitching hay. *vt* **1** lift and throw with a pitchfork. **2** assign work or responsibility to hastily or roughly.

pitch[2] *n* black viscous tarry liquid that sets hard on cooling and is used for roads, paths, etc. *vt* apply pitch to.

piteous *adj* arousing pity; pathetic.

pith *n* **1** core of spongy tissue in plant stems, feathers, etc. **2** white fibre inside the rind of oranges, lemons, etc. **3** essence; concentrated meaning; importance. **4** physical strength; mastery. **pithy** *adj*.

pittance *n* meagre allowance or portion.

pituitary gland *n* small gland in the brain that controls or influences hormone action.

pity *n* **1** compassion for suffering and the misfortunes of others; mercy. **2** cause of disappointment or regret. *vt* feel pity for. **pitiful** *adj* **1** arousing pity; pathetic; miserable. **2** contemptible. **pitifully** *adv*. **pitiless** *adj* merciless; cruel.

pivot *n* **1** pin or fixed point on which something turns. **2** person or thing on which all depends. *vt,vi* mount or turn on a pivot. *vi* depend on.

pizza *n* Italian dish consisting of a breadlike base with a topping of tomato sauce, cheese, and garnishes.

placard *n* public notice; written or printed display. *vt* **1** publicize by a placard. **2** fix a placard to.

placate *vt* appease the hostility or resentment of.

place *n* **1** geographical point; location; area. **2** position; state; rank. **3** space; room; seat. **4** house; residence. **5** duty; right. **6** job; appointment. **7** relative position in a race. **go places** *inf* become successful. **out of place** unsuitable; inappropriate. **in place of** instead of. **take place** occur; happen. ~*vt* **1** put or set in a particular or suitable position or order. **2** identify by some past link. **3** make; put. **4** appoint. **place with** put under the care of.

placenta *n* mass of tissue within the womb by which a connection is made between the foetus and the mother and which is discharged after birth. **placental** *adj*.

placid *adj* calm; unruffled. **placidly** *adv*.

plagiarize *vt,vi* steal from writings or ideas of another and use as one's own. **plagiarism** *n*. **plagiarist** *n*.

plague *n* **1** deadly highly infectious epidemic disease. **2** calamity; curse. **3** troublesome or annoying person or thing. *vt* be a persistent trouble to; pester.

plaice *n* edible flatfish having a brown body marked with orange spots.

plaid *n* cloth with a tartan or a chequered pattern.

plain *n* **1** tract of level land; open country. **2** simple knitting stitch. *adj* **1** level; flat; even. **2** clear; obvious. **3** simple; not ornate, decorated, or embellished. **4** neither beautiful nor ugly. **5** outspoken; straightforward. *adv also* **plainly** distinctly; bluntly; frankly. **plain-clothes** *adj* (of police, etc.) wearing ordinary clothes as opposed to a uniform. **plain sailing** *n* smooth and unhindered progress.

plaintive *adj* mournful; lamenting; complaining. **plaintively** *adv*.

plait *n* braid in which three or more strands or bunches of hair, etc., are passed over one another in turn. *vt* braid; intertwine.

plan *n* **1** scheme; project; method. **2** map of an area. **3** diagram of a structure. *vt,vi* (-nn-) **1** make a plan of or for; devise methods of doing. **2** regulate by a central authority.

plane[1] *n* **1** level or even surface. **2** level of existence or standard of performance, etc. **3** short for **aeroplane.** *adj* level; flat. *vi* skim over a water surface.

plane[2] *n* tool for levelling or smoothing surfaces, cutting grooves, etc. *vt* **1** use a plane on. **2** shave off by means of a plane.

planet *n* nonluminous celestial body that orbits around a star, esp. the nine bodies, including earth, that orbit around the sun. **planetary** *adj*.

plank *n* long broad length of cut timber. *vt* cover or supply with planks.

plankton *n* small animals and plants that inhabit the surface of a body of water and on which many larger animals feed.

plant *n* **1** living organism that synthesizes its own food from inorganic substances and lacks sense organs and powers of locomotion. **2** any herbaceous plant, as distinct from a tree or shrub. **3** factory; manufacturing works. **4** *inf* person or thing introduced into a group, place, etc., to throw guilt on innocent people. *vt* **1** put in the ground to grow. **2** establish; fix. **plantation** *n* large estate, esp. in tropical countries, where crops are grown. **planter** *n* **1** owner or supervisor of a plantation. **2** decorative holder for a house plant.

plaque 1 ornamental plate or disc intended to be mounted or hung for display. **2** hard white deposit that forms around the teeth.

plasma *n* clear yellowish fluid part of blood or lymph in which cells are suspended.

plaster *n* **1** mixture of sand, lime, and water that is applied to walls and ceilings to make them smooth. **2** self-adhesive bandage for minor wounds. *vt* cover or coat with or as if with plaster. **plaster of Paris** *n* hard refined plaster suitable for use in sculptures, casts, etc.

plastic *n* widely used synthetic material that can be moulded into a desired shape when soft. *adj* **1** made of plastic. **2** pliable; elastic. **3** easily influenced. **plastic surgery** *n* surgery concerned with the repair, sometimes cosmetic, of external tissue.

Plasticine *n Tdmk* soft modelling material.

plate *n* **1** shallow dish or receptacle. **2** thin coating of metal, esp. gold or silver. **3** item or items coated with gold or silver. **4** illustration or print in a book. **5** thin sheet, esp. of glass. *vt* coat with a thin layer of metal. **platelayer** *n* person who lays and maintains railway tracks.

plateau *n* **1** large level area of high land. **2** long stable period during development.

platform *n* **1** raised area, as for a speaker at a meeting. **2** waiting area at a railway station, etc. **3** statement of policy or plan of a political party, etc.

platinum *n* pliable silvery precious metal that is very durable and much used, esp. in jewellery.

platonic *adj* without physical desires.

platter *n* large dish or plate, used esp. for serving food.

plausible *adj* reasonable, likely, or believable. **plausibility** *n*. **plausibly** *adv*.

play *vt,vi* **1** occupy or amuse oneself (in a game, sport, etc.). **2** fill a particular role in a team game. **3** act as; imitate. **4** operate a musical instrument, radio, record player, etc., or be operated. *vt* **1** compete with. **2** act the part of. **3** give a dramatic performance of. *n* **1** drama; dramatic production. **2** games, diversions, etc. **3** manner or way of playing. **4** fun; lightheartedness. **5** liberty of action; scope. **playable** *adj*. **player** *n*. **playboy** *n* man who devotes himself to the pursuit of irresponsible pleasures. **playground** *n* outdoor area for children to play in. **playgroup** *n* nursery group for very young children. **playhouse** *n* **1** theatre for live drama. **2** toy house for children. **playing card** *n* one of a pack of fifty-two cards having a set value in one of the four suits into which the cards are divided. **playing field** *n* field used for playing team games. **playmate** *n* companion in play, esp. for children. **playschool** *n* playgroup. **playwright** *n* writer of plays; dramatist.

plea *n* **1** sincere claim or appeal. **2** something pleaded on behalf of a defendant in a legal trial.

plead *vt,vi* **1** appeal (to); beseech; implore. **2** offer an argument (for). *vt* **1** give as an excuse or justification. **2** declare oneself as being (guilty or not guilty) in a court of law.

pleasant *adj* pleasing; agreeable; enjoyable. **pleasantly** *adv*. **please** *vt,vi* gratify or delight (someone). *adv* used in making polite requests, asking favours, etc. **pleasure** *n* **1** delight; happiness; enjoyment. **2** something giving these things.

pleat *n* permanent fold or repeated crease in a fabric, esp. in skirts or dresses. *vt* make pleats in.

plectrum *n,pl* **plectrums** *or* **plectra** ('plektrə) implement or pick for plucking a musical string.

pledge *n* **1** solemn oath or promise. **2** guarantee; security. **3** token; symbol. *vt,vi* **1** promise solemnly. **2** give as a pledge. *vt* bind or secure by a pledge.

plenty *n* **1** enough; adequate supply. **2** abundance; profusion; large number. *adj* enough; very many. **plentiful** *adj*.

pliable *adj* **1** flexible; easily bent. **2** compliant; yielding; manageable.

plight *n* dilemma; difficult situation.

plimsoll *n* rubber-soled canvas shoe worn for sport.

plod *v* (-dd-) *vt,vi* walk along in a slow dogged manner. *vi* work slowly and steadily. *n* act or sound of plodding.

plonk *n inf* cheap wine.

plop *n* sound made by dropping an object into water. *v* (-pp-) *vt,vi* drop or make fall with a plop. *vi* make a plop.

plot[1] *n* **1** secret plan; outline; scheme. **2** story of a play, novel, etc. *v* (-tt-) *vt,vi* plan or conspire secretly. *vt* chart (a course) or make a map of.

plot[2] *n* small patch of ground.

plough *n* device for turning over soil when planting crops. *vt,vi* till or make a furrow with a plough.

pluck *vt* **1** pick off (feathers, flowers, etc.) from. **2** draw sound from (the strings) of (a musical instrument) by pulling them. **3** pull; tug. *n* courage. **plucky** *adj* brave; courageous.

plug *n* **1** piece of material used to fill a hole or stop up a gap. **2** device that connects an electrical appliance to an electricity supply. **3** *inf* unscheduled advertisement for or mention of a product. *vt* (-gg-) **1** attach to an electricity supply by means of a plug. **2** stop up or fill. **3** *inf* mention favourably or advertise.

plum *n* small tree bearing purple or green fruit with an oval stone. *adj inf* comfortable; pleasant.

plumage *n* feathers on a bird.

plumb *n* lump of heavy material, esp. when attached to a length of string (**plumbline**) and used to ensure that a wall, etc., is vertical. *vt* measure the depth of (the sea, etc.) with or as if with a plumb.

plumber *n* person who installs and repairs water pipes, baths, sinks, etc. **plumbing** *n* **1** profession of a plumber. **2** pipes and other appliances connected with the supply of water to a building.

plume *n* feather, esp. a long ornamental one.

plump[1] *adj* fleshy; chubby; fat. *vt,vi* make or become plump.

plump[2] *vi* fall or drop heavily or noisily. **plump for** choose; select.

plunder *vt,vi* steal (from) by force; rob. *n* **1** anything stolen or taken by force; loot. **2** act of plundering.

plunge *vt,vi* **1** thrust or be thrust, esp. into a liquid. **2** bring or be brought suddenly (into a certain condition). **3** rush madly in a certain direction. **4** throw oneself enthusiastically (into). *n* **1** act of plunging. **2** leap; mad dash.

plural *adj* consisting of or relating to more than one. *n* **1** linguistic number category in which plural nouns are placed. **2** plural form of a noun.

plus *prep* added to; with. *adv* or more. *n also* **plus sign** sign indicating addition.

plush *adj also* **plushy** very comfortable and expensive; luxurious.

Pluto *n* ninth and furthest known planet from the sun.

ply[1] *vt* **1** travel regularly around (an area) selling (goods, etc.). **2** supply continuously. **3** work at; engage in.

ply[2] *n* layer of material, esp. wood, or a strand of yarn. **plywood** *n* material consisting of layers or strips of wood glued together.

pneumatic *adj* relating to or operated by air, esp. compressed air.

pneumonia *n* disease marked by inflammation of the lungs, usually caused by bacteria or a virus.

poach[1] *vi,vt* **1** catch or take (game, fish, etc.) illegally. **2** trespass; encroach. **3** steal; pinch. **poacher** *n*.

poach[2] *vt* cook in gently boiling liquid.

pocket *n* **1** small pouch or bag, esp. one sewn into a garment. **2** cavity; hollow. **3** isolated area of group of people. **out of pocket** having made a financial loss. ~*vt* steal; appropriate. **pocket money** *n* small weekly sum of money given by parents to a child.

pod *n* fruit of the pea, bean, and related plants.

poem *n* composition usually written in regular rhythmic lines and often employing rhyme, metaphor, etc., to stimulate the imagination. **poetic** *adj*. **poet** *n* writer of poems. **poetess** *n f*. **poetry** *n* **1** verse. **2** art or work of a poet. **3** poetic qualities.

point *n* **1** sharp tapering end. **2** any projection, esp. a tapering one, such as a piece of land jutting out into the sea. **3** mark or dot made by something with a sharp point. **4** punctuation mark or accent used in writing, esp. a full stop. **5** something that has a position but no spatial extent. **6** definite place on a scale; specific moment. **7** stage in a course of action, procedure, etc., esp. an important or decisive stage. **8** element or part of something, esp. the most essential part, as of a topic, joke, etc. **9** reason; aim; meaning; significance. **10** unit of counting used in scoring games; mark. **on the point of** about to commit the act of. **make a point of** insist on as being important. **point of view** outlook; personal position or attitude. **stretch a point** be prepared to make an exception to one's usual practice. **to/off the point** relevant/irrelevant. **point-blank** at a range so close that one cannot miss; directly. ~*vt,vi* direct or aim (one's finger, etc.) at. *vt also* **point out 1** indicate the position of. **2** turn someone's attention to. *vi* indicate or face in the direction of. **pointed** *adj* **1** having a point. **2** referring obviously to someone or something; emphatic; incisive. **pointer** *n* **1** something used for pointing. **2** indicator on a dial. **3** hint; suggestion. **4** breed of hunting dog. **pointless** *adj* lacking relevance, meaning, significance, etc.

poise *n* **1** calmness of manner; composure. **2** balance; stability. *vt,vi* **1** balance or be balanced. **2** hold a position, esp. in mid-air; hover.

poison *n* substance that causes illness or death because of its chemical properties. *vt* **1** kill or injure by administering poison. **2** put poison into (food, water, etc.). **poisonous** *adj*.

poke *vt,vi* **1** probe; prod; pierce. **2** push or thrust. *n* prod; push; thrust.

poker[1] *n* metal rod used for stirring the embers of a fire.

poker[2] *n* gambling card game.

pole[1] *n* long usually slender cylindrical rod used for support, measurement, propulsion, etc. **pole-vault** *n* athletic event in which a competitor propels himself over a high bar by means of a pole. *vt,vi* perform the pole-vault over a barrier.

pole[2] *n* **1** either of the two extreme ends of the axis of a planet or other globe. **2** two ends of a magnet, terminals of an electric battery, etc. **Pole Star** star almost directly over the earth's North Pole. **polar** *adj*. **polarize** *vt,vi* form into two or more distinct opposing groups.

polemic *n* controversial dispute or argument or an article, essay, etc., containing this. *adj also* **polemical** of or concerning a polemic.

police *n* **1** authority in a country responsible for keeping order, preventing crime, and enforcing laws. **2** *pl* members of this authority. *vt* control or keep law and order in. **policeman** *n, pl* **-men** police officer. **police station** *n* headquarters of a local branch of the police.

policy[1] *n* **1** course or line of action, esp. one adapted by a government in running state affairs. **2** wise or sensible way of doing things.

policy[2] *n* document stating the details of a contract between an individual and an insurance company.

polio *n also* **poliomyelitis** acute infectious disease, usually of children, that can paralyse various muscle groups.

polish *vt,vi* put a shine on something. *vt* improve (one's language, manners, etc.). *n* **1** substance applied to something to make it smooth or shiny. **2** shine or smoothness resulting from polishing. **3** act of polishing. **4** elegance or superior quality, as of a person's behaviour.

polite *adj* **1** demonstrating good manners and good behaviour; courteous. **2** refined and elegant. **politely** *adv*. **politeness** *n*.

politic *adj* **1** wise. **2** clever; cunning.

political *adj* **1** of or connected with politics or a party in politics. **2** of or relating to a state government or its administration. **politically**

adv. **politician** *n* person concerned with politics, esp. one who holds a public office in a government. **politics** *n* **1** *s* science or profession concerned with government. **2** *pl* political affairs, principles, or ideas.

polka *n* **1** lively Bohemian dance. **2** music composed for this dance. *vi* dance a polka.

poll *n* **1** mass vote, as at an election. **2** number of votes cast. **3** list of people drawn up for voting or taxation purposes. **4** *also* **opinion poll** process in which a selection of people are interviewed as a means of assessing public opinion. *vt* **1** receive votes in an election. **2** interview to test public opinion.

pollen *n* dustlike material produced by flowering plants that serves as a fertilizing agent. **pollinate** *vt* transfer pollen to (a plant) for purposes of fertilization. **pollination** *n*.

pollute *vt* **1** make foul or poisonous; contaminate. **2** corrupt the morals of. **pollutant** *n* something that pollutes. **pollution** *n*.

polygamy *n* practice of marrying or the situation of being married to more than one woman at a time. **polygamist** *n*. **polygamous** *adj*.

polygon *n* geometric figure having three or more sides.

polymer *n* substance containing long chains of atoms joined together, as in cellulose, plastics, synthetic fibres, etc.

polyp *n* **1** type of individual of such organisms as corals or sea anemones, having tentacles and a mouth. **2** *also* **polyps** small pathological growth, as in the nose.

polytechnic *n* type of college of higher education originally set up to teach scientific subjects but now also teaching social sciences.

polythene *n* widely used type of plastic. *adj* made of polythene.

pomegranate *n* large round usually red fruit with a tough rind and inner parts divided into chambers containing edible seeds.

pommel *n* **1** raised front end of a saddle. **2** knob on the top of a sword.

pomp *n* **1** stately splendour. **2** ostentatious or empty show; vain display. **pompous** *adj* **1** overdignified; self-important. **2** ostentatious or inflated. **pompously** *adv*.

pond *n* small lake; pool.

ponder *vt,vi* reflect or think deeply; meditate.

pony *n* small horse.

poodle *n* breed of dog having thick curly hair.

pool[1] *n* **1** small body of water; pond; puddle. **2** any small amount of liquid. **3** still deep part in a river.

pool[2] *n* **1** group or association of mutually cooperative members. **2** combination of things, esp. a set of services or financial facilities shared by a number of people or groups. **3** all the stakes in a game. *vt,vi* combine to form a pool. **the pools** *n* system of betting on the results of football matches.

poor *adj* **1** having or characterized by little wealth or resources. **2** deficient in something necessary or desirable; inferior; unsatisfactory; scanty. *n* **the poor** poor people in general. **poorly** *adv* badly. *adj inf* ill.

pop[1] *v* (-pp-) *vt,vi* **1** make or cause to make a short sharp sound. **2** burst open or cause to burst open with a pop. *vi* come or go quickly. *n* **1** popping sound. **2** nonalcoholic fizzy drink. **pop off 1** depart. **2** die suddenly. **pop the question** propose marriage. ~*adv,interj* with or expressing a popping sound. **popcorn** *n* type of maize that bursts and puffs up when roasted.

pop[2] *n* type of music usually having a distinctive and persistent rhythmic beat and making extensive use of electronically aided instruments.

Pope *n* head of the Roman Catholic Church.

poplar *n* tall tree of the willow family having a spirelike appearance.

poppy *n* plant bearing red, orange, or white flowers.

popular *adj* **1** liked or enjoyed by a large number of people. **2** of or connected with the people. **3** normal among or suitable for the people. **popularity** *n*. **popularly** *adv*. **populate** *vt* **1** live in; inhabit. **2** introduce a population into; people. **population** *n* people considered collectively, esp. all the people living in a town, city, country, etc.

porcelain *n* type of delicate pottery; china.

porch *n* **1** exterior roofed entrance to a house. **2** veranda.

porcupine *n* animal of the rodent family whose body is covered with stiff sharp spines or quills.

pore[1] *v* **pore over** think or ponder deeply about; study.

pore[2] *n* tiny opening, esp. in the skin or a leaf, to allow the passage of perspiration or other moisture.

pork *n* flesh or meat obtained from pigs. **porker** *n* pig being fattened for slaughter.

pornography *n* literature or art dealing with obscene subjects and intended to arouse sexual desires. **pornographic** *adj*.

porous *adj* full of little holes like a sponge, which allow the passage of water or air.

porpoise *n* aquatic mammal with a blunt snout, related to the whale.

porridge *n* breakfast dish consisting of oatmeal, water, and often milk.

port[1] *n* a place, city, etc., where ships may load or unload cargoes.

port[2] *n* left side of a ship or aeroplane for someone facing towards the front.

port[3] *n* sweet fortified usually dark red wine.

portable *adj* able to be carried easily by hand. *n* portable object.

porter[1] *n* person employed to carry people's luggage, as at a railway station or hotel.

porter[2] *n* dark bitter ale.

portfolio *n* **1** large flat case for carrying documents, drawings, etc. **2** collection of documents concerned with a government department. **3** office of a government minister. **4** list of securities held by a person, bank, etc.

porthole *n* opening in a ship's side fitted with glass to let in air and light.

portion *n* **1** piece; share. **2** amount of food served to one person. *vt* **1** give as a share. **2** divide or share.

portrait *n* **1** picture of a person, usually a painting. **2** lively written description of a person. **portraiture** *n* **1** art of producing portraits. **2** portraits collectively.

portray *vt* **1** play the part of (someone), as in a play. **2** describe a person or his character. **portrayal** *n*.

pose *n* **1** way of standing or behaving deliberately adopted to give an effect. **2** pretence. *vi* **1** act (as something one is not). **2** stand or sit in a certain way to be photographed or painted. *vt* ask (a question); present (a problem).

posh *adj inf* **1** smart; showing style. **2** upper-class; snobbish.

position *n* **1** place. **2** situation or condition. **3** opinion; attitude. **4** way of standing, sitting, etc. **5** job; employment; office; rank. *vt* **1** put into place. **2** find the place of. **positional** *adj*.

positive *adj* **1** definite. **2** certain; sure. **3** real, true, or actual. **4** useful or helpful. **5** hopeful; optimistic. **6** denoting numbers greater than zero. **7** designating or having the electric charge of a proton. **8** (of a photograph) corresponding in colour or tone to the scene photographed. *n* positive photograph, electric terminal, etc. **positively** *adv*.

possess *vt* have or control; own. **possessed** *adj* mad or frenzied, esp. when under the control of an evil spirit. **possession** *n* **1** something one owns. **2** act of possessing or state of being possessed. **3** condition of occupying property. **4** overseas colony. **possessive** *adj* **1** concerning possession. **2** selfishly dominating or controlling a person. **3** denoting the case or form of a word used to indicate possession. *n* possessive case or a pronoun in it.

possible *adj* **1** able to exist, occur, be done, etc. **2** that may perhaps happen. **3** potential. *n* person or thing that is possible. **possibly** *adv*. **possibility** *n* something that is possible. **possibilities** *pl n* likely prospects.

post[1] *n* **1** stout wooden pole driven into the ground, esp. to support a roof, gate, or door. **2** place where a race starts or ends. *vt* **1** put up (a notice) on a wall, etc. **2** announce to the public by putting up a notice or sign.

post[2] *n* **1** job or duty. **2** place where a soldier carries out his duties. **3** fort or military camp. **4** remote settlement. *vt* **1** assign a task or duty to. **2** send to (a military camp). **3** appoint to (a certain job).

post[3] *n* **1** national system or organization for carrying letters, parcels, etc. **2** letters and parcels handled for delivery; mail. **3** act or time of collecting or delivering mail. *vt* send through the post. **keep posted** keep informed. **postage** *n* money paid for the use of the post. **postal** *adj*. **postal order** *n* money order that can be bought or cashed only at a post office. **postbox** *n* box in which letters are placed for collection. **postcard** *n* card, sometimes having a picture on one side, used to send short messages. **postman** *n, pl* **-men** official who delivers letters.

poster *n* placard, esp. used as an advertising announcement.

posterior *adj* placed or following behind something else. *n* buttocks.

posterity *n* future generations.

postgraduate *adj* relating to studies carried out

by a student who has already gained his first degree. *n* postgraduate student.

posthumous *adj* **1** happening or produced after a person's death. **2** published after an author's death. **posthumously** *adv*.

postmortem *n* **1** medical examination of a corpse to find out the cause of death. **2** analysis of reasons for failure of a plan, etc., of something after it is over. *adj,adv* after death.

postpone *vt* delay; put off; defer. **postponement** *n*.

postscript *n* additional note added at the end of a letter or document, after the signature.

postulate *n* ('pɔstjulit) **1** idea or principle temporarily adopted as the basis of an argument, etc.; assumption. **2** unproved or self-evident scientific statement. *vt* ('pɔstjuleit) **1** claim; demand. **2** adopt as a postulate.

posture *n* **1** way of standing or walking. **2** situation or condition. *vi* act in an unnatural way to achieve an effect.

posy *n* small bunch of flowers.

pot[1] *n* **1** round vessel or container. **2** vessel used for cooking food or from which tea or coffee is served. **3** jar. **go to pot** fall into a state of ruin. **pot shot** easy shot with a gun, etc. ~*v* (-tt-) *vt,vi* **1** place plants, etc., in a pot. **2** put food in jars to preserve it. *vt* strike (a billiard ball) into a pocket.

pot[2] *n* marijuana.

potassium *n* soft silvery-white metallic element whose compounds are much used in drugs and fertilizers.

potato *n, pl* **potatoes** tuber of certain plants used as a vegetable.

potent *adj* **1** powerful; strong; influential. **2** (of men) able to perform sexually. **potency** *n*.

potential *adj* **1** capable of existing, becoming effective, etc. **2** not yet using one's power. *n* capacity or ability not yet realized or used. **potentiality** *n*. **potentially** *adv*.

pothole *n* **1** small pit in a road. **2** deep hole in rock, often large enough to be explored. **potholer** *n*.

potion *n* drink of a medicinal, magical, or poisonous nature.

potter[1] *n* person who makes pottery.

potter[2] *vi* move or act aimlessly.

pottery *n* **1** earthenware vessels. **2** material from which such vessels are made. **3** factory where pots are made.

pouch *n* **1** small bag, esp. one for carrying money, food, tobacco, etc. **2** baglike or pocket-like part of the body on certain animals, esp. the one in which kangaroos, wallabies, etc., carry their young.

poultice *n* soft moistened mass applied to the body for medicinal purposes. *vt* place a poultice on.

poultry *n* domesticated fowls. **poulterer** *n* person who sells poultry and game.

pounce *vi* leap suddenly (upon); swoop. *n* sudden leap or swoop.

pound[1] *vt,vi* beat with a succession of heavy blows. *vt* reduce to dust; crush. *vi* thump; throb. *n* thump.

pound[2] *n* **1** unit of weight, divided into sixteen ounces, equivalent to 0.45 kilograms. **2** basic unit of British currency or the system of currency used in Great Britain (**pound sterling**) and several other countries.

pound[3] *n* enclosure, esp. one for sheltering, confining, or catching animals.

pour *vt,vi* **1** flow or cause to flow out. **2** emit or cause to emit continually and quickly. **3** rain heavily.

pout *vi* push out the lips as when angry, sullen, etc. *vt* say in a sulky manner. *n* **1** act or gesture of pouting. **2** sulk.

poverty *n* state or condition of being poor; lack of wealth. **poverty-stricken** *adj* without means; destitute.

powder *n* **1** solid substance in the form of tiny loose particles, usually produced by grinding or crushing. **2** type of powder used as a cosmetic, medicine, etc. *vt,vi* make into or become a powder; crush or be crushed. *vt* apply powder to. **powdery** *adj*.

power *n* **1** ability or means to do something. **2** capacity of mind or body. **3** strength, energy, or force. **4** control; influence; authority. **5** country or state having international influence. **6** divine or supernatural being. **7** rate at which work is done or energy is transferred. *vt* **1** provide energy, force, etc., for. **2** provide with an engine or motor. **powerful** *adj*. **powerfully** *adv*. **powerless** *adj*.

practicable *adj* able to be done or used.

practical *adj* **1** concerned with practice or action. **2** capable of or suitable for use. **3** concerned with the ordinary activities in the world. **4** inclined towards actual or useful work; not philosophical or interested in theory.

5 aware of possibilities; experienced. **practically** *adv* **1** almost; nearly. **2** in a practical manner.

practice *n* **1** custom; habit. **2** exercises done to gain skill in something. **3** action that corresponds to a theory. **4** work or clients of a lawyer, doctor, etc. **practise** *vt,vi* **1** do as a habit or do repeatedly to gain skill. **2** train (at). **3** take an action that corresponds to a theory. **4** work as a lawyer, doctor, etc. **practitioner** *n* person who works at a profession, esp. a doctor.

pragmatic *adj* **1** making judgments based on causes and results. **2** acting in a practical manner. **pragmatically** *adv*.

prairie *n* large usually fertile area of grassland without trees.

praise *vt* **1** show approval or admiration for. **2** give glory to (God, etc.). *n* **1** admiration or approval. **2** glory or homage expressed to God. **praiseworthy** *adj*.

pram *n* wheeled carriage for a baby.

prance *vi* **1** jump or move by jumping from the hind legs, as a horse does. **2** walk about pompously; swagger. *n* jump; spring; swagger.

prank *n* childish trick.

prattle *n* meaningless chatter. *vi* chatter meaninglessly.

prawn *n* edible marine animal resembling but larger than a shrimp.

pray *vt,vi* make an earnest request for, esp to God or a god; make a prayer. **prayer** *n* **1** earnest request made to God or a god. **2** special set of words used in praying. **3** strong wish or desire.

preach *vt,vi* **1** speak publicly on a religious theme or in support of a religion. **2** give strong moral encouragement (to); advocate. **3** give unwelcome moral advice (to). **preacher** *n*.

precarious *adj* insecure; unsafe; uncertain. **precariously** *adv*. **precariousness** *n*.

precaution *n* action taken to stop something unpleasant or dangerous from happening. **precautionary** *adj*.

precede *vt* **1** go in front of. **2** be earlier than. **3** be more important or of higher rank than. **precedence** *n* **1** act of preceding. **2** relative importance or rank. **3** right resulting from rank, birth, or important office. **precedent** *n* earlier case or decision that is taken as guidance in dealing with subsequent situations.

precept *n* rule or guide for behaviour; maxim.

precinct *n* enclosed area, esp. the grounds of a cathedral, school, etc.

precious *adj* **1** valuable; of great price. **2** well loved. **3** affected; excessively refined. *adv* very. **preciously** *adv*.

precipice *n* high, vertical, and steep cliff.

precipitate (priˈsipiteit) *vt* **1** cause to happen before required or expected; hasten. **2** throw down; hurl. **3** cause dissolved matter to separate from solution in solid form. *n* (priˈsipitit) solid precipitated matter. **precipitation** *n*.

précis *n* shortened form of a longer statement, document, etc. *vt* make a summary of.

precise *adj* **1** accurate; exact. **2** clear; definite. **precisely** *adv*. **precision** *n*.

precocious *adj* advanced in development.

preconceive *vt* form an opinion beforehand. **preconception** *n*.

predator *n* **1** animal that lives by hunting and killing other animals for food. **2** plunderer; thief. **predatory** *adj*.

predecessor *n* person who precedes someone else in a particular office, job, or duty.

predestine *vt* decide the fate of beforehand. **predestination** *n*.

predicament *n* awkward or dangerous situation.

predicate *n* (ˈpredikit) **1** part of a sentence that contains what is said about the subject. **2** statement relating to something. *vt* (ˈpredikeit) declare as a characteristic. **predication** *n*. **predicative** *adj*.

predict *vt* describe future events before they happen; foretell; prophesy. **predictable** *adj*. **prediction** *n*.

predominate *vi* **1** be the most numerous. **2** have the most power or strength. **predominance** *n*. **predominant** *adj*.

pre-eminent *adj* better than anyone or anything else; excellent; very distinguished. **pre-eminence** *n*. **pre-eminently** *adv*.

preen *vt,vi* **1** (of a bird) clean and straighten the feathers with the beak. **2** prepare or dress oneself tidily. **3** show self-satisfaction.

prefabricate *vt* manufacture parts or sections of (a building, etc.) ready for assembling and erection.

preface *n* **1** written introduction in a book; foreword. **2** similar introduction to a speech or play. *vt* introduce with a preface. **prefatory** *adj.*

prefect *n* senior pupil with some authority over other pupils at a school.

prefer *vt* (-rr-) **1** like better. **2** give special attention to. **3** present or make (a statement, charge, etc.). **4** promote. **preferable** *adj.* **preference** *n* **1** preferring or being preferred. **2** something preferred. **3** advantage or right granted to particular people, countries, etc. **preferential** *adj.*

prefix *n* affix added to the beginning of a word to alter or otherwise affect its meaning. *vt* attach at the beginning of something.

pregnant *adj* **1** (of a woman or female animal) being with child or young. **2** full of; abounding in. **3** very significant. **pregnancy** *n.*

prehistoric *adj* of or occurring in the period before history was written down.

prejudice *n* **1** judgment or opinion reached prematurely or on insufficient evidence. **2** unfavourable opinion or bias. *vt* **1** cause to be prejudiced; bias. **2** injure; harm. **prejudicial** *adj.*

preliminary *adj* occurring beforehand; introductory. *n* first action or occurrence; introductory or preparatory step, event, etc.

prelude *n* **1** short piece of music, esp. introducing an opera, suite, or fugue. **2** any introduction. *vt* form a prelude or introduction to.

premarital *adj* before marriage.

premature *adj* before the right time; too early.

premeditate *vt* think of or decide upon beforehand; plan. **premeditation** *n.*

premier *adj* of the highest importance; first; leading. *n* prime minister.

premiere *n* first showing or performance of a film, play, etc.

premise *n* **1** *also* **premiss** assumption. **2** introduction to a document, such as a lease. **premises** *pl n* house or other building, including the grounds. ~*vt* state as a premise.

premium *n* **1** prize; bonus. **2** additional payment to a standard rate, wage, etc. **3** amount paid periodically to renew an insurance policy. **at a premium** very valuable. **premium bond** government bond that pays no interest but offers the chance of monthly cash prizes.

preoccupied *adj* **1** concentrating on one thought above others; engrossed; absorbed. **preoccupation** *n.*

prepare *vt,vi* **1** make or become ready or suitable for something. **2** make; manufacture; construct. **3** equip. **preparatory** *adj.* **preparation** *n* **1** preparing or being prepared. **2** something prepared, esp. a medicine or cosmetic. **3** *also inf* **prep** school work done by a pupil at home; homework.

preposition *n* word placed before a noun or pronoun indicating relationship in time, space, etc. **prepositional** *adj.*

preposterous *adj* ridiculous; stupid; absurd. **preposterously** *adv.*

prerogative *n* privilege; right.

Presbyterian *adj* relating to a Protestant Church governed by elders (presbyters), traditionally following the teachings of Calvin. *n* member of such a Church.

prescribe *vt,vi* **1** order or require (medicine, treatment, etc.). **2** make certain rules about. **prescription** *n* **1** written instructions issued by a doctor indicating required medicine, treatment, etc. **2** act of prescribing.

presence *n* **1** state or condition of being present. **2** closeness; nearness. **3** demeanour; bearing. **4** dignity; importance. **presence of mind** ability to act quickly and intelligently when faced by difficulty or danger.

present[1] ('prezənt) *adj* **1** being here within sight or hearing. **2** being at a particular place at a certain time. **3** existing now; indicating this time now. *n* **1** time being lived through now. **2** tense in a language indicating this. **presently** *adv* soon; before long. **present participle** *n* verb form functioning as an adjective or used with an auxiliary verb to denote continuous action, e.g. *changing, living,* or *speaking.*

present[2] *n* ('prezənt) gift. *vt* (prə'zent) **1** give, esp. formally; bestow. **2** introduce, esp. in a formal way. **3** organize (a performance, etc.). **4** show to the public. **5** offer or put forward for consideration, etc. **6** raise (a weapon) in salute. **presentation** *n.* **presentable** *adj* fit to be introduced, displayed, etc.

preserve *vt* **1** keep safe or undamaged. **2** save from decay, change, etc. *n* **1** preserved food, such as jam. **2** area of country protected or kept private, as for hunting. **3** right; privilege. **preservation** *n.* **preservative** *n,adj.*

president *n* **1** person having highest authority in a republic. **2** someone presiding over an assembly, society, company, etc. **presidency**

n. **preside** *vi* **1** sit in authority over a meeting, debate, etc. **2** exercise control or authority.

press[1] *vt,vi* **1** apply weight, force, or pressure to, so as to squeeze, crush, flatten, etc. **2** obtain liquid, juice, oil, etc., by pressure. **3** hold close; grasp. **4** attack hard, as in battle. **5** insist on; compel; urge; entreat. **6** oppress; harass. **7** iron. **press on** continue with an activity. ~*n* **1** machine for printing. **2** newspapers and magazines collectively. **3** machine for exerting pressure, as in extracting liquids. **4** large crowd of people. **press stud** *n* fastener for clothes having two parts pressed together.

press[2] *vt* force into service, esp. military service. **pressgang** *n* men formerly employed to force people into the army or navy. ~*vt* force (someone) into doing something.

pressure *n* **1** act of pressing. **2** force exerted by pressing; force per unit area acting on a surface. **3** compulsion; constraint. **4** cause of distress; burden. **pressure group** *n* group of people seeking to influence public opinion, government, etc. **pressure cooker** *n* special pot in which food is cooked at a high temperature under pressure. **pressurize** *vt* **1** maintain normal air pressure in (an aircraft cabin, etc.). **2** urge or compel, esp. to a course of action.

prestige *n* **1** high reputation gained through success, rank, etc.; status. **2** power to influence and impress. **prestigious** *adj.*

presume *vt,vi* **1** assume; suppose. **2** dare or venture, esp. with excessive boldness. **presumption** *n.* **presumable** *adj.* **presumably** *adv.*

pretend *vt,vi* **1** feign or affect (to do or be something). **2** lay claim to, esp. dubiously. **3** state or profess falsely. **4** venture; attempt. **5** fancy or imagine oneself as being. **pretender** *n* **1** claimant to a throne, inheritance, etc. **2** someone who pretends. **pretence** *n.*

pretentious *adj* **1** claiming or attempting things beyond one's ability. **2** affecting dignity, importance, etc. **3** ostentatious; showy. **pretentiousness** *n.* **pretentiously** *adv.* **pretension** *n* **1** laying claim to something. **2** dubious or unsupportable claim, esp. made indirectly, to some merit, importance, etc. **3** pretentiousness.

pretext *n* pretended reason or motive that conceals the real one; excuse.

pretty *adj* **1** attractive, charming, or appealing in a delicate way. **2** neat; dainty. **3** *inf* fine; good. **4** *inf* considerable. **a pretty penny** great deal of money. ~*adv* fairly; quite. **prettily** *adv.* **prettiness** *n.*

prevail *vi* **1** be or prove dominant, effective, superior, etc.; be victorious. **2** be used or exist widely; predominate. **prevail on** persuade.

prevalent *adj* used or occurring widely; common. **prevalence** *n.*

prevaricate *vi* make misleading statements; answer evasively. **prevarication** *n.*

prevent *vt* make impossible; hinder; stop. **prevention** *n.* **preventive** *adj.*

preview *n* advance showing of a play, film, exhibition, etc., before presentation to the public. *vt* see in advance.

previous *adj* **1** before something else in time or position; prior. **2** *inf* too early; premature. **previously** *adv.*

prey *n* **1** animal hunted for food. **2** habit of hunting for prey. **3** victim, as of an enemy, illness, etc. *v* **prey on** **1** hunt for food. **2** make profits out of; exploit. **3** have a destructive or depressing influence (on); weigh heavily (on).

price *n* **1** amount of money, goods, etc., for which something is bought or sold. **2** cost at which something is acquired. **3** value; worth. *vt* **1** set a price on. **2** estimate or find out the price of. **priceless** *adj* **1** valuable beyond price; invaluable. **2** *inf* very funny or absurd. **pricey** *adj inf* expensive.

prick *vt* pierce; puncture; make holes in with a sharp point. *vi,vt* feel or cause to feel sharp mental or physical pain; sting. **prick up one's ears** listen attentively. ~*n* **1** pricking or being pricked. **2** small injury or puncture caused by a sharp point. **3** sharp painful sensation. **4** *sl* penis. **prickle** *n* **1** small sharp thorn or spine. **2** tingling or prickling sensation. *vt,vi* tingle. **prickly** *adj.*

pride *n* **1** self-respect based on a true sense of personal worth. **2** arrogance about or exaggerated belief in one's own merits, achievements, etc. **3** satisfaction. **4** source of pride, esp. something splendid. **5** group of lions. **take pride in** be proud about.

priest *n* minister who officiates at religious

ceremonies and rituals. **priestess** *f n*. **priesthood** *n*.

prim *adj* excessively formal or proper in attitude or behaviour.

primary *adj* **1** first or most important. **2** simple; elementary; basic; fundamental. **primarily** *adv*. **primary colours** *pl n* three colours, for example red, green, and blue, that can be combined to give any other colour. **primary school** *n* school for children below the age of eleven (or sometimes nine).

primate *n* **1** high-ranking clergyman, such as an archbishop. **2** member of the order of mammals that includes man, apes, and monkeys.

prime *adj* **1** first or most important; primary. **2** excellent; very good. **3** necessary; essential. *n* period when something is at its best or strongest, usually the earliest period. *vt,vi* **1** put explosive into. **2** fill with food. **3** supply with information. **prime minister** *n* chief minister; leader of the government. **prime number** *n* number, such as seven, able to be divided only by itself and one. **primer** *n* **1** book for beginners. **2** cap or tube containing explosive used to set off a charge. **3** first coat of paint.

primitive *adj* **1** at the beginning of development. **2** barbarous; savage. **3** not sophisticated; rough; simple. *n* primitive person or thing.

primrose *n* wild plant bearing pale yellow flowers. *n,adj* pale yellow.

prince *n* **1** son or close male relative of a king or queen. **2** nobleman. **3** ruler of a minor state. **princely** *adj*. **princess** *n* **1** daughter or close female relative of a king or queen. **2** wife of a prince.

principal *adj* **1** chief; main. **2** of the highest rank. *n* **1** person who plays a leading part in an activity. **2** head of a university, college, or school. **3** capital sum that is borrowed or lent at interest. **principally** *adv*.

principality *n* rule of a prince or the country or state over which he rules.

principle *n* **1** basic rule, esp. one that governs one's life. **2** fundamental truth or doctrine. **3** important element of something. **4** moral behaviour.

print *vt,vi* **1** produce (letters, text, pictures, etc.) by pressing inked types, plates, etc., directly onto paper. **2** publish (a book, magazine, etc.) in this way. **3** write in separated letters or block capitals. **4** produce a picture from a negative. **5** leave (a mark, etc.) by or as if by pressing or stamping. *n* **1** printed text. **2** picture produced from an engraved or etched plate or a photographic negative. **3** cloth with a pattern printed on it. **4** mark made by or as if by pressure. **out of print** (of a book, etc.) sold out; not available. **printable** *adj* fit to appear in print. **printer** *n*.

prior[1] *n* head of a monastery.

prior[2] *adj* **1** coming before; earlier. **2** of greater importance. **prior to** before; previous to. **priority** *n* **1** greater importance; superiority. **2** state of being earlier. **3** condition of being or right to be dealt with earlier.

priory *n* religious house presided over by a prior, often attached to an abbey.

prise *vt* lift or open by means of a lever, etc.

prism *n* **1** solid figure usually having rectangular sides and triangular ends of equal size. **2** triangular prism of transparent material, used esp. for splitting light into its component colours. **prismatic** *adj*.

prison *n* **1** building used for the confinement of convicted criminals. **2** any place of confinement. **prisoner** *n* criminal or other captive kept in prison.

private *adj* **1** not public or official; secret; confidential. **2** connected with an individual; personal. **3** out of the way; isolated. *n* soldier of the lowest army or marine rank. **privacy** *n*. **privately** *adv*.

privet *n* evergreen shrub commonly used for hedges.

privilege *n* **1** right granted to a person or group. **2** advantage connected with such a right. *vt* grant a privilege to; give a special advantage to.

prize[1] *n* **1** reward won in a competition. **2** something valuable captured in war, etc.

prize[2] *vt* hold in high estimation; place a high value on.

probable *adj* likely to occur or be true. **probability** *n* likelihood, esp. when mathematically calculated. **probably** *adv*.

probation *n* **1** period during which a person is tested for his ability or suitability. **2** system by which a convicted offender is set free on condition that he reports regularly to an official and behaves well. **probationary** *adj*.

probe *vt,vi* seek for information; investigate; examine. *n* **1** investigation. **2** surgical instrument used to probe wounds, etc. **3** spacecraft capable of exploration.

problem *n* **1** difficult issue or situation. **2** matter deserving profound consideration. **3** question requiring a solution by calculation. **problematic** *adj*.

procedure *n* **1** method of doing something; technique. **2** established manner of behaviour in a given situation. **3** rules governing the conduct of business, as in parliament. **procedural** *adj*.

proceed *vi* **1** go forward; advance. **2** start or continue a course of action. **proceed from** be the result of. **proceed against** bring a legal action against. **proceeds** *pl n* profit from a sale, etc.

process *n* **1** series of connected actions; course of action. **2** method by which legal action is conducted. **3** method of making or manufacturing something. **4** bone, organ, or part that sticks out or projects. *vt* **1** preserve (food), as by drying, freezing, etc. **2** use special methods to manufacture or do something.

procession *n* **1** large number of people moving along in an ordered manner. **2** long series of things or events.

proclaim *vt* announce or make known officially or openly. **proclamation** *n*.

procreate *vt,vi* give birth to or produce (offspring). **procreation** *n*. **procreator** *n*.

procure *vt* **1** get; obtain. **2** bring about; cause. **procurement** *n*.

prod *vt* (-dd-) **1** poke; nudge. **2** urge; encourage; rouse; stir. *n* **1** poke; nudge. **2** reminder.

prodigy *n* **1** wonder; marvel; miraculous event or thing. **2** person, esp. a child, having exceptional ability or talent. **prodigious** *adj* **1** enormous. **2** extraordinary; wonderful.

produce *v* (prəˈdjuːs) *vt,vi* bring forth; bear; yield. *vt* **1** cause; bring into existence. **2** manufacture or make. **3** organize or finance (a play, film, etc.). **4** bring out; show. *n* (ˈprɔdjuːs) anything that is produced, brought forth, or made, esp. fruit or crops. **producer** *n*. **production** *n*. **product** *n* **1** something produced. **2** result of multiplying two or more numbers. **productive** *adj* able to produce, esp. effectively or efficiently. **productivity** *n*.

profane *adj* **1** showing contempt or disrespect for sacred or holy things. **2** vulgar or coarse, esp. in language. *vt* **1** defile or otherwise spoil (something holy, sacred, or pure). **2** treat with callous disrespect. **profanely** *adv*. **profanity** *n*.

profess *vt* **1** declare or claim in public. **2** pretend; declare falsely.

profession *n* **1** job or career for which special training and mental skills are required. **2** body of people in a particular profession. **3** public declaration or claim. **professional** *adj* **1** connected with a profession or those who practise it. **2** earning one's living by playing a sport. *n* professional person.

professor *n* **1** head of a teaching department in a university or similar institution. **2** someone who professes a religious belief.

proficient *adj* skilled; capable; expert; experienced. **proficiency** *n*.

profile *n* **1** view or drawing of a face seen from the side. **2** outline or sectional drawing. **3** journalistic character outline of someone; brief biography. *vt* give, present, or draw an outline of.

profit *n* **1** advantage; benefit. **2** money left over after the necessary expenses of a transaction have been paid. *vt,vi* **1** gain advantage (from). **2** be of advantage. **3** obtain profits. **profitable** *adj*.

profound *adj* **1** extremely deep. **2** felt deeply; strong; intense. **3** requiring considerable concentration; obscure; difficult. **profoundly** *adv*. **profundity** *n*.

profuse *adj* **1** unrestrained; lavish; generous. **2** very plentiful; abundant to the point of excess. **profusely** *adv*. **profusion** *n*.

programme *n* **1** list of items or events in a theatrical performance, concert, etc., or at a meeting. **2** performance consisting of several items or parts. **3** radio or television broadcast. **program** *n* list of operations and data used in or prepared for a computer. *vt,vi* (-mm-) prepare data for a computer. **programmer** *n*.

progress *n* (ˈprougres) **1** forward motion. **2** advance; development; increase or growth. *vi* (prəˈgres) **1** move forward; advance. **2** improve; get better. **progression** *n*. **progressive** *adj* **1** characterized by progress. **2** supporting political or social reforms; enlightened. **3** increasing regularly; accumulative. *n* person supporting social and political reform. **progressively** *adv*.

prohibit *vt* forbid or prevent, esp. by law; stop; ban; restrict. **prohibition** *n*. **prohibitive** *adj*.

project *n* (ˈprɔdʒekt) scheme being planned or

already being worked on. *v* (prə'dʒekt) *vt,vi* stick out; protrude; jut out. *vt* **1** throw; thrust; drive forward. **2** cast (the mind) forward to think about the distant future; plan ahead. **3** shine light or an image on something, as with a film projector. **projection** *n*. **projectile** *n* object propelled through the air; missile. **projectionist** *n* person who works a projector at a cinema. **projector** *n* machine for projecting films or picture slides on a screen.

proletariat *n* social class that owns no property and earns its living by the sale of its labour; working class.

proliferate *vt,vi* bring or come forth in increasing abundance; produce or reproduce more and more. **proliferation** *n*. **prolific** *adj* **1** plentiful; abundant. **2** producing much. **3** having numerous offspring.

prologue *n* **1** section of a book, play, poem, etc., that comes before the main part; introduction. **2** any preliminary to something more important.

prolong *vt* make longer in time or space.

promenade *n* **1** place along which one may walk, esp. near the sea. **2** short walk; stroll. *vi* walk along freely; stroll.

prominent *adj* **1** famous; well-known. **2** obvious; clear. **3** projecting; sticking out. **prominence** *n*. **prominently** *adv*.

promiscuous *adj* **1** indiscriminate, esp. in sexual relations. **2** confused; lacking order; casual. **promiscuity** *n*. **promiscuously** *adv*.

promise *n* **1** declaration; vow. **2** assurance given to do or not to do something. **3** grounds or hope for future excellence, achievement, etc. *vt,vi* make a promise (of).

promote *vt* **1** advance to a higher or more important rank, position, etc. **2** encourage the development, progress, or growth of. **3** work to make successful, acceptable, or popular. **promotion** *n*.

prompt *adj* **1** quick to act, respond, or do. **2** punctual. **3** acted on or accomplished without delay. *vt* **1** instigate; incite. **2** inspire. *vi,vt* provide or help by providing cues or suggestions. *n* act of prompting or something that prompts. **promptly** *adv*.

prone *adj* lying with the face or front of the body downwards; stretched out. **prone to** liable, inclined, or disposed (to).

prong *n* pointed end, as of a fork; spike; narrow projection.

pronoun *n* word such as *you, my, who,* or *someone,* used as a substitute for a noun.

pronounce *vt,vi* make a speech sound, esp. in a specific manner; utter; articulate. *vt* state formally; declare officially. *vi* voice an opinion (on). **pronounced** *adj* obvious; marked. **pronouncement** *n* declaration. **pronunciation** *n* act or manner of making speech sounds, esp. with regard to correctness.

proof *n* **1** irrefutable evidence, reasoning, or facts. **2** anything that serves to establish validity or truth. **3** trial; demonstration; test. **4** alcoholic strength proved or maintained by certain standards. *adj* of standard or proved strength or quality. **proof against** unable to be penetrated; invulnerable. **proofread** *vt,vi* (-read) read and correct (trial printed matter).

prop[1] *n* **1** rigid support, such as a beam or pole. **2** person or thing giving support. *vt* (-pp-) **1** *also* **prop up** prevent from caving in or falling; support. **2** place or rest against something.

prop[2] *n* object placed on stage or used by actors.

propaganda *n* false, biased, or self-serving information, usually designed to harm or discredit another person, group, etc.

propagate *vt* **1** cause to increase or multiply. **2** reproduce or transmit in reproduction. **3** spread. *vi* **1** breed; multiply. **2** move (through); be transmitted. **propagation** *n*.

propel *vt* (-ll-) cause to move forwards; drive. **propeller** *n* powered device, usually consisting of blades mounted on a revolving shaft, for propelling aircraft, ships, etc.

proper *adj* **1** suitable, appropriate, right; apt. **2** having good manners; correct. **3** within the technical or strict meaning of a term, etc. **properly** *adv*. **proper noun** *n also* **proper name** noun that refers to a specific person, place, or thing.

property *n* **1** possession(s). **2** piece of land; estate. **3** ownership. **4** quality or characteristic associated with something.

prophecy ('prɔfisi) *n* **1** prediction. **2** divine revelation. **3** prophetic declaration. **prophesy** ('prɔfisai) *vt* **1** predict; proclaim; foretell. **2** reveal by divine inspiration. *vi* declare what is to come. **prophet** *n* **1** person who speaks by divine inspiration. **2** person who predicts future events, etc. **3** inspired leader, etc. **prophetic** *adj*.

proportion *n* **1** relative size or magnitude; ratio;

comparative relation. **2** symmetry; harmony. **3** part of a whole; share; portion. **proportions** *pl n* size. ~*vt* adjust or arrange proportions of. **proportional** *adj*.

propose *vt* **1** submit for consideration; suggest. **2** recommend for membership, office, etc. **3** intend; plan to do. *vi* make a proposal of marriage. **proposal** *n* **1** act of proposing. **2** plan; scheme. **3** offer of marriage.

proposition *n* **1** suggested plan; scheme. **2** statement; assertion. **3** point or subject offered for discussion. *vt* suggest a plan, scheme, etc., to.

proprietor *n* person who owns a business.

propriety *n* **1** suitability; correctness; aptness. **2** good conduct.

propulsion *n* **1** act of propelling or state of being propelled. **2** impulse; force.

prose *n* speech, writing, or printed matter, esp as distinguished from poetry.

prosecute *vt* bring legal action against. *vi* seek legal redress. **prosecutor** *n*. **prosecution** *n* **1** act of prosecuting or state of being prosecuted. **2** lawyers acting for the Crown in a criminal lawsuit.

prospect *n* **1** expectation; probability; future outlook. **2** scenic view; outlook. **prospects** *pl n* chances of success, good fortune, etc. ~*vt,vi* search, esp. for oil or valuable minerals; explore. **prospective** *adj* anticipated; expected; likely.

prospectus *n* statement or pamphlet giving details of a coming event or of school or academic courses or describing an organization, etc.

prosperous *adj* **1** successful; flourishing. **2** having plenty of money; well-off. **3** favourable; promising. **prosperity** *n* wealth; success. **prosper** *vi* be successful; thrive.

prostitute *n* woman who charges money for sexual intercourse. *vt* **1** offer (oneself) for sexual intercourse for money. **2** sell for immediate gain; put to a base or unworthy use. **prostitution** *n*.

prostrate *adj* ('prɔstreit) **1** lying with the face downwards. **2** helpless; defenceless; exhausted. *vt* (prɔ'streit) **1** throw (oneself) down in an act of submission, humility, etc. **2** force or throw to the ground. **3** render helpless; overcome.

protagonist *n* leading character, actor, participant, spokesman, etc.

protect *vt* guard; defend; shield from harm, etc. **protection** *n*. **protective** *adj*.

protégé *n* person under the protection or guidance of another.

protein *n* type of complex organic compound, found esp. in meat, eggs, and milk, essential for metabolism.

protest *n* ('proutest) **1** serious or formal objection, disapproval, or dissent. **2** act of objecting or declaring formally. *vt,vi* (prou'test) **1** object; complain. **2** affirm seriously or solemnly.

Protestant *n* member or adherent of any of various Christian Churches outside the Roman Catholic Church.

protocol *n* etiquette, esp. in formal or diplomatic situations.

proton *n* stable positively charged particle that occurs in the nucleus of an atom.

prototype *n* first model, design, or pattern; original.

protrude *vt,vi* project or thrust out. **protuberance** *n*.

proud *adj* **1** feeling intensely pleased with an achievement, etc. **2** showing or having self-esteem, often excessive. **3** very creditable. **proudly** *adv*. **proudness** *n*.

prove *vt* **1** demonstrate to be true or genuine. **2** test; verify; demonstrate by using, etc. **3** show to be as expected or specified. *vi* turn out (to be).

proverb *n* short common saying, expressing a general truth. **proverbial** *adj*.

provide *vt* **1** equip; supply; furnish. **2** yield. *vi* supply money or means of support (for). **providing** *conj also* **provided** on condition (that).

province *n* **1** administrative division of a country. **2** area of learning, interest, or activity. **provinces** *pl n* parts of a country distinct from the leading financial, cultural, or government centres. **provincial** *adj* **1** relating to a province; not national. **2** lacking sophistication; rustic. *n* unsophisticated person.

provision *n* **1** supplying of something needed. **2** arrangement in advance. **3** stipulation. **4** something provided. **provisions** *pl n* food and other necessities. **provisional** *adj* temporary; serving only a limited function, need, etc.

proviso *n* condition; stipulation.

provoke *vt* **1** make angry; irritate; enrage. **2**

arouse; move to action. **3** cause to happen; induce. **provocation** *n*. **provocative** *adj*.

prow *n* front part of a ship or boat; bow.

prowess *n* **1** bravery; courage. **2** accomplishment, esp. showing unusual ability.

prowl *vt,vi* move about stealthily, esp. in search of something. *n* act of prowling.

proximity *n* nearness; near neighbourhood.

prude *n* person who is excessively prim or modest. **prudish** *adj*.

prudent *adj* **1** wisely cautious or careful. **2** showing caution, good judgment, etc. **prudence** *n*.

prune[1] *n* dried plum, dark brown in colour.

prune[2] *vt* **1** trim; cut off, esp. from trees and shrubs. **2** remove (excesses, etc.).

pry *vi* look inquisitively; enquire closely or furtively; examine with intrusive curiosity.

psalm *n* religious song or hymn.

pseudonym *n* false name used by a writer, etc., to conceal his identity.

psychedelic *adj* relating to or producing a joyful state of expanded consciousness.

psychiatry *n* branch of medicine concerned with treating mental illness. **psychiatric** *adj*. **psychiatrist** *n*.

psychic *adj* **1** relating to the mind or mental activities. **2** relating to unusual mental powers, such as telepathy. **3** involving a nonphysical force or influence.

psychoanalysis *n* technique or system of bringing subconscious conflicts into awareness. **psychoanalyst** *n*. **psychoanalyse** *vt* treat by psychoanalysis.

psychology *n* scientific study of mental attitudes and human or animal behaviour. **psychologist** *n*. **psychological** *adj* **1** relating to psychology. **2** arising in the mind; irrational.

psychopath *n* person suffering from severe mental and emotional instability. **psychopathic** *adj*.

psychosis *n* serious mental illness. **psychotic** *adj*.

psychosomatic *adj* relating to a physical disorder that is caused or aggravated by the emotional state.

pub *n inf also* **public house** building licensed for the sale and consumption of alcoholic drinks. **publican** *n* person responsible for running a pub.

puberty *n* age at which a person becomes sexually mature.

public *adj* **1** relating or belonging to the people of a community, country, etc. **2** general; available to all; not private. *n* **1** people in general. **2** followers; admirers. **public relations** *n* business or activity of promoting goodwill for an organization, individual, etc. **public school** *n* private independent fee-paying school.

publication *n* act or product of publishing.

publicity *n* **1** state or condition of being generally known. **2** business, activity, or methods of informing the public about a person, product, campaign, etc.

publicize *vt* make public; bring to general notice.

publish *vt,vi* produce and issue (books, etc.) for sale. *vt* make known to the public. **publisher** *n*.

pucker *vt,vi* gather into wrinkles or folds. *n* uneven fold; wrinkle.

pudding *n* **1** cooked dish of various ingredients, such as suet or sponge with fruit or meat. **2** course following the main meal; sweet; dessert.

puddle *n* small pool of water or other liquid.

puff *n* **1** brief burst of air, smoke, vapour, etc.; gust of wind. **2** draw at a cigarette, cigar, or pipe. *vi,vt* **1** send out puffs of air, smoke, etc. **2** *also* **puff up** *or* **out** swell; inflate. **3** smoke. *vi* breathe in short gasps; pant.

pull *vt,vi* tug (at) forcefully; haul; jerk. *vt* **1** move forward by means of or using force; draw. **2** tear or rip (apart, out, etc.). **3** remove from the natural or normal position by pulling. **pull apart** criticize severely. **pull faces** grimace. **pull a fast one** trick; deceive. **pull in 1** draw into a station, kerb, etc., and stop. **2** attract. **pull off** succeed in accomplishing something. **pull oneself together** regain self-control. **pull one's weight** make a significant contribution towards a common task. **pull out** withdraw; abandon; leave. **pull someone's leg** tease. **pull strings** use personal influence. **pull through** recover. **pull up 1** stop. **2** draw level in a race. ~*n* act or force of pulling. **pullover** *n* sweater; jumper.

pulley *n* wheel for raising weights by pulling downwards on a cord, etc., passing over its grooved rim.

pulp *n* **1** mass of soft moist matter. **2** moist

mixture of wood particles, rags, etc., from which paper is made. *vt,vi* reduce or be reduced to pulp.

pulpit *n* raised stand or platform from which a clergyman preaches.

pulsate *vi* beat or throb, esp. rhythmically; quiver; vibrate. **pulsation** *n*. **pulse** *n* **1** periodic throbbing of the arteries, caused by successive contraction and relaxation of the heart. **2** transient change in voltage, current, etc.

pulverize *vt,vi* grind or pound to a fine powder or be so reduced. *vt* demolish.

pump *n* machine for forcing liquids or gases to a different level, container, etc., for reducing fluid pressure, etc. *vt,vi* raise, clear, inflate, etc., with a pump. *vt* **1** move up and down repeatedly. **2** elicit by repeated questioning. **3** question for information.

pumpkin *n* large orange-coloured edible gourd.

pun *n* play on words, esp. those with similar sounds. *vi* (-nn-) make puns.

punch[1] *n* **1** sharp forceful blow, esp. with the fist. **2** forcefulness; drive. **3** tool for stamping, piercing, etc. *vt* **1** hit sharply, esp. with the fist. **2** prod; poke. **3** stamp, pierce, etc., with a punch.

punch[2] *n* drink usually made in quantity by mixing wine or spirits with fruit, spices, etc.

punctual *adj* on time; prompt. **punctuality** *n*.

punctuate *vt* **1** mark (sentences, etc.) with full stops, commas, brackets, etc. **2** give emphasis to; stress. **3** interrupt at intervals. *vi* use punctuation. **punctuation** *n* **1** various marks inserted in sentences, etc., to clarify meaning. **2** act of punctuating.

puncture *n* **1** tiny hole made by pricking or piercing. **2** loss of pressure in a tyre resulting from this. *vt* **1** prick; pierce. **2** deflate by a puncture.

pungent *adj* **1** smelling or tasting sharp or acrid. **2** caustic; biting. **pungency** *n*. **pungently** *adv*.

punish *vt* **1** inflict a penalty on; make to suffer for some offence, fault, etc.; discipline. **2** hurt; injure. **punishment** *n*.

punt[1] *n* boat with a flat bottom, moved by aid of a pole. *vt,vi* propel (a boat) by using a pole.

punt[2] *vi,n* gamble; bet.

pup *n* young dog, seal, or similar animal.

pupa *n, pl* **pupae** ('pju:pi:) inactive stage of development of an insect, between larva and adult forms. **pupal** *adj*.

pupil[1] *n* student; schoolchild.

pupil[2] *n* variable aperture in the iris of the eye through which light enters.

puppet *n* **1** figure with movable limbs controlled by strings or wires; marionette. **2** person, group, etc., under the control of another.

puppy *n* **1** young dog. **2** conceited young man.

purchase *vt* buy; obtain by payment. *n* **1** something bought. **2** act of buying. **3** leverage. **4** hold; grip. **purchase tax** *n* tax levied on purchased goods, being added to the selling price.

pure *adj* **1** not contaminated; free from mixture with anything else. **2** simple; not complicated. **3** innocent; chaste. **4** mere. **purely** *adv* entirely; solely. **purity** *n*.

purgatory *n* **1** place where souls of the dead go for punishment of earthly sins before entering heaven. **2** state or condition of temporary pain, suffering, etc.

purge *vt* **1** cleanse; remove by cleaning. **2** rid of waste, unwanted elements, etc.; clear; eliminate; remove. *vi* become cleansed, purified, etc. *n* **1** act of purging. **2** something that purges. **3** *also* **purgative** drug or agent aiding defecation.

purify *vt,vi* make or become pure. *vt* free from undesirable elements, etc. **purification** *n*.

Puritan *n* member of an extreme reform group of 16th- and 17th-century Protestants. **puritan** person who is excessively strict, esp. in matters of religion or morals. **puritanical** *adj*.

purl *n* knitting stitch that is an inverted plain stitch. *vt,vi* knit in purl.

purple *n,adj* reddish-blue or bluish-red. **purplish** *adj*.

purpose *n* **1** end or aim towards which any view, action, etc., is directed; intention. **2** reason. **on purpose** intentionally.

purr *n* low murmuring sound, as made by a contented cat. *vi* utter such a sound.

purse *n* small pouch or bag for holding coins, etc.

pursue *vt* **1** trail; follow closely; chase. **2** attend. **3** seek to gain or accomplish. **4** continue (with or on). **pursuit** *n* **1** act of pursuing. **2** hobby; pastime.

pus *n* yellowish-white matter discharged from an infected wound.

push *vt,vi* **1** press (against) forcefully; impel by

pressure. **2** urge; promote. *vt* thrust (away, through, forward, etc.) with or by force. **pushed (for)** *inf* short of. ~*n* **1** act of pushing. **2** *inf* drive; self-assertion. **3** *inf* special effort. **4** *inf* dismissal. **pushchair** *n* small chair on wheels for carrying infants.

pussy *n inf* cat.

put *vt* (-tt-; put) **1** place, deposit, lay, set, or cause to be in any position, situation, or place. **2** render; transform. **3** express; propose. **put across** *or* **over** communicate. **put (it) at** estimate (it) as. **put away 1** store. **2** save. **3** imprison; lock up. **put down 1** record; write. **2** quell. **3** kill (an animal). **put forward** suggest; propose. **put off 1** delay; defer. **2** discourage. **3** switch off. **put on 1** dress in. **2** assume; adopt. **3** wager; bet. **4** switch on. **put out 1** annoy; disturb. **2** extinguish; switch off. **put up 1** build. **2** accommodate. **3** provide; give. **put up with** tolerate. **stay put** remain; not move.

putrid *adj* **1** rotten; decaying. **2** having a foul smell. **3** *inf* awful; of poor quality. **putrefy** *vi,vt* rot; decompose. **putrefaction** *n*.

putt *vt,vi* hit a golfball so that it rolls towards the hole. *n* putted stroke. **putting** *n* game like golf involving putted strokes only.

putty *n* pliable material that sets rigid, used for holding panes of glass in frames, etc. *vt* repair, fill, etc., with putty.

puzzle *vt,vi* confuse or perplex or be confused or perplexed. **puzzle over** strain to discover a solution; expend effort to find a meaning. ~*n* **1** something that poses a problem to be worked out. **2** something that perplexes. **3** jigsaw.

PVC *n* polyvinyl chloride: man-made plastic material, either flexible or rigid, with a wide variety of uses.

Pygmy *n* member of a central African hunting people of small stature. **pygmy** very small person.

pyjamas *pl n* loose trousers and jacket for sleeping in.

pylon *n* tall structure, used esp. to convey high-voltage electric cables over open country.

pyramid *n* **1** solid figure consisting usually of a square base and triangular sloping faces that meet at the top. **2** enormous pyramid-shaped stone monument, esp. of ancient Egypt.

Pyrex *n Tdmk* heat-resistant glass or glassware.

python *n* large snake that kills its prey by squeezing.

Q

quack[1] *n* harsh cry of a duck. *vi* make such a sound.

quack[2] *n* medical practitioner who is unqualified or unreliable.

quadrangle *n* **1** quadrilateral. **2** *also inf* **quad** quadrilateral courtyard, esp. within a school. **quadrangular** *adj*.

quadrant *n* quarter section of a circle.

quadrilateral *n* figure with four sides and four angles. *adj* having four sides and four angles.

quadruped *n* animal with four legs. *adj* having four legs.

quadruple *vt,vi* increase fourfold. *adj* **1** four times as much. **2** having four members, parts, etc.

quadruplet *n* **1** *also inf* **quad** one of four children born at the same time to the same mother. **2** group having four members or parts.

quail[1] *n* small game bird.

quail[2] *vi* shrink with dread or fear; tremble.

quaint *adj* pleasingly odd or old-fashioned. **quaintly** *adv*.

quake *vi* tremble or shake. *n inf* short for **earthquake.**

Quaker *n* member of a pacifist Christian sect advocating simplicity of worship, dress, etc.

qualify *vt,vi* make or become suitable, appropriate, or acceptable (for). *vi* reach a required standard or level. *vt* **1** restrict or modify (a statement, proposal, etc.). **2** temper or moderate. **qualification** *n*.

quality *n* **1** distinguishing attribute or characteristic. **2** degree of fineness or excellence. **3** excellence. **4** accomplishment. **qualitative** *adj*.

qualm *n* pang of conscience; misgiving.

quandary *n* dilemma; perplexed turmoil.

quantify *vt* assess or ascertain the amount of. **quantification** *n*.

quantity *n* **1** amount. **2** large amount.

quarantine *n* careful isolation imposed on people, animals, etc., to prevent the spread of an infectious disease. *vt* put into quarantine; isolate.

quarrel *n* **1** disagreement or dispute. **2** cause for complaint. *vi* (-ll-) argue or disagree; squabble; dispute.

quarry[1] *n* shallow mine or pit from which stone, slate, etc., is excavated. *vt* mine (stone, etc.) from a quarry.

quarry[2] *n* animal, person, or other object of pursuit; game; prey.

quart *n* liquid or dry measure equal to two pints (approx. 1.1 litres) and one quarter of a bushel respectively.

quarter *n* **1** one of four equal parts or portions; one divided by four. **2** *US* twenty-five cents or a coin having this value. *vt* **1** cut or divide into quarters. **2** place or provide someone, esp. soldiers, with lodgings. **quarterly** *adj,adv.* **quarterdeck** *n* rear section of the upper deck of a ship, often reserved for officers. **quartermaster** *n* **1** petty officer on a ship responsible for steering, signals, etc. **2** officer, esp. in the army, responsible for the provision of food, clothing, lodging, etc. **quarters** *pl n* living accommodation.

quartet *n* group of four persons or things, esp. four singers or musicians.

quartz *n* common colourless crystalline mineral.

quash *vt* **1** subdue; suppress. **2** annul or invalidate (a decision, law, etc.).

quaver *n* musical note lasting one eighth the time of a semibreve. *vi* quiver; quake; tremble.

quay *n* man-made landing place to which ships may come to load or unload; wharf.

queasy *adj* **1** feeling or causing nausea; sickly. **2** ill at ease. **queasily** *adv.* **queasiness** *n.*

queen *n* **1** female monarch or wife of a king. **2** woman, thing, etc., regarded as very fine or outstanding. **3** fertile female in a colony of wasps, bees, ants, etc. **4** court card whose value is higher than the jack and lower than the king. **5** most powerful chess piece able to move any distance in a straight or diagonal line. **6** *sl* homosexual male. **queenly** *adj.*

queer *adj* **1** odd; peculiar; strange. **2** *sl* homosexual. *n sl* homosexual. *vt sl* ruin or spoil. **queerly** *adv.*

quell *vt* suppress; subdue; calm.

quench *vt* **1** satisfy (a thirst, etc.). **2** extinguish or smother something such as a fire.

query *n* **1** question. **2** point of doubt. **3** question mark. *vt,vi* raise (a question); ask for (an answer or clarification).

quest *n* search or hunt, esp. one carried on fervently. *vi* engage in a quest; search.

question *n* **1** request for information, a decision, clarification, etc. **2** point of doubt; uncertainty. **3** problem or matter for discussion; issue. *vt,vi* ask questions (of). *vt* cast doubt upon; challenge. **beyond question** indisputable. **call into question** cast doubt upon. **out of the question** impossible. **question mark** *n* mark (?) used at the end of a sentence, phrase, or word to indicate a question. **questionnaire** *n* written list of questions used to gather information, obtain opinions, etc.

queue *n* line of people or things waiting their turn to do or obtain something. *vi* form or wait in a queue.

quibble *n* trivial or petty objection, criticism, evasion, etc. *vi* argue about trivial points; evade by petty criticism or objection.

quick *adj* fast or sudden; swift. *adv* rapidly; swiftly. *n* sensitive flesh at the edge of a fingernail or toenail. **the quick and the dead** the living and the dead. **cut to the quick** hurt or offend deeply. **quicken** *vt,vi* **1** hasten; accelerate. **2** stimulate; revive. **quicksand** *n* soft wet sand into which objects are liable to sink. **quicksilver** *n* mercury. **like quicksilver** moving very swiftly. **quickstep** *n* **1** quick marching step. **2** fast ballroom-dancing step. **quick-tempered** *adj* having a hasty or hot temper; easily angered. **quick-witted** *adj* thinking swiftly; alert.

quid *n, pl* **quid** *sl* pound (money).

quiet *adj* **1** free from harsh noise or disturbance. **2** tranquil; calm. **3** subdued; restrained. *n* calmness; stillness; tranquillity. **quietly** *adv.* **quieten** *vt,vi also* **quiet** make or become quiet; subdue; ease.

quill *n* **1** large feather from the wing or tail of a bird. **2** such a feather made into a pen for writing. **3** one of the spines of a hedgehog, porcupine, etc.

quilt *n* bed covering made of two layers of material filled with some soft fabric and sewn together. *vt,vi* make a quilt (of).

quinine *n* alkaline substance originally obtained from the bark of a tree and used medicinally, esp. in treating malaria.

quintet *n* group of five persons or things, esp. five singers or musicians.

quirk *n* **1** unusual or odd trait or characteristic. **2** sudden twist or turn.

quit *vt,vi* (-tt-; quitted *or* quit) **1** stop; cease. **2**

give up; relinquish; resign. **3** discharge (a debt, etc.). **4** depart (from); leave.

quite *adv* **1** wholly or entirely. **2** *inf* fairly; moderately. **3** positively. *interj* expression of agreement or concurrence.

quiver[1] *vi* shake; tremble; quake. *n* act of quivering; tremble.

quiver[2] *n* case or sheath for holding arrows.

quiz *n* series of questions, often taking the form of a competition between two or more people. *vt* (-zz-) question closely.

quizzical *adj* **1** comical or odd. **2** questioning; perplexed. **3** teasing. **quizzically** *adv*.

quoit *n* ring of rubber, metal, etc., used in a game by being thrown at an upright peg in an attempt to encircle it.

quota *n* prescribed share or amount of something that is allotted to or expected from a person, group, etc.; allotment.

quote *vt* **1** repeat (a passage, sentence, etc.) from a written or spoken source. **2** cite as an example. **3** state the price or cost of. *vi* use a quotation or quotations. *n* quotation. **quotation** *n* **1** *also* **quote** something quoted. **2** act of quoting. **quotation marks** *pl n* punctuation marks ' and ' or " and " used to enclose and indicate a quotation.

R

rabbi *n* **1** Jewish priest. **2** scholar and teacher of the Jewish law.

rabbit *n* small burrowing animal of the hare family with long ears, a short tufty tail, and soft fur. *vi* hunt rabbits.

rabble *n* noisy crowd or throng; mob.

rabid *adj* **1** fervent; wildly enthusiastic. **2** raging; violent. **3** relating to or having rabies.

rabies *n* fatal viral disease that is transmitted by the bite of an infected animal, esp. a dog.

race[1] *n* **1** contest of speed between people or animals in running, swimming, driving, etc. **2** any contest in which people compete to be the first to do or achieve something. *vi* **1** take part in a race. **2** hurry; go quickly. *vt* **1** run a race or compete with. **2** cause (a horse, car, etc.) to take part in a race. **racecourse** *n* track on which races, esp. horseraces, are held. **racehorse** *n* horse trained and used for racing.

race[2] *n* **1** group of people connected by common ancestry or blood. **2** subdivision of mankind to which people belong by virtue of their hereditary physical characteristics. **3** any group of people, plants, or animals regarded as a distinct class. **race relations** *pl n* relationships between people of different races, esp. within a single society. **racial** *adj* of or relating to race or races. **racially** *adv*.

rack *n* **1** framework, holder, or container; storage or display unit. **2** former instrument of torture on which people were tied and stretched. *vt* **1** torture on the rack. **2** torment. **3** arrange on or in a rack. **rack one's brains** strive to remember or understand something.

racket[1] *n* **1** noisy disturbance; uproar. **2** *sl* any illegal or dishonest scheme, activity, business, etc.

racket[2] *n* bat used in tennis, squash, etc., consisting of a rounded frame across which strings are stretched. **rackets** *n* kind of tennis played in a walled court.

radar *n* system for determining the presence and position of an object, such as a ship, by transmitting a beam of radio waves and measuring the direction and time taken for the echo to return from the object.

radial *adj* **1** branching out from a central point; radiating. **2** of or relating to a radius.

radiant *adj* **1** glowing with heat or brightness; shining. **2** glowing with happiness, joy, hope, etc. **3** emitted in rays.

radiate *v* ('reidieit) *vt,vi* **1** emit radiation. *vt* transmit or give out a particular emotion or feeling. *vi* spread or branch out from a central point. *adj* ('reidiit) having rays or radiating from a centre. **radiation** *n* **1** emission of energy in the form of light, heat, sound, electrons, etc. **2** energy so emitted and propagated. **3** radiate arrangement. **radiator** *n* **1** heating device through which hot air, water, steam, etc., passes. **2** device by which a car engine is kept cool.

radical *adj* **1** basic; fundamental. **2** essential; complete. **3** favouring fundamental political, social, or other reforms. **4** of or arising from a root. *n* person favouring radical reforms.

radio *n* **1** transmission of information by waves transmitted through the atmosphere. **2** device for receiving radio broadcasts; wireless. **3** broadcasts so received. *vt,vi* transmit a message, etc., by radio.

radioactivity *n* spontaneous disintegration of

unstable atomic nuclei with the emission of radiation. **radioactive** *adj* undergoing or relating to radioactivity.

radish *n* small crisp white or red root of a plant of the mustard family, usually eaten raw.

radium *n* radioactive metallic element.

radius *n, pl* **radii** (ˈreidiai) *or* **radiuses** **1** line from the centre of a circle or sphere to its perimeter or surface. **2** length of such a line. **3** any radiating or raylike part. **4** circular area defined by the length of its radius. **5** range or extent of experience, influence, activity, etc.

raffia *n* fibre obtained from the leafstalks of a Madagascan palm, used for weaving baskets, matting, etc.

raffle *n* scheme for raising money in which tickets give the purchaser the chance of winning a prize, the winning tickets being randomly selected. *vt* offer as a prize in a raffle.

raft *n* buoyant material, such as logs, fastened together into a platform to transport goods or people by water.

rafter *n* sloping timber or beam on which a roof is supported.

rag[1] *n* **1** scrap of cloth; torn, dirty, or worthless fragment. **2** *sl* newspaper or magazine, esp. one of poor quality. **rags** *pl n* old or tattered clothing. **ragged** *adj* **1** rough, tattered, or torn. **2** uneven; jagged. **3** irregular or imperfect.

rag[2] *vt* (-gg-) **1** tease or play jokes on. **2** scold. *n* **1** joke or escapade. **2** organized series of games, events, etc., by students to publicize the collection of money for charity.

rage *n* **1** extreme anger; fury. **2** violence or intensity of fire, wind, disease, etc. **3** intensity of emotion, appetite, or enthusiasm. **4** anything arousing widespread enthusiasm. *vi* **1** display violent anger. **2** move, continue, prevail, etc., with great intensity or violence.

raid *n* surprise attack, esp. one undertaken to capture goods, personnel, etc. *vt,vi* make a surprise attack (on).

rail *n* **1** horizontal bar of wood or metal acting as a barrier, support, etc. **2** fence. **3** one of a pair of parallel metal bars laid as a track for trains, etc. **4** railway transportation. *vt* enclose with a rail; fence. **railing** *n* fence or framework of rails. **railway** *n* **1** permanent track of rails on which trains may transport passengers, goods, etc. **2** complete network of such tracks together with stations, land, etc.

rain *n* **1** drops of water falling from clouds, condensed from atmospheric water vapour. **2** an instance of this; shower. **3** rapid heavy fall or occurrence of anything. *vt,vi* fall or cause to fall as or like rain. *vt* give (praise, gifts, etc.) in large quantities. **rain cats and dogs** rain very heavily. **rainbow** *n* banded arc of spectral colours visible in the sky during or just after a shower of rain. **rainfall** *n* **1** fall of rain; shower. **2** amount of water falling as rain, snow, etc., in a given area within a given period of time.

raise *vt* **1** elevate; lift up. **2** build; erect. **3** bring up for consideration. **4** initiate or inspire; provoke. **5** bring up (children, etc.); rear. **6** collect or gather. **7** increase in degree, size, intensity, etc. **8** evoke; suggest. **9** promote in rank, dignity, etc. **10** summon up. **11** bring back to life. **12** remove or lift (a ban, siege, etc.).

raisin *n* sweet dried grape.

rajah *n* king, prince, or chief, esp. in India.

rake *n* tool with a long handle and teeth or prongs at one end used for gathering leaves, etc. *vt* **1** gather, collect, or smooth with a rake. **2** gather in or collect up. **3** search through carefully. *vi* use a rake. **rake up** bring up or reveal (something, esp. from the past).

rally *vt,vi* **1** reassemble. **2** bring or come together for some common purpose. *vi* **1** gather to support or assist a person, cause, etc. **2** regain strength or vigour; recover. *n* **1** recovery. **2** gathering of people supporting a cause, taking part in a sporting event, etc.

ram *n* **1** male sheep. **2** device used to batter, crush, or drive against something. *vt* (-mm-) **1** strike or crash against with great force. **2** force, cram, or press.

ramble *vi* **1** wander about; stroll. **2** grow in or follow a meandering course. **3** talk or write aimlessly or incoherently. *n* walk taken for pleasure. **rambler** *n*.

ramp *n* sloping surface joining two levels.

rampage *vi* rush about wildly or destructively. *n* wild, violent, or destructive behaviour. **on the rampage** very angry; engaged in destructive behaviour.

rampant *adj* **1** rife; unchecked. **2** violent in opinion, action, etc.

rampart *n* **1** mound of earth, usually surmounted by a parapet, fortifying a castle, fort, etc. **2** any defence or protection.

ramshackle *adj* loosely constructed or held together; shaky; derelict.

ran *v pt of* **run.**

ranch *n* large farm, esp. in America, for rearing cattle, horses, or sheep. **rancher** *n*.

rancid *adj* having an unpleasant stale smell or taste; rank.

rancour *n* angry resentment; bitterness.

random *adj* happening, done, etc., without aim or purpose; chance; haphazard. *n* **at random** without choice, purpose, method, etc. **randomly** *adv*.

rang *v pt of* **ring.**

range *n* **1** limits within which variation is possible. **2** extent or scope. **3** possible distance of movement, flight, etc. **4** place with targets for shooting practice. **5** chain of mountains. **6** row or line. **7** class, set, or series. **8** large cooking stove. *vt* **1** arrange in order, esp. in rows or lines. **2** dispose or place in a particular group, class, etc. **3** travel through or over; roam. *vi* **1** vary within specified limits. **2** extend or run, esp. in a given direction. **3** roam or wander (over). **4** occur within a certain area or time. **5** have a particular range.

rank[1] *n* **1** position or standing in a scale or graded body. **2** row or line, esp. of soldiers. *vt* **1** arrange in a row or rank. **2** assign to a certain position, station, class, etc. *vi* hold a certain position. **rank and file** *n* body of soldiers in an army or people in any other organization, as opposed to the officers or leaders. **ranks** *pl n* soldiers as opposed to officers.

rank[2] *adj* **1** growing vigorously or producing luxuriant vigorous growth. **2** having a strong unpleasant smell or taste. **3** utter; complete. **rankly** *adv*. **rankness** *n*.

rankle *vi* annoy; hurt one's pride.

ransack *vt* **1** search thoroughly or energetically. **2** plunder.

ransom *n* **1** redeeming of a kidnapped person, captured goods, etc., for a price. **2** price paid or demanded. *vt* release from captivity, detention, etc., by paying the price demanded.

rant *vi* shout angrily; rage.

rap *vt,vi* (-pp-) **1** knock, strike, or tap, esp. quickly. **2** *also* **rap out** say sharply. *n* **1** quick light blow; tap. **2** sound of this. **3** *sl* blame or punishment, esp. a prison sentence.

rape *n* **1** crime of having sexual intercourse with a woman without her consent. **2** act of taking by force. *vt,vi* commit rape (on). **rapist** *n*.

rapid *adj* quick; fast; swift. **rapids** *pl n* part of a river where the water flows very swiftly. **rapidity** *n*. **rapidly** *adv*.

rapier *n* sword with a slender pointed blade used for thrusting.

rapt *adj* **1** enthralled; enchanted. **2** totally absorbed or engrossed.

rapture *n* ecstatic delight; joy; pleasure. **rapturous** *adj*.

rare[1] **1** seldom occurring, found, experienced, etc. **2** remarkable or unusual, esp. in excellence. **3** of low density. **rarely** *adv*. **rarity** *n*.

rare[2] *adj* not completely cooked; underdone.

rascal *n* **1** scoundrel; rogue. **2** mischievous child or animal. **rascally** *adj,adv*.

rash[1] *adj* hasty in speech or action; reckless.

rash[2] *n* skin eruption, as of spots.

rasher *n* thin slice of bacon.

rasp *vt,vi* grate; sound harsh. *n* harsh grating sound.

raspberry *n* shrub of the rose family producing small juicy red edible fruit.

rat *n* **1** long-tailed rodent resembling but larger than the mouse. **2** *sl* despicable person. **smell a rat** be suspicious about. ~*v* (-tt-) **rat on** *sl* desert or betray (friends, a cause, etc.).

rate *n* **1** quantity, amount, degree, etc., relative to a unit of something else. **2** price. **3** speed of movement, action, etc. **4** tax paid by householders, companies, etc., to cover the supply of local services and amenities. *vt* **1** appraise the value or worth of. **2** esteem; consider. **3** deserve. **4** determine (prices, etc.) at a certain rate. *vi* **1** be classed or ranked. **2** have status, value, position, etc.

rather *adv* **1** more readily; preferably. **2** somewhat; quite. **3** with more reason, justice, etc. **4** more accurately or properly. **5** on the contrary.

ratio *n* fixed numerical relation between two similar magnitudes; proportion.

ration *n* fixed allowance; share. *vt* **1** apportion; share out. **2** restrict to or provide with rations.

rational *adj* **1** of, relating to, or based on reason. **2** able to reason. **3** reasonable; sensible. **rationality** *n*. **rationally** *adv*. **ration-**

alize *vt* **1** make rational; justify unconscious behaviour. **2** make (an industry, process, etc.) more efficient; streamline. *vi* think in a rational manner; reason.

rattle *vi,vt* make or cause to make a series of short sharp sounds; vibrate noisily. *vi also* **rattle on** chatter. *vt* **1** say or do rapidly. **2** *sl* confuse or disturb (someone). *n* **1** rapid succession of short sharp sounds. **2** device producing a rattling sound, such as a baby's toy.

raucous *adj* rough or harsh sounding. **raucously** *adv*.

ravage *n* **1** violent destructive action. **2** devastation; damage. *vt* damage or devastate. *vi* cause great damage.

rave *vi,vt* talk or utter wildly or incoherently. *vi also* **rave about** talk or write very enthusiastically (about). *n* **1** act of raving. **2** extravagant praise.

raven *n* large bird of the crow family with shiny black plumage and a harsh cry. *adj,n* shiny black.

ravenous *adj* **1** extremely hungry. **2** greedy for praise, recognition, etc. **ravenously** *adv*.

ravine steep valley; gorge; canyon.

ravioli *n* small pieces of pasta enclosing chopped meat, etc., usually served in a tomato sauce.

ravish *vt* **1** seize and carry away forcibly. **2** rape. **3** enrapture.

raw *adj* **1** not cooked. **2** in a natural state; unprocessed. **3** inexperienced. **4** painfully open or exposed, as a wound. **5** crude; vulgar. **6** harsh; unfair; unpleasant. **rawness** *n*.

ray *n* **1** narrow beam of light, etc. **2** tiny amount of hope, comfort, etc.; spark. **3** line or structure radiating from a centre. *vi,vt* radiate.

rayon *n* man-made textile or fibre made from cellulose.

raze *vt* demolish or destroy (buildings, etc.) completely.

razor *n* instrument fitted with cutting edges, used esp. for shaving hair.

reach *vt* **1** get to; arrive at; attain; come to. **2** establish contact with. **3** amount to; total. *vt,vi* extend as far as. **reach for** stretch up or out for in order to grasp and bring closer. ~*n* **1** act of reaching. **2** range; extent covered.

react *vi* **1** reciprocate. **2** respond to a stimulus. **3** act in opposition or in reverse. **4** interact. **reaction** *n* **1** reciprocal action, movement, or tendency. **2** response to a stimulus. **3** response to an event, idea, etc. **4** tendency or movement in politics towards extreme conservatism. **5** interaction between chemicals. **reactionary** *adj* relating to reaction, esp. in politics. *n* reactionary person.

read *v* (read) *vt,vi* **1** apprehend the meaning of (letters, words, etc.). **2** *also* **read out** utter (printed or written matter) aloud. **3** be occupied in reading. **4** study (a subject). **5** learn of by reading. *vt* **1** interpret. **2** register; indicate. **3** predict; foretell. *vi* have a certain wording. **read between the lines** deduce an implied meaning not openly stated. ~*n* act of reading. **reader** *n*.

readjust *vt* adjust again or afresh; rearrange; readapt.

ready *adj* **1** fully prepared. **2** willing. **3** prompt; quick. **4** inclined; apt. **5** likely or liable (to). **6** immediately available. **get ready 1** prepare. **2** dress oneself. *n* **at the ready** in position. **readily** *adv* willingly; without delay.

real *adj* **1** true; genuine; authentic. **2** actual; not imaginary or fictitious. **really** *adv* **1** in fact; actually. **2** truly; genuinely. **reality** *n*. **realism** *n* interest in or concern for the real or actual. **realist** *n*. **realistic** *adj*. **realistically** *adv*.

realize *vt,vi* comprehend; appreciate; be aware. *vt* **1** bring to fruition. **2** convert into cash. *vi* be sold for; bring as proceeds; gain. **realization** *n*.

realm *n* **1** kingdom; domain. **2** region or sphere in which something rules or predominates.

reap *vt,vi* cut or harvest (grain). *vt* obtain as a result or recompense.

rear[1] *n* **1** back part of anything. **2** position behind or in the rear. **3** buttocks. *adj* of, at, or in the rear. **rear admiral** *n* naval officer ranking immediately below a vice-admiral. **rearguard** *n* military detachment that brings up and protects the rear, esp. in retreat.

rear[2] *vt* **1** care for and bring to maturity. **2** lift up; erect. *vi* rise up on the hind legs. **rear up** rise up in anger, resentment, etc.

reason *n* **1** ground, cause, or motive. **2** justification; explanation. **3** mental ability of logical argument. **4** good sense. **5** sanity. *vi,vt* **1** think or argue logically (about). **2** conclude or infer (that). **3** urge or persuade by reasoning. **reasonable** *adj* **1** amenable to reason. **2** based on reason; sensible or sound. **3** able to reason. **4** not excessive; moderate. **reasonably** *adv.*

reassure *vt* allay (fears, doubts, etc.); restore confidence or tranquillity to. **reassurance** *n.*

rebate *n* return of part of an amount paid for goods, a service, etc.

rebel *n* ('rebəl) person who defies authority or control. *vi* (ri'bel) (-ll-) resist; oppose. **rebel against** show or feel strong aversion (for). **rebellion** *n.* **rebellious** *adj.*

rebound *vt,vi* (ri'baund) spring back or cause to spring back. *n* ('ri:baund) act of rebounding; recoil.

rebuff *vt* treat scornfully; turn away; snub. *n* rejection; abrupt dismissal.

rebuke *vt,n* reprimand.

recalcitrant *adj* unwilling to submit; wayward; wilful; stubborn. **recalcitrance** *n.*

recall *vt* **1** remember. **2** call back. **3** revoke or withdraw. *n* **1** act or instance of recalling. **2** memory.

recede *vi* **1** move back; retreat. **2** become more distant. **3** slope backwards. **4** withdraw from a bargain, promise, etc. **5** decline in value, etc.

receipt *n* **1** written acknowledgement of payment or delivery. **2** act of receiving; fact of being received. *vt* mark (a bill) as paid. *vt,vi* write or give a receipt for. **receipts** *pl n* amount received.

receive *vt* **1** take into one's possession; gain; get. **2** encounter, experience, or undergo. **3** bear; sustain. **4** gain knowledge of; learn. **5** welcome; admit. *vi* **1** receive something. **2** buy and sell stolen goods. **receiver** *n* **1** someone or something that receives. **2** device for converting electrical signals into their desired form.

recent *adj* occurring, appearing, done, etc., just before the present time; fresh; not remote. **recently** *adv.*

receptacle *n* **1** container. **2** portion of a plant stem bearing a flower or flower head.

reception *n* **1** act of receiving or being received. **2** manner of being received. **3** formal social gathering. **4** area in an office, hotel, etc., where visitors are received. **5** quality attained in receiving radio signals, etc. **receptionist** *n* person employed to receive visitors, answer the telephone, etc. **receptive** *adj* able, quick, or willing to receive suggestions, requests, etc.

recess (ri'ses, 'ri:ses) **1** part or area that is set back; alcove. **2** *also* **recesses** secluded inner place or area. **3** *US* temporary break; holiday. *vt* **1** place in a recess. **2** make a recess in or of.

recession *n* **1** withdrawal. **2** receding part. **3** decline or falling off in business activity.

recipe *n* formula or method, esp. for preparing a dish in cookery.

recipient *n* person who receives.

reciprocal *adj* **1** given, felt, etc., on both sides; mutual. **2** given, done, etc., in return. *n* reciprocal relationship; equivalent; counterpart. **reciprocate** *vt,vi* **1** do, feel, etc., (something similar) in return. **2** give and receive; interchange.

recite *vt,vi* repeat aloud, as from memory. *vt* read or narrate before an audience. **recital** *n* **1** musical performance, poetry reading, etc. **2** detailed account; statement; description.

reckless *adj* careless of consequences; heedless; rash. **recklessly** *adv.*

reckon *vt,vi* add (up); calculate. *vt* consider; regard as; think. **reckon with 1** settle accounts with. **2** take into consideration.

reclaim *vt* **1** render useable for cultivation, habitation, etc. **2** recover from waste products. **3** bring back from error, sin, etc. **reclamation** *n.*

recline *vi,vt* lean back or cause to lean back. **reclinable** *adj.*

recluse *n* hermit.

recognize *vt* **1** identify; know again. **2** perceive; realize. **3** acknowledge or accept the existence, truth, etc., of. **4** show appreciation of by a reward, etc. **recognition** *n.* **recognizable** *adj.*

recoil *vi* **1** draw or shrink back, as in fear, horror, etc. **2** spring back when released, as a firearm. **3** rebound or react upon. *n* act or instance of recoiling.

recollect *vt,vi* recall; remember. **recollection** *n.*

recommend *vt* **1** speak or write of favourably; commend. **2** urge as advisable; advise. **3** entrust to. **4** make acceptable or likeable. **recommendable** *adj.* **recommendation** *n.*

recompense *vt* **1** compensate, repay, or reward. **2** compensate for (a loss, etc.). *n* compensation; repayment; remuneration.

reconcile *vt* **1** make no longer opposed or hostile. **2** settle. **3** make consistent or compatible. **reconciliation** *n.*

reconstruct *vt* **1** rebuild. **2** recreate from surviving information. **reconstruction** *n.*

record *v* (ri'kɔ:d) *vt* **1** set down for future reference, esp. in writing. **2** produce in a lasting form, as on magnetic tape. **3** register; indicate. *vi* record music, etc. *n* ('rekɔ:d) **1** written account. **2** something preserving evidence of the past. **3** aggregate of past achievements, actions, etc.; career. **4** attainment, occurrence, etc., that surpasses all others. **5** flat disc with a spiral groove played on a gramophone to reproduce music, etc. **6** list of a person's crimes. **on record** stated or known publicly. **recorder** *n* wind instrument similar to the flute.

recount *vt* **1** relate or tell in detail. **2** enumerate.

recover *vt* **1** regain; retrieve; reclaim. **2** secure compensation for; make up for. *vi* **1** regain health, composure, balance, etc. **2** get back to a former or normal position, state, etc. **recovery** *n.*

recreation *n* **1** refreshment and relaxation afforded by exercise, a pastime, etc. **2** hobby, exercise, or other diversion providing this. **recreational** *adj.*

recriminate *vi* accuse one's accuser. **recrimination** *n.*

recruit *n* recently enlisted member, esp. of the armed forces. *vt,vi* enlist (new personnel, etc.). **recruitment** *n.*

rectangle *n* four-sided figure with four right angles. **rectangular** *adj.*

rectify *vt* set or put right; remedy; correct. **rectification** *n.*

rector *n* clergyman of a parish formerly returning tithes. **rectory** *n* residence of a rector.

rectum *n* lower end of the intestine.

recuperate *vi* recover from illness or fatigue. *vt* recover (financial losses). **recuperation** *n.*

recur *vi* (-rr-) **1** occur again; be repeated. **2** return to the mind, in conversation, etc. **recurrence** *n.*

red *n* **1** colour of the spectrum that is the colour of fresh blood, ripe tomatoes, etc. **2** *also* **Red** someone who is radical in politics, esp. a communist. **in the red** in debt. **see red** become very angry. ~*adj* of the colour red. **reddish** *adj.* **redness** *n.* **redcurrant** *n* shrub bearing small red edible berries. **redden** *vt,vi* make or become red. *vi* blush. **red-handed** *adj,adv* in the act of performing a deed, committing a crime, etc. **red tape** *n* complicated official or administrative procedure.

redeem *vt* **1** buy or get back; recover; pay off. **2** convert (bonds, etc.) into cash. **3** fulfil (a pledge, etc.). **4** make amends for. **5** deliver from sin. **redemption** *n.*

redress *vt* set right; remedy; repair; adjust. *n* compensation; reparation.

reduce *vt,vi* make or become smaller or less; diminish; decrease. *vt* **1** bring or force into a certain state, form, etc. **2** lower; weaken; subdue. **reduction** *n.*

redundant *adj* **1** excessive; superfluous; unnecessary. **2** deprived of a job through being superfluous, etc. **redundancy** *n.*

reed *n* **1** hollow straight stem of any of various tall grasses. **2** vibrating piece of cane or metal in some wind instruments. **3** wind instrument that sounds by means of a reed.

reef *n* narrow ridge of sand, rocks, etc., at or just under the surface of water.

reek *vi* smell strongly or unpleasantly; stink. *vt* emit (smoke, etc.). *n* strong unpleasant smell.

reel[1] *n* cylinder, frame, or spool on which thread, wire, film, etc., may be wound. *vt* wind on a reel. **reel off** say, write, or produce easily and quickly.

reel[2] *vi* sway; rock; stagger; whirl. *n* act of reeling; stagger.

refectory *n* large communal dining hall.

refer *v* (-rr-) *vt,vi* direct attention, etc., (to). *vt* submit; assign. **refer to 1** be concerned with; relate to. **2** resort to for help, information, etc. **3** mention or allude (to). **referee** *n* **1** person to whom something is referred for decision. **2** umpire in certain games. **3** person who supplies a written reference. *vi* act as a referee. **reference** *n* **1** act of referring. **2** mention or allusion. **3** direction of attention to a person or thing. **4** written statement as to character, abilities, etc. **5** relation; regard. **referendum** *n, pl* **referendums** *or* **referenda** (refə'rendə) referring of legislative measures to the direct vote of the electorate for approval or rejection.

refine *vt,vi* **1** make or become fine; purify; separate out. **2** make or become more polished, elegant, etc. **refined** *adj.* **refinement** *n.* **refinery** *n* establishment for refining oil, sugar, etc.

reflation *n* government action taken to stimulate the economy. **reflationary** *adj.*

reflect *vt,vi* **1** cast or throw back light, heat, etc.

2 produce an image (of). *vt* 1 mirror; express; reproduce. 2 rebound; bring as a consequence. *vi also* **reflect on** 1 think about; contemplate. 2 cast credit, dishonour, etc., on. **reflection** *n*. **reflector** *n* surface or device that reflects light, heat, sound, etc.

reflex *n* involuntary reaction; automatic response. **reflexive verb** *n* verb having an identical subject and direct object.

reform *vt* improve by removing abuses, inequalities, etc.; change for the better. *vi,vt* abandon or cause to abandon (evil habits, crime, etc.). *n* act or instance of reforming; improvement. **reformation** *n*.

refract *vt,vi* appear to bend or be bent by the action of light or other waves. **refraction** *n*.

refrain[1] *vi* keep oneself from; forbear.

refrain[2] *n* recurring phrase or verse.

refresh *vt,vi* revive; restore; renew. *vt* stimulate or revive (the memory). **refreshment** *n* food or drink. **refreshments** *pl n* light meal.

refrigerator *n* cabinet in which food, drink, etc., may be kept at a low temperature. **refrigerate** *vt,vi* freeze, chill, or keep cool in a refrigerator. **refrigeration** *n*.

refuge *n* 1 shelter or protection from danger, trouble, etc. 2 place or person affording this. **refugee** *n* person who flees from warfare, persecution, etc., esp. to a foreign country.

refund *vt* (ri'fʌnd) pay back; reimburse. *n* ('ri:fʌnd) repayment; sum repaid.

refuse[1] (ri'fju:z) *vt* decline to do, accept, give, grant, etc. *vi* withhold or decline acceptance, consent, compliance, etc.

refuse[2] ('refju:s) *n* rubbish; waste.

refute *vt* prove to be false or in error.

regain *vt* 1 win or get back; recover. 2 reach or attain again.

regal *adj* 1 of, like, or befitting a king; royal. 2 stately; dignified; elegant.

regard *vt* 1 consider; look upon; take into account; heed. 2 have or display respect for; esteem. 3 relate to; concern. *vt,vi* look steadily (at). *n* 1 attention; heed. 2 respect; esteem. 3 reference; connection. **regards** *pl n* greetings. **regardless** *adj* heedless or careless (of). *adv* without regard for expense, difficulties, etc.

regatta *n* event in which yachts and other boats are raced.

regent *n* person ruling in a kingdom during the minority, illness, incapacity, etc., of the sovereign. **regency** *n,adj*.

regime *n* 1 system or method of government. 2 prevailing system or authority.

regiment *n* ('redʒimənt) 1 military unit of ground forces commanded by a colonel. 2 large quantity. *vt* ('redʒiment) organize strictly, esp. into disciplined groups. **regimentation** *n*.

region *n* 1 part; area; district. 2 range; scope. 3 sphere of activity. **regional** *adj*.

register *n* 1 official record or list of names, items, etc. 2 book in which this is kept. 3 range of a voice or an instrument. *vt,vi* 1 enter in a register. 2 record. 3 show by facial expression, reaction, etc. **registration** *n*. **registrar** *n* official keeper of a register or record.

regress *vi* 1 move or go backwards. 2 revert to a former, esp. worse, state. **regression** *n*. **regressive** *adj*.

regret *vt* (-tt-) 1 feel sorrow or remorse for. 2 remember with sadness or remorse. 3 mourn. *n* 1 remorse. 2 sorrow or grief, esp. for a loss. **regretful** *adj*. **regrettable** *adj*.

regular *adj* 1 usual; normal. 2 conforming to a rule, principle, etc. 3 symmetrical. 4 recurring at fixed times or distances; unvarying; periodic. 5 habitual. *n* 1 soldier in a permanent army. 2 habitual customer or visitor of a place. **regularity** *n*. **regularly** *adv*.

regulate *vt* 1 control by rule, principle, etc. 2 adjust to function accurately, conform to some standard, etc.; put in order. **regulatory** *adj*. **regulation** *n* 1 rule; law; requirement. 2 control; adjustment.

rehabilitate *vt* 1 restore to normal by treatment or training. 2 restore to a former position or standing. **rehabilitation** *n*.

rehearse *vt,vi* practise in private before giving a public performance. **rehearsal** *n*.

reign *n* 1 period of rule, esp. of a sovereign. 2 dominance or rule. *vi* 1 rule as a sovereign. 2 prevail; predominate.

reimburse *vt* repay or refund, esp. for expense incurred, time lost, etc. **reimbursement** *n*.

rein *n* 1 long narrow strap fastened to a bit for controlling a horse. 2 restraint; curb. **give free rein to** allow complete freedom or licence. ~*vt* 1 put a rein on. 2 check; guide.

reincarnation *n* 1 belief that the soul returns after death in a new bodily form. 2 rebirth of the soul in a new body. **3** new bodily form taken.

reindeer *n, pl* **reindeer** large deer having branched antlers, found in arctic regions.

reinforce *vt* strengthen; give support to; stress. **reinforcement** *n*.

reinstate *vt* restore to a former state or position.

reject *vt* (riˈdʒekt) refuse to take, keep, accept, grant, etc. *n* (ˈriːdʒekt) something rejected as imperfect, useless, etc. **rejection** *n*.

rejoice *vt,vi* make or become joyful; gladden.

rejuvenate *vt,vi* make or become young again; restore or be restored in vigour, freshness, etc. **rejuvenation** *n*.

relapse *vi* **1** fall or slip back to a former state or condition. **2** become ill again after apparent recovery. *n* act of relapsing.

relate *vt* **1** tell of; recount. **2** establish or perceive connection or relationship. *vi* refer to; have relation to. **relation** *n* **1** connection; association. **2** kinship. **3** relative. **4** reference; respect. **5** narration. **relations** *pl n* connections, feelings, etc., between people, countries, etc. **relationship** *n* connection; relation; mutual response.

relative *adj* **1** considered or existing in relation to something else; comparative. **2** related to; connected with. **3** relevant. **4** proportionate. *n* someone connected to another by birth or marriage. **relatively** *adv*. **relative pronoun** *n* word, such as *who* or *which*, that introduces a subordinate clause and refers back to a previous word or words.

relax *vt,vi* **1** make or become less rigid, tense, or firm. **2** make or become less strict, severe, or intense. **3** rest from or cease (work, effort, worry, etc.). **relaxation** *n*.

relay *n* **1** fresh supply or group of horses, men, etc., relieving others. **2** *also* **relay race** race between teams, each member covering part of the distance before being relieved by another. **3** broadcast; transmission. *vt* broadcast; transmit.

release *vt* **1** free; let go; give up; surrender. **2** permit to be issued, published, etc. **3** discharge. *n* **1** act of releasing; discharge. **2** something released for public sale, exhibition, publication, etc.

relent *vi* become less severe, firm, or harsh; soften; abate. **relentless** *adj* ruthless.

relevant *adj* to the point; pertinent. **relevance** *or* **relevancy** *n*.

reliable *adj* dependable; trustworthy. **reliability** *n*. **reliant** *adj* dependent; trusting. **reliance** *n*.

relic *n* **1** something associated with or surviving from the past. **2** object treasured in remembrance. **3** something associated with a saint, martyr, etc., revered as holy.

relief *n* **1** easing or alleviation of pain, distress, etc. **2** feeling resulting from this. **3** anything that eases. **4** aid; assistance. **5** pleasing change. **6** release from a post or duty. **7** person taking over. **8** raising of a siege. **9** elevation of figures, forms, etc., from a flat surface or the appearance of this. **10** distinct contrast. **relieve** *vt* **1** ease; lessen; alleviate. **2** help; aid. **3** free from anxiety, etc. **4** break the monotony of. **5** bring into relief; provide contrast. **6** release from duty; take over the duties of. **7** deprive.

religion *n* **1** belief in and worship of a god or gods. **2** a particular system of belief and worship. **3** associated ritual, conduct, doctrines, etc. **4** anything revered or zealously pursued. **religious** *adj* **1** relating to religion. **2** pious. **3** conscientious; scrupulous. **religiously** *adv*.

relinquish *vt* **1** give up; abandon. **2** let go, release. **3** surrender.

relish *vt* take delight in; enjoy; look forward to. *n* **1** enjoyment; keen anticipation. **2** appetizing taste or flavour. **3** sauce; spicy food.

relive *vt* experience again through the imagination or memory.

reluctant *adj* unwilling; marked by unwillingness. **reluctance** *n*. **reluctantly** *adv*.

rely *v* **rely on** trust in; depend on; have confidence in.

remain *vi* **1** stay behind in a place. **2** be left over or behind. **3** continue to be. **remains** *pl n* **1** remnants; relics; surviving fragments. **2** dead body; corpse. **remainder** *n* **1** something remaining or left over. **2** quantity remaining after subtraction or division.

remand *vt* send (a prisoner or accused person) back to prison pending further inquiries or proceedings. *n* act of remanding or state of being remanded. **remand home** *n* home for juvenile offenders.

remark *n* comment; observation. *vt,vi* say; comment (about). *vt* notice; perceive. **remarkable** *adj* worthy of notice; striking; unusual. **remarkably** *adv*.

remedy *n* **1** medicinal cure or treatment. **2** cure or correction for a wrong, evil, etc. **3** legal redress. *vt* **1** cure or heal. **2** put right; correct; redress. **remedial** *adj.*

remember *vt* retain in or recall to the memory. *vi* hold in one's memory. **remembrance** *n* memory; keepsake.

remind *vt* cause to remember or think of again. **reminder** *n* thing that reminds.

reminiscence *n* thing remembered or act of evoking old memories. **reminiscent** *adj.*

remiss *adj* negligent; at fault.

remission *n* **1** forgiveness; pardon. **2** reduction of a prison sentence.

remit *v* (-tt-) *vt* **1** send, esp. money. **2** pardon; refrain from inflicting (a sentence, etc.). *vt,vi* slacken. **remittance** *n* money sent; payment.

remnant *n* fragment; remainder; relic.

remorse *n* feeling of deep regret, guilt, etc. **remorseful** *adj.* **remorseless** *adj* **1** relentless. **2** not penitent.

remote *adj* **1** far away; removed; isolated. **2** slight; unlikely. **remotely** *adv.*

remove *vt* **1** take away or off; withdraw. **2** dismiss from a post or appointment. **removal** *n.*

remunerate *vt* grant as earnings, reward, etc.; pay or repay. **remuneration** *n.* **remunerative** *adj.*

renaissance *n* revival, esp. of learning. **the Renaissance** *n* period of radical artistic, scientific, and social development in Europe from the 14th to 16th centuries.

renal *adj* relating to the kidney.

render *vt* **1** give back; return. **2** serve; present for approval, action, etc.; supply with. **3** give a version or interpretation of; represent. **4** melt down. **rendition** *n.*

rendezvous *n* meeting place or time of meeting. *vi* meet by appointment.

renew *vt,vi* make or become new again; revive. *vt* **1** restore; replace; repair; renovate. **2** grant for a further period. **3** begin again. **renewal** *n.*

renounce *vt* **1** give up; abandon, esp. formally. **2** disown; break ties with. **renunciation** *n.*

renovate *vt* make fit or habitable again; restore. **renovation** *n.*

renown *n* fame; great distinction; notoriety.

rent *n* regular payment for the use of land, a house, buildings, etc. *vt* grant or use in exchange for rent; hire. **rental** *n* amount charged or paid in rent.

rep *n* short for (sales) **representative** or **repertory** (company).

repair *vt* **1** mend; restore; renew. **2** make up for; make good; remedy. *n* **1** mend. **2** act or process of repairing. **reparation** *n* compensation; amends; remedy.

repartee *n* witty reply or retort.

repatriate *vt* send (someone) back to his own country. **repatriation** *n.*

repay *vt,vi* (-paid) **1** pay back; refund. **2** return (a kindness, compliment, etc.).

repeal *vt* annul; revoke; cancel. *n* annulment; cancellation.

repeat *vt* say or do again; reproduce; echo. *n* second performance; something repeated. **repeatedly** *adv.*

repel *vt* (-ll-) **1** drive or force back or away; resist. **2** disgust. **repellent** *adj* **1** revolting; disgusting. **2** unpleasant. *n* substance used to keep flies, pests, etc., away.

repent *vi,vt* feel penitent (about); regret (one's sins). **repentance** *n.* **repentant** *adj.*

repercussion *n* **1** indirect or unintended consequence or result. **2** recoil.

repertoire *n* stock of plays, songs, etc., that a theatrical company, singer, etc., can offer.

repertory *n* **1** theatrical company performing a selection of plays, operas, etc., over a relatively short period. **2** repertoire; stock.

repetition *n* **1** act of repeating or being repeated. **2** something said or done again. **repetitious** *adj* repeated in a boring manner. **repetitive** *adj* **1** having a constant rhythm or beat. **2** characterized by repetition.

replace *vt* **1** put back. **2** find or be a substitute for. **replacement** *n.*

replenish *vt* fill up or supply again.

replica *n* copy or reproduction, esp. of a work of art.

reply *vi,vt* answer; respond. *n* answer; response.

report *vt,vi* **1** relate. **2** make, give, or bring back an account (of). **3** take down or write for publication. *vt* name as an offender; inform against. *vi* present (oneself); register (with). *n* **1** rumour. **2** account of something. **3** bang; sharp noise. **reporter** *n* person who reports, esp. for a newspaper.

repose *vi,vt* take rest or give rest to; recline; relax. *n* **1** rest; sleep; relaxed state. **2** tranquillity; composure.

represent *vt* **1** depict; stand for; symbolize. **2** act as a deputy or agent for. **3** portray; describe. **representation** *n*. **representative** *adj* serving to represent; typical. *n* **1** person or thing that represents or typifies. **2** *also* **sales representative** person selling a company's products. **3** agent; delegate.

repress *vt* keep down or under. **repressive** *adj*. **repression** *n* **1** restraint. **2** exclusion of thoughts and tendencies from consciousness.

reprieve *vt* **1** suspend execution of. **2** relieve temporarily from harm, punishment, etc. *n* **1** respite from punishment. **2** temporary relief.

reprimand *n* sharp rebuke; severe scolding. *vt* give a reprimand to.

reprint *vt* print again; print a new copy of. *n* reproduction or copy of something previously printed.

reprisal *n* retaliation; vengeful action.

reproach *vt* scold; rebuke. *n* scolding; rebuke. **reproachful** *adj*.

reproduce *vt* **1** produce again. **2** make a copy of; duplicate; imitate. *vt,vi* produce (offspring). **reproduction** *n*. **reproductive** *adj*.

reptile *n* cold-blooded egg-laying vertebrate, such as a snake, lizard, or turtle. **reptilian** *adj*.

republic *n* form of state in which supreme power rests in the people and their elected representatives. **republican** *adj,n*.

repudiate *vt* **1** reject. **2** disown; cast off. **repudiation** *n*.

repugnant *adj* distasteful; offensive. **repugnance** *n*.

repulsion *n* distaste; aversion. **repulsive** *adj*.

reputation *n* **1** what is generally thought about a person or thing. **2** good repute. **reputable** *adj* of good repute; respectable. **repute** *n* reputation, esp. a favourable one. **reputed** *adj* considered; reckoned.

request *n* act of asking for something or a thing asked for; demand. *vt* ask for (something) or ask (someone) to do something, esp. a favour.

requiem *n* **1** mass for the dead. **2** music composed for this.

require *vt* **1** need. **2** demand; order. **requirement** *n*.

rescue *vt* save or deliver from danger, etc. *n* delivery or release from harm or danger.

research *n* investigation, esp. into a scientific field in order to discover facts. *vt,vi* investigate. **researcher** *n*.

resemble *vt* look like or be similar to. **resemblance** *n*.

resent *vt* feel indignant at; dislike; be bitter about. **resentful** *adj*. **resentment** *n*.

reserve *vt* **1** hold back; set apart; keep for future use. **2** book (tickets, seats, etc.) in advance. *n* **1** something reserved. **2** part of an army, etc., kept back for use in emergency. **3** self-restraint; lack of familiarity. **in reserve** kept back for future use. **reservation** *n* **1** act of reserving; something reserved. **2** advance booking. **3** qualification; limitation. **reserved** *adj* **1** set aside for future use; held back. **2** booked in advance. **3** quiet; self-restrained; reticent.

reservoir *n* **1** place functioning as a store. **2** place for holding a large quantity of water.

reside *vi* dwell; have as one's home; live. **reside in** live in; be present or inherent. **residence** *n* state of residing or the place where a person resides. **resident** *adj* residing. *n* person staying in a place permanently or for a long time. **residential** *adj* relating to housing, residences, etc.; not commercial.

residue *n* what is left over; remainder. **residual** *adj*.

resign *vt* give up; surrender; relinquish. *vi* give up an office, commission, employment, etc. **resign oneself** (**to**) accept as unavoidable. **resignation** *n*.

resilient *adj* **1** elastic; rebounding. **2** capable of recovering quickly from a shock, injury, etc. **resilience** *n*.

resin *n* **1** sticky substance manufactured or obtained from various plants or trees. **2** synthetic substance used in making plastics, varnish, etc.

resist *vt,vi* **1** withstand; oppose. **2** overcome (a temptation). **resistance** *n*. **resistant** *adj*.

resit *vt* (-tt-; -sat) take (an examination) again after failing it.

resolute *adj* firm; determined. **resolutely** *adv*.

resolution *n* **1** firmness; determination; resolve. **2** act or state of resolving or being resolved. **3** decision of a court. **4** vote of an assembly, etc. **5** explanation; solution.

resolve *vt* **1** make clear. **2** determine; decide. **3** form by a vote or resolution. **4** find a solution to (a problem, etc.). **5** agree to (an action, course, etc.) formally. *vt,vi* separate into component parts; analyse. *n* **1** something resolved. **2** determination; strong intention.

resonance *n* increase or prolonging of vibrations, as of sound. **resonant** *adj*. **resonate** *vi,vt* undergo or cause resonance.

resort *vi also* **resort to** go for help to; turn to. *n* holiday or recreation place.

resound *vi* echo; ring; continue sounding.

resource *n* skill in devising means. **resources** *pl n* **1** means of supplying a want. **2** supplies, etc., that can be drawn on. **resourceful** *adj*.

respect *n* **1** reference; relation. **2** deference; esteem. **3** point or aspect. *vt* treat with esteem; admire. **respectable** *adj*. **respectability** *n*. **respectful** *adj*. **respective** *adj* relating to two or more persons or things regarded individually. **respectively** *adv* individually in the order mentioned.

respite ('respit) *n* **1** delay. **2** period of rest or relief. **3** suspension of execution; reprieve.

respond *vi* **1** answer; reply. **2** react. **response** *n*.

responsible *adj* **1** liable to answer for something. **2** of good credit or position. **responsibility** *n*.

responsive *adj* **1** answering; making reply. **2** acting in response.

rest[1] *n* **1** quiet repose; sleep. **2** refreshing break from activity. **3** freedom or relief. **4** calm; tranquillity. **5** stopping or absence of motion. **6** prop or support; something that steadies. **7** pause in music, rhythm, etc. *vi,vt* **1** take rest or give rest to. **2** support or steady or be supported or steadied. **restful** *adj*. **restless** *adj* **1** unable to remain at rest. **2** uneasy; unquiet. **3** never still or motionless. **4** without rest. **5** characterized by constant activity.

rest[2] *n* **1** remainder; that which is left. **2** others; everyone else. *vi* remain; continue to be.

restaurant *n* place where meals are bought and eaten.

restore *vt* **1** build up again; repair; renew. **2** establish again. **3** give back. **restoration** *n*. **restorative** *adj,n*.

restrain *vt* check; hold back; repress. **restraint** *n*.

restrict *vt,vi* place limits (on); confine; restrain. **restriction** *n*. **restrictive** *adj*.

result *n* **1** thing caused or produced; effect; outcome; consequence. **2** solution; answer. **3** final score. *vi* be the result. **result in** end in.

resume (ri'zju:m) *vt,vi* start to take up again after an interval or pause. *vt* occupy (a seat) again. **resumption** *n*.

résumé ('rezju:mei) *n* summary, esp. of one's career or background.

resurrect *vt* **1** bring to life again. **2** use again; express new interest in. **resurrection** *n*.

retail *n* sale of goods in small quantities to the public, usually through a shop; not wholesale. *adv* sold in such a way. *vt,vi* sell or be sold by retail. **retailer** *n*.

retain *vt* **1** keep back; continue to hold. **2** hold in the mind or memory. **3** continue to employ; keep for future use. **retention** *n*. **retentive** *adj*.

retaliate *vi* fight back; answer an attack. **retaliation** *n*.

retard *vt* hold back or slow down the development of; delay. **retardation** *n*.

retch *vi* attempt or begin to vomit.

reticent *adj* reserved; modest; shy; not forthcoming. **reticence** *n*.

retina *n, pl* **retinas** *or* **retinae** ('retini:) membrane of the eyeball that is sensitive to light and transmits images to the brain.

retire *vi* **1** leave one's employment at the end of one's working life. **2** go to bed. **3** leave or withdraw. *vt* cease to employ after a certain age. **retirement** *n*.

retort[1] *vi,vt* reply rudely or abruptly; answer back. *n* rude or angry reply.

retort[2] *n* round glass vessel with a long neck attached at an angle, used esp. in a laboratory for distilling or heating certain substances.

retrace *vt* **1** follow (a route) again in exactly the same way. **2** go over again; recount or recall.

retract *vt,vi* **1** draw or pull inwards. **2** withdraw (an earlier statement, promise, etc.); go back on. **retractable** *or* **retractible** *adj*. **retraction** *n*.

retreat *vi* **1** move back, esp. from an advancing army. **2** seek shelter or refuge. *n* **1** act of retreating. **2** safe place; refuge; haven; sanctuary.

retribution *n* punishment; revenge.

retrieve *vt* **1** fetch, find again; recover; regain. **2** rescue from difficulty or harm. **retrieval** *n*.

retrograde *adj also* **retrogressive** **1** moving or pointing backwards; reverse. **2** tending to retrogress or decline into a worse condition. **retrogress** *vi* **1** move backwards; recede. **2** revert; decline; deteriorate. **retrogression** *n*.

retrospect *n* **in retrospect** looking back in time; with hindsight. **retrospective** *adj*.

return *vi* **1** come or go back to a former place,

situation, etc. 2 reappear. 3 reply; answer back. *vt* 1 give, send, or take back. 2 respond to; react to; acknowledge. 3 yield as a rate of interest. 4 elect by voting. *n* 1 act of coming or going back. 2 yield on investment; revenue. 3 reappearance. 4 form to be filled in for tax purposes. **returnable** *adj*.

reveal *vt* 1 display; show. 2 divulge; disclose; betray. **revelation** *n* dramatic or sudden disclosure of the truth, esp. as revealed by God to mankind.

revel *v* (-ll-) **revel in** derive enormous satisfaction or pleasure from; bask in. **revels** *pl n also* **revelry** merrymaking; festivities.

revenge *n* act of retaliation to offset a previous crime or wrong; vengeance. *vt* avenge; retaliate for.

revenue *n* income, esp. from taxation or goods sold.

reverberate *vi* vibrate noisily; resound; echo. **reverberation** *n*.

reverence *n* feeling or act of deep respect, esp. towards something sacred. **Reverence** title used when addressing a priest or high-ranking clergyman. **reverent** *adj*. **revere** *vt* treat with reverence; idolize or worship.

reverse *vt* 1 change the direction or order of; turn back. 2 revoke; alter (a former decision, attitude, etc.). *vi* drive or move backwards. *n* 1 opposite side of a coin, sheet of paper, etc. 2 gear engaged on a vehicle for moving backwards. 3 opposite of what has been stated. *adj* opposite. **reversal** *n* 1 turning round; reversing. 2 revoking of a law, etc.; cancellation.

revert *vt* return to a former state or condition. **reversion** *n*.

review *vt* 1 look back over; examine, check, or consider again. 2 give a critical report of (a book, play, etc.). *n* 1 critical report. 2 general analysis or report; survey. **reviewer** *n*.

revise *vt* 1 alter (one's attitudes, opinions, etc.). 2 rewrite. *vi,vt* study in preparation for an examination. **revision** *n*.

revive *vt,vi* 1 bring or return to consciousness. 2 introduce again; restore. **revival** *n*.

revoke *vt* cancel, esp. a law or rule; repeal.

revolt *vi* rebel; protest or act against authority. *vt* disgust; repel. *n* rebellion; uprising; mutiny. **revolting** *adj* disgusting; repulsive.

revolution *n* 1 large-scale rebellion resulting in the overthrowing of those in power and radical social and political change. 2 dramatic change. 3 movement around a point or axis; orbit or rotation. **revolutionary** *n* person in favour of or working for political revolution. *adj* 1 relating to political revolution. 2 radical, changing dramatically. 3 revolving or rotating. **revolutionize** *vt* cause a radical change in; alter dramatically.

revolve *vt,vi* move around a point or axis; orbit or rotate. **revolve around** be centred on or totally engaged with. **revolver** *n* small firearm capable of discharging several shots before reloading.

revue *n* light entertainment with music, satirical or comic sketches, etc.

revulsion *n* 1 repugnance; feeling of extreme distaste or hatred. 2 violent withdrawal or recoil.

reward *n* 1 something, such as a sum of money or prize, awarded in acknowledgment of a particular deed, act of service, etc. 2 profit; gain; benefit. *vt* repay; give a reward to. **rewarding** *adj* satisfying.

rhetoric *n* 1 art of public speaking; oratory. 2 eloquence. **rhetorical** *adj* 1 relating to rhetoric. 2 concerned more with style or effect of language than with meaning or content. **rhetorical question** *n* question to which no answer is required, used esp. as a literary device for its dramatic effect.

rheumatism *n* inflammation of the muscles, joints, etc. **rheumatic** *adj*.

rhinoceros *n* large mammal inhabiting tropical or subtropical regions, having one or two horns and a tough hide.

rhododendron *n* evergreen shrub having showy red, pink, or white flowers.

rhubarb *n* plant with large flat leaves and edible pink stalks.

rhyme *n* 1 identical or similar form of sounds occurring esp. at the end of two or more words, e.g. *try* and *buy* or *relieve* and *believe*. 2 verse using rhymes. *vi,vt* occur or make use of as a rhyme.

rhythm *n* 1 alternation of strong and weak stress or beats in music, speech, etc. 2 recurring pattern or form of movement, flow, etc. **rhythmic** *or* **rhythmical** *adj*.

rib *n* 1 one of the curved bones forming the wall of the chest. 2 anything resembling such a bone. 3 ridged stitch in knitting. *vt* (-bb-) 1 knit using alternate plain and purl stitches. **2** *inf* tease; make fun of in a gentle way.

ribbon *n* **1** strip of satin, cotton, etc., used for decoration, trimming, etc. **2** long narrow strip of land, water, etc. **3** narrow band impregnated with ink for use on a typewriter or similar machine.

rice *n* type of grass whose grains are used as a staple food.

rich *adj* **1** having a large amount of money; wealthy. **2** having an abundant supply. **3** sumptuous; luxurious. **4** having a high proportion of cream or fat. **5** having a full flavour or consistency. **6** of a deep or vivid colour. **richly** *adv*. **richness** *n*. **riches** *pl n* wealth; valuable possessions.

rickety *adj* liable to collapse or break.

rickshaw *n* two-wheeled passenger vehicle drawn by hand, traditionally used in parts of Asia.

rid *vt* (-dd-; rid *or* ridded) free; clear away completely. **get rid of** dispose of entirely; do away with; banish or abolish. **good riddance (to)** *n* welcome relief (from).

riddle[1] *n* complicated puzzle or problem in the form of a verse or question, employing puns, hidden meaning, etc.

riddle[2] *vt* make a series of holes in.

ride *v* (rode; ridden) *vi* **1** be carried on the back of a horse, donkey, etc. **2** travel in a vehicle. **3** *inf* continue without interference. *vt* **1** travel by sitting on an animal's back. **2** drive or propel (a vehicle). *n* journey on horseback, in a vehicle, etc. **take for a ride** swindle; defraud. **rider** *n* **1** person who rides. **2** additional remark, observation, etc.

ridge *n* **1** long elevated stretch of land; range. **2** furrow; raised or projecting section. **3** area of high atmospheric pressure between two depressions.

ridicule *n* mockery; scorn. *vt* treat as absurd; mock; deride. **ridiculous** *adj* stupid; extremely silly; absurd; ludicrous. **ridiculously** *adv*.

rife *adj* prevalent; rampant; widely distributed.

rifle[1] *n* firearm that is effective over a relatively long range, having spiral grooves cut inside a long barrel.

rifle[2] *vt* ransack; loot; plunder.

rift *n* **1** crack or opening caused by a geological fault. **2** split or disagreement.

rig *vt* (-gg-) **1** equip (a vessel) with sails, masts, etc. **2** fix (prices, an election, etc.) by fraudulent means. **rig up** construct or set up, esp. in a makeshift fashion. ~*n* **1** arrangement of sails, masts, etc. **2** equipment or installation used in drilling for oil or gas. **rigging** *n* ropes, chains, etc., supporting sails or masts on a ship.

right *adj* **1** correct; accurate. **2** true; of an expected standard. **3** suitable; appropriate. **4** normal. **5** on the side of the body opposite the heart. **6** conservative or reactionary. *adv* **1** accurately; correctly; properly. **2** directly; all the way. **3** completely; totally. **4** towards the right side. **5** immediately. *n* **1** legal or moral entitlement; due. **2** direction, location, or part that is on the right side. **3** conservative or reactionary group. *vt* correct; restore. *vt,vi* make or become upright again. **rightly** *adv*. **rightful** *adj* proper; entitled; justified. **right angle** *n* angle of 90°. **right-hand** *adj* on the side towards the right. **right-handed** *adj* using the right hand for writing, etc. **right wing** *n* political group representing conservative attitudes. *adj* **right-wing** relating to the right wing.

righteous ('raitʃəs) *adj* virtuous; pious; upright. **righteousness** *n*.

rigid *adj* **1** straight and stiff; not flexible. **2** strict; not allowing variation. **rigidity** *n*. **rigidly** *adv*.

rigour *n* harshness; severity; hardship. **rigorous** *adj*. **rigorously** *adv*.

rim *n* outer or top edge of a container, wheel, etc.

rind *n* **1** tough outer skin of certain fruits; peel. **2** hard layer or coating of a piece of bacon or cheese.

ring[1] *n* **1** circle. **2** band worn on the finger. **3** circular course, track, route, etc. **4** group of people in a circle. **5** circular arena, esp. for a circus performance. **6** raised platform for a boxing match. *vt,vi* **1** encircle; surround. **2** fit rings on (birds, etc.) for identification. **ringleader** *n* main organizer, esp. of crime, etc. **ringlet** *n* long curl of hair. **ringside** *n* seats nearest the ring at a boxing or wrestling match.

ring[2] *v* (rang; rung) *vt,vi* **1** produce a clear metallic sound. **2** sound (a bell). **3** *also* **ring up** telephone; call. *vi* **1** resound. **2** experience a vibrating hum in the ears. **ring true/false** sound right/wrong. ~*n* **1** sound produced by a bell, telephone, etc. **2** echo. **3** telephone call. **4** quality; characteristic; hint.

rink *n* building or arena used for ice-skating.

rinse *vt* wash through in water, esp. in order to remove soap. *n* **1** application of clean water. **2** temporary dye for the hair; tint.

riot *n* **1** public disturbance causing a breakdown of law and order; uprising. **2** showy display; blaze. **3** *inf* hilarious occasion or person. *vi* participate in a riot. **rioter** *n*. **riotous** *adj* uproarious; disorderly.

rip *vt,vi* (-pp-) tear clumsily or violently. *n* torn part; split. **rip off** *sl* **1** cheat; overcharge. **2** steal. **rip-off** *n sl* **1** swindle. **2** exploitation for profit.

ripe *adj* **1** ready to be eaten or harvested. **2** fully matured. **3** having reached the appropriate stage of development. **ripen** *vi,vt* become or make ripe.

ripple *n* **1** slight movement of liquid; small wave. **2** continuous gentle sound. *vi* **1** form small waves; undulate. **2** gently rise and fall.

rise *vi* (rose; risen) **1** move upwards; ascend. **2** stand up; arise. **3** get out of bed. **4** progress to a higher rank or status. **5** become more cheerful, animated, etc. **6** increase in price or value. **7** rebel; revolt. **8** be able to tackle or cope. *n* **1** pay increase. **2** upward movement or progression; ascent. **3** slope; incline. **give rise to** cause; produce.

risk *n* possibility of harm, loss, etc.; gamble; chance. *vt* take a chance on; gamble; hazard. **risky** *adj*.

rissole *n* ball of minced meat fried with a coating of egg and breadcrumbs.

rite *n* formal ceremony having deep religious or cultural significance. **ritual** *adj* relating to rites. *n* **1** formalized procedure for performing certain rites or ceremonies. **2** rigid routine.

rival *n* person, organization, etc., in competition with others. *vt* (-ll-) **1** compete with. **2** be equal to. **rivalry** *n*.

river *n* **1** body of fresh water flowing usually into the sea or a lake. **2** flow; stream.

rivet *n* short bolt or nail. *vt* fasten with rivets. **riveted** *adj* unable to move or avert one's gaze; fixed.

road *n* **1** *also* **roadway** stretch of prepared land for vehicles. **2** street. **3** way.

roam *vi,vt* wander freely (over); travel widely. *n* leisurely walk; ramble. **roamer** *n*.

roar *vi* (esp. of lions) utter a loud noise. *vi,vt* **1** bellow; produce a loud angry or wild sound. **2** burn fiercely. *n* **1** loud cry of a lion, bull, etc. **2** angry or wild noise of a crowd, the wind, etc. **roaring trade** brisk profitable trade.

roast *vt,vi* **1** cook in an oven. **2** brown, scorch. *n* joint of meat for roasting.

rob *vt* (-bb-) **1** steal from. **2** deprive of. **robbery** *n* stealing by force or by threat of violence. **robber** *n*.

robe *n* long loose gown, often signifying office held. *vt,vi* dress, esp. officially.

robin *n* small brown songbird, the male of which has a red breast.

robot *n* man-like machine capable of performing certain human tasks and functions.

robust *adj* strong; healthy; vigorous. **robustly** *adv*.

rock[1] *n* **1** large solid mass of minerals. **2** cliff; boulder; large stone. **3** hard stick of sugar. **on the rocks 1** in serious financial trouble. **2** served with ice-cubes. **rock-bottom** *n* lowest possible level. **rockery** *n also* **rock garden** area in which small plants grow between specially placed rocks. **rocky** *adj* having or strewn with rocks.

rock[2] *vt,vi* sway; move gently from side to side; shake. **rocker** *n* curved wooden or metal support for a rocking-chair, cradle, etc. **off one's rocker** mentally unbalanced. **rocky** *adj* shaky; unsteady.

rocket *n* cylindrical object propelled at speed into the sky to launch spaceships, direct bombs, or act as a warning or decorative firework. *vi* move like a rocket.

rod *n* **1** long straight stick of wood, bar of metal, etc. **2** *also* **fishing rod** rod used to suspend a line over water.

rode *v pt of* **ride.**

rodent *n* mammal, such as a rat, vole, or squirrel, with four strong incisors for gnawing and no canine teeth.

roe *n* **1** *also* **hard roe 1** mass of eggs in a female fish. **2** *also* **soft roe** sperm of a male fish.

rogue *n* villain; rascal; scoundrel; criminal. **roguery** *n*. **roguish** *adj*.

role *n* **1** actor's part. **2** function; task.

roll *vt,vi* **1** move along by rotating; turn over. **2** move on wheels. **3** billow; undulate. **4** rotate; move up and down. **5** sway or move from side to side. **6** form into a ball or cylinder; coil. **7** produce a loud noise; roar. *vi* pass; move onwards. *vt* use a roller on. **roll in** *or* **up**

arrive; turn up. ~*n* **1** act of rolling. **2** something rolled into a cylinder or ball. **3** small round or oblong of baked dough. **4** undulation. **5** roar. **6** rapid drumbeat. **rollcall** *n* calling of names to check attendance. **rolling pin** *n* cylindrical kitchen utensil for rolling pastry, dough, etc.

roller *n* **1** cylindrical part of a machine for pressing, rolling, winding, etc. **2** small cylindrical hair-curler. **3** long swelling wave. **roller-skate** *n* skate with wheels. *vi* move on roller-skates.

Roman Catholic *n* member of that part of the Christian Church owing allegiance to the Pope. *adj* relating to the Roman Catholic Church. **Roman Catholicism** *n*.

romance *n* **1** love affair; idealized love. **2** inclination for adventure, excitement, etc. **3** atmosphere of mystery, nostalgia, etc. **4** love story, esp. remote and idealized. **5** heroic medieval legend, verse, etc. **6** flight of imagination or fancy. *vi* tell extravagant or untrue stories. **romantic** *adj* **1** concerned with or given to romance. **2** fantastic, extravagant; imaginative. *n* person with romantic views. **romanticize** *vt,vi* attach romantic qualities to an otherwise unromantic object, story, etc.

romp *vi* frolic and play together, esp. boisterously. **romp home** win easily. ~*n* boisterous game. **rompers** *pl n* one-piece garment for a young child.

roof *n* **1** upper covering of a building, vehicle, etc. **2** top limit; highest point. **hit the roof** become furious. **raise the roof 1** complain noisily. **2** cause confusion. ~*vt* cover with a roof.

rook[1] **1** black raucous gregarious type of crow. **2** *sl* swindler; cheat. *vt sl* swindle; cheat; overcharge. **rookery** *n* tree-top colony of rooks.

rook[2] *n also* **castle** chess piece that can move forwards, backwards, or sideways over any number of empty squares.

room *n* **1** unoccupied space. **2** partitioned part of a building with a specific purpose. **3** opportunity; scope. **make room** clear a space; bring about an opportunity. **roomy** *adj* spacious.

roost *n* bird's perch or sleeping place. **rule the roost** be in charge; dominate. ~*vi* settle for sleep.

root[1] *n* **1** part of a plant anchoring it to the ground and through which it absorbs water and nutrients. **2** essential element; basic part or cause; origin. **3** one of a specified number of equal factors of a number or quantity. *vi* **1** form roots; become established. **2** have a basis or origin (in). **root out 1** dig out. **2** remove; destroy.

root[2] *v* **root about** *or* **around** search (for).

rope *n* thick twisted cord. **give enough rope** allow enough freedom. **know the ropes** be familiar with the method, rules, etc. ~*vt* catch or tie with rope. **rope in** persuade to take part; enlist. **rope off** partition or enclose with a rope. **ropy** *adj sl* meagre; of poor quality.

rosary *n* **1** series of Roman Catholic prayers, counted on a string of beads. **2** beads so used.

rose[1] *n* **1** prickly shrub or climbing plant having red, yellow, pink, or white flowers, often fragrant. **2** rose-shaped ornament, window, etc. *n,adj* deep pink. **bed of roses** luxurious state. **through rose-coloured spectacles** *or* **glasses** with unjustified optimism. **rosette** *n* **1** cluster of ribbons in the shape of a rose, often worn or presented as a trophy. **2** carving in the shape of a rose. **rosy** *adj* **1** rose-coloured. **2** promising; hopeful.

rose[2] *v pt of* **rise.**

rot *vi,vt* (-tt-) decay or cause to decay; deteriorate, putrefy. *n* **1** decay; corruption. **2** disease causing localized decay in plants, animals, timber, etc. *n,interj inf* nonsense! rubbish!

rota *n* list of duties, names, etc., which may be performed or used in rotation.

rotate *vt,vi* **1** move or cause to move on an axis; spin. **2** recur or cause to recur in regular succession. **rotation** *n*. **rotary** *adj* **1** turning like a wheel; moving round an axis. **2** acting by rotation. **rotor** *n* rotating part of a machine.

rotten *adj* **1** unsound; decayed; putrefied. **2** corrupt; contemptible. **3** *inf* unfortunate; annoying; badly done.

rouge *n* pink cosmetic powder for the cheeks.

rough *adj* **1** not smooth; coarse; uneven. **2** turbulent; violent. **3** unkind; rude. **4** harsh; grating. **5** unfinished; casual. **rough and ready** primitive but effective. **rough and tumble** *or* **rough house** disorderly brawling behaviour. **rough diamond** person who is worthy but lacking refinement. **rough on 1** unfortunate for. **2** severe towards. ~*n* **1** rough ground. **2** preliminary sketch, stage, etc. *v* **rough it** live primitively. **rough up 1** *sl* attack; beat up. **2** produce a preliminary sketch, etc. **roughen** *vt,vi* make or become rough. **roughly** *adv* **1** in a rough way **2** approximately. **roughness** *n*.

roulette *n* gambling game in which bets are laid on which numbered socket a ball will find when dropped onto a rotating wheel.

round *adj* **1** circular; ring-shaped; spherical; curved. **2** complete; whole. *n* **1** habitual journey; single circuit, turn, session, etc. **2** meeting; session. **3** outburst; volley. **4** distribution of drinks to members of a group. **5** song in which voices sing in turn. *adv,prep* **1** continuously. **2** around; about; from place to place. **3** in a reverse or sideways direction. **4** with a circular movement. **5** so as to arrive. **6** so as to be conscious again. **round the bend** crazy. **get round** persuade; overcome. ~*vt,vi* make or become round, curved, etc. *vt* go or move around. **round off** bring to completion. **round on** attack, esp. verbally. **round up** gather or collect together. **roundup** *n* gathering; collection.

roundabout *n* **1** merry-go-round at a fairground. **2** road junction where traffic circulates in only one direction. *adj* indirect; circuitous.

rouse *vt,vi* **1** waken from sleep; stir. **2** incite to fury, passion, etc.; provoke. **rousing** *adj* exciting; thrilling; vigorous.

route *n* course or way to be followed to a destination. *vt* direct along or plan (a particular route).

routine *n* regular unvarying repeated course of action.

rove *vt,vi* stray; wander; ramble.

row[1] (rou) *n* line of several persons, objects, etc.

row[2] (rou) *vt,vi* propel by oars. *vt* carry or transport in a boat propelled by oars. *vi* take part in races in such a boat. *n* act or instance of rowing.

row[3] (rau) *n* **1** noisy brawl; squabble. **2** disturbance; noise; din. *vi* quarrel noisily.

rowdy *adj* noisily boisterous and exuberant. **rowdiness** *n*.

royal *adj* **1** of or relating to a king or queen; regal; majestic. **2** splendid; lavish; magnificent. **royally** *adv*. **royalty** *n* **1** the rank of a king or queen. **2** member(s) of a reigning family. **3** share of profits made on the sale of books, records, etc., paid to the author, composer, etc.

rub *vt,vi* (-bb-) **1** move a hand, cloth, etc., briskly or forcefully over the surface (of); polish; smooth. **2** irritate; grate. **rub (it) in** emphasize. **rub off on** affect through association. **rub out** obliterate; erase. **rub up** polish; improve. **rub up the wrong way** annoy. ~*n* act of rubbing; massage.

rubber *n* **1** elastic material made from the milky juice of certain tropical trees or synthesized. **2** piece of rubber used to erase pencil marks, etc.

rubbish *n* **1** waste materials; litter. **2** nonsense.

rubble *n* loose fragments of stone, rock, etc. esp. from demolished buildings.

ruby *n* deep red precious stone. *n,adj* deep red.

rucksack *n* large bag carried on the back by walkers, etc.

rudder *n* vertical pivoted piece of wood, metal, etc., at the stern of a boat or aircraft, used to steer it.

rude *adj* **1** impolite; impertinent. **2** primitive; unsophisticated. **3** vulgar; coarse. **rudely** *adv*. **rudeness** *n*.

rudiments *pl n* **1** basic elements; first principles of a subject. **2** undeveloped form. **rudimentary** *adj* undeveloped, primitive; elementary.

rueful *adj* regretful; repentant. **ruefully** *adv*.

ruff *n* **1** starched lacy collar or frill. **2** prominent growth of feathers or hair around the neck of a bird or animal.

ruffian *n* rogue; villain; bully.

ruffle *vt,vi* **1** disturb; wrinkle; rumple. **2** annoy or become annoyed. **3** erect (feathers) in anger or display. *n* frill at the neck or wrist.

rug *n* **1** small thick carpet. **2** thick woollen blanket.

rugby *n also* **rugby football** *or* **rugger** form of football in which players may use their hands to carry the ball or to tackle opponents.

rugged *adj* **1** uneven; rough; craggy. **2** strong; unbending; harsh. **ruggedly** *adv*. **ruggedness** *n*.

ruin *n* **1** collapse; devastation; total destruction. **2** complete loss of social, financial, or moral reputation. *vt* bring to ruin; spoil; destroy. **ruins** *pl n* remains of a partly destroyed or derelict building, etc. **in ruins** destroyed; decayed. **ruinous** *adj*.

rule *n* **1** regulation; law; maxim; code of discipline; procedure. **2** period of control, authority, etc. **as a rule** generally. **work to rule** decrease efficiency or output by observing rules precisely. ~*vt,vi* **1** govern; dominate. **2** decree (that); decide officially (that). *vt* draw a straight line. **rule out** exclude. **ruler 1** person who rules. **2** instrument for measuring, drawing straight lines, etc.

rum *n* alcoholic drink distilled from sugar cane.

rumble *vi* make a low rolling noise, as of distant thunder. *vt sl* see through; guess correctly. **rumble along** *or* **past** move or pass making a rumble. ~*n* low rolling noise.

ruminant *n* any of various cud-chewing, hoofed animals, such as the cow, sheep, or deer. **ruminate** *vi* **1** chew the cud. **2** meditate; ponder; consider carefully.

rummage *vt,vi* ransack; search (through).

rumour *n* hearsay; gossip; unverified talk.

rump *n* rear part of a person or animal; buttocks.

rumple *vt,vi* crease; crumple; ruffle.

run *v* (-nn-; ran; run) *vi* **1** proceed on foot at a fast pace. **2** gallop or canter. **3** make a quick journey. **4** function; operate. **5** be valid; endure or last. **6** go; proceed. **7** be inherited from. **8** fall in a stream; flow. **9** spread; become diffused. *vt* **1** do whilst running. **2** roll; push; drive. **3** cover quickly. **4** operate; manage; control. **5** be affected by. **6** cause to flow. **run across** *or* **into** meet unexpectedly. **run away** escape; abscond. **run down 1** slow down. **2** find or capture. **3** criticize; speak badly of. **run for** seek election for. **run out** become exhausted; have no more. **run to** be adequate for. ~*n* **1** act or pace of running; race. **2** continuous series. **3** sort; type. **4** unlimited freedom or access. **5** strong demand. **6** score of one in cricket. **in the long run** eventually; after a long while. **on the run** escaping from the police, etc.

rung[1] *n* bar forming a spoke of a wheel, step of a ladder, crosspiece on a chair, etc.

rung[2] *v pp* of **ring.**

runner *n* **1** person that runs; athlete. **2** lateral shoot of a plant. **3** narrow strip of wood, metal, or cloth on which something is supported or runs. **runner bean** *n* climbing bean plant with scarlet flowers and long edible green pods. **runner-up** *n* competitor finishing just after the winner.

running *adj* **1** continuous; without interruption. **2** taken at a run. **3** moving easily; flowing. *n* **1** condition of the ground on a race course. **2** management; operation. **in/out of the running** with a/no chance of winning.

runny *adj* discharging liquid; streaming.

runway *n* **1** long wide track used by aircraft for landing or taking off. **2** ramp. **3** channel; groove.

rupture *n* act of bursting; state of being burst or broken; breach; split. *vt,vi* break; burst.

rural *adj* **1** of the countryside. **2** rustic.

rush[1] *vi,vt* hurry or cause to hurry; hasten; proceed recklessly. *vi* come, flow, etc., quickly. *vt* make a sudden attack on. *n* sudden speedy advance. **rush hour** *n* time of day when traffic is heaviest.

rush[2] *n* plant growing in wet places, the stems of which can be used for chair seats, baskets, etc.

rust *n* powdery brownish coating formed on iron and steel by the action of air and moisture. *vi,vt* become or make rusty; corrode. **rusty** *adj* **1** covered in rust; corroded. **2** inefficient through disuse; spoilt by neglect. **rustiness** *n.*

rustic *adj* unsophisticated; rural; simple. *n* **1** country dweller. **2** unsophisticated person.

rustle *vi,vt* make or cause to make a soft sound, as of dry leaves, silk, etc. *vt* steal (cattle, etc.). **rustle up** improvise; procure hastily. ~*n* rustling sound.

rut *n* **1** sunken furrow in a path or track; groove. **2** dreary or boring way of life.

ruthless *adj* without mercy or pity; cruel; heartless. **ruthlessly** *adv.* **ruthlessness** *n.*

rye *n* cereal grain used as animal fodder and for making flour and whisky.

S

Sabbath *n* day set aside for rest and worship, Saturday for Jews and Sunday for Christians.

sabotage *n* deliberate destruction for political, military, or private ends. *vt* destroy or disrupt by sabotage. **saboteur** *n.*

saccharin *n* intensely sweet powder used as a non-fattening sugar substitute. *adj* cloyingly sweet.

sachet *n* small sealed bag containing perfume, shampoo, etc.

sack *n* **1** large coarse bag made of flax, hemp, etc., used for coal, flour, corn, etc. **2** *inf* dismissal from employment. *vt inf* dismiss from employment.

sacrament *n* religious ceremony (Baptism, Matrimony, Holy Orders, etc.) regarded as conferring an outward sign of inward divine grace. **sacramental** *adj*.

sacred *adj* holy; dedicated to God; inviolate. **sacredly** *adv*. **sacredness** *n*.

sacrifice *vt* **1** give up (something) so that greater good or a different end may result. **2** offer to or kill in honour of a deity. *n* **1** offering of something to a god. **2** giving or offering up (anything), esp. with a worthy motive. **sacrificial** *adj*.

sacrilege *n* desecration of a sacred place, person, or thing. **sacrilegious** *adj*.

sad *adj* **1** sorrowful; dejected; downcast. **2** unfortunate. **sadly** *adv*. **sadness** *n*. **sadden** *vt,vi* make or grow sad.

saddle *n* rider's seat fitted to a horse, bicycle, etc. *vt* **1** put a saddle on. **2** load or burden (with).

sadism *n* perversion in which pleasure, esp. sexual pleasure, is derived from inflicting pain. **sadist** *n*. **sadistic** *adj*.

safari *n* expedition, esp. for hunting big game.

safe *adj* **1** secure; free from danger. **2** dependable; reliable. **safe and sound** unharmed. ~*n* strong box for keeping valuables secure against theft. **safely** *adv*. **safeguard** *n* proviso; precaution. *vt* protect; guard. **safekeeping** *n* custody.

safety *n* security; freedom from danger or risk. **safety belt** *n* strong strap to secure a passenger in the seat of an aircraft, car, etc. **safety pin** *n* bent pin with the point protected by a guard. **safety valve** *n* **1** machine valve that opens when pressure becomes too great for safety. **2** harmless outlet for anger, passion, etc.

sag *vi* (-gg-) **1** droop; bend; sink. **2** give way under weight or pressure.

saga *n* **1** heroic prose tale in old Norse literature. **2** long chronicle, esp. of generations of one family.

sage[1] *n* very wise man. *adj* of great wisdom, discretion, prudence, etc. **sagacity** *n*. **sagely** *adv*.

sage[2] *n* grey-green aromatic herb widely used in cookery.

Sagittarius *n* ninth sign of the zodiac, represented by the Archer.

said *v pp* and *pt* of **say.**

sail *n* **1** large sheet of canvas, etc., spread to catch the wind and propel a boat. **2** arm of a windmill. **3** trip in a sailing vessel. *vt,vi* **1** move by sail power; travel by sea. **2** glide or pass smoothly and easily. **set sail** start on a voyage. **sail close to the wind** narrowly avoid danger, ruin, etc. **sailor** *n* member of ship's crew. **good/bad sailor** one not/very liable to seasickness.

saint *n* holy person canonized or famous for extreme virtue. **saintly** *adj*.

sake *n* purpose; benefit; behalf. **for the sake of** for the advantage or purpose of; in order to help, protect, etc.

salad *n* cold meal of vegetables seasoned and served raw. **fruit salad** mixture of raw fruits. **salad dressing** *n* mixture of oil, vinegar, seasoning, herbs, etc., used to flavour salad.

salamander *n* lizard-like creature of the newt family.

salary *n* fixed payment given periodically for non-manual work. **salaried** *adj* earning a salary.

sale *n* **1** exchange of goods for money. **2** fast disposal of unwanted stock at reduced prices or by auction. **saleable** *adj* easy to sell. **salesman** *n, pl* **-men** person employed to sell. **saleswoman** *f n*. **salesmanship** *n* skill in persuading customers to buy.

saline *adj* of or containing salt. **salinity** *n*.

saliva *n* spittle; colourless odourless juice secreted into the mouth, esp. for moistening food. **salivate** *vi* produce saliva, esp. in excess. **salivation** *n*.

sallow *adj* **1** with skin of a pale yellow colour. **2** unhealthy looking.

salmon *n, pl* **salmon** *or* **salmons** large fish, popular as a food, that goes up rivers to spawn. **salmon pink** *n,adj* orange-pink colour of salmon flesh.

salon *n* **1** large elegant reception room. **2** regular gathering of distinguished guests. **3** exhibition of paintings. **4** premises or shop where dressmakers, hairdressers, etc., receive clients.

saloon *n* **1** large public room in a hotel, ship, train, etc. **2** *also* **saloon bar** more comfortably furnished bar room in a public house. **3** car with an enclosed body.

salt *n* **1** white crystalline compound, sodium chloride, used as food seasoning, preservative, etc. **2** any crystalline compound formed from an acid and base. *vt* season or treat with salt. **salt-cellar** *n* small container for holding salt. **saltpetre** *n* nitrogen compound used in explosives, fertilizers, etc.

salute *n* gesture of greeting, recognition, or respect. *vt,vi* make a salute (to).

salvage *n* act of or reward for saving a ship, property, etc., from destruction or waste. *vt* save from loss or destruction.

salvation *n* act of saving from loss, destruction, or sin.

salve *vt* anoint, heal, or soothe. *n* ointment; balm; whatever soothes or heals.

same *adj* **1** identical. **2** indicating no change. *adv* **the same** in an identical manner; with no change. **all the same** even so; in spite of that; nevertheless. ~*pron* that same or identical thing or person.

sample *n* specimen; example; small quantity showing properties of something. *vt* test or try a sample.

sanatorium *n, pl* **sanatoria** (sænə'tɔ:riə) *or* **sanatoriums 1** hospital, esp. for convalescent, tubercular, mentally unbalanced, or chronically ill patients. **2** place where sickness is treated in a school, college, etc.

sanctify *vt* make holy or sacred; revere.

sanction *vt* allow; authorize; confirm. *n* **1** penalty or reward intended to enforce a law. **2** confirmation; authorization; permission.

sanctity *n* holiness; sacredness.

sanctuary *n* **1** recognized place or right of refuge. **2** part of a church beyond the altar rails. **3** protected reserve for birds, animals, etc.

sand *n* mass of tiny fragments of crushed rocks covering deserts, seashores, etc. *vt* rub with sandpaper. **sandpaper** *n* heavy paper coated with sand or other abrasive and used for smoothing, polishing, etc. **sandy** *adj* **1** covered in sand. **2** of the colour of sand.

sandal *n* open shoe secured by straps.

sandwich *n* two slices of bread enclosing jam, meat, etc. *vt* squeeze (one thing) between two others.

sane *adj* of sound mind; sensible; rational. **sanely** *adv*. **sanity** *n*.

sang *v pt* of **sing.**

sanitary *adj* concerning or conducive to health, esp. in regard to cleanliness and hygiene. **sanitary towel** *n* absorbent pad for use during menstruation. **sanitation** *n* sanitary methods and equipment, esp. concerning sewage disposal, drainage, clean water, etc.

sank *v pt* of **sink.**

sap *n* vital juice, esp. of plants. *vt* (-pp-) drain the sap or energy from. **sapling** *n* young tree.

sapphire *n* gemstone, usually brilliant blue, akin to the ruby. *adj* brilliant blue.

sarcasm *n* mocking, sneering, or ironic language. **sarcastic** *adj*. **sarcastically** *adv*.

sardine *n* young pilchard often packed tightly with others and tinned in oil.

sari *n* Indian or Pakistani woman's garment, worn over a blouse, consisting of a long bolt of cloth that is wrapped around the waist and over the shoulder.

sash[1] *n* band of material worn around the waist or over the shoulder.

sash[2] *n* sliding frame holding panes of glass in a window.

sat *v pt* and *pp* of **sit.**

Satan *n* the Devil. **satanic** *adj*.

satchel *n* small bag with shoulder straps, esp. for holding school books.

satellite *n* **1** heavenly body or spacecraft revolving round a planet or star. **2** disciple; hanger-on; underling.

satin *n* glossy closely woven silk fabric. *adj* of or like satin.

satire *n* **1** use of irony, ridicule, or sarcasm to mock or denounce. **2** literary work exhibiting this. **satirical** *adj*.

satisfy *vt,vi* fulfil the needs or wishes of. *vt* be sufficient for; give enough to; appease. **satisfaction** *n*. **satisfactory** *adj*.

saturate *vt* imbue or soak completely; cause to be thoroughly absorbed in. **saturation** *n*.

Saturday *n* seventh day of the week.

Saturn *n* outer giant planet lying between Jupiter and Uranus and having a system of rings around its equator.

sauce *n* **1** liquid poured over food to add piquancy or relish. **2** *inf* cheeky impudence. **saucy** *adj* **1** cheeky; impertinent; bold. **2** smart; pert. **saucily** *adv*. **sauciness** *n*.

saucepan *n* long-handled cooking pan.

saucer *n* **1** shallow indented dish placed under a cup. **2** anything of similar shape.

sauna *n also* **sauna bath 1** steam bath. **2** room used for this.

saunter *vi* wander idly; stroll; amble. *n* gentle stroll; ramble.

sausage *n* short tube, esp. of animal gut, stuffed with minced seasoned meat.

savage *adj* ferocious; violent; uncivilized. *n* **1** primitive person. **2** one with savage characteristics; brute. *vt* attack and wound.

save[1] *vt* rescue or protect from evil, danger, loss, damage, etc. *vt,vi* **1** store up; set aside for future use. **2** be economical or thrifty. **savings** *pl n* sum of money set aside for future use.

save[2] *prep* except; not including.

saviour *n* one who saves another person, etc., from serious trouble; redeemer. **Saviour** *n* Christ.

savoury *adj* not sweet but with a pleasant appetizing taste. *n* savoury course of a meal.

saw[1] *n* tool with a long toothed metal blade used for cutting wood, etc. *vt,vi* use a saw (on). **sawdust** *n* tiny fragments of wood produced by sawing and used in packaging, etc.

saw[2] *v pt of* **see.**

saxophone *n* brass wind instrument with a single reed and about twenty keys. **saxophonist** *n*.

say *vt,vi* (said) **1** state, utter, or speak in words. **2** declare; tell; repeat. **3** assume; take as an example. *n* **1** chance or turn to speak. **2** authority. **saying** *n* maxim; proverb; something commonly said.

scab *n* **1** crust formed over a healing wound. **2** *sl* blackleg.

scaffold *n* **1** temporary raised platform, esp. for supporting workmen. **2** platform on which criminals are executed. **scaffolding** *n* scaffold or system of scaffolds.

scald *vt* **1** burn with hot liquid. **2** clean or cook with boiling water. **3** bring (milk, etc.) almost to boiling point. *n* burn caused by hot liquid.

scale[1] *n* **1** graded table used as a scheme for classification or measurement. **2** series of musical notes ascending at fixed intervals. **3** range; compass; scope. *vt* clamber up; climb. **scale down** make smaller proportionately.

scale[2] *n* **1** one of the small thin plates protecting fish, reptiles, etc. **2** thin film or layer. *vt,vi* peel off (scales). **scaly** *adj* dry; flaky; hard.

scale[3] *n* **1** dish forming one side of a balance. **2** *also* **scales** weighing machine.

scalp *n* skin covering the head. *vt* tear off scalp and hair from.

scalpel *n* small surgical knife.

scampi *pl or s n* large prawns.

scan *v* (-nn-) *vt* **1** scrutinize carefully. **2** glance briefly over. **3** cast a beam over. **4** classify (verse) by metre. *vi* follow metrical pattern. *n* act of scanning.

scandal *n* **1** act or behaviour outraging public opinion. **2** malicious gossip; slander. **scandalize** *vt* shock by scandal. **scandalous** *adj*. **scandalously** *adv*.

scant *adj* scarcely enough; not plentiful. **scanty** *adj* meagre; inadequate.

scapegoat *n* one forced to bear the blame for others' faults.

scar *n* mark left by a wound. *vt* (-rr-) mark with a scar.

scarce *adj* in short supply; rare. **make oneself scarce** *inf* go away. **scarcely** *adv* **1** hardly; barely; only just. **2** not quite. **scarcity** *n*.

scare *vt* startle; frighten away; alarm. *n* sudden or unreasonable panic. **scary** *adj inf* frightening. **scarecrow** *n* device, often resembling a man, to frighten birds away from crops.

scarf *n, pl* **scarves** piece of material worn over the head or around the neck.

scarlet *adj* brilliant red.

scathing *adj* scornful; showing contempt.

scatter *vt* strew; sprinkle; throw loosely about. *vi* disperse; separate. **scatter-brained** *adj* easily distracted; unable to concentrate.

scavenge *vt,vi* search through litter and rubbish and take (anything of value). **scavenger** *n*.

scenario *n* outline of the plot of a film or play.

scene *n* **1** setting for an action, play, film, etc. **2** short division of an act in a play or film. **3** description of an incident. **4** noisy public outburst. **behind the scenes** not for public view or knowledge. **scenery** *n* **1** theatrical backdrops, properties, etc. **2** natural features of landscape. **scenic** *adj* **1** concerning natural scenery. **2** dramatic; theatrical.

scent *n* **1** individual smell, aroma, or fragrance. **2** mixture of fragrant essences; perfume. **3** sense of smell. *vt* **1** perceive odour of. **2** sense; suspect. **3** impart scent to.

sceptic *n* one unwilling to believe and inclined to question or doubt. **sceptical** *adj*. **scepticism** *n*.

sceptre *n* staff carried as a symbol of regal or imperial power.

schedule *n* **1** timetable; order of events. **2**

inventory or list. *vt* make a schedule of; plan; arrange. **on schedule** as arranged; on time.

scheme *n* **1** planned systematic arrangement. **2** cunning plot. *vt,vi* plan; contrive; plot.

schizophrenia *n* psychosis marked by delusions and inability to distinguish fantasy from reality and often leading to a double personality. **schizophrenic** *adj,n.*

scholar *n* **1** learned person. **2** student or holder of a scholarship. **scholarly** *adj* studious; learned; intellectually thorough. **scholarship** *n* **1** grant awarded to a promising student. **2** erudition; learning.

school[1] *n* **1** place of education, esp. for children. **2** group of students of a particular branch of learning. **3** followers or imitators of a particular theory, artist, etc. *vt* **1** instruct. **2** control. **scholastic** *adj* of schools, learning, etc.

school[2] *n* large body of fish, whales, etc.

schooner *n* **1** swift two-masted sailing ship. **2** large beer or sherry glass.

science *n* knowledge or branch of knowledge obtained by experiment, observation, and critical testing. **science fiction** *n* fiction based on imagined sensational changes or developments of environment, space travel, etc. **scientific** *adj* **1** to do with science. **2** systematic, careful, and exact. **scientist** *n.*

scissors *pl n* cutting tool with two pivoted blades.

scoff[1] *vi* mock or jeer; show scorn and derision. *n* expression of contempt.

scoff[2] *vt sl* eat greedily, ravenously, or quickly. *n sl* food.

scold *vt* find fault with; reprimand.

scone *n* small round plain cake eaten with butter and jam.

scoop *n* **1** small short-handled shovel. **2** journalist's exclusive story. *vt* hollow out or lift as with a scoop.

scooter *n* **1** child's two-wheeled vehicle with handles and a platform, propelled by pushing against the ground with one foot. **2** small low-powered motorcycle.

scope *n* range; extent; field of action.

scorch *vt,vi* **1** burn slightly, so as to discolour but not destroy. **2** dry up with heat; parch.

score *n* **1** tally or record of relative charges, achievements, or points gained. **2** incised line. **3** written musical composition. **4** set of twenty. *vt* **1** gain and record points. **2** furrow or mark with lines. **3** orchestrate. *vi inf* achieve a success. **know the score** know the hard facts. **scoreboard** *n* board on which a score is recorded.

scorn *vt* **1** despise; hold in contempt. **2** refuse contemptuously; disdain to. *n* derision; contempt; mockery. **scornful** *adj.* **scornfully** *adv.*

Scorpio *n* eighth sign of the zodiac, represented by a scorpion.

scorpion *n* member of the spider family with pincers and a joined head and thorax.

scoundrel *n* rascal; villain; rogue.

scour[1] *vt* clean or polish thoroughly by rubbing. *n* act of scouring. **scourer** *n.*

scour[2] *vt* search thoroughly through.

scout *n* one sent out or ahead to bring back information. *vi* act as scout. **Scout** *also* **Boy Scout** boy belonging to an organization founded to encourage high principles, self-reliance, etc.

scowl *vi* frown angrily or sullenly. *n* bad-tempered sullen frown.

scramble *vi* make one's way fast and awkwardly, esp. as to race others to a goal. *vt* **1** mix or muddle. **2** alter the frequencies of (a radio message, etc.) so as to render it unintelligible. *n* **1** undignified rush. **2** motorcycle race over rough ground. **scrambled eggs** eggs beaten and cooked.

scrap *n* **1** morsel; fragment. **2** rubbish; leftovers. **3** *inf* fight; quarrel. *vt* (-pp-) discard; throw away. **scrapbook** *n* blank book into which newspaper cuttings, photographs, etc., are pasted. **scrap iron** *n* fragments of metal useful only for remelting.

scrape *vt* smooth or damage by rubbing with a sharp edge. **scrape through** succeed by a narrow margin. **scrape up** *or* **together** gather with difficulty, diligence, or thrift. ~*n* **1** scratch. **2** *inf* awkward predicament.

scratch *vt,vi* **1** mark or cut with something sharp or be susceptible to such marking. **2** rub the nails over (the skin) to relieve itching. *vt* cancel; erase. *n* mark or sound made by scratching. **from scratch** from the very beginning. **up to scratch** *inf* acceptable; up to standard. **scratchy** *adj* **1** marked with scratches. **2** ragged; irregular. **3** irritable.

scrawl *vt,vi* scribble; write fast and unintelligibly. *n* illegible writing.

scream *vt,vi* shriek or cry out in a high loud

voice. *n* **1** piercing cry. **2** *inf* hilarious joke. **screamingly** *adv* hilariously.

screech *vi* cry out in a harsh shrill voice. *n* sound made by screeching.

screen *n* movable board or partition acting as a room divider, surface to project films, protection from heat or observation, etc. *vt* **1** hide or shelter. **2** display on a cinema or television screen. **3** subject to tests to determine weakness, disease, qualities, etc. **screenplay** *n* script for a film.

screw *n* spiral grooved metal shaft used as a fastening device. **have a screw loose** be mentally deficient. **put the screws on** extort by blackmail. ~*vt* fasten; tighten; compress with a screw. *vt,vi tab* have sexual intercourse (with). **screw up 1** tighten firmly with a screw. **2** twist; distort; crumple. **3** summon up. **screwdriver** *n* tool with metal wedge-shaped blade, which slots into the groove on the head of a screw to turn it. **screwy** *adj sl* crazy.

scribble *vt,vi* write carelessly, fast, or meaninglessly. *n* careless or meaningless writing. **scribbler** *n*.

script *n* **1** text of a film, play, speech, etc. **2** handwriting or print resembling it. **scriptwriter** *n* one who writes scripts, dialogues, television series, etc.

scripture *n* the Bible. **scriptural** *adj*.

scroll *n* **1** roll of parchment or paper. **2** ornamental design resembling a scroll.

scrounge *vt,vi inf* cadge; sponge; wheedle or scrape together. **scrounger** *n*.

scrub[1] *vt,vi* (-bb-) clean by rubbing hard with a brush and water. *n* act of scrubbing.

scrub[2] *n* landscape of low stunted trees, bushes, and shrubs.

scruffy *adj* untidy; unkempt; messy. **scruffily** *adv*. **scruffiness** *n*.

scruple *n* moral doubt or hesitation. *vi* hesitate because of scruple.

scrupulous *adj* conscientious; attentive to details. **scrupulously** *adv*.

scrutinize *vt* examine closely, critically, or in great detail. **scrutiny** *n*.

scuffle *n* close confused struggle or fight. *vi* fight in a disorderly manner.

scullery *n* small room for rough kitchen work, dish washing, etc.

sculpture *n* **1** art of making figures, statues, etc., by carving or moulding. **2** work or works made in this way. **sculpt** *vt,vi* make a sculpture (of). **sculptor** *n*.

scum *n* **1** foam on the surface of a liquid. **2** worthless or disgusting residue.

scurf *n* crust of small flakes of dead skin, esp. on the scalp; dandruff.

scythe *n* implement with a large curved blade for cutting grass. *vt* cut with a scythe.

sea *n* **1** continuous expanse of salt water that covers most of the earth's surface. **2** large body of salt water partially bounded by land. **3** large lake. **4** condition, turbulence, waves, etc., of an ocean or sea. **5** something suggestive of the sea in being vast or overwhelming. **at sea 1** on the ocean. **2** confused. **go to sea 1** become a sailor. **2** start an ocean voyage. **put to sea** leave port.

sea anemone *n* common marine animal whose arrangement of tentacles resembles a flower.

seacoast strip of land bordering on an ocean or sea.

seafront *n* area of a seaside resort directly facing the sea and having a promenade, hotels, etc.

seagull *n* gull frequenting the sea or coast.

seahorse *n* **1** marine fish that swims in an upright position and has a head shaped like that of a horse. **2** walrus.

sea-kale vegetable having broad green leaves.

seal[1] *n* **1** impression on wax or metal serving as an authorization, guarantee, etc. **2** anything used to close tightly to prevent leaking or opening. *vt* mark, attest, or close firmly with a seal. **set the seal on** formally conclude.

seal[2] *n* carnivorous marine mammal with flippers, a short tail, and a long body covered in dense fur. **sealskin** *n* close short furry hide of the seal, sometimes used for clothing.

sea-level *n* level of the sea midway between high and low tide.

sea-lion *n* large seal having visible external ears.

seam *n* join formed by sewing together or attaching two pieces of material. **seamy** *adj* squalid.

seaman *n, pl* **-men** sailor, esp. below the rank of officer. **seamanship** *n* skill or techniques of ship management, operation, and navigation.

seaplane *n* aeroplane equipped to land on or take off from the water.

search *vt,vi* examine, probe, or investigate closely hoping to find something. *n* investigation; exploration; enquiry. **search me!** *sl* I have no idea! **searchlight** *n* lamp emitting a strong beam of artificial light used to scan an area, the sky, etc.

seashore *n* seacoast.

seasick *adj* nauseated by the movement of a vessel at sea. **seasickness** *n*.

seaside *n* seacoast. *adj* relating to or located at the seacoast.

season *n* **1** one of the four climatic divisions of the year. **2** appropriate time; short spell. **in season 1** (of game, fish, foxes, etc.) allowed to be legally hunted or caught. **2** ripe; ready for use. ~*vt* **1** flavour with salt, pepper, etc. **2** accustom; mature. **seasonable** *adj* appropriate to the moment or occasion; timely. **seasonal** *adj* occurring at or changing with the season. **seasoned** *adj* **1** experienced. **2** flavoured; tempered. **seasoning** *n* **1** food flavouring, such as salt, pepper, or herbs. **2** processing of timber. **season ticket** *n* ticket valid for repeated use over a set period.

seat *n* **1** chair or part of a chair; place to sit. **2** position in Parliament, a council, etc., to which one is elected or appointed. **3** basis; central location or site. **4** manner of sitting (on a horse, etc.). **5** buttocks; bottom. *vt* place on a seat; accommodate in a chair or chairs. **seat-belt** *n* safety belt.

seaweed *n* plant or alga growing in the ocean.

seaworthy *adj* (of a vessel) fit for sailing. **seaworthiness** *n*.

secluded *adj* hidden or shut off from observation or company. **seclusion** *n* privacy; solitude.

second[1] *adj* **1** coming between the first and the third. **2** another; additional; extra. **3** alternate; alternative. *adv* in second place. *n* person or thing in second place. *vt* support (another's proposal or nomination). **secondly** *adv*. **second best** *adj* inferior to the best. **second-class** *adj* of second or inferior class, quality, etc. **second-hand** *adj* not new; having belonged to another. **second nature** *n* habit or tendency that has become automatic or instinctive. **second-rate** *adj* of inferior quality or value; shoddy.

second[2] *n* **1** period of time equal to one sixtieth of a minute. **2** moment; instant. **3** unit by which time is measured.

secondary *adj* subordinate; of less importance; coming second. **secondary school** *n* school teaching children over the age of eleven.

secret *adj* concealed; hidden; private; not made known. *n* whatever is made or kept secret. **secrecy** *n*. **secretly** *adv*. **secret agent** *n* spy.

secretary *n* **1** one employed to help with correspondence, keep records, etc. **2** principal assistant to a minister, ambassador, etc. **secretarial** *adj*.

secrete *vt* (of a gland, cell, etc.) produce and release (substances such as saliva, etc.). **secretion** *n*.

secretive *adj* reticent; given to undue secrecy; uncommunicative.

sect *n* group of people following a particular leader or holding specific views. **sectarian** *n,adj*.

section *n* division or portion; part. *vt* cut or separate into parts.

sector *n* **1** part of a circle bounded by two radii and an arc. **2** area; part; scope of activity.

secular *adj* temporal; lay; not spiritual or monastic. *n* priest bound by no monastic rule.

secure *adj* **1** safe; free from danger. **2** reliable; certain. **3** not movable. *vt* **1** make safe, certain, or sure. **2** obtain. **securely** *adv*. **security** *n* **1** safety; freedom from anxiety, danger, or want. **2** pledge, document, or certificate of ownership; bond or share. **3** precautions against espionage, theft, etc.

sedate *adj* **1** calm; placid; tranquil. **2** staid; dignified. **sedately** *adv*. **sedateness** *n*. **sedation** *n* act of calming or state of calmness induced by sedatives. **sedative** *adj* calming; soporific. *n* sedative drug.

sediment *n* dregs or residue at the bottom of a liquid. **sedimentary** *adj*.

seduce *vt* **1** entice, lure, or tempt, esp. into evil. **2** persuade to have sexual intercourse. **seducer** *n*. **seduction** *n*. **seductive** *adj*.

see[1] *v* (saw; seen) *vi* **1** have the power of sight. **2** find out, investigate. **3** attend (to). *vt* **1** look at; perceive; be aware of; observe. **2** experience. **3** visit. **4** realize; consider. **5** discover. **6** consult. **7** make sure; check; take care. *vt,vi* understand; comprehend. **see through 1** fail to be deceived by. **2** finish; remain with until completion.

see[2] *n* office or diocese of a bishop.

seed *n* **1** tiny cell containing an embryonic plant. **2** germ; first principle. *vt* **1** sow. 2

remove the seed from. **run to seed** deteriorate; decay. **seedling** *n* young plant grown from seed.

seedy *adj* shabby.

seek *vt,vi* (sought) look for; try to find; search (for).

seem *vi* appear to be; give the impression of being. **seeming** *adj* apparent. **seemingly** *adv*. **seemly** *adj* appropriate; decent.

seep *vi* ooze; percolate; leak through. **seepage** *n*.

seesaw *n* plank so balanced that children seated on either end can ride up or down alternately. *vi* move or vacillate like a seesaw.

seethe *vi* surge or be agitated (with extreme fury, excitement, etc.).

segment *n* **1** part of a circle bounded by a chord and arc. **2** section; portion. *vt,vi* divide into segments. **segmentary** *adj*. **segmentation** *n*.

segregate *vt* separate from others; isolate; group apart, esp. racially. **segregation** *n*.

seize *vt* take possession of, esp. suddenly or by force. **seize up** become jammed or stuck. **seizure** *n* **1** act of seizing. **2** sudden attack of illness; fit.

seldom *adv* rarely; only occasionally.

select *vt* choose; pick out for preference. *adj* choice; exclusive. **selection** *n* **1** act or result of choice; discrimination. **2** item or items selected. **3** scope or range of selected items. **selective** *adj* **1** able to select or discriminate. **2** tending to select very carefully. **selectively** *adv*.

self *n, pl* **selves 1** person or thing regarded as individual. **2** personality or ego.

self-assured *adj* confident; not shy. **self-assurance** *n*.

self-aware *adj* able to view oneself objectively. **self-awareness** *n*.

self-centred *adj* preoccupied with oneself; selfish. **self-centredness** *n*.

self-confident *adj* having confidence in oneself. **self-confidence** *n*.

self-conscious *adj* shy; embarrassed. **self-consciously** *adv*. **self-consciousness** *n*.

self-contained *adj* **1** reserved; absorbed in oneself. **2** (of accommodation) complete; not approached through another's property.

self-defence *n* protection of oneself or one's rights, property, etc.

self-discipline *n* control of one's own behaviour, emotions, etc. **self-disciplined** *adj*.

self-employed *adj* working for oneself; freelance.

self-expression *n* voicing or demonstrating one's own personality or beliefs.

self-interest *n* desire for benefit or advantage to oneself.

selfish *adj* motivated by self-interest; showing little regard for others. **selfishly** *adv*. **selfishness** *n*.

self-pity *n* pity for oneself; feeling of being sorry for oneself. **self-pitying** *adj*.

self-portrait *n* picture painted by an artist of himself.

self-respect *n* pride; dignity; integrity.

self-righteous *adj* excessively confident in one's own merits, judgment, etc.; hypocritical. **self-righteously** *adv*. **self-righteousness** *n*.

self-sacrifice *n* subordination of one's own desires or rights to another's.

selfsame *adj* (the) very same; exactly the same.

self-satisfied *adj* smug; conceited.

self-service *adj* (of a restaurant, shop, etc.) where the customer serves himself.

self-sufficient *adj* **1** needing nothing from outside oneself. **2** economically independent. **self-sufficiency** *n*.

self-will *n* obstinacy. **self-willed** *adj*.

sell *vt* (sold) **1** exchange for money. **2** betray for an ignoble motive. **3** extol; praise the virtues of. **sell off** sell cheaply to clear stock. **sell out 1** sell whole stock in trade. **2** betray for profit. **sell up 1** sell a debtor's goods in settlement. **2** sell a business.

Sellotape *n Tdmk* transparent adhesive cellulose tape. *vt* attach, stick down, etc., with adhesive tape.

selves *n pl* of **self**.

semaphore *n* means of signalling by flags. *vt,vi* signal using flags.

semen *n* fluid and cells produced by the male reproductive organs.

semibreve *n* musical note equal to two minims or four crotchets.

semicircle *n* half a circle. **semicircular** *adj*.

semicolon *n* punctuation mark (;) showing a sentence division that is stronger than a comma but less marked than a colon.

semiconductor *n* substance whose electrical conductivity increases with added impurities, used in transistors and other electronic components.

semidetached *adj* (of a house) joined to another on one side.

semifinal *n* last round of a tournament before the final. **semifinalist** *n*.

seminar *n* class of advanced students working on a specific subject.

semiprecious *adj* (of stones) valuable, but not rare or valuable enough to be classed as precious.

semiquaver *n* musical note half the length of a quaver.

semitone *n* musical interval between a note and its sharp or flat.

semolina *n* particles of fine hard wheat used for making milk puddings, pasta, etc.

senate *n also* **Senate 1** legislative or governing body of ancient Rome, modern British universities, etc. **2** upper house of government of the US, Australia, Canada, etc. **senator** *n*.

send *vt* (sent) **1** cause (mail, goods, a message, etc.) to be transmitted or taken. **2** direct; convey. **3** drive or force into a particular condition or state. **send for** ask to come; demand the services of.

senile *adj* weak or deteriorating through old age. **senility** *n*.

senior *adj* older, higher, or more experienced or advanced. *n* one who is senior. **seniority** *n*.

sensation *n* **1** feeling; perception through the senses. **2** public or melodramatic excitement. **sensational** *adj* exciting; thrilling; startling. **sensationally** *adv*.

sense *n* **1** faculty of sight, hearing, smell, touch, or taste. **2** sensation; feeling. **3** awareness; perception. **4** intelligence; common sense. **5** meaning or definition, esp. of a word or phrase. **make sense** be logical, reasonable, or coherent. ~*vt* **1** feel; be aware of. **2** comprehend, esp. intuitively. **senseless** *adj* **1** meaningless; motiveless; foolish. **2** unconscious.

sensible *adj* **1** wise; reasonable; practical. **2** aware. **3** appreciable by the senses. **sensibly** *adv*. **sensibility** *n* delicacy or capacity of emotional, mental, or moral responses.

sensitive *adj* **1** easily affected by another's emotions, actions, plight, etc. **2** easily irritated by certain stimuli. **sensitively** *adv*. **sensitivity** *or* **sensitiveness** *n*.

sensual *adj* **1** relating to the senses. **2** seeking pleasure or gratification of the senses. **3** voluptuous; licentious. **sensuality** *n*. **sensually** *adv*.

sensuous *adj* relating or pleasing to the senses. **sensuously** *adv*. **sensuousness** *n*.

sent *v pt* and *pp* of **send.**

sentence *n* **1** number of words forming a grammatical unit, usually containing a subject, predicate, and finite verb. **2** punishment allotted to an offender in court. *vt* pronounce judgment on (a person) in a court of law.

sentiment *n* thought or opinion at least partly dictated by emotion. **sentimental** *adj* **1** overemotional; mawkish. **2** having romantic or tender feelings. **sentimentality** *n*.

sentry *n* soldier, etc., posted to stand guard.

separate *v* ('sepəreit) *vt* set or keep apart; divide. *vi* go, move, or live apart. *adj* ('seprit) distinct; divided; individual. **separable** *adj*. **separately** *adv*. **separation** *n*.

September *n* ninth month of the year.

septic *adj* putrefying because of the presence of bacteria.

sequel *n* result; consequence; whatever succeeds, follows, or happens next.

sequence *n* **1** order of succession; series. **2** scene from a film. **sequential** *adj*. **sequentially** *adv*.

sequin *n* tiny sparkling piece of foil used to decorate clothing.

serenade *n* piece of music traditionally played at night by a lover under his lady's window. *vt* entertain with a serenade.

serene *adj* tranquil; calm; placid. **serenely** *adv*. **serenity** *n*.

serf *n* medieval farm labourer or peasant bound to the land. **serfdom** *n*.

sergeant *n* **1** noncommissioned officer ranking above a corporal. **2** police officer ranking between constable and inspector. **sergeant-major** *n* highest grade of noncommissioned officer.

serial *adj* forming a series; in instalments. *n* story told in instalments. **serialize** *vt* divide (a story, film, etc.) into instalments or episodes.

series *n, pl* **series** sequence; succession of things, episodes, etc., with similar characters, subjects, or purposes.

serious *adj* solemn; grave; earnest; not comic or frivolous. **seriously** *adv*. **seriousness** *n*.

sermon *n* speech, esp. one delivered from a pulpit, with a strong scriptural or moral lesson.

serpent *n* snake. **serpentine** *adj* **1** relating to serpents. **2** twisting; convoluted.

servant *n* person employed to serve another.

serve *vt,vi* **1** work for; wait upon. **2** be of use to; help. **3** act or offer as a host. **4** deliver (the ball) in certain games. **5** spend (a specified period of time, enlistment, etc.). *vt* **1** obey or honour. **2** deliver (a summons, etc.) to. **serve someone right** be an appropriate punishment. ~*n* act or turn of delivering the ball in certain games.

service *n* **1** work, position, or duty of a servant. **2** religious rite or ceremony. **3** supply, maintenance, or repair. **4** set of dishes, etc. **5** act of serving or turn to serve the ball in tennis, etc. **6** supply or system of a public utility. **7** branch of government or public employment. **8** help; assistance. (**the**) **services** *pl n* Army, Navy, and Air Force. ~*vt* do maintenance work on. **serviceable** *adj* useful; durable but not decorative. **service station** *n* roadside garage providing petrol and repair services.

serviette *n* table napkin.

servile *adj* **1** of servants or slaves. **2** menial; cringing. **servility** *n*.

session *n* period during which a court, Parliament, etc., sits, universities function, or meetings or interviews take place.

set *v* (-tt-; set) *vt* **1** place; position; put. **2** cause or prompt. **3** fix; regulate; mend. **4** make firm or hard. **5** put (hair) in rollers, etc., to produce waves or curls. **6** bring into contact with fire; ignite; light. **7** establish as a standard, record, etc. **8** require the completion of (an examination, task, etc.). *vi* **1** become firm or hard; solidify. **2** (of the sun) fall below the horizon. **3** (of bones, etc.) mend. **set about** begin to deal with. **set in** become established. **set off** *or* **out** begin a journey; leave. **set up** start (a business, scheme, etc.); establish; found. ~*adj* **1** fixed; settled; determined; not alterable. **2** ready; prepared. *n* **1** group of people; class. **2** number of things that match or are designed to be used together. **3** scenery used for a play. **4** studio or area used when making a film, TV broadcast, etc. **setback** *n* relapse; check; halt. **setting** *n* frame, background, scenery, environment, etc., in which anything is set.

settee *n* long upholstered seat with a back and arms; couch; sofa.

settle *vt* **1** place at rest or in comfort, peace, order, etc. **2** decide finally. **3** give money to; resolve (debts). *vi* **1** subside; come to rest; sink. **2** take up residence. **3** reach a decision. **settle down** take up a settled normal established way of life. **settle for** agree to accept. **settle in** adapt to a new environment, circumstances, etc. **settle up** balance accounts; pay. **settlement** *n* **1** act or state of settling, paying, etc. **2** group of social workers in an underprivileged community. **3** newly established colony. **4** sinking or subsidence.

seven *n* **1** number equal to one plus six. **2** group of seven persons, things, etc. **3** *also* **seven o'clock** seven hours after noon or midnight. *adj* amounting to seven. **seventh** *adj* coming between sixth and eighth in sequence. *n* **1** seventh person, object, etc. **2** one of seven equal parts; one divided by seven.

seventeen *n* **1** number that is seven more than ten. **2** seventeen things or people. *adj* amounting to seventeen. **seventeenth** *adj,adv,n*.

seventy *n* **1** number equal to seven times ten. **2** seventy things or people. *adj* amounting to seventy. **seventieth** *adj,adv,n*.

sever *vt,vi* separate; cut; end. **severance** *n*.

several *adj* **1** more than one; a few. **2** separate; distinct; various.

severe *adj* **1** harsh; strict; violent. **2** grave; serious. **3** unadorned; plain; austere. **severely** *adv*. **severity** *n*.

sew *vt,vi* (sewed; sewn *or* sewed) work on, fasten, join, embroider, etc., with a needle and thread; stitch.

sewage *n* used water supply containing domestic refuse and waste matter. **sewer** *n* underground pipe or drain for carrying sewage. **sewerage** *n* provision or system of sewers.

sex *n* **1** characteristics distinguishing male from female. **2** males or females. **3** sexual desires, instincts, or intercourse.

sextet *n* **1** group of or work composed for six musicians. **2** group of six.

sexual *adj* relating to sex or sex organs. **sexuality** *n* awareness of one's own sexual characteristics.

sexy *adj* sexually attractive or stimulating. **sexily** *adv*. **sexiness** *n*.

shabby *adj* **1** worn; dilapidated; ragged. **2** despicable; dishonourable. **shabbily** *adv*. **shabbiness** *n*.

shack *n* rough hut.

shade *n* **1** comparative darkness caused by shelter from light or sun. **2** screen against light. **3** gradation of colour. **4** small amount; tiny degree. *vt* shield from light; darken. **shady** *adj* **1** out of bright sunlight. **2** *inf* dishonest; of dubious reputation.

shadow *n* **1** dark outline of an object placed in front of light or sun. **2** mere insubstantial copy. **3** constant companion. *vt* **1** shade from light. **2** follow closely and secretly. **shadowy** *adj*. **shadow cabinet** *n* group of leading Opposition politicians determining policy should their party return to power.

shaft *n* **1** long straight narrow rod, handle, beam of light, column, etc. **2** vertical passage into a mine.

shaggy *adj* unkempt; tangled. **shaggily** *adv*.

shake *v* (shook; shaken) *vt* agitate; move with small fast gestures. *vi* tremble; be agitated. **shake off** get rid of. **shaky** *adj* unreliable; precarious; wobbling.

shall *v aux* used to express future probability or intention.

shallot *n* small onion similar to but milder than garlic.

shallow *adj* **1** not deep. **2** not profound; superficial. **shallowness** *n*.

shame *n* **1** feeling of humiliation caused by guilt, failure, disgrace, etc. **2** sense of modesty, pride, or dignity. **3** disappointing or unlucky event. *vt* bring shame upon. **put to shame** cause to feel inferior. **shameful** *adj*. **shamefully** *adv*. **shamefaced** *adj* embarrassed; humiliated; ashamed.

shampoo *n* preparation for washing hair, carpets, upholstery, etc. *vt* rub clean with shampoo.

shamrock *n* type of small three-leaved plant, used as the Irish emblem.

shandy *n* drink made by mixing beer with lemonade or ginger beer.

shanty[1] small roughly built cabin or shack.

shanty[2] *n* rousing sailors' song.

shape *n* **1** external appearance of an object or figure; outline; form. **2** condition; situation; state. **take shape** begin to develop or take on a definite form. ~*vt* **1** make a particular shape of. **2** develop; fit. **shapeless** *adj* not having the proper or appropriate shape. **shapely** *adj* well shaped.

share *n* **1** part; portion or division given to or contributed by an individual. **2** fixed equal part of a company's capital. *vt* divide into shares. **share out** distribute; allot. **shareholder** *n* one holding a share, esp. in a company.

shark *n* large long-bodied voracious and often dangerous marine fish.

sharp *adj* **1** having a fine edge or point; cutting; piercing. **2** acid; shrill; painful; intense. **3** clear-cut. **4** quick; lively. **5** artful; dishonest. **6** (in music) above true pitch; a semitone higher than the note. *adv* **1** punctually. **2** too high in pitch. **look sharp** hurry. **sharp-sighted** *adj* **1** having excellent eyesight. **2** shrewd; sharp-witted. **sharpen** *vt,vi* become or make sharp.

shatter *vt,vi* **1** smash or break into fragments. **2** wreck; exhaust; destroy.

shave *vt,vi* scrape off a superficial layer, esp. of facial hair. *n* act of shaving. **close shave** narrow escape; near miss.

shawl *n* folded square of material worn loosely around the shoulders or wrapped around a baby.

she *pron* female person; the 3rd person singular as the subject.

sheaf *n, pl* **sheaves** **1** large bundle of cereal crops tied together after reaping. **2** bundle of papers.

shear *vt* (sheared; shorn *or* sheared) clip or cut off hair or wool, esp. from sheep. **shears** *pl n* cutting implement resembling large scissors.

sheath *n* tightly fitting case or covering for a blade, insects' wings, etc. **sheathe** *vt* enclose in a sheath.

shed[1] *vt* (-dd-; shed) cast off; let fall; pour out. **shed light on** reveal; illuminate.

shed[2] *n* small simple building; hut.

sheen *n* glow; radiance; lustre.

sheep *n, pl* **sheep** wild or domesticated ruminant mammal reared for meat and wool. **black sheep** rogue. **sheepish** *adj* embarrassed through being wrong, etc. **sheepishly** *adv*. **sheepdog** *n* dog trained to herd sheep. **sheepskin** *n* skin of a sheep used for rugs, coats, etc.

sheer[1] *adj* **1** perpendicular; very steep. **2** unqualified; complete; utter. *adv* **1** vertically. **2** outright.

sheer[2] *vi* swerve; deviate. **sheer off** **1** move away. **2** snap off with a clean break.

sheet[1] **1** large thin rectangle of cotton, linen,

nylon, etc., for a bed. **2** thin rectangular piece of paper, metal, etc.

sheet[2] *n* rope attached to a sail of a boat.

sheikh *n* head of an Arab family or tribe. **sheikhdom** *n* area ruled by a sheikh.

shelf *n, pl* **shelves** horizontal board set into a wall, bookcase, cupboard, etc. **on the shelf** (usually of a woman) not married and unlikely to be so.

shell *n* **1** hard outer case enclosing an egg, nut, shellfish, tortoise, etc. **2** framework; outline. **3** explosive device fired from heavy guns. *vt* **1** remove shell from. **2** bombard. **shell out** *inf* pay. **shellfish** *n* aquatic mollusc or crustacean with a shell.

shelter *n* place or thing providing safety from weather, attack, danger, etc. *vt* shield; protect. *vi* take cover.

shelve *vt* **1** provide with or put on a shelf. **2** postpone indefinitely.

shepherd *n* one who guards and herds sheep. *vt* guide and herd like a shepherd. **shepherdess** *f n*.

sherbet *n* fizzy drink or powder for making it.

sheriff *n* chief Crown officer of a county, responsible for keeping the peace, administering courts, etc.

sherry *n* fortified wine, esp. from Spain.

shield *n* **1** broad piece of armour carried to protect the body. **2** anything serving as shelter, protection, or defence. *vt* protect; screen.

shift *vt,vi* move; change position (of). *vi* manage; make do. *n* **1** movement; change of position. **2** period of work on a rota or relay system. **3** undergarment.

shilling *n* former British coin or unit of currency worth five new pence.

shimmer *vi* glisten; gleam with faint diffuse light. *n* faint light.

shin *n* **1** front of the human leg below the knee. **2** beef from the lower part of the leg. *vi* climb up (a tree, rope, etc.) quickly, using only the arms and legs.

shine *vi* (shone) **1** give off or reflect light; beam; glow. **2** excel; be conspicuous or animated. *vt* (shined) polish (shoes, etc.). *n* sheen; lustre. **shiny** *adj*.

ship *n* large floating sea-going vessel. *vt* (-pp-) carry or send by ship. **shipment** *n* **1** cargo; goods shipped together. **2** shipping goods. **shipping** *n* **1** business of transporting goods by sea. **2** number of ships, esp. of a country or port. **shipshape** *adj* well-ordered; clean; neat. **shipwreck** *n* destruction or loss of a ship at sea. *vt,vi* cause or suffer shipwreck; ruin. **shipyard** *n* dock or yard where ships are built and repaired.

shirk *vt,vi* evade (duties or obligations). **shirker** *n*.

shirt *n* loose garment covering the top half of the body, esp. with sleeves, collar, and cuffs. **shirty** *adj sl* bad-tempered; irritable.

shiver *vi* tremble or quiver with cold, excitement, or fear. *n* tremble; shivering motion.

shock[1] *n* **1** alarming startling experience. **2** violent collision or impact. **3** bodily condition of near or complete collapse because of rapid falling of blood pressure. **4** *also* **electric shock** condition resulting from bodily contact with a strong electric current. *vt* shake or alarm by violent impact, frightening experience, improper outrageous behaviour, etc. **shock absorber** *n* device for diminishing vibration in vehicles.

shock[2] *n* thick shaggy mass, esp. of hair.

shoddy *adj* of inferior quality; cheap and nasty. *n* cloth made from scraps of other materials. **shoddily** *adv*. **shoddiness** *n*.

shoe *n* **1** outer covering for the foot. **2** anything resembling a shoe. *vt* (shod) provide shoes for.

shone *v pt* and *pp* of **shine.**

shook *v pt* and *pp* of **shake.**

shoot *v* (shot) *vt,vi* **1** fire (a gun). **2** propel (a bullet, arrow, etc.). **3** send out suddenly; project. **4** sprout; put out buds. **5** photograph or film. *vt* injure or kill with a gun. *vi* hunt game for sport with a gun. *n* **1** young branch or sprout. **2** hunting or shooting party. **3** inclined plank or trough down which water, rubbish, coal, etc., may be thrown; chute. **good/bad shot** good/bad marksman.

shop *n* **1** place where goods are sold. **2** place where industrial work is carried out. **on the shop floor** amongst the workers in a factory, workshop, etc. **talk shop** discuss one's own occupation or job. ~*vi* (-pp-) visit shops to buy goods. **shop around** compare values at different shops. **shopkeeper** *n* owner or manager of a shop. **shoplifter** *n* one who steals goods from a shop. **shoplifting** *n*. **shop steward** *n* trade union's elected departmental delegate.

shore[1] *n* land bordering a river, lake, or sea.

shore[2] *vt* support or prop up (a building, ship, etc.). *n* prop.

shorn *v pp* of **shear.**

short *adj* **1** of relatively little length; not long or tall. **2** lasting for a little while; brief. **3** brusque; abrupt; curt. **4** not plentiful; sparse; inadequate; insufficient. **5** abbreviated; cut. *adv* abruptly. *n* **in short** as a summary; briefly. **shorts** *pl n* short trousers, worn esp. when participating in certain sports. **shortness** *n.* **shortage** *n* lack; deficiency. **shortbread** *n* crisp biscuit made from butter, flour, and sugar. **shortcoming** *n* failure; deficiency. **shorten** *vt,vi* decrease; reduce. **shorthand** *n* system of symbols used for writing at speed. **shorthanded** *adj* short of staff; undermanned. **shortlived** *adj* transitory; brief. **shortly** *adv* **1** soon; in a short time. **2** briefly; abruptly. **short-sighted** *adj* **1** unable to see clearly at a distance. **2** without imagination or foresight. **short-sightedly** *adv.* **short-sightedness** *n.* **short-tempered** *adj* liable to lose one's temper easily; irritable. **short-term** *n* immediate future.

shot *n* **1** act of shooting or the missile shot. **2** photograph. **3** attempt; try. **4** hypodermic injection. **be/get shot of** be/get rid of. **like a shot** with great speed. **shot in the arm** encouragement. **shot in the dark** mere guess. *~adj* of changing colour. *v pt* and *pp* of **shoot. shotgun** *n* smooth bore gun firing small shot.

should *v aux* **1** used to express obligation, duty, or likelihood. **2** used to form the conditional tense. **3** used in indirect speech.

shoulder *n* **1** part of the body where the arm is attached. **2** corresponding part in animals and birds. **3** prominent part of a hillside, bottle, vase, etc. **4** roadside verge. **give the cold shoulder to** snub. **rub shoulders with** mix with; get to know. *~vt* **1** push, lift, or jostle with the shoulder. **2** accept (responsibility). **shoulder-blade** *n* broad flat bone of the upper back.

shout *n* loud cry or call. *vt,vi* utter (with) a shout.

shove *vt,vi* push; thrust; jostle. *n* hard push. **shove off 1** push a boat away from the shore. **2** *sl* leave.

shovel *n* broad often short-handled spade for lifting coal, earth, etc. *vt* (-ll-) move with or as if with a shovel.

show *v* (showed; shown) *vt* **1** display; allow to be seen. **2** conduct; guide. **3** reveal; indicate. **4** demonstrate; instruct. **5** prove; give evidence of. *vi* **1** be able to be seen; be revealed or displayed. **2** be evident; prove. **show off** behave in a pretentious way. *~n* **1** exhibition or display. **2** entertainment with dancers, singers, etc. **show business** *n* profession of theatrical entertainers, variety artists, etc. **showcase** *n* glass-fronted display cabinet. **showdown** *n* open conflict or challenge. **show-jumping** *n* horse-jumping displayed in competition. **showmanship** *n* skill in displaying goods, theatrical productions, etc., to the best advantage. **showroom** *n* room in which goods may be viewed.

shower *n* **1** short fall of rain, bullets, blows, etc. **2** large supply; abundant flow. **3** bathroom fitting from which water is sprayed from above. *vt* fall or pour out, as in a shower. **showery** *adj.* **showerproof** *adj* impervious to showers.

shrank *v pt* of **shrink.**

shred *n* strip; fragment. *vt* (-dd-; shredded *or* shred) cut or tear into shreds.

shrew *n* **1** small mammal resembling a mouse and also having an elongated snout. **2** bad-tempered woman.

shrewd *adj* **1** discerning; astute; wise. **2** cunning; sly. **shrewdly** *adv.* **shrewdness** *n.*

shriek *n* high piercing cry or scream. *vt,vi* utter (with a shriek).

shrill *adj* high-pitched, piercing, and insistent. *vt,vi* utter in a shrill manner. **shrillness** *n.* **shrilly** *adv.*

shrimp *n* **1** tiny edible crustacean smaller than and similar to a prawn. **2** *inf* small person.

shrine *n* **1** place hallowed by associations with a saint. **2** casket containing holy relics.

shrink *vi* (shrank; shrunk *or* shrunken) become smaller; contract, esp. when wet. **shrink (back) from** recoil or flinch from; shun.

shrivel *vi* (-ll-) *also* **shrivel up** become shrunken, withered, and wrinkled.

shroud *n* **1** sheet wrapped around a dead body. **2** anything that veils or wraps round. **3** set of ropes forming part of a ship's rigging. *vt* cloak or cover (in secrecy, antiquity, etc.).

Shrove Tuesday *n* day of confession and subsequent merrymaking before Lent.

shrub *n* low bush with no central trunk. **shrubbery** *n* area or group of shrubs.

shrug *vt,vi* (-gg-) raise the shoulders to express indifference, doubt, or dislike. *n* act of shrugging. **shrug off** shake off with indifference.

shrunk *v* a *pp* of **shrink.**

shrunken *v* a *pp* of **shrink.**

shudder *n* shiver, esp. with horror, fear, etc. *vi* **1** tremble as with horror. **2** vibrate.

shuffle *vt,vi* **1** move slowly without lifting the feet from the ground. **2** mix randomly, esp. playing cards. *n* act of shuffling.

shun *vt* (-nn-) avoid; stay away from.

shunt *vt,vi* **1** divert (a train) to another track. **2** bypass; sidetrack. *vi inf* move; go away. *n* **1** act of shunting. **2** electrical conductor diverting current.

shut *v* (-tt-; shut) *vt* **1** move (a door, the eyes, mouth, etc.) so as to be no longer open; close. **2** fasten; secure; lock or bolt. **3** cease to operate, trade, etc. *vi* become closed. **shut up 1** become silent. **2** lock up or in. **shutter** *n* **1** wooden or metal window covering. **2** device controlling light admitted to a camera lens.

shuttlecock *n* small piece of cork, plastic, etc., stuck with feathers and struck by a racket in badminton, etc.

shy *adj* bashful; timid; lacking self-confidence. *vi* move (away from); recoil (from). **shyly** *adv*. **shyness** *n*.

sick *adj* **1** unwell; ill. **2** inclined to vomit. **3** gruesome; macabre. **sick of** tired of; bored with. **sicken** *vi,vt* become or make sick, weary, or disgusted. **sickening** *adj* nauseating; annoying. **sickly** *adj* **1** prone to ill-health; feeble. **2** so sweet as to be nauseating. **sickness** *n* **1** illness; disease. **2** vomiting; nausea.

side *n* **1** one of the surfaces of an object. **2** that part of something other than the top and bottom or back and front. **3** surface of a piece of paper, cloth, etc. **4** left or right part of the body, face, etc. **5** area to the left or right of the centre of something. **6** one of the teams or groups in a match, competition, debate, etc. **7** facet; aspect; part. **side by side** together; in juxtaposition. **take sides** favour one side more than the other in a dispute. *v* **side with** take sides with one rather than the other. **sideboard** *n* piece of dining-room furniture holding or displaying plates, cutlery, etc. **sideboards** *pl n* side whiskers on the face. **side effect** *n* secondary unplanned and often undesirable effect of an action, drug, etc. **sideline** *n* subsidiary or additional occupation. **sideshow** *n* minor show or fairground entertainment. **sidestep** *vt* (-pp-) neatly evade; avoid or step aside from. **sidetrack** *vt* lead away from a subject; divert. **sideways** *adv, adj* on or towards one side. **siding** *n* short stretch of railway track used for shunting.

sidle *vi* **1** move sideways; edge along. **2** fawn; cringe.

siege *n* attempt to conquer a fortified place by surrounding and preventing access to it.

sieve *n* utensil with a perforated container for straining liquids, separating coarse from fine grains, or pulping solids. *vt* put through a sieve; sift.

sift *vt* **1** pass through or separate with a sieve. **2** examine minutely.

sigh *n* long deep breath expressing weariness, sadness, relief, etc. *vt,vi* utter (with) a sigh.

sight *n* **1** ability or power to see; vision. **2** something seen or viewed. **3** something that is messy, ugly, or untidy; mess. **4** appearance. **5** *inf* a lot; much more. **at first sight** on the first occasion of seeing. ~*vt* see; observe; spot. **sightless** *adj* blind. **sightread** *vt,vi* (-read) read, play, or sing music at first sight. **sightseeing** *n* visiting tourist attractions, beauty spots, etc. **sightseer** *n*.

sign *n* **1** symbol. **2** gesture; gesticulation. **3** hint; implication; clue; trace. **4** recognizable symptom. **5** advertisement or notice. *vt,vi* **1** write one's name or signature (on). **2** signal; communicate with signs. **sign on** *or* **up** enrol; enlist.

signal *n* visible or audible sign, esp. prearranged or well-known. *vt,vi* (-ll-) make signals (to).

signature *n* **1** signed name, esp. for use as authentication. **2** act of signing. **3** mark showing key and time at the beginning of a musical score. **signature tune** *n* tune used to announce and identify a particular performer or programme on stage, radio, television, etc.

significant *adj* meaningful; noteworthy; important. **significance** *n*. **significantly** *adv*. **signify** *vt* mean; indicate; be a sign of. *vi* matter; be important.

silence *n* absence of sound, speech, or communication. *vt* make silent; suppress. **silencer** *n* device rendering car exhaust, a gun, etc., more quiet. **silent** *adj* without a sound; noiseless; quiet. **silently** *adv*.

silhouette *n* outline figure, esp. in black on a white background. *vt* show in silhouette.

silk *n* fine soft fibre spun by silkworms and woven into fabric. **silkworm** *n* caterpillar of the mulberry-eating moth, which spins silk. **silky** *adj* soft, fine, and gleaming like silk. **silkiness** *n*.

sill *n* ledge or slab below a window or door.

silly *adj* foolish; fatuous; imprudent; unwise. **silliness** *n*.

silo *n* granary.

silt *n* sediment left by water in a river, harbour, etc. *vt,vi* fill (up) with silt.

silver *n* **1** white shining malleable valuable metallic element, widely used in coinage, jewellery, tableware, electrical contacts, alloys, etc. **2** *also* **silverware** cutlery, dishes, etc., made from silver or an alloy of silver. *adj* **1** made of silver. **2** of the colour of silver. **silver wedding** *n* twenty-fifth wedding anniversary. **silvery** *adj* **1** looking like silver. **2** having a clear soft sound.

similar *adj* like; resembling; exactly the same. **similarity** *n*. **similarly** *adv*.

simile *n* figure of speech in which two apparently unlike things are compared.

simmer *vt,vi* **1** cook slowly at boiling point. **2** have emotions (esp. anger) barely in check. **simmer down** calm down. ~*n* state of simmering.

simple *adj* **1** easy; plain; ordinary. **2** not complex. **3** mere. **simple-minded** *adj* ingenuous; foolish. **simple-mindedly** *adv*. **simple-mindedness** *n*. **simplicity** *n* condition of being simple. **simplify** *vt* make less complicated; clarify. **simplification 3** absolutely.

simulate *vt* feign or reproduce (a situation, condition, etc.). **simulation** *n*.

simultaneous *adj* occurring at the same time. **simultaneously** *adv*.

sin *n* moral or religious offence. *vi* (-nn-) commit a sin. **sinful** *adj*.

since *adv* from that time until now; subsequently; ago. *prep* after; from the time of. *conj* **1** from the time that. **2** because; seeing that.

sincere *adj* honest; straightforward; genuine. **sincerely** *adv*. **sincerity** *n*.

sinew *n* tendon joining a muscle to a bone. **sinewy** *adj* wiry; muscular.

sing *vi,vt* (sang; sung) **1** utter (words or a tune) melodiously; produce musical notes. **2** celebrate in poetry. **singer** *n*.

singe *vt,vi* scorch or burn (the surface, edge, or end of). *n* slight burn.

single *adj* **1** individual; only one. **2** separate; solitary. **3** unmarried. **4** unique. *n* **1** short gramophone record played at 45 revolutions per minute. **2** one-way train or bus ticket. **3** single thing, event, etc. **singles** *pl n* tennis match, etc., between two players. *v* **single out** select from many for a specific purpose. **singly** *adv*. **single-handed** *adj* alone; unaided. **single-minded** *adj* intent; with one driving force or set aim. **single-mindedly** *adv*. **single-mindedness** *n*.

singular *adj* **1** indicating a single person, place, or thing. **2** odd; extraordinary; unusual. **singularity** *n*. **singularly** *adv*.

sinister *adj* malignant; suggestive of evil.

sink *v* (sank; sunk) *vt,vi* **1** submerge. **2** drop; lower. **3** lower or become lower in cost, value, etc. *vi* **1** pass (into) a state, condition, etc. **2** become weaker, unwell, etc. *vt* drive (a stake, post, etc.) into the ground. *n* fitted basin for washing, etc. **sink or swim** fail or succeed.

sinner *n* one who commits sin.

sinus *n* bodily cavity or passage, esp. communicating with the nose. **sinusitis** *n* inflammation of the sinus.

sip *vt,vi* (-pp-) drink in small mouthfuls. *n* small mouthful of liquid.

siphon *n* **1** bent pipe or tube for drawing off liquids. **2** bottle for dispensing soda water, etc., by means of a siphon. *vt,vi* draw (off) using a siphon.

sir *n* title used in a formal letter or to address a knight, baronet, or a man superior in age, rank, dignity, etc.

siren *n* apparatus producing a loud wailing noise or signal.

sirloin *n* upper part of a loin of beef.

sister *n* **1** daughter of the same parents as another. **2** nun. **3** nurse in charge of a hospital ward. **sisterhood** *n* community of nuns or other women. **sister-in-law** *n, pl* **sisters-in-law** brother's wife or husband's or wife's sister. **sisterly** *adj*.

sit *v* (-tt-; sat) *vi* **1** be in the position of having one's buttocks resting on the ground, a chair, etc. **2** be placed; rest. **3** be a member (of a committee, etc.). *vt* **1** seat; place in a sitting position. **2** allocate a place at table to. *vt,vi* take (an examination). **sit-in** *n* mass occupation of premises as a form of protest.

site *n* place, setting, or ground on which a building, town, etc., stands. *vt* locate.

sitting *n* **1** session; business meeting. **2** time spent posing for a portrait, etc. **sitting room** *n* room used for sitting comfortably; living room.

situated *adj* **1** located; sited. **2** placed with respect to money, housing, or other considerations. **situation** *n* **1** position; condition. **2** job.

six *n* **1** number equal to one plus five. **2** group of six persons, things, etc. **3** *also* **six o'clock** six hours after noon or midnight. **at sixes and sevens** confused; in a muddle. ~*adj* amounting to six. **sixth** *adj* coming between fifth and seventh in sequence. *n* **1** sixth person, object, etc. **2** one of six equal parts; one divided by six. *adv* after the fifth.

sixteen *n* **1** number that is six more than ten. **2** sixteen things or people. *adj* amounting to sixteen. **sixteenth** *adj,adv,n.*

sixty *n* **1** number equal to six times ten. **2** sixty things or people. *adj* amounting to sixty. **sixtieth** *adj,adv,n.*

size *n* **1** extent; dimensions; importance. **2** measurement categorizing individual proportions. *vt* categorize by size. **size up** judge roughly; weigh up. **sizable** *adj* of considerable size or importance.

sizzle *vi* **1** hiss and splutter as during frying. **2** *inf* be very hot. *n* sizzling noise.

skate[1] *n* boot fitted with a blade or wheels allowing the wearer to glide smoothly over ice or other hard surfaces. *vi* move on or as if on skates. **skate on thin ice** deal with or be in a precarious situation. **skater** *n.*

skate[2] *n* large flatfish with an elongated snout.

skeleton *n* **1** framework of bones within a human or animal body. **2** outline, sketch, nucleus, or framework of anything. **skeleton in the cupboard** secret domestic disgrace.

sketch *n* **1** rough or unfinished drawing, draft, or outline. **2** very short usually amusing play. *vt,vi* draw or outline roughly. **sketchy** *adj* incomplete; rough; inadequate. **sketchily** *adv.*

ski *n* **1** one of two long narrow pointed pieces of wood, metal, etc., attached to boots allowing wearer to slide quickly over snow. **2** short for **water-ski.** *vi* (skiing; skied *or* ski'd) travel on skis. **skier** *n.* **ski-lift** *n* seats slung on a cable transporting skiers up slopes.

skid *n* **1** wooden or metal support on which a ship, aeroplane, car, etc., may be rested, moved, or slid. **2** act of skidding. *vi* (-dd-) (of a vehicle, etc.) slide sideways, esp. out of control. **skid row** haunt or condition of vagrants, drunkards, etc.

skill *n* accomplishment; craft; expert knowledge. **skilled** *adj.* **skilful** *adj.* **skilfully** *adv.*

skim *vt* (-mm-) **1** remove scum, cream, etc., from the surface of a liquid. **2** pass over lightly, scarcely touching. **skim over** *or* **through** read cursorily; glance at. **skimmed milk** milk without cream.

skin *n* **1** tissue forming the outer covering of the body. **2** outer covering of a fruit. **3** leather pelt obtained from an animal. **4** layer; thin coating. *vt* (-nn-) remove the skin of or from. **skinny** *adj* unpleasantly thin. **skin-tight** *adj* extremely close-fitting.

skip *vt,vi* (-pp-) **1** jump or hop lightly, esp. from one foot to the other or over a twirling rope. **2** omit; leave out. *n* skipping movement.

skipper *n* captain of a ship, aircraft, etc.

skirmish *n* small unplanned fight or clash, as between hostile armies, etc. *vi* engage in a skirmish.

skirt *n* **1** woman's garment extending downwards from the waist or this part of a dress. **2** edge; extremity; border. *vt* pass around or along the edge of.

skittle *n* bottle-shaped target used in ninepin or tenpin bowling.

skull *n* bony framework of the head enclosing the brain.

skunk *n* small carnivorous black North American mammal with bushy tail, white-striped back, and a gland that sprays a powerful offensive scent.

sky *n* upper atmosphere; heavens; apparent canopy of air seen from the earth. **sky-high** *adj,adv* extremely high. **skylark** *n* lark that sings while hovering in the air. *vi inf* indulge in practical jokes, frolics, etc. **skyscraper** *n* very tall building of many storeys.

slab *n* thick flat piece of stone, metal, cake, chocolate, etc.

slack *adj* **1** loose; not taut or stretched; limp. **2** lazy; remiss. *n* slack part of a rope. **slacks** *pl n* trousers for casual or informal wear.

slacken *vi,vt* **1** make or become slack(er). **2** relax; abate; delay.

slam *vt,vi* (-mm-) shut or put down violently and noisily. *n* noise of something slammed.

slander *n* false, defamatory, or injurious report. *vt* injure by spreading false malicious gossip. **slanderer** *n*. **slanderous** *adj*.

slang *n* colloquial language not regarded as good, educated, or acceptable. *vt* berate abusively. **slanging match** bitter exchange of verbal insults.

slant *vt,vi* **1** slope; turn obliquely. **2** write or present (material) in a biased or prejudiced manner. *n* **1** slope. **2** angle of approach; attitude.

slap *n* blow with hand or anything flat. **slap in the face** insult; rebuff. ~*vt* (-pp-) smack; strike with a slap. **slapdash** *adj* careless; haphazard. **slapstick** *n* rough boisterous comedy.

slash *vt,vi* **1** cut with long violent random strokes. **2** economize or reduce drastically. *n* long cut or slit.

slat *n* narrow strip of wood, metal, etc.

slate *n* **1** dull grey fine-grained rock that can be split into smooth even pieces. **2** thin piece of this used as a writing tablet, roofing tile, etc.

slaughter *n* killing, esp. of many people or animals at once; massacre. *vt* **1** kill or slay ruthlessly, esp. in large numbers. **2** kill (an animal) for market. **slaughterhouse** *n* place where animals are killed for market; abattoir.

slave *n* **1** person legally owned by another. **2** person forced to work against his will. **3** person under the control or influence of someone or something. *vi* work like a slave. **slavery** *n* **1** state or condition of being a slave. **2** extremely hard unrewarding work.

sledge *n* vehicle on runners for transporting goods or people over snow; sleigh.

sledgehammer *n* large heavy hammer.

sleek *adj* **1** smooth and glossy. **2** suave; elegant. *vt* make smooth and glossy. **sleekly** *adv*. **sleekness** *n*.

sleep *n* resting state during which the body is relaxed and consciousness is suspended. *vi* (slept) take rest in sleep. **sleep on it** postpone a decision overnight. **sleepless** *adj*. **sleepily** *adv*. **sleepiness** *n*. **sleepy** *adj*. **sleeper** *n* **1** one who sleeps. **2** horizontal beam supporting the rails of a railway track. **3** sleeping car or compartment on a train.

sleepwalk *vi* walk while asleep. **sleepwalker** *n*.

sleet *n* rain falling as half-melted hail or snow. *vi* fall as sleet.

sleeve *n* **1** part of a garment covering the arm. **2** tube covering a rod, pipe, etc. **3** cover for gramophone record. **up one's sleeve** held secretly in reserve.

sleigh *n* sledge, esp. one pulled by horses.

slender *adj* **1** slim; thin. **2** meagre; insufficient.

slice *n* **1** thin flat piece cut from something. **2** utensil for lifting and serving fish, etc. *vt* **1** cut into slices. **2** cut a slice from. **3** hit (a golfball, tennis ball, etc.) so that it curves in flight.

slick *adj* **1** sleek; smooth. **2** deft; cunning. **slickness** *n*.

slide *v* (slid) *vt,vi* **1** move or glide smoothly over a surface. **2** move or be moved unobtrusively. *vi* **1** pass gradually. **2** slip or fall. **let slide** allow to take a natural course. ~*n* **1** transparent photograph. **2** smooth inclined surface for children, goods, etc., to slide down. **3** clasp for the hair. **slide-rule** *n* mechanical device used for calculating.

slight *adj* **1** frail; slim; flimsy. **2** insignificant; unimportant. *n* snub; hurtful act. *vt* disregard; treat as if of no importance. **slightly** *adv* a little; somewhat.

slim *adj* **1** slender; thin. **2** small; slight; meagre. *vi* (-mm-) try to lose weight by means of diet, exercise, etc. **slimmer** *n*. **slimness** *n*.

slime *n* thin oozing mud or anything resembling it. **slimy** *adj* **1** resembling or covered with slime. **2** vile; repulsive.

sling *n* **1** piece of material for supporting an injured arm, hand, etc. **2** band or pocket attached to strings for throwing stones, hoisting or supporting weighty objects, etc. *vt* (slung) **1** throw casually. **2** support with or hang from a sling.

slink *vi* (slunk) move stealthily and quietly; sneak. **slinky** *adj* **1** close-fitting. **2** sinuous and graceful.

slip[1] *v* (-pp-) *vi* **1** slide; glide. **2** become unfastened or less secure. **3** lose one's balance, grip, etc. **4** become less efficient, careful, etc. **5** move quietly or without being noticed. **6** forget; make a mistake. *vt* **1** pull or push easily or hastily. **2** drop; let fall. **slip up** make a mistake. ~*n* **1** sliding; act of slipping. **2** mistake; small error. **3** petticoat. **slipway** *n* sloping area from which a vessel is launched.

slip[2] *n* narrow strip of wood, paper, etc.
slipper *n* loose comfortable indoor shoe.
slippery *adj* **1** so smooth, greasy, etc., as to make slipping likely. **2** elusive; unstable. **slipperiness** *n*.
slit *n* **1** long cut. **2** narrow opening. *vt* (-tt-) **1** make a long cut in. **2** cut into long strips.
slither *vi* slide unsteadily.
slog *vi,vt* (-gg-) **1** hit violently. **2** work hard and determinedly. *n* **1** long spell of hard work. **2** heavy blow.
slogan *n* catchy word or phrase used in advertising, etc.
slop *n* **1** liquid waste. **2** semiliquid unappetizing food. *vt,vi* (-pp-) spill carelessly and messily. **sloppy** *adj* **1** messy; careless; untidy. **2** muddy, slushy, or watery. **3** sentimental; maudlin. **sloppily** *adv*. **sloppiness** *n*.
slope *n* **1** inclined surface. **2** deviation from the horizontal; slant. *vi* have or take a sloping position or direction.
sloshed *adj inf* drunk.
slot *n* groove, channel, or slit into which a bolt, coin, etc., may fit or be inserted. *vt* (-tt-) **1** make fit into. **2** provide with or pass through a slot. **slot together** fit neatly together.
slovenly *adj* **1** careless; slipshod. **2** lazy and dirty. **slovenliness** *n*.
slow *adj* **1** taking a long time. **2** not quick; gradual. **3** behind correct time. **4** dull-witted or unresponsive. *vt* delay; retard. **slow down** *or* **up** lessen; slacken in speed. **slowly** *adv*. **slowness** *n*.
slug small shell-less mollusc, destructive to garden plants.
sluggish *adj* lazy; slow-moving. **sluggishly** *adv*. **sluggishness** *n*.
sluice *n* sliding gate or valve controlling a flow of water in a channel, drain, etc. *vt,vi* flush or wash down with running water.
slum *n* squalid overcrowded housing.
slump *n* **1** sudden fall or decline. **2** economic depression. *vi* **1** collapse in a heap. **2** suddenly lose value.
slung *v pt* and *pp* of **sling.**
slunk *v pt* and *pp* of **slink.**
slur *vt,vi* (-rr-) **1** sound (words) indistinctly. **2** pass over lightly. **3** disparage. *n* **1** smudge; blur. **2** indistinct noise. **3** slight, insult, or blame.
slush *n* **1** watery mud or snow. **2** excessive sentimentality. **slushy** *adj*.
sly *adj* **1** cunning. **2** devious; deceitful. **slyly** *adv*. **slyness** *n*.
smack[1] *vt* strike sharply with the palm of the hand. **smack the lips** make a smacking sound with the lips. ~*n* act or sound of smacking. *adv inf* immediately; directly.
smack[2] *n* slight trace or flavour. *vi* suggest; have the flavour (of).
small *adj* not large; of little size, strength, importance, quantity, etc. **feel small** feel humiliated. **small talk** polite trivial conversation. ~*n* narrow part (of the back, etc.). **smallness** *n*. **smallholding** *n* small farm or rented plot of agricultural land. **small-minded** *adj* petty; narrow-minded. **smallpox** *n* serious contagious disease causing eruptions and subsequent scars on the skin.
smart *adj* **1** fashionable; elegant. **2** clever; ingenious; witty. *vi* feel sharp pain or resentment. **smartly** *adv*. **smartness** *n*. **smarten** *vt* make cleaner, tidier, more fashionable, etc.
smash *vt,vi* **1** shatter; break into fragments. **2** hit or throw violently. *n* **1** sound or act of smashing. **2** violent collision, esp. of motor vehicles. **smashing** *adj inf* wonderful; excellent.
smear *n* **1** dirty greasy mark. **2** slur on one's reputation. **3** specimen taken for pathological testing. *vt* **1** spread or cover with something thick or greasy. **2** discredit publicly. **3** blur by smearing.
smell *n* **1** odour; stink; fragrance. **2** ability to distinguish smells. **3** suggestion; hint. *vt* detect or distinguish by the sense of smell. *vi* give off a smell. **smell out** discover by investigation. **smell a rat** become suspicious. **smelly** *adj* having a strong or unpleasant smell.
smile *vi* turn up the corners of the lips to express pleasure, approval, amusement, etc. *n* act of smiling; happy expression. **smilingly** *adv*.
smirk *vi* give an unpleasant, knowing, silly, or self-satisfied smile. *n* act of smirking; smirking expression.
smock *n* full long loose shirt.
smog *n* combination of smoke and fog. **smoggy** *adj*.
smoke *n* **1** visible cloud of fine particles given off during burning. **2** cigarette, cigar, etc. *vi* give off smoke. *vi,vt* inhale fumes of burning

tobacco in a cigarette, pipe, etc. *vt* cure (meat, fish, etc.) by treatment with smoke. **smoker** *n* **1** person who smokes tobacco. **2** train compartment where smoking is allowed. **smoky** *adj*.

smooth *adj* **1** having an even surface. **2** level; even. **3** unruffled; calm. **4** easy; comfortable. *vt,vi also* **smoothen** make or become smooth. *vt* **1** soothe; comfort. **2** facilitate; make easy or easier. **smoothly** *adv*. **smoothness** *n*.

smother *vt* **1** suffocate; prevent access of air with a thick covering, heavy smoke, etc. **2** suppress or conceal.

smoulder *vi* **1** burn slowly without a flame. **2** exist in a suppressed or undetected condition.

smudge *n* smear; dirty mark. *vt* mark or be marked with a smudge; smear.

smug *adj* self-satisfied; complacent. **smugly** *adv*. **smugness** *n*.

smuggle *vt,vi* import or export (goods) illegally. *vt* bring or take in secretly or illegally. **smuggler** *n*.

smut *n* **1** particle of soot or dust. **2** small dark mark. **3** bawdiness; obscenity. **smutty** *adj*.

snack *n* light quick meal.

snag *n* small problem, hitch, drawback, etc. *vt* (-gg-) **1** hinder; prevent. **2** catch or tear on a small sharp protuberance.

snail *n* small slow-moving hard-shelled mollusc.

snake *n* **1** long scaly legless reptile with a forked tongue and neither eyelids nor ears. **2** treacherous deceitful person.

snap *vt,vi* (-pp-) **1** bite suddenly. **2** speak sharply or irritably. **3** shut or break suddenly. **snap up** seize hastily. ~*n* **1** act or sound of snapping. **2** simple card game. **3** *inf* snapshot. **snapshot** *n* informal photograph.

snarl *vi* growl, speak, or show the teeth threateningly or angrily. *n* act, sound, or expression of snarling.

snatch *vt,vi* seize or grab suddenly, violently, or when an opportunity arises. *n* **1** act of snatching. **2** fragment or bit.

sneak *vi* move or creep in a furtive cowardly or underhand way. *vt* take secretly; steal. *n* one who sneaks.

sneer *n* cynical contemptuous expression or remark. *v* **sneer at** scorn; mock.

sneeze *vi* eject sudden convulsive involuntary breath through the nose. **not to be sneezed at** not to be treated as insignificant. ~*n* act or sound of sneezing.

sniff *vi* inhale sharply and noisily through the nose. *vt* smell. **sniff at** show scorn. ~*n* act or sound of sniffing.

snip *vt,vi* (-pp-) clip or cut off with or as with scissors. *n* **1** act of snipping. **2** small piece snipped off.

snipe *vi* shoot at an enemy or enemies from a concealed position. *n* long-billed wading bird. **sniper** *n*.

snivel *vi* (-ll-) **1** have a runny nose. **2** whine or whimper tearfully. *n* act or sound of snivelling. **sniveller** *n*.

snob *n* one who admires and imitates those he considers his superior in class, wealth, or rank and who despises his inferiors. **snobbish** *adj*. **snobbery** *n*.

snooker *n* game resembling billiards using fifteen red balls and six of other colours.

snoop *vi* pry; investigate secretly. **snooper** *n*.

snooty *adj* supercilious; haughty; disdainful. **snootily** *adv*. **snootiness** *n*.

snooze *n* short sleep; cat nap. *vi* doze; take a snooze.

snore *vi* breathe noisily while asleep. *n* act or sound of snoring.

snort *vi* exhale noisily and sharply through the nose, often in anger. *n* act or sound of snorting.

snout *n* **1** animal's projecting nose. **2** part of machinery, etc., resembling a snout.

snow *n* atmospheric vapour frozen and falling as flakes of white crystals. *vi* shower or fall as snow. **snowed under** overwhelmed with work, problems, etc. **snowed up** confined in a house, car, etc., by fallen snow. **snowy** *adj*.

snowdrop *n* tiny white-flowered bulbous plant of early spring.

snub *vt* (-bb-) humiliate or slight pointedly or sarcastically. *n* snubbing act or rebuff. **snub-nosed** *adj* having a short turned-up nose.

snuff[1] powder (esp. tobacco) inhaled through the nose.

snuff[2] *vt* extinguish (a candle).

snug *adj* cosy, comfortable, and warm. **snugly** *adv*.

snuggle *vt,vi* cuddle closely together or into blankets, etc., for warmth and comfort.

so *adv* **1** to such an extent; very. **2** in such a manner. **3** consequently; then. **4** also; as well. **and so on** and continuing; et cetera. ~*pron* **1** something similar. **2** as anticipated. *adj* correct; right; true. **so-and-so** *n* **1** particular but unnamed person. **2** awkward or difficult person; nuisance.

soak *vt,vi* steep or be steeped in liquid. *vt* drench; permeate. **soak up** draw into itself; absorb. ~*n* **1** act of soaking. **2** heavy downpour.

soap *n* substance used for cleansing, forming a lather with water. **soap opera** *n* serialized drama, esp. broadcast on daytime television. ~*vt* **1** rub with soap. **2** *inf* flatter. **soapy** *adj.*

soar *vi* rise upwards; fly or glide at great height. *n* act of soaring.

sob *v* (-bb-) *vi* catch one's breath noisily in involuntary spasms as a result of emotion; weep; cry. *vt* utter while sobbing. *n* act of sobbing.

sober *adj* **1** not drunk. **2** temperate in the use of intoxicants. **3** moderate; well-balanced. **4** serious; sedate. *vt,vi* make or become sober. **soberly** *adv.* **sobriety** *or* **soberness** *n.*

sociable *adj* **1** friendly. **2** fond of or conducive to social interaction. **sociability** *n.* **sociably** *adv.*

social *adj* **1** of or concerning interaction or relations between persons. **2** forming a society, group, or community. **3** gregarious; convivial. **4** pertaining to fashionable circles. *n* gathering for companionship. **socially** *adv.* **social class** *n* members of a community sharing a similar position in economic and social structure. **social security** *n* scheme(s) providing for the welfare of the public. **social work** *n* social service to improve the welfare of the public. **social worker** *n.*

socialism *n* political and economic theory of society which tends towards centralized planning and ownership of the means of production, distribution, and exchange and operation of the free market. **socialist** *adj,n.*

society *n* **1** group sharing territory, language, customs, laws, and political and economic organization. **2** fellowship; companionship. **3** any group of people organized for a purpose. **4** rich, aristocratic, and exclusive social group.

sociology *n* study of human societies, their structure, organization, and customs. **sociological** *adj.* **sociologist** *n.*

sock[1] *n* short stocking. **pull one's socks up** make greater efforts.

sock[2] *vt,n sl* punch; hit.

socket *n* **1** device which receives an electric plug. **2** natural or artificial indentation functioning as a receptacle.

soda *n* term applied to compounds of sodium. **soda-water** *n* aerated solution of sodium bicarbonate.

sodium *n* soft silvery reactive metallic element.

sofa *n* upholstered couch with a back and arms.

soft *adj* **1** yielding; malleable; smooth. **2** gentle. **3** lenient. **4** tender; sympathetic. **5** (of sound) low in volume. **6** (of colour) not very bright. **7** *inf* feeble-minded; foolish. **softly** *adv.* **softness** *n.* **soften** *vt,vi* make or become soft(er). **soft-hearted** *adj* easily moved to tenderness, pity, etc. **soft-heartedly** *adv.* **soft-heartedness** *n.* **software** *n* written or printed data used in the operation of computers; program.

soggy *adj* soaked; marshy; sodden. **soggily** *adv.* **sogginess** *n.*

soil[1] *n* top layer of the earth, composed of organic and inorganic substances; ground.

soil[2] *vt,vi* make or become dirty, stained, or polluted.

solar *adj* **1** of or from the sun. **2** measured by the movement of the earth relative to the sun. **3** radiating like the sun's rays. **solar system** *n* our sun with the planets, asteroids, comets, etc., that revolve round it. **solar plexus** *n* network of nerves radiating from behind the stomach.

sold *v pt* and *pp* of **sell.**

solder *n* alloy with a low melting temperature used for joining metals. *vt* join, mend, or patch with solder.

soldier *n* noncommissioned member of an armed force. *v* **soldier on** keep fighting or struggling towards something. **soldierly** *adj.*

sole[1] *n* flat underside of a foot, shoe, etc. *vt* put a sole on.

sole[2] *n* edible flatfish.

sole[3] *adj* only; single; solitary. **solely** *adv.*

solemn *adj* **1** grave; serious. **2** marked by formal or religious ceremony; arousing awe and reverence. **3** impressive; dignified; pompous. **solemnity** *n.* **solemnly** *adv.*

solicit *vt,vi* **1** ask (for) persistently. **2** make unlawful sexual offers or requests (to).

solicitor *n* lawyer who prepares deeds, manages cases, and who acts in lower courts only but prepares cases for barristers.

solicitous *adj* considerate; concerned; eager; anxious. **solicitude** *n.*

solid *adj* **1** firm; compact. **2** having three dimensions; not hollow. **3** heavy; strongly built. **4** reliable; steady. **5** unanimous. *n* solid substance; substance that is neither liquid nor gaseous. **solidity** *n*. **solidly** *adv*. **solidarity** *n* unanimous whole-hearted coherence in action or attitude. **solidify** *vt,vi* make or become solid.

solitary *adj* **1** existing, living, or going without others. **2** happening, done, or made alone. **3** secluded. **4** lonely; single; sole. **solitary confinement** *n* isolation of a prisoner from all others. **solitude** *n* absence of company; seclusion.

solo *n* **1** musical composition for a single voice or instrument. **2** card game in which players act individually and not in partnership. **3** flight during which the pilot is unaccompanied. *adv* alone; by oneself. **soloist** *n*.

solstice *n* time of year when the sun reaches its farthest points north and south of the equator, producing the shortest or longest day.

soluble *adj* **1** capable of being dissolved in liquid. **2** capable of being solved. **solubility** *n*.

solution *n* **1** method or process of solving a problem. **2** explanation or answer. **3** liquid containing a dissolved solid.

solve *vt* find the correct solution to; settle; clear up; explain.

solvent *adj* **1** able to pay debts. **2** able to dissolve another substance. *n* liquid capable of dissolving another substance. **solvency** *n* ability to pay off debts.

sombre *adj* dark; dismal; gloomy. **sombrely** *adv*. **sombreness** *n*.

sombrero *n* wide-brimmed hat with a tall crown, traditionally worn in Spain and Latin America.

some *adj* **1** certain (people or things). **2** a few; a number; an amount or quantity. **3** particular proportion. *pron* a number of people or things. *adv* about; approximately. **somebody** *pron* **1** particular but unnamed person. **2** important or famous person. **somehow** *adv* **1** in some way or other. **2** for some reason. **someone** *pron* somebody. **something** *pron* particular but unnamed thing, action, characteristic, etc. **something like** approximately; about; almost. *adv* to a certain extent. **sometime** *adv* on some occasion; at some time. **sometimes** *adv* occasionally; from time to time. **somewhat** *adv* to a certain extent; rather. **somewhere** *adv* **1** in or to some particular but unspecified place. **2** placed approximately.

somersault *n* **1** leap or roll in which one turns heels over head. **2** complete reversal of opinion or attitude. *vi* make a somersault.

son *n* **1** male offspring, esp. in relation to his parents. **2** any male descendant. **son-in-law** *n, pl* **sons-in-law** daughter's husband.

sonata *n* musical composition of three or four movements and featuring a solo instrument.

song *n* **1** musical piece that is sung. **2** songs in general. **3** characteristic call of certain birds. **song and dance** *inf* fuss.

sonic *adj* **1** relating to sound. **2** having a speed approximately equal to the speed of sound.

sonnet *n* poem of fourteen lines with a set rhyming pattern.

soon *adv* in a short time; without delay; quickly. **as soon as** at the moment that.

soot *n* black powdery substance given off by burning coal, wood, etc. **sooty** *adj*.

soothe *vt* calm; comfort; allay.

sophisticated *adj* **1** refined or cultured in taste and manner; urbane. **2** attractive to refined tastes. **3** over-refined; unnatural. **4** (of machines, etc.) complex. **sophistication** *n*.

soprano *n* **1** highest range of an adult female voice. **2** singer capable of this range of notes. **3** part written for this voice.

sordid *adj* **1** filthy; squalid. **2** degrading; base. **3** greedy or selfish. **sordidly** *adv*. **sordidness** *n*.

sore *adj* **1** painful; tender; inflamed. **2** grieved, vexed, or bitter. *n* injured or diseased spot; wound. **soreness** *n*. **sorely** *adv* severely; distressingly; greatly.

sorrow *n* mental pain caused by loss or misfortune. **sorrowful** *adj*. **sorrowfully** *adv*.

sorry *adj* **1** feeling pity, regret, sadness, sympathy, etc. **2** pitiful; miserable. **3** poor; shabby. *interj* expression of apology.

sort *n* **1** class; kind; type. **2** character; nature. **sort of** *inf* in some way; rather. **out of sorts** not in good health or spirits. ~*vt,vi* **1** classify. **2** group (with). **sort out 1** separate out. **2** solve (a problem); resolve (a situation). **3** *inf* punish; reprimand.

soufflé *n* light fluffy dish made with eggs.

sought *v pt* and *pp* of **seek.**

soul *n* **1** immortal spiritual part of man. **2** innermost depth, being, or nature; core. **3**

nobler feelings and capacities of the human being; conscience. **4** person. **5** music derived from Black American gospel singing. **soul-destroying** *adj* eroding identity; sapping effort or vigour; making inhuman. **soulful** *adj* having, expressing, or affecting deep or lofty feelings. **soulfully** *adv.* **soulless** *adj* inhuman; mechanical; lacking emotion or identity.

sound[1] *n* **1** noise perceptible to the ear. **2** mere noise without meaning. *vt,vi* **1** cause or emit a sound. **2** signal by a sound. *vi* seem; give an impression of being. **soundless** *adj.* **soundlessly** *adv.*

sound[2] *adj* **1** in good condition; healthy; whole and complete. **2** reasoned; prudent; reliable. **3** (of sleep) deep; unbroken. **soundly** *adv.* **soundness** *n.*

soup *n* liquid food made by boiling meat or vegetables in water. **in the soup** *sl* in trouble or difficulties.

sour *adj* **1** sharp or acid to the taste; not sweet. **2** turned or rancid. **3** embittered; morose. **sour grapes** pretending to dislike what one cannot have. **sourly** *adv.* **sourness** *n.*

source *n* **1** spring; origin; starting point or cause. **2** document or work providing authority, validity, or inspiration.

south *n* **1** one of the four cardinal points of the compass situated to the right of a person facing the sunrise. **2** part of a country, area, etc., lying towards the south. *adj also* **southern** of, in, or facing the south. *adv,adj also* **southerly** **1** towards the south. **2** (of winds) from the south. **southerner** *n.* **southeast** *n* point situated midway between the south and east. *adj also* **southeastern** of, in, or facing the southeast. *adv,adj also* **southeasterly** **1** towards the southeast. **2** (of winds) from the southeast. **southward** *adj* facing or moving towards the south. **southwards** *adv* in the direction of the south. **southwest** *n* point situated midway between south and west. *adj also* **southwestern** of, in, or facing the southwest. *adv,adj also* **southwesterly** **1** towards the southwest. **2** (of winds) from the southwest.

souvenir *n* memento or keepsake by which memory of some person, place, or event is cherished.

sovereign *n* **1** monarch; supreme ruler. **2** former English gold coin worth a pound. *adj* **1** supreme; utmost. **2** excellent. **sovereignty** *n.*

sow[1] (sou) *v* (sowed; sown *or* sowed) *vt,vi* scatter or put (seeds, plants, etc.) in the ground. *vt* disseminate; suggest. **sower** *n.*

sow[2] (sau) *n* adult female pig.

soya bean *n* seed of an east Asian plant, rich in oil and protein.

spa *n* resort having mineral water springs in its locality.

space *n* **1** three-dimensional expanse. **2** period of time or the distance between events, places, etc. **3** blank or unused area. **4** universe; area beyond the earth's atmosphere. *vt* arrange at or divide into intervals. **spacecraft** *n* vehicle launched into space for research purposes, exploration, etc. **spacious** *adj* having ample room; extensive; wide. **spaciously** *adv.*

spade[1] *n* digging tool with a broad flat blade.

spade[2] *n* playing card of the suit marked with a black heart-shaped pip and a stem or the symbol itself.

spaghetti *n* pasta in the form of long thin cords.

span *n* **1** extent of something stretched out; stretch of space or time. **2** distance between two points, as between pillars, supports of arches, bridges, etc. *vt* **1** extend; stretch across. **2** measure with an extended hand.

spaniel *n* breed of medium-sized dog with long drooping ears and a silky coat.

spank *vt* strike with the open hand, a slipper, etc., esp. on the buttocks; slap. *n* blow or series of blows with the flat of the hand, etc.; smack.

spanner *n* tool for manipulating nuts and bolts. **spanner in the works** deliberate hindrance; sabotage.

spare *vt* **1** be merciful to; refrain or release from punishment, suffering, etc. **2** give away freely; be able to do without. *adj* **1** left over; not used or needed; extra. **2** freely available; kept in reserve. **3** lean; thin. **4** scanty; meagre. *n* spare part. **sparing** *adj* thrifty; economical.

spark *n* **1** glowing particle thrown out by a burning substance. **2** brief flash of light, as that accompanying an electric discharge. **3** vitality; life. *vi* emit sparks. *vt* **1** produce (sparks). **2** kindle; excite.

sparkle *vi* **1** glitter; twinkle; emit sparks or flashes. **2** be gay, clever, or witty. *n* **1** act of glittering; brilliance. **2** gaiety; wit; lively intelligence. **3** appearance of effervescence, as in champagne.

sparrow *n* any of various small brown birds.

sparse *adj* thinly distributed; scanty. **sparsely** *adv.* **sparseness** *or* **sparsity** *n.*

spasm *n* **1** involuntary muscular contraction. **2** strong but short-lived movement, action, or emotion. **spasmodic** *adj* **1** intermittent; not continuous. **2** relating to spasms. **spasmodically** *adv.*

spastic *adj* suffering from spasms and lack of muscular control due to damage to the brain. *n* person who suffers so.

spat *v pt* and *pp* of **spit.**

spatial *adj* of, in, or concerning space or the placement of objects in space. **spatially** *adv.*

spatula *n* broad blunt-bladed knife or flattened spoon.

spawn *n* eggs of fish, frogs, molluscs, etc., laid in water. *vt,vi* deposit (eggs).

speak *v* (spoke; spoken) *vi* **1** utter words; talk. **2** give a speech, lecture, sermon, etc. *vt* declare; pronounce. **nothing to speak of** nothing worth mentioning. **so to speak** as one might put it. **speak for** speak on behalf of. **speak for oneself** express personal views. **speak up** speak so as to be sure to be heard. **speak up for** speak in favour of; defend. **speaker** *n.*

spear *n* **1** long weapon consisting of a shaft with a sharp pointed head. **2** anything so shaped. *vt,vi* kill or pierce with a spear.

spearmint *n* aromatic garden mint or the flavour of this.

special *adj* **1** distinctive; peculiar; for a particular purpose. **2** detailed; exceptional. *n* special thing or person. **specially** *adv.* **specialist** *n* person having comprehensive knowledge of a subject, etc.; authority. **speciality** *n* particular characteristic, product, etc., for which a person, shop, etc., is renowned. **specialize** *vi* limit oneself to one particular area for intensive study. **specialization** *n.*

species *n, pl* **species** group of animals or plants of the same genus, capable of interbreeding.

specific *adj* **1** of or particular to one definite kind or type. **2** explicit; precise; exact. **specifically** *adv.* **specify** *vt* **1** make explicit; mention particularly. **2** set down as a requisite. **specification** *n.*

specimen *n* individual, object, or portion regarded as typical or a sample for purposes of study or collection.

speck *n* small spot; minute particle. *vt* mark with specks.

spectacle *n* **1** exhibition; show; pageant. **2** unusual or ridiculous sight. **spectacles** *pl n* glasses worn to correct vision, etc. **spectacular** *adj* impressive; outstanding; amazing. *n* flamboyant show. **spectacularly** *adv.*

spectator *n* person watching a show, contest, etc.; onlooker.

spectrum *n* **1** range of colours in order of wavelength produced when sunlight is split into colours on passing through a prism. **2** wide range; graduated series. **spectral** *adj.*

speculate *vi* **1** theorize; reflect; make conjectures. **2** take risks, esp. in buying and selling, in the hope of quick gain. **speculation** *n.* **speculative** *adj.* **speculator** *n.*

speech *n* **1** that which is spoken; language. **2** act or faculty of speaking; manner of speaking. **3** oration; talk addressed to an audience. **speechless** *adj* **1** temporarily deprived of speech. **2** unable to speak.

speed *n* rate of movement; quickness; velocity. *v* (sped *or* speeded) *vi,vt* move rapidly or quickly. *vi* drive a vehicle at high speed or in excess of the speed limit. *vt* **1** further; hasten. **2** send forth with good wishes. **speedy** *adj.* **speedily** *adv.*

spell[1] *v* (spelt *or* spelled) *vt,vi* say or write in order the letters that constitute (a word). *vt* **1** (of letters) form; make up. **2** amount to. **spell out** explain in very simple and exact terms.

spell[2] *n* **1** magical formula or incantation. **2** enchantment; irresistible attraction. **spellbound** *adj* under a spell or influence; fascinated.

spell[3] *n* short period of time; bout.

spend *vt* (spent) **1** give; pay out. **2** expend; use; exhaust. **3** pass (time). **spendthrift** *n* person who wastes money.

sperm *n* **1** semen. **2** male reproductive cell.

sphere *n* **1** ball; globe. **2** scope; range. **3** field of activity or influence; world. **spherical** *adj.*

spice *n* **1** strong aromatic and pungent seasoning of vegetable origin. **2** that which adds excitement or interest. *vt* season with spice. **spicy** *adj.* **spicily** *adv.* **spiciness** *n.*

spider *n* eight-legged insect-like animal that spins webs to catch prey. **spidery** *adj* **1** spider-like. **2** having thin angular lines.

spike *n* sharp pointed rod, esp. of metal. *vt* fix or pierce with a spike. **spiky** *adj.*

spill *vt,vi* (spilt *or* spilled) **1** allow (liquid) to fall, esp. by accident. **2** overflow or cause to overflow. **spill the beans** reveal a secret. ~*n* **1** fall from a vehicle, horse, etc. **2** spilling.

spin *vt,vi* (spun) **1** rotate rapidly. **2** draw out and twist (wool, etc.) into thread. **3** (of spiders, etc.) form webs or cocoons. *n* **1** act or speed of rotating. **2** *inf* pleasure drive in a vehicle, etc.

spine *n* **1** backbone surrounding and protecting nerve tissue. **2** long thin ridge. **3** spiked extremity on a plant, fish, etc. **4** bound edge of a book. **spinal** *adj.* **spiny** *adj.* **spine-chilling** *adj* terrifying. **spineless** *adj* **1** having no spine. **2** weak; irresolute.

spinster *n* unmarried woman.

spiral *n* **1** curve that winds around and away from a fixed point or axis. **2** upward or downward trend in prices, wages, etc. *adj* resembling a spiral; twisting. *v* (-ll-) *vt,vi* take or make into a spiral course or shape. *vi* increase or decrease with ever-growing speed.

spire *n* **1** tall slender tower tapering to a point. **2** long slender flower or stalk; shoot.

spirit *n* **1** moving force; inner life; soul. **2** underlying meaning; true significance. **3** vitality; courage. **4** mood. **5** any distilled alcoholic beverage. **6** active essence of a drug, compound, etc. **spirited** *adj* lively; animated. **spirited away** *adj* mysteriously or secretly carried off.

spiritual *adj* **1** of or like a spirit or soul. **2** religious; sacred. **3** ideal; unworldly; not materialistic. *n* American Negro religious song originating in the time of slavery. **spiritually** *adv.*

spit[1] *n* saliva. *v* (-tt-; spat *or* spit) *vt,vi* eject (something) from the mouth. *vi* drizzle lightly and irregularly.

spit[2] *n* spike for roasting meat.

spite *n* malevolence; vindictiveness; desire to injure. **in spite of** notwithstanding; in defiance of. ~*vt* injure or grieve maliciously. **spiteful** *adj.* **spitefully** *adv.*

splash *vt,vi* **1** scatter or cause (a liquid) to scatter; spatter. **2** fall or cause to fall on in drops or waves. *n* **1** act or sound of splashing. **2** liquid splashed. **3** mark so made. **make a splash** cause a sensation.

splendid *adj* **1** magnificent; brilliant. **2** *inf* excellent; very good. **splendidly** *adv.* **splendour** *n* glory; brilliance; magnificence.

splint *n* rigid piece of wood tied to a limb to keep a broken bone in place. *vt* support with splints.

splinter *n* sliver of wood, glass, metal, etc. *vt,vi* break up into splinters. **splinter group** *n* members who break away from a main group.

split *vt,vi* (-tt-; split) **1** break or divide into separate pieces, groups, etc. **2** break off from a whole. **3** tear; rend. **4** separate because of disharmony, disagreement, etc. **5** share or divide among persons. **6** *sl* go away; leave. *n* **1** act or process of splitting. **2** result of splitting; division; gap.

splutter *vi* **1** gasp and spit jerkily. **2** speak incoherently as in rage. **3** eject drops of liquid. *n* act or noise of spluttering.

spoil *v* (spoilt *or* spoiled) *vt* **1** damage, destroy, or impair the beauty, usefulness, or value of. **2** cause (a child, etc.) to become selfish by excessive indulgence. *vi* deteriorate. **spoils** *pl n* plunder; booty. **spoil-sport** *n* person who spoils the enjoyment of others.

spoke[1] *v pt* of **speak.**

spoke[2] *n* **1** bar radiating from the hub towards the rim of a wheel. **2** rung of a ladder.

spoken *v pp* of **speak.**

spokesman *n, pl* **-men** person authorized to speak on behalf of others.

sponge *n* **1** pad of any porous elastic substance. **2** marine animal with fibrous skeleton. **3** act of applying or removing liquid with a sponge. **4** light baked or steamed pudding. *vt,vi* **1** apply a sponge to absorb; wipe off. **2** *inf* live or obtain by presuming on the generosity of others. **spongy** *adj.*

sponsor *vt* **1** vouch for good character of; act as surety. **2** act as godparent. **3** finance; fund. *n* person who sponsors. **sponsorship** *n.*

spontaneous *adj* **1** impulsive; uninhibited; unconstrained. **2** produced of itself without external cause. **spontaneity** *n.* **spontaneously** *adv.*

spool *n* small cylinder, bobbin, or reel for winding yarn, photographic film, etc., on.

spoon *n* utensil consisting of a small bowl on a handle. *vt,vi* transfer with or as if with a spoon.

sporadic *adj* occasional; occurring irregularly. **sporadically** *adv.*

sport *n* **1** activity or game indulged in for pleasure. **2** amusement; fun; joke. **3** *inf* good-humoured person. *vt* wear conspicuously.

sporty *adv.* **sportive** *adj* merry; playful. **sports car** *n* low-bodied usually two-seater car with high acceleration. **sportsman** *n* **1** person fond of sport. **2** one who bears defeat, inconvenience, etc., cheerfully. **sportsmanship** *n.*

spot *n* **1** small mark or patch. **2** small area or quantity. **3** skin blemish. **in a spot** in difficulties. **soft spot** liking; fondness. ~*vt* (-tt-) **1** mark with spots. **2** notice; observe; discover. **spotless** *adj* **1** without blemish. **2** very clean. **spotlight** *n* strong beam of light focused on one spot. **spotty** *adj* having spots, esp. on the face.

spouse *n* wife or husband of someone.

spout *n* **1** narrow projecting tube through which contents of a vessel are poured. **2** jet of liquid. *vt,vi* pour out conspicuously.

sprain *vt* twist or wrench muscles or ligaments (of a foot, hand, etc.) without dislocation of a joint. *n* **1** act of spraining muscles. **2** swelling and pain caused by this.

sprang *v pt* of **spring.**

sprawl *vi* **1** lie or sit with stretched-out limbs. **2** be spread untidily over a wide area. *n* **1** act or position of sprawling. **2** untidy spread, esp. of buildings.

spray[1] *n* **1** fine drops of liquid blown through the air. **2** apparatus for doing this. *vt,vi* squirt, disperse, or become spray.

spray[2] small shoot or branch of a plant; sprig.

spread *vt,vi* (spread) **1** extend or cause to extend or cover widely; stretch or be stretched. **2** circulate. *n* **1** extent. **2** act or degree of spreading or the area covered. **3** feast. **4** substance for spreading on bread, etc.

spree *n* lively outing; session of reckless activity or amusement.

sprig *n* small shoot; twig.

sprightly *adj* vivacious; brisk; lively. **sprightliness** *n.*

spring *v* (sprang; sprung) *vi* **1** leap; jump. **2** bounce; rebound; recoil. **3** move suddenly or violently. **4** have as a cause; originate; start. **5** produce shoots, leaves, etc.; sprout. *vt* **1** leap over; jump. **2** produce suddenly. *n* **1** leap; jump; bounce. **2** season following winter and preceding summer. **3** coil of wire, metal, etc., that cushions impact, causes movement of parts in a mechanism, etc. **4** natural flow of water forced by pressure from underground. **spring-clean** *n* thorough house-cleaning associated with springtime. *vt* clean in this way. **springy** *adj* **1** elastic; resilient; well-sprung. **2** able to leap or recoil.

springbok *n* African antelope.

sprinkle *vt,vi* scatter in small drops. *n* small quantity dispersed in drops; light shower.

sprint *vi* race or run very fast for a short distance. *n* short race at full speed.

sprout *vt* develop (shoots or buds). *vi* begin to grow; send forth. *n* **1** young bud or shoot. **2** short for Brussels sprout.

sprung *v pp* of **spring.**

spun *v pt* and *pp* of **spin.**

spur *n* **1** spiked or pointed device on the heel of a rider's boot for urging a horse on. **2** incitement; stimulus. **3** projecting small branch or hill range. **on the spur of the moment** on impulse. ~*vt,vi* (-rr-) goad; hasten.

spurt *vt,vi* **1** make a sudden intense effort. **2** send out a sudden jet or stream; spout. *n* **1** brief spell of intense activity. **2** sudden jet of liquid.

spy *n* secret agent watching others and collecting information. *vi* **1** watch. **2** ascertain; detect.

squabble *vi* dispute in a noisy way. *n* petty quarrel; wrangle. **squabbler** *n.*

squad *n* **1** small group of soldiers. **2** group or working party acting together.

squadron *n* **1** group of military aircraft. **2** group of warships forming part of a fleet.

squalid *adj* sordid; dirty; uncared for. **squalidly** *adv.* **squalor** *n* state of being squalid; repulsive dirtiness.

squander *vt* spend carelessly and wastefully.

square *n* **1** right-angled figure having four equal sides. **2** total obtained by multiplying a number by itself. **3** area of land, courtyard, etc., usually bounded on four sides by buildings. *adj* **1** of the shape of a square. **2** broad and straight. **3** relating to a measurement of area. **4** equal or fair. *adv* so as to be square. *vt* **1** form into a square. **2** multiply (a number) by itself. **3** make equal or fair. **square with** be equal or in agreement with; match up to. **squarely** *adv.* **squareness** *n.*

squash *vt,vi* crush or become crushed into or as if into a pulp. *n* **1** drink made from diluted fruit juice. **2** ball game played with racquets. **3** crushed mass or tight-packed crowd.

squat *vi* (-tt-) **1** sit down with knees bent up and heels against buttocks; crouch. **2** occupy a building or land without the consent of the legal owner. *adj* short and thick. **squatter** *n*.

squawk *vi* utter a loud raucous cry. *n* loud harsh cry.

squeak *vi* emit shrill note or cry. *n* shrill weak cry or grating noise. **squeaky** *adj*. **squeakiness** *n*.

squeal *vi* utter a long shrill cry of pain, terror, or excitement. *n* long shrill cry.

squeamish *adj* easily distressed, shocked, or disgusted; too sensitive.

squeeze *vt,vi* **1** subject or be subjected to pressure; press or be pressed out. **2** pack tightly; cram. **3** extort by threats. *n* **1** act of squeezing; state of being tightly pressed or packed. **2** government restrictions placed on commercial or financial activities.

squid *n* edible marine mollusc having a slender body and triangular tail fins.

squiggle *n,vi* twist; wriggle.

squint *vi* **1** be unable to focus both eyes in the same direction. **2** look obliquely; glance. *n* **1** defect in the alignment of the eyes. **2** sidelong or stealthy glance.

squire *n* country landowner, esp. of an old established family. *vt* attend or escort (a lady).

squirm *vi* **1** twist and turn; wriggle. **2** feel embarrassed or humiliated. *n* wriggling movement.

squirrel *n* **1** small nimble bushy-tailed rodent. **2** *inf* person who hoards.

squirt *vt,vi* eject or be ejected in a stream. *n* jet; stream.

stab *v* (-bb-) *vt* **1** wound or pierce with a pointed weapon. **2** give a sharp throbbing pain. *vt,vi* jab or strike (at). *n* act of stabbing; blow or wound.

stable[1] *adj* **1** firmly established or steady; unchanging. **2** not easily upset or overturned; constant. **stably** *adv*. **stability** *n* quality or state of being stable; steadiness. **stabilize** *vt,vi* make or become stable or permanent. **stabilizer** *n*.

stable[2] *n* **1** building where horses, etc., are kept. **2** group of horses, etc., kept by a particular owner or trainer. *vt,vi* provide with or keep in a stable.

stack *n* orderly pile or heap. *vt* **1** place in a stack; heap. **2** load; fill. **stack the cards** dishonestly or unfairly arrange (something) against the interests of others.

stadium *n, pl* **stadiums** *or* **stadia** ('steidiə) sports arena.

staff *n, pl* **staffs** *or* (for 3–6) **staves** **1** people employed by a company, individual, authority, etc. **2** officers appointed to assist a commanding officer. **3** rod; stick. **4** flag pole. **5** something capable of sustaining or supporting. **6** series of horizontal lines used in musical notation. *vt* provide with a staff.

stag *n* adult male deer. **stag party** *n* social gathering of men only.

stage *n* **1** elevated or allocated arena on which a performance takes place. **2** theatrical profession. **3** stopping place on a journey. **4** level or period of development. *vt* **1** put (a play, etc.) on the stage before an audience. **2** do for effect; contrive dramatically. **3** arrange and carry out. **stage manager** *n* person who organizes rehearsals, scenery, staging, etc., of a play.

stagger *vi,vt* move or walk unsteadily; totter. *vt* **1** startle; shock. **2** arrange at intervals. *n* unsteady movement; tottering gait. **staggeringly** *adv*.

stagnant *adj* **1** still; not flowing. **2** foul; putrid from standing still. **3** inert; languid. **stagnantly** *adv*. **stagnate** *vi* **1** cease to flow; putrefy. **2** fail to develop; become sluggish. **stagnation** *n*.

stain *n* **1** discoloration; spot; blemish. **2** dye or tint. *vi,vt* soil or discolour. *vt* **1** taint. **2** colour or dye. **stainless** *adj*. **stained glass** *n* glass coloured by metallic pigments fused into its surface.

stair *n* one in a series of steps. **stairs** *pl n* series of steps from one level to another. **staircase** *n* flight of stairs usually having a banister and containing structure.

stake[1] *n* **1** pointed stick or post for fixing into the ground. **2** post to which persons were tied and burnt to death. *vi* **1** tie or join with or to a stake. **2** mark a boundary with stakes. *vt* **1** register (a claim) to a plot of land, rights, etc. **2** support by tying to a stake.

stake[2] *n* **1** money risked in gambling. **2** amount that may be won. **at stake** in danger of being lost; at risk, at issue. ~*vt* bet; wager; risk.

stale *adj* **1** (of food, etc.) not fresh; altered by age. **2** out of condition or practice. **staleness** *n*.

stalemate *n* **1** one type of draw in a game of

chess. **2** deadlock. *vt* cause to suffer a stalemate.

stalk[1] *n* **1** stem of a plant. **2** slender support; shaft.

stalk[2] *vt,vi* **1** walk stealthily (after); go after (prey). **2** walk stiffly or haughtily.

stall *n* **1** place for a single animal in a stable. **2** bench, table, booth, or barrow for displaying goods for sale. **3** theatre seat on the ground floor. **4** church seat, esp. for the choir. **5** covering for a finger or toe. *vt,vi* **1** stop (a car, motor, etc.) or make stop because of incorrect adjustment or handling. **2** put off; evade; delay.

stallion *n* male horse, esp. one kept for breeding.

stamina *n* power of endurance; strength.

stammer *n* speech defect in which particular sounds are uttered falteringly and sometimes repeated involuntarily. *vi,vt* speak or say with a stammer; utter brokenly.

stamp *vt,vi* crush or tread (on) heavily with the feet. *vt* **1** make a mark, symbol, or design on. **2** affix a postage stamp to. **3** make a deep impression; scar. **stamp out** suppress or abolish completely. ~*n* **1** heavy tread or pressure with the feet. **2** *also* **postage stamp** small piece of paper printed with a design, for affixing to mail as proof of postage paid. **3** seal, symbol, or mark. **4** device for producing a particular symbol or mark. **5** characteristic quality.

stampede *n* **1** sudden rush of frightened animals. **2** any impulsive action by a mass of people. *vi,vt* flee or cause to flee in panic. *vt* press a person into rash action.

stand *v* (stood) *vi* **1** be erect with the feet supporting the weight of the body. **2** move into such a position; rise; get up. **3** be positioned or located. **4** have a particular point of view. **5** remain; stay; adhere (to). **6** be a candidate; be nominated. *vt* **1** place; position; rest. **2** take the strain of; bear. **3** tolerate; put up with. **4** treat; pay for. **5** be subjected to (a trial). **stand by 1** be ready to act if needed. **2** remain loyal to. **stand down** give up a post, claim, etc. **stand for** represent; tolerate. **stand out** be conspicuous or prominent. **stand up for** defend; protect; fight for. ~*n* **1** platform. **2** article or piece of furniture for supporting something. **3** stall at a market, exhibition, etc. **4** position or point of view to be defended. **stand-by** *n* person or thing that may be relied upon in an emergency. **standing** *n* **1** rank; status; reputation. **2** duration; length of experience, etc. *adj* **1** erect. **2** permanent or continuing. **3** stagnant. **standstill** *n* complete cessation of movement or progress.

standard *n* **1** guideline; example. **2** principle; integrity. **3** flag; banner; emblem. **4** commodity on which a monetary system is based. **5** fruit or rose tree having a straight stem and no lower branches. *adj* serving as or conforming to a standard; average; accepted. **standardize** *vt* cause to conform to a standard; remove variations from. **standardization** *n*.

stank *v pt* of **stink.**

stanza *n* group of lines of verse forming a division of a poem.

staple[1] *n* bent length of wire for fastening. *vt* fasten with a staple or staples. **stapler** *n*.

staple[2] *n* **1** basic essential food. **2** grade of fibre in wool, flax, etc. *adj* basic; indispensable; standard.

star *n* **1** incandescent body in outer space seen in the night sky as a twinkling light. **2** figure with five or six pointed rays. **3** highly popular public entertainer. **4** asterisk. **5** planet influencing one's luck according to astrology; fate. *vt* (-rr-) **1** mark or cover with stars. **2** play the leading part or present as the leading performer. **3** mark with an asterisk. **starfish** *n* star-shaped invertebrate fish. **starry** *adj*.

starboard *n,adj* right-hand side of a vessel when one is facing forward.

starch *n* **1** carbohydrate present in many plants and vegetables. **2** this substance used as a stiffener after laundering fabrics. *vt* stiffen with starch. **starchy** *adj*. **starchily** *adv*. **starchiness** *n*.

stare *vi* look with fixed eyes. *n* act of staring.

stark *adj* **1** bleak; harsh; grim. **2** unelaborated; blunt. *adv* completely. **starkly** *adv*. **starkness** *n*.

starling *n* small gregarious bird with blackish feathers.

start *vt* **1** begin; set up. **2** set in motion. *vi* jump involuntarily as because of fright. *n* **1** beginning. **2** jerk; jump. **starter** *n*.

startle *vt* give a shock to; alarm; take aback. *vi* feel slight shock or alarm; be taken aback. **startlingly** *adv*.

starve *vi,vt* **1** die or make die from lack of food. **2** suffer or make suffer from hunger. *vi* be very hungry. **starvation** *n*.

state *n* **1** condition; situation; circumstances. **2** form; structure. **3** political community under a government. **4** status; rank. **5** splendour; dignified style. **6** *inf* distressed or anxious condition. *vt* declare; specify; utter. **stately** *adj* imposing; magnificent; dignified. **stateliness** *n*. **statement** *n* **1** act of stating. **2** something stated. **3** formal account. **4** financial account in detail.

statesman *n* wise revered politician. **statesmanlike** *adj*. **statesmanship** *n* skill and abilities involved in being a statesman.

static *adj* **1** at rest; unmoving. **2** not causing movement. **3** relating to interference in reception of radio signals. *n* disturbance in radio or television reception caused by electrical disturbances.

station *n* **1** fixed stopping place for a bus, train, etc. **2** position; status. **3** office or headquarters of the police, etc. *vt* assign a place or post to. **station-master** *n* official in charge of a railway station.

stationary *adj* fixed; still; permanently located.

stationer *n* person who sells writing materials, etc. **stationery** *n* writing materials, esp. notepaper and envelopes.

statistics *pl n* numerical data used to make analyses. *s n* study of the analysis of numerical data. **statistical** *adj* relating to numerical data. **statistically** *adv*. **statistician** *n* expert in statistics.

statue *n* sculpture or representation of a person, group, or an animal.

stature *n* **1** height of a person or animal standing upright. **2** moral or intellectual greatness.

status *n* **1** official or social position. **2** prestige; high rank. **status quo** the existing situation. **status symbol** object desired or owned for prestige purposes.

statute *n* **1** act, law, or decree made by Parliament or some other legislative body. **2** rule laid down by an institution or authority. **statutory** *adj* prescribed; authorized by statute.

stave *n* **1** strip of wood, esp. on the side of a barrel. **2** series of five lines on which music is written. **staves** *pl* of **staff** (defs 3–6).

stay[1] *vi* remain or be (for a time). *vt* check; delay. **stay the course** be able to finish in spite of difficulties. ~*n* **1** period of time spent; visit. **2** postponement.

stay[2] *n* support; prop; rope or cable supporting a ship's mast, etc. **stays** *pl n* corsets.

steadfast *adj* **1** unwavering. **2** resolute; loyal. **steadfastly** *adv*. **steadfastness** *n*.

steady *adj* **1** firmly balanced or supported. **2** regular; controlled; fixed. **3** constant. **4** reliable; sober. *vt,vi* make or become steady. **steadily** *adv*. **steadiness** *n*.

steak *n* thick slice of meat or fish.

steal *v* (stole; stolen) *vt* **1** unlawfully take away (another person's property). **2** obtain secretly; snatch. *vi* **1** thieve. **2** move quietly and unobtrusively; creep. **stealth** *n* furtive behaviour; secrecy; evasion. **stealthy** *adj*. **stealthily** *adv*.

steam *n* **1** vapour produced by boiling water. **2** mist left by water vapour. **get up steam** become excited or emotional. **let off steam** release pent-up emotion or energy harmlessly. ~*vi* **1** emit steam. **2** move by steam power. *vt* cook, iron, etc., using steam. **steamy** *adj*.

steel *n* **1** widely used strong hard alloy of iron and carbon. **2** quality of toughness. **3** steel weapon, esp. a sword. *vt* toughen; strengthen. **steel oneself** prepare oneself (to do something difficult or unpleasant). **steely** *adj* **1** of or like steel. **2** unwavering.

steep[1] *adj* **1** rising or sloping sharply; precipitous. **2** exorbitant; outrageous. **steeply** *adv*. **steepness** *n*. **steepen** *vi* become steep(er).

steep[2] *vt* soak thoroughly; immerse.

steeple *n* spire. **steeplechase** *n* horse race in which ditches, fences, etc., must be jumped.

steer *vt* guide; direct the course of (a vehicle, etc.). *vi* manoeuvre; guide. **steer clear of** keep away from.

stem[1] *n* **1** stalk of a plant. **2** anything resembling a stalk, such as the shaft of a pipe or wine glass. **3** unchanging part of a word to which inflexions are added. *v* (-mm-) **stem from** arise out of.

stem[2] (-mm-) *vt* stop the flow of; plug.

stencil *n* sheet of card, paper, or metal in which patterns or lettering have been cut in order to transfer the design to a further sheet or sheets. *vt* (-ll-) use or apply with a stencil.

Sten gun *n* lightweight machine gun.

step *n* **1** movement made by lifting the foot;

pace. **2** manner of walking, dancing, etc. **3** single section of a flight of stairs. **4** single grade or stage on a scale. **5** short distance. **step by step** gradually. **take steps (to)** begin to control; initiate action (on). ~*vi* (-pp-) move by steps; walk. **step on 1** trample on; walk on or rest the foot on. **2** *inf* accelerate; go fast. **step up** increase; intensify activity. **step-ladder** *n* folding ladder with wide flat rungs.

stepbrother *n* son of one's stepmother or stepfather by another marriage.

stepdaughter *n* daughter of one's spouse by another marriage.

stepfather *n* man married by one's mother after the death or divorce of one's father.

stepmother *n* woman married by one's father after the death or divorce of one's mother.

stepsister *n* daughter of one's stepmother or stepfather by another marriage.

stepson *n* son of one's spouse by another marriage.

stereo *adj* short for **stereophonic.** *n* apparatus for reproducing stereophonic sound. **stereophonic** *adj* (of music, etc.) recorded through separate microphones and relayed through separate loudspeakers to give an impression of natural distribution of sound.

stereotype *n* **1** conventionalized idea, conception, or person that lacks variation or individuality. **2** solid metal printing plate cast from a mould made from movable type.

sterile *adj* **1** free from live bacteria. **2** unable to produce offspring, seeds, or crops; barren; unproductive. **sterility** *n*. **sterilize** *vt* **1** destroy bacteria in. **2** render incapable of producing offspring, seeds, or crops. **sterilization** *n*.

sterling *adj* **1** relating to British money. **2** (of silver) conforming to a special standard. **3** valuable; reliable; excellent. *n* British money.

stern[1] *adj* strict; severe; grim. **sternly** *adv*. **sternness** *n*.

stern[2] *n* **1** back section of a ship or aircraft. **2** rear; rump.

stethoscope *n* medical instrument for listening to the sounds of the body.

stew *vt* cook by long slow boiling or simmering. *n* dish, usually of meat, cooked by stewing.

steward *n* **1** person organizing the catering, seating, and sleeping arrangements, esp. on a ship; passenger attendant. **2** estate or household manager; organizer or helper at a public function, etc. **stewardess** *n* female attendant on a ship or airliner.

stick[1] *v* (stuck) *vt* **1** join or attach by using glue, paste, nails, pins, etc. **2** pierce; prod; thrust. **3** put or place carelessly or absent-mindedly. *vi* **1** become fixed, attached, or jammed; wedge. **2** remain close to. **stick out 1** protrude; jut. **2** be conspicuous. **stick to** concentrate on for a length of time; adhere to. **stick up for** defend or support (a person, one's rights, etc.). **sticky** *adj* **1** tending to stick. **2** covered with glue, paste, etc. **3** *inf* awkward; tricky.

stick[2] *n* **1** wooden rod; thin detached branch; staff or cane. **2** rod used in certain sports. **3** anything resembling a stick in shape.

stiff *adj* **1** difficult to move, bend, or twist; rigid; not flexible. **2** (of persons) not moving easily; formal; not at ease socially. **3** strong. **4** (of prices) high. **stiff upper lip** stoicism. ~*n sl* corpse. **stiffly** *adv*. **stiffness** *n*. **stiffen** *vt,vi* make or become stiff. **stiffening** *n* substance used to stiffen something.

stifle *vt* **1** suffocate; choke. **2** suppress; put down. *vi* **1** die from suffocation; choke. **2** have a suffocating impression.

stigma *n* **1** mark or sign of disgrace; social blot. **2** that part of a flower that receives pollen. **stigmata** *pl n* marks of Christ's crucifixion. **stigmatize** *vt* denounce; brand.

stile *n* permanent set of steps or railings for climbing over a hedge, fence, etc.

still[1] *adv* **1** even now; yet. **2** even more. *conj* in spite of that. *adj* **1** quiet; hushed; calm; not agitated. **2** not fizzy. *vt* calm; subdue. *n* single photograph taken from a film. **stillborn** *adj* **1** born dead. **2** (of ideas, etc.) conceived but not put into practice. **still life** *n* painting or photograph of inanimate things.

still[2] *n* apparatus for distilling liquids by vaporizing and condensing.

stilt *n* **1** one of a pair of poles with platforms for the feet for walking above the ground. **2** supporting pole or pillar for a house, pier, etc.

stilted *adj* stiff; artificial; pompous.

stimulate *vt* **1** persuade; encourage; arouse. **2** inspire; excite mental activity in. **3** increase. **stimulation** *n*. **stimulant** *n* **1** anything, esp. a drink or drug, that produces extra mental or physical activity. **2** stimulus; spur. **stimulus** *n, pl* **stimuli** ('stimjulai) something that encourages, persuades, spurs on, or excites a response.

sting *vt,vi* (stung) **1** hurt by piercing the skin and secreting poison. **2** feel or cause to feel a piercing pain. **3** hurt (a person's feelings). **4** *sl* extort money (from), esp. by overcharging. *n* **1** act of or pain from stinging. **2** part of an insect, fish, or plant that causes a sting.

stink *vi* (stank *or* stunk; stunk) **1** smell disgusting or offensive. **2** *inf* (of a situation) be offensive or unpleasant. *n* disgusting smell. **stinker** *n* offensive person or thing.

stint *n* fixed amount; quota (of work). *vt* give small amounts to reluctantly; be ungenerous towards.

stipulate *vt,vi* insist (on) as a condition of agreement; require. **stipulation** *n*.

stir *v* (-rr-) *vt* **1** move or agitate (a mixture) with a spoon, etc. **2** move (slightly). **3** rouse; incite. *vi* move; become active. *n* **1** stirring movement. **2** disturbance; sensation.

stirrup *n* hooped metal footrest hanging either side of a horse's saddle.

stitch *n* **1** one unit in a row of sewing or knitting. **2** particular kind of stitch. **3** loop of thread used in surgery to close a wound, etc. **4** *inf* piercing pain in one's side. *vt,vi* sew using stitches.

stoat *n* small fur-covered mammal similar to but larger than a weasel.

stock *n* **1** store or supply of goods. **2** persons, animals, etc., having a common ancestor. **3** livestock. **4** unspecified number of shares. **5** liquid derived by cooking meat, bones, etc., in water. **6** flower having purple or white scented flowers. *vt* keep in supply; store. **stockbreeding** *n* breeding and rearing of livestock. **stockbroker** *n* person whc deals professionally in stocks and shares. **stock exchange** *n* place or association for the buying and selling of stocks and shares. **stockpile** *n* store set aside for future use. *vt,vi* build a stockpile (of). **stocktaking** *n* making of an inventory of goods or assets in a shop or business.

stocking *n* tight-fitting nylon, woollen, or cotton covering for the leg and foot.

stodge *n inf* heavy not easily digestible food. **stodgy** *adj* thick and heavy; unpalatable; turgid.

stoical *adj* bearing suffering without showing pain or emotion; being resigned to one's lot. **stoically** *adv*. **stoicism** *n*.

stoke *vt,vi* tend and pile fuel into (a fire or furnace).

stole[1] *v pt of* **steal.**

stole[2] *n* woven or knitted shawl, scarf, or fur collar worn round the shoulders.

stolen *v pp of* **steal.**

stomach *n* **1** principal digestive organ lying between the gullet and the intestines. **2** appetite. *vt* **1** digest. **2** bear; tolerate.

stone *n* **1** hard compact rock material, used in building, etc. **2** lump of rock. **3** jewel. **4** hard-shelled part of certain fruit. **5** anything resembling a stone or made of stone. **6** unit of weight equal to 14 pounds (6.3 kilograms). *adj* made of stone. *vt* **1** throw stones at. **2** remove stones from. **stony** *adj* **1** made of, covered with, or like stone(s). **2** hostile; cold. **stony broke** completely penniless.

stood *v pt* and *pp* of **stand.**

stool *n* **1** backless seat for one person; footstool. **2** solid excreta.

stoop *vt,vi* bend (one's head and body) forward and down. *vi* lower oneself morally; demean oneself. *n* **1** act of stooping. **2** habitually bent posture.

stop *v* (-pp-) *vt,vi* cease; bring or come to an end; halt. *vt* **1** discontinue; cut off; prevent. **2** prevent the passage of air, liquid, etc., through; block; plug. **stop off** call (at); visit. ~*n* **1** halt; end; finish. **2** place at which a bus, train, etc., stops to let passengers enter or leave. **3** full stop. **stopgap** *n* temporary measure or substitute in an emergency, etc. **stoppage** *n* **1** act of stopping; state of being stopped. **2** obstruction. **3** cessation of work. **stopper** *n* **1** person or thing that stops. **2** plug for a bottle or vessel. *vt* close with a stopper. **stopwatch** *n* watch that can be stopped and restarted for timing races, etc.

store *n* **1** stock set aside for future use; reserve supply; accumulation. **2** shop with several departments. **3** place where stock is kept. **in store 1** expected to happen. **2** set aside. **set store by** value greatly. ~*vt* make a store of. **store up** reserve for a future occasion; stock up. **storage** *n* keeping of stocks of goods for future use.

storey *n* floor or level of a building.

stork *n* large long-legged long-billed wading bird.

storm *n* **1** weather condition including a strong wind and often rain and thunder. **2** sudden outburst of noise, feelings, etc. **storm in a teacup** a lot of fuss over something unimportant. **take by storm 1** capture (a fortress) by a sudden massed attack. **2** bowl over; captivate. ~*vt* attack and capture suddenly. *vi* rage. **stormy** *adj* violent; tempestuous; relating to or portending a storm.

story *n* **1** tale; short narrative. **2** plot of a novel, etc. **3** *inf* lie; fib.

stout *adj* **1** fat; portly. **2** strong; sturdy. **3** brave. *n* strong dark ale. **stoutly** *adv*. **stoutness** *n*.

stove *n* device for cooking or heating, using gas, electricity, paraffin, etc.

stow *vt* put away; store. **stowaway** *n* person who hides on a ship or aircraft in order to avoid paying the fare.

straddle *vt,vi* stand or sit with one leg on either side (of); stand or sit astride.

straggle *vi* **1** sprawl; be scattered. **2** fall behind the main group; continue in small irregular groups.

straight *adj* **1** not crooked or curved. **2** direct. **3** rigid or erect. **4** honest; correct. *adv* **1** directly; in a straight line. **2** honestly. **straight away** immediately. **straighten** *vt,vi* make or become straight. **straighten out 1** make straight. **2** sort out or deal with (a problem). **straightforward** *adj* **1** uncomplicated; not difficult. **2** honest; open.

strain[1] *vt,vi* harm by stretching, exerting force, etc.; stress. *vt* **1** filter (a liquid). **2** make tense; demand excessive effort of. *n* tension; stress; act or instance of straining; demand.

strain[2] *n* **1** breed. **2** hereditary trait or tendency.

strand[1] *n* single thread from a wire, rope, etc.

strand[2] *vt,vi* run aground; beach. **stranded** *adj* abandoned; cut off; left helpless. ~*n* beach; shore.

strange *adj* **1** odd; peculiar. **2** unfamiliar; unusual; extraordinary. **3** foreign. **strangely** *adv*. **strangeness** *n*. **stranger** *n* person foreign to or not familiar with a particular place, area, or society.

strangle *vt* kill by throttling. **strangler** *n*. **stranglehold** *n* **1** choking grip. **2** force that suppresses freedom of movement or growth.

strap *n* thin strip, esp. of leather and with a buckle, for holding objects together. *vt* (-pp-) **1** bind with a strap. **2** beat with a strap.

strategy *n* overall plan of attack or campaign, esp. military; set of tactics. **strategic** *adj* relating to or important to an overall strategy.

stratum *n, pl* **strata** ('strɑːtə) *or* **stratums 1** layer of rock. **2** level of society.

straw *n* **1** single dried stem of grain. **2** such stems used as a material for baskets, mats, etc., for packing, or as bedding for cattle, etc. **3** narrow tube of paper or plastic used for drinking. **the last straw** a final blow that makes a situation no longer tolerable.

strawberry *n* creeping plant bearing soft reddish edible fruit.

stray *vi* wander; digress; err; go astray. *n* homeless animal or child. *adj* strayed; lost; scattered.

streak *n* **1** narrow irregular stripe (of colour, etc.). **2** flash (of lightning). **3** slight surprising tendency or trace. *vt* mark with streaks. *vi* **1** dash. **2** *inf* run naked in public in order to amuse or shock. **streaky** *adj*. **streakiness** *n*.

stream *n* **1** flow (of water, blood, etc.); current. **2** brook. **3** educational division according to ability. *vi* **1** flow in a steady stream; pour out. **2** (of hair, a flag, etc.) wave in the air. *vt* divide (children) into educational groups according to ability. **streamline** *vt* **1** design (cars, aircraft, etc.) in a smooth narrow shape to give minimum air resistance. **2** remove inefficient areas from an operation or process.

street *n* road with houses along one or both sides. **streets ahead** wholly superior. **up one's street** in one's line or area of interest.

strength *n* **1** quality of being strong; power; force. **2** support; aid. **3** effectiveness. **4** potency; degree of concentration. **on the strength of** based on; relying on. **strengthen** *vt,vi* make or become strong(er).

strenuous *adj* vigorous; diligent; energetic. **strenuously** *adv*. **strenuousness** *n*.

stress *n* **1** anxiety or distress caused by pressure or tension. **2** importance; weight; emphasis. **3** emphasis put on a word or syllable. **4** deforming force applied to an object. *vt* emphasize; put the stress on.

stretch *vt* pull or push out; extend; pull taut. *vi* **1** extend. **2** be elastic. **3** flex one's muscles. *n* **1** act of stretching. **2** expanse. **3** continuous period of time. **4** *sl* term of imprisonment. **stretcher** *n* framework covered in canvas, etc., and used for transporting the sick or injured.

strict *adj* **1** accurate; precisely defined. **2** stern;

severe; requiring complete obedience. **strictly** *adv*. **strictness** *n*.

stride *n* long step. **take in one's stride** cope with easily and without worrying. ~*vt,vi* (strode; stridden) walk (over) in strides.

strident *adj* harsh; grating.

strike *v* (struck) *vt* **1** hit; touch violently; collide with; beat. **2** light (a match). **3** occur to; remind; seem to. **4** reach suddenly or unexpectedly. *vt,vi* chime. *vi* **1** attack. **2** collide. **3** take part in a strike. **strike out 1** delete; cross out. **2** embark on a new venture. **strike up** begin; set up; establish. ~*n* **1** stoppage of work by employees in support of a claim, etc. **2** discovery of oil, etc.

string *n* **1** twine or cord used for tying, binding, etc. **2** string-like object, such as a tendon or fibre. **3** taut cord of wire, catgut, etc., fitted to a musical instrument and producing a note when caused to vibrate. **4** linked series; chain; line. **strings** *pl n* stringed instruments of an orchestra. **no strings attached** with no restricting factors or conditions. **pull strings** use influence in order to better oneself. ~*vt* (strung) fit strings to; thread. **string along** keep happy with false promises. **string out 1** spread out over a long area. **2** make (something) last a long time.

stringent *adj* strict; harsh; rigorous. **stringency** *n*. **stringently** *adv*.

strip[1] *v* (-pp-) *vt* **1** remove (the covering, outer layer, or clothes) from; lay bare. **2** take (an engine, etc.) apart. *vi* remove one's clothes. **striptease** *n* cabaret act in which the performer seductively removes clothing piece by piece.

strip[2] *n* narrow band; long piece. **strip cartoon** cartoon made up of a sequence of drawings.

stripe *n* **1** band of contrasting colour or texture. **2** band worn to show military rank. **striped** *adj* marked with stripes.

strive *vi* (strove; striven) try hard; endeavour; labour (to do something).

strode *v pt* of **stride.**

stroke[1] *n* **1** hit; blow. **2** single controlled movement in sports such as tennis, golf, etc. **3** style of swimming. **4** individual mark made by a brush or pen. **5** one of a series of movements. **6** apoplexy; damage to the brain's blood supply causing paralysis. **7** oarsman facing the cox. **8** chime of a clock.

stroke[2] *vt* caress with the hand; smooth. *n* act of stroking.

stroll *vi* walk for pleasure; saunter. *n* leisurely walk.

strong *adj* **1** physically powerful; forceful; difficult to break down, overcome, capture, or injure. **2** sound; healthy; vigorous. **3** positive; persuasive; drastic; effective; convincing. **4** concentrated; intense. *adv* **going strong** doing well; flourishing. **strongly** *adv*. **stronghold** *n* **1** fortress; garrison. **2** area where something prevails or has gained control. **strong-minded** having a powerful will; able to resist temptation.

struck *v pt* and *pp* of **strike.**

structure *n* **1** way in which things are put together; internal organization; make-up. **2** something constructed, esp. a building. *vt* give structure or form to; organize. **structural** *adj*. **structurally** *adv*.

struggle *vi* **1** fight hand to hand; wrestle; grapple. **2** labour; make great efforts; endeavour. *n* fight; strenuous effort.

strum *vt,vi* (-mm-) play (a stringed instrument) idly; sound a few chords (on).

strung *v pt* and *pp* of **string.** *adj* **highly strung** very nervous or tense.

strut[1] *vi* (-tt-) walk proudly to show off; swagger. *n* pompous gait.

strut[2] *n* supporting bar of wood, iron, etc., slat; rung.

stub *n* piece left after something has been used or worn down, esp. a cigarette end or counterfoil of a ticket or cheque. *vt* (-bb-) accidentally strike (one's foot or toe) against. **stub out** crush and extinguish (a cigarette).

stubborn *adj* obstinate; difficult to persuade or influence; strong-willed. **stubbornly** *adv*. **stubbornness** *n*.

stuck *v pt* and *pp* of **stick** .

stud[1] *n* **1** ornamental heavy-headed nail or peg; flat knob. **2** button-like device for fastening collars or fronts to shirts. **3** threaded pin or bolt. *vt* (-dd-) **1** put studs into. **2** dot or cover (with jewels, stars, etc.).

stud[2] *n* **1** establishment for breeding pedigree animals, esp. horses. **2** horse or group of horses kept for breeding.

student *n* person who studies, esp. one following a course at a college or institute of further education.

studio *n* **1** artist's or craftsman's workroom. **2**

place where broadcasts, recordings, or films are made. **studio couch** sofa that doubles as a bed.

studious *adj* **1** hard-working; fond of studying. **2** deliberate.

study *vt* **1** examine closely; peer at. **2** give special attention to; learn about; devote oneself to (a particular subject). *vi* follow a course of instruction; devote oneself to learning from books. *n* **1** act or process of studying; learning. **2** book, etc., produced by study. **3** room intended for study, reading, etc. **studied** *adj* deliberate; intentional; carefully considered; elaborately executed.

stuff *n* any type of material or substance. *vt* **1** cram full; overfill. **2** fill with stuffing. *vi* overeat. **stuffing** *n* **1** material with which objects are stuffed. **2** seasoned filling for meat, poultry, vegetables, etc.

stuffy *adj* **1** close; poorly-ventilated; oppressive. **2** *inf* prim and proper; easily shocked. **stuffily** *adv*. **stuffiness** *n*.

stumble *vi* trip and lose one's balance. **stumble on** *or* **across** discover by chance; come across. ~*n* act of stumbling. **stumbling block** obstacle; something that causes hesitation or doubt.

stump *n* **1** portion remaining after the main part of a limb or tree has been removed. **2** one of the three posts of a cricket wicket. *vt inf* puzzle; outwit. *vi* walk slowly and heavily. **stump up** *inf* produce or come up with (money).

stun *vt* (-nn-) **1** knock senseless; make unconscious. **2** amaze or shock. **stunning** *adj inf* extremely attractive.

stung *v pt* and *pp* of **sting.**

stunk *v pt* and *pp* of **stink.**

stunt[1] *vt* impede the growth or development of.

stunt[2] *n* dangerous, sensational, or acrobatic feat; anything done to attract attention or publicity. **stunt man** *n* person employed to perform dangerous feats in films or for entertainment.

stupid *adj* foolish; silly; not clever; dim-witted. **stupidity** *n*. **stupidly** *adv*.

sturdy *adj* strong; stout; solid. **sturdily** *adv*. **sturdiness** *n*.

sturgeon *n* large edible fish whose roe is eaten as caviar.

stutter *n* speech impediment causing hesitation or constant repetition of a word or syllable; stammer. *vt,vi* speak or say with a stutter.

sty[1] *n* pen for pigs.

sty[2] *n* small inflamed swelling on an eyelid.

style *n* **1** characteristic manner or fashion, esp. of practising a particular art, craft, or sport. **2** fashion; mode. **3** elegance; luxury; grandeur. **4** form; kind; sort. **5** title; mode of address. *vt* fashion or shape (hair, clothes, etc.). **stylist** *n*. **stylistic** *adj* relating to artistic style. **stylish** *adj* fashionable; smart.

stylus *n* **1** sapphire or diamond point used as a gramophone needle. **2** pointed writing or engraving instrument.

subconscious *n* area of one's mind, memory, and personality of which one is not aware. *adj* unconscious; stemming from the subconscious. **subconsciously** *adv*.

subcontract *n* (sʌbˈkɔntrækt) agreement assigning part of the work specified in a contract to another party. *vt,vi* (ˈsʌbkəntrækt) make a subcontract (regarding). **subcontractor** *n* person accepting a subcontract.

subcutaneous *adj* situated or introduced beneath the skin.

subdue *vt* suppress; put down; quieten.

subject *n* (ˈsʌbdʒikt) **1** something dealt with; object of study, analysis, discussion, examination, etc.; topic. **2** citizen under the authority of a state or ruler. **3** grammatical term for word(s) about which something is predicated or for the noun or pronoun acting as the doer of the verb in a sentence. **4** central musical theme of a composition. **subject to** *adj* **1** liable or prone to. **2** owing allegiance to. **3** conditional; dependent. *adv* conditionally. ~*vt* (səbˈdʒekt) **1** force to experience or undergo. **2** bring under the control (of). **subjection** *n*. **subjective** *adj* **1** influenced by or arising from personal feelings rather than external evidence. **2** (in grammar) of the subject. **subjectively** *adv*.

sublime *adj* **1** of great moral or spiritual worth; majestic; awe-inspiring; supreme. **2** utter; extreme. *n* anything majestic or inspiring awe. *vt,vi* change directly from a solid to a gas. **sublimely** *adv*.

submachine gun *n* lightweight automatic gun.

submarine *n* vessel that can operate underwater. *adj* relating to or intended for use below water level.

submerge *vt* place under water; flood; cover

with liquid. *vi* dip or go under water. **submergence** *or* **submersion** *n*.

submit *vt,vi* (-tt-) **1** surrender; yield. **2** put forward for consideration; suggest. **submit to** give in to; allow oneself to be under the control of. **submission** *n* **1** act of submitting. **2** suggestion. **submissive** *adj* timid and yielding.

subnormal *adj* mentally handicapped; below average intelligence.

subordinate *adj* (sə'bɔːdinit) **1** junior; inferior in rank, position, or importance. **2** (in grammar) subsidiary; dependent on a main clause. *n* (sə'bɔːdinit) person in an inferior position or rank. *vt* (sə'bɔːdineit) **1** reduce to a lower rank or position; assign to a lesser place. **2** subdue. **subordination** *n*.

subscribe *vt,vi* pledge a regular sum of money (to). *vi* **subscribe to 1** agree to buy (a magazine, etc.) regularly. **2** approve of; agree with. **subscriber** *n*. **subscription** *n* **1** act of subscribing. **2** amount subscribed. **3** regular monetary contribution.

subsequent *adj* later; following or coming afterwards. **subsequently** *adv*.

subservient *adj* **1** showing exaggerated feelings of humility; obsequious. **2** serving an end; useful as a means. **subservience** *n*.

subside *vi* **1** sink in; collapse. **2** die down; decrease. **subsidence** *n*.

subsidiary *adj* supporting; supplementary; secondary. *n* thing that is subsidiary, esp. a company that is part of a group.

subsidy *n* state grant for an industry, cultural organization, etc.; official financial assistance. **subsidize** *vt* support with a subsidy; assist financially.

substance *n* **1** stuff; matter; material. **2** chief part; importance; essence; gist. **3** worth; value; foundation. **substantial** *adj* **1** ample; large; considerable. **2** solid; well-established; wealthy. **substantially** *adv*. **substantiate** *vt* provide proof of (a claim, charge, etc.); establish; show to be true.

substitute *vt* put (one person or thing) in place of another. *vi* serve as. *n* person or thing substituted. **substitution** *n*.

subtitle *n* **1** title, often explanatory, subsidiary to the main one. **2** caption translating dialogue in a foreign film. *vt* provide a subtitle for.

subtle *adj* **1** delicate; slight; not gross; hard to detect or perceive. **2** ingenious; perceptive; complex. **subtlety** *n*. **subtly** *adv*.

subtract *vt* take (an amount) away from; deduct. **subtraction** *n*.

suburb *n* residential area on the outskirts of a town or city. **suburban** *adj* **1** conventional; narrow-minded. **2** relating to a suburb.

subway *n* **1** underground passage enabling pedestrians to cross a busy road. **2** *US* underground railway.

succeed *vi* achieve one's purpose; be able; manage. *vt* come after; follow and take the place or position of.

success *n* **1** achievement of one's purpose. **2** achievement of fame and wealth. **3** triumph; anything that succeeds. **successful** *adj*. **successfully** *adv*.

succession *n* **1** series of things coming one after another. **2** act or process of succeeding to a title or position. **successive** *adj* happening one after another or in sequence. **successively** *adv*. **successor** *n* person taking over the position or rank of another.

succulent *adj* **1** juicy. **2** fleshy-leaved, as a cactus. **succulence** *n*. **succulently** *adv*.

succumb *vi* **1** yield or give in, esp. to powerful persuasion. **2** die.

such *adj* **1** of a particular kind. **2** so much or so many. *pron* **1** those who or that which. **2** the same. **as such 1** by or in itself. **2** in that role or capacity. **such as** for example; like. ~*adv* this or that amount of. **suchlike** *pron* things of a similar sort. *adj* similar; of that sort.

suck *vt,vi* draw (liquid) into the mouth by action of the lips and tongue. *vi* **1** draw milk (from a mother's breast, an udder, etc.). **2** absorb; draw up (liquid). **3** hold in the mouth and lick. **4** make sucking actions. *n* act of sucking. **sucker** *n* **1** person that sucks. **2** *sl* person easily deceived. **3** device or organ, usually disc-shaped, that sticks to surfaces by suction. **4** shoot growing from the root of a plant.

suckle *vt,vi* give or suck milk from the breast.

suction *n* **1** action or process of sucking. **2** force causing a flow of liquid or gas or the adhesion of two surfaces.

sudden *adj* unexpected; happening quickly or without warning. *n* **all of a sudden** unexpectedly. **suddenly** *adv*. **suddenness** *n*.

suds *pl n* froth on the surface of soapy water; lather.

sue *vt,vi* take legal action (against). **sue for** beg; petition (for).

suede *n* soft leather with a velvety surface.

suet *n* hard fat found round the kidneys of sheep and cattle.

suffer *vt,vi* **1** endure; undergo mental or physical pain. **2** bear; tolerate. **suffer from** be ill, usually periodically, with. **suffering** *n* mental or physical pain; anguish.

sufficient *adj* enough; adequate for the purpose. **sufficiency** *n*. **sufficiently** *adv*.

suffix *n* letter(s) or syllable(s) put at the end of a word to change its part of speech, meaning, or grammatical inflexion.

suffocate *vt* kill by preventing or restricting breathing; smother. *vi* suffer restriction of one's breathing; die through lack of air; stifle. **suffocation** *n*.

sugar *n* sweet crystalline white or brown carbohydrate obtained from plants such as sugar cane or sugar beet. *vt* sweeten or coat with sugar. **sugary** *adj*. **sugar beet** *n* plant from the roots of which sugar is obtained. **sugar cane** *n* tall tropical grass from the canes of which sugar is obtained.

suggest *vt,vi* **1** propose; submit for consideration. **2** imply; intimate. **3** evoke; bring to mind; make (a person) think of. **suggestible** *adj* easily persuaded by suggestion. **suggestion** *n* **1** proposal; act of suggesting. **2** hint; trace. **3** implication. **4** production of an idea through association. **suggestive** *adj* **1** provoking thoughts (of). **2** having sexual overtones or implications.

suicide *n* **1** act of intentionally killing oneself. **2** person who has committed suicide. **3** action likely to ruin oneself or one's interests. **suicidal** *adj*.

suit *vt* **1** be convenient for; be acceptable to; satisfy. **2** (of clothes, colours, etc.) look attractive on or with. **3** be or make appropriate. **4** equip; adapt. *n* **1** matching jacket and trousers or skirt. **2** matching set or series, esp. of playing cards. **3** court case involving a claim. **4** wooing. **follow suit** copy; follow the example. **suitable** *adj* appropriate; proper; fitting. **suitably** *adv*. **suitability** *n*. **suitor** *n* **1** one who courts a woman. **2** petitioner. **suitcase** *n* portable case for luggage.

suite *n* **1** set of rooms. **2** set of furniture designed for one room. **3** group of attendants; retinue. **4** musical work of several connected movements, esp. based on dance forms.

sulk *vi* show offence or resentment by refusing to speak or cooperate. *n* act of sulking. **sulky** *adj* glumly withdrawn; sullen. **sulkily** *adv*. **sulkiness** *n*.

sullen *adj* silently unfriendly or uncooperative; morose and resentful; gloomy. **sullenly** *adv*. **sullenness** *n*.

sulphur *n* yellow nonmetallic element, used in making sulphuric acid. **sulphurous** *adj*.

sultan *n* Moslem ruler, esp. the head of the Turkish empire.

sultana *n* **1** sweet seedless raisin. **2** wife, mother, or daughter of a sultan.

sultry *adj* **1** hot and humid. **2** sexually exciting; voluptuous.

sum *n* **1** result obtained from addition; total or whole. **2** amount of money. **3** simple arithmetical problem. *vt* (-mm-) find the sum of. **sum up** make a summary; review; appraise; judge. **summary** *n* review of the main points; précis. *adj* hasty and unceremonious. **summarily** *adv*. **summarize** *vt* make a summary of.

summer *n* season of the year between spring and autumn. **summery** *adj* characteristic or suggestive of summer.

summit *n* **1** highest point; peak. **2** zenith; highest point, esp. of a career. **summit conference** *n* high level discussion(s) between governments.

summon *vt* demand the presence of; call forth; call upon. **summons** *n* order to appear, esp. in court. ~*vt* issue a summons to.

sumptuous *adj* lavish; luxurious. **sumptuously** *adv*.

sun *n* star about which the earth rotates and from which it receives heat and light. *v* (-nn-) **sun oneself** expose one's body to the sun's warmth. **sunflower** *n* tall plant with large yellow flowers. **sunglasses** *pl n* spectacles with tinted lenses for protection from the sun's rays. **sunny** *adj* **1** exposed to the sun; full of or characterized by sunshine. **2** cheerful. **sunrise** *n* **1** daily appearance of the sun above the eastern horizon. **2** time when this occurs. **sunset** *n* **1** daily disappearance of the sun below the western horizon. **2** time when this occurs. **sunshine** *n also* **sunlight** light and warmth received from the sun.

Sunday *n* first day of the week; day of Christian worship.

sundry *adj* various; miscellaneous. **sundries** *pl n* miscellaneous articles; extras.

sung *v pp* of **sing.**

sunk *v pt* and *pp* of **sink. sunken** *adj* **1** situated below the surface; lying underwater; hollowed into the ground or floor. **2** fallen in.

super *adj inf* splendid; wonderful; first-rate.

superannuation *n* retirement pension. **superannuated** *adj* obsolete; out of date; antiquated.

superb *adj* excellent; splendid. **superbly** *adv*.

superficial *adj* shallow; perfunctory; of or on the surface; not probing or thorough. **superficiality** *n*. **superficially** *adv*.

superfluous (suː'pəːfluəs) *adj* more than is wanted; unnecessary; left over. **superfluity** *n*. **superfluously** *adv*.

superhuman *adj* greater or more intense than seems humanly possible.

superimpose *vt* place (something) on top of something else.

superintendent *n* **1** official in charge of an institution, department, building, etc. **2** high-ranking police officer. **superintend** *vt* supervise; direct.

superior *adj* **1** greater; higher; better. **2** excellent; of high quality; high-ranking. **3** disdainful; conceited; indifferent. *n* person above one in rank or status. **superiority** *n*.

supermarket *n* large self-service food store.

supernatural *adj* **1** existing outside or beyond the laws of nature; magical; ghostly. **2** unnatural. *n* **the supernatural** supernatural creatures and happenings.

supersonic *adj* travelling faster than sound.

superstition *n* irrational or uninformed belief or fear, esp. in or of the supernatural or magic. **superstitious** *adj*. **superstitiously** *adv*.

supervise *vt,vi* **1** direct (work and workers); control. **2** act as a tutor (to). **supervision** *n*. **supervisor** *n*.

supper *n* light evening meal.

supple *adj* easily bent or manipulated; physically agile; flexible. **suppleness** *n*.

supplement *n* ('sʌplimənt) **1** something added to complete or extend something else. **2** additional section of a book, newspaper, etc. *vt* ('sʌpliment) add to; make supplements to. **supplementary** *adj*.

supply *vt* **1** provide; keep provided with. **2** fulfil; satisfy. *n* **1** stock; amount stored; something supplied. **2** availability or production of goods, esp. in relation to demand. **supplies** *pl n* stored goods; provisions.

support *vt* **1** hold up; bear the weight of. **2** back; stand up for; favour the cause of; assist. **3** maintain financially; provide for. **4** tolerate. *n* **1** act of supporting. **2** person or thing that supports. **supporting** *adj* secondary; not principal.

suppose *vt,vi* imagine; be inclined to think; assume. **supposition** *n*. **supposed** *adj* presumed. **supposed to** expected or obliged to. **supposedly** *adv* said or thought to be.

suppress *vt* **1** put down; crush. **2** keep concealed; withhold; stifle. **suppression** *n*. **suppressive** *adj*.

supreme *adj* most powerful; absolute; highest; greatest. **supremely** *adv*. **supremacy** *n* state of being supreme; dominance.

surcharge *n* extra amount added to the main bill, total, or cost. *vt* **1** impose a surcharge. **2** overload.

sure *adj* **1** convinced; having no doubt; confident. **2** certain; inevitable. **3** reliable; proven. **make sure (of) 1** satisfy oneself (about); check. **2** make certain. ~*interj inf* certainly! of course! **surely** *adv* **1** in a sure way. **2** certainly; without doubt. **surety** *n* **1** pledge; guarantee; guarantor. **2** certainty.

surf *n* foam made by waves breaking along the shoreline; breakers. *vi* engage in surfing. **surfing** *n* sport of riding large waves while balancing on a board.

surface *n* **1** topmost or outer covering, layer, or edge. **2** outward appearance. *vt* provide with a surface; improve the surface (of). *vi* rise to the surface; emerge.

surfeit *n* excessive or superfluous amount; overabundance; excess, esp. of food consumed.

surge *vi* drive or press forward in a rush or flood. *n* surging action; gush; swell; onrush.

surgeon *n* **1** doctor who performs medical operations. **2** military or police doctor. **surgery** *n* **1** medical treatment involving operations. **2** doctor's consulting-room; hours for visiting a doctor. **surgical** *adj* used in or relating to surgery.

surly *adj* bad-tempered and unhelpful; sullen.

surmount *vt* overcome (an obstacle or problem);

climb over. *vt,vi* be above; place on top of. **surmountable** *adj*.

surname *n* hereditary family name.

surpass *vt* excel; outdo; exceed; transcend. **surpassing** *adj* extraordinary.

surplus *n* **1** excess amount. **2** portion that remains after needs have been supplied, expenses subtracted, etc. *adj* extra; left over; no longer needed.

surprise *vt* **1** astonish; amaze. **2** take unawares. *n* **1** something unexpected. **2** amazement; astonishment. **surprised** *adj* revealing or expressing surprise. **surprising** *adj* causing surprise. **surprisingly** *adv*.

surrender *vt,vi* yield; give in; give up; abandon. *n* act of surrendering.

surreptitious *adj* done clandestinely; furtive; deliberately concealed. **surreptitiously** *adv*. **surreptitiousness** *n*.

surround *vt* encircle; extend right round; crowd around. **surrounding** *adj* situated around or nearby. **surroundings** *pl n* environment; objects or area immediately surrounding one.

survey *vt* (sə'vei) **1** scan; look over carefully. **2** measure and record the area, elevations, and other geographical features of a piece of land. **3** make a detailed inspection of the condition of a building, etc. *n* ('sə:vei) **1** act or process of surveying. **2** review; analysis. **3** surveyor's report. **surveying** *n* study or practice of surveying land. **surveyor** *n* person employed to survey areas of land or buildings.

survive *vt,vi* continue to exist (following); come through; outlive. **survival** *n*. **survivor** *n*.

susceptible *adj* **1** prone (to); easily affected or influenced (by). **2** easily stricken by emotion; sensitive. **susceptibility** *n* **1** quality of being susceptible to. **2** weakness (for).

suspect *vt,vi* (sə'spekt) **1** believe to be true without proof; have a feeling (about); suppose. **2** be doubtful about. **3** think (a person) guilty of. *n* ('sʌspekt) person thought to have committed a crime, etc. *adj* ('sʌspekt) dubious; arousing suspicion.

suspend *vt* **1** hang (one object from another); hang from above. **2** postpone; defer; delay; keep unresolved. **3** remove temporarily from office, etc.; withdraw (someone's privileges). **suspension** *n* **1** act of suspending; condition of being suspended. **2** postponement; temporary dismissal. **3** mixture consisting of one substance dispersed in small particles in another. **suspension bridge** *n* bridge suspended from steel cables hung between two towers.

suspense *n* feeling of tension; state of uncertainty.

suspicion *n* **1** act of suspecting; doubt or mistrust. **2** hint; trace; vague idea. **suspicious** *adj* **1** dubious; likely to cause suspicion. **2** mistrustful; doubtful; likely to suspect. **suspiciously** *adv*.

sustain *vt* **1** keep alive; maintain. **2** support; hold up. **3** endure; suffer; bear. **4** give strength to. **sustenance** *n* nourishment; food.

swab *n* **1** piece of cotton wool, etc., used in medicine to absorb liquid, blood, etc., or to take specimens. **2** mop; cloth used for washing floors, etc. *vt* (-bb-) mop up; wash down.

swagger *vi* strut about; show off; behave conceitedly. *n* swaggering walk or manner.

swallow[1] *vt,vi* **1** take into the stomach through the throat; gulp. **2** *inf* believe or accept (something unlikely). **swallow up** consume; engulf. ~*n* act of swallowing.

swallow[2] *n* small migratory bird with a forked tail.

swam *v pt* of **swim.**

swamp *n* permanently waterlogged ground, often overgrown. *vt* **1** drench with water; fill with water and sink. **2** overwhelm; flood. **swampy** *adj*.

swan *n* large long-necked water-bird. **swansong** final appearance; last work or contribution.

swank *vi* boast; show off. *n* **1** person who swanks. **2** act of swanking. **swanky** *adj*.

swap *vt,vi* (-pp-) *also* **swop** *inf* exchange (one thing for another). *n* **1** act of exchanging. **2** thing exchanged.

swarm *n* **1** dense mass of insects, esp. bees. **2** large crowd or throng. *vi* **1** flock or surge; be crowded (with). **2** (of bees) leave the hive in a swarm with a new queen.

swat *vt* (-tt-) strike or slap (an insect, etc.) with the hand, a newspaper, etc. *n* sharp slap.

sway *vt,vi* **1** swing, move, or bend to and fro; lean to one side. **2** persuade; influence. *n* **1** act of swaying. **2** rule; power. **hold sway** rule (over); be in control; dominate.

swear *vi* (swore; sworn) **1** use obscene or insulting language; utter curses or oaths. **2** declare or promise solemnly; make a binding legal promise or oath. **swear by 1** take an oath on (a sacred object, etc.). **2** rely on absolutely. **swearword** *n* socially unacceptable word; profane or obscene word.

sweat *n* **1** moisture secreted from the pores of the skin; perspiration. **2** *inf* hard work; trouble. *vi* **1** exude sweat; perspire. **2** *inf* work hard; labour.

sweater *n* woollen garment covering chest, back, and arms; jersey; jumper; pullover.

swede *n* pale orange root vegetable related to the turnip.

sweep *vi,vt* (swept) **1** clean or clear with a broom, brush, etc. **2** proceed or move rapidly (through). **3** extend; curve. *n* **1** sweeping movement. **2** person who cleans chimneys. **sweeper** *n*.

sweet *adj* **1** tasting sugary; not sour. **2** kind; likeable; charming; cute. *n* **1** any type of small confection made principally from sugar. **2** pudding; dessert. **sweetly** *adv*. **sweetness** *n*. **sweeten** *vt* **1** make sweet(er). **2** make more acceptable. **sweetheart** *n* person who loves and is loved in return; darling. **sweet pea** *n* climbing garden plant with sweet-smelling flowers.

swell *vt,vi* (swelled; swollen) expand; bulge out; increase in size, volume, etc. *n* **1** act of swelling. **2** waves; action of waves when not breaking. **3** gradual increase in sound. **swelling** *n* **1** act of swelling. **2** something swollen, esp. a bruised or infected area of the body. **swollen-headed** *adj* conceited.

swerve *vi* make a sudden or abrupt sideways turn. *n* act of swerving.

swift *adj* speedy; rapid; prompt. *n* small widely distributed bird capable of fast sustained flight. **swiftly** *adv*.

swig *inf vt,vi* (-gg-) swallow; take gulps (from). *n* draught; gulp.

swill *vt,vi* **1** drink large quantities (of). **2** wash or slop down. *n* liquid food for animals, esp. pigs.

swim *v* (swam; swum) *vi* **1** move in or under water by movement of the body, limbs, tail, or fins, etc. **2** float; drift; appear to swim. **3** feel dizzy; swirl. *vt* cross by swimming. *n* act or period of swimming.

swindle *vt,vi* obtain by fraud; cheat; exploit unfairly. *n* instance of swindling. **swindler** *n*.

swine *n, pl* **swine 1** pig. **2** brutish or beastly person.

swing *vt,vi* (swung) **1** move; sway; rock back and forth. **2** whirl about. **3** veer; turn. **swing round** turn suddenly in a sweeping movement. ~*n* **1** swinging movement or action. **2** seat suspended on ropes, etc., on which a person can swing himself.

swipe *n* lunging blow. *vt,vi* **1** make a swipe (at). **2** *inf* seize; steal.

swirl *vi* move round in a slow whirl, eddy, or series of curves. *n* **1** swirling action. **2** eddy; whirl.

swish *n* whistling sound as of a thin rod swung through the air; rustle; hiss. *vi,vt* make a swishing sound (with).

switch *vt,vi* exchange; transfer; shift; make a change. **switch on/off** turn on/off (an electric appliance, etc.). ~*n* **1** act of switching. **2** device for turning an electrical appliance, etc., on or off. **3** thin flexible cane or whip. **switchboard** *n* device fitted with many switches, esp. one used for relaying telephone calls.

swivel *vt,vi* (-ll-) turn (round) on a pivot. *n* device for joining two objects to allow one to move independently of the other.

swollen *v pp* of **swell.**

swoop *vt,vi* plunge or sweep down (on), as of a bird of prey, esp. to attack or carry off. *n* act of swooping.

swop *vt,vi,n* swap.

sword *n* weapon with a long pointed blade set in a handle. **swordfish** *n* edible marine fish with a long pointed jaw resembling a sword. **swordsman** *n* person skilled in the use of a sword.

swore *v pt* of **swear.**

sworn *v pp* of **swear.**

swot *vt,vi* (-tt-) *inf* study hard, esp. for an examination. *n* person who swots.

swum *v pp* of **swim.**

swung *v pt* and *pp* of **swing.**

sycamore *n* any of various kinds of deciduous tree having large indented leaves.

syllable *n* word or part of a word uttered as a single unit of sound.

syllabus *n, pl* **syllabuses** *or* **syllabi** ('siləbai) outline of work to be studied; summary of a course.

symbol *n* sign or object that represents something else, esp. something abstract. **symbolic** *adj*. **symbolically** *adv*. **symbolism** *n* the use of symbols to express abstract concepts, esp. in the arts. **symbolize** *vt* represent; stand for; act as a symbol of

symmetry *n* harmonious balance between parts; regularity or correspondence of a pattern within a whole. **symmetrical** *adj*.

sympathy *n* quality of feeling for people's suffering or understanding their attitude; compassion; understanding. **sympathetic** *adj* **1** having sympathy. **2** understanding; congenial. **sympathetically** *adv*. **sympathize** *vi* share a person's feelings, esp. during suffering; have understanding; show sympathy. **sympathizer** *n* one who approves of or sanctions a cause, political party, etc., without being a member or an active supporter.

symphony *n* major orchestral composition in three or more movements.

symptom *n* **1** physical or mental change indicative of or due to a malfunction. **2** any sign indicative of a change, disorder, or condition. **symptomatic** *adj*.

synagogue *n* place of worship and instruction for members of the Jewish religion.

synchronize *vt,vi* work, operate, or occur at the same time or in harmony. **synchronization** *n*. **synchronous** *adj*.

syndicate *n* **1** association of people carrying out a business or joining in an enterprise. **2** agency that sells articles, etc., to several newspapers for simultaneous publication. *vt* publish through a syndicate.

syndrome *n* combination of symptoms or signs indicating a certain condition or disorder.

synopsis *n, pl* **synopses** (si'nɔpsi:z) brief summary, précis, or outline, esp. of the plot of a novel, play, etc.

synthesis *n, pl* **syntheses** ('sinθəsi:z) combination or fusing of parts into a whole; whole thus formed. **synthetic** *adj* **1** artificial; false; man-made. **2** produced by or relating to a synthesis. **synthesize** *vt*.

syphilis *n* serious contagious type of venereal disease. **syphilitic** *adj*.

syringe *n* device for sucking in liquid and/or forcing it out in a spray or jet, esp. one used for injecting fluid into the body. *vt* clean out or spray using a syringe.

syrup *n* thick solution of sugar and water or juice; treacle. **syrupy** *adj*.

system *n* **1** group of coordinating parts forming a whole. **2** carefully organized set of related ideas or procedures. **systematic** *adj* methodical; regular; following a system.

T

tab *n* small flap or strip of cloth, paper, etc. **keep tabs on** keep a check or watch on.

tabby *adj* (of cats) brown or grey with dark stripes or blotches. *n* tabby cat.

table *n* **1** piece of furniture with a flat top and legs or supports, usually high enough to sit at. **2** organized list, chart, index, etc. **turn the tables on** place in an inferior or losing position. *~vt* put forward for future discussion. **tablespoon** *n* large spoon used for serving food. **table tennis** *n* game played with round bats and a small light ball on a table fitted with a low net.

tablet *n* **1** pill. **2** inscribed stone slab or plaque. **3** cake (of soap).

taboo *n also* **tabu** act, object, or word that is forbidden in a particular society or religion. *adj* forbidden.

tack *n* **1** large-headed short nail for fastening things. **2** direction taken by a sailing ship according to the angle of the wind. **3** method of approach; course of action. *vt* **1** fasten with tacks. **2** sew together with loose temporary stitching; gather together loosely. *vi* steer a course along a different tack.

tackle *n* **1** gear or equipment, esp. for fishing. **2** set of ropes used in a pulley system. **3** (in rugby football) act of seizing a player's legs so that he will give up the ball. **4** attempt to get the ball from another player in football. *vt* **1** attempt or attack (something difficult). **2** approach or deal with (a difficult or unwilling person, situation, etc.). **3** perform a tackle on in football.

tact *n* sensitivity to other people's feelings or to situations that require delicate and discreet handling. **tactful** *adj*. **tactfully** *adv*.

tactic *n* manoeuvre, act directed towards a goal. **tactics** *pl n* strategy, plan of action. **tactical** *adj*. **tactically** *adv*.

tadpole *n* completely aquatic stage in a frog's or toad's life during which the legs develop and the tail and gills disappear.

taffeta *n* strong stiff satin-like cloth.

tag *n* small label or indentity disc. *vt* (-gg-) label;

identify. **tag along** accompany; go along (with).

tail *n* **1** end part of an animal's body that is an elongation of the backbone. **2** back or end part, section, or projection. **turn tail** flee; run away. ~*vt,vi* **1** follow and observe (a person's actions), esp. without being noticed. **2** take the tail from. **tail off** gradually diminish or deteriorate. **tails** *s n* side of a coin not bearing the sovereign's head.

tailor *n* **1** person employed to make garments which require careful fitting, esp. those for men. **2** person selling men's clothes. *vt,vi* **1** make and fit (suits, etc.). **2** adapt; alter to suit individual needs.

taint *n* trace of some defect, infection, corrupting influence, etc. *vt* infect; stain; poison; spoil.

take *vt* (took; taken) **1** receive or accept (something offered). **2** bring into one's possession; help oneself to; remove. **3** accompany to a particular destination. **4** capture; seize. **5** grasp; grip; hold. **6** eat, drink, or swallow (medicine, tablets, etc.). **7** steal. **8** select; use. **9** transmit; transport; convey. **10** keep a record of. **11** last; be the time required for. **12** require; be necessary for. **13** have accommodation for. **14** regard; consider. **15** subtract; deduct. **16** study. **take in** deceive; swindle. **take off 1** remove. **2** become airborne. **3** impersonate; mimic. **take on** accept as a duty or commitment. **take out 1** extract; delete. **2** escort. **3** acquire (a licence, insurance, etc.). **take over** assume control. **take to** find pleasure in; develop a liking or skill for. **take up** pursue; adopt; become involved in. **take-off** *n* **1** act of jumping or lifting off the ground. **2** satirical imitation. **take-over** *n* act of taking over and assuming control, esp. of a business, government, etc. **takings** *pl n* money obtained in the course of business during a particular period.

talcum powder *n* very fine scented body powder.

tale *n* story; narrative; legend. **tell tales 1** report another's misdoings. **2** tell lies.

talent *n* ability; skill; special gift or aptitude.

talk *vi,vt* **1** communicate by means of speech. **2** discuss; express by speaking. **3** chatter; gossip. *n* **1** manner of speaking. **2** speech or brief lecture. **3** gossip. **talkative** *adj* tending to talk a lot; chatty.

tall *adj* large in height; not small. **tall order** difficult commission. **tall story** *or* **tale** *n* unlikely or exaggerated account or story.

tally *vi* correspond; agree. *vt* add up; reckon. *n* **1** reckoning; score; bill. **2** notched stick for recording numbers.

talon *n* claw, esp. of a bird of prey.

tambourine *n* small shallow drum with metal discs, which clink when shaken.

tame *adj* **1** (of animals) not wild; not aggressive towards or frightened of humans. **2** unexciting; unadventurous. *vt* make tame.

tamper *vi* interfere; meddle.

tan *n,adj* light brown. *n* skin browned by the sun. *vt,vi* (-nn-) **1** make or go brown. **2** turn (hides) into leather.

tang *n* sharp taste.

tangent *n* straight line that touches but does not intersect a curve. **go off at a tangent** digress; change the subject or line of thought. **tangential** *adj* **1** relating to tangents. **2** connected but irrelevant.

tangerine *n* type of small sweet orange.

tangible *adj* **1** able to be touched. **2** visible; factual; real.

tangle *n* muddle; confused web of knots; intricate mass. *vt,vi* make into a tangle; muddle.

tango *n* Latin-American ballroom dance.

tank *n* **1** large container for keeping or storing liquids. **2** large armour-plated military vehicle.

tankard *n* large mug with a handle, used esp. for beer.

tanker *n* ship or lorry built for carrying liquids in bulk.

tantalize *vt* tease by offering or presenting something desirable that cannot be attained.

tantrum *n* hysterical fit of bad temper.

tap[1] *vt,vi* (-pp-) strike a quick gentle blow (on). *n* tapping action or sound. **tap dancing** *n* style of dancing involving complicated heel and toe tapping steps.

tap[2] *n* device with a screw and washer for controlling the flow of liquid from a pipe or container. **on tap** constantly available. ~*vt* (-pp-) **1** sap; drain off; extract. **2** fit a bugging device to (a telephone, etc.) so as to intercept or overhear calls.

tape *n* **1** strip of flexible resistant material for binding, mending, etc. **2** length of tape stretched across the finishing line of a race track or cut symbolically to open a fête, etc. **3** strip of plastic magnetized recording tape. *vt* **1**

bind or stick together with tape. **2** record on tape. **tape-measure** *n* length of tape marked off with measurements; flexible rule. **tape-recorder** *n* device for recording sound on magnetic tape.

taper *vt,vi* make or become gradually thinner at one end; tail off. *n* very thin candle.

tapestry *n* heavy fabric having a picture or design,woven by hand in coloured threads.

tar *n* thick black sticky coal-based substance used in road building, wood preserving, etc. *vt,vi* (-rr-) cover with tar.

target *n* **1** object or person to be aimed at or attacked. **2** goal or objective.

tariff *n* **1** tax or list of taxes levied on imported goods. **2** fixed schedule of charges or prices.

tarnish *vt,vi* spoil the shine or lustre (of). *n* loss of shine or lustre.

tart[1] *adj* **1** sharp to the taste; acid. **2** sarcastic.

tart[2] *n* **1** small pie or flan with a sweet filling. **2** *sl* prostitute.

tartan *n* woollen plaid fabric in different patterns and colours corresponding to those of various Highland Scottish clans.

task *n* particular job or piece of work; chore. **take to task** reprove; censure.

tassel *n* ornamental knot with a bunch of loose threads.

taste *vt,vi* **1** sense the flavour (of) with one's tongue. **2** try; have a short experience of. **3** have the flavour (of). *n* **1** flavour. **2** sense by which one perceives flavour. **3** ability to make aesthetic judgment; discernment. **4** fineness or elegance of style, manners, etc. **5** particular preference. **6** small amount; trace; hint. **tasteful** *adj* elegant; fitting. **tasteless** *adj* **1** not strongly flavoured; insipid. **2** not tasteful; tactless. **tasty** *adj* good to eat.

tattoo[1] *vt* permanently mark (the skin) by putting indelible stains into pricked designs. *n* design made by tattooing.

tattoo[2] *n* **1** military entertainment involving marching and music, usually at night. **2** signal sounded on a drum or bugle recalling soldiers to their quarters for the night. **3** continuous drumming.

taught *v pt* and *pp* of **teach.**

taunt *vt* jeer at; provoke; tease. *n* jeer; insulting remark.

Taurus *n* second sign of the zodiac, represented by the Bull.

taut *adj* tightly stretched; having no slack; tense. **tautness** *n*.

tavern *n* public house; inn.

tax *n* **1** money demanded by law to be paid according to income, assets, goods purchased or imported, etc. **2** difficult or onerous obligation, demand, etc.; burden. *vt* **1** impose a tax on. **2** put a burden on; strain. **taxation** *n* system of imposing taxes or the amount of tax payable.

taxi *n* car with a driver for public hire. *vi* (of aircraft) move along the ground on landing or before take-off. *vt* cause (an aircraft) to taxi.

tea *n* **1** evergreen shrub grown in East Asia for its pungent leaves. **2** drink made from infusing dried tea leaves in boiling water. **3** meal between lunch and supper at which tea is drunk. **tea-cloth** *n also* **tea-towel** cloth for drying dishes.

teach *vt,vi* (taught) instruct; give lessons (in); show (a person) how to do something. **teacher** *n*. **teaching** *n* **1** ability to teach; knowledge or practice of teaching. **2** set of doctrines.

teak *n* large tree found in SE Asia with hard orange-brown wood, used for furniture, etc.

team *n* **1** group of people working together, esp. in order to compete against others. **2** group of horses, dogs, etc., pulling together. *v* **team up with** join with in order to pool resources and work in harmony.

tear[1] (tiə) *n also* **teardrop** drop of salty liquid that falls from the eye. **tearful** *adj* **1** liable to cry. **2** sad. **tear-gas** *n* type of gas that makes the eyes water, used to disperse rioting crowds, etc.

tear[2] (tɛə) *v* (tore; torn) *vt,vi* divide; split; rip. *vi* hurry; rush. **tear down** pull down; destroy. **tear off 1** pull or pluck off, esp. violently. **2** *inf* do in a great hurry. **tear up 1** divide into small pieces, strips, etc. **2** pull up; destroy. ~*n* torn hole; slit.

tease *vt,vi* **1** torment by joking; mock; make fun of. **2** draw out; comb out; disentangle. *n* person given to teasing others.

teat *n* **1** nipple. **2** feeding nipple on a baby's bottle.

technical *adj* **1** relating to a technique, method, or skill. **2** relating to specialized industrial or mechanical skills and crafts or to technology. **technically** *adv*.

technician *n* person skilled in the technical

processes of a particular craft, science, or industry.

technique *n* **1** method of performing some skill; system of practical procedures. **2** practical skill.

technology *n* **1** application of scientific ideas to industry or commerce. **2** methods and equipment so used. **technological** *adj*. **technologist** *n*.

tedious *adj* **1** boring; monotonous. **2** tiresome. **tediously** *adv*. **tedium** *n*.

tee *n* **1** small peg that supports a golf ball for the first stroke at each hole. **2** elevated area from which this stroke is played. *v* **tee off 1** drive the ball from the tee. **2** start.

teenager *n* person aged between 13 and 19; adolescent.

teeth *n pl* of **tooth. get one's teeth into** begin to cope with or tackle seriously. **teethe** *vi* (esp. of babies) produce teeth.

teetotal *adj* refusing to drink or serve alcoholic drinks. **teetotaller** *n* teetotal person.

telegram *n* message transmitted by telegraph.

telegraph *n* method of or apparatus for transmitting messages using radio signals or electric impulses sent along wires. *vt,vi* send a telegram to. **telegraphy** *n*.

telepathy *n* human communication through scientifically inexplicable channels; mind-reading. **telepathic** *adj*.

telephone *n* system or apparatus for verbal communication over a distance, usually using electric impulses sent back and forth along a wire. *vt,vi* call or talk to by telephone; phone. **telephonist** *n* operator of a telephone switchboard.

telescope *n* **1** optical instrument using lenses or mirrors to magnify distant objects. **2** instrument, esp. one using radio or light waves, to study astronomical bodies. *vt,vi* make or become shorter, compressed, or crushed. **telescopic** *adj*.

television *n* **1** process of or apparatus for using high-frequency radio waves to transmit and receive visual images with accompanying sound. **2** radio broadcasts received on a television. **televise** *vt,vi* record or broadcast by means of television.

telex *n* telegraph service or apparatus for transmitting printed messages.

tell *v* (told) *vt,vi* inform; let know. *vt* **1** relate; recount; express in words; describe. **2** order; instruct. **3** disclose; reveal; confess. *vi* reveal secrets; inform against someone. **can tell** be able to discover, understand, distinguish, etc. **tell off** scold. **telltale** *adj* betraying; serving to reveal something hidden. *n* person given to informing on others.

temper *n* **1** state of mind; mood. **2** angry fit; rage; tendency to become angry. *vt* **1** modify; moderate; alleviate. **2** strengthen (metal) by sudden changes of temperature.

temperament *n* nature; disposition; person's style of thinking and behaviour. **temperamental** *adj* **1** given to violent changes of mood; excitable. **2** unreliable.

temperate *adj* **1** mild in temperature. **2** moderate; restrained; even-tempered.

temperature *n* **1** measured or approximate degree of hotness of something. **2** fever.

tempestuous *adj* stormy; violent.

temple[1] *n* **1** place of worship dedicated to a particular deity. **2** sacred place.

temple[2] *n* flat area on either side of the forehead.

tempo *n* speed at which a conductor or performer chooses to play a piece of music.

temporal *adj* existing in or limited by time; not spiritual; earthly. **temporally** *adv*.

temporary *adj* intended to be used for a short time; not permanent; passing. **temp** *n inf* person not employed on a permanent basis. **temporarily** *adv*.

tempt *vt* persuade or induce (a person) to try or do something undesirable; attract; seduce; influence. **temptation** *n*.

ten *n* **1** number equal to one plus nine. **2** group of ten persons, things, etc. **3** *also* **ten o'clock** ten hours after noon or midnight. *adj* amounting to ten.

tenacious *adj* holding or sticking firmly; stubbornly persisting. **tenaciously** *adv*. **tenacity** *n*.

tenant *n* person who occupies a house, flat, farm, etc., for payment of rent. **tenancy** *n* state of being a tenant or the period during which this occurs.

tend[1] *vt* look after; care for.

tend[2] *vi* be inclined or likely (to); have the effect of. **tendency** *n*.

tender[1] *adj* **1** soft; delicate; not hardy. **2** gentle; loving; compassionate. **3** painful when touched; sensitive. **4** easily chewed. **5** youthfully innocent; vulnerable. **tenderly** *adv*. **ten-**

derness *n*. **tender-hearted** *adj* easily moved to pity. **tenderize** *vt,vi* make (food) soft and easy to chew.

tender[2] *vt,vi* offer for acceptance or settlement. *n* offer of goods or services at a fixed rate.

tendon *n* band or sheet of fibrous tissue by which muscle is attached to bone.

tendril *n* threadlike shoot of a plant enabling it to cling to a support while climbing.

tenement *n* **1** rented room or flat in a block, esp. one in a poor quarter of a city. **2** property held by a tenant.

tennis *n* game for two or four players played by hitting a ball over a net with rackets.

tenor *n* **1** general meaning; tone; direction. **2** instrument or male voice with a range between that of baritone and alto.

tense[1] *adj* **1** anxious; in suspense; overwrought. **2** taut; strained; stretched. *vt* make tense. **tensely** *adv*. **tenseness** *n*. **tensile** *adj* able to be stretched. **tension** *n* **1** stretching or state of being stretched or strained. **2** excitement; suspense. **3** anxiety or unease caused by suppressed emotion.

tense[2] *n* form of a verb indicating the time of action.

tent *n* canvas portable shelter for camping, etc.

tentacle *n* slender flexible organ of various invertebrates, used for feeding, grasping, etc.

tentative *adj* **1** hesitating; cautious. **2** provisional.

tenth *adj* coming between ninth and eleventh. *n* **1** tenth person, object, etc. **2** one of ten equal parts; one divided by ten. *adv* after the ninth.

tenuous *adj* **1** thin; slender; flimsy. **2** subtle; weak.

tenure *n* holding of land or office.

tepid *adj* **1** slightly warm; lukewarm. **2** unenthusiastic.

term *n* **1** period of time for which something occurs or is in force, as a period of teaching in a college, school, etc. **2** word used in specialized field. **3** end of pregnancy. **terms** *pl n* **1** conditions of an agreement, bargain, etc. **2** relationships between people. **come to terms** form an agreement; reconcile. **in terms of** as expressed by. ~*vt* define (something) as; call.

terminology *n* set of terms specific to any particular field of study. **terminological** *adj*.

terminate *vt,vi* bring or come to an end. **termination** *n*. **terminal** *adj* of, at, or marking an end or limit; final. *n* **1** end of a transport route. **2** either end of an open electrical circuit. **terminally** *adv*.

terminus *n, pl* **termini** ('tɜːminai) *or* **terminuses** **1** boundary points; final point reached. **2** end of a railway, airline, or bus route.

terrace *n* **1** raised bank or walk in a garden. **2** flat area cut into a slope, often for crop cultivation. **3** balcony; flat rooftop. **4** row of similar adjoined houses.

terrestrial *adj* **1** of or on earth; earthly. **2** living or growing on land rather than in the sea or air.

terrible *adj* **1** causing terror; appalling; very bad. **2** *inf* excessive; outstanding. **terribly** *adv*.

terrier *n* small dog of various breeds originally used in hunting out animals underground.

terrific *adj* **1** frighteningly large; instilling terror. **2** *inf* amazingly good; enjoyable. **terrifically** *adv*.

terrify *vt* cause terror in; frighten.

territory *n* area regarded as owned by the state or a social group or individual or animal. **territorial** *adj*. **territorially** *adv*.

terror *n* **1** extreme fear. **2** anything causing fear or dread. **3** *inf* nuisance; troublesome person. **terrorist** *n* person employing organized violence and intimidation to obtain political objectives. **terrorism** *n*. **terrorize** *vt* manipulate by inspiring terror.

terse *adj* concise; curt.

Terylene *n Tdmk* type of synthetic fibre used as textile yarn.

test *n* any critical trial or examination to determine the merit or nature of something. *vt* conduct a test on; examine. **test case** *n* legal case that establishes a precedent. **test match** *n* international cricket match. **test-tube** *n* glass tube used in conducting chemical experiments.

testament *n* **1** one of the two major divisions of the Bible (the Old Testament and the New Testament). **2** act of testifying, as to religious faith. **3** (in law) will.

testicle *n* one of two glands in males producing sperm and male sex hormones.

testify *vi,vt* bear witness; affirm; give evidence.

testimony *n* evidence; proof; declaration. **testimonial** *n* **1** written testimony of character.

2 gift presented as a tribute or token of respect.

tether *n* rope or chain by which an animal is secured. **at the end of one's tether** at the end of one's patience or ability to withstand. ~*vt* fasten with a tether; tie.

text *n* **1** main section of written or printed words of a book as distinguished from illustrations, the index, etc. **2** passage from the Bible. **textual** *adj*. **textbook** *n* book used as a standard source for a particular course of study.

textile *n* woven fabric or cloth.

texture *n* **1** surface, arrangement of strands, etc., of a material, esp. as perceived by the sense of touch. **2** quality, esp. of music.

than *conj* **1** expressing the second stage of a comparison. **2** expressing an alternative after *rather, sooner,* etc.

thank *vt* **1** express gratitude to. **2** blame. **thankful** *adj*. **thankless** *adj*. **thanks** *pl n, interj* expression of gratitude, relief, etc.

that *adj* relating to the person or thing specified, esp. one further away than or different from another. *pron* **1** the particular person or thing so specified. **2** who(m) or which. *adv* so; to such an extent. *conj* introducing a noun clause. **that's that** there is no more to be said or done.

thatch *n* arrangement of straw, reeds, etc., used as a roof covering. *vt,vi* cover with a thatch.

thaw *vt,vi* **1** melt after being frozen. **2** make or become less hostile, frigid, etc. *n* period or process during which snow or ice melts.

the *def art* preceding a noun. *adv* used for emphasis or to express a comparative amount or extent.

theatre *n* **1** building in which plays, operas, etc., are performed. **2** lecture hall. **3** *also* **operating theatre** room equipped for carrying out surgery. **4** drama. **5** business of working in or for a theatre. **theatrical** *adj*.

theft *n* crime of stealing another's property.

their *adj* belonging to them. **theirs** *pron* those things belonging to them.

them *pron* those people or things. **themselves** *r pron* **1** their own selves. **2** their normal selves.

theme *n* **1** main idea or concept with which a work of art, discussion, etc., is concerned; topic. **2** recurring melody.

then *adv* **1** at the particular time referred to. **2** immediately afterwards; next. **3** in that case. *adj* functioning at that time. *n* that time.

theology *n* study of religion and the nature of God. **theological** *adj*. **theologian** *n*.

theorem *n* statement that is to be proved by logical reasoning.

theory *n* **1** system or formula as an explanation of a particular phenomenon. **2** body of abstract ideas or principles, esp. as distinguished from practice. **theoretical** *adj*. **theoretically** *adv*. **theorize** *vi* speculate; formulate a theory.

therapy *n* course of treatment designed to cure various disorders of the body or mind. **therapeutic** *adj*. **therapist** *n*.

there *adv* **1** in, to, at, or towards that place. **2** at that point. *pron* used with forms of *be, can,* etc., to introduce a sentence or clause. *n* that position. *interj* expression of consolation, victory, pride, etc. **thereabouts** *adv also* **thereabout** in that approximate place or position. **thereafter** *adv* after that time; from then on. **thereby** *adv* thus; by those means. **therefore** *adv* so; consequently; for that reason. **thereupon** *adv* at which point; after which.

thermal *adj* of or relating to heat. *n* rising current of warm air.

thermodynamics *n* study of the relationships between work, heat, and other forms of energy.

thermometer *n* any instrument used to measure temperature.

thermonuclear *adj* involving fusion of two atomic nuclei, with consequent production of large amounts of heat. **thermonuclear bomb** *n* hydrogen bomb.

Thermos flask *n also* **Thermos** *Tdmk* container with double walls enclosing a vacuum to prevent heat transfer, used for keeping food or drink hot or cold.

thermostat *n* automatic device to maintain a room, enclosure, etc., at a constant temperature. **thermostatic** *adj*. **thermostatically** *adv*.

these *adj* form of **this** used with a plural noun.

thesis *n, pl* **theses** ('θi:si:z) **1** original work submitted by a candidate for an academic degree. **2** hypothesis; proposition.

they *pron* **1** two or more persons or things when used as the subject in a sentence or clause. **2** people in general.

thick *adj* **1** relatively deep, wide, or fat; not thin. **2** measured by width or diameter. **3** densely layered, arranged, etc. **4** not watery or runny. **5** *inf* stupid. **6** having a broad accent. **a bit thick** unfair; unreasonable. **through thick and thin** throughout both good and bad periods. *adv also* **thickly** so as to be thick. **thickness** *n*. **thicken** *vt,vi* make or become thick(er). **thick-skinned** *adj* **1** insensitive, esp. to criticism. **2** having a thick hide or outer layer.

thief *n, pl* **thieves** person committing theft. **thieve** *vt,vi* commit theft; steal.

thigh *n* that part of the leg above the knee.

thimble *n* small cap worn over the fingertip whilst sewing.

thin *adj* **1** relatively narrow; not thick. **2** slim; slender; not fat. **3** not densely layered, arranged, etc.; sparse. **4** watery or runny. **5** lacking depth of quality; not rich. *adv also* **thinly** so as to be thin. *vt,vi* (-nn-) **1** make or become thin(ner). **2** dilute. **thinness** *n*. **thin-skinned** *adj* sensitive, esp. to criticism.

thing *n* **1** inanimate object; entity. **2** course or action; act; deed. **3** person or animal, esp. when referred to with affection, sympathy, etc. **have a thing about** be preoccupied with. **the thing** fashionable trend. **things** *pl n* **1** possessions. **2** points; matters; ideas. **3** conditions or circumstances.

think *v* (thought) *vi* use one's mind or power of reason. *vt,vi* **1** believe; consider. **2** be aware (of); regard. **think about 1** reflect or ponder on. **2** *also* **think of** have an opinion of. **think of 1** bring to mind; imagine or remember. **2** plan; anticipate; consider. ~*n inf* concentrated effort to examine or analyse an idea, suggestion, etc.

third *adj* coming between second and fourth in sequence. *n* **1** third person, object, etc. **2** one of three equal parts; one divided by three. **3** gear above second on a motor vehicle. *adv* **1** after the second. **2** *also* **thirdly** as a third point. **third party** *n* person only marginally involved in a case or affair. **third person** *n* category of pronouns or verbs other than the person speaking or addressed. **third rate** *adj also* **third-class** of a very poor standard; mediocre.

thirst *n* **1** desire for water or other liquids. **2** craving; yearning. *vi* have a thirst (for). **thirsty** *adj*.

thirteen *n* **1** number that is three more than ten. **2** thirteen things or people. *adj* amounting to thirteen. **thirteenth** *adj,adv,n*.

thirty *n* **1** number equal to three times ten. **2** thirty things or people. *adj* amounting to thirty. **thirtieth** *adj,adv,n*.

this *adj* relating to the person or thing specified, esp. one closer than or different from another. *pron* the particular person or thing so specified. *adv* to a specified extent.

thistle *n* plant with a purple flower and prickly leaves.

thong *n* thin strip of leather used in a whip, as a fastening, etc.

thorax *n, pl* **thoraxes** *or* **thoraces** ('θɔːrəsiːz) **1** part of the body containing the heart, lungs, etc.; chest. **2** part of an insect bearing the wings and legs.

thorn *n* **1** sharp woody point occurring on a stem or leaf. **2** bush, esp. the hawthorn, having thorns. **thorny** *adj* **1** having thorns. **2** difficult to solve.

thorough *adj* **1** completed carefully and painstakingly; meticulous. **2** utter; absolute. **thoroughly** *adv*. **thoroughness** *n*. **thoroughbred** *n* animal of a pure breed; pedigree. *adj* relating to such an animal. **thoroughfare** *n* **1** road or street. **2** access; passage.

those *adj* form of **that** used with a plural noun.

though *conj* in spite of the fact that; although. **as though** as if. ~*adv* nevertheless; on the other hand.

thought *v pt* of **think.** *n* **1** idea, notion, concept, etc., produced by thinking. **2** act or process of thinking. **3** attention; consideration. **4** body of ideas relating to a particular period, movement, etc. **thoughtful** *adj* **1** considerate. **2** engaged in thought. **thoughtfully** *adv*. **thoughtfulness** *n*. **thoughtless** *adj* tactless; careless; inconsiderate. **thoughtlessly** *adv*. **thoughtlessness** *n*.

thousand *n* **1** number equal to ten times one hundred. **2** thousand people or things. **thousands** *pl n* huge number. *adj* amounting to a thousand. **thousandth** *adj,adv,n*.

thrash *vt* **1** flog; whip; beat. **2** defeat overwhelmingly. *vi* make a violent movement with the arms or legs, esp. in water. **thrash out** settle by debate or intense discussion. ~*n* beating; violent blow.

thread *n* **1** strand of cotton, yarn, wool, etc. **2** spiral groove of a screw, bolt, etc. **3** central idea running through a story, argument, etc. *vt* **1** pass (a thread) through (a needle). **2** make (a way) through (obstacles, etc.). **threadbare** *adj* **1** worn; having no pile or nap. **2** shabby; poor.

threat *n* **1** statement or indication of future harm, injury, etc. **2** person or thing likely to cause harm, injury, etc.; danger. **threaten** *vt,vi* make threats (to); be a threat (to); menace.

three *n* **1** number equal to one plus two. **2** group of three persons, things, etc. **3** *also* **three o'clock** three hours after noon or midnight. *adj* amounting to three. **three-dimensional** *adj also* **3-D** having three dimensions; solid or apparently solid. **threesome** *n* group of three; trio.

thresh *vt,vi* beat or shake (corn) so as to separate the grain from the husks. **thresher** *n* person or machine that threshes.

threshold *n* **1** slab or board placed at a doorway or entrance. **2** starting point or verge. **3** point at which a stimulus produces an observable effect.

threw *v pt of* **throw.**

thrift *n* economic or careful use of resources. **thrifty** *adj*.

thrill *n* **1** tingle of excitement; flush of enthusiasm; intense emotion or sensation. **2** event causing this. *vt,vi* cause or experience a thrill. **thriller** *n* book, film, etc., arousing strong excitement and suspense.

thrive *vi* **1** grow healthily and well. **2** prosper.

throat *n* **1** front of the neck. **2** passage connecting the mouth and stomach. **3** narrow part, passage, or opening. **cut one's throat** pursue a disastrous course. **jump down someone's throat** attack verbally with sudden vehemence. **ram down someone's throat** assert or force upon without allowing response. **throaty** *adj* hoarse, as if with a sore throat.

throb *vi* (-bb-) beat strongly and rhythmically. *n* strong pulsating beat.

throne *n* **1** monarch's, pope's, or bishop's seat. **2** sovereign power.

throng *n* crowd; mass of people. *vi,vt* form or fill with a throng.

throttle *n* valve that regulates an engine's fuel supply. *vt* **1** choke; strangle. **2** regulate or restrict (power supply).

through *prep* **1** along the length of; from one end to the other of. **2** in one side and out of the other side of. **3** during; from the beginning to the end of. **4** via. **5** with the influence of; by the means or agency of. **6** because of. *adv* **1** from one side or end to another. **2** from start to finish. **3** throughout; completely. **4** no longer functioning or successful. **throughout** *prep* right through; during the whole of. *adv* in every part.

throw *v* (threw; thrown) *vt,vi* **1** send (a missile) through the air. **2** toss; fling. *vt* **1** baffle; perplex; confuse; take aback. **2** place in a particular situation. **throw away** discard as useless; reject; get rid of. **throw out 1** eject; remove by force. **2** expel; dismiss. **throw up 1** vomit. **2** produce unexpectedly. **3** leave or reject (a job). ~*n* **1** act of throwing. **2** toss; pitch.

thrush *n* songbird with brown plumage and speckled underparts.

thrust *vt,vi* **1** push with force. **2** stab; pierce. **3** force (a situation) upon (someone). *n* **1** violent lunge or push. **2** force of the propulsion of an engine. **3** *inf* ruthless drive to succeed.

thud *n* dull heavy sound of impact. *vi* (-dd-) make such a sound.

thumb *n* **1** short thick digit of the human hand. **2** corresponding digit in other mammals. **rule of thumb** practical method based on experience. **under the thumb of** under (someone's) control. ~*vt* **1** mark or touch with the thumb. **2** use the thumb as a signal, esp. as a hitch-hiker.

thump *n* **1** dull heavy blow. **2** sound made by such a blow. *vt,vi* strike; pound; beat.

thunder *n* loud rumbling noise caused by movement of air after lightning. *vi,vt* **1** make a sound like thunder; roar. **2** speak loudly and angrily. **thunderous** *adj*. **thunderstorm** *n* thunder and lightning accompanied by heavy rain.

Thursday *n* fifth day of the week.

thus *adv* **1** in the meantime. **2** to this extent or degree. **3** therefore.

thwart *vt* prevent; frustrate.

thyme (taim) *n* fragrant herb with a minty odour.

thyroid *n also* **thyroid gland** gland whose hormones regulate metabolism and growth.

tiara *n* jewelled head ornament worn by women.

tick[1] *n* **1** light tapping or clicking noise of a watch, clock, etc. **2** mark or symbol used to indicate approval or acknowledgment of having been noted. *vi* make a ticking sound. *vt* mark with a tick. **tick off** rebuke; scold. **tick over** (of an engine) idle.

tick[2] *n* any of a number of parasites of warm-blooded animals.

ticket *n* **1** card or slip indicating right to entry, service, etc. **2** price label. **3** slip issued for any of certain motoring offences.

tickle *vt* **1** touch lightly so as to cause laughter, pleasure, etc. **2** amuse; please. *vi* tingle; be the location of an itching sensation. *n* itching sensation. **ticklish** *adj* **1** susceptible or sensitive to tickling. **2** precarious; difficult to handle.

tide *n* **1** twice daily movement of the sea caused by the gravitational pull of the moon. **2** turning point in time. *v* **tide over** enable to cope until help or relief comes. **tidal** *adj*.

tidy *adj* neat; orderly. *vt,vi* make tidy. **tidily** *adv*. **tidiness** *n*.

tie *v* (tying) *vt* **1** fasten with a knot, bow, etc. **2** bind or secure with string, rope, etc. **3** restrict the freedom or mobility of. *vi* **1** fasten. **2** obtain an equal score or number of marks as someone else; draw. *n* **1** fastening such as string or rope. **2** obligation; restriction of freedom, etc.; commitment. **3** draw; equal score. **4** shaped piece of material worn with a shirt, fastened in a large knot at the throat.

tier *n* **1** row (of seats, etc.) above and slightly behind another or others. **2** level; layer.

tiger *n* Asiatic feline mammal with a yellow and black striped coat.

tight *adj* **1** taut; not loose. **2** fitting snugly; constricting. **3** compact. **4** strict; hard. **5** *inf also* **tight-fisted** stingy; mean; miserly. **6** *inf* drunk. **tightly** *adv*. **tightness** *n*. **tighten** *vt,vi* make or become tight(er). **tightrope** *n* taut rope or wire on which an acrobat performs. **tights** *pl n* close fitting sheer garment covering the lower part of the body, legs, and feet.

tile *n* thin flat slab used for covering roofs, floors, etc. *vt* cover with tiles.

till[1] *prep* until.

till[2] *n* box or receptacle into which money is put behind the sales counter in a shop, etc.

till[3] *vt* cultivate or work (land). **tillable** *adj*.

tiller *n* lever attached to a rudder.

tilt *vi,vt* incline; slant; lean. *n* slope; inclination.

timber *n* wood cut into planks for use in building. *vt* provide with timber.

time *n* **1** system that relates successive events, occurrences, or changes in terms of the past, present, or future. **2** measurement by means of a clock. **3** period; age. **4** period for which something lasts; duration. **5** tempo. **6** instance; moment. **7** experience of an event, emotion, etc. **8** leisure; freedom from other tasks or duties. **9** period allotted or taken to complete something. **10** occasion. **from time to time** occasionally. **in time** not late or overdue. **on time** at precisely the time fixed; punctual. ~*vt* **1** keep a record of (the amount of time needed or taken). **2** fix the time of. **time bomb** *n* bomb detonated by a timing device. **timekeeper** *n* person or mechanism that records time. **timely** *adj* happening at a fortunate or suitable time. **times** *prep* multiplied by. *pl n* period; era. **timetable** *n* schedule of times of events, arrivals, departures, etc.

timid *adj* easily frightened; shy. **timidity** *n*. **timidly** *adv*.

timpani *pl n* kettledrums.

tin *n* **1** soft silvery metal. **2** container for food, etc., made of iron and plated with tin. *vt* (-nn-) **1** cover with tin. **2** preserve (food) in airtight containers.

tinge *vt* colour faintly. *n* **1** faint colour or tint. **2** small trace; hint.

tingle *vi* experience a prickling or mildly vibrating sensation. *n* prickling feeling; mild vibration.

tinker *n* itinerant craftsman who mends or sells pots and pans. *vi* **1** work as a tinker. **2** work in a haphazard fashion. **3** meddle; interfere (with).

tinkle *n* light metallic bell-like sound. *vi,vt* make or produce such a sound.

tinsel *n* ornamental string of glittering metal threads used as a festive decoration.

tint *n* **1** shade of a colour produced by mixture with white. **2** dye; pigment. *vt* give a tint to; colour; dye.

tiny *adj* very small; minute.

tip[1] *n* end; extremity, esp. of anything tapering to a point. **tiptoe** *vi* walk very quietly. *n* **on tiptoe** standing or walking on the balls of the feet; straining to reach up.

tip[2] *v* (-pp-) *vt,vi* lean or tilt to one side. *vt* **1** pour out or dump by tipping the container. **2**

touch or raise (one's hat). **tip over** topple; overturn. ~*n* place where rubbish is dumped.

tip[3] *n* **1** extra payment in appreciation of services rendered. **2** useful hint or advice. *vt,vi* (-pp-) give a tip (to). **tip off** give a tip-off to. **tip-off** *n* advance warning or confirmation of advantage to the recipient.

tipsy *adj* inebriated; tight; slightly drunk.

tired *adj* **1** weary; suffering from fatigue; sleepy. **2** bored; fed up; no longer interested. **tire** *vt,vi* make or become tired. **tireless** *adj* unwearying. **tiresome** *adj* wearying; trying; irritating.

tissue *n* **1** finely woven thin paper. **2** substance consisting of cells forming the structure of plants and animals.

tithe *n* (formerly) tenth part of agricultural produce, levied as a tax.

title *n* **1** name by which a person or thing may be distinguished. **2** heading by which a novel, play, etc., is known. **3** position or mode of address, esp. of a member of the nobility. **4** legal right to possess something.

to *prep* **1** in the direction of. **2** as far as. **3** into the state of. **4** giving the result of. **5** near or in contact with. **6** in comparison with. **7** with the extent of. **8** conforming with. **9** for use with or on. **10** in the opinion of. **11** until. **12** into the possession of. **13** used before the infinitive form of a verb. *adv* **1** fixed; closed. **2** into consciousness. **to and fro** alternately backwards and forwards. **to-do** *n* fuss; bother; commotion.

toad *n* **1** small tailless greenish-brown amphibian with a dry warty skin. **2** unpleasant person. **toadstool** *n* umbrella-shaped fungus living on dead organic matter.

toast[1] *n* slice of bread browned by heat on each side. *vt,vi* crisp; brown under heat.

toast[2] *vt* drink to the health of (a person, etc.). *n* drink in honour of a person, country, etc., or words proposing such a drink.

tobacco *n* **1** tall annual plant with large broad leaves. **2** cured leaves of this plant used in cigarettes, cigars, etc. **tobacconist** *n* person or shop selling tobacco.

toboggan *n* small sledge used on snow slopes for winter sport. *vi* ride on a toboggan.

today *n* this present day. *adv* **1** now; on this very day. **2** nowadays; at the present time.

toddle *vi* walk with an unsteady uneven gait, as a child learning to walk. **toddle along** *inf* go at an easy unhurried pace. **toddler** *n* child between the ages of one and three approximately, who is beginning to walk.

toe *n* **1** digit of the foot. **2** part of a shoe, stocking, etc., covering this. *v* **toe the line** obey; do as one is told. **toenail** *n* nail covering the toe.

toffee *n* sweet made of boiled sugar. **toffee-apple** *n* apple coated in toffee. **toffee-nosed** *adj sl* snobbish; conceited.

together *adv* **1** in close proximity. **2** in the company of one or more other persons. **3** simultaneously; at the same time.

toil *vi* **1** work hard and long. **2** proceed slowly and with difficulty. *n* labour; hard work.

toilet *n* **1** process of washing, combing one's hair, etc. **2** lavatory; W.C. **toilet water** *n* dilute solution of perfume.

token *n* **1** something used to represent or serve as a substitute. **2** symbol; gesture. **3** small gift; memento. **4** metal or plastic voucher used in place of money. *adj* **1** serving as a token. **2** in name only; having little practical effect.

told *v pp* and *pt* of **tell.**

tolerate *vt* allow; permit; endure. **tolerable** *adj* bearable. **tolerably** *adv* moderately; to a certain extent. **tolerance** *n* **1** *also* **toleration** forbearance; fair-mindedness; freedom from bigotry. **2** degree to which something can withstand specified conditions, etc.

toll[1] *n* **1** payment exacted for use of a bridge, road, etc., in certain circumstances. **2** price paid; number or amount sacrificed.

toll[2] *vt,vi* ring or cause to ring with slow heavy strokes.

tomato *n, pl* **tomatoes** juicy red fruit usually served as a vegetable with seasoning.

tomb *n* place where the dead are buried or laid out in a hollow chamber.

tomorrow *n* **1** the day after today. **2** the future. *adv* on the day after today.

ton *n* measure of weight equivalent to 2240 pounds (approx. 1016 kilograms).

tone *n* **1** quality of a musical note. **2** pure musical note. **3** manner of speaking, writing, etc., indicating attitude or emotion. **4** general physical or moral condition. **5** shade of colour; tint. *v* **tone down** reduce; soften; calm. **tonal** *adj*. **tonality** *n* system of musical keys, esp. in traditional Western music.

tongs *pl n* instrument consisting of two hinged arms for grasping objects.

tongue *n* **1** flexible organ in the mouth used in eating and in forming speech. **2** language; method or tone of speaking. **3** anything shaped like a tongue. **tongue in cheek** insincerely or ironically. **tongue-tied** *adj* **1** suffering from a speech defect. **2** speechless; inarticulate. **tongue-twister** *n* phrase or sentence that is difficult to pronounce because of unusual sound combinations.

tonic *n* **1** medicine used to stimulate and invigorate. **2** anything with this effect. **3** key on which a musical work is primarily based.

tonight *n* the night of the present day. *adv* on this night or evening.

tonsils *pl n* pair of oval-shaped organs situated on each side of the back of the throat. **tonsillitis** *n* enlargement or inflammation of the tonsils due to infection.

too *adv* **1** also; in addition; as well. **2** to an excessive extent.

took *v pt of* **take.**

tool *n* **1** instrument used in making or doing something; implement. **2** person used to serve another's purpose. **3** useful device; means. *vt,vi* use a tool (on).

tooth *n, pl* **teeth 1** hard projection in the jaws of humans and most vertebrates, used for biting, chewing, etc. **2** any similar projection, as on a comb. **toothbrush** *n* brush used for cleaning the teeth.

top[1] *n* **1** highest point; peak. **2** upper part. **3** highest position. **4** cap or cover of a bottle, jar, box, etc. **blow one's top** lose one's temper. ~*adj* best; highest. *vt* (-pp-) **1** take the top off. **2** cover or form the top of. **3** surpass. **top up** add extra liquid to so as to fill. **top hat** *n* tall cylindrical hat worn by men on formal occasions. **top-heavy** *adj* **1** disproportionately heavier or thicker above than below and thus unstable. **2** with too much emphasis on certain parts. **topmost** *adj* highest. **topsoil** *n* uppermost and most fertile layer of the earth's crust.

top[2] *n* small shaped object made to balance by spinning on a point, used esp. as a toy.

topic *n* subject; theme. **topical** *adj* of current interest.

topography *n* detailed geographical description or representation of the features of an area.

topple *vi,vt* fall or cause to fall over; overturn. *vt* overthrow; depose.

topsy-turvy *adj,adv* **1** upside down. **2** confused; muddled.

torch *n* **1** burning material held on a stick. **2** device carried by hand for giving light, usually operated by a battery.

tore *v pt of* **tear**.

torment *n* ('tɔːment) severe mental or physical distress; anguish. *vt* (tɔː'ment) **1** torture; distress. **2** pester; harass.

torn *v pp of* **tear**.

tornado *n, pl* **tornadoes** *or* **tornados** violent storm of short duration with a characteristic rotating movement and funnel-shaped cloud.

torpedo *n, pl* **torpedoes** self-propelled missile carried by a submarine for use against ships. *vt* hit with or as if with a torpedo.

torrent *n* **1** rapidly flowing stream of large quantities of water. **2** any copious rapid flow, as of words, abuse, etc. **torrential** *adj.*

torso *n* trunk of the human body.

tortoise *n* slow-moving reptile with a bony shell and scaly head and legs.

tortuous *adj* **1** twisting; winding; snakelike. **2** devious; unnecessarily complicated.

torture *n* **1** severe pain inflicted as a punishment or method of persuasion. **2** any extreme physical or mental distress. *vt* **1** inflict torture on. **2** cause extreme agony, pain, or distress in. **torturous** *adj.*

Tory *n* supporter of the Conservative party. *adj* belonging or relating to this party.

toss *vt* **1** throw into the air. **2** move (the head, hair, etc.) upwards with a jerk. *vt,vi* **1** move about or up and down quickly and in an irregular manner; pitch; jerk. **2** move restlessly, as in sleep. **3** *also* **toss up** spin (a coin) in the air to decide something. **toss off** finish quickly. ~*n* act of tossing or being tossed.

tot[1] *n* **1** small child. **2** small measure of alcoholic liquor.

tot[2] *v* **tot up** (-tt-) add up; count.

total *n* **1** complete whole as compared with a part. **2** final figure obtained by addition. *adj* **1** complete; final. **2** absolute; unrestrained. *vt,vi* (-ll-) add up (to).

totalitarian *adj* (of a government) characterized by absolute authority; allowing no opposition. **totalitarianism** *n.*

totem *n* object, esp. an animal, regarded as having special significance for a clan, tribe, etc. **totem-pole** *n* carved post used as a totem by North American Indians.

totter *vi* **1** walk unsteadily. **2** be in a precarious state.

touch *vt,vi* **1** bring or come into contact with. **2** bring the hand into contact with; feel. **3** *also* **touch (up)on** allude to; mention in passing. *vt* **1** affect; influence. **2** deal with; be associated with. **3** *sl* borrow money from. *n* **1** sense by which objects in contact with the body are felt. **2** act of touching, esp. a light brush or blow. **3** small amount of something. **4** knack; ability. **5** *sl* act of borrowing money or the person borrowed from. **in touch 1** aware. **2** having correspondence or contact (with). **touched** *adj* **1** emotionally moved. **2** slightly mad. **touching** *adj* producing pity or sympathy; moving. **touchy** *adj* easily offended.

tough *adj* **1** strong; hard-wearing. **2** hardy; robust; capable of suffering hardship. **3** (of food) difficult to chew. **4** stubborn; uncompromising. **5** difficult. **6** vicious; rough. *n* ruffian; lout. **toughness** *n*. **toughen** *vt* make tough(er); strengthen.

toupee *n* small patch of false hair worn to cover a bald spot.

tour *n* journey through several places, usually for sightseeing. *vt,vi* make a tour (through). **tourism** *n* business catering for the needs of tourists. **tourist** *n* person, esp. a holidaymaker, visiting a city, foreign country, etc.

tournament *n* **1** medieval contest between armed horsemen. **2** organized competition involving several matches, as in tennis, chess, etc.

tow *vt* pull along behind, as with a rope. *n* act of towing.

towards *prep also* **toward 1** in the direction of. **2** close to; in the vicinity of. **3** as a contribution to.

towel *n* cloth or paper for drying things. **throw in the towel** surrender; concede. ~*vt,vi* (-ll-) dry with a towel. **towelling** *n* type of absorbent cloth used for towels.

tower *n* tall cylindrical or square-shaped construction, forming part of a church, castle, etc. **tower of strength** strong reliable person. **in an ivory tower** insulated from reality. ~*vi* rise up to great heights. **tower above** *or* **over 1** be much higher than. **2** be greatly superior to.

town *n* **1** group of houses, shops, etc., larger than a village and smaller than a city. **2** inhabitants of a town. **go to town** act in a wholehearted or unrestrained manner. **town clerk** *n* official in charge of civic records. **town hall** *n* public building used as the administrative centre of a town.

toxic *adj* poisonous.

toy *n* **1** plaything of a child. **2** trifle; something treated lightly. *adj* **1** relating to or like a toy. **2** (esp. of a dog) bred specially to be smaller in size than average. *v* **toy with 1** play or trifle with. **2** consider; ponder about.

trace *vt* **1** follow (a track, path, etc.). **2** discover or find by careful searching. **3** copy by overlaying a transparent sheet and marking the lines. **4** draw; sketch. *n* **1** trail; track. **2** sign showing former presence of something. **3** small amount; vestige.

track *n* **1** mark or marks left by the passage of something; trail. **2** path. **3** path designed for guiding something, as in a railway. **4** course on which races are held. **5** series of metal plates fitted instead of wheels to vehicles such as tractors, tanks, etc. *vt,vi* follow the track of. **track down** find by searching. **tracksuit** *n* loose-fitting garment fastened at the neck, wrists, and ankles, worn by athletes in training.

tract[1] *n* **1** large area of water or land; expanse. **2** bodily structure or system serving a specialized function. **3** bundle of nerve fibres.

tract[2] *n* treatise or pamphlet.

tractor *n* vehicle with large wheels or tracks, for use esp. on farms.

trade *n* **1** business; commerce. **2** interchange of goods and money on an agreed basis. **3** skilled manual craft. *vt,vi* exchange for money or other goods; barter. *vi* engage in a business. **trade in** give in part exchange for something. **trade on** exploit. **trader** *n*. **trademark** *n* **1** mark or name registered by a manufacturer for a product. **2** characteristic trait. **tradesman** *n, pl* **-men 1** person engaged in trade, esp. a small shopkeeper. **2** skilled worker. **trade union** *n* association of people engaged in the same trade pledged to protect standards of wages, working conditions, etc.

tradition *n* beliefs and practices passed down from earlier generations. **traditional** *adj*. **traditionally** *adv*.

traffic *n* **1** motor vehicles using a road. **2** movement of ships, aircraft, etc. **3** trade; commerce. *vi* (-ck-) trade (in), esp. illicitly.

tragedy *n* **1** prose or drama with an inevitable unhappy ending. **2** sad event; great misfortune. **tragic** *adj* **1** in the style of a tragedy. **2** sad; moving; calamitous. **tragically** *adv*.

trail *n* track left behind by a person, animal, or thing. *vt* **1** drag or pull behind. **2** track; pursue. **3** hang loosely. *vi* **1** walk wearily with lagging steps. **2** hang or grow downwards. **trailer** *n* **1** vehicle attached to and pulled by another. **2** series of short extracts used to advertise a film.

train *n* **1** number of railway carriages or wagons coupled together and drawn by an engine. **2** succession of things, persons, or events. **3** part of a gown or robe trailing behind. *vt* **1** impart skill or knowledge to. **2** teach (an animal) to obey commands or perform tricks. **3** encourage (plants) to grow as required. **4** point (a gun, camera, etc.) at. *vi* **1** receive instruction. **2** exercise regularly to increase fitness. **trainee** *n*. **trainer** *n*.

traipse *vi* trudge; follow a long or circuitous route; wander about aimlessly; trek. *n* long tiring walk or journey.

traitor *n* person who betrays a trust, esp. one who commits treason. **traitorous** *adj*.

tram *n* passenger car running on a metal track on a road. **tramlines** *pl n* **1** tracks on which trams run. **2** parallel lines on a tennis court marking the boundaries of the singles court.

tramp *vi* walk with heavy tread. *vi,vt* walk (a certain distance), as for recreation. *n* **1** itinerant vagrant living by casual work or begging. **2** sound of someone tramping. **3** walk, esp. a long recreational walk.

trample *vt,vi* tread under foot; crush with the feet.

trampoline *n* gymnasium apparatus consisting of a sheet attached to a framework by springs, used for jumping, performing somersaults, etc. *vi* exercise on a trampoline.

trance *n* dreamlike semi-conscious state produced by hypnotism, drugs, etc.

tranquil *adj* calm; peaceful; unruffled. **tranquillity** *n*. **tranquillize** *vt* make tranquil; calm down. **tranquillizer** *n* drug used to reduce anxiety.

transact *vt,vi* perform; carry out (something, esp. a business deal). **transaction** *n*.

transatlantic *adj* **1** across or beyond the Atlantic Ocean. **2** relating to North America.

transcend *vt,vi* excel; surpass; exceed. **transcendent** *adj*. **transcendental** *adj* of or connected with the philosophy of seeking after truth by exploring the inner self. **transcendentalism** *n*.

transcribe *vt* copy out in writing. **transcription** *n*.

transfer *vt,vi* (træns'fəː) (-rr-) **1** move from one place to another. **2** change from one position, job, responsibility, etc., to another. **3** make over (power, responsibility, etc.) to another. *n* ('trænsfəː) **1** act of transferring. **2** prepared design or picture on paper that can be transferred to another surface.

transform *vt,vi* change in character, nature, shape, etc. **transformation** *n*.

transfusion *n* transfer of blood from one person to another or injection of other fluids to make up loss of blood. **transfuse** *vt* give a transfusion of.

transient *adj* transitory.

transistor *n* small electronic component made of certain solid materials. **transistorized** *adj* (of a piece of electronic equipment) using transistors rather than valves.

transit *n* **1** act of crossing or being conveyed from one place to another. **2** act of moving across. **transition** *n* **1** change from one place or set of circumstances or conditions to another. **2** process of continuous change or development. **transitory** *adj* changing; of limited duration.

transitive *adj* designating a verb that takes a direct object.

translate *vt,vi* **1** express in another language. **2** interpret; explain the meaning of. **translation** *n*. **translator** *n*.

translucent *adj* allowing light to pass through but not allowing a clear image of an object to be seen.

transmit *vt* (-tt-) **1** send across; pass on; communicate. **2** act as a condition or medium for. **transmission** *n*. **transmitter** *n* device used to broadcast radio or television signals.

transparent *adj* **1** transmitting rays of light; clear. **2** easily seen or detected. **transparently** *adv*. **transparency** *n* **1** quality of being transparent. **2** transparent photographic print projected or viewed by transmitted light.

transplant *vt* (træns'plɑːnt) **1** dig up and plant elsewhere. **2** transfer (living tissue or an organ) from one person to another. *n* ('trænsplɑ:nt) act of transplanting or something transplanted.

transport *n* ('trænspɔ:t) **1** means of conveying a person or thing from one place to another. **2** vehicle used for this purpose. *vt* (træn'spɔ:t) **1** carry; move from one place to another. **2** carry away, as with emotion.

transpose *vt* **1** cause to exchange positions. **2** rewrite (music) in a different key. **transposition** *n*.

trap *n* **1** device for catching an animal. **2** trick to place someone in an unfavourable position. **3** hazard; pitfall. **4** device to prevent passage of gas, impurities, etc. **5** light open horse-drawn carriage. **6** stall from which greyhounds are released for a race. **7** *also* **trap door** door in a floor or ceiling. *vt* (-pp-) catch or remove by means of a trap. **trapper** *n* person who traps animals for fur.

trapeze *n* apparatus used by gymnasts or acrobats, consisting of two suspended ropes carrying a horizontal crossbar.

trash *n* **1** rubbish; refuse. **2** anything considered worthless or shoddy.

trauma *n* violent emotional shock or experience. **traumatic** *adj*.

travel *v* (-ll-) *vi* **1** go on a journey; make a trip. **2** go abroad frequently or regularly. **3** move; proceed. **4** move from place to place selling goods. *vt* cover (a specified distance). **traveller** *n* **1** person who travels. **2** person employed to travel in goods; travelling salesman. **travels** *pl n* trips or journeys, esp. abroad.

traverse *vt,vi* cross from one side or corner to another. *n* act of crossing over or through.

trawl *n* large net pulled behind a boat to catch fish. *vi,vt* catch (fish) with a trawl. **trawler** *n* fishing boat equipped with a trawl.

tray *n* flat piece of wood, metal, etc., often with a raised edge, for carrying objects.

treacherous *adj* **1** deceitful; betraying a trust. **2** dangerous; hazardous. **treachery** *n*.

treacle *n* thick sticky syrup obtained by refining sugar.

tread *v* (trod; trod *or* trodden) *vi,vt* put the foot down on (something) or apply pressure to (something) with the foot. *vi* walk. *vt* **1** walk on (a path, road, etc.). **2** mark a floor with (mud, dirt, etc.) carried on the feet. **tread on** **1** oppress. **2** crush; stamp out. ~*n* **1** act or manner of treading. **2** part of a tyre that makes contact with the ground, usually having a patterned surface to improve the grip. **3** horizontal part of a step.

treason *n* disloyalty to a sovereign or the state.

treasure *n* object or collection of objects of value. *vt* value or regard greatly; cherish. **treasurer** *n* person in charge of funds of a society, group, etc. **treasury** *n* storehouse for treasure. **the Treasury** government department responsible for finance.

treat *vt* **1** deal with; handle. **2** prescribe medicine or medical care for. **3** act towards or regard. **4** buy something for. **5** act upon; apply a process to. *n* **1** entertainment or a gift paid for by someone else. **2** something producing joy or pleasure. **treatment** *n* **1** act or manner of treating a person or thing. **2** course of medical care.

treaty *n* formal agreement between nations.

treble *vt,vi* multiply or be multiplied by three. *n* soprano or a voice or instrument in this range. *adj* threefold; multiplied by three.

tree *n* perennial plant with a thick trunk of wood topped by branches and leaves.

trek *vi* (-kk-) make a long slow journey, esp. through difficult country. *n* journey of this kind.

trellis *n* framework of criss-crossed bars used as a plant support, decorative screen, etc.

tremble *vi* **1** shake or quiver, as from cold, fear, etc. **2** be afraid. **3** vibrate. *n* act or an instance of trembling.

tremendous *adj* **1** overpowering; astonishing. **2** *inf* great; considerable. **tremendously** *adv*.

tremor *n* trembling; shaking; quivering.

trench *n* **1** narrow ditch dug in the ground. **2** ditch with soil parapets, used by soldiers during battle. *vi,vt* dig a trench (in).

trend *n* **1** movement or tendency in a particular direction. **2** *inf* fashion. **trendy** *adj inf* up-to-date; fashionable.

trespass *vi* **1** intrude upon private property without permission. **2** encroach upon. *n* act of trespassing. **trespasser** *n*.

trestle *n* structure consisting of a beam with hinged legs, used to support a plank, table top, etc.

trial *n* **1** test; experiment. **2** trying experience; hardship. **3** formal inquiry in court.

triangle *n* **1** plane figure bounded by three straight lines. **2** steel musical instrument of this shape sounded by striking with a small rod. **triangular** *adj*.

tribe *n* **1** group of people, usually primitive, with a common ancestry, culture, etc. **2** group of related animals or plants. **tribal** *adj*.

tribunal *n* **1** court of justice. **2** board or group appointed to settle any matter in dispute.

tributary *n* small river flowing into a larger one.

tribute *n* **1** payment in money or kind made by one ruler or country to another as an act or submission. **2** mark or expression of respect.

trick *n* **1** action or device intended to deceive. **2** skill; knack. **3** prank; joke. **4** cards played in one round. *vt,vi* deceive; delude; cheat. **trickery** *n*. **tricky** *adj* **1** crafty; deceitful. **2** difficult; complicated.

tricycle *n* vehicle with three wheels propelled with pedals.

trifle *n* **1** small object. **2** matter of little value or importance. **3** cold dessert sweet consisting of layers of cream, custard, fruit, and sponge. *v* **trifle with** act insincerely towards.

trigger *n* **1** device releasing the spring mechanism of a gun. **2** any device that sets off or initiates something. *vt also* **trigger off** set off; cause; initiate.

trill *n* high-pitched vibrating sound. *vi,vt* utter or sing with a trill.

trim *vt* (-mm-) **1** make neat or tidy, as by clipping. **2** cut away (superfluous material) from. *adj* **1** neat; tidy. **2** smart; in good condition. *n* **1** correct condition; good order. **2** act of trimming, esp. the hair. **trimmings** *pl n* additional decoration or garnish.

trio *n* group of three, esp. three singers or musicians.

trip *n* **1** journey; excursion. **2** stumble or fall. **3** mistake; slip. **4** sudden starting of a mechanism. *v* (-pp-) *vi,vt* **1** stumble or cause to stumble. **2** make or cause to make a mistake. **3** release (a mechanism) or (of a mechanism) be released. *vi* dance; skip.

tripe *n* **1** white lining of the stomach of a ruminant, used for food. **2** *sl* rubbish; worthless material.

triple *adj* **1** three times as great; threefold. **2** of three parts or kinds. *n* anything that is a group of three. *vt,vi* multiply or be multiplied by three. **triplet** *n* **1** one of three children born at the same birth. **2** any one of a group of three.

tripod *n* stand with three legs, for supporting a camera, etc.

trite *adj* commonplace; hackneyed.

triumph *n* **1** victory. **2** notable achievement; great success. *vi* **1** gain a victory; win. **2** achieve great success. **3** rejoice in something; exult. **triumphant** *adj* **1** victorious. **2** exultant.

trivial *adj* insignificant; of no account. **triviality** *n*.

trod *v pt* and a *pp* of **tread. trodden** *v* a *pp* of **tread.**

trolley *n* **1** small hand-drawn wheeled vehicle for carrying goods, dishes, etc. **2** wheel on the end of a pole running on an overhead cable, used to draw electric current to drive a bus (trolleybus) or tram.

trombone *n* long brass instrument, usually having a moving slide to control the notes. **trombonist** *n*.

troop *n* **1** body of soldiers. **2** group of people or animals. *vi* march or proceed in a group. **troops** *pl n* soldiers.

trophy *n* memento of a victory; prize; award.

tropic *n* one of two lines of latitude, either 23°28' north (tropic of Cancer) or 23°28' south (tropic of Capricorn) of the equator. **tropical** *adj* relating to the tropics. **tropics** *pl n* region between these lines of latitude.

trot *n* **1** pace between walking and running. **2** pace of horses with diagonal pairs of legs moving together. *vi* (-tt-) move with a trot. **trot out** produce; introduce. **trotter** *n* **1** horse bred for trotting. **2** foot of a pig or certain other animals.

trouble *n* **1** disturbance; uneasiness. **2** affliction; distress. **3** person or thing causing trouble or worry. **4** care; pains; effort. *vt* afflict; annoy; inconvenience. *vi* take pains; bother; make an effort.

trough (trɔf) *n* **1** long narrow vessel holding food or drink for animals. **2** area of low barometric pressure.

troupe *n* group of performers.

trousers *pl n* garment designed to cover the legs and lower part of the body.

trout *n, pl* **trout** *or* **trouts** brownish speckled edible fish of the salmon family.

trowel *n* **1** flat-bladed tool with a pointed tip, used to spread mortar. **2** hand tool used by gardeners. *vt* (-ll-) use a trowel on.

truant *n* child absenting himself from school without permission. **truancy** *n*.

truce *n* temporary cessation of hostilities by mutual agreement.

truck *n* strong vehicle for carrying heavy loads.

trudge *vi* walk wearily. *n* long or tiring walk.

true *adj* **1** relating to truth; in accordance with facts; not false. **2** legitimate; rightful. **3** real; genuine. **4** exact; precise; correct. **5** faithful; reliable. **truly** *adv* **1** sincerely; honestly; truthfully. **2** really; absolutely.

trump *n* card of a suit ranking above the others for the duration of a game or round. *vt,vi* defeat by playing a trump.

trumpet *n* long funnel-shaped brass wind instrument, usually having three valves. *vi* make a loud noise similar to that of a trumpet. **trumpeter** *n*.

truncheon *n* short wooden club used esp. by policemen.

trundle *vt,vi* roll along or propel on or as if on wheels or castors.

trunk *n* **1** large strong box with a hinged lid for storing or transporting goods. **2** main stem of a tree. **3** human body, excluding the head and limbs; torso. **4** main telephone line. **5** long flexible snout of an elephant. **trunk call** *n* long distance call on a main telephone line.

trust *n* **1** belief in someone's honesty or something's reliability. **2** responsibility. **3** good faith. **4** association of companies combining for trade. **hold in trust** take legal charge for benefit of another. ~*vt,vi* place or have trust (in). **trustee** *n* person holding property or money in trust for another. **trustworthy** *adj* deserving of trust; reliable; dependable.

truth *n* fact, statement, or concept that is known to be true or can be verified. **truthful** *adj* given to speaking the truth. **truthfully** *adv*.

try *vt,vi* **1** attempt or make an effort to do (something). **2** test, as by experiment. *vt* **1** irritate; strain. **2** subject to a trial. **try on** put (a garment) on to test the fit. ~*n* **1** attempt; effort. **2** score of four points in rugby made by grounding the ball behind the opponent's line.

tsar *n also* **czar** Russian emperor.

T-shirt *n* short-sleeved shirt without buttons or collar.

tub *n* **1** small barrel. **2** bath, esp. one filled by hand. **tubby** *adj* shaped like a tub; chubby; rotund.

tuba *n* large low-pitched brass instrument.

tube *n* **1** long hollow cylinder. **2** narrow flexible container for toothpaste, etc. **the Tube** London's underground railway. **tubular** *adj*.

tuber *n* thick underground stem of certain plants on which buds are formed at or below ground level.

tuberculosis *n* disease produced by bacteria attacking body tissues, esp. the respiratory tract.

tuck *vt,vi* **1** fold under. **2** push or fit into a small space. **3** draw (the legs or arms) in close to the body. **4** make folds in (a material). **tuck in** eat heartily. ~*n* **1** small fold sewn into a garment. **2** position in which the knees are drawn up close to the chest.

Tuesday *n* third day of the week.

tuft *n* bunch of strands, hairs, etc.

tug *vt,vi* (-gg-) pull sharply or with force. *n* **1** act of tugging. **2** small boat used to tow larger boats. **tug-of-war** *n, pl* **tugs-of-war** sporting contest between two teams, each holding one end of a rope and trying to pull the other over a line between them.

tuition *n* instruction; teaching.

tulip *n* bulb producing a brightly coloured bell-shaped flower on a single upright stem.

tumble *vi,vt* **1** fall or cause to fall; topple. **2** move in an ungainly manner. **3** roll or toss about. **4** decrease or lose value sharply. *n* fall. **tumbler** *n* **1** acrobat who performs somersaults, etc. **2** stemless drinking glass.

tummy *n inf* stomach.

tumour *n* local swelling from a benign or malignant growth.

tumult ('tju:mʌlt) *n* noisy or violent disturbance, as of a crowd; uproar. **tumultuous** *adj*.

tuna *n also* **tunny** large ocean fish of the mackerel family with pinkish edible flesh.

tune *n* **1** sequence of musical notes forming a melody. **2** piece of music, song, etc. **out of/in tune** having the incorrect/correct pitch. **out of/in tune with** unsympathetic/sympathetic to. ~*vt* **1** adjust (a musical instrument) so as to obtain the correct pitch. **2** adjust (a radio, etc.) so as to obtain the correct setting. **3** adjust (a car engine) to improve performance. **tune in** adjust a radio to receive a particular programme. **tune up** (of an orchestra) check instruments to ensure that they are in tune before performing. **tuneful** *adj* melodious. **tunefully** *adv*. **tuning fork** *n* device with two prongs, which produce a sound of a set pitch when vibrated.

tunic *n* loose-fitting kneelength garment.

tunnel *n* underground passage. *vi,vt* (-ll-) make a tunnel (through).

turban *n* **1** headdress consisting of a long scarf wound around a cap, traditionally worn by men in parts of N Africa, India, etc. **2** woman's hat resembling this.

turbine *n* engine in which a wheel is turned by the direct force of steam, water, etc.

turbulent *adj* **1** restless; disturbed; tumultuous. **2** (of liquids) not flowing smoothly; agitated. **turbulence** *n*.

tureen (tju'ri:n) *n* large dish from which soup is served.

turf *n, pl* **turves** *or* **turfs** **1** ground covered with short close-growing springy grass. **2** single piece of grass and soil cut from the ground. **the turf** horseracing. ~*vt* cover with turf. **turf accountant** *n* bookmaker; person who takes legal bets on horseraces.

turkey *n* large domesticated bird used for food.

turmoil *n* state of confusion or anarchy; turbulence.

turn *vt,vi* **1** rotate; move around; spin. **2** face or cause to face a different direction. **3** go around (a corner). **4** move in a different direction. **5** change (into a specified state or condition); transform. *vt* **1** move (a page) over so as to display the other side. **2** dig or plough (the soil). **3** shape on a lathe. **4** reach (a specified age). *vi* **1** become sour, rancid, etc. **2** change colour. **turn away** send away; refuse. **turn down** **1** refuse. **2** reduce the volume or intensity of. **3** fold down. **turn in** **1** hand in; deliver. **2** go to bed. **3** finish; give up. **turn off** **1** branch off; deviate. **2** cause to stop operating. **3** *sl* repel; disgust. **turn on** **1** cause to operate. **2** produce automatically. **3** *sl* arouse; attract. **4** attack without warning. **5** *sl* initiate, esp. into the use of drugs. **turn out** **1** stop (a light, gas burner, etc.) operating. **2** produce; make. **3** expel. **4** become; develop into. **5** assemble; gather. **6** dress; array. **7** clear out the contents of. **turn over** **1** move so as to reverse top and bottom; shift position. **2** start (an engine). **3** deliver; hand over. **4** (of an engine) function correctly. **5** handle (a specified amount of stock or money) in a business. **turn tail** run away; flee. **turn to** have recourse to; seek help from. **turn up** **1** appear; attend. **2** be found or discovered as if by chance. **3** increase the volume or intensity of. **4** point upwards. ~*n* **1** act or instance of turning. **2** one of a number of successive periods during which different people have the right or responsibility of doing something. **3** short spell of work, etc. **4** distinctive style. **5** something done to affect someone. **6** need; requirement. **7** *inf* shock; surprise. **8** short walk. **at every turn** on all occasions; in all directions. **to a turn** perfectly. **turn-off** *n* road branching off from a main road. **turn-out** *n* **1** group of people appearing at a gathering. **2** output. **3** style in which someone is dressed or something is equipped. **4** act of clearing out the contents of something. **turnover** *n* **1** small pastry containing fruit or jam. **2** amount handled, produced, used, etc., during a specified period. **turntable** *n* **1** revolving circular table of a record player. **2** revolving platform for turning a locomotive. **turnup** *n* **1** cloth folded up at the bottom of a trouser leg. **2** chance occurrence.

turnip *n* vegetable having a rounded purplish edible root.

turpentine *n also inf* **turps** oily resin of several types of conifers, used in mixing paints.

turquoise *n* opaque greenish-blue stone. *adj,n* blue-green.

turret *n* **1** small round or square tower attached to a larger building. **2** revolving structure for a gun on a ship, tank, etc.

turtle *n* large marine reptile similar to a tortoise.

turves *n* a *pl* of **turf.**

tusk *n* long pointed tooth of an elephant, walrus, etc., protruding from the closed mouth.

tussle *vi,n* struggle; scuffle; fight.

tutor *n* **1** private teacher. **2** university teacher in charge of the studies of individual students or small groups. **tutorial** *n* teaching session run by a university tutor.

twang *n* resonant sound of the type produced by plucking a string. *vi,vt* produce a twang.

tweed *n* rough woollen fabric made from interwoven colours, used esp. for clothing.

tweezers *pl n* small metal tongs, used to lift small objects or pull out splinters, hairs, etc.

twelve *n* **1** number equal to one plus eleven. **2** group of twelve people, things, etc. **3** *also* **twelve o'clock** noon or midnight. *adj* amounting to twelve. **twelfth** *adj* coming between eleventh and thirteenth in sequence. *adv* after the eleventh. *n* **1** twelfth person, thing, etc. **2**

one of twelve equal parts; one divided by twelve.

twenty *n* **1** number equal to twice ten. **2** twenty things or people. *adj* amounting to twenty. **twentieth** *adj,adv,n*

twice *adv* **1** two times. **2** multiplied by two. **3** on two occasions. **4** doubly; two times as much or many.

twiddle *vt,vi* twirl; turn to and fro; fidget (with).

twig *n* small shoot of a branch of a tree or bush. *vt* (-gg-) *inf* catch the significance of.

twilight *n* evening light as the sun is setting; dusk.

twin *n* **1** one of two children born at one birth. **2** one of any identical or closely related pair. *adj* relating to a twin or pair. *vt* (-nn-) bring together as a couple or pair; match exactly.

twine *n* string made up of twisted strands. *vt,vi* wind; coil; entwine.

twinge *n* **1** sudden shooting pain. **2** sudden pang as of conscience, regret, etc.

twinkle *vi* **1** sparkle; glitter; flash intermittently. **2** move lightly and rapidly. *n* single flash; gleam.

twirl *vt,vi* revolve or cause to revolve; turn in rapid circles. *n* single rapid turn or flourish.

twist *vt,vi* **1** alter in shape by a rotating or screwing motion; wrench; contort. **2** wind or twine. *vt* **1** alter or misinterpret the meaning of. **2** *inf* deceive; cheat. *vi* **1** rotate or turn sharply. **2** writhe. *n* **1** twisting movement; turn; rotation. **2** anything twisted, as in a spiral. **3** unexpected turn of events.

twitch *vt,vi* **1** make spasmodic or convulsive muscle movements. **2** pull; jerk; pluck. *n* act of twitching; jerk.

twitter *vi,vt* chirp; produce a continuous chattering sound. *vi* tremble.

two *n* **1** number equal to one plus one. **2** group of two persons, things, etc. **3** *also* **two o'clock** two hours after noon or midnight. *adj* amounting to two. **two-faced** *adj* hypocritical; deceitful. **twosome** *n* **1** pair; couple, esp. when exclusive of others. **2** game with two players. **two-way** *adj* **1** operating in two directions. **2** reciprocal; of mutual benefit.

tycoon *n* wealthy powerful businessman.

type *n* **1** kind; sort. **2** class; category. **3** block of material carrying relief characters for printing. **4** printed characters considered collectively. *vt,vi* use a typewriter (for). *vt* assign to a type; classify. **typecast** *vt* (-cast) cast (an actor) in a part similar to parts he has played before. **typewriter** *n* machine for printing characters on paper, operated by pressing keys, which strike an ink-impregnated ribbon. **typical** *adj* **1** characteristic; normal or average. **2** showing the essential properties of a category. **typically** *adv*. **typify** *vt* represent; be typical of. **typist** *n* person who uses a typewriter, esp. a person employed to type.

typhoid *n also* **typhoid fever** infectious intestinal disease caused by bacilli growing in contaminated food or water.

typhoon *n* violent cyclonic storm occurring in the W Pacific Ocean.

tyrant *n* harsh ruler or master; despot. **tyranny** *n*. **tyrannical** *adj*. **tyrannize** *vt* treat tyrannically; terrorize.

tyre *n* solid or air-filled rubber tube held round the circumference of a vehicle wheel.

U

ubiquitous *adj* present everywhere. **ubiquity** *n*.

udder *n* external organ of cows, goats, etc., through which milk is secreted.

ugly *adj* **1** unpleasant to look at; repulsive; offensive. **2** threatening; angry. **ugliness** *n*.

ukulele *n* four-stringed instrument resembling but smaller than a guitar.

ulcer *n* open sore on the skin or an internal membrane, which is slow to heal.

ulterior *adj* **1** further away in time or space; distant. **2** not disclosed; deep-seated.

ultimate *adj* **1** last; final. **2** most desirable or significant. *n* **1** basis; final stage. **2** best; greatest; most desirable. **ultimately** *adv* eventually; in the end. **ultimatum** *n* final proposal of terms whose rejection will cancel further negotiations; deadline.

ultraviolet *n* invisible radiation having wavelengths between that of violet light and x-rays.

umbrella *n* portable collapsible object used as protection against rain or sun.

umpire *n* impartial person who enforces rules and settles disputes in cricket, tennis, etc. *vt,vi* act as umpire (for).

umpteen *adj inf* large number of; countless.

unaccompanied *adj* **1** alone. **2** singing or playing without instrumental accompaniment.

unanimous *adj* having the support and agreement of all concerned. **unanimity** *n*. **unanimously** *adv*.

unarmed *adj* without weapons.

unavoidable *adj* inevitable.

unaware *adj* ignorant; not aware. **unawares** *adv* by surprise; without warning or previous knowledge.

unbalanced *adj* not sane; mentally disturbed.

unbearable *adj* intolerable; beyond endurance. **unbearably** *adv*.

unbend *vt,vi* (-bent) **1** straighten. **2** *inf* relax or become relaxed, friendly, etc. **unbending** *adj* **1** stiff; rigid. **2** stubborn; formal.

unbutton *vt,vi* **1** undo the buttons (of). **2** *inf* unbend.

uncalled-for *adj* unwarranted; out of place; gratuitously rude.

uncanny *adj* weird; strange; irrational.

uncertain *adv* doubtful; undecided; variable; unpredictable. **uncertainty** *n*.

uncle *n* brother of one's father or mother; aunt's husband.

uncomfortable *adj* **1** not comfortable. **2** uneasy; awkward; embarrassing.

unconscious *adj* **1** unaware; unintentional. **2** having lost consciousness; insensible; in a faint, coma, etc. *n* part of the mind concerned with instincts, impulses, repressed feelings, etc., not normally accessible to the conscious mind. **unconsciously** *adv*.

unconventional *adj* not conforming; bizarre; eccentric.

uncouth *adj* ill-mannered; awkward; boorish.

uncut *adj* **1** entire; not abridged. **2** natural; unpolished and without facets.

undecided *adj* uncertain; hesitant; in two minds.

undeniable *adj* definite; obviously true. **undeniably** *adv*.

under *prep* **1** below the surface of; beneath; in a lower position than. **2** covered or concealed by. **3** lower in rank than; inferior to. **4** less in price or value than. **5** with the classification of. **6** in; according to. **7** influenced by; subject to. *adv* **1** in or to a lower or inferior place or position. **2** younger than. **3** less than. *adj* lower; low; inferior.

underclothes *pl n* underwear.

undercoat *n* coat of paint below the top or final coat. *vt* apply an undercoat to.

undercover *adj* secret; disguised.

undercut (-tt-; -cut) *vt,vi* sell at lower prices than competitors.

underdeveloped *adj* **1** not fully developed; developing; of unrealized potential. **2** primitive; backward.

underdone *adj* lightly cooked; rare.

underestimate *vt* (ʌndər'estimeit) estimate at too low a value; underrate. *n* (ʌndər'estimət) estimate that is too low.

underfoot *adv* **1** under the feet; on the ground. **2** in a subservient position.

undergo *vt* (-goes; -went; -gone) experience; submit oneself to; endure; suffer.

undergraduate *n* student who has not yet taken a degree.

underground *adj,adv* **1** below ground level. **2** secret; hidden. *n* **1** secret political resistance movement. **2** underground railway.

undergrowth *n* shrubs and plants growing under trees in a wood, etc.

underhand *adj* sly; dishonest; furtive. *adv* secretly; fraudulently.

underline *vt* **1** draw a line under. **2** stress; emphasize.

undermine *vt* **1** tunnel beneath; wear away. **2** destroy or weaken by subtle or insidious methods.

underneath *adv,prep* below; beneath; lower than. *n* lower part.

underpants *pl n* man's undergarment covering the waist to the thighs.

underpass *n* road or path crossing underneath another road, a railway, etc.; subway.

underrate *vt* underestimate; rate too low.

understand *v* (-stood) *vt,vi* know or grasp the meaning (of); comprehend; realize. *vt* **1** infer; believe. **2** sympathize with; tolerate. **understanding** *n* **1** sympathy. **2** comprehension; intelligence. **3** agreement; pact. *adj* sympathetic; wise.

understatement *n* expression with less force or completeness than merited or expected. **understate** *vt* express by understatement; minimize.

understudy *n* actor or actress prepared to take another's part when necessary. *vt* be ready to act as understudy to; learn a part as understudy.

undertake *vt* (-took; -taken) commit oneself (to); attempt to; accept; promise. **undertaker** *n* person who arranges funerals. **undertaking** *n* **1** task; venture. **2** promise.

undertone *n* **1** low, suppressed, or hidden tone of voice or feeling. **2** pale or subdued colour.

undervalue *vt* place too low a value on.

underwear *n* clothing worn under outer clothing, next to the skin; underclothes.

underweight *adj* of less than average or required weight.

underwent *v pt* of **undergo.**

underworld *n* **1** place of departed spirits. **2** section of society controlled by criminals, gangsters, etc.

underwrite *vt* (-wrote; written) accept liability; insure; guarantee. **underwriter** *n*.

undesirable *adj* not desirable; unpleasant; offensive.

undo *v* (-does; -did; -done) *vt,vi* open; loosen; unfasten. *vt* **1** cancel; reverse. **2** ruin the reputation of.

undoubted *adj* certain; sure **undoubtedly** *adv.*

undress *vt,vi* remove the clothes (of). *n* state of being naked or partly clothed.

undue *adj* excessive; unnecessary. **unduly** *adv.*

undulate *vi* move in a wavelike or rolling manner. **undulation** *n*

unearth *vt* dig up; uncover; reveal; bring to light. **unearthly** *adj* **1** ethereal; supernatural; uncanny. **2** ridiculous; unreasonable.

uneasy *adj* anxious; apprehensive; uncomfortable; awkward. **uneasily** *adv.*

unemployed *adj* **1** out of work. **2** not in use. *n* those without jobs. **unemployment** *n*. **unemployment benefit** *n* regular payments made to the unemployed; dole.

unequal *adj* not equal, similar, or uniform; not evenly balanced. **unequal to** lacking necessary strength, ability, etc., to. **unequalled** *adj* supreme; without rivals. **unequally** *adv.*

uneven *adj* **1** not level or straight; rough. **2** not uniform or well balanced; patchy. **3** odd; not divisible by two. **unevenly** *adv.*

unfailing *adj* dependable; continuous; certain.

unfair *adj* not fair; unjust; dishonest. **unfairly** *adv.* **unfairness** *n*.

unfaithful *adj* **1** not faithful; disloyal. **2** adulterous. **3** inaccurate; unreliable.

unfamiliar *adj* strange; not known or experienced. **unfamiliar with** having little knowledge of.

unfit *adj* **1** not fit; unhealthy. **2** unsuitable; incapable; not worthy.

unfold *vt,vi* **1** spread or open out. **2** reveal or be revealed; relate; develop.

unfortunate *adj* unlucky; unsuccessful; undesirable; regrettable. **unfortunately** *adv.*

ungainly *adj* awkward; gauche; clumsy.

unhappy *adj* **1** not happy; sad; miserable. **2** unfortunate; unlucky. **3** tactless. **unhappily** *adv.* **unhappiness** *n*.

unhealthy *adj* **1** not healthy; sick; diseased; abnormal. **2** threatening physical, mental, or moral damage; harmful.

unicorn *n* fabulous animal resembling a white horse with a single horn projecting from its forehead.

uniform *adj* exactly similar in appearance, quality, degree, etc.; unvarying; regular. *n* distinctive outfit worn by all members of a school, nursing staff, police force, etc. **uniformity** *n*. **uniformly** *adv.*

unify *vt,vi* make or become one; unite. **unification** *n*.

unilateral *adj* one-sided; of, affecting, or carried out by one side only.

uninterested *adj* not interested; bored. **uninteresting** *adj* arousing no interest; dull.

union *n* **1** act or condition of becoming united or joined together. **2** association or confederation of people, companies, countries, etc., formed for the common good. **3** trade union. **Union Jack** *n* national flag of Great Britain, combining the crosses of the patron saints Andrew, Patrick, and George.

unique *adj* **1** single; sole. **2** unequalled; remarkable. **uniquely** *adv.* **uniqueness** *n*.

unison *n* **in unison 1** sounding or speaking the same notes or words simultaneously. **2** in agreement.

unit *n* **1** single item; undivided entity. **2** standard amount such as the metre or second, by which a physical quantity, such as length or time, may be measured. **3** small part of a larger scheme, organization, etc. **4** apparatus; mechanical assembly; functional system.

unite *vt,vi* **1** join together; combine; cooperate. **2** unify; come or bring to agreement. **unity** *n* **1** state of being united; amalgamation; continuity; harmonious agreement. **2** the number one.

universe *n* **1** whole system of matter, energy, and space, including the earth, planets, stars, and galaxies. **2** field of human experience. **universal** *adj* **1** relating to all mankind, to nature, or to every member of a specific group. **2** widespread; general; applicable to most situations, conditions, etc.

university *n* institution of higher education empowered to confer degrees and having research facilities.

unkempt *adj* not cared for; neglected; untidy; messy.

unkind *adj* not kind; inconsiderate; hurtful. **unkindly** *adv*. **unkindness** *n*.

unknown *adj* not known, recognized, or identified. *n* unknown thing, state, etc.

unlawful *adj* against the law; illegal.

unless *conj* except on condition or under the circumstances that.

unlike *adj* not like; dissimilar; different. *prep* not like; not typical of.

unlikely *adj* not likely; improbable.

unload *vi,vt* remove a load (from). *vt* sell in bulk.

unlucky *adj* not successful; unfortunate; bringing misfortune or failure.

unnatural *adj* **1** not natural; artificial; unusual; abnormal; forced. **2** wicked; vile.

unnecessary *adj* not necessary; superfluous.

unofficial *adj* not official or confirmed; informal. **unofficially** *adv*.

unorthodox *adj* not orthodox; unconventional.

unpack *vt,vi* remove (items) from a case, box, package, etc.

unpleasant *adj* not pleasant; nasty; impolite; disagreeable. **unpleasantly** *adv*. **unpleasantness** *n*.

unravel *v* (-ll-) *vt* **1** disentangle; undo a piece of knitting. **2** sort out; straighten. *vi* become unravelled.

unreasonable *adj* not guided by reason; not justified; excessive; illogical.

unrest *n* state of discontent; disturbance; anxiety.

unruly *adj* difficult to control; not disciplined; wild; disorderly.

unscrew *vt* **1** unfasten or loosen by turning a screw. **2** loosen or detach by rotating. *vi* become unscrewed.

unsettle *vt* disturb; make uncertain or insecure; upset.

unsightly *adj* unpleasant to look at; ugly.

unsound *adj* not stable or reliable.

unstable *adj* **1** not firm or reliable, esp. mentally or emotionally. **2** decomposing spontaneously; radioactive. **3** readily decomposing into other chemicals.

unsteady *adj* not steady or firm; rocky; precarious. **unsteadily** *adv*.

untidy *adj* not tidy; disordered; slovenly. *vt* make untidy; mess up. **untidily** *adv*. **untidiness** *n*.

untie *vt* (-tying) unfasten; undo (a knot).

until *prep* during the time preceding; up to the time of. *conj* up to the time or stage that. **not...until** only...when.

untrue *adj* **1** not true; incorrect; false. **2** unfaithful. **3** diverging from a standard, rule, etc. **untruth** *n* lie; falsehood. **untruthful** *adj* **1** given to lying. **2** untrue.

unusual *adj* not usual or common; strange; remarkable. **unusually** *adv*.

unwarranted *adj* uncalled for; unnecessary.

unwell *adj* sick; ill.

unwieldy *adj* difficult to handle or use; awkward; clumsy; cumbersome.

unwind *vt,vi* (-wound) **1** unroll; uncoil; slacken; untangle. **2** relax; calm down.

unworldly *adj* **1** unearthly; spiritual. **2** not sophisticated; not materialist.

unworthy *adj* not worthy or deserving; lacking merit. **unworthily** *adv*.

unwrap *vt* (-pp-) remove the wrapping from.

up *adv* **1** in or to a higher position; further away from the ground. **2** in or to a higher status or rank. **3** into a hotter condition. **4** into a more intense emotional state. **5** no longer in bed. **6** so as to be equal to. **be up to 1** be the responsibility of. **2** be secretly engaged in. **up against** involved in a struggle with; face to face with. **up to date 1** modern; fashionable; current. **2** complete up to the present time; not in arrears. ~*prep* **1** to a higher position on. **2** further along. **3** to a place level with. *adj* moving or directed towards the top or north. *n* **ups and downs** fluctuations; alternate good and bad periods. ~*v* (-pp-) *vi* rise; get or stand up. *vt* make larger; increase or raise.

upbringing *n* education and rearing of children.

upheaval *n* great disturbance; commotion; eruption.

uphill *adj* **1** going or sloping upwards. **2** very difficult and exhausting. *adv* upwards; towards higher ground.

uphold *vt* (-held) maintain or defend against opposition; sustain.

upholstery *n* **1** coverings, padding, springs,

etc., of chairs, sofas, etc. **2** business, trade, or skill of upholstering. **upholster** *vt,vi* provide or work with upholstery. **upholsterer** *n*.

upkeep *n* **1** maintenance; keeping in good condition. **2** cost of maintenance.

uplift *vt* **1** elevate; raise. **2** raise spiritually, morally, etc.; exalt. *n* **1** raising; elevation. **2** improvement; encouragement; enlightenment. **3** moment of joy.

upon *prep* on; on top of.

upper *adj* **1** higher in position, rank, status, etc. **2** further upstream or inland. **upper hand** position of control. ~*n* upper part of a shoe, boot, etc., above the sole. **on one's uppers** reduced to desperate poverty. **uppermost** *adj* highest in position, power, etc. *adv* in the highest position, rank, etc.

upright *adj* **1** vertical; erect. **2** honest; worthy; righteous. *adv* vertically. *n* **1** vertical post, beam, etc. **2** *also* **upright piano** piano with vertical strings.

uproar *n* **1** loud clamorous noise. **2** angry protest. **uproarious** *adj* **1** hilarious. **2** accompanied by uproar; tumultuous. **uproariously** *adv*.

uprising *n* revolt; rebellion.

uproot *vt* **1** dig up by the roots. **2** displace or remove from native surroundings. **3** destroy.

upset (-tt-; -set) *vt,vi* **1** overturn; knock or be knocked over; spill. **2** distress; disturb; confuse. **3** make or become ill. *n* **1** act of upsetting. **2** quarrel; disturbance. *adj* **1** annoyed; unhappy; disturbed. **2** overturned. **3** ill; sick.

upshot *n* consequence; outcome.

upside down *adj* **1** turned over completely; inverted. **2** confused; chaotic. *adv* in an upside down position or fashion.

upstairs *adv* up the stairs; to, in, or on a higher level. *n* upper part or floor.

upstream *adv,adj* against the current of a river; nearer or towards the source.

upward *adj* facing or moving towards a higher place, level, etc. **upwards** *adv* **1** to or towards a higher place, level, etc. **2** onwards; further along a scale. **upwards of** more than.

uranium *n* radioactive metallic element, used in nuclear reactors.

Uranus *n* outer giant planet lying between Saturn and Neptune.

urban *adj* relating to a town or city.

urbane *adj* sophisticated; suave; refined.

urge *vt* **1** entreat; plead with; press; strongly advise. **2** drive or force forward. *n* impulse; strong tendency; yearning. **urgent** *adj* pressing; demanding immediate action or attention. **urgency** *n*. **urgently** *adv*.

urine *n* fluid containing waste products excreted by the kidneys that is stored in the bladder before being discharged from the body. **urinate** *vi* discharge urine. **urination** *n*.

urn *n* **1** large metal container for heating and dispensing tea, etc. **2** vase or vessel, esp. for holding the ashes of a dead person.

us *pron* form of **we** when used as the object.

use *vt* (ju:z) **1** employ; put to some purpose. **2** handle; treat. **3** exploit. **4** expend; consume. *v aux* **used to** expressing past habits or regular occurrences. **use up** finish; exhaust. **used to** *adj* accustomed to; in the habit of. ~*n* (ju:s) **1** act of using; state of being used; usage. **2** right of using. **3** need; purpose; point of using. **4** custom; familiar practice. **usage** *n* manner of use; employment; treatment. **useful** *adj* of use; convenient; serviceable; helpful. **usefully** *adv*. **usefulness** *n*. **useless** *adj* of no use or help; incompetent; hopeless.

usher *n* **1** person employed to show people to their seats. **2** minor official at a law court, parliament, etc. *vt* **1** act as usher to; escort; lead in or to. **2** precede; herald. **usherette** *n* female usher in a cinema, theatre, etc.

usual *adj* habitual; customary; ordinary. **usually** *adv*.

usurp *vt* oust or take forcibly; seize without legal authority. **usurper** *n*.

utensil *n* tool or implement, esp. used in cookery.

uterus *n* womb; organ in female mammals where an embryo develops.

utility *n* **1** usefulness. **2** something useful or practical. **3** *also* **public utility** public service, such as the railway or electricity supply. **utilize** *vt* make practical or worthwhile use of.

utmost *adj also* **uttermost** furthest; outermost; maximum; most extreme. *n* greatest possible amount, degree, extent, etc.; best.

utter[1] *vt,vi* give audible voice to; say or speak.

utter[2] *adj* extreme; complete; total; absolute. **utterly** *adv*.

V

vacant *adj* **1** empty; unoccupied; not in use. **2** blank; stupid. **vacantly** *adv*. **vacancy** *n* **1** position, job, etc., that is not yet filled. **2** stupidity; blankness. **vacate** *vt* make empty; leave. **vacation** *n* holiday period for universities, law courts, etc.

vaccinate *vt* produce immunity against a specific disease by inoculating with vaccine. **vaccination** *n*. **vaccine** *n* dead microorganisms used in vaccination to produce immunity by stimulating antibody production.

vacillate *vi* **1** oscillate; fluctuate. **2** waver; hesitate; prevaricate. **vacillation** *n*.

vacuum *n* **1** space devoid of air or containing air or other gas at very low pressure. **2** feeling of emptiness. **vacuum cleaner** *n* equipment for removing dust, etc., by suction. **vacuum flask** *n* container in which the contents are kept at constant temperature by means of the insulating effect of the vacuum between its two walls.

vagina (və'dʒainə) *n* passage from an exterior orifice to the uterus in female mammals. **vaginal** *adj*.

vagrant *n* person with no fixed abode or job; tramp. *adj* wandering; unsettled; erratic. **vagrancy** *n*.

vague *adj* lacking precision or clarity; uncertain; indefinite. **vaguely** *adv*. **vagueness** *n*.

vain *adj* **1** conceited; excessively proud of one's appearance, possessions, etc. **2** useless; futile; worthless; empty. **in vain** to no purpose. **vainly** *adv*

valiant *adj* brave; strong; heroic. **valiantly** *adv*.

valid *adj* based on truth; logically sound; having legal force. **validity** *n*. **validate** *vt* confirm; make valid. **validation** *n*.

valley *n* **1** trough between hills, often containing a river. **2** land area drained by a river.

value *n* **1** worth; market price; fair equivalent. **2** quality that makes something estimable, desirable, or useful. **3** degree of this quality. *vt* **1** assess the value of; assign a value to. **2** esteem; prize. **valuable** *adj* **1** of great worth; costing much money. **2** very useful; having admirable qualities, etc. *n* article of high value.

valve *n* **1** device or structure that seals, opens, or regulates fluid flow, usually in one direction. **2** electronic device in which current flows in one direction only, used esp. to amplify signals. **3** device on some brass instruments by which the tube length and hence pitch may be varied.

vampire *n* creature of folklore that rises by night from the grave to suck the blood of humans.

van *n* **1** covered motor vehicle for transporting or delivering goods. **2** railway wagon for luggage, goods, etc.

vandal *n* person who deliberately destroys or spoils something of value. **vandalism** *n*. **vandalize** *vt* destroy by vandalism.

vanilla *n* flavouring obtained from the bean of a tropical climbing orchid.

vanish *vi* disappear; become invisible; cease to exist.

vanity *n* **1** exaggerated opinion of oneself; conceit; excessive pride. **2** worthlessness; futility.

vapour *n* **1** moisture in the air, seen as mist, smoke, clouds, etc. **2** substance in a gaseous state, esp. when its temperature is below its boiling point. **vaporize** *vt,vi* turn into or become a vapour.

variable *adj* liable to change; not constant; inconsistent; unreliable. *n* something that can change value, etc.

variant *adj* showing discrepancy or difference; varying. *n also* **variance** different form of the same thing; variation; deviation.

variation *n* **1** change; modification. **2** departure from a standard type or norm.

variety *n* **1** state or quality of having many forms or versions; diversity; versatility. **2** different form or version of something. **3** assorted collection. **4** theatrical presentation of assorted turns.

various *adj* several; of different kinds; displaying variety. **variously** *adv*.

varnish *n* **1** oil-based solution that dries to provide a hard glossy skin. **2** glossy surface so produced. **3** superficial attractiveness. *vt* **1** coat with varnish. **2** conceal under superficial gloss.

vary *vt* make different; alter; diversify; modify. *vi* become different or altered; disagree; deviate.

vase *n* ornamental container, often used for holding flowers.

vasectomy *n* sterilization of men by surgical cutting of the spermatic duct.

vast *adj* boundless; immense; exceedingly great. **vastly** *adv*. **vastness** *n*.

vat *n* large vessel or cask for holding or storing liquids.

Vatican *n* **1** palace and principal residence and administrative centre of the Pope, in Rome. **2** Papal authority.

vault[1] *vi,vt* spring; leap over, esp. with the aid of the hands or a pole. *n* act of vaulting.

vault[2] *n* **1** underground room, often a burial chamber. **2** arched roof or ceiling. **3** strong-room in which valuables may be safely stored. **vaulted** *adj* arched. ~*vt,vi* cover with, construct, or curve like a vault.

veal *n* calf's flesh, prepared as food.

veer *vi,vt* change direction or course; swing round.

vegetable *n* **1** plant having various parts that may be used for food. **2** *inf* person entirely dependent on others due to loss of mental faculties, etc.

vegetarian *n* person who eats no meat but only vegetable foods and sometimes fish, eggs, and dairy produce. **vegetarianism** *n*.

vegetation *n* plants in a mass; plant life. **vegetate** *vi* lead a boring, empty, inactive life.

vehement *adj* marked by strong feelings; forceful; passionate; emphatic. **vehemence** *n*. **vehemently** *adv*.

vehicle *n* **1** means of transport or communication; conveyance. **2** medium for conveying or expressing ideas, etc. **vehicular** *adj*.

veil *n* **1** covering for a woman's head or face. **2** something flat that covers or conceals. *vt* cover with a veil; conceal; disguise.

vein *n* **1** vessel conducting oxygen-depleted blood to the heart. **2** fluid-conducting vessel in plant leaves. **3** fine tube in the framework of an insect's wing. **4** streak in marble, wood, etc. **5** trait in a person's character.

velocity *n* speed; rate of change of position; rate of motion.

velvet *n* **1** silk, cotton, or nylon fabric with soft thick pile on one surface. **2** soft smooth surface or covering.

vendetta *n* private feud; rivalry.

veneer *n* **1** thin layer of wood, plastic, etc., bonded to a surface. **2** superficial covering. *vt* cover with veneer.

venerate *vt* worship; have great respect or reverence for. **veneration** *n*.

venereal disease *n* disease transmitted by sexual intercourse.

vengeance *n* infliction of injury in return for injury suffered; revenge. **with a vengeance** thoroughly. **vengeful** *adj* vindictive; desiring revenge.

venison *n* deer's flesh prepared as food.

venom *n* **1** poison, esp. that of a snake. **2** spite. **venomous** *adj*.

vent *n* narrow opening or outlet; ventilating duct. **give vent to** allow free expression of. ~*vt* give expression to.

ventilate *vt* **1** allow free passage of air into; drive stale or foul air out. **2** expose to public examination and discussion. **ventilation** *n*.

venture *n* hazardous or speculative course of action; attempt. *vt* **1** risk. **2** dare to put forward. *vi also* **venture out** brave the dangers of something.

Venus *n* conspicuous bright planet, lying between Mercury and the earth.

veranda *n also* **verandah** covered terrace along the outside of a house.

verb *n* word expressing action, occurrence, or existence. **verbal** *adj*. **verbally** *adv*. **verbatim** *adj* word for word. **verbiage** *n* excess of words. **verbose** *adj* using an excessive number of words. **verbosity** *n*.

verdict *n* conclusion of a jury; decision.

verge *n* **1** limit; boundary; edge; margin. **2** grass border. *v* **verge on** approach; border on.

verger *n* person acting as an official attendant and usher in a church.

verify *vt* ascertain or confirm the truth of. **verifiable** *adj*. **verification** *n*.

vermin *pl n* **1** animals, esp. rodents, that are destructive or dangerous to man. **2** obnoxious people; scum.

vermouth *n* white wine flavoured with aromatic herbs.

vernacular *n* **1** spoken language or dialect of a people. **2** jargon or idiom.

versatile *adj* capable of many activities or uses; adapting readily. **versatility** *n*.

verse *n* **1** subsection of a poem; stanza. **2** metrical composition of a line of poetry. **3** poetry as opposed to prose. **4** unit into which chapters of the Bible are divided. **versed** *adj* acquainted with; skilled in.

version *n* one of a number of possible accounts, renderings, or interpretations.

vertebrate *n* animal having a backbone. *adj* having a backbone.

vertex *n, pl* **vertexes** *or* **vertices** ('vəːtisiːz) apex; topmost point; meeting point of two intersecting lines.

vertical *adj* **1** upright; at right angles to the horizon. **2** extending at right angles from a surface; directly above or overhead. *n* vertical line or position. **vertically** *adv*.

verve *n* vigour; zest.

very *adv* used to add emphasis to an adjective. *adj* used with a noun to give emphasis to a quality inherent in the meaning of the noun.

vessel *n* **1** container or receptacle, esp. for a liquid. **2** ship or boat, usually large. **3** tube for conducting fluid in animals or plants.

vest *n* undergarment covering the upper half of the body. *vt* invest, confer on, or endow with (rights, property, etc.). **vest in** place in the control of.

vestige *n* faint trace or hint of proof, evidence, etc.

vestment *n* ceremonial garment as worn by clergy.

vestry *n* room in or attached to a church where vestments and church documents are kept.

vet *n* short for **veterinary surgeon.** *vt* (-tt-) examine; check.

veteran *n* **1** person with great or long experience in something. **2** old and experienced soldier. **veteran car** *n* old car constructed before 1905 or sometimes before 1919.

veterinary surgeon *n also* **vet** person having specialized medical training in the treatment of sick or injured animals.

veto *vt* forbid absolutely; withhold assent; reject. *n, pl* **vetoes 1** right to veto, esp. the passing of a law. **2** act of vetoing.

vex *vt* distress; tease; annoy; agitate. **vexation** *n*.

via *prep* through; by way of.

viable *adj* **1** capable of sustaining existence. **2** capable of being effected, validated, etc.; feasible; workable. **viability** *n*.

viaduct *n* structure bridging a valley, etc., bearing a road or railway.

vibrate *vt,vi* **1** move rapidly to and fro; oscillate; quiver. **2** resound; resonate. **vibration** *n*.

vicar *n* clergyman of a parish having the same spiritual status as a rector. **vicarage** *n* residence of a vicar.

vicarious *adj* deriving one's own pain, pleasure, etc., from another's experiences. **vicariously** *adv*.

vice[1] *n* evil practice or trait; wickedness; immorality; bad habit.

vice[2] *n* adjustable tool for gripping an object that is being worked on.

vice-chancellor *n* active head of a university.

vice-president *n* president's immediate deputy.

vice versa *adv* conversely.

vicinity *n* surrounding or adjacent area; neighbourhood; proximity.

vicious *adj* wicked; cruel; violent; harsh; spiteful. **viciously** *adv*. **viciousness** *n*.

victim *n* object of attack; person suffering from an accident or from ill treatment by others. **victimize** *vt* make a victim of. **victimization** *n*.

victory *n* defeat of an enemy; success in a contest or struggle. **victor** *n* person gaining victory; winner. **victorious** *adj*.

video-tape *n* magnetic tape on which television programmes, films, etc., may be recorded for subsequent transmission.

view *n* **1** act of seeing or observing; examination; inspection. **2** prospect of the surrounding countryside, etc. **3** range or field of vision. **4** mental attitude; opinion. **5** survey. **6** intention. **in view of** considering. ~*vt,vi* watch, esp. a film or television; inspect; judge. **viewer** *n*. **view-finder** *n* device in a camera through which the area to be photographed can be established.

vigil *n* act of or time spent keeping watch, esp. at night. **vigilance** *n* alertness; watchfulness. **vigilant** *adj*.

vigour *n* energy; power; strength; forcefulness; good health. **vigorous** *adj*. **vigorously** *adv*.

vile *adj* **1** disgusting; despicable. **2** abominable; shameful; sinful. **3** unpleasant; objectionable. **vilify** *vt* speak ill of; abuse. **vilification** *n*.

villa *n* luxurious house, esp. one by the sea or in the country.

village *n* **1** group of rural dwellings with a smaller population than that of a town. **2** inhabitants of a village. **villager** *n*.

villain *n* **1** wicked person; scoundrel; evil-doer. **2** character whose evil is central to the plot in a story, play, etc. **villainous** *adj*.

vindictive *adj* vengeful; spiteful. **vindictively** *adv*.

vine *n* woody climbing plant, esp. one bearing grapes. **vineyard** *n* plantation of grapevines.

vinegar *n* sour-tasting acidic liquid used for pickling, as a seasoning, etc.

vintage *n* **1** age as an indication of quality. **2** time of origin. **3** harvesting or harvest of grapes and the making of wine. **4** wine obtained from grapes grown in a specified year, esp. one of good quality. *adj* **1** old and of good quality. **2** dated. **vintage car** *n* old car, esp. one built between 1919 and 1930.

vinyl *adj* containing an organic group of atoms that form the basis of many plastic and resins.

viola *n* four-stringed instrument resembling but slightly larger than a violin.

violate *vt* **1** do violence to; abuse; defile; treat disrespectfully. **2** rape or assault. **3** disregard or break (a rule, promise, etc.). **violation** *n*.

violence *n* **1** assault; use of excessive unrestrained force. **2** great force; intensity; fervour. **violent** *adj* **1** impetuously forceful; overwhelmingly vehement. **2** using or needing great physical strength. **violently** *adv*.

violet *n* **1** small purple spring flower. **2** spectral colour of a bluish-purple hue. *adj* of a violet colour.

violin *n* musical instrument having a hollow wooden waisted body and four strings, played with a bow. **violinist** *n*.

viper *n* small venomous snake; adder.

virgin *n* person, esp. a woman, who has never had sexual intercourse. *adj* **1** *also* **virginal** pure; chaste. **2** in the original condition; untouched; not yet used, cultivated, etc. **virginity** *n*.

Virgo *n* sixth sign of the zodiac, represented by the Virgin.

virile *adj* sexually potent; displaying traditional masculine characteristics. **virility** *n*.

virtual *adj* existing in effect or essence, but not in fact. **virtually** *adv* in effect; practically.

virtue *n* **1** goodness; moral excellence. **2** chastity; sexual purity. **by virtue of** by reason of; on the grounds of. **virtuous** *adj*.

virus *n* microorganism causing various infectious diseases. **viral** *adj*.

visa *n* stamp or endorsement on a passport permitting the bearer to enter a particular country.

viscount ('vaikaunt) *n* nobleman ranking between a baron and an earl in the British peerage. **viscountess** *n* wife or widow of a viscount.

viscous *adj* thick; sticky; slow to flow. **viscosity** *n*.

visible *adj* **1** capable of being seen. **2** apparent; obvious. **visibility** *n* **1** state of being visible. **2** clearness of the atmosphere; range of vision.

vision *n* **1** act or power of seeing; sight; range of sight. **2** beautiful person or object. **3** mystical experience or prophetic dream. **4** imagination; foresight.

visit *vt,vi* go or come to see for pleasure, business, etc.; call (on). *n* act of visiting; call. **visitor** *n*.

visual *adj* of or by sight; capable of being seen; visible. **visually** *adv*. **visualize** *vt* form a clear mental image of.

vital *adj* **1** necessary to or sustaining life; living. **2** lively. **3** very important; essential. **vitality** *n* strength; vigour; energy. **vitally** *adv* critically.

vitamin *n* substance found in food and essential in small quantities to health.

vivacious *adj* lively; sprightly; full of vitality. **vivaciously** *adv*. **vivacity** *n*.

vivid *adj* **1** very bright; intense. **2** graphic; distinct; clear. **3** vigorous; lively. **vividly** *adv*.

vivisection *n* practice of performing surgical operations on living animals, esp. for medical research.

vixen *n* female fox.

vocabulary *n* **1** total number of words used or understood by a person, group, etc., or contained in a language. **2** listing of words or phrases given with meanings, translations, etc.

vocal *adj* **1** relating to or produced by the voice. **2** readily disposed to express opinions; outspoken. **vocalist** *n* singer. **vocal cords** *pl n* vibrating membranes in the larynx that are responsible for vocal production.

vocation *n* **1** course of action or occupation to which a person feels called by God, duty, or conscience. **2** profession or occupation, esp. when viewed as a career. **vocational** *adj*.

vodka *n* traditional Russian alcoholic drink distilled from rye or potatoes.

voice *n* **1** sound produced by the vocal cords. **2** tone, quality, etc., of a voice; person's characteristic speech sounds. **3** musical sound of a singing voice. **4** faculty of speech or singing. **5** expression of opinion. *vt* express.

void *adj* **1** empty; vacant. **2** not binding; null; invalid. *vt* make empty, invalid, or ineffective.

n **1** empty space. **2** painful awareness of a lack of something or someone.

volatile *adj* **1** changeable; lively but unstable. **2** readily forming a vapour.

volcano *n, pl* **volcanoes** *or* **volcanos** outlet in the earth's crust for erupting subterranean matter (lava, rocks, dust, and gases), which forms into a conical mountain. **volcanic** *adj*.

vole *n* small rodent resembling a rat.

volition *n* power or exercise of the will.

volley *n* **1** series of things discharged simultaneously or rapidly. **2** return of a ball in cricket, tennis, etc., before it bounces. *vt,vi* **1** return (a ball) before it bounces. **2** discharge in a volley.

volt *n* unit for measuring voltage. **voltage** *n* force producing an electric current in a circuit.

volume *n* **1** measure of the space occupied by or enclosed inside something; quantity; amount. **2** intensity of sound. **3** book; one of a series of books forming one work. **voluminous** *adj* **1** sufficient to fill many volumes. **2** ample; large.

voluntary *adj* **1** done willingly or by one's own choice or desire; not compulsory. **2** given or offered for no payment; supported by donations. **voluntarily** *adv*. **volunteer** *vi,vt* freely offer (oneself, one's help, etc.) for something; enlist for service without compulsion. *n* person who makes a voluntary offer or enlists voluntarily.

voluptuous *adj* full of or suggesting sensual pleasure; alluring; provocative. **voluptuously** *adv*.

vomit *vi,vt* eject the contents of the stomach through the mouth. *n* **1** matter ejected. **2** act of vomiting.

voodoo *n* religious cult, esp. of Negroes in Haiti, involving belief in spirits, who possess the worshippers, and other rituals.

vote *n* **1** indication of preference or opinion; formal decision. **2** right to express such. **3** act of voting. *vt* **1** determine, decide on, or elect by a vote or general opinion. **2** *inf* suggest. *vi* express one's preference, etc., by a vote. **voter** *n*.

vouch *vi also* **vouch for** guarantee; confirm; bear witness to. **voucher** *n* **1** written evidence supporting a claim. **2** ticket acting as a substitute for cash.

vow *n* solemn promise; pledge. **take vows** enter and commit oneself to a religious order. ~*vt,vi* make a vow (that); solemnly promise (to).

vowel *n* speech sound represented by the letters a, e, i, o, u, or a combination of these.

voyage *n* journey of some distance, esp. by water. *vi* make a voyage.

vulgar *adj* **1** lacking in taste; crude; coarse; unrefined. **2** of the common people. **vulgarity** *n*.

vulnerable *adj* open to attack or injury; easily hurt. **vulnerability** *n*.

vulture *n* **1** large predatory bird, feeding mainly on dead flesh. **2** person who preys on others.

vulva *n, pl* **vulvae** (**'vʌlvai**) *or* **vulvas** external female genitals.

W

wad *n* **1** mass of soft material. **2** bundle; roll. *vt,vi* (-dd-) pack, pad, or stuff with a wad. **wadding** *n* material for padding, packing, etc.

waddle *vi* take short steps, swaying from side to side. *n* swaying walk.

wade *vi* **1** step forward through water, mud, etc. **2** progress with difficulty; labour. *vt* cross by wading.

wafer *n* **1** thin light crisp biscuit. **2** thin disc of bread or biscuit used in the Eucharist.

waft *vi,vt* convey or cause to move smoothly through the air, over water, etc. *n* **1** whiff or scent carried through the air. **2** rush of air.

wag *vt,vi* (-gg-) move or cause to move from side to side or up and down. *n* act of wagging.

wage *n* rate of pay for a job, manual work, etc. *vt* engage in; carry on. **wager** *n,vt,vi* bet; stake. **wages** *pl n* payment for a job; earnings.

waggle *vt,vi,n* wag.

wagon *n* four-wheeled vehicle, such as a cart or open lorry.

wail *vi* lament; moan; express grief in long plaintive cries. *n* cry of grief.

waist *n* **1** narrowest part of the human body between the ribs and hips. **2** *also* **waistband** part of a garment covering the waist. **3** narrow middle part of an object, such as a violin. **waistcoat** *n* sleeveless close-fitting garment covering the chest and back. **waistline** *n* **1** junction of the skirt and bodice of a garment. **2** level of or length around a waist.

wait *vt,vi* defer action; remain in the same place

(until, for, etc.); delay or be delayed. *vi* act as a waiter or waitress. *n* act or period of waiting. **lie in wait** prepare an ambush. **waiter** *n* male person employed to serve meals and wait at table in restaurants, etc. **waitress** *f n.*

waive *vt* refrain from insisting on, claiming, or enforcing; defer.

wake[1] *vi,vt* (woke; woken) *also* **wake up** disturb or be disturbed from sleep or inactivity; arouse; excite. *n* vigil beside a corpse before the funeral. **waken** *vt,vi* rouse or be roused; wake.

wake[2] *n* **1** disturbed water waves produced by a moving boat, etc. **2** disturbed track left by a hurricane, etc.

walk *vi* **1** move, pass through, or travel to on foot at a moderate pace. **2** stroll; ramble; hike. *vt* **1** pass through, pace, or traverse on foot. **2** cause to walk; accompany. **walk out** *v* **1** go on strike. **2** leave or abandon as a protest. **walkout** *n* industrial strike. **walk out on** *inf* abandon; desert. **walk over** *v* **1** beat or win easily. **2** *inf* take advantage of. **walkover** *n* easy victory; unopposed win. ~*n* **1** act or manner of walking. **2** leisurely excursion. **3** path; route.

wall *n* **1** upright construction of brick, stone, etc., forming part of a room or building, marking a boundary, etc. **2** containing surface or membrane. **3** barrier. *vt* surround, divide, fortify with, or confine within a wall. **wallflower** *n* **1** cultivated plant with fragrant yellow, brown, or red flowers. **2** *inf* spectator at an essentially participatory event. **wallpaper** *n* paper, usually decorated, for pasting to a wall or ceiling. *vt,vi* cover with wallpaper.

wallet *n* folding case for bank notes, etc.

wallop *inf vt,vi* beat soundly; thrash. *n* heavy blow.

wallow *vi* **1** indulge or delight (in). **2** roll about in mud, etc. *n* act of wallowing.

walnut *n* tree yielding highly esteemed hardwood for furniture, etc., and a nut with a wrinkled shell and edible kernel.

walrus *n* amphibious mammal related to the seal, having two long tusks.

waltz *n* **1** dance in three-four time performed in pairs. **2** music for this dance or having this rhythm. *vi* dance the waltz.

wand *n* slender and supple stick used as symbol of power or authority.

wander *vi* **1** roam without purpose or plan; stroll; meander. **2** deviate from the line of argument. **3** become delirious; talk incoherently. *n* ramble. **wanderer** *n.* **wanderlust** *n* urge to travel.

wane *vi* diminish in observed size, esp. after a peak; decrease; decline. *n* act of waning.

wangle *inf vt,vi* manipulate to suit oneself; use craft or irregular means to achieve ends. *n* act or instance of wangling.

want *vt* feel a need for; long for. *vt,vi* need; desire. **want for** lack. ~*n* **1** something wanted. **2** lack; shortage. **in want** destitute; requiring help.

war *n* **1** armed conflict between nations, groups of people, etc. **2** bitter conflict; hostility. *vi* (-rr-) make war; fight. **warfare** *n* act or process of waging war. **warlike** *adj* **1** hostile; belligerent. **2** military.

warble *vi,vt* sing with trills. *vi* produce a quavering note. *n* sound of such singing.

ward *n* **1** hospital room with beds for patients. **2** area of a city, borough, etc., for administrative purposes. **3** minor entrusted to the care of a guardian or a court of law. **ward off** protect against. **warden** *n* **1** guardian; guard; custodian. **2** superintendent or head of certain colleges and schools. **warder** *n* person in charge of prisoners in a gaol. **wardress** *f n.*

wardrobe *n* **1** cupboard in which clothes are kept. **2** range and extent of clothing or costumes of an individual or theatrical group.

warehouse *n* building used for storage of goods before their sale, distribution, etc. **wares** *pl n* goods for sale.

warm *adj* **1** having or maintaining a pleasant temperature; moderately hot. **2** affectionate; kind. **3** enthusiastic; passionate; lively. **4** red, yellow, or orange coloured. **5** near to discovery, guessing, etc. *vt,vi* **1** *also* **warm up** raise or be raised to medium temperature. **2** make or become livelier or happier. **warm to** become enthusiastic about or friendly towards. ~*n* process of warming. **warm up 1** make receptive to a performance on television, etc. **2** exercise before a sporting contest. **3** run until operating conditions are achieved. *n* **warm-up** process of warming up. **warmly** *adv.* **warmth** *n.* **warm-blooded** *adj* able to maintain a constant body temperature. **warm-hearted** *adj* generous; sympathetic; kindly.

warn *vt,vi* **1** give an indication of approaching

danger, adverse results, etc.; threaten. **2** advise against or in advance. **warning** *n* indication of a likely course of events or state of affairs; caution.

warp *vt,vi* **1** twist or cause to twist out of shape; distort. **2** make or become full of misconceptions; pervert. *n* **1** threads running along the length of woven material. **2** distortion of wood, etc., caused by heat, damp, etc.

warrant *n* **1** authorization, esp. for police to make an arrest, search property, etc. **2** guarantee. *vt* authorize; guarantee. *vt,vi* declare; affirm. **warrant officer** *n* officer in the armed services holding a rank, authorized by warrant, between commissioned and non-commissioned officers.

warren *n* **1** interconnecting underground tunnels inhabited by rabbits. **2** overcrowded living quarters.

warrior *n* man who is skilled in or experienced in warfare or fighting.

wart *n* horny protuberance on the skin. **warty** *adj.*

wary *adj* cautious; careful of deception or danger. **warily** *adv.* **wariness** *n.*

was *v* 1st and 3rd person form of **be** in the past tense.

wash *vt,vi* make or become clean using water and usually soap. *vt* **1** remove with soap and water. **2** flow over. **3** cover with a thin layer of paint, etc. *vi inf* bear examination. **wash away** move or remove by the force of water. ~*n* **1** act of washing. **2** collection of articles for washing. **3** flow or wake of water. **4** medical lotion. **washing** *n* clothes, etc., washed or to be washed. **wash-out** *n inf* total failure.

washer *n* flat ring under a bolt head or nut to distribute pressure or provide a seal.

wasp *n* winged stinging insect, usually with black and yellow stripes on its body.

waste *vt* use carelessly; squander. **waste away** deteriorate in health; dwindle. ~*n* **1** misuse; neglect; act of wasting. **2** something squandered, neglected, discarded, worthless, superfluous, etc. **3** rubbish. **wasteful** *adj* causing or tending to waste.

watch *vt,vi* **1** look (at) or observe carefully or closely. **2** wait attentively (for); keep a look-out (for). **3** guard. *vi* keep guard or vigil. *n* **1** small mechanism, worn esp. on the wrist, registering the passage of time. **2** act or instance of watching; period of vigil. **3** person or persons performing this duty. **watchdog** *n* dog kept for guarding property. **watchful** *adj* vigilant; awake.

water *n* colourless liquid that consists of hydrogen and oxygen and forms ice below its freezing point and steam above its boiling point. **2** impure water, as found in rivers, oceans, etc. **3** large expanse of water. **4** solution of something in water. *vt* **1** supply or add water to; make wet. **2** irrigate. **3** dilute. *vi* **1** (of the mouth) secrete saliva at the sight of food. **2** (of the eyes) secrete tears.

watercolour *n* **1** painting in water-soluble pigments. **2** those pigments.

watercress *n* freshwater plant with edible leaves.

waterfall *n* precipitous descent of water in a river course.

watering-can *n* vessel with a handle, spout, and nozzle for watering plants, etc.

water lily *n* aquatic plant whose large leaves and showy flowers float on the surface of water.

waterlogged *adj* saturated with water.

watermelon *n* melon plant bearing large edible fruit with reddish watery flesh.

waterproof *adj* not allowing water through. *n* waterproof garment; raincoat. *vt* make waterproof.

water-ski *vi* travel over the surface of water on skis holding a rope pulled by a speedboat. *n* ski used for this purpose. **water-skier** *n.*

watertight *adj* **1** impervious to water. **2** irrefutable; allowing no points of dispute.

waterworks *n* **1** establishment for supplying water to a community. **2** *sl* shedding of tears. **3** *sl* urinary system.

watery *adj* **1** of, like, or containing water. **2** weak; pale; insipid.

watt *n* unit of electrical, mechanical, and thermal power.

wave *n* **1** undulation on the surface of a liquid, esp. the sea. **2** any undulation, as in the hair. **3** oscillating disturbances by which radio energy, sound energy, light energy, etc., is carried through air or some other medium. **4** surge of events, emotions, people, etc. **5** to-and-fro movement of the hand expressing greeting, etc. *vt,vi* move or cause to move to and fro. *vi* greet or signal by a wave. *vt* **1** direct by a wave. **2** set waves in (hair).

waveband *n* range of wavelengths used in radio transmission. **wavelength** *n* distance between two successive peaks of an energy wave. **wavy** *adj* undulating; full of waves; swaying to and fro.

waver *vi* **1** be unsteady. **2** oscillate; vary. **3** hesitate; falter.

wax[1] *n* solid or viscous insoluble natural substance that softens at low temperatures. *vt* smear or rub with wax. **waxy** *adj*.

wax[2] *vi* become larger or apparently larger; increase.

way *n* **1** route; direction; path. **2** progress; distance; journey. **3** manner; style; method; characteristic behaviour, etc. **4** condition; state. **by the way** incidentally. **give way (to) 1** yield. **2** stop for. **in a way** in certain respects. **in the way** impeding progress. **out of the way 1** so as not to obstruct. **2** unusual. **3** not easily accessible. **under way** in progress; in motion. **wayside** *n* edge of a road or route.

waylay *vt* **1** intercept so as to attack; ambush. **2** detain in order to speak with.

wayward *adj* wilful; capricious; selfish.

we *pron* used as the subject to refer to oneself and another person or all other people including oneself.

weak *adj* **1** not strong; frail. **2** very diluted; insipid. **3** below expected standard. **4** lacking moral, mental, or political strength. **weakly** *adv*. **weakness** *n*. **weaken** *vt, vi* make or become weaker; reduce or be diminished in stature, strength, or resolve. **weak-kneed** *adj* lacking resolution or firmness; timid. **weakling** *n* person or animal that gives way easily or lacks strength. **weak-minded** *adj* **1** mentally deficient. **2** lacking resolution; easily persuaded. **weak-willed** *adj* easily deterred, dissuaded, or distracted.

wealth *n* **1** aggregate of valuable property; affluence; riches. **2** abundance. **wealthy** *adj*.

weapon *n* object, device, or other means used for attack or defence or to injure another.

wear *v* (wore; worn) *vt* **1** be dressed in; have on. **2** carry; bear; display; present. *vt,vi* **1** produce or be produced by constant rubbing, long use, etc.; impair or deteriorate. **2** reduce or be reduced to a certain condition. *n* **1** act of wearing. **2** clothing. **3** damage; wastage caused by use. **4** lasting quality. **wearable** *adj*.

weary *adj* **1** tired; reduced in strength or patience. **2** tedious; causing or caused by fatigue. *vt,vi* make or become tired or impatient. **wearily** *adv*. **weariness** *n*.

weasel *n* **1** small nimble carnivorous animal with a long slender brownish body. **2** treacherous, furtive, or sharp-featured person.

weather *n* local current atmospheric conditions of temperature, humidity, cloudiness, rainfall, wind, etc. *vt* come safely through. *vt,vi* expose or be exposed to the air or the weather.

weave *v* (wove *or* weaved; woven *or* weaved) *vt,vi* **1** interlace by passing threads alternately below and above other threads. **2** make fabric in this way. **3** create or move by winding in and out. *vt* **1** construct; fabricate. **2** introduce; combine. *n* texture or pattern of a woven fabric. **weaver** *n*.

web *n* **1** something woven. **2** fine filmy net spun by a spider to trap its prey. **3** membrane between the digits of a bat, duck, etc. **webbed** *adj*.

wedding *n* marriage ceremony.

wedge *n* **1** piece of solid material tapering towards one end. **2** anything of this shape. *vt* **1** fix firmly by positioning a wedge. **2** split; force apart. *vt,vi* squeeze or be squeezed into a space.

Wednesday *n* fourth day of the week.

weed *n* **1** wild prolific plant, esp. one growing where it is not wanted by man. **2** *inf* person of puny stature. **3** *sl* tobacco; cigarette. *vt,vi* remove weeds from (ground).

week *n* **1** period of seven days, usually from Sunday to Saturday. **2** working days of the week. **weekday** *n* any day of the week except Sunday and usually Saturday. **weekend** *n* period from Friday night to Sunday night.

weep *v* (wept) *vi,vt* **1** shed tears of sorrow, joy, etc; grieve (for). **2** exude moisture. *n* act of grieving or crying.

weft *n* threads running across the width of woven material.

weigh *vt* **1** ascertain the weight of. **2** compare against; counterbalance. **3** have a weight of. **4** estimate weight by holding or balancing in the hands. **5** consider carefully. **6** draw in an anchor. *vi* **1** have weight; be heavy. **2** be considered important or to have value. **weigh down** press down; oppress. **weigh out** measure by weight. ~*n* process of weighing.

weighbridge *n* machine for weighing vehicles and their loads.

weight *n* **1** heaviness. **2** standardized piece of metal used for weighing. **3** force by which a mass is attracted by gravity to the earth. **4** anything heavy or oppressive. **5** power; impressiveness; significance. *vt* load with a weight. **weighty** *adj*. **weight-lifting** *n* sport consisting of competitive attempts at lifting increasingly heavier weights.

weird *adj* odd; uncanny; unreal. **weirdly** *adv*.

welcome *n* cordial greeting or reception. *adj* agreeable; giving pleasure; gladly received; willingly permitted. **make welcome** treat hospitably. ~*vt* greet cordially; be glad of.

weld *vt* join (metals, plastics, etc.) by applying heat or pressure; unite. *vt,vi* bring or be brought together. *n* welded joint or union.

welfare *n* **1** well-being; state or condition of life; freedom from want, sickness, or ignorance. **2** work or plans to improve people's welfare.

well[1] *n* **1** underground source of water; spring. **2** deep sunken shaft through which oil, water, gas, etc., may be extracted. *vi* pour forth; flow; gush.

well[2] *adv* **1** satisfactorily; correctly; thoroughly. **2** intimately. **3** clearly; easily. **4** with reason or consideration. **5** fully; abundantly. **6** generously; kindly; with care. **as well** also; too; in addition. *adj* **1** healthy. **2** right; favourable; satisfactory. *interj* expression of surprise, etc. **well-being** *n* state of good health, happiness, etc.; good. **well-bred** *adj* of good stock; properly reared; having good manners, etc. **well-built** *adj* of generous proportions and stature. **well-known** *adj* celebrated; famous; notorious. **well-off** *adj* rich; fortunate. **well-spoken** *adj* **1** speaking with a sociably acceptable accent. **2** spoken fittingly or appropriately. **well-worn** *adj* **1** thoroughly used. **2** trite; hackneyed.

wellington *n also* **wellington boot** knee-length footwear, esp. of rubber.

went *v pt* of **go.**

wept *v pt* and *pp* of **weep.**

were *v* **1** 2nd person singular and 1st, 2nd, and 3rd person plural form of **be** in the past tense. **2** form of **be** in the subjunctive.

west *n* **1** one of the four cardinal points of the compass situated to the rear of a person facing the sunrise. **2** part of a country, area, etc., lying towards the west. *adj also* **western** of, in, or facing the west. *adv,adj also* **westerly 1** towards the west. **2** (of winds) from the west. **western** *n* story, film, etc., taking place in the American West during pioneering times. **westerner** *n*. **westward** *adj* facing or moving towards the west. **westwards** *adv* in the direction of the west.

wet *adj* **1** covered or saturated with liquid; not yet dry. **2** rainy. **3** *inf* sentimental; feeble; lacking spirit; naive. *vt* (-tt-) make wet. *n* rain; moisture; dampness. **wetness** *n*.

whack *vt* strike; hit. *n* **1** sharp blow or the sound of this. **2** *inf* share. **whacked** *adj inf* exhausted. **whacking** *n* beating. *adj inf* very large.

whale *n* very large marine mammal that breathes through a blowhole on its head. *vi* hunt whales.

wharf *n, pl* **wharves** *or* **wharfs** landing-stage for mooring, loading, and unloading boats. *vt,vi* **1** berth. **2** unload (cargo).

what *adj,pron* used as an interrogative to request further information. *adj* that which. *interj* exclamation of surprise, dismay, etc. **whatever** *pron* **1** anything or all that. **2** what. *adj,pron* whichever; no matter which. *adj* at all.

wheat *n* cereal grass or its grain used for flour to make bread, etc.

wheedle *vt,vi* persuade by devious means; cajole.

wheel *n* **1** circular frame attached by radial supports to a central axis around which it rotates, used to aid movement, transportation, etc. **2** thing of similar shape or function. *vt,vi* **1** move on wheels; push along. **2** change direction; pivot. **wheelbarrow** *n* barrow supported on one wheel in front and two legs behind, which may be lifted by two handles. **wheelchair** *n* chair on two wheels, used by invalids, etc.

wheeze *vi* breathe with difficulty, making a rattling or hissing sound. *n* **1** sound of difficult breathing. **2** *inf* ruse; clever scheme; dodge.

whelk *n* edible marine mollusc with a snail-like shell.

when *adv* **1** at what time. **2** in or during which period. *conj* at the time that. *pron* from or until what time. **whenever** *conj,adv* at any or whatever time that. *adv* when.

where *adv* **1** in, at, or to what or which place or position. **2** from which place. *conj* to or in the place or situation that. **whereabouts** *adv* in what place; near where. *n* place where something or someone is located or hidden. **whereas** *conj* but; though; while. **whereby** *adv* by which means. **whereupon** *conj,adv* at which point. **wherever** *conj,adv* in or to any or whatever place that. *adv* where.

whether *conj* used to introduce an indirect question, esp. implying an alternative or choice and sometimes substitutable by 'if'.

which *adj,pron* used as an interrogative to request further information, esp. so as to distinguish between things. *pron* used to introduce a relative clause when referring to inanimate objects. **whichever** *adj,pron* **1** any one(s) that. **2** no matter which.

whiff *n* **1** puff; gust. **2** slight smell. *vt,vi* **1** puff. **2** smell.

while *conj also* **whilst** as long as; during the time that; at the same time as; although. *n* space of time. *v* **while away** spend or pass idly.

whim *n* caprice; fancy. **whimsical** *adj* capricious; fanciful.

whimper *n* feeble cry; whine. *vi* utter a whimper; plaintively moan or whine.

whine *n* **1** wailing high-pitched cry or note. **2** undignified complaint. *vi,vt* make or utter in a whine.

whip *v* (-pp-) *vt* **1** beat with a lash to punish or cause (a horse, etc.) to move forward. **2** whisk into froth. *vi* move or act quickly. **whip out** produce suddenly. ~*n* **1** lash on a handle for whipping. **2** stroke of a lash. **3** person responsible for a political party's discipline. **4** call on members to vote according to party policy. **5** confection of whipped ingredients. **whip-round** *n* informal collection of money for a present, etc.

whippet *n* thin long-legged dog similar to a greyhound.

whir *vi* (-rr-) move rapidly with a buzzing sound.

whirl *vi,vt* **1** move or cause to move in a circle; spin very fast. **2** move away quickly. *vi* swing round quickly. *n* **1** rapid circular movement; rush; agitation. **2** state of bewilderment. **whirlpool** *n* circular current of water. **whirlwind** *n* moving spiral of air into which surrounding air can be drawn.

whisk *vt* **1** move or remove swiftly and lightly; brush, swing, or toss briskly. **2** beat lightly introducing air so as to make froth. *vi* move or pass quickly. *n* **1** rapid sweeping motion. **2** light stiff brush. **3** instrument for beating eggs, etc.

whisker *n* **1** firm sensitive hair at the side of an animal's mouth. **2** hairs on a person's upper lip or side of the face.

whisky *n* alcoholic drink, distilled esp. from malted barley.

whisper *vi,vt* **1** speak in very low tones; murmur. **2** converse in secret. *vi* spread rumours. *n* **1** soft speech; murmur; rustle. **2** hint; rumour.

whist *n* card game played in pairs.

whistle *vi* make a shrill sound by forcing breath through almost sealed lips or teeth, or air through a crack, etc. *vt* use this method for rendering a tune. *n* **1** sound of whistling. **2** device making a similar sound.

white *n* **1** colour of fresh snow, having no hue. **2** something coloured or characteristically white. *adj* **1** of the colour white or nearly white; pale; colourless. **2** pure; unblemished. **White** *n* person with a pale skin colour, esp. a European. *adj* having skin colour of Europeans. **whiten** *vt* make white. *vi* grow pale. **whitewash** *n* substance for whitening walls, etc. *vt* **1** cover with whitewash. **2** *inf* gloss over; conceal (errors, faults, etc.).

whiting *n* marine food fish.

Whitsun *n* **1** *also* **Whit Sunday** seventh Sunday after Easter when the Christian Church celebrates Pentecost, the inspiration of the disciples by the Holy Spirit. **2** week following Whit Sunday.

whiz *vi,vt* (-zz-) **1** move quickly, making a buzzing whirring sound. **2** *inf* move or go rapidly. *n* buzzing sound.

who *pron* **1** what or which person. **2** used to introduce a relative clause when referring to a person or people. **whoever** *pron* **1** anyone at all that. **2** no matter who. **3** who.

whole *adj* complete; total; undamaged; healthy. *adv* in a complete or unbroken piece. *n* entire or undivided thing; total of all parts. **wholehearted** *adj* sincerely and enthusiastically felt, done, etc. **wholeheartedly** *adv*. **wholesale** *n* sale of goods in bulk rather than retail selling. *adj* **1** relating to sales in bulk. **2** large-scale; indiscriminate. *adv* on a wholesale basis. **wholesome** *adj* **1** containing good value. **2** healthy in body, mind, morals, etc. **3**

conducive to such. **wholly** *adv* completely; altogether.

whom *pron* form of **who** as the object.

whooping cough *n* infectious disease characterized by bouts of coughing, respiratory difficulties, etc.

whore (hɔ:) *n* female prostitute.

whose *pron* belonging to whom; of whom or which.

why *adv,conj* for what reason; from what cause.

wick *n* stringlike cord that burns in a candle.

wicked *adj* **1** sinful; evil; extremely bad. **2** mischievous; roguish. **wickedly** *adv*. **wickedness** *n*.

wickerwork *n* craft of making furniture, etc., from twisted twigs or branches, or the objects so made.

wicket *n* **1** three pointed stumps with two bails resting on top, at which the bowler aims in a game of cricket. **2** strip of turf between two wickets. **3** batsman or batsman's turn. **4** small gate or door. **wicketkeeper** *n*.

wide *adj* **1** broad; of considerable dimension from side to side. **2** roomy; extensive; including much. *adv* **1** to the full extent. **2** widely. **widely** *adv* over a large area or extent; considerably; spreading far from. **widen** *vt,vi* make or grow wide(r). **widespread** *adj* found over a considerable area; distributed far.

widow *n* woman whose husband has died and who has not remarried. **widower** *m n*.

width *n* **1** distance or measurement between sides. **2** state of being wide.

wield *vt* hold and use; possess; exercise.

wife *n, pl* **wives** female partner in a marriage; married woman. **wifely** *adj*.

wig *n* hairpiece for the whole head made of artificial or real hair.

wiggle *vt,vi* move or cause to move to and fro jerkily. *n* wiggling movement.

wigwam *n* light conical dwelling used by North American Indians.

wild *adj* **1** uncivilized; undomesticated or uncultivated. **2** uncontrolled; boisterous; extremely excited or angry. **3** untidy; dishevelled. **4** lacking judgment; random; erratic; fantastic. **wildly** *adv*. **wildness** *n*. **wildlife** *n* animals, birds, plants, etc., that are undomesticated and live in their natural habitat.

wilderness *n* large desolate area; uncultivated and uninhabited region.

wilful *adj* headstrong; obstinately self-willed. **wilfully** *adv*.

will[1] *v aux* **1** used to form the future tense. **2** used to emphasize an intention. **3** used to express willingness or ability. **4** used to express probability or likelihood.

will[2] *n* **1** faculty by which decisions are made. **2** conscious choice; intention; inclination; moral strength. **3** intended distribution of one's property at death. **4** legal document expressing this. *vt,vi* **1** bequeath in a will. **2** compel by using the will; desire. **willpower** *n* strength of mind; firmess; control.

willing *adj* without reluctance; in agreement; eager; cooperative. **willingly** *adv*. **willingness** *n*.

willow *n* tree with slender pliant branches and long slender leaves, often found near rivers. **willowy** *adj* flexible; graceful; slender.

wilt *vt,vi* droop, as through lack of moisture, energy, etc.; fade.

win *v* (-nn-; won) *vi* reach a goal, esp. before anyone else; come first. *vt* secure or gain by effort or contest; obtain by gambling. **win over** persuade. ~*n* act of winning; victory; success. **winner** *n*.

wince *vi* draw back; flinch. *n* involuntary movement resulting from pain, etc.

winch *n* hauling or hoisting machine consisting of a drum on a rotating axle.

wind[1] (wind) *n* **1** current of air usually moving with speed. **2** gas produced in the alimentary canal. **3** empty meaningless words. **4** wind instruments in an orchestra. **5** *inf* hint; suggestion. **get/put the wind up** become frightened or alarmed/frighten or alarm. **in the wind** about to happen. ~*vt* cause to be short of breath. **windbag** *n* **1** *sl* person who talks a lot but says little of interest. **2** bag in bagpipes from which air can be squeezed to maintain a continuous sound. **windfall** *n* **1** fruit blown off a tree. **2** unexpected good fortune, often a receipt of money. **wind instrument** *n* musical instrument played by blowing or using an air current. **windmill** *n* mill with rotating sails driven by wind power. **windpipe** *n* passage between the mouth and lungs through which breath is inhaled or exhaled. **windscreen** *n* protective plate of glass in front of a vehicle. **windswept** *adj* exposed to or disordered by wind. **windy** *adj* like, characterized by, or exposed to wind.

wind[2] (waind) *v* (wound) *vt* **1** turn; twist; **2** *also* **wind up** tighten the spring of (a watch, etc.) by turning something. **3** make into a ball; coil. *vi* change direction constantly; meander.

windlass *n* machine with a revolving cylinder for hauling or hoisting. *vt* hoist by means of a windlass.

window *n* **1** opening in a wall, etc., to let in air and light. **2** frame of a window or the glass in it. **window-dressing** *n* **1** displaying of goods in a shop window. **2** art of doing this. **3** skill in emphasizing the best features of something. **window-shop** *vi* (-pp-) scrutinize goods in shop windows without buying.

wine *n* alcoholic drink made from fermented grape juice or sometimes from other fruits.

wing *n* **1** limb or organ by which a bird, insect, etc., flies. **2** similarly shaped structure on an aeroplane. **3** any side structure, as of a building or stage. **4** player on the extreme right or left of the forward line in football, etc. **wing-commander** *n* airforce officer similar in rank to lieutenant colonel or naval commander. **wingspan** *n* length from tip to tip of wings.

wink *vi,vt* **1** rapidly shut and open (one or both eyes), often to convey complicity, etc. *n* act or instance of winking.

winkle *n* edible shellfish. *v* **winkle out** extract with difficulty.

winter *n* coldest season of the year. *adj* of, like, happening, used, or sown in winter. *vi* spend the winter (in). *vt* feed and shelter (animals) through winter. **wintry** *adj*.

wipe *vt* clean or dry by drawing a cloth over or rubbing lightly. **wipe out** obliterate. ~*n* act of wiping; clean; rub.

wire *n* **1** flexible strand or rod of metal or a group of strands plaited or twisted together. **2** insulated wire for carrying an electric current. **3** *inf* telegram. *vt* join, fasten, support, protect, equip, etc., with wire. *vi* telegraph. **wireless** *n* radio. **wiry** *adj* sinewy; tough.

wise *adj* **1** having knowledge, perception, or judgment; clever. **2** sensible; discreet. **3** *sl* knowing the whole situation; warned about. **wisdom** *n*. **wisely** *adv*.

wish *vt* **1** desire; long for. **2** request; want. *vt,vi* express or have a desire for. *n* **1** desire. **2** thing desired. **wishful** *adj* desirous; hoping.

wisp *n* **1** thin strand or streak of something. **2** small bundle of straw, hay, etc.

wisteria *n* climbing plant with blue flowers hanging in clusters.

wistful *adj* yearning, with little hope of satisfaction; thoughtful. **wistfully** *adv*.

wit *n* **1** ability to think quickly and pertinently and say clever amusing things. **2** person with this ability. **3** *also* **wits** intelligence; resourcefulness.

witch *n* **1** woman believed to have supernatural powers through contact with evil spirits. **2** ugly malevolent woman. **witchcraft** *n* craft or practice of supernatural powers for evil purposes.

with *prep* **1** in the company of. **2** by means of; using. **3** bearing; possessing. **4** displaying; showing. **5** in relation to. **6** among; in the midst of. **7** at the same time as.

withdraw *v* (-drew; -drawn) *vi* draw back or away; retire. *vt* take out; take back; retract; remove. **withdrawal** *n*. **withdrawn** *adj* unsociable; very reserved.

wither *vi,vt* shrivel; dry (up); fade; decay. **withering** *adj* crushingly sarcastic.

withhold *vt* (-held) keep from; hold back; restrain; refuse to grant.

within *adv* inside; internally; indoors. *prep* **1** not out of or beyond. **2** in; inside; to the inner part of.

without *adv* outside. *prep* **1** outside. **2** not having; free from; in the absence of. **3** beyond the limits of. *conj* unless; but.

withstand *vt* (-stood) maintain; endure; oppose successfully.

witness *n* **1** person who is present and perceives a fact or event. **2** person who gives evidence, esp. in court. **3** person who attests another's signature. *vt,vi* give testimony; observe personally; act as witness. **witness box** *n* place in a lawcourt where witnesses give evidence.

witty *adj* capable of verbal wit; amusing. **wittily** *adv*.

wives *n pl* of **wife.**

wizard *n* **1** man having supernatural powers; magician. **2** ingenious person; expert. **wizardry** *n*.

wobble *vi* **1** move unsteadily; rock; shake; tremble. **2** be uncertain; vacillate. *n* unsteady motion. **wobbly** *adj*.

woke *v pt* of **wake. woken** *v pp* of **wake.**

wolf *n, pl* **wolves** **1** gregarious carnivorous predatory animal of the dog family. **2** person who is greedy and cunning. **cry wolf** raise a false alarm. ~*vt also* **wolf down** eat rapidly and ravenously.

woman *n, pl* **women 1** adult female human being. **2** women collectively. **womanhood** *n.* **womanly** *adj.*

womb *n* uterus.

won *v pt* and *pp* of **win.**

wonder *n* **1** emotion of delighted surprise and admiration. **2** object or person that excites this. **no wonder** not surprising(ly). **work wonders** achieve great results. ~*vt,vi* **1** be curious or seek to find out (about). **2** doubt. **3** marvel (at). **wonderful** *adj* **1** amazing. **2** *inf* very good; marvellous. **wonderfully** *adv.*

wonky *adj sl* unsound; shaky; not right or well.

wood *n* **1** collection of growing trees and other plants over an extensive area. **2** hard fibrous material in the trunks and branches of trees, used as a building material, in furniture, etc. **woody** *adj.* **wooden** *adj* **1** made of wood. **2** stiff; clumsy. **3** showing no emotion. **4** stupid; insensible. **woodpecker** *n* bird with a chisel-like bill, which it uses for drilling the bark of trees for insects. **woodwind** *n* section of an orchestra containing wind instruments with the exception of brass instruments. **woodwork** *n* anything made of wood; carpentry. **woodworm** *n* **1** larva of certain beetles laid in, boring through, and eating wood. **2** resulting damage in wooden furniture, etc.

wool *n* **1** hair-covering of sheep and other animals. **2** yarn spun from this. **3** garment, etc., made from the yarn. **woollen** *adj* made from wool. *n also* **woollens** woollen cloth or garments. **woolly** *adj* **1** made of or like wool. **2** lacking clearness or precision. *n* jersey.

word *n* **1** unit of spoken language or a written symbol of this, expressive of some object, idea, or relation. **2** brief conversation; remark. **3** news; message. **4** decree; promise; recommendation. **have words** argue. **in a word** in short. ~*vt* express in words; phrase. **wordy** *adj* using too many words. **word-perfect** *adj* memorized accurately.

wore *v pt* of **wear.**

work *n* **1** effort exerted in purposeful activity; expenditure of energy. **2** task; occupation for gain; employment. **3** product of one's efforts; creation. **4** place of employment or where activity takes place. *vt* **1** bring into action; effect. **2** handle; shape. *vi* **1** labour; expend energy; be occupied; be employed (at or in). **2** behave in a desired way when started; operate; function. **worked up** *adj* angry; excited. **work out** solve; develop. **working class** *n* workers, usually implying those in manual work. **workman** *n, pl* **-men** labourer; skilled manual worker. **workmanlike** *adj* efficient; of a high standard. **workmanship** *n* level of competence or skill in a product. **workshop** *n* place where goods are made, manual work is carried on, etc.

world *n* **1** universe; all that exists. **2** earth and its inhabitants; part of the earth. **3** mankind; public; society. **4** present state of existence; public life; sphere of interest or activity; environment. **5** materialistic standards or system; secular life. **6** large amount or quantity. **worldly** *adj* **1** familiar with public life and the ways of society. **2** adhering to materialistic standards; not idealistic or religious. **worldliness** *n.* **worldwide** *adj* extending over or applying to the whole planet.

worm *n* **1** long slender usually limbless invertebrate animal, esp. an earthworm. **2** internal parasite. *vt* wriggle; squirm; make (one's way) slowly or secretly; extract insidiously.

worn *v pp* of **wear.** *adj* **1** well used; long used; exhausted. **2** worried; haggard.

worry *vi* be anxious; fret. *vt* make anxious; disturb; pester; harass; be a trouble to. *n* **1** act of worrying. **2** cause of this.

worse *adj* less good; poorer in health; more inferior or severe in condition or circumstances. *adv* in a worse way; with more severity. **worsen** *vt,vi* make or become worse.

worship *v* (-pp-) *vt* **1** accord religious honour and supreme esteem to. **2** adore; idolize. *vi* attend religious worship. *n* **1** act of worshipping; religious service. **2** adoration; devotion.

worst *adj* of the extreme degree of badness. *adv* in the worst way. *n* worst part, state, etc.; least good part. *vt* get an advantage over; defeat.

worth *adj* **1** having a value of. **2** deserving; justifying. *n* intrinsic value; value in money; merit. **worthwhile** *adj* warranting the time, effort, etc; sufficiently important. **worthy** *adj* of sufficient merit; deserving; commendable. **worthily** *adv*.

would *v aux* form of **will**[1] in the past tense, conditional, or subjunctive.

wound[1] *vt,vi* (wu:nd) hurt; injure. *n* injury.

wound[2] *v* (waund) *pt* and *pp* of **wind**[2].

wove a *pt* of **weave. woven** a *pp* of **weave.**

wrangle *vi* argue; dispute doggedly. *n* angry dispute.

wrap *vt* (-pp-) cover; fold round or together; wind; envelop in. *vi* **1** enfold. **2** package. *n* **1** covering, such as a shawl or rug. **2** single turn or fold.

wreath *n* **1** arrangement, often circular, of intertwined leaves and flowers, often in memory of a deceased person; garland. **2** wisp or curl of smoke or vapour. **wreathe** *vt,vi* twist; entwine; interweave.

wreck *vt* ruin; damage or destroy; sabotage. *n* **1** ship that has foundered or sunk. **2** broken or damaged remains after a disaster; destruction. **3** person enfeebled mentally or physically. **wreckage** *n* **1** act of wrecking. **2** remains of a wrecked thing or person.

wren *n* small brown songbird with short erect tail.

wrench *vt* pull sharply and with a twist; force by violence; sprain; distort. *vi* undergo violent pulling, tugging, or twisting. *n* **1** act of wrenching; twist; sprain. **2** difficult parting; pain at parting. **3** adjustable spanner.

wrestle *vi,vt* struggle to overcome. *vi* contend in an organized fight by holding and throwing, without punching. *n* bout of wrestling; struggle. **wrestler** *n*. **wrestling** *n*.

wretch *n* **1** miserable unfortunate person. **2** worthless despicable person. **wretched** *adj* **1** miserable; dismal. **2** of poor quality; contemptible.

wriggle *vi,vt* squirm or make short twisting movements. **wriggle into/out of** *inf* insinuate oneself deviously into or extricate oneself out of. *n* act, motion, or shape of wriggling movement.

wring *v* (wrung) *vt,vi* twist and squeeze out moisture (from). *vt* **1** twist. **2** clasp in anguish. **3** grip in a friendly manner. **4** extract. *n* act of wringing.

wrinkle *n* small ridge or furrow on a surface; crease. *vt,vi* crease.

wrist *n* **1** joint between the hand and lower arm. **2** part of a garment covering this. **wristwatch** *n* watch worn at the wrist.

writ *n* legal or formal document summoning or requiring a person to take some course of action.

write *v* (wrote; written) *vt,vi* **1** mark letters, words, numbers, etc., usually on paper, to communicate ideas, thoughts, etc. **2** correspond (with) by letter. **3** be an author (of). *vt* state in a letter, book, etc. **write down** *or* **out** put in writing. **write off** consider a loss or failure. **write-off** *n* complete loss or failure; wreck. **write up** describe or bring up to date in writing. **write-up** *n* written account in a newspaper, etc., of a book, film, etc.; review. **writing** *n* **1** written work, book, etc. **2** act of writing. **3** style of handwriting.

writhe *vi* **1** twist or roll about as if suffering pain; squirm. **2** suffer mentally.

wrong *adj* **1** not correct, accurate, or true; mistaken. **2** wicked; unjust. **3** not suitable; not wanted. *n* injustice; wrong action. **in the wrong** mistaken. *adv also* **wrongly** in a wrong way. **get wrong 1** misunderstand. **2** produce an incorrect answer. ~*vt* do injustice or harm to; think ill of unjustifiably. **wrongdoing** *n* improper, illegal, or immoral action. **wrongdoer** *n*.

wrought iron *adj* malleable pure iron, often drawn out into decorative shapes.

wry *adj* **1** twisted; contorted. **2** ironical; dryly humorous. **wryly** *adv*.

X

xenophobia *n* irrational fear or hatred of foreigners or things foreign or strange.

xerography *n* copying process in which images are produced using electrically charged surfaces.

Xerox *n Tdmk* process or machine employing xerography.

Xmas *n* Christmas.

X-ray *n* **1** wave of radiation of considerable energy that can penetrate matter, used esp. in medical diagnosis and treatment. **2** image, esp. of bone structure, produced on film sensitive to X-rays. *vt,vi* irradiate with X-rays.

xylophone *n* musical instrument consisting of a graduated series of wooden bars struck by wooden hammers.

Y

yacht *n* light sailing vessel for racing, cruising, etc. *vi* sail in a yacht. **yachtsman** *n, pl* **-men** person who keeps or sails a yacht.

yank *vt,vi* pull sharply; jerk. *n* sharp tug.

yap *n* short sharp high-pitched bark; yelp. *vi* (-pp-) **1** bark in yaps. **2** *inf* chatter stupidly or at length.

yard[1] *n* **1** unit of length, equivalent to 0.91 metres (three feet). **2** piece of material of this length. **yardstick** *n* **1** graduated stick, one yard long, used for measuring. **2** any standard used for comparison.

yard[2] *n* enclosed area, usually adjoining a building and having a hard surface.

yarn *n* **1** continuous thread made from twisted fibres of wool, cotton, synthetic materials, etc. **2** story spun out to some length. *vi* tell stories.

yawn *vi* **1** breathe in through a wide open mouth, usually as a result of tiredness or boredom. **2** be open wide. *n* act of yawning.

year *n* **1** *also* **calendar year** period of time of 365 days (or 366 in a leap year) from Jan 1 to Dec 31. **2** period of twelve months. **3** period of time (365.256 days) taken by the earth to complete one orbit of the sun. **yearly** *adj,adv*.

yearn *vi* **1** have a great longing; crave. **2** feel pity or tenderness. **yearning** *n*.

yeast *n* fungus or a preparation of this fungus, used in brewing and for raising bread.

yell *vi,vt* scream; shout loudly. *n* scream of anger, pain, or excitement; loud cry.

yellow *n* spectral colour, as that of gold or a daffodil. *adj* **1** of the colour yellow. **2** *inf* cowardly.

yelp *n* short sharp cry of pain, surprise, or excitement, esp. by a dog. *vi* utter a yelp.

yes *adv,interj* expression of affirmation, consent, etc. *n* affirmative reply.

yesterday *n* day before today. *adv* **1** on or during yesterday. **2** not long ago.

yet *adv* **1** up to that or this time. **2** now; at this moment. **3** still; even. *conj* but; nevertheless; however.

yew *n* coniferous tree with dark needle-shaped leaves and red cones.

yield *vt* **1** produce; supply. **2** give up under pressure; concede. *vi* submit; give way under pressure; comply. *n* amount yielded; product.

yodel *vi,vt* (-ll-) alternate in singing between a normal and falsetto voice. *n* song in this style. **yodeller** *n*.

yoga *n* philosophy and practice of type of oriental meditation. **yogi** *n* person who practises yoga.

yoghurt *n also* **yogurt, yoghourt** thickly clotted milk curdled by bacteria.

yoke *n* **1** wooden neckpiece holding together two draught oxen. **2** something resembling this. **3** fitted part of a garment, esp. for the chest and shoulders. **4** oppressive force; slavery. **5** bond of union. *vt* put a yoke on; join together.

yolk *n* yellow centre of an egg.

yonder *adv* over there. *adj* distant but in sight.

you *pron* **1** used to refer to one or more persons addressed directly, excluding the speaker. **2** people in general; one.

young *adj* having lived a relatively short time; undeveloped; immature; not old. *pl n* young people; offspring. **youngster** *n* young person or animal.

your *adj* belonging to you. **yours** *pron* something or someone that belongs to or is associated with you. **yourself** *r pron, pl* **-selves** **1** of your own self. **2** your normal self.

youth *n* **1** age between childhood and adulthood; early life. **2** quality or condition of being young, inexperienced, etc. **3** young man. **4** young people collectively. **youthful** *adj* fresh; vigorous; optimistic; buoyant.

Z

zeal *n* enthusiasm; fervour; passionate ardour.

zebra *n* black-and-white striped animal of the horse family, originating in Africa. **zebra crossing** *n* black-and-white striped path used by pedestrians to cross a road.

zero *n* nought; nothing; nil; figure 0; point separating positive and negative values or quantities, as on a temperature scale.

zest *n* **1** gusto; keen interest; obvious enjoyment. **2** anything that gives added zest.

zigzag *n* **1** line that forms a series of sharp alternately right and left turns. **2** something having this form. *vt,vi* (-gg-) move or cause to move along such a line.

zinc *n* hard bluish-white metal, used esp. in alloys and in galvanizing iron.

zip *n* **1** interlocking fastener for openings in clothes. **2** whizzing sound. **3** energy; vigour. *v* (-pp-) *vt also* **zip up.** fasten with a zip. *vi* **1** hurry or rush (through, etc.). **2** move with a whizzing sound.

zither *n* musical instrument consisting of numerous strings stretched over a wooden frame.

zodiac *n* belt or zone of the heavens divided into twelve parts, each accorded a sign, in which the paths of the sun, moon, and planets appear to lie.

zone *n* area; region; belt; characteristic or distinctive section, as of the earth. *vt* divide into or mark with zones.

zoo *n* enclosure where wild animals are kept for display to the public, for breeding, etc.

zoology *n* scientific study of animals and animal life. **zoological** *adj.* **zoologist** *n.*

zoom *vi,vt* produce a loud buzzing noise. *vi* move or rise rapidly.